Literature and Film

Edited by

Robert Stam
Alessandra Raengo

Literature
and Film

A Guide to the Theory and Practice of Film Adaptation

Blackwell
Publishing

BLACKWELL PUBLISHING
350 Main Street, Malden, MA 02148-5020, USA
108 Cowley Road, Oxford OX4 1JF, UK
550 Swanston Street, Carlton, Victoria 3053, Australia

First published 2005 by Blackwell Publishing Ltd

Library of Congress Cataloging-in-Publication Data

Literature and film : a guide to the theory and practice of film adaptation / edited
by Robert Stam and Alessandra Raengo.
p. cm.
Includes bibliographical references and index.
ISBN 0–631–23054–8 (alk. paper) — ISBN 0–631–23055–6 (pbk. : alk. paper)
1. Film adaptations—History and criticism.   2. Motion pictures and literature.
I. Stam, Robert, 1941–   II. Raengo, Alessandra.

PN1997.85.L515 2005
791.43'6—dc22
2004015927

A catalogue record for this title is available from the British Library.

Set in 9.75/14pt Bell Gothic
by Graphicraft Limited, Hong Kong
Printed and bound in the United Kingdom
by TJ International, Padstow, Cornwall

For further information on
Blackwell Publishing, visit our website:
www.blackwellpublishing.com

Contents

Contents

Illustrations

Notes on Contributors

Melissa Anderson is a writer living in Brooklyn. Her film criticism and essays have appeared in *The Village Voice, The New York Times, Film Comment, Studies in French Cinema, Quarterly Review of Film and Video*, and other publications. She is currently working on a book about the films of François Ozon.

Paul Arthur is Professor of English and Film Studies at Montclair State University. He is a regular contributor to *Film Comment* and *Cineaste* magazines and is co-editor of *Millennium Film Journal. A Line of Sight*, a collection of his essays on avant-garde film, is forthcoming.

Mbye Cham is Professor of Literature and Film in the Department of African Studies at Howard University, Washington, DC. He is the author of numerous essays on African and Caribbean literature and film, editor of *EX-ILES: Essays on Caribbean Cinema*, and co-editor of *Blackframes: Critical Perspectives on Black Independent Cinema* and *African Experiences of Cinema*.

Patrick Deer is Assistant Professor of English at New York University. He is currently completing the manuscript of *Modernism in Camouflage: War Culture and British Literature*. His research interests include modernism, the twentieth-century novel and film, war culture, and cultural and postcolonial studies.

Jacquelyn Kilpatrick is Chair of Humanities and Social Sciences at California State University Channel Islands. She is the author of *Celluloid Indians: Native Americans in Film* and a variety of essays on literature and film. She has edited a volume of essays entitled *Louis Owens: Literary Reflections on his Life and Work*.

Bliss Cua Lim is Assistant Professor of Film Studies at the University of California, Irvine. Her research centers on Filipino and Hong Kong cinemas, postcolonial feminist criticism, taste cultures, and the politics of genres. She is currently working on a book on fantastic cinema, temporality, and the philosophy of history.

Mia Mask holds an MA and PhD in Cinema Studies from New York University. She is currently Assistant Professor of Film at Vassar College where she teaches African American cinema, documentary film history and aesthetics, and non-Western film. As a freelance film critic, she is a contributor to *IndieWire.com*, and has published in *The Village Voice*, *Abafazi*, and *Resident Publications*. Her criticism also appeared in *Best American Movie Writing* (1999).

Paula J. Massood is Associate Professor of Film Studies in the Film Department at Brooklyn College/CUNY. She is the author of *Cities in Black: Visualizing African American Urban Experiences in Film*. Her articles have appeared in *Cinema Journal*, *African American Review*, and *Cineaste*.

Ranjani Mazumdar is an independent filmmaker, film scholar, and visiting faculty at the AJK Mass Communication Research Center at Jamia Millia Islamia, New Delhi. She received her PhD in Cinema Studies from the Tisch School of the Arts, New York University in 2001. She is a co-founder member of *Mediastorm,* a collective of six women filmmakers. Her publications and films focus on women's issues, popular cinema, politics, and everyday lives. She is currently working on an historical study of the Bombay film poster and a co-authored book on the contemporary Indian film industry.

Dianna C. Niebylski teaches at the University of Kentucky. Her publications include *The Poem on the Edge of the Word: The Limits of Language and the Uses of Silence in the Poetry of Mallarmè, Rilke and Vallejo* (1993) and *Humoring Resistance: Laughter and the Excessive Body in Latin American Women's Fiction* (2004).

Richard Porton is on the editorial board of *Cineaste* magazine. He is the author of *Film and the Anarchist Imagination*. His book on prostitution and cinema is forthcoming.

Jessica Scarlata holds a PhD in Cinema Studies from New York University, and is currently Visiting Assistant Professor at Florida Atlantic University. She teaches and writes on cinema and postcolonial studies, gender, national identity, and the body as a site and weapon of struggle in Irish culture.

Alexandra Seibel holds a Master's Degree in German Literature from the University of Vienna and is currently a PhD candidate in Cinema Studies at New York University. Her main areas of research include representations of the city of Vienna in international filmmaking from 1920 to 1950, teen films, and youth culture with a special focus on girl culture. Her most recent publications are on Luchino Visconti's *La Terra Trema* and Glauber Rocha's *Barravento*, contemporary feminist film and video practices, and the Austrian director Georg Tressler and his films on German youth culture in the 1950s.

Vivian C. Sobchack is Associate Dean and Professor of Film and Television Studies at the UCLA School of Theater, Film, and Television. Her work focuses on film and media theory and its intersections with philosophy, perceptual studies, and historiography. Her books include *Screening Space: The American Science Fiction Film*, *The Address of the Eye: A Phenomenology of Film Experience*, two edited anthologies, *The Persistence of History: Cinema, Television and the Modern Event* and *Meta-Morphing: Visual Transformation and the Culture of Quick Change*, and a collection of her essays entitled *Carnal Thoughts: Embodiment and Moving Image Culture*.

Robert Stam is University Professor at New York University. His many books include *Reflexivity in Film and Literature* (1992), *Tropical Multiculturalism* (1997), and *Film Theory: An Introduction* (Blackwell 2000). He is also author, with Ella Shohat, of *Unthinking Eurocentrism: Multiculturalism and the Media* (1994), which won the Katherine Singer Kovacs "Best Film Book Award." With Toby Miller, he is the editor of *Film and Theory* (Blackwell 2000) and *The Blackwell Companion to Film Theory* (2000).

Kirsten Thompson is Assistant Professor of Film at Wayne State University, Detroit. She is co-editor (with Terri Ginsberg) of *Perspectives on German Cinema*, and has published articles on animation and New Zealand cinema. Her other research interests include American cinema, the blockbuster, and crime.

Tim Watson teaches in the English Department at Princeton University. He is currently completing a book on humanitarianism and imperialism in the anglophone Caribbean.

Preface

Literature and Film forms part of a three-volume series devoted to literature and film, and, more specifically, to the history, theory, and practice of the filmic adaptations of novels. This volume consists of a wide range of essays, virtually all previously unpublished, covering a broad spectrum of subjects and problematics. My introductory essay, "The Theory and Practice of Adaptation," is followed by a variety of essays concerning single novels/adaptations, essays that both illustrate and problematize the methodologies.

A second volume, *Literature Through Film: Realism, Magic, and the Art of Adaptation*, treats the history, theory, and practice of the filmic adaptations of novels, and, more broadly, the relation between filmic and literary writing. This book approaches the subject from the specific angle of the history of the novel. Arranged according to the chronology of the literary source texts rather than that of their filmic adaptations, *Literature Through Film* highlights key moments and trends in the history of the novel from *Don Quixote* and *Robinson Crusoe* to Nabokov's *Lolita* and Carpentier's *Concierto barroco*. All the novels are treated in their own terms, as novels, but also as seen through their various filmic adaptations. In each case, I stress the historical importance of the novel, its central narrative and aesthetic strategies, and its verbal texture, before moving to the "re-readings" of these same novels as "performed" by film. In sum, I provide an historicized overview of privileged moments in the development of the novel, but as refracted and "rewritten" in the form of cinematic adaptations.

The third book in the series, *A Companion to Literature and Film*, complements the first two volumes by exploring the broader question of the interface between the literary and the filmic. More specifically, the *Companion* features theoretical and analytical essays, again previously unpublished, concerning such issues as: (1) **the narratology of adaptation;** (2) **adaptation in the oeuvre of single directors** (for example, Alfred Hitchcock);

(3) **hidden intertextualities** (for example, the unacknowledged presence of *Les Liaisons dangereuses* in the work of Eric Rohmer; and (4) **thematic/generic essays** on such topics as apocalyptic fiction/film, cross-cultural adaptation, the Hollywood novel/film, *noir* novels and films, and the Bible as cultural object in popular cinema. The *Companion* moves the discussion beyond adaptation per se into broader questions of transtextuality and intermediality.

Although the essays in the two anthologies do not conform to any a priori theory or model, they all share a reflexive awareness of key orienting questions or "problematics." In diverse ways, they mingle the methods of literary theory, semiotics, narratology, cultural studies, and media theory. The totality of the essays moves adaptation discourse forward, through a tour de force of sophisticatedly literate (and cine-literate) readings, performed so as to reconfigure the field of literature/film studies. Cumulatively, the work is highly international, covering novels/films from England, the United States, France, Italy, Germany, Spain, Ireland, Russia, China, India, Egypt, Senegal, Cuba, Brazil, Argentina, Mexico, and Venezuela. The work represented in all three volumes points the way, it is hoped, toward a richly theorized and complexly contextualized and transformalist approach to adaptation. While paying homage to the classics of world literature, the work also highlights the contemporary relevance of adaptation studies in the age of the Internet.

Acknowledgments

The editors and publisher gratefully acknowledge the permission granted to reproduce the copyright material in this book:

Chapter 5: Vivian C. Sobchack, "*The Grapes of Wrath*: Thematic Emphasis through Visual Style." This chapter was first published as "*The Grapes of Wrath* (1940): Thematic Emphasis Through Visual Style," in *American Quarterly* 31:5, Special Issue on Film and American Studies (Winter, 1979), 596–615. © 1979 by The American Studies Association. Reprinted with permission of The Johns Hopkins University Press.

Chapter 9: Paula J. Massood, "*Boyz N the Hood* Chronotopes: Spike Lee, Richard Price, and the Changing Authorship of *Clockers*." A longer version of this chapter entitled "Taking the A-Train: The City, the Train, and Migration in Spike Lee's *Clockers*" appears in Paula J. Massood, *Black City Cinema: African American Urban Experiences in Film* (Philadelphia: Temple University Press, 2003). © 2003 by Temple University. All rights reserved. Reprinted with permission of Temple University Press.

Every effort has been made to trace copyright holders and to obtain their permission for the use of copyright material. The publisher apologizes for any errors or omissions in the above list and would be grateful if notified of any corrections that should be incorporated in future reprints or editions of this book.

Introduction: The Theory and Practice of Adaptation

Robert Stam

I will take as my point of departure for discussion one of those rare feature films that not only **is** an adaptation, but is also **about** adaptation, and that is also actually **entitled** *Adaptation*, to wit the recent film (2002) directed by Spike Jonze and written by Charlie Kaufman. The film adapts Susan Orlean's *The Orchid Thief*, a non-fiction account of a flower poacher, named La Roche (played by Chris Cooper), working out of the Florida Everglades. The giddily reflexive film focuses less on the poacher than on the book's adapter struggling to write a screenplay about adapter Charlie Kaufman (played by Nicolas Cage) struggling to write an adaptation. In real life, the flesh-and-blood screenwriter Charles Kaufman did indeed have a contract to adapt the Orlean book, but he developed a severe case of writer's block, broken only when he conceived the idea of thematizing the screenwriting struggle itself. Thus *Adaptation* is simultaneously an adaptation and an original screenplay, one which turns a non-fiction book into a fictional adventure.

Rather like a Catskill writers' colony, *Adaptation* is crowded with writers working on their writing: (1) Susan Orlean (Meryl Streep) as she writes *The Orchid Thief*; (2) Charles Kaufman writing the adaptation of *The Orchid Thief*; (3) Charles's twin brother Donald (also played by Nicolas Cage) writing formulaic, commercial scripts; and (4) Charles Darwin, shown in the process of writing *The Origin of Species*. Even the auto-didact poacher La Roche dabbles at writing. Still another writer in the film – script guru Robert McKee (played by Brian Cox), the real-life author of *Story: Substance, Structure, Style, and the Principles of Screenwriting*[1] – lectures large audiences about screenwriting and adaptation. More important, the film foregrounds the **process** of writing. We see Susan Orlean at her computer, surrounded by the various sources – encyclopedias, botanical books, histories – that feed into her own text. And we see Charles Kaufman, trying to adapt her book, panicked and sweating before the blank computer screen. Film, we are reminded, is a form of writing that borrows from other forms of writing.

Although the source book of *Adaptation* is a work of non-fiction, the discussion in the film proceeds as if that source **were** in fact a work of fiction. Charles aims at fidelity: "I want to be true to the *New Yorker* piece." But he has to translate fact into fiction, find new forms and equivalencies. Thus a person who is not even a "character" in the source book – Charlie Kaufman – becomes the main character of the film. The portrayal of Charlie's work suggests that adaptation consists of the reading of a book – we see him reading the Orlean text – and the writing of the scenario of a film. The two twin brothers, furthermore, spend much of their time arguing about screenwriting and adaptation; Charlie defends the sensitive, Sundance-style Hollywood-lite values of the independent art film, while Donald defends clichéd Hollywood blockbuster entertainment. In fact, Donald speaks in the kind of formulaic hype – "It's *Psycho* meets *The Silence of the Lambs*!" – mocked in Robert Altman's reflexive *The Player* (1992). Charlie begins by stating all the clichés he detests and plans to avoid – plot-driven narrative, character epiphanies, happy ending – precisely the clichés that his alter-ego brother defends with naïve enthusiasm.

While Charlie is a hypercerebral, insecure, masturbatory, Dostoevskyan Underground Man, Donald is a breezily confident womanizer. Together the twins manifest the split personality of many screenwriters, torn between the art film and the blockbuster, between complexity and facile appeal. All the various writers and their theories about writing are webbed together in a complex Pirandellian maze of doubles. Charlie wonders if he should play himself in the film, and worries that the producers will choose Depardieu, with "that awful accent." He contemplates writing an alternative film about orchids, *sans* romance, violence, and car chases, but the joke of the film is that his script ends up providing all of them in good measure, following the script guru's advice to "wow them in the end."

Indeed, it is revealing to "test" the film against McKee's stated principles in *Story*, a book that argues virtually all of the positions that I dispute in this chapter. For the neo-Aristotelian McKee, stories should be about realities, not about the mysteries of writing, yet the mysteries of writing are precisely the focus of *Adaptation*.[2] For McKee, a mature artist "never calls attention to himself," yet in *Adaptation* a whole gallery of artists call attention to themselves. For McKee, films are not good at depicting inner life, yet *Adaptation* does reveal Charlie Kaufman's inner life: indeed, it begins with Charlie's voice-over ruminations superimposed on a dark screen. For McKee, Aristotle provides the standard: strong, noble characters, cause–effect logic, catharsis. *Adaptation*, in contrast, features weak, masturbatory characters, a digressive, non-linear plot, absurd improbabilities, and a tongue-in-cheek feint at catharsis. Such is the film's reflexivity that the character Charles Kaufman quotes McKee's line "God Help You if you use voice-over" – but does it, paradoxically, in voice-over.

Adaptation leaves us, then, with a Florida swamp-like profusion of suggestive metaphors for the adaptational process: novel and adaptation as twins like Don and Charlie, or adaptations as parasites, as hybrids, or adaptations as evidencing split personality, or as demonstrating the interdependence of species or genres. Most significantly, the film brings out the Darwinian overtones of the word "adaptation" itself, evoking adaptation as a means of evolution and survival. Ironically, the adapter in the film himself – nervous, sexually inept, paralyzed by insecurity – has trouble "adapting" to everyday life. Hardly among the "fittest," he looks as if he might not even survive, much less evolve. Significantly, the digital montage sequence that traces the birth of the planet and the origin of the species, culminating in Charlie Kaufman's birth, is set in "Hollywood, California," just as part of the poacher story is set in "Hollywood, Florida." And what could be more Darwinian than the dog-eat-dog ethos of Hollywood? The block-buster aesthetic, in this sense, forms the end-point of the commercial "survival of the fittest."

Yet if mutation is the means by which the evolutionary process advances, then we can also see filmic adaptations as "mutations" that help their source novel "survive." Do not adaptations "**adapt to**" changing environments and changing tastes, as well as to a new medium, with its distinct industrial demands, commercial pressures, censorship taboos, and aesthetic norms? And are adaptations not a hybrid form like the orchid, the meeting place of different "species?" For La Roche, creating a hybrid is like playing at being God Almighty. But La Roche also invokes the metaphor of the parasite, a trope typically deployed **against** adaptations, seen as parasitical on their source texts and on the A-list prestige of literature. La Roche speaks of giant flower parasites that devour and kill their host tree, much as critics speak of adaptations which overwhelm and vampirize their sources, "suck-ing the life" out of their "hosts." Even the metaphor of murder is invoked. "We have to kill him," the Susan Orlean character says of her adapter, "before he murders my book."

The Roots of a Prejudice

The film *Adaptation* calls up the question of how we speak about the filmic adaptation of novels. The conventional language of adaptation criticism has often been profoundly moralistic, rich in terms that imply that the cinema has somehow done a **disservice** to literature. Terms like "infidelity," "betrayal," "deformation," "violation," "bastardiza-tion," "vulgarization," and "desecration" proliferate in adaptation discourse, each word carrying its specific charge of opprobrium. "Infidelity" carries overtones of Victorian prudishness; "betrayal" evokes ethical perfidy; "bastardization" connotes illegitimacy; "deformation" implies aesthetic disgust and monstrosity; "violation" calls to mind sexual violence; "vulgarization" conjures up class degradation; and "desecration" intimates religious sacrilege and blasphemy.

As *Adaptation* demonstrates, one might easily imagine any number of positive tropes for adaptation, yet the standard rhetoric has often deployed an elegiac discourse of loss, lamenting what has been "lost" in the transition from novel to film, while ignoring what has been "gained." In a 1926 diatribe, Virginia Woolf, for example, excoriated the adaptations that reduced a novel's complexly nuanced idea of "love" to "a kiss," or rendered "death," literal-mindedly, as a "hearse."[3] Too often, adaptation discourse subtly reinscribes the axiomatic superiority of literature to film. Too much of the discourse, I would argue, has focused on the rather subjective question of the **quality** of adaptations, rather than on the more interesting issues of (1) the theoretical **status** of adaptation, and (2) the analytical **interest** of adaptations. My goal here, then, is not to correct erroneous evaluations of specific adaptations, but rather to deconstruct the unstated doxa which subtly construct the subaltern **status** of adaptation (and the filmic image) vis-à-vis novels (and the literary word), and then to point to alternative perspectives.

Although the persuasive force of the putative superiority of literature to film can be partially explained by the undeniable fact that many adaptations based on significant novels **are** mediocre or misguided, it also derives, I would argue, from deeply rooted and often unconscious assumptions about the relations between the two arts. The intuitive sense of adaptation's inferiority derives, I would speculate, from a constellation of substratal prejudices. First, it derives from the a priori valorization of historical **anteriority** and **seniority**: the assumption, that is, that **older** arts are necessarily **better** arts. Through what Marshal MacLuhan calls "rear view mirror" logic, the arts accrue prestige over time. The venerable art of literature, within this logic, is seen as inherently superior to the younger art of cinema, which is itself superior to the even younger art of television, and so forth ad infinitum. Here literature profits from a double "priority": (a) the general historical priority of literature to cinema, and (b) the specific priority of novels to their adaptations. The procedural corollary of the seniority bias is the deployment of rigged criteria when evaluating the status of adaptation; literature at its best is compared to the cinema at its worst. Critics lambast filmic "betrayals" of modernist novels, for example, while forgetting the filmic "redemption" of many non-modernist novels. They denounce the Joseph Strick version of Joyce's *Ulysses*, but forget to laud Hitchcock's innovative transmogification of du Maurier's story "The Birds," or Kubrick's unforgettable satiric reconversion of Peter George's *Red Alert*.

A second source of hostility to adaptation derives from the **dichotomous thinking** that presumes a bitter rivalry between film and literature. The writer and the filmmaker, according to an old anecdote, are traveling in the same boat but they both harbor a secret desire to throw the other overboard. The inter-art relation is seen as a Darwinian struggle to the death rather than a dialogue offering mutual benefit and cross-fertilization. Adaptation becomes a zero-sum game where film is perceived as the upstart enemy storming the ramparts of literature. This is not to suggest that there was no institutional rivalry between the two media. Leo Tolstoy saw film as "a direct attack on the old methods of literary art," which obliged writers, in a symptomatic choice of words, to "adapt" to the new medium.[4] Even today, sophisticated proponents of "visual culture," such as W. J. T. Mitchell, speak of the "protracted struggle for dominance between pictorial and linguistic signs."[5] Filmic embodiment is seen as making literature obsolescent, retroactively revealing mere words as somehow weak and spectral and insubstantial. In Freudian terms, film is seen in terms of Bloom's "anxiety of influence," whereby the adaptation as Oedipal son symbolically slays the source-text as "father."[6]

A third source of hostility to adaptation is **iconophobia**. This deeply rooted cultural prejudice against the visual arts is traceable not only to the Judaic–Muslim–Protestant prohibitions of "graven images," but also to the Platonic and Neoplatonic depreciation of the world of phenomenal appearance. The *locus classicus* of this attitude is in the Second Commandment forbidding the making of idols in the form of anything in heaven above or on earth beneath or in the waters below. Within the Platonic view, meanwhile, the irresistible allure of the spectacle overwhelms reason.[7] Plato's polemic against poetry thus gets subliminally enlisted in an attack on contemporary visual arts and the mass media, seen as corrupting the audience through dangerously delusional fictions.[8] (Ironically, for Plato's mentor Socrates it was **writing** that corrupted the mind by substituting fixed and visible letters for the subtle movements of the mind.) Contemporary theorists hostile to the cinema often replay, whether consciously or not, Plato's rejection of the fictive arts as nurturing illusion and fomenting the lower passions. In the nineteenth century, Baudelaire worried about photography's corrupting influence on the arts, and even today a sophisticated and film-literate theorist like Fredric Jameson, perhaps picking up on the stigmatization of the visual in 1970s' apparatus theory, sees the filmic image as "essentially pornographic," since it demands that we "stare at the world as though it were a naked body."[9] In Lacanian terms, film's iconic "imaginary signifier" (Metz) is seen as triumphing over the *logos* of the symbolic written word, of which literature remains the most prestigious form. Film and other visual media seem to threaten the collapse of the symbolic order, the erosion of the powers of the literary fathers, patriarchal narrators, and consecrated arts.[10]

Images and the debates about images, then, trigger inordinate passion. Adaptations, for example in the case of the Brazilian film *City of God* (2002), at times provoke an outrage not provoked by the source book. Images provoke passion to the point, as Bruno Latour writes, "that destroying them, erasing them, defacing them, has been taken as the ultimate touchstone to prove the validity of one's faith, of one's science, of one's critical acumen, of one's artistic creativity."[11] Is it possible, then, that iconoclastic assaults on the "imaging" of literary texts derives, at some deep cultural level, from a desire to affirm one's faith, in literature for example? Thus the image takes on the qualities of the scapegoat, hated for its presumed vicious qualities but loved for its unifying function. Yet the same images that are hated always return, partially because they are already there as a dimension of the verbal text. The features of a biblical spectacular film – miracles, plagues, parted seas, burning bushes – are already there in the Jewish Bible. The icons are never definitively broken. In words that resonate with some of the recent passions provoked by Mel Gibson's *The Passion of the Christ* (2004), which is, after all, an adaptation, Latour speaks of iconoclastic Protestants who broke the limbs of the dead Christ in a *Pieta*: "What is a dead Christ if not another broken icon, the perfect image of God, desecrated, crucified, pierced and ready to be entombed . . . what does it mean to crucify a crucified icon?"[12]

Indeed, *The Passion of the Christ* brings up many of the key issues concerning fidelity in adaptation. As an adaptation of the ultimate Ur-text, the sacred word of Holy

Scriptures, not only did Mel Gibson proclaim his goal to be complete fidelity, he also claimed to have attained it. Backed up by a (later withdrawn) papal blurb, Gibson claimed that "It is as it was." Gibson raised the stakes of his adaptation, first, by assuming, in a rather absolutist manner, that the source text was infallible (despite the contradictions between the various accounts) and, second, by claiming full, literal fidelity to the text.

A fourth, related source of hostility to film and adaptation is the obverse form of iconophobia, to wit **logophilia**, or the valorization of the verbal, typical of cultures rooted in the sacred word of the "religions of the book." It is symptomatic, in this sense, that many littérateurs reject films based on literature, that most historians reject films based on history, and that some anthropologists reject films based on anthropology. The common current, coming from such different disciplinary angles, is the nostalgic exaltation of the written word as the privileged medium of communication.

A fifth source of hostility to film and adaptation — and here we move in more speculative directions — is **anti-corporeality**, a distaste for the unseemly "embodiedness" of the filmic text; the "seen," to recycle a venerable pun, is regarded as **obscene**. Film offends through its inescapable materiality, its incarnated, fleshly, enacted characters, its real locales and palpable props, its carnality and visceral shocks to the nervous system. In an essay on the cinema, Virginia Woolf describes film spectators, in terms that borrow from racist discourse, as twentieth-century "savages," whose eyes mindlessly "lick up" the screen.[13] Unlike film, literature is seen as channeled on a higher, more cerebral, transsensual and out-of-body plane. While novels are absorbed through the mind's eye during reading, films directly engage the various senses. As the cognitive theorists point out, films have impact on our stomach, heart, and skin, working through "neural structures" and "visuo-motor schemata."[14] Vivian Sobchack, following on Merleau-Ponty, calls film the "expression of experience by experience," which deploys kinetic, haptic, and sensuous modes of embodied existence.[15] Although novel reading as well as film spectatorship constitutes a purely mental event, novels are not literally seen through lenses, projected on wide screens, or heard in sounds measurable in decibels, sounds which can break glass or damage eardrums.

Films, then, are more directly implicated in bodily response than novels. They are felt upon the pulse, whether through the in-your-face gigantism of close-ups (which shocked Griffith's contemporaries), the visual impact of "flicker effects," or the vertiginous effect of Cinerama-style roller-coaster sequences, or the bodily register of jiggly, hand-held camera movements or "thrill cam" plunges. (The thumping, whooshing sound tracks and adrenaline-fueled editing of action blockbusters clearly exploit this corporeal side of cinema.) Kinetic and kinesthetic, films can provoke physical nausea or mental disorientation. Montage specialist Slavko Vorkapich spoke of motor impulses "passed through joints, muscles, and tendons so that at the end we duplicate internally whatever it is we are watching."[16] Filmic mimesis generates a contagious energy; reading a book about the dancing of Gene Kelly does not necessarily make us want to dance, but actually seeing him perform means we feel like we "gotta dance." In film, to kidnap Gloucester's words in *King Lear*, we "see it feelingly." The important point is that for some literary minds the cinema's engagement with bodies – the body of the performer, the body of the spectator, and even the "skin" and the "haptic visuality" of the "body" of the film itself[17] – discredits it as a serious, transcendent, art form. The body–mind hierarchy which informs the image–word prejudice then gets mapped onto other binaristic hierarchies such as surface–depth, so that films are dismissed as dealing in surfaces, literally "superficial."[18]

A sixth source of hostility to adaptation is what I would call **the myth of facility**, the completely uninformed and somewhat puritanical notion that films are suspectly easy to make and suspectly pleasurable to watch. This myth relays, first of all, a cliché about production: "a director merely films what's there." This idea is subliminally linked to what might be called "apparatusism," the by-now-discredited and technologically deterministic assumption that the cinema, as a mechanical means of reproduction, merely registers external appearances, and therefore cannot be art. At the same time, "facility" relays a cliché about reception: the idea, as one of my literature professors once put it, that "it takes no brains to sit down and watch a film." This is rather like saying that it takes no brains to sit down and turn the pages of a novel; what matters, in both cases, is understanding what one sees or reads. On the production side, the facility myth ignores the diversified talents and Herculean efforts required actually to make films. On the reception side, it ignores the intense perceptual and conceptual labor – the work of iconic designation, visual deciphering, narrative inference, and construction – inherent in film. Like novels of any complexity, films too bear "rereading," precisely because so much can be missed in a single viewing. That is also why we can see a film like Hitchcock's *Rear Window* (1954), also an adaptation, over and over, long after the "suspense" has faded, for the music-like beauty of its forms.

A seventh source of the hostility to the cinema and adaptation is a subliminal form of **class prejudice**, a socialized form of guilt by association. The cinema, perhaps unconsciously, is seen as degraded by the company it keeps – the great unwashed popular mass audience, with its lower-class origins in "vulgar" spectacles like sideshows and carnivals. Through a class-based dichotomy, literature pays indirect, and begrudging, homage to film's popularity, while film pays homage to literature's prestige. Adaptations, in this view, are the inevitably "dumbed down" versions of their source novels, designed to gratify an audience lacking in what Bourdieu calls "cultural capital," an audience which prefers the cotton candy of entertainment to the gourmet delights of literature. The frequent charge against adaptations that they have "vulgarized" – from the Latin "vulgus" or "people" – bears the etymological traces of this prejudice, which is also stereotypically split along gender lines, projecting, on the one hand, a crude, boisterous, male, working-class spectator, and, on the other, a passive, distracted, dreamy, female spectator.

A final source of hostility to adaptation is the charge of **parasitism**. Adaptations are seen as parasitical on literature; they burrow into the body of the source text and steal its vitality. How often have journalistic reviews claimed that an adaptation has "drained the life out" of the original?[19] Yet adaptations are seen are mere illustrations of the novel, and reviewers constantly trot out the same hackneyed put-down — that an adaptation is only "the Classics Illustrated" version of the novel. As Kamilla Elliot points out, adaptations are perceived as doubly "less;" they are less as novels because they are only copies of the original, but they are also less as films because they do not represent "pure film;" they lack "representational fluency on [their] own grounds."[20] Adaptation criticism purveys a series of such "double binds" and "Catch 22s." A "faithful" film is seen as uncreative, but an "unfaithful" film is a shameful betrayal of the original. An adaptation that updates the text for the present is upbraided for not respecting the period of the source, but respectful costume dramas are accused of a failure of nerve in not "contemporizing" the text. If an adaptation renders the sexual passages of the source novel literally, it is accused of vulgarity; if it fails to do so, it is accused of cowardice. The adapter, it seems, can never win.

Robert Stam

The Impact of the Posts

Structuralist and poststructuralist theoretical developments, meanwhile, subvert many of these prejudices and hierarchies, and thus indirectly have an impact on our conversation about adaptation. The structuralist semiotics of the 1960s and 1970s treated all signifying practices as shared sign systems productive of "texts" worthy of the same careful scrutiny as literary texts, thus abolishing the hierarchy between novel and film. The intertextuality theory of Kristeva (rooted in and literally translating Bakhtin's "dialogism") and the "transtextuality" theory of Genette, similarly, stressed the endless permutation of textualities rather than the "fidelity" of a later text to an earlier model, and thus also impact on our thinking about adaptation. Roland Barthes's provocative leveling of the hierarchy between literary criticism and literature, by the same token, worked by analogy to rescue the film adaptation as a form of criticism or "reading" of the novel, one not necessarily subordinate to or parasitic on its source.

Although intertextuality theory certainly reshaped adaptation studies, other aspects of poststructuralism have not yet been marshaled in the rethinking of the status and practice of adaptation. Derridean deconstruction, for example, undid overly rigid binarisms in favor of notions of "mutual invagination." Deconstruction also dismantled the hierarchy of "original" and "copy." In a Derridean perspective, the auratic prestige of the original does not run counter to the copy; rather, the prestige of the original is **created** by the copies, without which the very idea of originality has no meaning. The film as "copy," furthermore, can be the "original" for subsequent "copies." A film adaptation as "copy," by analogy, is not necessarily inferior to the novel as "original." The Derridean critique of origins is literally true in relation to adaptation. The "original" always turns out to be partially "copied" from something earlier: *The Odyssey* goes back to anonymous oral formulaic stories, *Don Quixote* goes back to chivalric romances, *Robinson Crusoe* goes back to travel journalism, and so on ad infinitum.

Introduction

The poststructuralist interrogation of the unified subject, meanwhile, fissured the author as point of origin of art. In the Lacanian view, the self is an "ego-artifact," a discursive fiction based on a bric-a-brac of identificatory impulses, always on the verge of dissolution. The psyche only **seems** to be unified, consistent, and centered. Bakhtin's notion of author and character as multi-discursive and resistant to unification, similarly, problematized both author and character as stable and unitary entities. Unlike new criticism's notions of organic unity, poststructuralist criticism emphasized the fissures, aporias, and excesses of the text. And if authors are fissured, fragmented, multi-discursive, hardly "present" even to themselves, the analyst may inquire, how can an adaptation communicate the "spirit" or "self-presence" of authorial intention?

The Bakhtinian "proto-poststructuralist" conception of the author as the orchestrator of pre-existing discourses, along with Foucault's downgrading of the author in favor of a "pervasive anonymity of discourse," opened the way to a non-originary approach to all arts. Bakhtin's attitude toward the literary author as inhabiting "inter-individual territory" suggested a devalorization of artistic "originality." Despite the perennial comparisons of the artist to a god, demiurge, creator, or progenitor, the artist's actual role, for Bakhtin, is caught up in more modest, more typically human interactions. As what Bakhtin calls a "hybrid construction," the artistic utterance always mingles one's own word with the other's word. Adaptation too, in this view, can be seen as an orchestration of discourses, talents, and tracks, a "hybrid" construction mingling different media and discourses and collaborations. Complete originality is neither possible nor even desirable. And if "originality" in literature is downplayed, the "offense" in "betraying" that originality, for example through an "unfaithful" adaptation, is that much the less grave.

Speaking more generally, the move away from the "work" to more diffuse notions like "textuality," "écriture," and "the literary" facilitates a retracing of boundaries which allows for more inclusive categories, within which adaptation becomes simply another "zone" on a larger and more variegated map. As theory discovers the "literariness" of non-literary phenomena, qualities thought to be literary turn out to be crucial to non-literary discourses and practices. The inclusion of the subliterary into the literary, the rethinking of the very category of the literary as an unstable, open-ended configuration, in this sense, makes for a more tolerant view of what has often been seen as a "sub-literary" and "parasitic" genre – the adaptation.

Cultural Studies and Narratology

Other theoretical movements and trends also indirectly demote the literary text from its position of overweening authority and thus point to a possible reconceptualization of adaptation. The interdisciplinary field of "cultural studies," for example, has been less interested in establishing vertical hierarchies of value than in exploring "horizontal" relations between neighboring media. From a cultural studies perspective, adaptation forms part of a flattened out and newly egalitarian spectrum of cultural productions. Within a comprehensively textualized world of images and simulations, adaptation becomes just another text, forming part of a broad discursive continuum.

Narratology, meanwhile, grants cultural centrality to narrative **in general** as opposed to literary narrative alone. For narratology, human beings use stories as their principal means of making sense of things, not only in written fictions but all the time, and all the way down. Narratologists see story as kind of genetic material or DNA to be manifested in the body of specific texts; they speak of narrative kernels existing "below" specific media. Narrative is protean, taking varied forms, from personal narratives of everyday life, to the myriad public forms of narrative – cartoons, stories, TV commercials, the evening news and, of course, film.[21] Literature, and the novel, no longer occupy a privileged position; adaptation, by implication, takes up a legitimate place alongside the novel, as just one more narratological medium. (We will return to the narratology of adaptation below.)

Reception theory, too, indirectly authorizes more respect for adaptation as a form. For reception theory, a text is an event, whose indeterminacies are completed and actualized in the reading (or spectating). Rather than being merely portrayals of a pre-existing reality, both novel and film are communicative utterances, socially situated and historically shaped. Like poststructuralism, reception theory, too, undermines the notion of a semantic core, a nucleus of meaning, ascribable to novels, which adaptations are presumed to "capture" or "betray," and thus clears space for the idea of adaptation as supplementing the gaps of the literary text. Furthermore, contemporary theory assumes that texts do not know themselves, and therefore seeks out the unsaid (the **non-dit**) of texts. Adaptations, in this sense, might be seen as filling in the lacunae of the source novels, calling attention to their structuring absences. This "filling in" is especially common in adaptations of long-consecrated texts, such as *Robinson Crusoe*, where the passage of time has made readers/adapters skeptical about the novels' basic premises and assumptions.

Thinkers from other fields, such as philosophy, have also questioned the hierarchy that places literature and philosophy "above" cinema. For Gilles Deleuze, cinema is itself a philosophical instrument, a generator of concepts which renders thought in audiovisual terms, not in language but in blocks of movement and duration. The Deleuzian view rejects the long-held idea that cinema, unlike literature and philosophy, is "incapable of thought." Deleuze does not "apply" philosophical concepts to the cinema; rather, he works with the concepts that cinema itself gives rise to. In the cinema, thought-in-movement meets the image-in-movement. Indeed, Deleuze is interested in commensurabilities and intercuttings between the history of philosophy and the history of cinema, the conceptual moves that link Eisenstein to Hegel, for example, or modern cinema to Nietzsche or Bergson. At the same time, Deleuze points to a new possible language for speaking of adaptations in terms not of copy but of transformational energies and movements and intensities.

Performativity theory, for its part, offers an alternative language for addressing adaptation, by which both novel and adaptation become performances, one verbal and the other visual, verbal, and acoustic. The concept of the performative utterance, developed in the

1950s by British philosopher J. L. Austin, and subsequently reworked by Jacques Derrida and Judith Butler, is rooted in Austin's distinction between *constative* utterances, which make a statement, describe a state of affairs, and are true or false, and *performative* utterances, which are not true or false but actually perform the action to which they refer. Just as the literary utterance **creates** the state of affairs to which it refers – rather than merely imitating some pre-existing state of affairs – so the filmic adaptation might be said to create a new audiovisual–verbal state of affairs, rather than merely imitating the old state of affairs as represented by the source novel.[22]

Finally, the whole constellation of currents – multiculturalism, postcoloniality, normative race, queer theory, feminist standpoint theory – revolving around issues of identity and oppression, also have an impact on the theory of adaptation. What these currents have in common is their egalitarian thrust, their critique of quietly assumed, unmarked normativities which place whiteness, Europeanness, maleness, and heterosexuality at the center, while marginalizing all that is not normative. The implications for adaptation studies are multifold: (1) a revisionist view of the literary canon and the inclusion of minority, postcolonial, and queer writers; (2) a revisionist view of literary history which tends to have a Euro-diffusionist view of the evolution of the novel, whereby the novel begins in Europe (*Don Quixote, Robinson Crusoe*) and then "spreads" around the world, when in fact the novel as "prose fiction of a certain length" can be traced back to Egypt, Mesopotamia, Persia, India, and so forth; (3) a changed view of oral literature as a legitimate form of literature (see Mbye Cham in Chapter 14 of this volume); (4) a change in the protocols of reading both novels and films, in ways that are sensitive to the multicultural and racial dimensions of all texts; and (5) the possibility of revisionist adaptations, such as *Man Friday*, which take multicultural currents into account.

Adaptation in a Post-celluloid World

The sequence of innovations in film technology – sound, color, 3D, digital editing – have also clearly had an impact on the production and reception of cinema, and this too has implications for adaptation. In the contemporary period, VCRs and widely available "portable" videos have "domesticated" the conditions of film viewing, bringing them closer to the conditions of novel reading. Packaged videos even physically resemble books in size and format; the videoteque resembles the biblioteque. Adaptation must therefore also be considered in the light of this final "post," to wit the post-celluloid world of the new media: the Internet, electronic games, CD Roms, DVDs, virtual environments and interactive installations.[23] Just as Umberto Eco predicted that literature would be changed by the existence of word processors, so film production and consumption – and adaptation theory – will be irrevocably changed by the digital revolution.

One linguistic byproduct of the new media is the generation of new metaphors for speaking about adaptation. In new media lingo, "transcoding," for example, designates the translation of one "text" into a new format, an apt image for adaptation itself as a "reformatting" or "transcoding" of the novel. More importantly, the cinema in its long-heralded specificity now seems to be dissolving into the larger bitstream of the audiovisual media, whether photographic, electronic, or cybernetic. Since digital media potentially incorporate all previous media into a vast cyber archive, it makes less sense to think in media-specific terms. Novels, films, and adaptations take their place alongside one another as relative co-equal neighbors or collaborators rather than as father and son or master and slave.

The new technologies, and the theories associated with them, also undermine, in their way, ideas of purity and essence. Many analysts, such as Landow and Moulthrope, have noted a kind of convergence between poststructuralist theory and the new media.[24] Is it an accident that the term "hypertext" first emerged from literary theory? But, in broader terms, digital imaging "de-ontologizes" the indexical, Bazinian image. Images themselves are no longer "faithful" to any pro-filmic model. Within a regime of freeplay downloading and infinite reproducibility, there is no loss of quality since the images are stored as pixels, with no "original." Indeed, filmmakers no longer need a pro-filmic model in the world; like novelists, they can give artistic form to abstract dreams. No longer a copy, the image acquires its own dynamism within an interactive circuit, freed of the contingencies of location shooting, inclement weather, and so forth.

The new technologies have already impacted upon adaptation and will do so even more in the future. Raúl Ruiz's hypertext project, conducted while the director was teaching at Duke University, as Marsha Kinder points out, fed into Ruiz's adaptation of Proust in *Time Regained* (2000).[25] Digital media make spectacular effects inexpensive and thus "available" even to relatively low-budget films. Thus Atom Egoyan in his adaptation of Russell Banks's *The Sweet Hereafter* can send a virtual school bus skidding over a cliff onto a frozen lake, for a bare fraction of what it would have cost to film the same scene with an actual bus. The digital media have further undermined the notion of original and copy by making virtually everything "copyable," so that the language of "originality" gives way to a language of cut 'n' mix and sampling. At the same time, Siva Vaidhyanathan points to counter-currents, as theory and practice part ways when "intellectual property" laws reassert the rights either of authors or of the corporate owners of art. Copyright law is more and more about the rights of publishers and corporations, with both author and public in a subordinate position. "We can deconstruct the author for six more decades," Vaidyanathan points out, "and still fail to prevent the impending concentration of the content, ownership, control, and delivery of literature, music, and data."[26]

In another sense, the digital media have produced a kind of mutation in the very notion of filmic "writing." While the New Wave directors saw the shooting of the film as a form of improvisational **écriture**, with the camera as "pen," filmic writing in the digital age is more linked to hypertextual collaging and digital re-editing in the post-production phase. But, beyond that, the new media – for example, web-based hypertext fiction – will probably provoke a major mutation in writing generally. A hypertext like Shelley Jackson's *Patchwork Girl* (1995), as Tom LeClair points out, refigures both L. Frank Baum's

Patchwork Girl of Oz and Mary Shelley's *Frankenstein*. Such a hypertext already shares some features with film adaptations, since it is partially visual, combining pictures and words. The first image to come up on screen is that of a woman pieced together and crossed by a dotted line. The next link is a title page with collaborative authors: Mary Shelley and Shelley Jackson. This matrix then leads to various sequences of narrative and metafictional texts which counterpoint two stories, one about the female-companion monster created by Frankenstein but denied life at the last minute, the other the reflexive "story" of the composition of Patchwork Girl's body and personality and of the "patchwork" hypertext itself.[27]

How, then, might the new technologies facilitate new approaches to adaptation and to adaptation studies? While this is not the place for a thoroughgoing discussion, we can permit ourselves a few brief speculations. Laser disks and DVDs which include sequences cut from released versions of films implicitly cast doubt on the idea of the "original" or definitive text, revealing its status as the arbitrary result of constantly changing decisions about inclusion and exclusion. But apart from that, a CD-Rom, for example, might easily juxtapose all the filmic adaptations of a given passage from *Great Expectations*. Or a morphing technique could have all the actresses who have played Emma Bovary blend into one another, or help us imagine an actress of a different ethnicity. Digital environments might allow us to interact with revised versions of fictional characters through digitally created "synthespians" or "vactors" (i.e. virtual actors), "avatars" and "cyberstars." A literary character like Don Quixote could be inserted into cyber-space in the form of an intelligent agent programmed with a repertoire of behavioral traits (in Quixote's case, a penchant for attributing magical or demonic powers to innocuous objects) and then placed into new environments. A three-dimensional simulation might convey the atmosphere of a Victorian novel, or make us feel in our guts the symbiotic relationship between decor and character in Balzac's *Père Goriot*, or between mine and miner in Zola's *Germinal*. A cyber-maze version of *L'Année dernière à Marienbad* could add still another labyrinthine dimension to that already maze-like text. Disconnected lexias could render Joycean "streams of consciousness." Virtual reality and mobile spectatorship could amplify the kinesthetic dynamism of Proust's depiction of the steeples of Combray. Virtual reality could make it possible for spectators to "plug into" the experience of Emma Bovary's suicide, much as the spectator-characters in the film *Strange Days* (1995) inserted themselves into the personal traumas of strangers. A holodeck version of *In Remembrance of Things Past* could induce delusional sensations as a way of rendering obsessional jealousy. Multitrack sound could render the heteroglossia of voices and accents in Joyce's *Ulysses*. The magical duplication of crowds, the possibility of digitally "resurrecting" deceased actors, also bring new possibilities for the adaptation of, say, "magical realist" novels. The new media could also generate new forms of fiction, which would then through a feedback loop be susceptible themselves to innovative forms of adaptation. Given that filmmaking, as Jean-Pierre Geuens points out, is now losing its "aura" of difficulty, one wonders if digital media will make old-style celluloid filmmaking so obsolete that all the existing film adaptations of novels will have to be redone in digital formats?[28] Could old-style film adaptations become, as it were, a new form of "novel" vis-à-vis digital "adaptations?"

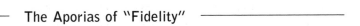

The Aporias of "Fidelity"

In the light of all these "posts," it is important to move beyond the moralistic and judgmental ideal of "fidelity." At the same time, we have to acknowledge at the outset that "fidelity," however discredited theoretically, does retain a grain of experiential truth. Fidelity discourse asks important questions about the filmic recreation of the setting, plot, characters, themes, and the style of the novel. When we say an adaptation has been "unfaithful" to the original, the very violence of the term gives expression to the intense sense of betrayal we feel when a film adaptation fails to capture what we see as the fundamental narrative, thematic, or aesthetic features of its literary source. The notion of fidelity gains its persuasive power from our sense that (a) some adaptations are indeed better than others, and (b) some adaptations fail to "realize" or substantiate what we most appreciated in the source novels. Words like "infidelity" and "betrayal" in this sense translate our feeling, when we have loved a book, that an adaptation has not been worthy of that love.

Russell Banks describes novelistic writing/reading as an intimate exchange between strangers, a secret sharing.[29] We read a novel "through" our introjected desires, hopes, and utopias, fashioning as we read our own imaginary *mise-en-scène* of the novel on the private sound stage of our mind. Interestingly, little has been written about the reverse sequence, when the spectator sees the adaptation **before** reading the novel. Does the reader then retrospectively project the actor's face (say Jeremy Irons's face in *Un amour de Swann*) onto the novel's character, in a kind of mental superimposition? Do readers who have seen the film *Jules and Jim* (1961) mentally "hear" the music track as they read the novel? Are the readers who encounter the adaptation first similarly disappointed that the source novel has not managed to capture the specific pleasures of the film version? Are they annoyed or agreeably surprised that the novel has "added" the unnecessary descriptions "edited out" of the film version? Does the film then become the experiential "original" betrayed by the actual original? Or is the reader, whose appetite has merely been whetted by the film, exhilarated to discover the incomparable riches of the verbal text?

The words of a novel have a virtual, symbolic meaning; we, as readers, fill in their paradigmatic indeterminances. A novelist's portrayal of a character induces us to imagine the person's features in our own imagination. While the reader moves from the printed word to visualizing the objects portrayed, the spectator moves in the opposite direction, from the flux of images to naming the objects portrayed and identifying the events recounted. A film actualizes the virtual through specific choices. Instead of a virtual, verbally constructed Madame Bovary open to our imaginative reconstruction, we are faced with an embodied performer, encumbered with nationality and accent, a Carol Lynley or a Dominique Swain. When we are confronted with someone else's phantasy of a novel, as Metz pointed out in the 1970s, we feel the loss of our own phantasmatic relation to the source text, with the result that the adaptation itself becomes a kind of "bad object." The clichéd response that "I thought the book was better" in this sense really means that our experience, our phantasy of the book was better than the director's.[30] Kubrick's Lolita, or Adrian Lyne's, was not the woman we had phantasized. To paraphrase the Georges Perec lines about films borrowed by Godard in *Masculin féminin* (1965): "We left the theatre sad. It was not the [adaptation] of which we had dreamed . . . It wasn't the [adaptation] we would have liked to make. Or, more secretly, that we would have liked to live."[31]

"Fidelity discourse" relies on essentialist arguments in relation to **both** media. First, it assumes that a novel "contains" an extractable "essence," a kind of "heart of the artichoke" hidden "underneath" the surface details of style. Hidden within *War and Peace*, there is an originary core, a kernel of meaning and events which can be "delivered" by an adaptation. But, in fact, there is no such transferable core: a single novelistic text comprises a series of verbal signals that can trigger a plethora of possible readings. An open structure, constantly reworked and reinterpreted by a boundless context, the text feeds on and is fed into an infinitely permutating intertext, seen through ever-shifting grids of interpretation. In fact, when critics refer to the "spirit" or "essence" of a literary text what they usually mean is the critical consensus within an "interpretative community" (Stanley Fish) about the meaning of the work.[32]

The question of fidelity also ignores the wider question of fidelity to what? Is the filmmaker to be faithful to the plot in its every detail? That might mean a thirty-hour version of *War and Peace*. Should one be faithful to the physical descriptions of characters? Perhaps so, but what if the performer who happens to fit the physical description of a character also happens to be a mediocre actor? Or is one to be faithful to the author's intentions? But what might **they** be, and how are they to be determined? In cases where an author, for example Nabokov, writes a screenplay for his own novel, should the filmmaker be faithful to the novel or the screenplay? What about cases where a novelist/filmmaker, for example the Senegalese novelist/filmmaker Sembène in *Xala*, is "unfaithful" to his **own** novel? And what about cases, such as the French **cine-roman**, where it is no longer an issue of adapting a prior text but rather one of engendering parallel, simultaneous, autonomous creations, one literary and the other filmic?

A fundamental unfairness plagues "fidelity" discourse, reflected in a differential and even prejudiced application of the very concept, depending on **which** art is being considered. It is adaptation in the cinema, particularly of novels, that has been especially castigated and held to an absurdly rigorous standard of "fidelity." The ideal of a single, definitive, faithful adaptation does not hold sway in other media. In the theater, conceptual reinterpretation and performative innovation – for example, in Orson Welles's modern-dress *Julius Caesar* or his Haiti-set "Voodoo" *Macbeth* – are seen as normal, even prized. Popular music, similarly, is endlessly sampled and "versioned." While filmic rewritings of novels are judged in terms of fidelity, **literary** rewritings of classical texts, such as Coetzee's rewriting of *Robinson Crusoe* are **not** so judged – change is presumed to be the point! Why should we assume that one director, for example John Houston, has said everything that needs to be said about *Moby Dick*? If one has nothing new to say about a novel, Orson Welles once suggested, why adapt it at all? Simply adapting a novel without changing it, suggested Alain Resnais, is like reheating a meal.

The Automatic Difference

Crucial to any discussion of adaptation is the question of media specificity. What can films do that novels cannot? Are some stories "naturally" better suited to some media rather than others? Are magical stories best rendered as animated cartoons? Can stories "migrate" from a less appropriate to a more appropriate medium? Do stories pre-exist their mediation? Is there a digital narrative code, based on binary bits, to be found in some ideal Platonic cybernetic realm, which archives, as it were, the diacritical differences that constitute *Cinderella* or *Little Red Riding Hood* prior to their being programmed within an actual medium?

The demand for fidelity ignores the actual processes of making films, the important differences in modes of production. While a novelist's choices are relatively unconstrained by considerations of budget – all the writer needs is time, talent, paper, and pen – films are from the outset immersed in technology and commerce. While novels are relatively unaffected by questions of budget, films are deeply immersed in material and financial contingencies. Thus grand panoramic novels like *War and Peace* are difficult to film on a low budget, while interiorized novellas like *Notes from Underground* seem more manageable. With the novel, questions of material infrastructure enter only at the point of distribution, while in the cinema they enter at the very start of the production of the film itself. While a novel can be written on napkins in prison, a film assumes a complex material infrastructure (camera, film stock, laboratories) simply in order to exist. While it costs almost nothing for a novelist to write "The Marquis left Versailles Palace at 5pm on a cold and wintry day in January 1763," the filmmaker requires substantial sums in order to stage, for example, a sumulacral Paris (or to shoot on location), to dress the actors in period costume, and so forth.

All this inevitably has an impact on what scenes can be filmed. Does one stage, or choose to ignore, the account of the Battle of Waterloo in Stendhal's *The Charterhouse of Parma*? At the same time, a larger budget is not always better. Godard has argued that big budgets **destroy** films by pushing them in reactionary, lowest-common-denominator directions, toward Manicheanism and sentimentality. When the budget exceeds a certain sum, Paul Schrader has said, the director "has to put white hats on the good guys."[33] The low-budget production values of dos Santos's adaptation of Ramos's novel *Vidas secas* (Barren Lives), in this sense, work to the film's advantage, fostering what Glauber

Rocha called an "aesthetics of hunger," a synchronicity between the poverty of the signifier (the lack of sophisticated crane or tracking shots, the contrasty black-and-white cinematography) and the poverty of the signified: the famished lives of poor people in the arid northeast of Brazil.

The shift, in adaptation, from a single-track, uniquely verbal medium such as the novel to a multitrack medium like film, which can play not only with words (written and spoken) but also with music, sound effects, and moving photographic images, explains the unlikelihood, and I would suggest even the **undesirability**, of literal fidelity. Along with the semiotic differences, practical and material contingencies also render fidelity in adaptation virtually impossible. A novel is, usually, produced by a single individual; the film, almost always, is a collaborative project, mobilizing at minimum a crew of four or five people and at maximum a cast and crew and support staff of hundreds. Nabokov once compared this process to a "communal bath where the hairy and the slippery mix in a multiplication of mediocrity."[34]

Apart from budgetary constraints or possibilities, there are issues of available talent, studio or producer pressures, censorship in terms of performers, screenwriters, editors, and so forth. The MGM studio style, in the case of Minnelli's *Madame Bovary* (1949), brings with it musical production numbers. The improvisational skills of certain actors, such as Peter Sellers and Robin Williams, push adaptations in a performative direction. Peter Sellers's shape-shifting performance as Quilty in *Lolita* (1962) is arguably the most "Nabokovian" feature of the Kubrick adaptation.[35]

For all these reasons, fidelity in adaptation is literally impossible. A filmic adaptation is **automatically** different and original due to the change of medium. Here we can take as our own Fritz Lang's response (in *Contempt*, 1963) to the producer Prokosch's accusation of infidelity to the script: "Yes, Jerry, in the script it's written, in a film it's a picture . . . a motion picture it's called." Even a "faithful" adaptation might take many forms. If one were to take a canonical realist novel such as *The Grapes of Wrath* and ask five "faithful" and "realist" directors to adapt it, the results would vary widely, for a very simple reason. Filmmaking generally, and adaptation in particular, involves thousands of **choices**, concerning performers, budget, locale, format, props, and so forth. It is unimaginable, therefore, that the five adaptations, even by directors with similar aesthetic inclinations, would even closely resemble one another: there would be an infinity of subtle differences.

The "automatic difference" between novel and film is evident even in fairly straightforward adaptations of specific novelistic passages by "realist" directors. In the case of the John Ford adaptation of *The Grapes of Wrath*, for example, a putatively realist director adopts a putatively realist/naturalist novel, just a few months after the novel's publication, in what most would regard as a "faithful" rendition, yet even here the "cinematization" generates an "automatic difference." Take, for example, the passage, from Steinbeck's *Grapes of Wrath*, in which Ma Joad contemplates her memorabilia just before leaving her Oklahoma home for California:

> She sat down and opened the box. Inside were letters, clippings, photographs, a pair of ear-
> rings, a little gold signet ring, and a watch chain braided of hair and tipped with gold swivels.
> She touched the letters with her fingers, touched them lightly, and she smoothed a news-
> paper clipping on which there was an account of Tom's trial.

In the film version of this passage, we do indeed see Ma Joad sit down, open the box, and look at letters, clippings, photographs, and so forth. But even here the "cinematization" generates an inevitable supplement. Where Steinbeck writes "photographs," Ford has to choose specific photographs. The mention of "earrings," in the novel, does not dictate Ford's choice of having Ma Joad try them on. The newspaper account of Tom's trial requires the choice of a specific newspaper, specific headlines, illustrations, fonts, none of which is spelled out in the original. But beyond such details of *mise-en-scène*, the very processes of filming – the fact that the shots have to be composed, lit, and edited in a certain way – generates an "automatic difference." The idea that film must always be reductively literal as compared to the novel is undercut by the synergistic interaction between tracks. Thus nothing in the novel prepares us for the idea that Ma Joad will look at the memorabilia by the light of a fire, the reflections of which will flicker over her face. Nothing dictates the point-of-view editing which alternates close shots of Ma Joad's face with what she sees, within a contemplative rhythm of shot/reverse shot. Nor does the Steinbeck passage mention music, yet the Ford version features a melancholy accordion version of the song "Red River Valley." Even if the text **had** mentioned "Red River Valley" that would still have been quite different from our actually hearing it performed. And even if the passage **had** mentioned both the music and the firelight, and the light's flickering over Ma Joad's face, that would still not have been anything like our seeing her face and hearing the music **at the same time.**[36]

Specificity and the Multiplication of Registers

Fidelity theory does not always name itself as such. It sometimes takes the disguised form of respect for the "spirit" but not the "letter" of the text (a notion that implicitly inscribes Christian notions of "going beyond" the literalism of the Jewish Bible). Or it can take the form of "equivalency" theory, the idea that the filmmaker finds the "equivalents" in a new medium for the novelist's style or techniques. But, in fact, there can be no **real** equivalence between source novel and adaptation. While a film can recapitulate the outlines of the basic story – a summary of *Great Expectations* and of David Lean's adaptation will have much in common – the actual resulting texts in their densely signifying materiality will be in many ways incommensurable. Everything in literature is an act of language; it does recount but it does not literally represent or enact. According to Andre Gardies, we should regard the source novel as a kind of databank, where the

Robert Stam

Introduction

data are variously diegetic (places, characters), thematic (romance), generic (comedy, or science fiction), and formal (point of view, structure, rhythm). The widely varying formulae for adaptation – "based on the novel by," "inspired by," "free adaptation of" – indirectly acknowledge the impossibility of any real equivalency.[37]

Another variation on "fidelity" discourse suggests that an adaptation should be faithful not so much to the source text but rather to the essential traits of the **medium** of expression. This "medium-specificity" approach assumes that every medium is inherently "good at" certain things and "bad at" others.[38] A cinematic essence is posited as favoring certain aesthetic possibilities and foreclosing others, as if specific aesthetic norms were inscribed on the celluloid itself. The essentialist view of cinema as an exclusively visual medium, for example, leads to neglect of the verbal dimension of film. The cinema, and especially the sound film, is remarkably adept at the *mise-en-scène* of actual speech situations, at the visual and aural contextualization of speech. It can render those phenomena that lie on the border of the verbal and the non-verbal, the spoken and the non-spoken. Film has special capacities for presenting the extraverbal aspects of discursive exchange. In the sound film, we do not only hear the words, with their accent and intonation, but we also witness the facial or corporeal expression that accompanies the words – the bodily postures of arrogance or resignation, the skeptically raised eyebrows, the look of distrust, the ironic glances – that modify the ostensible meaning. While a writer such as Proust can brilliantly evoke salon conversations through sinuous, elegant prose, a filmmaker like Cassavetes or Welles presents them, as it were, "in fact." For Bakhtin, words are saturated with "accents" and "intonations." Film directing consists in contextualizing the words not only through performance and *mise-en-scène*, but also through the other tracks (music, noise, written materials). Film is ideally suited for conveying the social and personal dynamics operating between interlocutors. Perhaps this is what Deleuze meant when he argued that of all the media only the cinema had managed to "grasp conversation for itself." For Deleuze, cinema invented "the sound conversation," something which had previously "escaped the theatre and the novel alike."[39]

In the novel, writers like Virginia Woolf and James Joyce tried to evoke "inner speech" or "stream of consciousness," through associative and fragmented forms, omitting verbs, pronouns, connectives, and articles, and leaving sentences uncompleted. A number of filmmakers, interestingly, have shown interest in cinematically rendering inner speech. Bakhtin's contemporary Eisenstein repeatedly expressed a desire to render the stream-of-consciousness monologues of Joyce's *Ulysses*, and Godard, in both *Une femme mariée* (1964) and *Two or Three Things I Know About Her* (1967), approximates inner speech through discontinuous and fragmentary voice-over commentaries. (The former film even echoes Joyce's rendition of Molly Bloom's orgasmic "yes, I said yes" as Charlotte's "oui, oui, oui.") Film spectatorship, according to Boris Eikhenbaum, is "accompanied by a constant process of internal speech," whereby images and sounds are projected onto a kind of verbal screen functioning as a "ground" for meaning.[40]

There is still another sense, however, in which film is "bathed by" and "suspended in" language. Films are saturated by language from the beginning to the end of their existence; they come from language and partially return to it. Films often initially take the form of verbal text or spoken performance: source play or novel, verbal synopsis, script, story conference. Upon completion, the film returns to language, again becoming the subject of verbal representation, in the form of verbal synopsis, "word of mouth" evaluations, journalistic reviews, scholarly text, classroom exegesis, *TV Guide* capsule summary, "thumbs up" Siskel-Ebert banter, and even "novelization." (This last, despised, subgenre of writing has generated such books as *The Mexican* and *The Gladiator*. Sean Penn's 1995 film *The Crossing Guard* was novelized by playwright David Rale in a version which some critics saw as superior to the film itself.) Filmic representations, in sum, which have never ceased to be partially linguistic, get translated back, by a rough exchange, once again into words. David Black speaks of "the synoptic tendency" whereby verbal recountability becomes a kind of gold standard for narrative exchange.[41] The fiction film too, then, exists within the powerful gravitational field of what Bakhtin calls "the word."

Despite fidelity criticism's discourse of loss, the cinema has not lesser but rather **greater** resources for expression than the novel, and this quite independent of what actual filmmakers have actually done with these resources. In a suggestive passage in Nabokov's *Lolita*, the narrator–protagonist Humbert Humbert expresses a kind of envy of the cinema. He laments the prodding deliberateness of prose fiction, its subordination to linear consecution, its congenital incapacity to seize the moment in its multifaceted simultaneity. Humbert deplores having to put "the impact of an instantaneous vision into a sequence of words." The "physical accumulation on the page," he complains, "impairs the actual flash, the sharp unity of impression."[42] But while Humbert Humbert lusts after the cinema's "fantastic simultaneousness," he might also envy its potential for **non**-simultaneity, its capacity for mingling apparently contradictory times and temporalities. While the novel is capable of the most supple forms of ironic double-voiced discourse, film's multitrack nature makes it possible to stage ironic contradictions between music and image. Thus the cinema offers synergistic possibilities of disunity and disjunction not immediately available to the novel. The possible contradictions and tensions between tracks become an aesthetic resource, opening the way to a multitemporal, polyrhythmic art form.[43]

Adaptation criticism has tended to emphasize the cinema's impairments and disabilities vis-à-vis the novel – its putative incapacity to convey tropes, dreams, memories, abstraction – yet, on almost any plane one might mention, cinematic adaptation brings, whether for good or ill, not an impoverishment but rather a **multiplication** of registers. Let us take, for example, the issue of "tense" in the cinema, about which a good deal of nonsense has been uttered. A common idea, purveyed even by a sophisticated writer like Robbe-Grillet, is that the cinema has only a single tense – the present – since in a film everything unrolls before our eyes, in the present. (Ironically, Robbe-Grillet's own films contradict his thesis, since they superimpose, in a heterochronotopic confusion, what Deleuze calls "sheets of time.") But on a phenomenological level, the same point could be made about reading novels: the action, even in an historical novel set in the distant past, always unrolls in the virtual present of our reading. Moreover, the cinema has tense even in the most literal sense, since its "languaged" tracks grant it all the moods and voices and tenses of verbal or written language. But quite apart from this linguistic capacity to mark tense, film offers myriad other ways of marking past time, or the passage of time, in non-verbal ways. In an earlier period, films used hackneyed visual tokens such as the flipping pages of a calendar. Or tense was indicated through conventional markers – a title, a lap-dissolve, or flashbacks – whether cued by a wavering image (as parodically invoked on the *David Letterman Show*) or by a change in lighting or color, or simply by the juxtaposition of a pensive face with a remembered image.

But the cinema can also convey "pastness" through a wide range of other means, notably: decor (a seventeenth-century chateau location); titles ("Paris, 1900"); color (sepia tints); undercranked cameras evocative of an earlier technology; make-up (the cosmetic aging of a character); archaic recording devices (*Zelig*, 1983); artificially "aged" footage (*Zelig* again); costume (as in any costume drama); music (from any period); paintings (from any period); props (vintage automobiles); and so forth. Furthermore, the cinema can deliberately scramble time periods by mingling the traces of two time periods within the same shot (*The Travelling Players*, 1975) where two epochs "invade," as it were, the same public square during the same continuous sequence shot), or by using the new technologies to scramble historical periods (*Forrest Gump*, 1994), or by using a single pan shot to link different time periods (*Lone Star*, 1996).

Furthermore, the cinema has available to it a remarkable mechanism through which it can "congeal" past time, to wit in the form of archival footage, i.e. images (and some-times sounds) literally registered in the past. In the novel *The Unbearable Lightness of Being*, Kundera refers to the "stills and motion pictures . . . stored in archives around the world" showing the 1968 Soviet invasion of Czechoslovakia. The Philip Kaufman adaptation of the Kundera novel, in contrast, includes actual TV reports on the invasion. The Truffaut adaptation of *Jules and Jim*, similarly, amplifies the novel's sparse allu-sions to the First World War by inserting archival footage of trench battles, thus affirming a pacifist dimension merely latent in the book. Films can even intermingle temporalities by mixing in various forms of congealed past time, such as past feature films (as in Resnais's *Mon oncle d'Amerique*, 1980) or documentaries and newsreels (as in *Zelig*). While novels such as Doctorow's *Ragtime* mix documentary and fictional materials, a film like *Zelig* can "quote" or even create fiction films, fake fiction films, real documentaries, and fake documentaries.

In sum, film is ideally equipped, thanks to its multitrack and multiformat nature, to magically multiply times and spaces. As a technology of representation, film has the capacity to mingle very diverse temporalities and spatialities. Produced within one con-stellation of times and spaces, the fiction film stages yet another diegetic constellation of times and spaces, and it is received in still another time and space (theater, home, classroom). The panoply of cinematic techniques further multiplies the possibilities. Unlike a novel, a film can be played backwards. Superimposition redoubles time and space, as do montage and multiple frames within the image. The fact that dominant cinema has largely opted for a linear and homogenizing aesthetic where track reinforces track within a Wagnerian totality cannot efface the equally salient fact that the cinema (and the new media) are infinitely rich in polyphonic potentialities.[44] The cinema makes it possible to stage temporalized cultural contradictions not only within the shot, through *mise-en-scène*, decor, costume, and so forth, but also through the interplay and contradictions between the diverse tracks, which can mutually shadow, jostle, undercut, haunt, and relativize one another. Each track can develop its own velocity; the image can be accelerated while the music is slowed, or the soundtrack can be temporally layered by references to diverse historical periods. A culturally polyrhythmic, heterochronic, multiple-velocity and contrapuntal cinema becomes a real possibility. Those who argue that cinema lacks "tense" forget these protean possibilities.

This same multiplication of tracts and registers also applies in relation to the filmic character. While no medium − whether theater, novel, film − really gives us direct access to a character, they do give us the forms of signification available to that particular medium − live performance in theater, verbal evocation in the novel, performance and *mise-en-scène* in film. Each medium deploys significant traces to trigger a sense of a character in the mind of the reader or spectator. Each medium, in this sense, brings gains and losses. Although filmic characters in adaptations lose some of the slowly evolving textured verbal complexity developed in a novel, they also gain an automatic "thickness" on the screen through bodily presence, posture, dress, and facial expression.

The absence of actors brings enormous advantages to the novelist: the author need not deal with performers' temper tantrums, pregnant actresses (as in Truffaut's *La Nuit Americaine*, 1973), or performers who inconveniently die (a recurring problem for Welles in relation to his *Don Quixote*). Unlike the purely verbal novelistic character, the cinematic character forms an uncanny amalgam of *photogenie*, body movement, acting style, gestures, locale, costume, accent and grain of voice, all amplified and molded by dialogue (what a character says and how he/she says it and what the other characters say about the character), lighting, props (*mise-en-scène*), and music. Like the filmmakers, performers too become, in their way, the adapters and interpreters of the novel, or at least of the screenplay, as they mold characters through gestural details, ways of walking or talking or smoking. Furthermore, filmic characters not only act, they also react and listen; they register surprise or boredom or curiosity, something usually left unspecified in a novel but absolutely crucial in film. Filmmakers, meanwhile, have the option of associating a given character with a specific kind of lighting, as when haloed backlighting gives a religious aura (for example, to the pious protagonist of Rohmer's *Ma nuit chez Maud*, 1969) or with a style of editing (as when Catherine, in *Jules and Jim*, is associated with fragmented, discontinuous, deliberately mis-edited shots, an intimation of her own "discontinuous" and capricious personality).

While novels have only a single entity − the character − filmic adaptations have both character (actantial function) and performer.[45] The doubleness of filmic representation allows for possibilities of interplay and contradiction denied a purely verbal medium. In the cinema, a single actor can play many characters − for example, Peter Sellers's multiple roles in *The Mouse that Roared*, 1959 or *Dr Strangelove*, 1964 − or, conversely, multiple performers can play a **single** character: the four incarnations of Christ in Rocha's

Robert Stam

Introduction

Age of the Earth (1977). The Pierre Louiys's novel *The Woman and the Puppet* features only one entity – the character Conchita – whereas the Buñuel adaptation of the novel, *That Obscure Object of Desire* (1977), features three (or even four) entities: the character Conchita; the **two** actresses (Angela Molina and Carole Bouquet) who play the role of Conchita; and the dubber who lends her voice to both actresses. The unity on the characterological plane is split on the performance plane; and then recast and reunified again on the plane of postsynchronization.

Decades ago, Christian Metz spoke of the "*rendezvous manqué*" between actor and spectator in the cinema; the actor, present during the production of the film, is absent during its reception in the theater. Although the filmic performer has a signal advantage denied the novelistic character – to wit, his or her bodily existence – that existence is mediated by film's imaginary signifier; it is turned into an absence, and thus made even more "available" for our projections. While literary characters are like ghastly, hologrammatic entities cued by the text and projected (and introjected) by readers, filmic characters are at once projected **and** embodied. Our projections spread themselves, as it were, not over the virtualities of the verbal text but rather "over" the actually existing body and performance of the actor, which cues and receives and resists our projections. (In the case of body doubles and stunt persons, we actually project a false unity over **two** bodies.) Adaptations of novels thus provoke a tension between the characters as constructed and projected during our reading, and the embodied actors/characters witnessed on screen. Our spectatorial impressions are further shaped by what we already know about the actors' performances, and even, in the case of stars, of what we know about their three-dimensional lives, their sexual relationships, and their opinions and feelings as channeled by the mass media, all of which feed into the reception of the performance.

The character/actor dynamic elicits a series of questions. Does the actor in the adaptation "fit" the verbal description of the character in the novel in terms of physical attributes, ethical traits, and so forth? How does the specific performer add to or detract from or change the character through intertextual or contextual echoes? Does the performer follow the script like Jeremy Irons or improvise like Robin Williams and Peter Sellers? How does Oprah Winfrey's status as celebrity talk-show host affect the reception of her performance in the film *Beloved* (1998)?[46] In her adaptation of Virginia Woolf's *Orlando*, Sally Potter wittily casts the flamboyantly effeminate Quentin Crisp as "Queen" Elizabeth. What is the impact of the performer's other roles? How do Jack Palance's earlier roles as gangsters and tough guys bleed into his role as producer in Godard's *Contempt*? Or think of the immense effort required for Robin Williams to erase his stand-up persona to be considered a serious actor.

The multiplication of registers also has to do with the fact that the cinema is both a synesthetic and a synthetic art. Film is synesthetic in its capacity to engage various senses (sight/hearing), while it is synthetic in its anthropophagic hunger to devour and digest and change antecedent arts. A composite language by virtue of its diverse matters of expression, the cinema "inherits" all the art forms associated with these matters of expression. It has available to it the visuals of photography and painting, the movement of dance, the decor of architecture, the harmonies of music, and the performance of theater. Adaptation, in this sense, creates an active weave, a relational tissue wrought from these various strands. Perhaps the relation between source novel and adaptation is less like that between original and copy than that between the sounds and styles and verbal snippets that are "sampled" in a rap CD, where what counts is not the "fidelity" but, rather, the automatically new interweaving that has taken place.

Summas by their very nature, both the novel and the fiction film have no essence; they are open to all cultural forms. But still even here the cinema has resources unavailable to the novel. The cinema can literally include painting, poetry, and music or it can meta-phorically evoke them by imitating their procedures; it can show a Picasso painting, or emulate cubist techniques, cite a Bach cantata, or create montage equivalents of fugue and counterpoint. Godard's *Passion* (1982) not only includes music (Ravel, Mozart, Ferre, Beethoven, Fauré) but is conceived musically. It not only shows animated tableaux based on celebrated paintings (Rembrandt's *Night Watch*, Goya's *The Third of May*) but also demonstrates a painterly sensitivity to light and color. The famous definitions of cinema in terms of other arts – "painting in motion" (Canudo); "sculpture in motion" (Vachel Lindsay); "music of light" (Abel Gance); "architecture in movement" (Elie Faure) – merely call attention to the synthetic multiplicity of signifiers available to the cinema. Adaptations can take advantage of this multiplicity by amplifying artistic references, as when Pasolini, in his *The Gospel According to Saint Matthew* (1964), draws not only on the Bible itself but also on the various forms of painting and music which the Bible inspired.[47]

------------------------- **From Fidelity to Intertextuality** -------------------------

We need, therefore, a new language and a new set of tropes for speaking about adapta-tion. If "fidelity" is an inadequate trope, what tropes might be more appropriate? Instead of denigrating terms for adaptation, such as "betrayal" and "infidelity," one might speak of a "Pygmalion" model, where the adaptation brings the novel "to life," or of a "ventriloqual" model, where the film "lends voice" to the mute characters of the novel, or of an "alchemical" model, where the adaptation turns verbal dross into filmic gold. Or, drawing on the West African religious tradition, one could speak of a "possession" model, whereby the **orixa** (spirit) of the literary text descends into the body/horseman of the film adaptation. Even Christian discourse is ambivalent about adaptation. On the one hand, the Second Commandment valorizes the sacred word; on the other, what some have demonized as the gross embodiment of the film medium could be "redeemed" through what Kamilla Elliott calls "the incarnational model," i.e. the very Christocentric idea that, thanks to adaptation, the "Word" of the novel is "made Flesh," while the Jewish Bible (in Christian parlance the "Old Testament") is "fulfilled" by the New Testament of the film.[48]

Adaptation theory by now has available a well-stocked archive of tropes and concepts to account for the mutation of forms across media: adaptation as reading, rewriting, critique, translation, transmutation, metamorphosis, recreation, transvocalization, resuscitation, transfiguration, actualization, transmodalization, signifying, performance, dialogization, cannibalization, reinvisioning, incarnation, or reaccentuation. (The words with the prefix "trans" emphasize the **changes** brought about in the adaptation, while those beginning with the prefix "re" emphasize the **recombinant** function of adaptation.) Each term, however problematic as a definitive account of adaptation, sheds light on a different facet of adaptation. The trope of adaptation as a "reading" of the source novel suggests that just as any text can generate an infinity of readings, so any novel can generate any number of adaptational readings which are inevitably partial, personal, conjunctural, interested.[49] The metaphor of translation, similarly, suggests a principled effort of intersemiotic transposition, with the inevitable losses and gains typical of any translation.[50]

Much of the discussion of intertextual aspects of adaptation goes under the label "genre," which constitutes an important current within the broader stream of intertextuality. While some genres (comedy, tragedy, melodrama) are broadly shared between novel and film, other genres are specifically filmic (for example, the animated cartoon) because they depend on specific cinematic procedures like the moving image, editing, and so forth. Since adaptations typically mingle literary and cinematic genres, the question is one of correlating the genres invoked by the novel and those invoked by the film.[51]

Adaptations, typically, carry over some of the literary genres and mix in some of the filmic genres. Tony Richardson's adaptation of Henry Fielding's *Tom Jones* provides a good example. Just as Fielding's novel draws on some very early, time-hallowed literary sources such as the epic, the film draws on early film history and specifically the slapstick comedies and melodramas of the silent period. Just as Fielding mimicked the procedures of Homeric epic in the novel, the opening sequence of the Richardson film mimics the procedures of silent cinema. In other cases, we find a clear shift in genre, as when Kubrick turned the "realistic" atomic war suspense novel *Red Alert* into the filmic satire of *Dr Strangelove*, foregrounding the absurd premises of the Cold War and its MAD ("Mutually Assured Destruction") policies.[52]

The complexity of these intertextual and generic negotiations becomes manifest in the case of the Spielberg adaptation of Alice Walker's *The Color Purple* (1985). As a kind of methodological demonstration or taxonomic delirium, we can try to locate the major intertextual elements in the novel and the adaptation. The novel interweaves any number of intertexts, literary and extraliterary: (1) **the epistolary novel** (implying an orchestration of multiple voices, along with such themes as class consciousness and patriarchal oppression (as in *Pamela* and *Clarissa*); (2) **the historical romance**, implying a past setting but here domesticated and rendered quotidian; (3) the **autobiographical slave narrative**, implying the personalization of social protest; (4) the **realistic novel**, with its connotations of democratization, stylistic dignity, and the respectful treatment of the everyday life of "lower" social strata; (5) the *Bildungsroman* or novel of development, evoked by Celie's coming-of-age story, her coming into herself; (6) the **reflexive novel**, found in the direct thematization of Celie's wrestling with language and writing; (7) the **fairy tale**, implied in the once-upon-a-time quality of the girl-child's fantasies; (8) **inspirational literature** (religious, secular, feminist), implied by the overall homiletic drift of the novel; (9) **self-help literature** (Celie as a role model for transcending victimization); and (10) **the blues**, cited literally and emulated figuratively as a vernacular art.

The Spielberg adaptation then picks up some of these literary cues, ignores others, and "adds" specifically filmic allusions and protocols. Spielberg maintains the conventions of the epistolary novel, with its multiple voices, but cinematizes the genre through specifically filmic techniques such as voice-over. In terms of specifically filmic genres, the film relays the stereotypical echoes of the "all-black musical" (for example, *Hallelujah*, 1928, and *Cabin in the Sky*, 1943), especially in the gospel sequences. Thus Spielberg's (rather uninformed) vision of black people is largely mediated by film, and specifically by three filmic tradition: (1) the tradition that makes the black rural community the locus of spiritual and physical vibrancy; (2) the more jazzistic tradition that renders blacks not as rural but rather as urban, sophisticated and Afro-modernist; and (3) the tradition of slapstick farce and minstrelsy, as exemplified by Harpo's repeated pratfalls and by "Mister's" ponderously comic efforts to cook for Shug.[53] At the same time, the film adds a surprising literary supplement through literary references **not** made in the source novel, notably through repeated references to Dickens's *Oliver Twist*.

Bakhtin, Genette, and Transtextuality

Virtually all of the theory and literary analysis directly or indirectly related to "intertextuality" – from Bakhtin's "dialogism" through the Brazilian modernists' idea of "anthropophagy," on to Henry Louis Gates's notion of "signifying" and Harold Bloom's "anxiety of influence" – bear relevance to film and adaptation. Here, however, I will concentrate on the analytical productivity of some concepts developed by Mikhail Bakhtin and Gérard Genette.

Many of Bakhtin's conceptual categories, although developed in relation to the novel, are equally germane to film and to adaptation. The Bakhtinian notion of the "chronotope," for example, also helps illuminate adaptation, allowing us to historicize our understanding of space and time in both film and novel. The chronotope, defined as "the necessary relation between time and space in the novel," helps us understand the ways in which spatio-temporal structures in the novel evoke the existence of a life-world cued by the text but also independent of it. The concept of the chronotope assumes that stories "take time" but they also "take space;" it avoids the absurd "Sophie's choice" **between** time and space. Since the chronotope provides diegetic fictional environments implying historically specific constellations of power, it is ideally suited to a medium like the cinema where "spatial and temporal indicators are fused into one carefully thought-out

Robert Stam

Introduction

concrete whole."[54] Paraphrasing Bakhtin, we could say that film, too, forms the textual site where time "thickens, takes on flesh, becomes artistically visible" and where "space becomes charged and responsive to the movements of time, plot and history."

In filmic terms, a chronotopic model of analysis evokes suggestive linkages between three elements: (1) typical decor in film (the bars, lounges and city streets of *film noir*, for example); (2) temporal articulations (in film the *faux raccords* of Resnais, or the slow pacing of Satyajit Ray); and (3) spatial articulations (the flattened perspectives of a Godard, the oblique angularity of a Welles). A chronotopic model might facilitate the construction of a more comprehensive model for the analysis of time–space in the cinema, one which would take into simultaneous account questions of history, genre, and the specifically cinematic articulation of space and time.[55]

Bakhtinian "dialogism," meanwhile, refers in the broadest sense to the infinite and open-ended possibilities generated by all the discursive practices of a culture, the matrix of communicative utterances which "reach" the text not only through recognizable citations but also through a subtle process of indirect textual relays. Any text that has "slept with" another text, as a postmodern wag once put it, has also slept with all the other texts that that other text has slept with. It is this textually transmitted "dis-ease" that characterizes the intertextual daisy-chain that Derrida called "dissemination."

Notions of "dialogism" and "intertextuality," then, help us transcend the aporias of "fidelity" and of a dyadic source/adaptation model which excludes not only all sorts of supplementary texts but also the dialogical response of the reader/spectator. Every text, and every adaptation, "points" in many directions, back, forward, and sideways. A text like *Don Quixote*, for example, points backward to chivalric romance, sideways to Lope de Vega, and forward to Kathy Acker and Orson Welles and *Man from La Mancha*. Building on Bakhtin's concept of "dialogism" and Kristeva's "intertextuality," Gérard Genette in *Palimpsestes* (1982) offers other useful analytic concepts.[56] While Genette does not address film, his concepts can be extrapolated for film and for adaptation. Instead of maintaining the term "intertextuality," Genette proposed the more inclusive term "transtextuality" to refer to "all that which puts one text in relation, whether manifest or secret, with other texts." Genette posits five types of transtextual relation, all of which are suggestive for the theory and analysis of adaptation.

The first type of transtextuality is "**intertextuality**," or the "effective co-presence of two texts" in the form of quotation, plagiarism, and allusion. Intertextuality, perhaps the most obvious of the categories, calls up the play of generic allusion and reference in film and novel. This intertext can be oral or written. As Mbye Cham points out in his essay on African cinema (see chapter 14), adaptations can be rooted in both orature and literature. Often the intertext is not explicit but is rather the taken-for-granted background reference. This is especially true of seminal cultural texts like the Jewish and Christian Bibles. Think, for example, of the presence of the Exodus story in *Grapes of Wrath*, or of all the comic/satiric variations on Christ's Last Supper (from Buñuel's *Viridiana*, 1961, to Mel Brooks's *History of the World Part I*, 1981, to *Monty Python Live at the Hollywood Bowl*, 1982).[57] "Allusion" in the cinema can also take distinct medium-specific forms. A camera movement can be an allusion, as we see in the long chain of virtuoso, even exhibitionistic, long-take crane and steadicam shots – moving from Welles's *Touch of Evil* (1958) to Altman's *The Player* (1992), and Paul Thomas Anderson's *Boogie Nights* (1997) – that have formed the flamboyant overtures of a whole series of films, each consciously referring to the earlier ones and each taking advantage of evolving technologies.[58]

Genette's second kind of transtextuality is "**paratextuality**," or the relation, within the totality of a literary work, between the text proper and its "paratext" – titles, prefaces, postfaces, epigraphs, dedications, illustrations, and even book jackets and signed autographs, in short all the accessory messages and commentaries which come to surround the text and which at times become virtually indistinguishable from it. In film, although Genette does not mention it, "paratextuality" might evoke all those materials close to the text such as posters, trailers, reviews, interviews with the director, and so forth. The new media, in fact, have fostered an explosion of paratextual materials. A number of DVD versions of films (for example, *Bridget Jones's Diary*, 2001) include sequences that were filmed but not included in the final version. This paratextual feature allows the DVD viewer to literally "envision" alternative versions of the adaptation, enabled to regret (or applaud) the loss of a filmed sequence. A Criterion DVD devoted to Godard's adaptation of the Moravia novel *Contempt*, for example, includes interviews with Godard, with cinematographer Raoul Coutard, with Fritz Lang, along with visual materials on actress Brigitte Bardot. Other laser-disks and DVDs reveal the scenes filmed by directors but excluded from the release versions – for example, the longer version of *Apocalypse Now* (1979) – thus giving a sense of the "director's cut." These paratextual materials inevitably reshape our understanding of the text itself. But the "paratext" also takes more commodified forms. In the case of Hollywood blockbusters, including those based on pre-existing sources like novels or comic books, the text becomes overwhelmed, as it were, by a commercial paratext. The film becomes a kind of franchise or brand, designed to generate not only sequels but also ancillary consumer products like toys, music, books, and other products of cross-media synergies. The *Harry Potter* film adaptations, for example, become what Peter Bart calls a "megafranchise," garnering billions of dollars.[59]

Genette's third type of intertextuality is "**metatextuality**" or the critical relation between one text and another, whether the commented text is explicitly cited or only silently evoked. Here we can emphasize either the "critical relation" or the "silently evoked" aspects of the category. The former term suggests all those adaptations which criticize or in some way express hostility either toward the source novel or toward previous adapters. Stephen Schiff and Adrian Lyne, for example, saw the antecedent Kubrick version of *Lolita* as an example of "everything to avoid" in their own version.[60] Thus "metatextuality" evokes the entire tradition of the critical rewritings, whether literary or filmic, of novels. Adaptations, in this sense, can be "readings" or "critiques" of their source novel. Every age, Bakhtin suggested, reaccentuates in its own way the works of the past. In the colonial and postcolonial eras, literature has often "written back" against empire, often in the form of critical rewriting of key texts from the European novelistic tradition. Jean Rhys's *The*

Wide Sargasso Sea (1966) retells Charlotte Brontë's *Jane Eyre* as the story of Bertha Mason, Mr Rochester's first wife and the by-now-celebrated "madwoman in the attic" of feminist criticism, leading us to reassess the racialized presentation of Bertha as a "creole savage."

Another recent trend within literature involves the rewriting of a novel from the perspective of secondary or even imaginary additional characters. Thus we get *Robinson Crusoe* rewritten from the perspective of Susan Barton (Coetzee's *Foe*), *Moby Dick* from the perspective of the wife of Captain Ahab (Sena Naslund's *Ahab's Wife*), *Lolita* from the perspective of Lolita (Pia Pera's *Lo's Diary*), *Don Quixote* from the perspective of a female Quixote (Kathy Acker's *Don Quixote*), and *Gone with the Wind* from the perspective of the enslaved (Alice Randall's *The Wind Done Gone*). Here the possible permutations become endless, since any novel could be rewritten from the perspective of a different character: an ecological rewriting of *Moby Dick* might give us Captain Ahab from the point of view of the whale. Filmic adaptations, I would argue, should be seen as existing on a continuum with these other "rewritings."

Sergio Giral's film *El otro Francisco* (1975), which adapts Cuba's first anti-slavery novel, Anselmo Suarez y Romero's *Francisco* (1837), constitutes a brilliant example of adaptation as critique. The novel, often called the Cuban *Uncle Tom's Cabin*, was an historical romance about a young slave who commits suicide when his fiancée reveals that she has been raped by her master. The original novel already formed part of a circuit of intertextual rewriting, and specifically of a set of anti-slavery novels sponsored by the abolitionist literary circle of Domingo del Monte. The Giral film, over a century later, further builds on this tradition of **recriture**, now in the very different context of the revolutionary 1960s and 1970s. The basic procedure of the Giral film is to critique the novel's rendition of slavery by dialectically counterpointing diverse generic styles. While the source novel is fundamentally a melodrama, the Giral adaptation promotes interplay between diverse generic modes of presentation: a parodically melodramatic approach, sarcastically "faithful" to the sentimental spirit of the novel; a staged (anachronistically verité) documentary about the novel's production context; and a realistic reconstruction of the historical life of the enslaved. Taken together, the three modes emphasize exactly what is suppressed in the novel: the economic motives behind the abolitionist movement, the catalyzing role of black rebellion, and the artistic mediation of the story itself.

The Giral film self-reflexively explores adaptation as demystificatory critique. Giral **parodies** the novel, for example in the opening pre-credit sequence, by exaggerating the novel's melodramatic conventions through their filmic equivalents: overwrought acting, haloed backlighting, soft-focus visuals, and lachrymose music. He **contextualizes** the novel, by revealing the social/artistic habitus out of which the novel was generated: to wit the upper-class, liberal del Monte salon. He **adds characters** to the novel by including the author Suarez y Romero himself (i.e. an actor impersonating him) in the film, informing us that the abolitionist author had himself inherited slaves and knew about slave rebellions. Turning film into a new kind of historiographical écriture, he stages what most frightened the Cuban elite: the history of black resistance in Cuba. Finally, he **transforms** the novel's docile central character – Francisco – into a revolutionary, the "other" Francisco of the title.

In terms of a source not mentioned or "silently evoked," meanwhile, "metatextuality" calls up those films which have a more diffuse, unstated relation to a source novel or even to a whole genre or body of literature. Maria Tortajada argues that Eric Rohmer's films, for example, rework the French tradition of **libertinage** as exemplified by Laclos's novel *Les Liaisons dangereuses*, even though Rohmer never adapted Laclos.[61] Buñuel's *L'Age d'or* (1931), similarly, is not an "adaptation" of the Marquis de Sade, yet Alan Weiss argues that *120 Days of Sodom* forms a source text/structuring absence in that film.[62] When Claude Chabrol was unable to secure the rights to the Patricia Highsmith story *The Talented Mr Ripley*, due to the fact that it had already been adapted by Clement as *Plein soleil* (1960), he simply switched the gender of the protagonists from male to female, so that his film *Les Biches* (1968) went unrecognized as an adaptation of Highsmith's novel.

"Metatextuality" also evokes the case of "unmarked adaptations." It has been a common practice of the commercial film industry in India to make "unmarked adaptations." According to Nitin Govil, in the 1990s three versions of *Pretty Woman* (1990) and four versions of *Ghost* (1990) were made.[63] Other examples might include the non-explicit intertextual relation between Charlotte Brontë and Jane Campion's *The Piano* (1993); or between *Forrest Gump* and Voltaire's *Candide*; or *Clueless* (1993) as an unstated (except in interviews) adaptation of Jane Austen's *Emma*. While *Emma* refers to a character in the Jane Austen novel, *Clueless* evokes the teenage slang of a particular Los Angeles milieu in a particular historical period. Some adaptations, such as Claire Denis's *Beau Travail* (1999), are barely recognizable **as** adaptations. Here the source novel – Melville's *Billy Budd* – becomes an inspirational matrix of thematic and stylistic motifs. Melville's "bronzed mariners" become the bare-chested soldiers, while the scene shifts to another point in the continuum of the Black Atlantic world – East Africa. The novel becomes the springboard less for an adaptation than for a stylized tone-poem, one mingled with allusions to other films (Godard's *Le Petit Soldat*, 1962) and other arts (Benjamin Britten's opera *Billy Budd*).

Genette's fourth type of intertextuality is "**architextuality**," or the generic taxonomies suggested or refused by the titles or subtitles of a text. At first glance, this category seems irrelevant to adaptation, since adaptations usually simply take over the title of the novel in question. But as we have seen, there are "unmarked adaptations" (*Clueless*) and diffuse generic adaptations (Rohmer). There are also renamed adaptations, as when Coppola adapts Conrad's *Heart of Darkness* as *Apocalypse Now* (1979), the title clearly a twist on the Living Theatre's counter-cultural *Paradise Now*. "Architextuality" also bears on the falsely or misleadingly labeled adaptation. Michael Snow's *Rameau's Nephew* (1974), for example, apparently has nothing to do with the Diderot dialogue-novel, thereby prodding the literate spectator to search for some other connection to Diderot. Godard's *Le Gai Savoir* (1968) draws its title-phrase from Nietzsche (*Fröhliche Wissenschaft*) but also claims to adapt Rousseau's *Emile*, with which it has little in common.

"Architextuality" also evokes the thorny legal issue of copyright. Interestingly, adaptations have played a crucial role in the development of copyright law. Before 1910, film companies like Biograph had released many films based on literary works in the public domain, but Griffith's *Ramona* (1910) was probably the first film to base itself on a literary source secured with permission and payment. By 1912, Congress decided to provide guidance on such issues, declaring that Griffith could control the rights to the film version of Dixon's *The Clansman* but not to other versions of the novel in other media. Lawsuits that claim that a given film was based on an unacknowledged source — for example, Barbara Chase Riboud's charge that Spielberg's *Amistad* (1997) stole scenes from her 1989 novel *Echo of Lions* — can also be seen as revolving around architextual issues, a claim that the filmmaker failed to **designate** a film **as** an adaptation. (In the case of *Amistad*, Dreamworks countered with another transtextual twist on the plagiarism theme, arguing that *Echo of Lions* itself failed to designate itself as an "adaptation," since it had borrowed materials from the 1953 history *Black Mutiny*.) All these quarrels revolve, in a sense, around the question of who "owns," as it were, a portion of the intertext.

While all of Genette's categories are suggestive, Genette's fifth type, "**hypertextuality**," is perhaps the type most clearly relevant to adaptation. "Hypertextuality," refers to the relation between one text, which Genette calls "hypertext," to an anterior text or "hypotext," which the former transforms, modifies, elaborates, or extends. In literature, *The Aeneid*'s hypotexts include *The Odyssey* and *The Iliad*, while the hypotexts of Joyce's *Ulysses* include *The Odyssey* and *Hamlet*. Both *The Aeneid* and *Ulysses*, along with Moravia's *Dizprezzo* (1954) and Godard's adaptation *Le Mépris* (1963), are hypertextual elaborations of a single hypotext, *The Odyssey*. Filmic adaptations, in this sense, are hypertexts derived from pre-existing hypotexts which have been transformed by operations of selection, amplification, concretization, and actualization. The diverse filmic adaptations of *Madame Bovary* (Renoir, Minnelli, Mehta) or of *La Femme et le pantin* (Duvivier, von Sternberg, Buñuel) can be seen as variant hypertextual "readings" triggered by the same hypotext. When Victorian novels are adapted scores of times, hypertextuality itself becomes a sign of canonical status; the "copies," within the logic elaborated by Jacques Derrida, create the prestige of the original. Indeed, the diverse prior adaptations of a novel can come to form a larger, cumulative hypotext available to the filmmaker who comes relatively "late" in the series. Filmic adaptations, then, are caught up in the ongoing whirl of intertextual reference and transformation, of texts generating other texts in an endless process of recycling, transformation, and transmutation, with no clear point of origin.[64]

Note ✓

——————————— **Proposals for Adaptation Studies** ———————————

In this final section, I would like to make some modest proposals for dealing with the narrative, thematic, and stylistic aspects of filmic adaptations of novels, something less grandly ambitious than a theory yet more substantive than a methodology. Here I will no longer be addressing the theoretical **status** of adaptation, but rather gesturing toward an analytical/practical **model** for addressing actual adaptations.

Many of the questions about adaptation have to do with the modifications and permutations of the story. Here we enter into the realm of narratology, or the study of the mechanics of narrative. Film narratologists have especially drawn on Genette's narratological analysis of novelistic time. In his literary work, Genette stresses the double schema engaged by novelistic fiction, i.e. the relation between the events recounted and the manner and sequence of their telling. Film narratologists have extrapolated three of Genette's principal categories: **order** (which answers the question "when?" and "in what sequence?"), **duration** (which answers the question "how long?"), and **frequency** (which answers the question "how often?").

The issue of **order** touches on questions of linear versus non-linear sequence. A story can respect the normal sequentiality of the putatively "real" events, proceeding from beginning through middle to end, or it can scramble that sequentiality. Both the Kubrick and the Lyne versions of *Lolita*, for example, adopt a circular structure which begins and ends with Humbert Humbert's murder of Quilty, something revealed only gradually in the novel. Eschewing linear development and tampering with sequentiality generates "anachronies" such as **analepses** (roughly, flashbacks) and **prolepses** (roughly flashforwards). Analepses are further divided into **external analepses** (flashback stories which extend back even earlier than the beginning point of the main narrative) and **internal analepses** (which begin at a point within the main narrative). **Mixed analepses** start at an earlier point but come to inflect or invade the "present" of the main narrative.

The interest of Genette's rather drily technocratic schema lies less in simply **naming** these phenomena than in reflecting on their correlation with stylistic tendencies. *Films noirs*, for example, favor analeptic strategies, usually relayed through restrospective off-screen narrators (for example, Joe Gillis in *Sunset Boulevard*, 1950). The French **cine-roman**, for its part, is fond of subjective prolepses (for example, the various premonitions in Resnais's *La Guerre est fini*, 1966, or Chris Marker's *La Jetée*, 1963), as well as mixed analepses (for example, the traumatic memories that repeatedly erupt into the putative "present" of *Hiroshima mon amour*, 1959).

"**Duration**" invokes all the complex relationalities between discourse time – the time it takes to read the novel or see the film – and those veristic imponderables about how long a fictional event "really" lasted. This relation defines the pace of narration. In temporal terms, some adaptations clearly condense the events of the novel. The two **years** portrayed in the Moravia novel *Contempt*, for example, become the two **days** of Godard's adaptation. Such changes bear on Genette's useful concept of narrative "speed" (the shifting ratios between story time and discourse time). Is an adaptation "slower" or "faster" than the novel in terms of density of incident and pace of action? Efficient exposition, density of information in the frame, rapid movement within the shot, staccato delivery of dialogue, all contribute to a sense of speed in the cinema.

Robert Stam

Introduction

Genette proposes an analytical fiction or norm called "constant speed" to suggest a relatively stable, "normal" speed of narrative in relation to which a given passage would be "fast" or "slow." The maximum speed in relation to this imaginary norm is "**ellipsis**," where major or minor events are completely skipped over. In the classical Hollywood film, ellipsis forms part of normal (analytic) editing and staging which gives us highly selective accounts of events. The minimum speed is **descriptive** "**pause**," a kind of suspension of story time, where the fiction stops, as it were, in its tracks. In the "**scene**," with its theatrical overtones, the narrative discourse time coincides with the imagined story time of the diegesis. In "**summary**," discourse time is less than story time; for example, the brief montage sequence in *Citizen Kane* (1941) which recounts Susan Alexander's meteoric rise and fall as an opera singer.

Frequency, finally, refers to the relationship between how many times an event occurs in the story and how many times it is narrated (or mentioned) in the textual discourse. Genette posits three main variants: (1) **singulative narration** (a single event is told a single time – the norm in the mainstream fiction film); (2) **repetitive narration** (an event is recounted many times, as in multiperspectival narrations such as *Rashomon*, 1951); (3) **iterative narration** (an event which occurred many times is told once); and (4) an event which occurred many times is told many times, which I would call **homologous narration**. But both film and novel offer a possibility not mentioned by Genette which combines (1) and (2), which might be called "cumulative narration," i.e. cases where a single causal event is gradually fleshed out through repeated flash-backs over the course of the film; for example the traumatic events generating Marnie's kleptomania in Hitchcock's *Marnie* (1964), or provoking Ballantine's amnesia in *Spellbound* (1945).

By way of example, we can elaborate on just one of Genette's types – the iterative. The iterative in the novel evokes the imperfect of Flaubertian prose in *Madame Bovary*, the tense of habitual repetition, and specifically the novelistic treatment of boredom in what Flaubert, long before *Seinfeld*, called "a book about nothing." In this same spirit, Italian neo-realist theorist/filmmaker Cesare Zavattini dreamed of filming ninety minutes in the life of a person to whom nothing happened. But what might be the ideal cinematic means for evoking the ennui that permeates a novel like *Madame Bovary*? One possibility would be to deploy the literal duration of a long-held shot-sequence, where real-time slowness would render the snail-like passage of time (a technique used in dos Santos's *Vidas secas*). Another would be to have the characters verbally comment on their boredom (Minnelli's solution), or deploy voice-over narration to literally borrow the words evoking ennui in the novel (Chabrol's solution). Or one might stage what Metz calls the "episodic sequence" (little scenelets showing a certain trajectory, in this case a trajectory toward boredom. Another approach would deploy visual metonymy: a dripping faucet to convey the slow and repetitious drip, drip, drip of time; or slow motion, or the dilation of a shot by editing (whereby the same gesture is repeated ad infinitum), or a well-chosen synecdochic gesture (e.g. distracted doodling). Each approach has its advantages and drawbacks.

The Theory and Practice of Adaptation

Introduction

Since it involves two semiotically distinct texts relaying the same narrative, adaptation necessarily brings up some issues not mentioned by Genette. The issue becomes one of **comparative** narratology, which asks such questions as the following. What events from the novel's story have been eliminated, added, or changed in the adaptation, and, more important, why? Although the fiction film has evolved a good deal since the five-minute silent versions of novels like Zola's *L'Assomoir*, adaptations today typically still trim down the events in the novel to produce a film of "normal" feature length. Many filmmakers, in this spirit, "streamline" the novel by focusing on certain characters and events rather than others. Most film versions of *Robinson Crusoe*, for example, skip over the early chapters in order to rush to what they see as the "core" elements of the story: the shipwreck, the island, and the encounter with Friday.

Apart from characters and events, many adaptations eliminate specific **kinds** of materials – the literary-critical commentaries in *Don Quixote* or *Tom Jones*, the intercalary essay chapters in *The Grapes of Wrath*, the meditative portions of *Moby Dick* – materials not seen as directly related to the story and therefore regarded as detracting from the onward drive of the narrative. At times, surprisingly, eliminations can be unintentional. When Kubrick adapted Anthony Burgess's *Clockwork Orange*, he worked with an American (rather than the British) edition of the novel, which was missing the final chapter, and therefore the protagonist's epiphany. Or filmmakers can **amplify** novelistic passages that offer tempting possibilities for particularly spectacular or "cinematic" shots. Thus a brief mention of Squire Western's love of hunting, in Fielding's *Tom Jones*, becomes in the film a long and elaborate hunt sequence, with galloping horses and air-borne crane shots. Some directors **add** materials simply for their own pleasure, as when Truffaut includes the song "Le Tourbillon de la Vie" sung by Jeanne Moreau in *Jules and Jim*. In very rare instances, a director throws out most of the events in the source novel, and constitutes the film uniquely out of new materials, the case of Godard's *Masculin féminin*, presumably based on a Guy de Maupassant story but which features little more than the names of the characters from the novel.

A comparative narratology of adaptation also examines the ways in which adaptations add, eliminate, or condense characters. Sometimes a constellation of groups of characters is reduced to a single group; the many Okie families in Steinbeck's *The Grapes of Wrath* become simply one family – the Joads. Or a single character in a film can gather together in herself the traits of a number of the novel's characters, as when Truffaut in *Jules and Jim* molds the character of Catherine as contradictory by amalgamating the features of a whole gallery of women from the novel. Characters can also be altered in terms of their ethnic identity, as when the white judge of *Bonfire of the Vanities* is turned into the black judge played by Morgan Freeman, perhaps as a hedge against the accusations of racism leveled against the Tom Wolfe novel. The important issue for adaptation studies is what principle guides the processes of selection or "triage" when one is adapting a novel? What is the "drift" of these changes and alterations? What principles orient the choices?

The history of the novel offers a wide sprectrum of narrators, from the first-person reporter–narrator of fictitious autobiographies like *Robinson Crusoe*, to the multiple letter-writers of epistolary novels like *Pamela*, to the amiable, digressive, outside-observer narrators of reflexive novels like *Don Quixote* and *Tom Jones*, to the variable-distance, infinitely flexible, at once intimate and impersonal, narrator of *Madame Bovary*, to the "stream-of-consciousness" narrators of Virginia Woolf's *Mrs Dalloway*, on to the intensely objective/subjective obsessional narrators of Robbe-Grillet.

The conventional terms of discussion, unfortunately, do not account for even this limited spectrum of styles of narration. The traditional analysis in both literature and film was rooted in concepts based in language and grammar, such as "first-person narrator" (subdivided into "first-person observer and first-person participant narrator) and "third-person" narrator (subdivided into omniscient, limited omniscient, and dramatic narrators). But such grammar-based terminology created more confusion than clarity, since designating a narrator "third person" actually tells us very little about specific narrational processes in novelistic texts. A strictly grammatical approach obscures the fact that a writer like Flaubert can shift person, moving easily from an occasional "I" or a "we" to a mixed **style indirect libre** (free indirect discourse), constantly changing the relation between the narrator and the fiction. More important than the grammatical "person" is authorial control of intimacy and distance, the calibration of access to characters' knowledge and consciousness, all issues which function above and beyond and below the issue of grammatical "person."[65]

Film complicates literary narration by practicing two parallel and intersecting forms of narration: the verbal narration, whether through voice-over and/or the speech of characters, and the film's capacity to show the world and its appearances apart from voice-over and character narration.[66] For André Gaudreault, filmic narration superimposes "monstration" (showing) – the gesture which creates the fictional world – and "narration" (telling) whereby editing and other cinematic procedures inscribe the activity of a filmic narrator who evaluates and comments on the fictional world. Films thus both tell stories (narration) and stage them (monstration). Thus *Citizen Kane* combines the various verbal recountings of Kane's life, alongside everything the film **shows** in tandem with these recountings. Leland recounts his memories of Kane, while the film shows Leland in his wheelchair telling the story, or shows the events that Leland is recounting. The film as "narrator" is not a person (the director) or character in the fiction but, rather, the abstract instance or superordinate agency that regulates the spectator's knowledge. The narrator has been variously called "le grand imagier" (Albert Laffay) and the "meganarrator" (André Gaudreault). The filmic equivalent of Wayne Booth's "implied author," this figure can be metaphorized as an orchestra conductor who takes charge of the various "instruments" of cinematic expression.[67]

Sound cinema thus makes possible a double play of forms. The classical realist film usually unifies the two levels, making them redundant and mutually reinforcing. Often, a voice-over narration gradually gives way to direct monstration, yet we somehow take what is "monstrated" to emanate from the initial narrative voice. In *Sunset Boulevard*, as Eric Smoodin points out, "even when we cannot hear the narrating voice of Joe Gillis, we suppose the scene to be a visual manifestation of his speech."[68] More modernist films amplify the gaps and contradictions between the two forms. Marguerite Duras's *India Song* (1975) shows silent, voiceless actions, while unidentified voices comment on and raise doubts about our perceptions of those actions. In *Last Year at Marienbad* (1961), the narrator's off-screen words about what we see – he speaks of these "empty corridors" – are contradicted by the shots of corridors crowded with people.

Ever since the advent of sound, the cinema has been "vococentric" (Chion), oriented toward the human voice. Voices in the cinema both provide information and provide a focus for spectatorial identification. While voice-over narrators address themselves to us as spectators, over the heads of the characters, as it were, the diegetic characters address one another while (usually) appearing to ignore us. Genette's "intradiegetic" narrator acts **and** tells a story to other characters within the fiction. Some adaptations dramatically shift the tenor of narration. Philip Kaufman's adaptation of Kundera's *The Unbearable Lightness of Being*, for example, eliminates the novel's first-person reflexive narrator, and with him the various philosophical debates that animate the novel.

Film theorists have not come to a consensus about whether film per se **can** narrate. Some theorists, such as David Bordwell and Edward Branigan, argue that the very idea that films can "narrate" is an anthropomorphic fiction. While films do develop processes of "narration," they can offer only a pathetic mimicry of a "narrator." But by this logic novelistic narrators as well offer only a pathetic mimicry of real-life, flesh and blood narrators. For André Gaudreault, theorists like Bordwell commit a disguised form of anthropomorphism, since in the end their abstract substantive "narration" does everything that a conventional "narrator" does. Still other theorists, like Christian Metz and Marie-Laure Ryan and Robert Burgoyne, see film as deploying "**impersonal**" narration, a word that resonates tellingly with the narrational project of such writers as Flaubert and James Joyce. In this form of narration, the narrator is both the illocutionary source of the fictional world and the agent that comments on that world. The impersonal narrator, in Burgoyne's words, "produces a type of discourse that is read directly as the facts of the 'real world' of the fictional universe."[69]

Narratology also addresses the relationship between the events told and the temporal standpoint or "home base," as it were, of the telling. Is the story in the novel or film told, as is most usually the case, **after** the events of the story (retrospective narration), **prior** to the event (as in oracular or prophetic narration), or **simultaneously** with the events of the story. Or are there **interpolated** events, set within the intervals between the moments of the main action? The question then becomes how these various temporal frameworks are translated within adaptations. In the case of "**embedded narration**," for example, one story is wrapped, as it were, "inside another," in a narrative **mise-en-abyme**.

Embedded narratives generate **hypodiegeses**, i.e. substories embedded within stories, like those to be found in Cervantes's *Don Quixote* (and in Orson Welles's adaptation of that novel), or in Buñuel's highly Cervantic *The Discreet Charm of the Bourgeoisie* (1972).[70]

Genette constitutes his typology of narrative levels around the term "diegesis" as referring to the spatio-temporal "surround" and the participants and the events in a narrative. A narrator, in Genette's terms, can be **auto-diegetic** (the narrator generates and tells his own story, à la *Robinson Crusoe*), **homodiegetic** (the narrator is part of the story but not the protagonist; for example, Ishmael in *Moby Dick*), or **heterodiegetic** (outside the story told; the case of the narrator of *Tom Jones*). The narrator, I would add, can be single, as in *Tom Jones*, or a collective, group narrator, such as the cohort of admiring male neighbors in Sophia Coppola's *The Virgin Suicides*. Off-screen narrators can be anonymous or named, single or multiple and even contradictory, as in *Citizen Kane* and *Rashomon*. We can even distinguish between living narrators – the norm – and those posited as dead, as occurs with Joe Gillis in *Sunset Boulevard* and with the narrator of the symptomatically titled Brazilian novel *Posthumous Memoirs of Bras Cubas*, by Machado de Assis (and the adaptation by André Klotzel).

As many analysts of narrative have pointed out, we react to narrators as we do to persons, finding them likeable or repulsive, wise or foolish, fair or unfair.[71] Narrators vary widely on a broad spectrum, not only in terms of likeability but also in terms of reliability. Some narrators are honest brokers, while others are pathological liars. On a scale of trustworthiness, narrators range from those who are almost completely suspect (e.g. Jason in *The Sound and the Fury*) to those who are more or less reliable (Nick in *The Great Gatsby*, Bras Cubas in *Posthumous Memoirs of Bras Cubas*) to those who serve as dramatized spokespersons for the implied author and whose values conform to the norms of the text (Conrad's Marlowe in *Heart of Darkness*). Some narrators, such as Nabokov's Humbert Humbert in *Lolita*, are reliable in terms of reportorial fact but not at all reliable in terms of moral evaluation.

The modern period has been especially fond of (1) changing narrators, and (2) unreliable narrators. Changing narrators alter their discourse and ideas as they narrate; they mutate before our eyes. This trait is especially true of the *Bildungsroman* or novel of development (for example, *Great Expectations*); part of the plot, in such novels, is not just **what** happens but how the narrator changes **in function of** what happens, for example when Pip learns about the true source of his fortune. Film adaptations almost inevitably condense and telescope these processes of development. In the case of unreliable narration, the challenge of reading consists in divining the narrator's inconsistencies and neuroses, penetrating the veil set up by the narrators to hide their vices (or even their virtues). Sometimes the reliability of a narrator, as with Ellen Dean in *Wuthering Heights* or of the governess in James's *Turn of the Screw*, becomes a "crux" in literary interpretation. The cinema also offers cases of "lying narration" (Hitchcock's *Stage Fright*, 1950) and multiple "tag-team" narration. Kurosawa's *Rashomon*, in which the story of a crime is told in four radically different yet equally plausible ways, constitutes a tour de force of multiple, problematic narration. The Russell Banks novel *The Sweet Hereafter* is told from the separate but linked points of view of four characters, each of whom, in relay-race fashion, picks up the story where the previous narrator has left off. Contrastingly, the Atom Egoyan adaptation, in Russell Banks's own account, runs "the several points of view horizontally, as it were, almost simultaneously, the relay runners running four abreast instead of sequentially," so that the story "moves back and forth in time and from place to place with unapologetic ease."[72]

The challenge, in adapting unreliable narration, is to somehow reproduce the hermeneutic mechanisms of textual ambiguity and readerly decipherment found in the novels, but on a distinct, cinematic register. Self-obsessed, neurotic narrators like those of Dostoevsky's Underground Man in *Notes from Underground* or Humbert Humbert in *Lolita*, interestingly, tend to be severely **relativized** by adaptation. While the narrator in the novel is "autodiegetic" – i.e. the author generates and narrates a story within which he is the main protagonist – the film's narrator is closer to what Genette calls "homodiegetic," i.e. the narrator is involved with the story but is no longer the only protagonist. What becomes clear in the film versions of *Lolita* is that filmic narrator/ characters drawn from novels featuring unreliable narrators must struggle against the grain of a basic feature of the film medium. The discursive power of unreliable narrators is almost automatically reduced by film, precisely because of film's multitrack nature. It is as if unreliable narrator/characters were thrown into a new and some ways hostile environment where they exercise less power and agency over the narration. In a novel, the narrator controls the **only** track available – the verbal track. In a film, the narrator can partially control the verbal track – through voice-over or character dialogue – but that control is subject to innumerable constraints: the presence of other characters/ performers and voices, the palpable and distracting "thereness" of decor and objects and so forth. In a film, the other characters instantly take on a physical presence denied them in a novel dominated by a narcissistic narrator. These characters cannot be safely "solipsized," as Humbert solipsizes Lolita, since they are now present as speaking, moving, gesticulating, performing characters. While it is not impossible to relay unreliable first-person narration in the cinema, it would require relentless subjectification on almost all the cinematic registers: foregrounded presence in the shot, uninterrupted voice-over, non-stop point-of-view editing, constantly motivated camera movements, always marked subjective framing, in a way that might approximate an extreme version of Pasolini's subjectivized "cinema of poetry."

Point of View

Other questions about adaptation have to do with *focalization* and *point of view*. The term "point of view" is somewhat problematic because it gestures in so many directions at once. At once cognitive and perceptual, "point of view" can refer to an ideological orientation (a "Marxist point of view") or an emotional stance (an empathetic point of view) or the angle from which a story is told (a character's point of view). While in literature the term "point of view" can be literal or figurative, in the cinema it is at least on one level literal, in that films require camera set-ups. On the other, it can also be figurative, transmitted through specifically cinematic means. In the cinema, we can sense authorial point of view even in films – such as Emilie de Antonio's *Point of Order* (1963) – composed uniquely of pre-existing materials and without voice-over. The narrator's point of view, in such cases, becomes the ensemble of shaping principles organizing the selection and sequencing of elements, the instance that shapes and orchestrates the pre-existing materials.

Any comprehensive theory of cinematic point of view must take into account film's multitrack and multiform nature. Each and every filmic track and procedure – camera angle, focal length, music, performance, *mise-en-scène*, and costume – can convey a point of view. A wide-angle or fish-eye lens, for example, can "adjectivally" render a character as grotesque and menacing from a character's (or the director's) point of view. Moreover, the various tracks can act redundantly and in tandem or in creative tension, and each choice inflects the point of view. If a romantic kiss is accompanied by saccharine music, haloed backlighting, and misty-eyed performance, we can assume that the narrational point of view is unified and redundant. If the same scene is accompanied by circus music and garish color, we suspect that the director is distancing us from the romantic sentiment of the scene. Unlike literary point of view, filmic point of view is usually quite precise and literal. We can look "with" a character, for example, or the director or actor can look directly at us, in a way unavailable to the literary author or character. As François Jost points out, it is ironic that notions of "point of view" and "focalization" were first worked out by **literary** theorists, even though within the novelistic field "vision" is metaphoric rather than actual. Thus literary theorists have gone to the cinema, as it were, to explain the functioning of vision in the novel. Yet too often, Jost argues, these same theorists end up speaking quite imprecisely about the role of vision in both media.[73]

The term "focalization," despite its cinematic ring, was originally coined in relation to literature (by Genette in *Figures III* in 1972) to reference the relationship between the knowledge of the character vis-à-vis that of the narrator. Already in the 1960s, Todorov made the seemingly obvious point that there were three possibilities in this domain: narrators could know **more than** the characters, **less than** the characters, or **as much as** the characters. (Although one might argue that Todorov's schema has an overly quantitative conceptualization of knowledge, since characters and narrators can also know **differently**.) For Genette, terms like "vision" and "point of view" are too ambiguous and exclusively visual. He distinguishes between narration (who speaks or tells) and focalization (who sees). He proposes a tripartite scheme to account for the field. "Zero focalization" occurs with omniscient narrators, those who know much more than any of the characters. "Internal focalization" refers to the filtering of events through a character, a concept close to Henry James's idea of "center of conciousness." That concept is usually further subdivided into "fixed" (when limited to a single character) or "variable" when passed from character to character. Flaubert's *Madame Bovary*, and Hitchcock's films, in this sense, develop "variable focalization." "External focalization," finally, occurs when the reader is denied access to point of view and motivations, and restricted instead to merely observing external behavior. (In *Narrative Discourse Revisited*, Genette clarifies that for him focalization ultimately applies not to the characters but to the narrative itself, which has the power to "focalize.")[74]

Narratologists André Gaudreault and François Jost have argued that Genette's terms require modification for the cinema.[75] They point out that the term "focalization" brings a certain clarity if one is discussing the novel, where vision is only metaphorical, but becomes problematic, paradoxically, in relation to a supposedly visual medium like the cinema. The sound film can simultaneously **show** what a character sees and **say** what a character thinks. The two narratologists therefore propose separating the two functions, using the term "ocularization" to characterize the relation between what the camera shows and what the character is supposed to be seeing, while retaining "focalization" for the cognitive point of view adopted by the story. They further distinguish between "internal primary ocularization" for cases where the filmic signifier suggests the look of a character through clear indices – soft focus, double or blurred images, or the superimposed form of binoculars – pointing to a special regard within the shot. "Internal secondary ocularization" is reserved for those cases where the act of looking is evoked only through point-of-view editing; for example, through eyeline matches, shot/counter shot and so on. "Zero ocularization," finally, refers to "nobody's shot," the shot which is not apparently "anchored" by any character within the diegesis.

Issues of point of view also intersect with issues of style. In stylistic/narrative terms, we can ask if the story is told in a direct, linear fashion or in a modernist, scrambled, multitemporal fashion? Adaptations are sometimes assumed to be always **less** modernist than their sources. Yet Buñuel's *That Obscure Object of Desire* modernizes and destabilizes the rather conventional Louiys source text (*La Femme et le pantin*) through various modernist devices: the confusion of identities through the use of two actresses, the deployment of the coitus interruptus structure, and so forth. In the case of Sally Potter's 1992 adaptation of Virginia Woolf's *Orlando*, the novel's modernism is not muffled but rather amplified. The novel begins with Orlando as a boy in the late sixteenth century and ends with her as a woman in 1928. While the narrator of the novel is very present, the film is sparing in its use of voice-over. In the film's opening scene, Orlando recites poetry as we hear the voice-over say "There can be no doubt about his sex, despite the feminine appearance" yet the voice continues to say "But when **he**," at which point Orlando (Tilda Swinton) interrupts and turns to the camera to say "that is I." The embodied character need not be characterized as a "he" or a "she," and the "shifter" word "I" simply points to the person speaking. In this sense, the film evokes the performative transcendence of rigid gender categories.

Other stylistic questions have to do with the handling of temporality. Are there instances of what Genette calls "pause" in the novel and the adaptation, in the form of montage sequences or static close shots without action? What is the usefulness of Christian Metz's eight syntagmatic types in the cinema (one-shot sequence or autonomous shot, parallel syntagma, bracket syntagma, descriptive syntagma, alternating syntagma, scene, episodic sequence, ordinary sequence) and what are the correlations (if any) with temporality in film? What is the role of description in novel and film? Is pure (unnarrativized) description possible in either medium? There is also the question of stylistic equivalences across the two media. Which features are "translatable" and which are not? What is the filmic equivalent of an "adjective" or "qualifier?" Lighting and music and angle, for example, could be seen as "adjectivally" placing characters "in a certain light," or seeing them from "a certain angle." Does a wide-angle or fish-eye lens on a face form the equivalent of the adjective "grotesque?" One can also ask if there is anything in the novel that might be called "proto-cinematic" (if written before the advent of cinema) or "cinematic" or "cinemorphic" (Millicent Marcus) if written after?[76] Conversely, is there anything about the film that might be called "novelistic?" What is the influence of other arts or media in the novel (for example, Hogarth in Fielding) or in the adaptation (for example, the role of painting in Kubrick's *Barry Lyndon*, 1975, or in Scorsese's *Age of Innocence*)?[77] What is needed, and what I have only begun to gesture toward here, is a thoroughgoing comparative **stylistics** of the two media.

The Limits of Formalism

Narratology is an indispensable tool for analyzing certain formal aspects of film adaptations. But an exclusively formal approach, which Edward Said compares in *Culture and Imperialism* to "describing a road without its setting in the landscape,"[78] risks foreclosing a more deeply historical analysis of the subject at hand. An important set of questions concerning adaptation has to do with **context**, i.e. the elements that go "with" or "alongside" the text. But this "alongside" is in a way a misleading spatial metaphor, since text and context are ultimately inseparable, "mutually invaginated" (in Derridean language).

One context is temporal. In some cases, the time of publication of the novel and the production of the film are very close. In the case of "bestsellers," producers hurry to take advantage of the commercial success of the novel. The John Ford *Grapes of Wrath* was rushed into production shortly after publication of the John Steinbeck novel, and was actually released within a year of the novel's publication. The Spielberg adaptation of *The Color Purple* (1985), similarly, was released just three years after the Alice Walker novel, and quickly became embroiled in a series of topical polemics linked to the moment of release, having to do with (1) **identity** (can a white male director adapt a novel by a black woman?); (2) **the canon** (which works of literature should be taught in schools?); (3) **race and gender** (does the film demonize black men?); and (4) **Oscar awards** (did racism, or anti-Spielberg prejudice, prevent the film from garnering more Oscars?).

In other cases, centuries or even millennia can elapse between the publication of the source novel and production of the adaptation, as in the case of Fellini's *Satyricon* (1969) or Pasolini's *The Decameron* (1979), or even *The Passion of the Christ* and *Troy*. The adaptations of novels like *Don Quixote* and *Robinson Crusoe* are necessarily filmed centuries after the original. As a result, the adapter enjoys more freedom to update and reinterpret the novel. The existence of so many prior adaptations relieves the pressure for "fidelity," while also stimulating the need for innovation. At times the adapter innovates by actualizing the adaptation, making it more "in synch" with contemporary discourses. The 1990s' adaptation of *Mansfield Park* envisions the Jane Austen novel "through" postcolonial critique à la Edward Said, foregrounding the Caribbean slavery largely backgrounded by the Jane Austen novel.[79] Many revisionist adaptations of Victorian novels, meanwhile, "de-repress them" in sexual and political terms; a feminist and sexual liberationist dynamic releases the sublimated libidinousness and the latent feminist spirit of the novels and of the characters, or even of the author, in a kind of anachronistic therapy or adaptational rescue operation. Postcolonial adaptations of colonialist novels like *Robinson Crusoe*, for example *Man Friday* (1976), meanwhile, retroactively liberate the oppressed colonial characters of the original.[80]

The term context also evokes issues of **censorship**, whether external or internal, conscious or unconscious. Thus the film *Grapes of Wrath* sheds not only the more explicitly "socialist" passages of the novel, but also the shocking naturalism of the passage where Rosasharn suckles a hungry man. In the case of *Madame Bovary*, Minnelli begins his adaptation with the staging of the trial for obscenity of the Flaubert novel, as if to warn **contemporary** censors that they should not be as shortsighted as Flaubert's philistine peers. Censorship, too, is medium specific; written media like the novel are generally granted more sexual freedom than a mass-mediated medium like film. Such considerations inevitably "color" the representation. Both film versions of *Lolita* had to wrestle with the threat of censorship. Working in the censorious, post-McCarthyite, postwar period, Kubrick so internalized the spirit of censorship that at one point he and screenwriter James Harris contemplated having Humbert **marry** Lolita – family values incest? – with an adult relative's blessing.[81] Decades later, the Adrian Lyne version came up against widespread concerns or "moral panics" about pedophilia and child pornography. But adaptation can also make the source **more** daring as well. Thus the tastefully euphemistic circumlocutions of Henry James give way to the carnal delights of Jane Campion's *Portrait of a Lady* (1996), where Isabel fantasizes about being caressed by Goodwood, Ralph Touchett, and Lord Warburton all at the same time; a costume drama becomes a disrobing drama. Minghella's version of the Patricia Highsmith story *The Talented Mr Ripley*, by the same token, is more explicit about homosexuality than is either the source novel or the earlier adaptation *Purple Noon* (*Plein soleil*).[82]

Many of the changes between novelistic source and film adaptation have to do with ideology and social discourses. The question becomes whether an adaptation pushes the novel to the "right," by naturalizing and justifying social hierarchies based on class, race, sexuality, gender, region, and national belonging, or to the "left" by interrogating or leveling hierarchies in an egalitarian manner. There are also "uneven developments" in this respect; for example, in adaptations which push the novel to the left on some issues (e.g. class) but to the right on others (e.g. gender or race). Film adaptations often "correct" or "improve on" their source texts, and from many different and even contradictory directions. Contemporary Hollywood films tend to be phobic toward any ideology regarded as "extreme," whether coming from left or right. In chapter 3 of this volume, Richard Porton shows how the adaptation of *House of Mirth* "cleaned up" the book's anti-Semitism. Hollywood adaptations often "correct" their sources by purging the source of the "controversial" (for example, the lesbianism of *The Color Purple*) or the revolutionary (the socialism of *The Grapes of Wrath*) or the difficult (the reflexive technique of *Lolita*) or the "uncinematic" (the philosophical/meditational passages of *Moby Dick*). The "reconciliation scene" between Shug and her preacher father, in Spielberg's *The Color Purple*, non-existent in the novel, nudges the film in a more patriarchal direction by making Shug less bisexual, less rebellious and independent.[83]

Many televisual or mainstream Hollywood adaptations perform what might be called an **aesthetic mainstreaming**. The various popular manuals on screenwriting and adaptation are quite illuminating in this regard. Most of the manuals show a radical aversion to all forms of experimentation and modernism. They almost invariably recommend adapting the source along the lines of the dominant model of storytelling (whether in its classical Hollywood or its Sundance Hollywood-lite version). The recycled, suburbanized Aristotelianism of the screenwriting manuals calls for three-act structures, principal conflicts, coherent (and often sympathetic) characters, an inexorable narrative "arc" and final catharsis or happy end. The schema is usually premised on combat between highly motivated, competitive characters, a paradigm often premised, as Raoul Ruiz points out, on "constant hostility" among human beings.[84] Everything becomes subordinated to a teleology as relentlessly purposeful as the Fate of classical tragedy. The best way to open your screenplay, Sid Field advises, is to "know your ending."[85] The goal seems to be to "de-literize" the text, as the novel is put through an adaptation machine which removes all authorial eccentricities or "excesses." Adaptation is seen as a kind of purge. In the name of mass-audience legibility, the novel is "cleansed" of moral ambiguity, narrative interruption, and reflexive meditation. Aesthetic mainstreaming dovetails with economic censorship, since the changes demanded in an adaptation are made in the name of monies spent and box-office profits required.

Adaptations of novels from another period confront the filmmaker with the choice of either creating a period piece or full-scale costume drama, on the one hand, or an update which actualizes the novel for a contemporary period on the other. Period pieces present special challenges, not only in terms of reconstructing an era but also in terms of avoiding temporal anachronisms such as TV antennas in Victorian England or airplanes in the skies of revolutionary France. But here an important distinction is sometimes missed. Some novels **begin** as costume dramas, in that they are set in the past even vis-à-vis the time of the production of the novel (the case of Machado de Assis's *Posthumous Memoirs of Bras Cubas*). Other novels, in contrast, **become** costume dramas only because of the passage of time. Kubrick's *Lolita*, made just seven years after the publication of the Nabokov novel, is not a period piece, but Lyne's *Lolita*, made over three decades later, **is** a period

The Theory and Practice of Adaptation

Introduction

piece, one which uses popular music and period props to push the story back into the late 1940s and early 1950s.

Some adaptations move **toward** the present without arriving there. Sarquis's adaptation of *Notes from Underground* (1980) moves the Dostoevsky novella forward in time, but only to the 1930s. The Merchant–Ivory adaptations of authors like Henry James (*The Bostonians*) and E. M. Forster (*Room with a View*) are all costume dramas, as are most adaptations of Jane Austen (*Emma, Pride and Prejudice, Mansfield Park*), but *Clueless* is an update, as is Alfonso Cuaron's 1998 *Great Expectations*. Some novels, like Laclos's *Les Liaisons dangereuses*, have been adapted **both** as period pieces and as updates. Two of the versions, Frears's *Dangerous Liaisons* (1988) and Forman's *Valmont* (1989) are costume dramas, but the versions by Roger Vadim and Roger Kumble are updates. Vadim in 1960 reset the novel in postwar New Wavish Paris, turning Laclos's **libertine** into a "liberated woman" enjoying an "open marriage." More recently, in *Cruel Intentions* (1999), Kumble transposed the novel into contemporary Manhattan, remodeling Laclos's adults into upscale teenagers. Rather than take advantage of e-mail as the contemporary equivalent of eighteenth-century correspondence, Kumble has the film's Valmont dismiss e-mail as good only for "geeks and pedophiles."

As the last two examples suggest, adaptations are inevitably inscribed in **national** settings. Is the adaptation set in the same locale as the novel, or is the locale changed? Coppola transforms the African jungles of Conrad's *Heart of Darkness* into the Vietnamese jungles of *Apocalypse Now*. *Clueless* transposes Austen's nineteenth-century Highwood into twentieth-century Beverly Hills. While the novel as genre allows complete flexibility of creation — the writer can evoke ancient times or "exotic" places at the stroke of the pen — the cinema has to work harder. But film also enjoys a resource unavailable to the novel – to wit, real locations; for example, the English country estates available for Jane Austen adaptations or the Manhattan brownstones and townhouses available for the Henry James films.

Many adaptations are cross-national: Minnelli adapts Flaubert; Claire Denis adapts Melville; Visconti adapts Thomas Mann; Bresson adapts Dostoevsky.[86] The question of cross-national adaptation brings with it questions of language and accent. What happens when a novel set in France like *Madame Bovary* is adapted in Hollywood by an American director like Minnelli or in Bombay by an Indian like Mehta?[87]

With international co-productions, the national and linguistic "scene" becomes even more uncertain. *Doctor Zhivago* (1965), for example, was based on a Russian novel, filmed in Spain, but featured Egyptian actors (Omar Sharif) alongside English ones (Julie Christie) speaking English. In the age of globalization, the national locale is impacted by bottom-line concerns of profitability and cost-effectiveness. While Melville's *Moby Dick* was already global in its scope and implications, featuring worldwide travel and the multicultural crew of the *Pequod*, the 1988 USA Network adaptation was global**ized**. While the cable channel and the novel were American, the film was an Australian/UK co-production in order to take advantage of favorable exchange rates, low labor costs, and tax incentives.

Robert Stam

Introduction

Since adaptations engage the discursive energies of their time, they become a barometer of the ideological trends circulating during the moment of production. Each re-creation of a novel for the cinema unmasks facets not only of the novel and its period and culture of origin, but also of the time and culture of the adaptation. Texts evolve over what Bakhtin calls "great time," and often they undergo surprising "homecomings." "Every age," Bakhtin writes, "reaccentuates in its own way the works of [the past]. The historical life of classic works is in fact the uninterrupted process of their social and ideological reaccentuation."[88] Adaptation, in this sense, is a work of reaccentuation, whereby a source work is reinterpreted through new grids and discourses. Each grid, in revealing aspects of the source text in question, also reveals something about the ambient discourses in the moment of reaccentuation. By revealing the prisms and grids and discourses through which the novel has been reimagined, adaptations grant a kind of objective materiality to the discourses themselves, giving them visible, audible, and perceptible form.

Conclusion

If adaptation studies at first glance seems a somewhat minor and peripheral field within cinematic theory and analysis, in another sense it can be seen as quite central and important. Not only do literary adaptations form a very high percentage of the films made (and an especially high proportion of prestige productions and Oscar winners), but also almost all films can be seen in some ways as "adaptations." While adaptation studies often assumes that the source texts are literary, adaptations can also have subliterary or paraliterary sources. Bio-pics adapt biographical writing about famous historical figures. Some films, like Hitchcock's *The Wrong Man* (1957), adapt newspaper stories. A film like *Spiderman* (2002) adapts a comic strip. Carlos Diegues's *Veja esta cancao* (See This Song, 1987) adapts Brazilian popular songs. History films like *Reds* (1981) adapt historical texts.[89] Other films (for example, Gilberto Dinnerstein's *War of the Children*, 1992) adapt non-fictional works, or explore the life and work of a philosopher (*Wittgenstein*, 1993), or of a painter (*Pollock*, 2001) or a novelist (*Iris*, 2001). Even non-adaptation fiction films adapt a **script**. The point is that virtually all films, not only adaptations, remakes, and sequels, are mediated through intertextuality and writing. Copyright law speaks of the "derivative works," i.e. those works that "recast, transform, or adapt" something that came before. But adaptations in a sense make manifest what is true of all works of art – that they are all on some level "derivative." And in this sense, the study of adaptation potentially impacts our understanding of **all** films.

In the case of filmic adaptations of novels, to sum up what has been argued thus far, source-novel hypotexts are transformed by a complex series of operations: selection, amplification, concretization, actualization, critique, extrapolation, popularization, reaccentuation, transculturalization. The source novel, in this sense, can be seen as a situated utterance, produced in one medium and in one historical and social context, and later transformed into another, equally situated utterance, produced in a different context and relayed through a different medium. The source text forms a dense informational network, a series of verbal cues which the adapting film text can then selectively take up, amplify, ignore, subvert, or transform.

The filmic adaptation of a novel performs these transformations according to the protocols of a distinct medium, absorbing and altering the available genres and inter-texts through the grids of ambient discourses and ideologies, and as mediated by a series of filters: studio style, ideological fashion, political and economic constraints, *auteurist* predilections, charismatic stars, cultural values, and so forth. An adaptation consists in an interested reading of a novel and the circumstantially shaped "writing" of a film. The filmic hypertext, in this sense, is transformational almost in the Chomskian sense of a "generative grammar" of adaptation, with the difference that these cross-media operations are infinitely more unpredictable and multifarious than they would be were it a matter of "natural language." Adaptations redistribute energies and intensities, pro-voke flows and displacements; the linguistic energy of literary writing turns into the audio-visual–kinetic–performative energy of the adaptation, in an amorous exchange of textual fluids.

The conventional language of the critique of adaptations ("infidelity," "betrayal," and so forth), to return to our starting-point, translates our disappointment that a film version of a novel has not conveyed the moral or aesthetic impact of the novel. By adopt-ing an intertextual as opposed to a judgmental approach rooted in assumptions about a putative superiority of literature, we have not abandoned all notions of judgment and evaluation. But our discussion will be less moralistic, less implicated in unacknowledged hierarchies. We can still speak of successful or unsuccessful adaptations, but this time oriented not by inchoate notions of "fidelity" but rather by attention to "transfers of creative energy," or to specific dialogical responses, to "readings" and "critiques" and "interpretations" and "rewritings" of source novels, in analyses which always take into account the gaps between very different media and materials of expression.

─────────────────────── Acknowledgments ───────────────────────

A much shorter and very different version of this chapter appeared in James Naremore's highly recommended collection, *Film Adaptation* (New Brunswick, NJ: Rutgers University Press, 2000). A slightly different version appears in the conference paper publication of the Udine Film Conference. I would like to thank the various academic audiences – at the University of California, Santa Cruz, at the Udine Conference in Italy, at the University of Tel Aviv, at the University of São Paulo, at the Federal University of Rio de Janeiro (Niteroi), and at the University of New Delhi – for useful feedback concerning these materials.

1 Robert McKee, *Story: Substance, Structure, Style, and the Principles of Screenwriting* (London: Methuen, 1998).

2 A recent book, Michael Tierno's *Aristotle's Poetics for Screenwriters: Storytelling Secrets from the Greatest Mind in Western Civilization* (New York: Hyperion, 2002), argues that *The Poetics* is still "the Bible" for Hollywood screenwriters. "The criteria that Hollywood executives use to evaluate screenplays," he informs us breathlessly, "are **exactly** those the legendary philosopher Aristotle thought were the nuts and bolts of ancient drama more than 2,000 years ago!" (p. xviii).

3 Quoted in Kamilla Elliott, "Through the Looking Glass," dissertation written for the English Department at the University of California, Berkeley, 2001. The dissertation has now been published as *Rethinking the Novel/Film Debate* (Cambridge: Cambridge University Press, 2003).

4 Cecile Star, *Discovering the Movies*, quoted in Kamilla Elliott, "Rethinking the Novel/Film Debate," unpublished manuscript, p. 53.

5 See W. J. T. Mitchell, *Iconology: Image, Text, Ideology* (Chicago: University of Chicago Press, 1980), p. 43.

6 For Harold Bloom's work on intertextual influence see *The Anxiety of Influence: A Theory of Poetry* (Oxford: Oxford University Press, 1997) and *A Map of Misreading* (Oxford: Oxford University Press, 2003).

7 Youssef Ishaghpour notes the paradox that the first "speaking film, *The Jazz Singer*, takes as its subject a central ceremony of a religion – Judaism – founded exclusively on the word and on the prohibition of the image." See "La Parole et l'interdit des images: *Le Chanteur de Jazz* et les Juifs de Hollywood," in Jacques Aumont (ed.), *L'Image et la parole* (Paris: Cinemateque Française, 1999), p. 141.

8 Countless theorists have pointed out the remarkable analogies between the cinematic apparatus and the scene depicted in Plato's allegorical "cave." In both the movie theater and in Plato's cave, an artificial light, cast from behind the prisoners/spectators, plays over effigies of people and animals, leading the deluded captives to confuse flimsy simulations with ontological reality.

9 See Fredric Jameson, *Signatures of the Visible* (London: Routledge, 1992), p. 1.

10 On the theological background to this suspicion, see Ella Shohat, "Sacred Word, Profane Image: Theologies of Adaptation," in Robert Stam and Alessandra Raengo (eds), *A Companion to Literature and Film* (Oxford: Blackwell, 2004), ch. 2. For an encyclopedic account of anti-visualism, consult Martin Jay's *Downcast Eyes: The Denigration of Vision in Twentieth-century French Thought* (Berkeley, CA: University of California Press, 1994).

11 See Bruno Latour, "Introduction" to *Iconoclash: Beyond the Image Wars in Science, Religion, and Art* (Cambridge, MA: MIT Press, 2002).

12 Ibid., p. 33. See also Ella Shohat on the taboo on graven images in "Sacred Word, Profane Image."

13 From "Pictures," included in *The Moment and Other Essays*, quoted in Elliott, "Rethinking the Novel/Film Debate," p. 55 (see note 3).

14 See, for example, Torben Grobal, *Moving Pictures: A New Theory of Film Genres, Feelings and Cognition* (Oxford: Oxford University Press, 1997), p. 1.

The Theory and Practice of Adaptation

Introduction

Robert Stam

Introduction

15 See Vivian Sobchack, *The Address of the Eye: A Phenomenology of Film Experience* (Princeton, NJ: Princeton University Press, 1992), pp. 3–50.

16 Slavko Vorkapich, "A Fresh Look at the Dynamics of Film-making," *American Cinematographer* (February 1972), 223.

17 See Laura U. Marks, *The Skin of the Film: Intercultural Cinema, Embodiment, and the Senses* (Durham, NC: Duke University Press, 2000).

18 Kamilla Elliott makes this argument in "Through the Looking Glass" (see note 3).

19 But in French "*parasite*" also refers to communicational "static," which Michel Serres sees as the "noise" which engenders systemic change. Tom LeClair develops this point in his on-line essay "False Pretenses, Parasites and Monsters" (http://www.altx.com/ebr/ebr).

20 Elliott, "Rethinking the Novel/Film Debate," p. 27.

21 Lyotard's postmodernism, interestingly, is formulated as a kind of anti-narratology, as the decline of "grand narratives" in favor of more relativized "*petits recits*" or little stories, much as filmmaker Claude Chabrol recommended the treatment of "*petits sujets*," a suburban love affair rather than Fabrice at Waterloo.

22 Francesco Casetti, in his essay "Adaptation and Mis-adaptations: Film, Literature, and Social Discourses," in Stam and Raengo (eds), *Companion to Literature and Film*, ch. 6, sees adaptations as "reprogramming" reception in a new "communicative situation."

23 Although they do not deal with adaptation per se, two books treat the narratological innovations brought by the new media: Janet H. Murray's *Hamlet on the Holodeck: The Future of Narrative in Cyberspace* (Cambridge, MA: MIT Press, 1997) and Lev Manovich, *The Language of New Media* (Cambridge, MA: MIT Press, 2001).

24 See, for example, George P. Landow, *Hypertext: The Convergence of Contemporary Critical Theory and Technology* (Baltimore, MD: The Johns Hopkins University Press, 1991) and Stuart Moulthrope, "Reading from the Map: Metaphor and Metonymy in the Fiction of Forking Paths," in G. P. Landow and P. Delaney (eds), *Hypermedia and Literary Studies* (Cambridge, MA: MIT Press, 1990).

25 See Marsha Kinder, "Hotspots, Avatars and Narrative Fields Forever: Buñuel's Legacy for New Digital Media," *Film Quarterly* 55: 4 (Summer 2002).

26 Siva Vaidhyanathan, *Copyrights and Copywrongs: The Rise of Intellectual Property and How it Threatens Creativity* (New York: New York University Press, 2001), p. 10.

27 For a thorough discussion, see LeClair, "False Pretenses."

28 See Jean-Pierre Geuens, "The Digital World Picture," *Film Quarterly* 55: 4 (Summer, 2002).

29 See Russell Banks, "No, but I Saw the Movie," *Tin House* 2: 2 (Winter 2001), 12.

30 See Christian Metz, *The Imaginary Signifier* (Bloomington, IN: Indiana University Press, 1977), p. 12.

31 Georges Perec, *Les Choses* (Paris: L. N. Julliard, 1965), p. 80 (my translation).

32 Stanley Fish, *Is There a Text in this Class?* (Cambridge, MA: Harvard University Press, 1983).

33 Quoted by Banks in "No, but I Saw the Movie."

34 Vladimir Nabokov, *Lolita: A Screenplay* (New York: Vintage, 1997).

35 For an extended discussion of *Lolita*, see my *Literature Through Film: Realism, Magic, and the Art of Adaptation*, ch. 5 (Oxford: Blackwell, 2005).

36 For a discussion of visual style in *The Grapes of Wrath*, see Vivian Sobchack's essay in chapter 5 of this volume.

37 See André Gardies, *Le Recit filmique* (Paris: Hachette, 1993), pp. 5–6.

38 For a critique of medium-specificity arguments, see Noel Carroll, *Theorizing the Moving Image* (Cambridge: Cambridge University Press, 1996).

39 Gilles Deleuze, *The Time-Image*, trans. Hugh Tomlinson and Robert Galeta (Minneapolis, MN: University of Minnesota Press, 1989), p. 231.

40 See Boris Eikhenbaum, "Problems of Film Stylistics," *Screen* 15: 3 (Autumn 1974), 7–32.

41 See David Black, "Narrative Film and the Synoptic Tendency," a doctoral dissertation now in the process of completion for the Cinema Studies Department at New York University.

42 Vladimir Nabokov, *Lolita* (New York: G. P. Putnam/Berkley Medallion, 1955), p. 91.

43 I do not want to give the impression that I am alone in "going beyond" fidelity discourse. Dudley Andrew, James Naremore, Judith Mayne, François Jost, André Gaudreault, Tom Gunning, Millicent Marcus, Brian McFarlane, and many others have all, in their distinct ways, gone beyond such a discourse.

44 Ella Shohat and I try to call attention to the vast corpus of films that explore these potentialities in our *Unthinking Eurocentrism: Multiculturalism and the Media* (London: Routledge, 1994).

45 Brian McFarlane, in his useful book *Novel to Film: An Introduction to the Theory of Adaptation* (Oxford: Clarendon Press, 1996), draws what strikes me as an overly neat distinction between narrative events (especially what Barthes calls "cardinal functions" and what Seymour Chatman calls "kernels") and enunciation, the expressive apparatus that governs the presentation of the narrative. But it is difficult to separate narrative from enunciation. McFarlane speaks of narrative functions in the novel as those that are "not dependent on language," but in a novel everything is in a sense dependent on language. The problem is that cinematic enunciation, as I have argued in other terms throughout this chapter, changes the narrative in an infinity of subtle ways. "Kernels" do not exist in the abstract. Genette's very title *Narrative Discourse* (at least in the English version) suggests the impossibility of separating narrative and enunciation. Can a narrative kernel as purveyed in a novel really be exactly the same kernel when it is presented in film? Only if one moves to an impossibly high level of abstraction. McFarlane's book suffers from a tension between its formalist structuralist aspect and its poststructuralist aspects, with the result that McFarlane ends up falling back on the same binaries and truisms that he has gestured at discrediting: that film has no past tense, that film is spatial and novel is temporal, and so forth.

46 See Mia Mask's essay on *Beloved* in chapter 13 of this volume.

47 For painterly influences on Scorsese's *The Age of Innocence* (1993), see Brigitte Peucker, "The Moment of Portraiture: Scorsese Reads Wharton," in Stam and Raengo (eds), *Companion to Literature and Film*, ch. 21.

48 See Elliott, "Rethinking the Novel/Film Debate," ch. 4, p. 25 (see note 3). Elliott develops a very useful taxonomy of models for speaking about adaptation: (1) **psychic** (a passing of the spirit of the text); (2) **ventriloqual** (the imposition of a new voice on an inert body); (3) **genetic** (a deep textual DNA is newly manifested in a new realm); (4) **de(re)composing** (the novel is decomposed into parts and recomposed at another level); (5) **incarnational** (word becomes flesh); and (6) **trumping** (i.e. film shows its superior capacities to tell the story). The issue of "incarnational" adaptation came up in relation to Mel Gibson's *The Passion of the Christ*. Where some saw anti-Semitism, and others a gratuitously sadistic imaging of the crucifixion, others saw the words of the gospel made flesh.

49 For a discussion of adaptation as critical reading, see Margaret Montalbano, "From Bram Stoker's *Dracula* to *Bram Stoker's 'Dracula'*," in Stam and Raengo (eds), *Companion to Literature and Film*, ch. 23.

50 For a systematic, even technical, exploration of adaptation as translation, see Patrick Cattrysse, *Pour une théorie de l'adaptation filmique: le film noir Americain* (Berne: Peter Lang, 1992).

51 On the interrelations between the two kinds of genre, see Julian Cornell's essay on apocalyptic fiction/film, "All's Wells that Ends Wells: Apocalypse and Empire in *The War of the Worlds*," in Stam and Raengo (eds), *Companion to Literature and Film*, ch. 25.

52 For a relational and "polysystemic" analysis of *film noir* as genre, see R. Barton Palmer, "The Sociological Turn of Adaptation Studies: The Example of *Film Noir*," in Stam and Raengo (eds), *Companion to Literature and Film*, ch. 16.

53 See James Naremore's chapter on *Cabin in the Sky* in his *The Films of Vincente Minnelli* (Cambridge: Cambridge University Press, 1993).

54 See Gary Saul Morson (ed.), *Literature and History: Theoretical Problems and Russian Case Studies* (Stanford: Stanford University Press, 1986), p. 265.

55 For examples of the chronotopic analysis of adaptation, see Bliss Cua Lim's essay on *Stepford Wives* (chapter 8 in this volume), Paula Massood's essay on Spike Lee's *Clockers* (chapter 9 in this volume), and Peter Hitchcock, "Running Time: The Chronotope of *The Loneliness of the Long Distance Runner*," in Stam and Raengo (eds), *Companion to Literature and Film*, ch. 19.

56 Gérard Genette, *Palimpsestes* (Paris: Seuil, 1982).

57 On the relation between the Bible and film, see Ella Shohat, "Sacred Word, Profane Image;" Gavriel Moses, "The Bible as Cultural Object(s) in Cinema;" and Pamela Grace, "Gospel Truth? From Cecil B. DeMille to Nicholas Ray," all in Stam and Raengo (eds), *Companion to Literature and Film*.

58 On intertextuality, see Raffaele De Berti's essay on the metamorphoses of Pinocchio ("Italy and America: Pinocchio's First Cinematic Trip") and Charles Musser's essay on the various "refigurations" of the novels of Horace McCoy ("The Devil's Parody: Horace McCoy's Appropriation and Refiguration of Two Hollywood Musicals") both in Stam and Raengo (eds), *Companion to Literature and Film*.

59 See Peter Bart, "Attack of the Clones," *GQ* (September 2002).

60 See Stephen Schiff, *Lolita: The Book of the Film* (New York: Applause, 1998).

61 See Maria Tortajada, "From Libertinage to Eric Rohmer: Transcending 'Adaptation'," in Stam and Raengo (eds), *Companion to Literature and Film*, ch. 20.

62 See Alan S. Weiss, "The Rhetoric of Interruption," in Stam and Raengo (eds), *Companion to Literature and Film*, ch. 11.

63 Nitin Govil, "Screening Copyright and Pirate Hollywood," chapter in a dissertation in progress for the Cinema Studies Department at New York University.

64 For an expanded discussion of this process as it operates in *Robinson Crusoe*, see my *Literature Through Film*, ch. 2.

65 For an extended discussion of these issues in relation to Cervantes, Fielding, Flaubert, Dostoevsky, and Nabokov, see my *Literature Through Film*.

66 See André Gaudreault and François Jost, *Le Recit cinematographique* (Paris: Nathan, 1999), p. 10.

67 See Wayne Booth, *The Rhetoric of Fiction* (Chicago: University of Chicago Press, 1961).

68 See Eric Smoodin, "The Image and the Voice in the Film: Spoken Narration," *Quarterly Review of Film Studies* 8: 4 (Fall, 1987).

69 See Robert Burgoyne, "The Cinematic Narrator: The Logic and Pragmatics of Impersonal Narration," *Journal of Film and Video* 42: 1 (Spring, 1990).

70 In some adaptations, a novel's form of embedded narrative is replaced by a different yet still embedded form. In the novel *The French Lieutenant's Woman*, John Fowles's narrator performs an analytical shuttle between a Victorian plot and a metacommentary on the nature of Victorian fiction. But the Karel Reisz adaptation introduces an altered form of embedded narration by intercutting a Victorian and a modern love story, with the former becoming a kind of film-within-the-film. Fowles's anachronistic references to Victorian science and political theory are largely discarded. Nor is there an equivalent in the film of the authorial persona of Fowles's narrator, costumed in Victorian frock coat and beard, sharing a train compartment with his protagonist, contrasting the conventions of Victorian fiction with those of the French New Novel, initiating us into the historical genealogy and the technical secrets of his craft. The film has neither a writer reflecting on writing nor a filmmaker reflecting on filmmaking. Instead the film gives us a bifurcated romance, two parallel love stories set in distinct referential time-frames. Although the two stories beautifully play off the trendily modern against the romanticized archaic, and although the transitions between them are often brilliant, their interaction merely generates an ambiguous Pirandellian touch, rather than a more thoroughgoing subversion of referentiality.

71 See, for example, Booth, *The Rhetoric of Fiction*.

72 See Banks, "No, but I Saw the Movie," 21.

73 See François Jost, "The Look: From Film to Novel. An Essay in Comparative Narratology," in Stam and Raengo (eds), *Companion to Literature and Film*, ch. 5.

74 See Gérard Genette, *Narrative Discourse Revisited*, trans. Jane E. Lewin (Ithaca, NY: Cornell University Press, 1988).

75 See their separate essays in Stam and Raengo (eds), *Companion to Literature and Film*.

76 Millicent Marcus, *Filmmaking by the Book: Italian Cinema and Literary Adaptation* (Baltimore, MD: The Johns Hopkins University Press, 1996).

77 As discussed by Brigitte Peucker in "The Moment of Portraiture."

78 Edward Said, *Culture and Imperialism* (New York: Alfred Knopf, 1994), p. 151.

79 See Tim Watson's essay on *Mansfield Park* in chapter 1 of this volume.

80 See chapter 2 of my *Literature Through Film*.

81 See Brian Boyd, *Vladimir Nabokov: The American Years* (Princeton, NJ: Princeton University Press, 1991), p. 387.

82 See Chris Straayer's essay, "The Talented Poststructuralist: Hetero-masculinity, Gay Artifice, and Class Passing," in Stam and Raengo (eds), *Companion to Literature and Film*, ch. 22, on the various adaptations of "Ripley."

83 For discussions of ideological shifts in adaptation, see Jacquelyn Kilpatrick's essay on "transmutations of the national" in *The Last of the Mohicans* (chapter 2 of this volume), and Patrick Deer's essay on *The English Patient* (chapter 10 of this volume), along with Noa Steimatsky's "Photographic *Verismo*, Cinematic Adaptation, and the Staging of a Neorealist Landscape," in Stam and Raengo (eds), *Companion to Literature and Film*, ch. 14.

84 See Raoul Ruiz, *Poetics of Cinema* (Paris: Editions Dis Voir, 1995).

85 Sid Field, *Screenplay: The Foundations of Screenwriting* (New York: Dell, 1979), p. 56.

86 For a discussion of cross-national adaptations in Chinese cinema, see Zhang Zhen's essay "Cosmopolitan Projections: World Literature on Chinese Screens," in Stam and Raengo (eds), *Companion to Literature and Film*, ch. 10.

87 For further discussion of the impact of national context, see Alexandra Seibel's essay on *The Lost Honor of Katharina Blum* (chapter 7 of this volume) and Jessica Scarlata's essay on *The Butcher Boy* (chapter 11 of this volume).

88 M. M. Bakhtin, "Discourse in the Novel," in *The Dialogical Imagination*, trans. Caryl Emerson and Michael Holquist (Austin: University of Texas Press, 1981), p. 421.

89 See Dudley Andrew, "Adapting Cinema to History: A Revolution in the Making," in Stam and Raengo (eds), *Companion to Literature and Film*, ch. 13.

Robert Stam

Introduction

Chapter 1

Improvements and Reparations at Mansfield Park

Tim Watson

When Miramax released *Mansfield Park* in 1999, the movie was greeted with outrage from critics and fans who found its emphasis on slavery unpalatable and unfaithful to the Jane Austen novel on which Patricia Rozema's film was based.[1] Customer reviews of the DVD version of the film on the amazon.com website carry many such expressions of anger: "I'm sure we all understand the vulgarity of slavery without needing to see it graphically displayed in a format that Austen herself would have refused to watch," wrote one viewer, referring to the scene in the film in which Fanny Price discovers Tom Bertram's sketchbook of brutal and pornographic scenes from the Bertram family's Antigua plantation; another viewer claimed, "The moral issue of slavery, not even addressed in the novel, is tossed in, seemingly on a whim."[2] "Rubbing slavery in the faces of the audience," wrote "hannah12," "misses what Ms Austen is about and why people still read her books. Ms Austen did not write about the political issues of the 18th–19th centuries. She wrote about relationships."[3] In other words, politics is still "what some read [and watch] Austen to avoid," as Claudia Johnson put it in her review of Rozema's film in the *Times Literary Supplement*.[4]

However, while outraged fans imagined Jane Austen rolling or spinning in her grave in response to Rozema's *Mansfield Park*,[5] in many ways the film's emphasis on the slavery subtext in Austen's novel was simply the logical outcome of the revisionist historiography and literary criticism of the past twenty years or so that has placed the question of slavery at the center of discussion of early nineteenth-century British history in general and of Austen's *Mansfield Park* in particular, and has placed this hitherto least appreciated of her novels at the center of the Jane Austen canon. While individual critics certainly disagree about both the importance and the meaning of Austen's references to the Bertrams' Antigua plantation in the novel, historicist interpretations of *Mansfield*

Park, in terms of its place in the discourses of slavery and imperialism, have become hegemonic in academia, even if they have made little headway in such forums of Jane Austen criticism as the massively popular Republic of Pemberley website.[6] Revisionist work on the history of slavery, abolition, and the rise of industrial capitalism has fed into Austen criticism. In *Culture and Imperialism*, the reference point for all later criticism of *Mansfield Park*, Edward Said cites the work of Robin Blackburn, C. L. R. James, and Eric Williams as enabling his own analysis of Jane Austen's novel.[7]

Historians have approached abolition and emancipation as many-sided phenomena, so that it is hardly controversial nowadays to argue, for instance, that emerging humanitarian and liberal attitudes in the late eighteenth and early nineteenth centuries – the hallmark of the abolitionist movement in Britain – helped to pave the way for new forms of imperialism, and in particular the "civilizing mission," of the later nineteenth century.[8] Consequently, the liberal and humanitarian Jane Austen was an obvious candidate for inclusion in this new complex historiography, as an exemplary recorder of the multiple relationships between domestic and colonial in the interregnum between the first and the second British empires, and of some of the ways in which colonial questions were actually central to the elaboration of new English cultures in the nineteenth century.[9] The sophistication and irony of this historiographical approach – in which it is sometimes hard to tell the good guys from the bad – appeared to match the intricacies and ironies of *Mansfield Park* itself. And so Rozema's film picked up on and validated this academic approach. As John Wiltshire puts it in his recent book on Austen adaptations, "The film is the apotheosis of these variously political readings of Jane Austen: it certainly represents a meeting point or site of infiltration by academic commentary into the mass media."[10]

However, while the film appears to validate academic hegemony over *Mansfield Park*, and over Jane Austen in general, against the middlebrow inhabitants of the Republic of Pemberley, in fact, if we read the Jane Austen criticism carefully, we can see a curious parallel between fan outrage at Rozema's film and academic disappointment with Austen's novel. Despite the undoubted importance of the revisionist histories of British slavery, and despite their formal analogy to the difficult structure of Austen's novel itself, it is nevertheless a common experience of modern readers of *Mansfield Park* that, for all its subtlety, what the novel lacks is precisely a simple, heroic narrative of abolition. Faced with the complexities of plot, character, and narrative point of view in the novel, readers often experience disappointment, loss, and even a sense of infidelity to an imaginary "original" story of slavery – just as viewers of film adaptations routinely complain of movies' unfaithfulness to "the book."

One of Jane Austen's heroes, the abolitionist Thomas Clarkson, provided one of the best-known versions of that simple historical narrative. In his *History of the Rise, Progress, and Accomplishment of the Abolition of the African Slave-Trade*, first published in 1808, the movement to outlaw the buying and selling of Africans in the transatlantic slave trade is famously likened to a river. A fold-out map of the history of abolition is included in Clarkson's book, with the names of famous abolitionists attached to streams or tributaries, linking up to form a large body of water: "The torrent which swept away the Slave-trade."[11]

Readers and critics of *Mansfield Park* have often longed for another kind of story, one as clear cut and sweeping as Clarkson's river. Austen's careful laying bare of the complex system of suppression, evasion, and silencing necessary for the comfortable life of the English gentry dependent on wealth derived from slavery – the careful staging of the silence of the Bertrams in response to Fanny's famous question about the slave trade, for example – actually carries the force of an active silencing, suppression, and evasion on the part of the novel.[12] If Jane Austen really "loved" Thomas Clarkson, as she once declared, then she should have made Fanny's opposition to slavery as explicit and courageous as her opposition to the attentions of Henry Crawford. "It would be silly," writes Edward Said, "to expect Jane Austen to treat slavery with anything like the passion of an abolitionist or a newly liberated slave."[13] And yet this is often precisely what modern readers wish for and expect. While we may recognize, and take pleasure in, the multiplicity and ambiguity of the events of this historical period and of Austen's novel, we still long for history as simple story – for Clarkson's river of justice running toward victory – just as viewers of Jane Austen adaptations sometimes long for history as an elegant and simple tale of "relationships," manners, and pretty country houses, validating the notion that "Jane Austen's novels have a pervading modesty."[14]

Thus, while academic viewers and readers are quick to scorn the popular language of "fidelity" as a way of understanding film adaptations – and quick therefore to dismiss fans' anger at Rozema's film's "betrayal" of Austen's tale – we ought also to be aware of our own investment in particular versions of history, and not necessarily the versions that are "good for us," or sanctioned by the protocols of academic historiography. Robert Stam points out that there is a "grain of truth" in the language of fidelity and betrayal in relation to film adaptations; that it speaks to a certain loss of "our own phantasmatic relation" to the cultural object that viewers of film versions of classic novels experience.[15] And what is crucial here is that this fantasy of control is itself a result of the fact that history is produced, disseminated, and consumed at many different sites, of which the academic discipline of history is only one, and often not the most important one, as Michel-Rolph Trouillot has usefully reminded us in his book *Silencing the Past*.[16] The genre of the Western lies behind Trouillot's rhetorical question: "Is it really inconsequential that the history of America is being written in the same world where few little boys want to be Indians?"[17] Likewise, film and television are undoubtedly the most influential elements in the establishment of slavery as a crime against humanity. Behind our contemporary dissatisfaction with Austen's version of Fanny Price, and with the novel's equivocation on the question of slavery, lie *Roots*, *Eyes on the Prize*, and images of civil rights protests in the US South in the 1950s, all of which helped to establish slavery as an unambiguous historical evil.

I believe, however, that a careful historical reading of Austen's novel will show that this apparently simple and unambiguous narrative of emancipation is, in fact, more complex than it seems; that the price we pay for agreeing that slavery was an historical evil is a complicity with an understanding of history that imagines the liberal subject as autonomous, self-fashioning, and always capable therefore of "improvement." An analysis of Austen's novel — in which "improvement" is a key figure — shows that the idea of "emancipation," which relies on this modern subject for its ethical charge, grows out of this Janus-faced figure of improvement, one employed by proslavery and abolitionist writers alike. In other words, a new reading of *Mansfield Park*, the novel, reveals the multiple and sometimes contradictory presuppositions that lie behind contemporary belief in the simple narrative of slavery. In this respect, this chapter endorses historical specificity and complexity over simple narratives, but in it I also hope to show that simple narratives always have complex and contradictory components.

However, I think that an emphasis on the complexities and ambiguities of the apparently straightforward narrative of emancipation might also have the unintended effect of causing us to overlook, marginalize, or dismiss an emergent common sense in the contemporary world: the simple narrative or logic of reparations for slavery. I imagine a future "new historicist" looking back at Rozema's film version of *Mansfield Park* would notice that it appeared in the midst of a great upsurge of interest and activism around the question of slavery reparations, just as critics of Austen's novel have repositioned it in the context of debates over emancipation in the 1810s and 1820s. In other words, perhaps an attentiveness to the new simple narrative of reparations will sometimes draw us away from the elitist pleasures of complexity and ambiguity. I conclude by arguing that Rozema's film constitutes both an evasion of, but also an engagement with, this new logic of reparations.

Improvements

Since the publication in rapid succession of Alistair Duckworth's *The Improvement of the Estate* (1971) and Raymond Williams's *The Country and the City* (1973), it has been a critical commonplace that the problem of "improvement" lies at the center of Jane Austen's *Mansfield Park*.[18] As has been often noted, improvement in the novel is ambiguous: careless improvements to country estates are deprecated, while the careful improvement of Fanny's mind is welcomed. Less frequently remarked upon is the fact that this confusion parallels and is informed by the contemporary debate over improvement in the British West Indies, in which the improvement or "melioration" of slaves' moral and material living conditions was linked to "improvements" in estate management and agricultural practices. Tracing these connections reveals some of the complicated beginnings of the modern figure of the autonomous liberal subject, who is crucially defined by his or her capacity for improvement, and the simple narrative of emancipation which requires this improvable subject as the precondition for the historical rejection of slavery.

Mansfield Park was published at the moment of emergence of a new form of historiography requiring this liberal subject as both its precondition and its endpoint — the form of historiography that became "common sense" to later readers. As noted by Mark Salber Phillips, this new historiography prefigured later social history by representing "worlds of social experience and inward feeling that were hard to translate into the traditional narrative conventions . . . Eighteenth-century narratives were already concerned with commercial life and everyday manners, with the experiences of women, 'primitives,' poets, and others not involved in statecraft."[19] Austen's novel stands at the crossroads of a new modernity, and a new understanding of history, one marked, as David Lloyd argues in an important essay on the Irish famine, by "a dominant historical conception of human development . . . [that] is not merely an ethical ideal but an end that regulates historical method and evaluation, from the selection and legitimation of archives and sources to the organizing modes of narrative."[20] A re-reading of the novel in this light allows us to see some of the complicated streams from which this historical river of common sense flowed.

The proper register for the evaluation of improvement – moral, intellectual, architectural, and political – is rarely present in *Mansfield Park*. The word is almost always presented to the reader in free indirect discourse, from which we need to disentangle character, narrator, and implied author's value judgments, often a thankless task. Are we meant to recoil at Sir Thomas Bertram's apparently lecherous and certainly acquisitive judgment of Fanny on his return from Antigua: he notices, with "decided pleasure," how Fanny has grown while he has been away, and when she blushes, finds himself "justified in his belief of her equal improvement in health and beauty" (p. 123)? If so, then the reader is compelled to question the invocation of improvement as a positive term to describe the changes in Fanny's mind and character after her transfer to Mansfield Park: the narrator comments that Fanny's cousin Edmund's attentions, and his book recommendations in particular, "were . . . of the highest importance in assisting the improvement of her mind, and extending its pleasures" (p. 18). Again, while clearly the bumbling aristocrat Rushworth is a fool for thinking that cutting down the avenue of trees at his Sotherton estate constitutes "improvement" (p. 40), on the other hand, what is the reader to make of Edmund's warm embrace of the "spirit of improvement abroad" (p. 230) amongst clergymen that allows them to preach more dramatically, and, perhaps, more effectively? Clearly, improvement is an ambiguous, even Janus-faced, figure in *Mansfield Park*: it looks toward both past and future, mediating them without allowing a stable point of reference. At times, the novel appears to endorse improvement as positive change; at others, improvement appears to be little more than a synonym for vandalism and social control. Through the figure of improvement, then, the novel stages the difficult problems of how and when to change inherited social and cultural forms without thereby undermining their power to stabilize family and community structures: how, in other words, to manage and govern the effects of the past in the present, without risking sudden and potentially revolutionary innovation and change.

We see this in a little-noticed moment of dialogue in the novel, an apparently casual conversation that in fact bears the weight of these questions of improvement, development, and the new historiography. After Sir Thomas's return from Antigua, Fanny and Mary Crawford strike up a new kind of intimacy, with Fanny paying frequent visits to her new friend at the parsonage owned by Mary's sister and brother-in-law, the Grants. Walking in the parsonage's shrubbery, Fanny suddenly breaks into her longest speech of the novel up to that point, in which she rhapsodizes on the improvements Mrs Grant has made since taking over the parsonage from the Norrises: "This is pretty, very pretty . . . every time I come into this shrubbery I am more struck with its growth and beauty. Three years ago, this was nothing but a rough hedgerow along the upper side of the field, never thought of as anything, or capable of becoming anything; and now it is converted into a walk, and it would be difficult to say whether most valuable as a convenience or an ornament" (p. 143). These are proper improvements: Fanny admires Mrs Grant's "taste" and comments: "There is such a quiet simplicity in the plan of the walk! Not too much attempted!" (p. 143). The conversation has a symbolic importance that the reader can only guess at this stage: the parsonage will eventually be the home of Fanny and Edmund at the end of the novel, and these improvements in fact represent the obliteration of all traces of the parsonage's previous tenants, Mr and Mrs Norris.

However, this particular narrative of improvement actually resonates little with modern readers – certainly to judge by the lack of attention this passage has received in writing on *Mansfield Park* – who, in this as in so many other aspects of the novel, in fact think more like Mary Crawford, who, "untouched and inattentive, had nothing to say" (p. 143) in response to Fanny's remarks about the shrubbery. I would suggest that an attentive reading of these passages, however, provides important clues for understanding the vexed question of improvements in relation to the narration of history. Fanny continues her speech with a disturbing meditation on the past and on memory: "Perhaps, in another three years, we may be forgetting – almost forgetting what it was before" (p. 144). She goes on to muse about "something more speakingly incomprehensible in the powers, the failures, the inequalities of memory . . . [which] is sometimes so retentive, so serviceable, so obedient; at others, so bewildered and so weak; and at others again, so tyrannic, so beyond controul!" (p. 144). But while Fanny worries about memory, Mary Crawford, the emerging modern subject, lives in the new register of history – which is always the history of the modern subject. While Fanny remembers the words of "my uncle's gardener" (p. 144) on the rich soil of the parsonage grounds – invoking customary practice, community memory, and a rural caste system – Mary replies, "To say the truth . . . I am something like the famous Doge at the court of Lewis XIV; and may declare that I see no wonder in this shrubbery equal to seeing myself in it" (p. 144). Mary's narcissistic self-insertion into the narrative of history – in keeping with her London roots and her modern tastes – is excessive enough to enable us to see that this is in fact the structure of all modern historical narratives.

Christopher Kent has made the important observation that the French Revolution "ushered in the age of historicism. Jane Austen lived and wrote at the threshold of this new era of and for history."[21] Here Mary Crawford reaches back before the French Revolution in the interests of a modern history, one entirely at odds with Fanny's invocation of the wonders of nature, or the local wisdom of her uncle's gardener.[22] The result is a particularly striking emblem of the ambiguous figure of improvement. On the one hand, the novel's emphasis on Fanny's education, moral and intellectual, and the creation of a modern, liberal subject through the discipline of *history* carries with it as its underside the creation of the egotistical, materialist modern subject, Mary Crawford; on the other hand, Fanny's emphasis on communal *memory*, estate improvements in accord with nature and social custom, carries with it as its shadow the preservation of a social and economic system that produces the likes of Mrs Norris, a heavy-handed, patriarchal gentry society that stifles and suppresses Fanny's creativity and imagination. This ambiguity becomes even more complicated and resonant when we factor in the debate over improvement taking place simultaneously in the pamphlet literature on abolition and emancipation in the Caribbean.

Just as in *Mansfield Park*, in both abolitionist and pro-slavery pamphlets and books, some of which Austen undoubtedly knew of and read, "improvement" also joins rather than separates land-based and subject-based discourses: the improvement of the West Indian estate becomes inseparable from the "improvement" of slaves' conditions, religious understanding, and level of civilization. For example, in James Stephen's *Reasons for Establishing a Registry of Slaves in the British Colonies*, published in 1814, the same year as *Mansfield Park*, this leading abolitionist writer sought to co-opt the position of West Indian planters who claimed that their chief interest was improving both the living and working conditions and the moral character of their slaves. He argued that abolitionists hoped to encourage ideas and practices that would "operate in the mind of the master; inclining him powerfully for his own sake, to promote the happiness, and improve the conditions of his slaves."[23] This "melioration" or improvement of the slaves' condition is seen as part of a more general improvement of the sugar estates, and thus ultimately of British power itself. In order to encourage the benevolent master who "would improve the moral conduct of his slaves, and render their lot more cheerful, by the all-powerful prospect of freedom" (p. 53), the British government needed to understand the economic circumstances of post-abolition planters who would have to make "great sacrifices" in order to:

> keep up or enlarge a declining gang [of slaves] by means of native increase. A great diminution of labour, especially among the females, is essential to that change: so are a more liberal and expensive sustenation [sic] of the slaves in general, [and] a more chargeable care of infants and invalids . . . It was not known or considered [before abolition of the slave trade], how few planters, comparatively, are in circumstances to afford such improvements, or have even the present capacity to make them. (p. 40)

It was this kind of abolitionist thinking that led, ultimately, to the large-scale compensation of West Indian planters in 1833 when slavery was finally abolished (although it was replaced for five years by the quasi-bondage of "apprenticeship"). Here, however, I cite it as a sign that *Mansfield Park* was hardly the only text in 1814 to link the improvement of the estate to the moral and material improvement of its subservient population, and to do so in the name of a benign form of social regulation, especially of female reproductive capacity. It is, we should remind ourselves, at the moment of Sir Thomas Bertram's return from Antigua, from dealing with the "recent losses" (p. 19) of his West Indian estates after abolition, that he comments so favorably on Fanny's improvement in health and beauty, and so quickly moves to sell her off in the gentry's marriage market.

In Rozema's film, this analogy between Fanny and Sir Thomas's slaves is made explicit: bridling at Sir Thomas's post-Antigua offer of a ball to showcase her value as a potential wife, Fanny flees, pursued by Edmund, to whom she declares, "I'll not be sold off like one of your father's slaves."[24] We should be wary, of course, of making too quick analogies between West Indian chattel slavery and the position of lower-class women in England in the early nineteenth century. Nevertheless, a "benign, though insensible revolution in opinions and manners," as Stephen summarizes the abolitionists' goal for West Indian slaves (p. 37), is also an apt description of the change Fanny goes through at Mansfield Park. The costly "improvements" that Stephen outlines for West Indian estates in the gradual transition to freedom are all necessary changes in Sir Thomas's estate management when back in Northamptonshire, especially in regard to Fanny: "a great diminution of labour, especially among the females . . . [and] a more liberal and expansive sustenation of the slaves in general" closely echo the novel's, and Sir Thomas's, escalating critique of Mrs Norris's parsimony (not allowing Fanny a fire in her room, for example) and unnecessary extraction of labor from Fanny. Readers' frustration with Fanny's apparent passivity stems from the challenge of a novel which denies to its protagonist the authority over her own destiny, and yet leads her to a kind of freedom all the same, just as Stephen hoped for "an emancipation, of which not the slaves, but the masters, should be the willing instruments or authors" (p. 37).

In retrospect, therefore — looking back from the period when emancipation became common sense — "improvement" comes to look like a perverse and ironic strategy for maintaining the status quo, for prolonging the brutality of slavery by a hypocritical cover of humanitarian interest in the slaves' bodies, minds, and labor conditions. Such a conclusion, for example, seems perfectly justified for the slave codes passed by planter-dominated Caribbean local assemblies in the late eighteenth and early nineteenth centuries, such as the one passed by Antigua and the other Leeward Islands in 1798, which spoke insistently of improvement but changed little or nothing on the ground.[25] However, historical hindsight may also be a kind of blindness — hindering us from seeing the extent to which the idea of improvement has become part of the structure of our own psyches and social lives, blocking our view of its historical emergence at a particular moment, and in a particular contest over its meaning and value. We are tempted to see only hypocrisy in proslavery discourse about improvement because in fact we need to maintain the fiction of the autonomous liberal subject of whom improvement is always possible. Instead, the tussle over subjecthood, enslavement, and improvement played out, albeit sometimes in diffuse and displaced forms, in *Mansfield Park*, allows us to rethink some of our own assumptions about these same questions, to undo some of the common sense that links narratives and ideas of human development/improvement, the autonomous subject, and the structures of power that produce and constrain that subject.

Not, of course, in order to endorse proslavery arguments, but in order to understand more clearly the ways in which the language of humanitarianism, education, and the improvable subject are in fact the preconditions for the new forms of suppression and exploitation emerging in the early nineteenth century, the new forms that come after that moment called "emancipation." James Ramsay, in one of the most famous early abolitionist tracts, makes this link strikingly clear. In the preface to his book, he states the goal of the abolitionist movement:

> To gain to society, to reason and religion, half a million of our kind, equally with us adapted for advancing themselves in every art and science, that can distinguish man from man, equally with us made capable of looking forward to and enjoying futurity . . . The people, whose improvement is here proposed, toil for the British state. The public, therefore, has an interest in their advancement in society. And what is here claimed for them? Not bounties, or gifts from parliament, or people; but leave to become more useful to themselves, their masters, and the state.[26]

What is so troubling, therefore, about *Mansfield Park* in the post-emancipation moment, but what also allows it to become the most important Austen text in the current critical matrix, is that it resists the lure of the improved, liberal subject (Mary Crawford) even as it also calls into question the values of a rural England that was passing away in the commercialization of agriculture in the early nineteenth century (Sir Thomas, Mrs Norris). The novel allows the reader to re-examine some of the presumptions of history as progress or improvement, without succumbing to the lure of the anti-historical nostalgia that imagines "Jane Austen" as a sign for a cozy, stable rural society.

Mansfield Park, in other words, allows us to see some of the complicities and complexities of our understanding of history – and to do so without undue reverence for the memory of what Mary Crawford calls "the sturdy independence of your country customs" (p. 43). In his essay on the aftermath of the Irish famine, David Lloyd argues that the "dominant historical conception of human development," which we have traced back to the moment of *Mansfield Park* and the debates over improvement and emancipation, "bears, moreover, an idea of the human subject which is the product of that narrative and the ideal of the discipline itself [i.e., history] – the disinterested subject of modern civil society. The legitimacy of any given historical utterance is proportional to its coherence with the emergence of such a subject."[27] So re-reading the novel allows us to glimpse the multiple, ambiguous lineaments of the apparently commonsensical, progressive narrative of history in which the triumph of the improvable bourgeois subject requires that "emancipation" appear at the beginning of the narrative – that rejecting slavery (as Austen's novel notoriously declines to do) is the *sine qua non* of modernity and the emergence of "the disinterested subject of modern civil society." Lloyd's essay also shows how popular memory, while inextricably overlaid and tied up with official historical narratives, nevertheless provides evidence of ways of surviving oppression and tyranny, ways of "living on," in Lloyd's terms.[28] The problem of *Mansfield Park* therefore is not merely the problem of slavery, or the problem of the novel's undecidable attitude toward slavery, but the problem of how we might recover alternative narratives to the narrative of liberal, humanitarian emancipation – different ways of "living on" – without losing our-selves in the wilds of Fanny's unkempt memory in the shrubbery, "bewildered," "weak," "tyrannic," and "beyond controul," as she describes it (p. 144). In the final section of this chapter, I suggest some ways in which an analysis of the film version of *Mansfield Park* might lead to an understanding of "reparations" as a form of living on – attentive to both history and to memory without reconstituting the "disinterested subject."

Reparations

Patricia Rozema's film *Mansfield Park* acknowledges a debt to recent revisionist history in many ways: while it is flagrantly unfaithful to its fictional predecessor (incorporating little of Austen's dialogue or narrative language, for example), the movie follows closely the main thrust of contemporary historiography. The project of social historians of all stripes to recover and represent the experience of "the people," rather than their political and military leaders, is sanctioned in Rozema's film in its rethinking of the traditional country-house costume drama: as Rozema put it in the commentary for the DVD version of the film, she began her screenplay by asking the question, "Who's paying for the party?"[29] The answer, made explicit in the film in an appropriately preachy moment from Edmund, is the slaves in Antigua: "We all live off the profits, Fanny, even you."[30] When the elder son, Tom, returns early, and drunk, from his and Sir Thomas's trip to Antigua, he falls from his horse, and in response to Edmund's question "What of Antigua?" replies: "Ah, Antigua and all the lovely people there paying for this party."[31] As the director put it in an interview, "I actually believe that this [*Mansfield Park*] was her [Austen's] meditation on servitude and slavery . . . She was kind of exploring what it is to treat humans as property, women, blacks, and the poor especially."[32]

Mansfield Park positions itself in explicit opposition to the nostalgic cult of the English country house, a genre drawn on by all other Austen adaptations, even those, such as Ang Lee and Emma Thompson's *Sense and Sensibility* (1995), that seek to temper such preciousness with careful attention to the place of servants' labor in maintaining such mansions.[33] Rozema's film uses a ruined manor house (Kirby Hall) for the exterior shots of Mansfield Park, and in its interior shots makes sure that some of the bleakness of even a grand house comes across to the viewer. (Nevertheless, a materialist reading of the conditions of production of the film would note that the film's producers thank in the credits both English Heritage and the National Trust, prime institutional movers in the heritage industry of which the film is ostensibly a critique.) In the first shot of the house at night, it bulks dark and foreboding in the distance, dwarfing its new inhabitant, Fanny Price. Once inside, the camera resists almost entirely the impulse of costume dramas to dwell on details of furnishing, dress, and decoration.[34] Fanny is given a whirlwind tour of the house by Mrs Norris in which rooms are pointed out but denied to both Fanny and the viewer, in which corridors and bare walls are swept through in an unsettling way, and in which one of the few moments of rest is provided by a view through a window to a section of the building in visible disrepair: "Oh, that's the west wing," Mrs Norris explains, "soon to be repaired, if Tom could set aside his horses and the dice for long enough."[35]

This problem of repair, of fixing the problems of the past in the present, is both a theme in the film (which ends with a shot of the west wing under reconstruction) and a precondition for the making of the movie in the first place, as it seeks to repair both the historical and historiographical errors of the past: building British and American societies on the profits of slavery, and then denying the fact in historical narratives of the past. Tom, the elder son, with abolitionist sympathies and a drinking problem, becomes the film's focal point for representing this dilemma. The film oscillates between treating Tom as a figure of playful fun, falling down drunk and pettishly rejecting his father's orders, producing the jagged but irreverent self-portrait on the landing that Mrs Norris dismisses on Fanny's house tour as "very modern," and Tom as a figure of emotional weight, caught in an intolerable position between his filial duty as heir and his abolitionist sympathies, producing the sketches of West Indian plantation life that so shock Fanny and the viewer with their frank depiction of the violence of slave societies, and lapsing into serious illness as a bodily sign of the psychic trauma he has endured. In this respect, Tom uncannily represents the paradoxical contemporary relation to the idea of history that political theorist Wendy Brown describes in her book *States of Injury*: on the one hand, we have become accustomed to the idea of historical narratives as arbitrary and playful, written from the point of view of particular interests, while, on the other hand, we experience the full weight of history as force, as "immeasurable heaviness" penetrating and even destroying the innermost recesses of the psyche: "We know ourselves to be saturated by history, we feel the extraordinary force of its determinations; we are also steeped in a discourse of its insignificance."[36]

Thus, on the one hand, Rozema's film version of *Mansfield Park* marks the heaviness of history, forcefully disrupting and denying the cozy image of elegant, prettified Jane Austen as a refuge from politics, while, on the other hand, the film registers the insignificance and arbitrariness of history and historical narrative, especially in its closing sequence in which the camera flies jauntily as it wraps up the stories of each character with Fanny's cheeky voice-over: "It could have turned out differently, I suppose . . . but it didn't . . ."[37] There is an especially severe disjunction between, on the one hand, this light-hearted, even sprightly voice-over, with the swooping pleasures of the helicopter-borne camera angles, and, on the other hand, the touching father–son reconciliation scene between Sir Thomas and Tom that immediately precedes this final sequence. The actual verbal content of Fanny's final voice-over emphasizes the fact that Mrs Norris has become an "hourly evil" – a rare example of Austen's original text appearing unaltered in Rozema's film – and that Sir Thomas has given up his business in Antigua only in order to "pursue some exciting new opportunities in tobacco."[38] History is made light of and even trivialized – "it could all have turned out differently, I suppose" – at the same time as it appears inescapable – "but it didn't" – and the damage done irreparable.

The slave-holder Sir Thomas's heartfelt apology to the abolitionist Tom, as the latter appears to be dying, which comes immediately before the playful closing sequences of the film, is explicitly designed as a resolution to the slavery subplot in the film, as Rozema acknowledges in her audio commentary for the DVD, where she says that she added the apology scene at the last minute because the question of slavery had been left without closure. "I'm sorry, Tom, I'm so sorry," are the last words of dialogue in the film before the camera takes off on its final spin to wrap things up – a moment of seriousness and historical weight, and a suggestion of the need to heal and repair emotional and historical wounds, even if the Antiguan slaves themselves who continue to pay for the party are still invisible offstage.[39] This gesture to the "immeasurable heaviness" of history is, however, immediately undercut by the film's comic resolution, in which Sir Thomas and Tom's reconciliation is made possible by their partnership in the new business venture in tobacco, another slave-grown crop. The latter moment, although played for laughs in the film, in fact ties the stereotypical "Englishness" of the Jane Austen phenomenon firmly to the realities of US consumption, since tobacco was predominantly a mainland American, rather than West Indian, crop – and thus the imagined afterlife of the film mimics its joint British (state) and US (corporate) funders, the BBC, the Arts Council of England, and Harvey Weinstein's Miramax company.

Tom's recovery from his illness is indicated by his position in the closing tableaux, working on the books of the new tobacco business, directly underneath the workers repairing the (still rather forlorn-looking) west wing of Mansfield Park. It would be easy, and doubtless partly correct, to read this closing image of repair and healing between the white father and son as an evasion, rather than a resolution, of the slavery theme: the Antiguan slaves themselves must remain offstage, content to be represented by Tom, the English abolitionist-businessman (in his sketches, and now in his account books), who earlier in the movie appeared unaccountably in blackface. However, the ironic comedy of the closing scene also undercuts the ostensible message: tobacco companies are the contemporary equivalent of "slave-holders" in British and American culture, and moreover, the massive damages awarded against tobacco companies in lawsuits brought against them in the late 1990s turn the theme of repair back against its apparent object in the film and raise the specter of slavery reparations. The legal claims against US tobacco companies explicitly form the basis for the movement in the United States to claim reparations for slavery in a major lawsuit to be filed against the federal government and US corporations that can be shown to have profited from slavery before 1865.[40]

The case for slavery reparations has been gathering strength in the past few years, prompted partly by the success of these tobacco lawsuits and the large damages won in court by black farmers against the US Department of Agriculture and by Jewish World War II slave laborers against German corporations in the late 1990s, and partly by the wave of public apologies offered by state actors for historical wrongs throughout the 1990s, such as Queen Elizabeth II's apology to New Zealand's Maori population, British prime minister Tony Blair's apology for the Irish famine, and President Bill Clinton's half-apology for the African slave trade.[41] In the United States, the debate was sparked by the publication in 2000 of Randall Robinson's book-length call for reparations, *The Debt: What America Owes to Blacks*.[42] But the case for reparations is a global phenomenon, and has potentially global consequences, as was amply demonstrated by the tortuous discussions of the need for Western apologies and reparations for slavery and colonialism at the United Nations World Conference Against Racism in Durban, South Africa, in September 2001.[43] The temporary result of the conference was to effectively sideline or suppress the call for reparations, in a compromise final declaration that stated that "slavery and the slave trade are crimes against humanity and should always have been so" – a form of words that avoided the more sweeping "slavery was a crime against humanity" and was designed to protect European and US interests from future lawsuits – and simply "noted" that "some States have taken the initiative of regretting or expressing remorse or presenting apologies" for slavery, a form of words that replaced an earlier text that specifically endorsed "reparations" themselves.[44] But it seems clear that reparations in some form will eventually be paid; reparations have become, or will soon become, the new common sense about slavery, race, and history, and Rozema's film can be interpreted as a partial response to this new cultural and historical imperative.

The danger, however, is that the search for reparations will merely reconsolidate the structures it appears to contest, leaving its beneficiaries forever attached to an image of themselves as historical victims, wounded subjects denied even the liberal promise of "improvement." The quest for reparations risks becoming, in Wendy Brown's terms, "a practice which reiterates the existence of an identity whose present past is one of insistently unredeemable injury. This past cannot be redeemed *unless* the identity ceases to be invested in it, and it cannot cease to be invested in it without giving up its identity as such, thus giving up its economy of avenging and at the same time perpetuating its hurt."[45] But Rozema's film, although on one level it evades the question of reparations altogether, as I argue above, also suggests a possible way out of Brown's double bind. The ironic invocation of "freedom" in the flight of the camera in the closing sequence of the film and the playful self-reflexivity of Fanny's "it could all have turned out differently, I suppose" at first suggest the constraints of any adaptation, compelled to retain some "fidelity" to its "original." However, I suggest that we might also take this statement at face value. It, history, *could* all have turned out differently. The film opens itself up to a certain freedom in its reference here to the arbitrariness both of the events of history, and of the way in which they are recorded and passed down. The possibility emerges of reparations that do not simply fix or freeze the subject: the momentary freezing of the subjects in the closing tableaux of Rozema's *Mansfield Park*, before they shake themselves and continue with their lives, represents therefore a moment of possibility rather than determinism.

Wendy Brown suggests the possibility of a model of subject formation that recognizes contingency in the form of desire, in the form of the "I want" rather than the "I am," a form of subjectivity that is neither the "disinterested subject" of modern civil society nor the frozen victim of reparations:

> What if "wanting to be" or "wanting to have" were taken up as modes of political speech that could destabilize the formulation of identity as fixed position, as entrenchment by history, and as having necessary moral entailments, even as they affirm "position" and "history" as that which makes the speaking subject intelligible and locatable[?] . . . The subject understood as an effect of an (ongoing) genealogy of desire, including the social processes constitutive of, fulfilling, or frustrating desire, is in this way revealed as neither sovereign nor conclusive, even as it is affirmed as an "I."[46]

Perhaps Brown's formulation might be productively applied to the debate over reparations. The complications of historical production, the modernist or postmodernist embrace of historical contingency, the recognition of the multiple sites of historical reconstruction, academic and mass market, film and novel – all these are implied and embraced in Brown's equation. And yet the "simple" ethical narrative is not thereby obliterated – it still exerts its power, just as it does when we lament the "unfaithfulness" of a film adaptation, or the "simplistic" understanding of history. We can still say, with Fanny/Jane Austen of Joan of Arc: "They should not have burnt her[,] but they did";[47] we can still say, of slavery, it is a debt as yet unpaid. Randall Robinson, in his book *The Debt*, compares the lack of attention paid to the history of slavery and the slave trade to the millions of dollars spent on historical costume dramas on film.[48] While clearly *Mansfield Park* qualifies as another diversionary "costume drama," it also suggests the possibility that film historiography is not always part of the problem, but can disrupt conventional historiographical wisdom and suggest new directions in the future for thinking about the past.

---------- Acknowledgments ----------

Thanks to Claudia Johnson and Robert Stam for helpful comments on an earlier version of this chapter. I am grateful to Paul Arthur, Janet Cutler, and Art Simon for generously responding to early, naïve queries about film adaptations and pointing me in the right direction. Thanks also to the staff and fellows at the John Carter Brown Library in Providence, Rhode Island, who helped to create a productive space for much of the research and writing of this chapter. My stay at the JCB was funded by an Andrew W. Mellon postdoctoral fellowship.

---------- Notes ----------

1 *Mansfield Park*, dir. and scr. Patricia Rozema (Miramax Films/HAL Films/BBC Films/Arts Council of England, 1999).

2 "Austen Rolling in her Grave!," June 28, 2001, and dharting, "Mansfield Park Meets Alice in Wonderland," June 28, 2001 (amazon.com customer reviews: *Mansfield Park*, accessed July 22, 2001).

3 hannah12, "Janie's Darkest Tale?," June 3, 2000 (amazon.com customer reviews: *Mansfield Park,* accessed July 22, 2001).

Tim Watson

Chapter 1

4   Claudia L. Johnson, "Run Mad, but Do Not Faint," *Times Literary Supplement* (December 31, 1999), 16–17, quotation on p. 16. See also Johnson, "Introduction," in Patricia Rozema, *Mansfield Park: Final Shooting Script* (New York: Talk Miramax, 2000), pp. 1–10, quotation on p. 4.

5   "This production had nothing in common with the book and must have Jane Austen spinning in her grave." Pat Martinson, "Pure Garbage!," December 17, 2000 (amazon.com customer reviews: *Mansfield Park*, accessed July 22, 2001).

6   See, for example, Fraser Easton, "The Political Economy of *Mansfield Park*: Fanny Price and the Atlantic Working Class," *Textual Practice* 12: 3 (1998), 459–88; Moira Ferguson, "*Mansfield Park*: Plantocratic Paradigms," in Moira Ferguson, *Colonialism and Gender Relations from Mary Wollstonecraft to Jamaica Kincaid: East Caribbean Connections* (New York: Columbia University Press, 1993), pp. 65–89; You-me Park and Rajeswari Sunder Rajan (eds), *The Postcolonial Jane Austen* (London: Routledge, 2000); Edward W. Said, *Culture and Imperialism* (New York: Knopf, 1993), pp. 80–97; Brian Southam, "The Silence of the Bertrams: Slavery and the Chronology of *Mansfield Park*," *Times Literary Supplement* (February 17, 1995), 13–14; Maaja A. Stewart, *Domestic Realities and Imperial Fictions: Jane Austen's Novels in Eighteenth-century Contexts* (Athens: University of Georgia Press, 1993); Ruth Vanita, "*Mansfield Park* in Miranda House," in Rajeswari Sunder Rajan (ed.), *The Lie of the Land: English Literary Studies in India* (Delhi: Oxford University Press, 1992), pp. 92–9. The Republic of Pemberley can be visited at www.pemberley.com. On "Janeites" more generally, see Claudia L. Johnson, "The Divine Miss Jane: Jane Austen, Janeites, and the Discipline of Novel Studies," in Deidre Lynch (ed.), *Janeites: Austen's Disciples and Devotees* (Princeton, NJ: Princeton University Press, 2000), pp. 25–44.

7   Said, *Culture and Imperialism*, pp. 94–5.

8   See, for example, Christine Bolt and Seymour Drescher (eds), *Anti-slavery, Religion, and Reform: Essays in Memory of Roger Anstey* (London: Wm Dawson; Hamden, CT: Archon Books, 1980). See also Robin Blackburn, *The Overthrow of Colonial Slavery, 1776–1848* (London: Verso, 1988). For a valuable collection of source material, see Peter J. Kitson and Debbie Lee, *Slavery, Abolition and Emancipation: Writings in the British Romantic Period*, 9 vols (London: Pickering and Chatto, 1999).

9   See, for example, Susanne Seymour, Stephen Daniels, and Charles Watkins, "Estate and Empire: Sir George Cornewall's Management of Moccas, Herefordshire and La Taste, Grenada, 1771–1819," *Journal of Historical Geography* 24: 3 (1998), 313–51.

10 John Wiltshire, *Recreating Jane Austen* (Cambridge: Cambridge University Press, 2001), p. 135.

11 Thomas Clarkson, *The History of the Rise, Progress, and Accomplishment of the Abolition of the African Slave-Trade by the British Parliament*, 2 vols (London: Longman, Hurst, Rees, and Orme, 1808), vol. 1, p. 259.

12 Fanny asks her uncle, Sir Thomas Bertram, about the slave trade after his return from Antigua, but the conversation goes nowhere: "There was such a dead silence!," as Fanny recalls in a subsequent conversation with her cousin Edmund. Jane Austen, *Mansfield Park: Authoritative Text, Contexts, Criticism*, ed. Claudia L. Johnson (1814; New York: Norton, 1998), p. 136. Further references to the novel are to this edition, and will be given parenthetically in the body of the chapter.

13 Said, *Culture and Imperialism*, p. 96.

14   jenn818, "Jane Austen Disrespected!," April 23, 2001 (amazon.com customer reviews: *Mansfield Park*, accessed July 22, 2001).

15   Robert Stam, "Beyond Fidelity: The Dialogics of Adaptation," in James Naremore (ed.), *Film Adaptation* (New Brunswick, NJ: Rutgers University Press, 2000), pp. 54–76, quotations on pp. 54, 55.

16   Michel-Rolph Trouillot, *Silencing the Past: Power and the Production of History* (Boston: Beacon Press, 1995), pp. 19–30. See also Robert A. Rosenstone (ed.), *Revisioning History: Film and the Construction of a New Past* (Princeton, NJ: Princeton University Press, 1995); Robert A. Rosenstone, *Visions of the Past: The Challenge of Film to our Idea of History* (Cambridge, MA: Harvard University Press, 1995); and Vivian Sobchack (ed.), *The Persistence of History: Cinema, Television, and the Modern Event* (New York: Routledge, 1996), especially Hayden White, "The Modernist Event," pp. 17–38.

17   Trouillot, *Silencing the Past*, p. 22.

18   Alistair M. Duckworth, *The Improvement of the Estate: A Study of Jane Austen's Novels* (Baltimore, MD: The Johns Hopkins University Press, 1971); Raymond Williams, *The Country and the City* (New York: Oxford University Press, 1973).

19   Mark Salber Phillips, *Society and Sentiment: Genres of Historical Writing in Britain, 1740–1820* (Princeton, NJ: Princeton University Press, 2000), pp. 342–3. See also Jonathan Lamb, *Preserving the Self in the South Seas, 1680–1840* (Chicago: University of Chicago Press, 2001), esp. ch. 1, "Political Theories of the Self," pp. 17–48.

20   David Lloyd, "Colonial Trauma/Postcolonial Recovery?," *Interventions* 2: 2 (2000), 212–28, quotation on p. 222.

21   Christopher Kent, "Learning History with, and from, Jane Austen," in J. David Grey (ed.), *Jane Austen's Beginnings: The Juvenilia and Lady Susan* (Ann Arbor: University of Michigan Press, 1989), pp. 59–72, quotation on p. 59.

22   See also Easton, "The Political Economy of *Mansfield Park*," p. 473.

23   [James Stephen,] "Reasons for Establishing a Registry of Slaves in the British Colonies," *The Pamphleteer* 7 (1816), 33–85, quotation on p. 37. Stephen's pamphlet was originally published in 1814, and reprinted in this journal two years later. Further references will be given parenthetically in the body of the chapter. Moira Ferguson also makes a connection between Austen's novel and the simultaneous campaign to establish a registry of all slaves in the British West Indian colonies. See Ferguson, *Colonialism and Gender Relations*, p. 67.

24   Rozema, *Mansfield Park: Final Shooting Script*, p. 63.

25   *An Act More Effectually to Provide for the Support and to Extend Certain Regulations for the Protection of Slaves; to Promote and Encourage their Increase, and Generally to Meliorate their Condition* (St John's, Antigua: John Hardcastle, 1799).

26   James Ramsay, *An Essay on the Treatment and Conversion of African Slaves in the British Sugar Colonies* (London: James Phillips, 1784), p. v.

27   Lloyd, "Colonial Trauma," p. 222.

28   Ibid., pp. 219–20, 223–28.

29   Patricia Rozema, "Audio Commentary," on *Mansfield Park*, dir. and scr. Patricia Rozema, DVD version, 2000. The critique of the "great house" is not new, but it has gathered steam since the "heritage industry," in both Britain and North America, has placed the manor house at the center of a particular version of Britain's past. See, for example, Ronald Fraser, *In Search of a Past: The Rearing of an English Gentleman, 1933–1945* (New York: Atheneum,

1984); Williams, *The Country and the City*; Patrick Wright, *On Living in an Old Country: The National Past in Contemporary Britain* (London: Verso, 1985). See also Kazuo Ishiguro, *The Remains of the Day* (New York: Knopf, 1989).

30 Edmund's line is quoted from the DVD version of the film. The text of the published screenplay is somewhat different, tending to emphasize Fanny's abolitionist sympathies. While Edmund is troubled by the "inroads" the abolitionists are making in Antigua, Fanny wonders about the slaves who "must miss their families," as she sometimes does herself. Edmund replies, "Their misery seems to require more than a few weighty sighs, but . . . at the same time Mansfield Park is entirely dependent on the profits of that operation . . . It's not, it's not . . . clear." Rozema, *Mansfield Park: Final Shooting Script*, p. 33 (ellipses in original).

31 Ibid., p. 45.

32 Randall King, "New Austen Film No Plain Jane," November 29, 1999, JAM Movies Database (www.canoe.ca/JamMoviesArtistsR/rozema_patricia.html, accessed July 22, 2001).

33 *Sense and Sensibility*, dir. Ang Lee, scr. Emma Thompson (Columbia Pictures/Mirage, 1995). See also Emma Thompson, *The Sense and Sensibility Screenplay and Diaries: Bringing Jane Austen's Novel to Film* (New York: Newmarket Press, 1995). Servants, usually silent and almost always unnoticed by the first-time viewer, appear in almost every shot of *Sense and Sensibility*, sometimes providing a subversive counterpoint to the prettiness of Lee and Thompson's film. An intriguing comparison would be to the omnipresent Japanese "tourists" in *The Spanish Prisoner*, David Mamet, dir. and scr. (Jean Doumanian Productions/Magnolia Films/Sweetland Films, 1997).

34 As Claudia Johnson notes, "Austen's novels are indifferent to this kind of specificity," Johnson, "Run Mad," p. 16.

35 Rozema, *Mansfield Park: Final Shooting Script*, p. 24.

36 Wendy Brown, *States of Injury: Power and Freedom in Late Modernity* (Princeton, NJ: Princeton University Press, 1995), p. 71.

37 Rozema, *Mansfield Park: Final Shooting Script*, p. 141 (ellipses in original). The phrase, slightly modified as "it could all have turned out differently, I suppose," is repeated in the completed film (although not in the published screenplay) as the camera pans up above the final tableaux of characters to focus on the sunlight streaming (but setting) through the still unrepaired gaps in the west wing of Mansfield Park.

38 Rozema, *Mansfield Park: Final Shooting Script*, pp. 140, 144. Austen's narrator describes the change in Sir Thomas's opinion of Mrs Norris: "He had felt her as an hourly evil" (Austen, *Mansfield Park*, p. 319).

39 Rozema, *Mansfield Park: Final Shooting Script*, p. 139.

40 Willie E. Gary et al., "Making the Case for Racial Reparations," *Harper's* (November 2000), 37–51.

41 On this spate of historical apologies, see Michel-Rolph Trouillot, "Abortive Rituals: Historical Apologies in the Global Era," *Interventions* 2: 2 (2000), 171–86.

42 Randall Robinson, *The Debt: What America Owes to Blacks* (New York: Penguin/Plume, 2000).

43 See, for example, Dennis Brutus and Ben Cashdan, "Reflections on Durban," *The Nation*, September 11, 2001 (www.thenation.com, accessed September 24, 2001); Serge Chalons et al., *De l'esclavage aux réparations* (Paris: Editions Karthala, 2000); Chris McGreal, "Give Them Hard Cash," *Guardian*, September 3, 2001 (www.guardian.co.uk, accessed September 6, 2001); Manning Marable, "An Idea Whose Time Has Come," *Newsweek*, August 27, 2001

(www.msnbc.com/news, accessed August 26, 2001); Faiza Rady, "Playing It Cool," *Al-Ahram Weekly*, September 13–19, 2001 (www.ahram.org.eg/weekly, accessed September 24, 2001); Dudley Thompson, "Reparation Is a Demand for Justice," *Jamaica Gleaner*, October 9, 2001 (http://jamaica-gleaner.com, accessed October 12, 2001).

44 Quotations taken from *Durban 2001: United Against Racism*, the official newsletter of the World Conference Against Racism Secretariat, issue 6 (October 2001), p. 4 (www.unhchr.ch, accessed November 26, 2001).

45 Brown, *States of Injury*, p. 73, emphasis in original.

46 Ibid., p. 75.

47 Rozema, *Mansfield Park: Final Shooting Script*, p. 29.

48 Robinson, *The Debt*, p. 54.

Chapter 2

Keeping the Carcass in Motion: Adaptation and Transmutations of the National in *The Last of the Mohicans*

Jacquelyn Kilpatrick

The Last of the Mohicans story has real staying power. Written by James Fenimore Cooper in 1826, it has been adapted, condensed, serialized, published, and re-published many times, and there are at least fourteen English language films of the story. It has captured the imagination of succeeding generations of readers and viewers for more than 175 years, which is quite impressive when one considers that Cooper's writing does not really rank among the very best of any generation. As Barker and Sabin (1995: 202–3) have noted, "Aside from sheer narrative thrill (of which there is some, but in truth not so very much in *Mohicans*) something has worked to keep the carcass moving."

What has kept that carcass moving in print and on the screen is, I think, a combination of three things: Cooper's conscious construction of an American mythology, developing and using uniquely American symbols which still resonate; his adherence to the Romantic tradition, which happened to fit his subject matter nicely and provided a kind of pattern with which readers could identify; and his working of the first two elements into a frame-work which fit his own complex, or perhaps confused, political views. It is this last trait, the complex and even contradictory nature of Cooper's ideas, that has made the story so adaptable by filmmakers and others who have made the story their own.

Cooper belonged to the Bread and Cheese club, a group of literary and visual artists who set about developing a uniquely American personality in the arts. Their goal was to manufacture an American mythology, what they referred to as an "indigenous culture." They were part of a larger movement to establish a strong national personality for America, with a mythology that tied the American people, a large percentage of whom were recent immigrants, into a cohesive whole with a unifying "history." *The Last of the Mohicans* is a mythological story that presents symbolically rich landscapes and characters whose actions and fates are thoroughly symbolic, a story of America that sets it firmly apart from any British/European roots. It is a part of the nationalist myth − the shared conceptions that create a common core and make the experience more than one merely of intellectual understanding. It is part of *the* story of what America is and of what stuff Americans are made. As film critic Peter Wollen (1969: 14) noted, "Nationalism depends crucially on the creation of an invented national history, with its monumental heroes, dramatic climaxes, narrative goals." Cooper probably did not envision his creation as a defining moment for America, but he and his friends did dedicate themselves to creating art that was intrinsically, quintessentially American.

For Cooper, the challenge in developing a nationalist mythology was twofold. He needed to create a uniquely American hero who functioned in a uniquely American setting, and his story would have to have a ring of elemental, if not always logical, "truth" to it. Of course, Cooper was not the first to do this, and in fact his hero, Nathaniel (Natty) Bumpo (a.k.a. Hawkeye, Leatherstocking, and La Longue Carabine), owes a great deal to the legends which grew up around Daniel Boone and other real and imagined frontiersmen. Bumpo is therefore not so much an individual as a specific type of proto-American. It is the settlers in the story who are the "general" proto-Americans, but they are represented or symbolized by Hawkeye. He is symbolic also of the transfer of power from one nation to the other as he takes over the best qualities of the British as well as the Indians.[1]

Cooper's attitudes toward the Native Americans and the British were not unusual for his time. Nostalgia for the indigenous past was rampant, and Indians of the "bloodthirsty savage" ilk, it was generally thought, were induced to violence by the British and/or the French who used them as pawns. The reality of the situation was that Euroamerican settlers were breaking treaties right and left, crossing into Native land and, as William Henry Harrison, governor of Indiana Territory reported, "A great many of the Inhabitants of the Fronteers [sic] consider the murdering of the Indians in the highest degree meritorious" (Edmunds, 1998: 142). Historian R. David Edmunds has noted that:

> Unwilling to admit that they were the authors of their own misfortune, American frontiersmen in the first decade of the nineteenth century blamed the British, whom they charged with inciting the Indians against them. Although the British did exercise considerable influence among the tribes, a close examination of these events indicates Indian resistance to American expansion was a natural, indigenous act . . . the Indians welcomed the technical and logistical support of the Crown, but their decision to resist the Americans was their own. (Edmunds, 1998: 142)

As settlers moved further west, British influence of course decreased, but the idea that Euroamerican expansion was a natural and even righteous act became even more ingrained. Nathaniel Bumpo is the culmination of the two ideas: he is a product of the wilderness and a "brother" to the Native peoples, and he is a white man capable of taming that wilderness, making it safe for others like him, meaning, of course, other

Euroamericans. In film adaptations of *The Last of the Mohicans*, these qualities have been variously manipulated, with emphases on one side or the other, as called for by the attitudes of the day or the desires of the producer/directors.

In the novel, Nathaniel Bumpo is illiterate but honest; man reduced to his purest form and outside the influences of civilization. He is not beholden to man-made laws, but he can interact ethically with those of his own race as well as with Cooper's "pure" Indians (the almost-gone Mohicans), who have ideals of justice instead of law, a kind of "natural" morality. He is physically and mentally tough and at home in the wild. He is a loner with a very long gun (La Longue Carabine) and the prototype for the Western hero of the dime novels and Western movies. Cooper's Bumpo can also be extremely violent or even bloodthirsty, as when he stabs the already-dead enemy after a battle. "So saying, the honest, but implacable scout, made the circuit of the dead, into whose senseless bosoms he thrust his long knife, with as much coolness, as though they had been so many brute carcasses" (Cooper, 1986: 114). This part of Hawkeye's persona shows that Cooper was not beyond incorporating even the "bloodthirsty-savage" stereotype into his adopted Indian, an element that filmmakers, for obvious reasons, have chosen not to replicate.

The wilderness is also mythologized in the novel. In fact, the greenery is as much a character in the book as are the humans. It represents a rejection of urbanization, industrialization, and commercialism in favor of a more natural, absolutely American existence. Cooper engenders a deep respect for the power of nature and presents the American wilderness as a dangerous place where only the brave can thrive. For the white men it is the ultimate proving ground, a place to test one's valor against Nature, whether represented by flora, fauna, or Native peoples. Interestingly, the Indians are presented as belonging to the land, as opposed to the settlers' point of view, which see the land as belonging to the man. The conflicts in the novel are over land ownership, and it is ultimately a story about the contest between the French and the British for North American soil, not about the Indians, "last" or not, except perhaps as attachments to the land, much like the trees, rocks, and the other dangerous wildlife.

In *The Legacy of Conquest*, Patricia Limerick (1988) makes the point that the intersection of races and the allocation of property unified Western history, since that history has been an "ongoing competition for legitimacy – for the right to claim for oneself and sometimes for one's group the status of legitimate beneficiary of Western resources" (Wexman, 1993: 71–6). From a Native American point of view, the very concept of the land as real estate was dishonorable and irrational. However, Cooper and most other Americans of his time saw the acquisition and subjugation of land as a cultural imperative and manifestly "right." In fact, the quest for land was one of the primary motivations for the migration of the first Europeans to the American continent, and it is the idea that everyone can own a piece of America that has made the American national identity so unique. It has been the primary motivating force in the growth of white America throughout the five hundred years since first contact and is directly responsible for the constant push westward and the firm belief in the idea of Manifest Destiny (see Kilpatrick, 1999).

For Cooper's story to become a nationalist myth, it had to be somehow believable. *The Last of the Mohicans* was sold as "history" and therefore did much to build the American myth and to develop conceptions of the American character as distinct from that of the British. It was more closely researched than most novels written in that time period, but Cooper took much of his information from Joseph Heckewelder's *History, Manners and Customs of the Indian Nations*, a less than reliable source, and he exercised literary license to change even that information. As Barker and Sabin (1995: 182) have noted:

one of the things that emerges when a myth is formed . . . is something akin to a cultural organism: a story-form which makes its own demands, resists perverse uses, and lingers on in the imagination long after its primary uses have passed away . . . myths can be studied for their capacity to speak a society's view of itself through symbols. Indeed, real events and characters can become mythic . . .

It is the mythic element of *The Last of the Mohicans* that has lasted through almost two centuries, the myth of the rugged American male who is part of the landscape and exists in the American wilderness in ways not possible for outsiders – in this case the French and English. By assuming an indigenous identity comfortable in the wilderness, Cooper's hero becomes the quintessential American. In adaptations for print and film, this is the mythic core of the story, the one element that has remained unchanged.

In a discussion of a scene in the 1990 film *Dances with Wolves* in which the white hero is introduced to his first Lakota man, Louis Owens makes a point critical to an understanding of novelists such as Cooper as well as a wide variety of filmmakers. This scene, he notes, "illuminates the crucial Euroamerican fantasy of being inseminated with Indianness, of absorbing and appropriating everything of value in the indigenous world as a prelude to eradicating and replacing the actual Native . . ." (Owens, 1995: 47, my translation). In effect, Cooper has done just that. He has created a character, Hawkeye, who has absorbed and appropriated the Mohican world, which leaves him to inherit when the "last" Mohican vanishes. In Cooper's day the assumption was that all such indigenous people would eventually be swept away.

It is also important to situate Cooper's novel within the traditions of the Romantic Movement, part of the intellectual mainstream in Europe and America from roughly 1790 to 1870. A reaction against neoclassicism and the Enlightenment as a whole, Romanticism emphasized Nature as an elemental force and focused largely on the testing of one's spirit, two "naturals" for Cooper's setting. It also stressed the rise and fall of nations and the importance of heroes and heroic deeds. The result for Cooper was a series of novels with a hero who was Euroamerican but raised as an Indian in the "untamed" wilderness of America just before the revolution.

But what has made the novel so attractive for adaptation, whether in *Readers' Digest* or as a feature film, is it malleability. As Barker and Sabin (1995: 201) stated:

The Last of the Mohicans, because of the particular circumstances under which it was written, balances with great precision on top of a nest of contradictions. Born of the cusp of a contradiction in Cooper's own politics, born at a time of the very fast transition in the image of Indians and of the wilderness, *Mohicans* holds within itself, in tension, a wealth of possibilities for subsequent use. To be brutally paradoxical, it has a coherent incoherence.

The coherence in the text is due in part to the mythology it establishes: that of the naturally good backwoodsman in concert with Nature and the indigenous people and quite at home in the New World. Its incoherence derives largely from the contradictions of Cooper's politics and philosophy.

By the time *The Last of the Mohicans* was written, the eastern seaboard was settled, with the "Indian problem" shifted to the Great Plains and the Southwest. The land was firmly in the hands of the settlers, due to bloody wars or insidious efforts like the one proposed by Thomas Jefferson in a letter to William Henry Harrison dated February 27, 1803, delineating the plan for achieving the sale of Native land: "To promote this disposition to exchange lands . . . we shall push our trading houses, and be glad to see the good and influential individuals among them run in debt, because we observe that when these debts get beyond what the individuals can pay, they become willing to lop them off by a cession of lands" (Lipscomb, 1990: 22–3).

Jefferson's ideas were shockingly cold-hearted, but in the early 1800s Euroamericans were increasing in power and number, and needed more land – Indian land. Acquiring that land was one of the most problematic issues of the early nineteenth century, made even more complicated by a nostalgic longing for the indigenous past. This nostalgia was largely responsible for the intensity of interest in Native Americans made apparent by the cult of the "Vanishing American." One of the effects of this interest was the publication of 40 novels about Indians between 1824 and 1834, of which *The Last of the Mohicans* was only one. The country was littered with Indian enthusiasts, but even they could not agree on what to do about the "Indian problem."

Cooper was obviously aware of the conflicting emotions and ideas surrounding Native American issues, which were clearly seen in the debate surrounding the Indian Removal Act of 1830, just four years after *The Last of the Mohicans* was published. This act provided for the removal of the eastern tribes to an area west of the Mississippi and was brought to a head by the efforts of the Cherokee to remain outside the control of (and the confiscation of land by) the state of Georgia. President Andrew Jackson came down heavily on Georgia's side and promoted the removal of the Cherokee and other tribes. In his 1830 Presidential address to Congress, Jackson asked "What good man would prefer a country covered by forests and ranged by a few thousand savages, to our extensive Republic, studded with towns and prosperous farms . . . and filled with the blessings of liberty, civilization, and religion?" (quoted in Barker and Sabin, 1995: 191). On the other side of the issue was Senator Frelinghuysen, who expressed embarrassment that the

The Last of the Mohicans

Chapter 2

government would disregard what he regarded as natural, human law. In an impassioned speech to the Senate, he made the case that "Indians are men, endowed with kindred faculties and powers with ourselves . . . and, with this conceded, I ask in what code of law of nations, or by what process of abstract deduction, their rights have been extinguished?" (Prucha, 1990: 49).

After reading even a synopsis of his novel, a reader would be likely to assume that Cooper was a Frelinghuysen supporter and be very surprised to find that he was, in fact, very much a Jacksonian. Cooper apparently believed that the Euroamericans treated the Native Americans very badly, and he was saddened by the prospect of the Native Americans, as he assumed, heading for extinction, but he apparently considered it simply the natural way of things. The Romantic Movement, which Cooper embraced, assumed the rise and fall of nations and the stratification of humanity. In *The Last of the Mohicans*, Indian/white relations become a metaphor for those ideas: no empire lasts forever, different races invariably enter into conflict, and it was, alas, time for the Indians to hand over the country to the invaders.

Like most people of his time, Cooper believed in the "purity" of the races, and Hawkeye repeatedly refers to himself as an "uncrossed" man. White and Indian were considered separate and not equal. To "cross," then, was to dilute or contaminate. Cooper repeatedly contrives situations where the Indians' lack of civilization is contrasted with that of their white counterparts. For instance, Magua is obsessed with revenge for being whipped by Munro, and Cooper indicates that Magua does not understand the concept of discipline — not that Magua questions Munro's *right* to discipline him. After the massacre of the British, Cooper's Hurons become so excited that they drink the blood of those they have killed. Cooper gave his fictional Indians a larger portion of respect than most authors of his day, albeit from a decidedly superior position, but he was not the "friend of the Indian" his detractors accused him of being.

Cooper was, on the one hand, a strong adherent of Jacksonian democracy, a philosophy dedicated to pushing the frontier ever westward and decidedly hostile to the old families of the Northeast. On the other hand, Cooper was a member of one of those old, Northeastern families blessed with old Northeastern money, and his extreme fondness for things European conflicted with his own political views. Born into a powerful, landholding family, he married even deeper into the same group, but he still enthusiastically embraced the Jacksonian idea of the "common man."

In defense of his Jacksonian political views, he wrote *Notions of the Americans* (1831), *The Bravo* (1831), and *A Letter to My Countrymen* (1834) in which he defended his ideals. However, shortly thereafter, his views seemed to have changed rather radically, partly in response to the "Three Mile Point Incident." The Cooper family owned some land that was very popular with picnickers, and after Cooper erected "No Trespassing" signs (1837), he found himself in a controversy in which he was labeled an "aristocrat," a terrible thing for a Jacksonian to be called. And in 1839, when tenants in the great New York estates strove for restructuring of their leases and the dissolution of the estates, Cooper spoke loudly against "anti-landlordism," and went on to write three polemical

In his novel *The Redskins*: *or, Indian and Injin*, the "Injins" are the anti-renters who carried out protests in the form of house burnings and the like but disguised themselves as "Injins." There are few actual Indians in the book – only a small band led by Susquesus who come to help the aristocratic landowner, Hugh Littlepage, resist the attacks. The "Injins" grunt and speak a silly pidgin English, but Susquesus speaks eloquently as he instructs the anti-rent rioters in the value and necessity of the law. The band of Indians he has with him stand ready, as Philip Deloria has said, "to literally pound home the moral of social stability embedded in what becomes Susquesus's death speech" (Deloria, 1998: 39). And, of course, it is a death speech because Cooper's Indians are always in the process of disappearing. Deloria continues,

> In *The Redskins*, Cooper responded by characterizing them [the anti-renters] as unreasonable savages who had corrupted new national ideals of political stability and economic continuity. For Cooper and other members of the new order, the injins' rebellious proclivity for murder, arson, cowardice, and bad manners (especially in contrast to the wise Susquesus and his gracious comrades) placed them outside the borders of American society, "skulking from and shirking the duties of civilization." Yet even as Cooper excluded the antirenters, they remained white, part of a racially defined American us that retained its citizenship and would no doubt return to the fold. (Deloria, 1998: 39)

It is important that Susquesus is dying and, in effect, bequeathing his very self, his identity and his inheritance, to Littlepage. Cooper seems to have believed that, when the "last" Indian disappears, the land that was theirs should naturally fall to the aristocrats, the leaders of the "common man," among the Euroamericans. For Barker and Sabin (1995: 194):

> Cooper's quite contradictory political views were only resolved through the construction of a nonsensical idea: the idea that holding property could induce a form of nobility . . . In sum, Hawkeye in *The Last of the Mohicans* is a living myth of private property. He inherits at its end, through his relation to Chingachgook, the once-perfect relation of the "good Indian" to the land.

Cooper achieved the founding myth he wanted, but he could not have anticipated the many ways in which his particular story would be adapted, particularly by Hollywood, arguably the most powerful myth-making machine on the planet. *The Last of the Mohicans* is an attractive novel for adaptation because it carries the legitimacy of being an "American classic," with built-in product awareness, and it certainly has an action-based plot, once the long speeches are removed. But aside from the quasi-historical central myth of the story, everything else in an adaptation is pretty much up for grabs. The myth is the vessel, but it simply yearns for a filmmaker to fill it, and each adaptation brings

The Last of the Mohicans

Chapter 2

forth the same story but with sometimes surprising differences. Barker and Sabin (1995: 29–33) stress the loose ends and ambiguities of the text:

> For one of the joys of *Mohicans* is that there are a great many loose ends. It constitutes a founding myth, certainly, but a myth with ambiguities. The book is in many ways a racist book, yet it incorporates a condemnation of racism. It raises the possibility of interracial sexual relations between two of its heroic characters, yet avoids consummation. It celebrates frontier qualities, yet it mourns the passing of the frontier . . . Hawkeye himself is a splendid and moral figure, yet he is also a loner, he is capable of real violence . . . All in all, *Mohicans* is a truly ambivalent tale . . . it is the book's very ambiguities that have made it so pliable to other people's uses.

Of the many films that have been made from Cooper's story, four especially stand out for the kind of choices that were made in their adaptations: Griffith's *Leatherstocking* (1909), Tourneur and Brown's *Last of the Mohicans* (1920), Seitz's 1936 blockbuster, and Mann's 1992 version. Clearly, the choices were shaped by the time, place, artistic inclinations, and politics of the filmmakers, and some of the choices would have probably thoroughly rattled Cooper's bones. Although close analysis of the four films is beyond the scope of this chapter, the recurring aspects of the story that appear in each of these films make for interesting contrasts.

It is not surprising that D. W. Griffith chose to make a film based on *The Last of the Mohicans* story, though he chose to title it the more Cooper-generic *Leatherstocking*. He made the film in the second year of his five-year stay at Biograph, one of the most prolific of the early production companies. It was fifteen minutes long, made in three days, and released within a month. Griffith was obviously drawn to the story by the heroic action (fifteen minutes does not provide much opportunity for in-depth plot or character development), and the nostalgic tragedy of the Indians' plight. As in the original, the wilderness in the film is presented as menacing, navigable only by those who belong there, Hawkeye (Henry Walthall) and the Indians. The women in the film appear as fragile, foolish, and in need of protection. There is no love story because Uncus has been cut out of the story altogether; it is left to Chingachgook to be the last of the last. It is a very violent film, even by modern standards, though Cora (Linda Arvidson) does make it through alive in this telling. The Hurons in the film definitely fit the bloodthirsty savage stereotype of the dime novels, and Chingachgook is definitely of the noble savage ilk.

A few years later, Griffith would make *Birth of a Nation* (1915), a cinematic landmark but ideologically racist and separatist, and evidently reflective of Griffith's actual racist attitudes; those attitudes are apparent in *Leatherstocking* as well. The Indians in the film are starkly divided into the good and the bad, and even the good Indians must remain separate from the Europeans, including the one raised by the Mohicans. In this story, Hawkeye does not remain with his adoptive father but leaves with his new white friends. The film closes with Chingachgook doing a dance of death, the ultimate separation.

> Griffith's 1915 film [*Birth of a Nation*] immediately came to symbolize racial division in America: One had to be for or against it. The film seemed to make an explicit argument for the irreconcilability of racial differences. The black, the nonwhite, was the enemy. Though we cannot be sure, we suspect that part of the appeal of *Mohicans* to Tourneur and Brown was the ability of that story to offer an answer to *Birth of a Nation* . . . What better way to seize the ascendancy than to make a riposte to the other master's film?

This "riposte" is a beautifully made film which pioneered lighting effects, cutting, and the use of panchromatic stock, which produced a tinted effect (each scene tinted a different color, presumably chosen for its emotional affect: red for the battles, pink for shots of the women, and green or blue for the nature shots). But more than that, Tourneur and Brown's film was an attempt to combat the racism apparent not only in Griffith's film but in American culture in general. Immigrants of the time were being turned away on the basis of putative inferiority, and separation of the races, was, to put it mildly, the rule rather than the exception.

The more liberal Tourneur and Brown were less interested in Cooper's adventure story than the issues surrounding the interactions of the races. However, they changed Cora (Barbara Bedford) from the racially mixed offspring of a white/black marriage to a thoroughly white lady, perhaps because they recognized that their white ticket-buying public would be less than willing to accept a mixed heroine. In Cooper's story, Cora's mixed blood, due to the "shocking" mix of a black mother and a British military officer father, was probably a device to make her attraction to Uncas (Albert Roscoe) more understandable for a white reading public, but that element of the story would have been politically explosive in 1920 and could have had an effect opposite to the one Tourneur and Brown had in mind. In their film, the love story between Uncas and Cora serves to show that love is possible across color lines, and their tragic deaths at the end make their love seem all the more heroic − although, of course, unconsummated. From the moment Cora sees Uncas, she is enthralled. She chooses him over the British officer, Randolph (an addition to the original story), and as Uncas dies, he takes her already dead hand in his. United in death is not the optimal result for a love affair, but for the time of this film it was important that this cross-racial couple could at least bring about a tragic sympathy for an American Romeo and Juliet.

The addition of Randolph to the story is also significant. He is a British officer, a profession generally depicted as intrinsically dashing in 1920s' films. However, he is a coward and a traitor who goes to the French as soon as he sees that defeat is probable; he is absolutely disgusted with Cora's attraction to an Indian, and audiences no doubt cheered when he was blown up while hiding in a munitions locker. He is the absolute opposite of the courageous, ethical, and loving Uncas, a very intentional comparison which makes the man of color, although played by a Euroamerican actor, a very attractive choice.

The Last of the Mohicans

Chapter 2

The rather unappealing Hawkeye (Harry Lorraine) and Chingachgook (Theodore Lerch) almost drop out of sight, becoming important only at the beginning and end of the film. The centerpiece is the relationship between Uncas, Cora, and the still villainous Magua (Wallace Beery), with issues of land and American myth taking a back seat to their story. While Cooper probably made Cora half black in order to make her attraction to Uncas more palatable for his readers, this all-white Cora stands defiantly in favor of an Indian man at a time when racial crossing was not well tolerated, especially not by a white *woman*.

By 1936, movies were talking, and in the case of George Seitz's film, talking and talking and talking. In the years since the Tourneur/Brown film, America had gone through a major crisis, the Great Depression, and the economy had not completely rebounded. Hollywood had become the Dream Factory whose films were made for escape from harsh reality as much as for entertainment. The star system produced films which revolved around the company's stars, in this case Randolph Scott as Hawkeye. Scott was considered the epitome of the heroic leading man, particularly in Westerns, which owed much to the dime novels and Wild West shows. It was therefore to be expected that the pre-revolutionary story would take on a definite Wild West feel, with Mohicans and Hurons whooping it up in Hollywood Indian style, wearing headdresses and attacking to the sound of the tom-tom. The changes did make the film more commercial, and in fact it was a huge success. The story of *The Last of the Mohicans* that most mid-twentieth-century Americans knew was the one depicted in the Seitz film.

Cooper's story was changed drastically in this adaptation, partly to accommodate its star's reputation and style, but mostly due to the political climate of the day. The Depression had strained America's belief in capitalism, and Europe was going into World War II. America was divided on the question of intervening in the European situation, with the isolationists and interventionists in heated debate once more. Therefore, Seitz brought the relations between the British and the colonists to the forefront.

The British in this film are enormously pompous, arrogant, and stupid. The film starts out with King George II, "German George," deciding capriciously on the question of whether or not to support the British forces in North America. Heywood is the British officer we know best, but for most of the film he is officious and patronizing, an account true to Cooper's own description of the English. "The imbecility of her military leaders abroad, and the fatal want of energy in her councils at home, had lowered the character of Great Britain from the proud elevation on which it had been placed by the talents and enterprise of her former warriors and statesmen" (Cooper, 1986: 13). However, in this film the English and the colonists learn to respect each other as the story goes on, and, in the end, as Hawkeye is pressed into service as a scout for the British, he says "After all, we are fighting for the same thing," and, as in Griffith's film, he leaves his Indian friends behind.

Hawkeye has been changed into a colonist/settler, as opposed to Cooper's more isolated man of the wilderness who would "inherit" the land. In fact, this Bumpo has a lot in common with a real-estate developer. Wilderness plays a small part in this film, and, at the end, Hawkeye talks to Alice (Binnie Barnes) of the never-ending supply of new trails in the country and says that he likes to imagine a new city growing up at the end of every one. This is the American Dream – a successive line of "frontiers" to expand into, a chance to start anew. In Cooper's story the Indians are a noble but vanishing impediment to settlement, a stance preserved in this film, but with a decidedly Wild West/New Deal twist.

In 1992, Michael Mann took on *The Last of the Mohicans*. In some ways, it is a remake of the Seitz version; in fact, he bought the rights to the 1936 screenplay. However, there are significant differences between Mann's film and both Seitz's film and Cooper's novel.

Though the beautiful musical score won an Academy Award, the most striking aspects of the film are visual. It is the most visual, or cinematic, of all the *Mohican* films. The wilderness, here the mountains of North Carolina, provide an imposing presence very much in line with Cooper's novel, with long, slow views of the panorama beginning and ending the film. Mann tells his story through images rather than with words, and because conversation has been pared down from earlier versions of the film, he is able to tell much of the story in relatively short lengths of action. For instance, a beautiful opening sequence shows three men, all dressed in Native garb, running through the forest. At first it is unclear why they are running, and a predictable first response would be that they are chasing or being chased. In fact, they are hunting, and when they bring down the deer, the scene ties together nicely: these are men of the woods, a natural element of the wilderness, not an intrusive force. This is made very clear when Chingachgook (Russell Means) thanks his brother the deer for giving his life and does so in a Native language. In a few short minutes we learn what Cooper took pages to convey, and we also learn something Cooper did not intend. We begin to understand what the remainder of the film supports – Nathaniel (Daniel Day Lewis) is at heart an Indian, although unfortunately he, like other white heroes in films with Native Americans, becomes a better Indian than the Indians. Unlike the other films in which Hawkeye remains absolutely white with Indian *abilities*, Mann's Nathaniel is essentially Native with white abilities. This is an important distinction largely because the film becomes one in which race is not the central issue. The Mohicans are unquestionably on a par with the whites of the film, though the Hurons fare rather badly.

British imperialism is as much a class-structure issue as a political issue in this film. The aristocratic Heywood (Steven Waddington) makes the statement that the colonists have behaved "without so much as a by your leave" to which Cora responds: "These people do not live *by your leave*." This is something she has been learning since they found the Cameron family slaughtered by Hurons. She asks Nathaniel why people would live in such a hostile country, and he tells her that, after seven years of indentured servitude, the family had come to the wilderness to make a home for themselves where they have to answer to no one. It is again the American Dream, and its inclusion in this film would at first seem odd. However, we have gotten to know this family in an earlier scene, during which it is made very obvious that Chingachgook and Uncas (Eric Schweig) are as much the Camerons' friends as Nathaniel is. The settlers accept and have been accepted by the "good" Indians, and in this way they would seem like the natural "inheritors" of the land after the Last Mohican is gone. But, more importantly, they are the underdogs. They and the other settlers are looked down upon by the English, they are former servants to the aristocratic class, and they are presented as the "noble common people," an over-turning of Cooper's ideas of the land passing "naturally" to the more aristocratic white people. The colonists are set in opposition to the British to a greater degree than in Seitz's film. In both films the settlers agree to fight only after the commanding officer of the British forces agrees that they can leave if their homes become endangered. In Mann's film this "bargaining" disgusts Heywood, who obviously thinks it below the dignity of the British army to negotiate with the locals.

In the Seitz film, it is Hawkeye who represents the colonists in this discussion, but Mann brings in other colonists to speak for them, keeping Nathaniel/Hawkeye on the fringe of the conversation. This is important because Seitz's Hawkeye is fighting for the American Dream — westward expansion and land for anyone who wants to work for it. Mann's Nathaniel understands this dream, but he is not directly a part of it, at least not in the time-frame of the film.

As Mann did his best to make the Mohicans seem real and to make their relationship with Nathaniel seem familial, this Nathaniel cannot say that he is "fighting for the same thing" as the British, as he does in Seitz's film. He and the two Mohicans try to help the colonists because they are friends and because it is the ethical thing to do. They come to the aid of the Munro women and their escorts because it is the ethical response, and they are honorable men. It would be difficult to see the passage of these Mohicans as the natural order in a rise and fall of nations or as bequeathing their place in this world, as did Cooper. It is also impossible to dismiss questions of whether the invasion of a continent was "right" or not, as did the Seitz film.

Seitz shot his film mostly on sets or in what looks like a park, thereby under-emphasizing the wilderness, but Mann's wilderness is overpoweringly spectacular. It is beautifully filmed, and what we see is even more important than what we hear. The characters of both races seem reticent to talk very much, except perhaps Heywood, whose continuing attempts to command with words sets him apart from the Mohicans, Hawkeye, and the women in the film. And the people in Mann's film do seem more real than in the previous *Mohican* films. The Mohicans are good-looking, friendly, and intelligent — Eric Schweig (as Uncas) is a fine actor, and Russell Means does an adequate job as Chingachgook. Magua is played by Wes Studi, a very talented actor who makes even the blatant stereotyping of his character as the bloodthirsty savage develop believably. Mann also worked hard for this: while Cooper gave a beating for drunkenness as a motive for Magua's vengeful fury, Mann gives him a much more understandable motive. His children have been killed, he was sold into slavery, and he lost his wife. He blames Munro for this and is determined to make him suffer the loss of his daughters before he dies a painful death. While Magua still seems bloodthirsty, especially when he rips Munro's beating heart out of his chest, at least his motives are more human than simply stereotypical.

Yet the film has serious shortcomings. Although Chingachgook and Uncas play affec-tionately and good-naturedly with the white settlers' children and are steadfast, courageous, and honorable, they remain firmly in the background. They speak well when they speak, a major improvement over the run-of-the-mill Hollywood movie Indian, but only the final scene makes any real statement about the Indian, which is that the Native American is almost extinct. Given that the idea is central to Cooper's story, this would be difficult to avoid in a remake, and probably Mann was relying on the very obvious presence of at least three (and there were more) Native American actors, one of whom is a well-known activist, to make the point that they did not *really* die off. This film is primarily a love story, and only secondarily about the British, French and proto-Americans, with the Indians as the dangerous obstacles or colorful backdrops and sidekicks for the hero. The Native Americans are very visible, leading an audience to think that they are also "heard," that there is a real interplay of voices and perspectives. In fact, the Mohican and the Huron experiences in Mann's film are again relayed through the alien and dominant white voice and white perspective. As the editors of *Nationalisms and Sexualities* have noted:

> a national identity is determined not on the basis of its own intrinsic properties but as a function of what it (presumably) is not. Implying "some element of alterity for its definition," a nation is ineluctably "shaped by what it opposes." But the very fact that such identities depend constitutively on difference means that nations are forever haunted by their various definitional others. (Parker et al., 1992: 5)

In *The Last of the Mohicans*, "the opposition" is two-fold: the British (though the settlers are still fighting on the British side against the French), and the "bad" Indians. The hero is an adopted Indian, so his opposition to the British, French, and Hurons sets him squarely as the "new" American, he who embodies the best of the two worlds and who is set to rule the continent. But this hero is indeed haunted by the "other."

Mann has received criticism for not following the story, for taking liberties with an American "classic" novel. But Mann obviously understands quite well the differences between the novel and the film, and he chose very deliberately to tell a story for the 1990s, as Cooper had told a story for the 1820s and Seitz told his story for the 1930s. Mann's changes probably have more to do with being politically/socially sensitive than anything else, and he obviously understands that an audience likes the leading man to connect with the leading woman, no matter what Cooper might have intended.

This Cora (Madeleine Stowe) is a brunette but not racially mixed, and Alice (Jodhi May) is again a blonde. However, in this version it is Alice that Uncas quite literally falls for, and Cora and Nathaniel develop a steamy love affair. Cooper would probably be amazed to see his Natty Bumpo turned into a rather elegant and sexy Nathaniel who stays at the fort instead of leaving with his friends because he refuses to leave Cora, even though her father has thrown him in jail and is planning to hang him. Although Nathaniel has lived all his life with the Mohicans and is presented as being as much Mohican as the equally eloquent Uncas, it is the white woman he stumbles upon who immediately becomes his soul mate.

The Last of the Mohicans

Chapter 2

Mixing emotions, mixing blood, and mixing identity have historically tended to provoke violence in Hollywood movies. Although miscegenation is and was an obvious fact, apparently it is an easier idea to deal with in film if presented as a tragic possibility rather than as a possible reality, even in the 1990s. Cinematic examples are numerous, including the death of Tom Jefford's wife, Sonseearay (*Broken Arrow*, 1950), Horse's Indian wife, who dies carrying their unborn child in *A Man Called Horse* (1970), and Little Big Man's Sunshine, who dies along with their newborn baby (*Little Big Man*, 1970). When a Hollywood Indian woman is loved by a white man, she is almost certain to die. But Mann's Nathaniel and Cora, as well as John Dunbar and Stands With a Fist in Costner's *Dances with Wolves* (1990), show that white men and white women go nicely together, even if one or the other has lived with Indians all his or her life. Uncas and Cora or Alice (whichever is his love interest in the particular re-telling) always die, in the original and all the adaptations (except Griffith's, where Uncas has been cut out altogether). When a same-race love affair is presented, whether between Heywood and Alice, or Hawkeye and Alice, or Cora and Nathaniel, the couple can survive, but it seems that, any way that it is arranged, miscegenation is still a very risky business.

All in all, Cooper's story has survived because it still plays into the nationalist mythology it helped to create, and that is the core part of the story that remains in every adaptation. It is the one immutable part of the story. However, the ways in which that myth have been interpreted and "dressed" vary considerably. The question is – why not just tell a new story; why make the same story over and over again, if it is going to be changed so radically? As Barker and Sabin (1995: 9) have noted, "freedom of interpretation" makes a source novel "a hollow vessel; everyone knows the title phrase, but it doesn't seem to tie you down. But whenever a conscious effort at reinterpretation is made, something seeps from the vessel into the contents, to color and flavor them." That which seeps from the vessel is the American myth, the way white Americans see themselves. Understandably, the view is a bit different each time the story is told, each time the carcass is reinvented and made to move again.

---------------------------------- Note ----------------------------------

1   I use the term "Indian" when referring to fictional characters and the term "Native American" for real people.

---------------------------------- References ----------------------------------

Barker, Martin and Sabin, Roger (1995) *The Lasting of the Mohicans: History of an American Myth*. Jackson: University Press of Mississippi.
Cooper, James Fenimore (1986) *The Last of the Mohicans*. New York: Penguin.
Deloria, Philip J. (1998) *Playing Indian*. New Haven, CT: Yale University Press.

Edmunds, R. David (1998) "National Expansion from the Indian Perspective," in Fredrick E. Hoxie and Peter Iverson (eds), *Indians in American History*. Wheeling: Harlan Davidson.

Kilpatrick, Jacquelyn (1999) *Celluloid Indians: Native Americans and Film*. Lincoln: University of Nebraska Press.

Limerick, Patricia Nelson (1988) *The Legacy of Conquest: The Unbroken Past of the American West*. New York: W. W. Norton.

Lipscomb, Andrew A. (ed.) (1990) "Writings of Thomas Jefferson," Register of Debates in Congress, 10: 369–71, in Francis Paul Prucha (ed.), *Documents of United States Indian Policy*, 2nd edn. Lincoln: University of Nebraska Press.

Owens, Louis (1995) "D'une disparition à l'autre," *Palestiniennes: Revue trimestrielle publiée l'Institut des études palestiniennes*, n.s. 3: 47.

Parker, Andrew, Russo, Mary, Summer, Doris and Yaeger, Patricia (eds) (1992) *Nationalisms and Sexualities*. New York: Routledge.

Prucha, Francis Paul (ed.) (1990) "Senator Frelinghuysen on Indian Removal," 6: 311–16 in *Documents of United States Indian Policy*, 2nd edn. Lincoln: University of Nebraska Press.

Wexman, Virginia Wright (1993) *Creating the Couple: Love, Marriage, and Hollywood Performance*. Princeton, NJ: Princeton University Press.

Wollen, Peter (1969) *Signs and Meaning in the Cinema*. Bloomington, IN: Indiana University Press.

Chapter 3

The Discreet Charm of the Leisure Class: Terence Davies's *The House of Mirth*

Richard Porton

In his classic study, *The Rise of the Novel*, Ian Watt observes that Samuel Richardson's pioneering eighteenth-century novel, *Clarissa*, as well as notable nineteenth-century descendants such as *Middlemarch* and *Portrait of a Lady*, underline "the all but unendurable disparity between expectation and reality that faces women in modern society, and the difficulties that lie before anyone who is unwilling to be used, or to use others, as a means."[1] Edith Wharton's *The House of Mirth* is nothing if not devoted to the collision between "reality and expectation" that confronts modern women. Lily Bart, like Richardson's heroine, is ultimately stymied by what Watt identifies as the twin snares of the authoritarian, patriarchal family and economic individualism. Yet, unlike the work of her mentor Henry James, with its finely modulated exploration of interiority, Wharton's novel is a supremely self-conscious, proto-feminist study of a woman who is not merely a victim of male strictures. Lily is, above all, a protagonist who has the ability to view her own reification by male society with detachment and implicitly acknowledge that her own ambivalence toward – and assimilation of – conformist values contributes to her own doom.

Wharton's biographers, fascinated – and to a certain extent mystified – by their subject's contradictions, grapple heroically with the legacy of a woman who had little but disdain for the bourgeois mores that entrapped Lily but who was nonetheless an archetypal product of the haute bourgeoisie. And a considerable amount of ink has been spilled in attempts to probe the motivations of a woman who spurned patriarchal values but could insist, however disingenuously, that "women were made for pleasure and procreation."[2]

Robert Stam has eloquently demonstrated how the specter of "fidelity" haunts evaluations of literary adaptations.[3] It is equally true that an ultra-auteurist impetus leads some commentators to assert that "strong" authors can eradicate, and triumph over, the burdensome anxiety of confluence, if not influence, that confronts directors who want to impose their own aesthetic or ideological perspective upon cherished source material. Terence Davies's adaptation of *The House of Mirth* polarized critics, and the mixed response to the film yielded more than the usual share of platitudinous verities. *The House of Mirth*'s devotees enshrined it as a pristine art film, a worthy successor to elegiac classics such as Welles's *The Magnificent Ambersons* and Mizoguchi's *The Life of Oharu*.[4] As much embalmed as praised by this reception, Davies's adaptation becomes unwittingly analogous to the objets d'art which decorate the overstuffed late Victorian parlors inhabited by Lily Bart and her cohorts. Conversely, given the fact that *The House* of *Mirth* has almost achieved iconic significance among Wharton's enthusiasts, particularly feminists, it is perhaps unsurprising that Davies has been castigated as something of an upstart (ironically akin to some of the nouveaux riches in the novel) by certain critics. *The New York Times* featured a prominent lament by cultural critic Margo Jefferson, who bemoaned the supposed limitations of Davies's minimalist approach and chided him for synthesizing two of the novel's supporting characters: Grace Stepney and Gerty Farish.[5] Dismissing the film with even less concealed vitriol, *Cineaste*'s Martha Nochimson found it an "unsavory" compote of melodramatic clichés and a disconcerting paean to female masochism.[6]

Both the attempts to elevate Davies's adaptation to the status of a "pantheon" film and the efforts to denigrate it as kitsch disguised as a respectful adaptation are red herrings. The screen version of *The House of Mirth*, despite a few inventive deviations from its source, is much more faithful to the novel than its harshest critics care to acknowledge. Nevertheless, Davies's faithfulness to the spirit of Wharton cannot be separated from its spirited dialogue with her text – a salutary recasting of the novel that offers a prismatic view of both the past's economic rapacity and current permutations of the consumer society. Lily Bart was both drawn to and repulsed by her own status as a female ornament and an analysis of the psychic violence lurking beneath the surface of a superficially placid film yields insights into what Bakhtin refers to as the "differentiated unity of the epoch's entire culture."[7] Untangling the strands of this "differentiated unity" indicate unsettling points of convergence between Wharton's epoch and our own, as well as a productive tension between them:

(a) Davies's appropriation of melodramatic cinematic conventions that mesh well with the novel's own subtly melodramatic imagination; and

(b) a constellation of historical issues (Wharton's genteel anti-Semitism versus Davies's philo-Semitism, the pertinence of the novel's Veblenesque orientation to a contemporary critique of "everyday life").

——— **Emersonian Optimism versus the Melodramatic Imagination** ———

As one of the most insightful commentaries on Wharton's novel observes, "the most brutal moment . . . dramatizes not so much the centrality of sex as the centrality of exchange."[8] The brutal moment in question is Lily's near-rape by her supposed friend, Gus Trenor,

Figure 3.1 An intimate interlude between Lily (Gillian Anderson) and her close friend, Lawrence Selden (Eric Stoltz)

a duplicitous businessman who expects sexual favors after helping her to make a small killing on the stock market. Bored and agitated by the limited options available to a *jeune fille à marier*, her half-hearted attempts to ensnare a rich husband are evidence of a reluctance to play the role of a docile plaything but also reveal that she has little inclination to defy the social order. Her conversations with Lawrence Selden, a lawyer and art connoisseur, are deft exercises in amorous circumlocution. In a maneuver that frustrates readers' expectations, theirs is a nascent romance (figure 3.1); Selden's relative penury makes him poor marriage material. Perilously wedged between the lures of Eros and Thanatos, Lily spends the novel considering hellish marriages while striving for a qualified autonomy. She passes most of her time pondering, and eventually rejecting, the advances of rich, but dull, potential husbands. Thanatos finally wins out as she dies from an overdose of chloral, an act that seems more a product of her quiescence than willful self-destruction.

Most of Wharton's feminist admirers, although initially perturbed by the death of *The House of Mirth*'s decidedly ambiguous heroine, do not view its ostensibly pessimistic conclusion as a conservative retreat from the possibility of female solidarity. Indeed, many of the novel's partisans, particularly Elizabeth Ammons and Elaine Showalter, construe Lily's death as ironically optimistic: the old, constricting femininity that imprisons her clears the way for the birth of a New Woman unencumbered by outdated mores (figure 3.2).

Figure 3.2 Lily Bart (Gillian Anderson) enjoys a rare happy moment in *The House of Mirth*

From this vantage point, Lily's weakness and self-deception are encouraging products of constructively negative thinking – proof positive that the jargon of empowerment might be construed as reactionary bad faith masquerading as progressive rhetoric. Wharton's stance was far from radical: a thoroughgoing lack of interest in reformist zeal distinguishes her from many of her feminist forebears and descendants. Her distaste for emotional uplift is far different from – to cite one representative example – the Transcendentalist rhetoric of Margaret Fuller, a nineteenth-century feminist whose outlook was indebted to Ralph Waldo Emerson's curious mixture of Nietzscheanism *avant la lettre* and mystical idealism. One of Emerson's best-known essays, "Self-reliance," encompasses many of the intriguing contradictions that permeate much of his – and subsequently Fuller's – work.

Emerson's self-reliance bears little resemblance to stereotypical American "rugged individualism." His metaphysics places equal emphasis on the cultivation of the self *and* what he termed the collective mind. In fact, Emerson's biographer credits him with achieving a "remarkably complete critique of romantic individualism."[9] This critique was, of course, well suited to his advocacy of liberal and radical causes, most notably abolitionism. Unfortunately, Fuller's appropriation of the Transcendentalist ethos often melded a truly radical agenda with inchoate metaphysics. As one of her most sympathetic critics observes, Fuller's commitment to female emancipation co-existed uneasily with Emerson's "transcendental moral egoism,"[10] a creed that may have successfully interrogated the American belief in asocial individualism but remains tethered to the vagaries of a muddled belief in Enlightenment perfectibility.

Just as the conservative Balzac's critique of the machinations of the French bourgeoisie were more acute than many of his "progressive" rivals, Wharton, less *engagé* and more hesitant in her opposition to American inequities than Fuller, is better equipped to assess the American class system and its entrenched sexism.

Wharton's visceral understanding of the cash nexus, coupled with her melodramatic flair, allow her to undermine American individualistic cant and enabled her to be, however unwittingly, an historical materialist par excellence. *The House of Mirth*'s withering portrait of a woman whose path to oblivion is inextricable from a desire to cultivate consumable "decorative" qualities (Selden at one point refers to Lily as a "wonderful spectacle" and Wharton herself once wrote an architectural treatise entitled *The Decoration of Houses*) proved irresistible to Davies.

For Peter Brooks, the melodrama of Balzac and Wharton's friend, Henry James, draws sustenance from the "surfaces of manners," creating a universe of discourse where "the signifiers of the text are indices pointing to hidden forces and truths, latent signifieds."[11] Wharton's propensity to create emotional intensity through the detailing of surfaces seems to be what drew Davies to the project; he is unabashed in admitting that Hollywood melodramas, particularly Max Ophuls's *Letter from an Unknown Woman*, served as stylistic reference points during his planning of the adaptation. In addition to his "sensuous attention to . . . marble mantels, mirrors, train-car windows speckled with afternoon sun,"[12] Davies punctuates the film's action with languorous dissolves and protracted, deliberate camera movements. Despite the Manichean struggles outlined in *The House of Mirth* — the vulnerable, foolish, but essentially good Lily pitted against antagonists who want to exploit and defame her — it is also a naturalistic chronicle of the vulgarity of the parvenu class. Both strands co-exist in Davies's conception of the novel, a conception that echoes Eric Bentley's description of melodrama as "the Naturalism of the Dream life."[13]

The fact that Bentley also notes melodrama's "affinities with infantile narcissism, its indulgence in self-pity and grandiose emotional states,"[14] pinpoints the ideological quandary personified by Lily's contradictions. However aware she may be of her oppression as a woman, she is only vaguely aware of how her own lassitude prolongs this oppression. In the tradition of Ophuls and Douglas Sirk, Davies's visual style complements his flawed heroine's double bind. Unlike the Emersonian subject whose freedom is achieved through an empowering dynamism that is implicitly male, many of the film's set pieces illustrate how Lily's consciousness is mired in stasis. For example, during a train journey when she begins to realize that her fair-weather friend, Bertha Dorset, is actually her nemesis, Davies shows us Lily's despondent face reflected in an adjacent window – an emblem of a woman who has achieved a certain self-consciousness that can never move beyond solipsism.

Brooks remarks that "there tends throughout melodramas, and most especially at the end of scenes . . . to be a resolution of meaning in *tableau*, where the characters' attitudes and gestures . . . give, like an illustrative painting, a visual summary of the emotional situation."[15] Davies appropriates this echt-melodramatic device in a distinctively modernist fashion by subtly transforming one of Wharton's key scenes. Lily's appearance as the cynosure of a *tableau vivant* derived from Joshua Reynolds's portrait of a society grande dame "Mrs Lloyd" has been cited as one of the key modern examples of *ekphrasis* – the verbal description of visual art in literature.[16] In a shift that ironizes Wharton, Davies's Lily sheds the stiff-upper-lip hauteur of Reynolds and emerges with considerably more sexual ripeness from a recreation of Watteau's *Summer*. The scene is an impeccable example of melodrama's ability to shatter repressive façades; the heroine's temporary lack of inhibition is witnessed (employing canny point-of-view shots) by Selden, her elusive near-paramour, and her jealous cousin, Grace Stepney. For critics who maintain that Davies's version of Wharton foregrounds female masochism, this scene is a cogent riposte. As the lusty embodiment of "Summer," Lily is equipped with a scythe. Complicit as she may be in this voyeuristic ritual, her flamboyance is nonetheless rooted in a society that thrives on spectacle and specularity. To complain that Davies's Lily Bart lacks the pluck of an autonomous "empowered" woman is as misguided as complaining that the street urchins of Buñuel's *Los Olvidados* steal and taunt beggars when they should instead be poring over Marx and Bakunin. The evocation of Watteau provides a glimpse (even a slightly utopian glimpse) of Lily's desire to escape from class-bound repression. Within a culture where women are reduced to their "exchange value," however, this desire can only be envisioned as a *tableau vivant* that provides onlookers with an opportunity to gawk and smirk.

Davies's ability to achieve temporal distension through camera movement emphasizes the stasis of the New York upper-class milieu and reiterates Lily's own inner paralysis. A prime example is a series of transitional shots that chronicles her summer migration from her aunt's funereal New York mansion to Monte Carlo. The Monte Carlo trip is a pivotal point in the narrative: venomous accusations about Lily lead inexorably to her banishment from the predatory ranks of "society." Davies undercuts the somber mood with a peculiarly lyrical, near-hallucinatory series of tracking shots that initially capture the ornate clocks and bric-a-brac on a mantelpiece, move on to furniture enveloped in sheets for the summer and torrential rains, and land on the eerily pristine surface of the Mediterranean. This sequence is, from one perspective, a reflexive meditation on Wharton's painstaking analysis of Lily's despondency and stasis; visual accompaniment to passages from the novel that almost clinically describe "the sparkle [that] had died out of her," when the "taste of life was stale on her lips . . . an inner desolation deeper than the loneliness about her." The dissolution of a coherent sense of self that these camera movements underscore might also be contrasted with the type of focalization featured in another great epic of upper-class venality, Proust's *In Search of Lost Time*. Marcel Proust's omnipresent narrator possesses – despite certain doubts and fissures – a supreme faith in the redemptive power of consciousness. For reasons that undoubtedly have everything to do with Lily – and Edith Wharton's – gender, it is impossible for *The House of Mirth* to mimic what Malcolm Bowie refers to as Proust's "exhilarating sense of moral purpose."[17] Ironically enough, Davies's stylistic flourishes imbue Wharton's late-Victorian narrative devices with a modernist, near-Proustian gloss. As in Proust, objects becomes talismans of memory – even if this process cannot bestow upon Lily, herself a venerated object, the sense that time has been regained and vanquished. "Self-reliance," defined in either a Proustian or an Emersonian manner, is beyond Lily's grasp.

The House of Mirth's inventive *mise-en-scène* and fluid camera movements help to exteriorize a novel that is primarily filtered through the consciousness of its protagonist. As Gillian Anderson, who plays Lily with understated bravura, remarks "the majority of [this] novel takes place inside Lily's head."[18] In many respects, Anderson and her co-stars' measured underacting – as well as our *lack* of access to Lily's introspection – helps the audience to understand the profound artificiality and hypocrisy of a rarefied society where forthrightness is taboo. These rigid norms force Wharton to cast her narrator/protagonist as a cagey performer. In Cynthia Griffin Wolff's formulation, "the most clearly gendered activity of the narrator is an exposure of society's 'make-believe' that could only come from a woman . . . the vigilance with which women must monitor the reactions of empowered males, and the range of petty deceptions and rigorous disciplines by which women must manage to appear 'naturally' appealing."[19] Anderson is well aware of this dynamic and conveys Lily's calculated opacity with a great deal of aplomb – the realization that "in every scene we are pretending to be something other than we really believe we are or want to be."[20] Anderson's low-key, but adamantly self-aware, performance seems designed to make most of her male foils (e.g. the oily Gus Trenor played by the comic actor Dan Aykroyd and Anthony La Paglia's ambitious businessman, Sim Rosedale) look transparent and one-dimensional (figure 3.3).

Wharton's novel is notable for subverting several of the motifs embraced by nineteenth-century women's "sentimental fiction." As Ann Douglas demonstrated in her seminal *The Feminization of American Culture*, sentimental fiction of the pre-Wharton era is, in many respects, a bridge between Calvinist self-abnegation and our contemporary consumer culture.[21] Wharton shares the scorn for male hypocrisy evinced by writers of this era, but thoroughly bypasses the celebration of domesticity and the "cult of motherhood" deified in the novels of Martha Finley and Harriet Beecher Stowe. Similarly, despite Davies's avowed indebtedness to the tradition of the "women's film," he does not simply incorporate a predigested version of the trope that taxonomists of Hollywood melodrama have christened the saga of the "Woman Alone."[22] Her suicide notwithstanding, Lily is not a self-sacrificing victim in the tradition of *Stella Dallas*. Lily's passivity is in fact a deceptively silent rebellion: a negation of the Emersonian strain of muscular, if "liberal," self-reliance (figure 3.4).

Figure 3.3 Gossipy Judy Trenor (Penny Downie) with her oily husband Gus (Dan Aykroyd)

Figure 3.4 Lily (Gillian Anderson) condemned to solitude

Although she hedged her bets in her attitudes toward feminism, Edith Wharton's fiction nevertheless addressed many of the suppressed yearnings of her women readers. Her absolute empathy with Lily Bart's plight (since Lily was one of Wharton's youthful nicknames, the seeming identification with her protagonist was far from accidental) still resonates with a contemporary audience. However much her indictment of female oppression looks forward to feminism's Second Wave, Wharton's characterization of Lily's acquaintance, the wily businessman Simon Rosedale, reflects the ingrained hostility to "vulgar" Jews shared by most members of the WASP elite at the beginning of the twentieth century. Like many of her compatriots, Wharton subscribed to a crude biological reductionism which identified Jews as a race that possessed identifiable traits and quirks. Of course, like much racial stereotyping, the "genteel" anti-Semitism of Wharton's milieu was riddled with incoherence. It is assumed, for example, that Rosedale benefits from an almost preternatural, hard-nosed gift for business dealings, while his "otherness" makes him exotic and almost sexually ambiguous – or "sexually problematic" in Meredith Goldsmith's formulation.[23] Despite Wharton's general revulsion toward Jews whose social ineptitude was apparently genetic,[24] she, like many of her peers, made exceptions for cultivated, assimilated individuals who could not be pigeonholed as ghetto-dwellers or upstart poseurs. As a case in point, both Wharton and her rabidly anti-Semitic friend Henry Adams were friendly with the famous Jewish art connoisseur (and Episcopalian convert) Bernard Berenson.

In fashioning his adaptation, Davies decided that "the anti-Semitism had to go"; he ardently believed that it "disfigured" the book.[25] This presumed, well-intentioned "solution" to an embarrassing dilemma – the effacement of Rosedale's ethnicity – is one of the adaptation's few miscalculations. For better or worse, Rosedale's Jewishness cannot be effaced, but resurfaces in a spectacular display of the "return of the repressed." The man who is regarded as a "pushy little Jew" by his gentile cohorts is distinguished in the novel by his status as an outsider. By casting an all-purpose ethnic (the Australian-Italian actor Anthony La Paglia) as Rosedale – pegged as fair-haired in the novel – Davies re-contextualizes the peculiar comradeship of Lily and her persistent (and persistently unsuccessful) Jewish suitor. Whereas Wharton deliquesced into honest condescension by imagining her "stage Jew"[26] as a gauche interloper, Davies's liberalism still retains, however inadvertently, the sense that Rosedale is both an outsider and an unwelcome "exotic."

While it would be absurd to reprimand Davies for being insufficiently anti-Semitic, his attempt to sanitize Wharton's novel ironically affirms Bryan Cheyette's contention that the figure of "the Jew" in literature evades "rigid racial hierarchies."[27] Cheyette argues that Jews played an ambivalent role in Victorian culture and frustrated racial taxonomists since they could not be categorized as either "black or white" – a frustration that manifests itself in both the novel and film version of The House of Mirth. Rosedale is neither a total outsider nor a bona fide insider. His colleagues and associates view him as either a nuisance or an obstacle. Lily's Aunt Julia, in a comic aside, castigates Rosedale for his audacity to make money at a time when others are losing their shirts. For Lily herself, Rosedale's frankness concerning financial dealings is unspeakably vulgar. Yet, ironically enough, his unvarnished regard for pecuniary values makes him one of the most admirable characters in both the novel and the film. (Davies readily endorses this view-point in interviews and a DVD commentary, although he is unaware of the paradox that this is true in both Wharton's anti-Semitic treatment and his bowdlerized, philo-Semitic variant.) In essence, Lily's disdain for Rosedale stems from his empathy for her own status as an ostracized woman. Confirming Freud's notion that hatred often originates in the "narcissism of minor differences," she dislikes him because he, not the apparently sensitive Selden, is her true kindred spirit. Davies, like Wharton, emphasizes the resem-blance between Rosedale's heartfelt marriage proposal and a business negotiation. Well aware of Lily's "fondness for luxury," he boasts that "whatever he enjoys he is prepared to pay for." Eminently consumable, Lily is unwilling to admit to herself that the cerebral Selden, with his gift for repartee and vaunted book collection, is no less a consumer than his apparently shadier Jewish rival. Rosedale is an intriguing shape-shifter – both despic-able and untainted with the pretentiousness of his WASP associates.

Wharton's disdain for (and barely suppressed attraction toward) Jews is difficult to expunge from a film adaptation; it exemplifies the dark, reactionary side of her anti-capitalist ethos. Like Henry Adams, she irrationally linked the passing of the old aristocratic order and the United States' embrace of modernity with the so-called Jewish menace. As with many men of his ilk, Adams associated "infernal Jewry" with moneylenders and inter-national bankers.[28] In the final analysis, *The House of Mirth*'s reactionary anti-capitalism is subsumed by its "progressive" animosity toward the commodification of women.

The less noxious aspects of Wharton's uneasiness with the capitalist order coincide with the work of Thorstein Veblen, maverick sociologist and "philosophical radical." Many feminist champions of *The House of Mirth* cite Veblen's observation that "the dress code imposed on women is one of capitalism's most blatant examples of 'conspicuous consumption.'" While the sardonic passages outlining this notion in *The Theory of the Leisure Class* (published in 1899, six years before *The House of Mirth*) and "The Economic Theory of Women's Dress" are unquestionably pertinent to both the preoccupations of the novel and film, Veblen's distinctive blend of satirical invective and hard-nosed economic analysis cannot be reduced to the doctrine of "conspicuous consumption." His critique of American culture was all-encompassing, yielding a "theory of value" that was as nuanced and radical as (if more pessimistic than) Marx's and a cynical view of the "productivist" ethic that predates Guy Debord and Jean Baudrillard's musings by many decades.[29]

At no point was Veblen more venomously witty than in his conviction that the leisure class retained its hegemony by its "conspicuous abstention from productive labor."[30] Wharton betrays a mordant familiarity with the leisure class's fear of productive labor and no moment in Davies's film is more shocking – and emblematic of his protagonist's fall from grace – than the scene chronicling Lily's pathetic attempts to execute the tasks of an apprentice milliner. The camera lingers on Anderson's face as her supervisor chides her for inept efforts to attach spangles to a hat and subtly captures her restrained devastation. Shortly after, her boss Madame Regina fires her and – in an archetypal Davies shot – the screen is bifurcated by her tormentor's sullen face reflected in a mirror and Lily's impassive countenance in the foreground. In Wharton's version, Lily's clumsiness with the spangles is intermingled with the voices of her colleagues' gossipy references to her former friends, the Trenors and the Dorsets. These murmured remarks demarcate a transition from a leisure-class existence, where labor is taboo, to a life of toil that is beyond her capabilities: "the strangest part of Lily's strange experience, the hearing of these names . . . the fragmentary and distorted image of the world she had lived in reflected in the mirror of the working girls' minds."[31] Davies's depiction of her cognitive dissonance is decidedly low key but, in some respects, more violent. (Wharton's Lily is not fired, but despondently drifts away from Madame Regina's.) Madame Regina's parting speech to Lily in the film – "Perhaps you will find a position more suited to your skills" – drives home Veblen's point that upper-class ladies and gentlemen were extremely skilled in the art of doing nothing at all.

This thumbnail sketch of a woman at the end of her tether grimly rhymes with another Davies embellishment – a much earlier scene in which Lily, decked out in a florid red dress, is besieged with stares from friend and foe alike as she stoically endures a performance of Mozart's *Cosi fan tutte*. Mozart's ode to playful flirtation co-exists uneasily with the more heavy-handed romantic stratagems of New York society. Of course, this uneasy mesh is surely behind Davies's highly calculated dramaturgy and *mise-en-scène*. (Lily in a Bette Davis-like red dress offsets the Mozart with proper ironic acerbity.) This night at the opera, moreover, reinforces Veblen's conclusion that "there is reason to believe that the institution of ownership [began] with the ownership of persons, primarily women" (figure 3.5). There may be something slightly incongruous about discussing this pampered woman's fate in the same breath as Veblen's claim that "the basis of the industrial system is chattel slavery and that the women are commonly slaves."[32] Nevertheless, the spectacle of Lily being ogled and denounced by a wide array of men (close-ups of the prissy Percy Gryce alternate with shots of Selden, Trenor, and Rosedale), as well as her imperious aunt and mousy cousin, vindicates *The Theory of the Leisure Class*'s assertion that upper-class women of his era, despite their privileges, often suffered from the privations of fashion: "the mutilations and handicaps endured by modern women, such as constricted waists and cumbrous skirts."[33] The Lily portrayed by Anderson dearly cherishes an autonomy that her society refuses to grant her – an imprisonment conveyed to us by her "constricted waists and cumbrous skirts."

The House of Mirth is a period film that, in taking a backward glance toward the age of the robber barons, illuminates our equally predatory contemporary economic environment. During Lily Bart's "Gilded Age," real and faux aristocrats were determined to differentiate themselves from hoi polloi. The dot.com magnates of recent memory believed that they were preaching a very different gospel by endorsing a supposedly egalitarian form of capitalism where every investor is a potential plutocrat.

Figure 3.5 Lily is ensnared at the opera by her benefactor and nemesis, Gus Trenor (Dan Aykroyd) and wealthy suitor Sim Rosedale (Anthony La Paglia)

In the aftermath of that duplicitous era and the Bush recession, it becomes easier to grasp that the reigning economic doctrine of the 1990s – referred to by Thomas Frank as "market populism" – had much in common with the credo of the Gilded Age. Of course, as opposed to the transparently stratified society of Wharton's era, the yuppie populists paying obeisance to "one market under God" "insisted that class was disappearing altogether."[34] In addition, the women's movement appears to have put an end to marriage being a necessary (in the words of Selden describing Lily's – and modern womanhood's – plight) "vocation." But at a time when conformist, if supposedly tongue-in-cheek, marriage manuals such as *The Rules* remain best sellers, Lily's anguish, and its ideological implications, is perhaps not completely outmoded. Terence Davies intuitively recognized the parallels between one turn of the century and the next, and brilliantly conveys *The House of Mirth*'s pertinence to postmodern sexual politics. Far from being quaint relics of a bygone age, Edith Wharton, and her alter ego Lily Bart, are fascinatingly contradictory and personify an all-too-contemporary "decentered" subjectivity: feminist and antifeminist, wary of consumer capitalism but clinging to conformist, even racist, social attitudes, nostalgic for a mythic past while half-aware that the glory of the past is something of a sham.

1   Ian Watt, *The Rise of the Novel: Studies in Defoe, Richardson, and Fielding* (Berkeley, CA: University of California Press, 1957), p. 225.

2   Wharton made this remark in a letter to Mary Berenson. See R. W. B. Lewis, *Edith Wharton: A Biography* (New York: Harper and Row, 1975), p. 486.

3   See Robert Stam, "Beyond Fidelity: The Dialogics of Adaptation," in James Naremore (ed.), *Film Adaptation* (New Brunswick, NJ: Rutgers University Press, 2000), pp. 54–76.

4   This is a summary of J. Hoberman's encomiums, quoted approvingly by Kent Jones in *Cinema Scope* 6 (Winter 2001), 24–5.

5   Margo Jefferson, "The Film of Taste: Just Add Soft Lighting and Close-ups," *The New York Times* (February 21, 2001).

6   Martha Nochimson. "The House of Mirth," *Cineaste* 26: 2 (2001), 41–3.

7   Bakhtin quoted in Stam, "Beyond Fidelity," p. 65.

8   Wai-chee Dimock, "Debasing Exchange: Edith Wharton's *The House of Mirth*," *PMLA: Publications of the Modern Language Association of America* 100 (October, 1985), 783.

9   Robert D. Richardson, Jr, *Emerson: The Mind on Fire* (Berkeley, CA: University of California Press, 1995), p. 258.

10 See David M. Robinson, "Margaret Fuller and the Transcendental Ethos: *Woman in the Nineteenth Century*," in Larry J. Reynolds (ed.), Margaret Fuller, *Woman in the Nineteenth Century*, Norton Critical Edition (New York: W. W. Norton, 1998), pp. 243–57.

11 Peter Brooks, *The Melodramatic Imagination: Balzac, Henry James, Melodrama, and the Mode of Excess* (New Haven, CT: Yale University Press, 1975), p. 199.

12 Jessica Winter, "Vanity Foul: Terence Davies takes on Manhattan," *Cinema Scope* 6 (Winter 2001), 21.

13 Bentley is quoted in Brooks, *Melodramatic Imagination*, p. 35.

14 This is Brooks's paraphrase of Bentley in ibid.

15 Ibid., p. 48.

16 Margaret Doody, *The True Story of the Novel* (New Brunswick, NJ: Rutgers University Press, 1994), p. 404. For another view of *ekphrasis*, see W. J. T. Mitchell, *Picture Theory* (Chicago: University of Chicago Press, 1994).

17 Malcolm Bowie, *Proust Among the Stars* (New York: Columbia University Press, 1998), p. 5.

18 Gavin Smith, "Gillian Anderson," *Film Comment* (January–February, 2000), 60.

19 Cynthia Griffin Wolff, *A Feast of Words: The Triumph of Edith Wharton* (New York: Oxford University Press, 1995), p. 435.

20 Smith, "Gillian Anderson," p. 61.

21 Ann Douglas, *The Feminization of American Culture* (New York: Knopf, 1977).

22 See, for example, Jackie Byars, *All That Hollywood Allows: Re-reading Gender in 1950s Melodrama* (Chapel Hill, NC: University of North Carolina Press, 1991).

23 For a summary of Wharton's brand of anti-Semitism and a summary of Goldsmith's critique of it, see the entry on "Anti-Semitism," in Sarah Bird Wright (ed.), *Edith Wharton A to Z: The Essential Guide to the Life and Work* (New York: Checkmark Books, 1998), pp. 10–11. See also Irene C. Goldman, "The Perfect Jew and *The House of Mirth*: A Study in Point of View," *Modern Language Studies* 23: 2 (1993), 25–35.

Richard Porton

Chapter 3

24 According to biographical accounts, Wharton also found Jews alluringly "exotic." In an unpublished erotic fragment (discovered years after her death) the female protagonist is described as "half-Levantine." According to R. W. B. Lewis, she used the word Levantine as a code word for Jew.

25 Karen Gordon, "Terence Davies: Inside *The House of Mirth*," *Screentalk* 1: 4 (May/June 2001), 42.

26 In the midst of placing *The House of Mirth* in a tradition of theatrical melodrama, Wolff terms Rosedale a "stage Jew." See Wolff, *Feast of Words*, pp. 413–36.

27 Bryan Cheyette, "Neither Black nor White: The Figure of 'the Jew' in Imperial British Literature," in Linda Nochlin and Tamar Garb (eds), *The Jew in the Text: Modernity and the Construction of Identity* (London: Thames and Hudson, 1995), p. 32.

28 For Adams's views on "infernal Jewry," see Ernest Samuels, *Henry Adams: The Major Phase* (Cambridge, MA: The Belknap Press of Harvard University Press, 1964), pp. 129–30.

29 For more on Veblen's foreshadowing of contemporary social and economic theory, see John P. Diggins, *The Bard of Savagery: Thorstein Veblen and Modern Social Theory* (New York: Seabury Press, 1978).

30 Joseph Dorfman, *Thorstein Veblen and his America* (New York: Augustus M. Kelley, 1961), p. 176.

31 Interestingly enough, Joan Scott traces "how crucial gender was to the formation of work identities" and political social movements by discussing the history of labor strife among Parisian seamstresses in the nineteenth century. Despite her empathy for the plight of milliners, this sort of salutary class-consciousness is not at all evident in Wharton's account. See "Work Identities for Men and Women: The Politics of Work and Family in the Parisian Garment Trades in 1848," in Joan Wallach Scott, *Gender and the Politics of History* (New York: Columbia University Press, 1999), pp. 93–112.

32 These quotes are from an excerpted chapter of *The Theory of the Leisure Class*, in Edith Wharton, *The House of Mirth*, ed. Elizabeth Ammons, Norton Critical Edition (New York: W. W. Norton, 1990), pp. 266–7.

33 Veblen, quoted in Dorfman, *Thorstein Veblen and his America*, p. 114.

34 Thomas Frank, *One Market under God: Extreme Capitalism, Market Populism, and the End of Economic Democracy* (New York: Doubleday, 2000), p. 201.

Terence Davies's *The House of Mirth*

Chapter 3

Chapter 4

In Search of Adaptation: Proust and Film

Melissa Anderson

In Harold Pinter's introduction to *The Proust Screenplay*, his distillation of the major themes of Marcel Proust's magnum opus, *A la recherche du temps perdu* (*In Search of Lost Time*), the playwright notes: "We knew we could in no sense *rival* the work. But could we be true to it?" (Pinter, 1977: x). This question of veracity unquestionably haunts most film adaptations of literary works. Adapting Proust's four-thousand-page grand novel, with its labyrinthine prose, plethora of characters, and multiple shifts in time, poses an even more daunting set of challenges to a filmmaker. Pinter completed *The Proust Screenplay* (written in collaboration with Joseph Losey and Barbara Bray) in 1973, yet his film was never made. That Pinter's project languished may be a sign of just *how* daunting a task adapting Proust to film is (or, at the very least, how reluctant producers were to support such an endeavor). Luchino Visconti and Bernardo Bertolucci were also foiled in their attempts to adapt Proust. Others, however, have been able to bring their film treatments of *A la recherche du temps perdu* to the screen: Volker Schlöndorff's *Un Amour de Swann* (*Swann in Love*, 1984), Raúl Ruiz's *Le Temps retrouvé* (*Time Regained*, 1999), and Chantal Akerman's *La Captive* (*The Captive*, 2000). Each film is distinguished by the radically different ways in which it interprets Pinter's notion of "being true" to the text — one that majestically explores, to name but a few themes, memory, sexuality, jealousy, art, high society, and gossip.

Proust is often considered the most influential writer of the twentieth century. Graham Greene noted: "For those who began to write at the end of the twenties or the beginning of the thirties, there were two great inescapable influences: Proust and Freud, who are mutually complementary" (quoted in White, 1999: 2). Proust began work on his multi-volume novel in 1908. *Du côté de chez Swann* (*Swann's Way*), the first volume, was published in 1913, followed by *A l'ombre des jeunes filles en fleurs* (*Within a Budding Grove*, 1919), *Côté de Guermantes* (*The Guermantes Way*, 1920), and *Sodome et Gomorrhe*

(*Sodom and Gomorrah*, 1921). Three remaining volumes were published after Proust's death on November 18, 1922: *La prisonnière* (*The Captive*, 1923), *La fugitive* (*The Fugitive*, 1925), and *Le temps retrouvé* (*Time Regained*, 1927).

Proust's grand novel is both an emotional and cerebral treatise; rather than being plot-driven, it focuses instead on interiority. Critic André Aciman (2002: 55) has eloquently noted that Proust "turned every moment, from the most rarefied to the most ordinary, into an occasion for boundless introspection. He took the private temperament and mental habits of someone accustomed to prolonged solitude and applied them to the world around him, giving, as would become his signature, an internal mold to anything external." One of the more celebrated examples of Proust's introspective style is the young narrator's description of dipping a madeleine into a cup of tea in *Du côté de chez Swann*:

> And soon, mechanically, dispirited after a dreary day with the prospect of a depressing morrow, I raised to my lips a spoonful of the tea in which I had soaked a morsel of the cake. No sooner had the warm liquid mixed with the crumbs touched my palate than a shiver ran through me and I stopped, intent upon the extraordinary thing that was happening to me. An exquisite pleasure had invaded my senses, something isolated, detached, with no suggestion of its origin. And at once the vicissitudes of life had become indifferent to me, its disasters innocuous, its brevity illusory – this new sensation having had the effect, which love has, of filling me with a precious essence; or rather this essence was not in me, it *was* me. I had ceased now to feel mediocre, contingent, mortal. Whence could it have come to me, this all-powerful joy? I sensed that it was connected with the taste of the tea and the cake, but that it infinitely transcended those savours, could not, indeed, be of the same nature. Where did it come from? What did it mean? How could I seize and apprehend it? (Proust, 1992: 60)

As this extract lushly demonstrates, the simplest physical action – taking a bite of cake – triggers a multitude of emotions. Proust's fastidious attention to the slightest nuances and shifts in feelings and memory frequently provide the narrative heft in *A la recherche*; the actual "events" of the characters in the novel are secondary to the exploration of the sprawling world of interiority.

Posing an even more daunting challenge to filmmakers wishing to adapt Proust's novel is the complex syntax used throughout *A la recherche*. Sentences often shift from the active to the passive voice and contain many different verb tenses. Time expands and contracts; narration of an event in the present tense is frequently interrupted by a passage devoted to a memory or an emotional state. Compounding the difficulty of adaptation is the expansion of one memory or sensory experience into many. In *Proust Among the Stars*, Malcolm Bowie (1998: xiv) observes:

> the narrator of the novel has a mania for multiplicity, wants the world to contain more things rather than fewer, and stands guard over an unstoppable transformational machine. He speaks of the hundreds, thousands and millions of opportunities for new perceptions that the world affords, and of the novelist as an insatiable traveller in outer and inner space, always on the move and always driven by the demon of imagination to actualise the potential forms of things.

Proust's writing, with its intricate web of subordinate clauses linking a spiral of memories, is undeniably difficult to translate to the screen. Yet *A la recherche du temps perdu* need not elude film adaptation; the key to a successful cinematic rendering is reconfiguring how to approach adaptation.

Un Amour de Swann

Volker Schlöndorff is certainly no stranger to the task of literary adaptation, having brought Günter Grass's novel *The Tin Drum* to the screen in 1979. *Un Amour de Swann* (1984) should be lauded for its significance as the first film to tackle adapting Proust, certainly a Herculean feat. Of the three film adaptations of Proust, *Un Amour de Swann* takes the most conventional approach in adapting a challenging literary source to the screen, one that imposes a more straightforward narrative structure on Proust's unwieldy prose. Although *Un Amour de Swann* is the least compelling of the three adaptations, its mis-steps are nonetheless highly instructive, for they serve as a primer on what *not* to do when adapting *A la recherche*. Successfully adapting Proust for the screen demands a creative approach to exploring temporality, memory, and emotional states; simply lifting passages from Proust's text and dramatizing them, as Schlöndorff does, is insufficient.

Schlöndorff, who co-wrote the screenplay of *Un Amour de Swann* with four others (including prominent theatrical director Peter Brook and frequent Luis Buñuel collaborator Jean-Claude Carrière), focuses on Part Two of the first volume of *Du côté de chez Swann*, which is primarily a chronicle of aesthete Charles Swann's obsessive love for the former courtesan Odette de Crécy, and which suggests more broadly that love is never reciprocated. What distinguishes this section of *A la recherche* from the rest of Proust's novel is the absence of the narrator – sometimes referred to elsewhere as Marcel and often thought to be the surrogate for Marcel Proust himself – from the actual scenes that unfold. Most of the scenes take place before the narrator's birth and are therefore recapitulated omnisciently. Although this section of the novel is well suited to the conventions of the costume drama, the absence of the narrator's subjectivity in the film is a profound one, since it is his highly personal, specific re-imagining of the past that gives *A la recherche* so much of its power. Furthermore – and this may be the greatest mis-step in *Un Amour de Swann* – Schlöndorff condenses this section of Proust's novel to one twenty-four-hour period plus an epilogue. By attenuating memory and time – two of the hallmarks of Proust's novel – Schlöndorff assigns more significance to the *actions* of Proust's characters.

Curiously, Schlöndorff is concerned with demonstrating the actual process of writing and its attendant anguish. An odd melding of personages occurs in *Un Amour de Swann*. In the opening scene, Jeremy Irons, as Swann, is seen writing in bed, looking forlorn, still in his nightgown, his voice-over narrating his own memoir-like prose: "My love for

Odette . . ." This image of Swann instantly evokes Proust's own legendary process of composing *A la recherche*, done while reclining in bed in a cork-lined room, often in a sickly, enervated state. Additionally, in the opening moments of the film, just before Swann's voice-over, the sounds of writing – the frantic pressure of ink being engraved onto parchment – and pages being turned dominate the audio, accompanying a sun-dappled tableau of letters and a satchel on a desk. Yet the conflation of a character with its own author, coupled with a rather clichéd filmic representation of writing, does little to elucidate Swann's anxiety over Odette, an emotional state that dominates the "Un Amour de Swann" section of Proust's novel.

Schlöndorff's film also suffers from the affectations of its performers. Jeremy Irons's Swann is all petulance and agitation; Ornella Muti as Odette limits her gestures to heaving her bosom and showing off her gapped-tooth smile. The supporting players are also leaden. Alain Delon, as Baron de Charlus, Swann's kohl-eyed homosexual friend, is incapable of finding his character's considerable wit; and Fanny Ardant, as the Duchesse de Guermantes, another friend of Swann's, struggles to convey imperiousness. This mannered rigidity and discomfort are greatly at odds with the sense of fluidity present in Proust's constellation of shape-shifting characters.

The stiff performing styles are but one aspect of the film's humorlessness, a fault most apparent in the scenes of physical intimacy between Swann and Odette. The "cattleyas" scene, for instance, which marks Swann and Odette's first erotic encounter, typifies Schlöndorff's mis-steps. In *Du côté de chez Swann*, after Swann has joined Odette in her carriage, Proust writes:

> She was holding in her hand a bunch of cattleyas, and Swann could see, beneath the film of lace that covered her head, more of the same flowers fastened to a swansdown plume. She was dressed, beneath her cloak, in a flowing gown of black velvet, caught up on one side to reveal a large triangle of white silk shirt, and with a yoke, also of white silk, in the cleft of the low-necked bodice, in which were fastened a few more cattleyas. She had scarcely recovered from the shock which the sight of Swann had given her, when some obstacle made the horse start to one side. They were thrown forward in their seats; she uttered a cry, and fell back quivering and breathless.
>
> "It's all right," he assured her, "don't be frightened." And he slipped his arm round her shoulder, supporting her body against his own. Then he went on: "Whatever you do, don't utter a word; just make a sign, yes or no, or you'll be out of breath again. You won't mind if I straighten the flowers on your bodice? The jolt has disarranged them. I'm afraid of their dropping out, so I'd just like to fasten them a little more securely. (Proust, 1992: 328–9)

A few moments later – and after more fumblings with Odette's cattleyas – Swann and Odette kiss. The funny, tender moment highlights Swann's anguish and punctiliousness, qualities that exacerbate his fits of jealousy. Yet in Schlöndorff's rendition of the "cattleyas" scene, the eroticism is made trite. "Let me arrange the orchids in your corsage," Swann purrs to Odette. As the camera pulls in for a tight close-up of Muti's bosom and Irons's caressing hand, heavy breathing is heard on the soundtrack. Schlöndorff jettisons the humor in this scene for fear, it would seem, that it would compromise the seriousness of his endeavor. Unfortunately, though, *Un Amour de Swann* is an endeavor that is compromised by its own solemnity in adapting Proust's novel.

Le Temps retrouvé

Raúl Ruiz's skillful rendering and direction of *Le Temps retrouvé* (1999) is exemplary primarily for *not* making Proust's work precious and *recherché*. Like *Un Amour de Swann*, *Le Temps retrouvé* showcases a fine assortment of period-specific costumes and millinery. Ruiz's films, most notably *Généalogies d'un crime* (*Genealogies of a Crime*, 1997), are marked by an elliptical sense of time, and here he smartly utilizes cinematic tricks to evoke the multiple layers of memory in Proust's writing, which in itself anticipates a cinematic sensibility. Rather than emphasizing the preciosity of his grand novel, Proust invites his readers to visualize temporality; film transforms this invitation into its sine qua non. For those who are unfamiliar with Proust's sprawling novel, Ruiz's film may seem somewhat impenetrable, since he wastes no time on exposition. True to Proust's aesthetic, Ruiz's film plunges immediately into a series of oneiric, time-bending episodes linked by the vagaries of memory.

Although not necessarily a summation of the previous volumes of *A la recherche* (Proust's writing remains, to the very end, adamantly antithetical to a conventional narrative arc), *Le Temps retrouvé* is nonetheless concerned with the irrevocable changes wrought by World War I – death, loss, reconciliation, and, above all, the ravaging effects of aging – themes that Ruiz, by occasionally borrowing incidents from the preceding volumes of the novel, handles quite adeptly. The film begins with an ailing Marcel Proust (Marcello Mazzarella), haggard and gaunt, painfully dictating from his bed to his maid, Céleste Albaret (who would later write an "as told to" memoir, *Monsieur Proust*, about her life with the writer). "Then, one day, everything changes," Proust utters wistfully, immediately introducing the themes of nostalgia and the inextricable link of the past with the present in *Le Temps retrouvé*. After this arduous exercise, Proust examines, with the aid of a magnifying glass, a series of sepia-toned photographs of the main characters in his vast novel, including Odette, the Verdurins, Robert de Saint-Loup, Gilberte, and himself as a boy. The importance of image – or, more specifically, the *moving pictures* of Proust's "scrapbook" – establishes how an innovative approach to filmmaking is required when adapting Proust's writing for the screen. Ruiz's creative intervention in the opening scenes of his film, in which the "reality" of Proust on his deathbed segues to – and is then eclipsed by – the fiction of his great novel, greatly contrasts with Schlöndorff's facile deference to the written word at the beginning of *Un Amour de Swann*.

The leitmotif of Proust's scrutinizing gaze is introduced in the opening scene: a meticulous, often ruthlessly vicious gift of observation bestowed upon the narrator (also played by Mazzarella), who is sometimes referred to as Marcel, Proust's literary alter-ego. As a chronicler of Paris's moribund aristocratic society, the narrator notes later in the film, "I was X-raying them," suggesting a gaze as penetrating as that afforded by a camera's tight close-up. Ruiz skillfully frames this insatiable voyeurism as a peepshow when the narrator, peering through a porthole-size window, spies on the sinisterly fey Baron de Charlus (John Malkovich) in the throes of passion as he's being whipped by a male prostitute. It is important to note that Malkovich, unlike Alain Delon in *Un Amour de Swann*, fully comprehends that Charlus's exaggerated mannerisms and idiosyncrasies are an integral part of this desiccated dandy. All of the actors in *Le Temps retrouvé* eschew the staid posturing that weighs down Schlöndorff's film in favor of nuanced performances that always communicate the comical, droll aspects of Proust's cast of characters.

Ruiz not only makes the connection between the narrator's voyeurism with that of a film spectator but also suggests that the narrator is a kind of cinematographer, one whose *mise-en-scène* is composed of memory, dreams, and childhood fantasies. In one scene the young Marcel (played by Georges du Fresne, the star of the 1996 *Ma Vie en rose*, in which he also played a sensitive young boy given to flights of fancy) maneuvers a magic lantern, casting a gorgeous spectacle of light and color onto several party guests who have suddenly turned to stone. As Marcel says of this pre-cinematic invention in *Du côté de chez Swann*, "it substituted for the opaqueness of my walls an impalpable iridescence, supernatural phenomena of many colors, in which legends were depicted as on a shifting and transitory window" (Proust, 1992: 10). Similarly, Marcel's memories of the "legends" of Parisian society are also shifting and transitory. During the party scene hosted by the Duchesse de Guermantes (Edith Scob), Marcel mistakes Gilberte (Emmanuelle Béart) for her mother, Odette (Catherine Deneuve), a mishap that suggests the conflation of characters and past and present within his memory.

In one of Ruiz's more adroit liberties with the text, the young Marcel is depicted as a film projectionist sitting high above the oblivious members of the aristocracy. His delicate face is alternately obscured and illuminated by the flickering of the images, which, appropriately enough, are early films by Georges Méliès, who, as the inventor of the "trick film," was as innovative in film language as Proust was in written language and narrative structure. Ruiz's own cinematic innovations are a glorious tribute to the moments in Proust's novel in which the laws of gravity and motion are obliterated by the more powerful laws of memory. During a recital at the Guermantes' party, entire rows of seated guests tilt left then right, trees mysteriously change position; the narrator himself remains stationary in front of the animated shifts from the past to the present. These kinesthetic movements recall a passage in the "Combray" section of *Du côté de chez Swann* in which the narrator describes "the feeling which makes us not merely regard a thing as a spectacle, but believe in it as in a unique essence," which is evoked by his memories of seeing the steeple of the church at Combray from different perspectives:

Whether one saw it at five o'clock when going to call for letters at the post-office, some doors away from one, on the left, raising abruptly with its isolated peak the ridge of house-tops; or whether, if one were looking in to ask for news of Mme Sazerat, one's eyes followed that ridge which had now become low again after the descent of its other slope, and one knew that it would be the second turning after the steeple; or again if, pressing further afield, one went to the station and saw it obliquely, showing in profile fresh angles and surfaces, like a solid body surprised at some unknown point in its revolution; or if, seen from the banks of the Vivonne, the apse, crouched muscularly and heightened by the perspective, seemed to spring upwards with the effort which the steeple was making to hurl its spire-point into the heart of heaven − it was always to the steeple that one must return, always the steeple that dominated everything else . . . (Proust, 1992: 90−1)

Similarly, Ruiz's film is no mere "spectacle" of period costumes; *Le Temps retrouvé* gracefully attempts to capture the "unique essence" of the vagaries of memory.

Making the themes of time and memory even more poignant is the casting in the film, which is as varied as the constellation of players in Proust's Parisian high society. It was particularly brilliant of Ruiz to cast Catherine Deneuve − who better represents the aristocracy of French actors? − and Marie-France Pisier, who appeared in three of the five films in François Truffaut's Proustian Antoine Doinel series, as Mme Verdurin. "The true paradises are the ones that we have lost," muses the narrator (in a voice-over provided by Patrice Chereau) toward the end of *Le Temps retrouvé*. Upon first seeing the older Deneuve and Pisier, one cannot help but reflect back on their youthful incarnations during the halcyon, lionized years of French film in the 1960s − a period that is not necessarily a paradise lost but one that is worshiped as an era of youthful exuberance, vitality, and possibility. The faces of Deneuve and Pisier, then, become the icons − much like Proust's renowned madeleine − that evoke our own cinematic memories. The very iconicity of Deneuve and Pisier is accentuated by the lusciously surreal recurrence, spaced about an hour apart in the film, of Odette's entrance into Mme Verdurin's salon after several years of absence from her "little clan." This brief reunion acts as a mnemonic device on two different levels, reminding the viewer both of the significance of the two formidable characters throughout Proust's epic *and* the regal status of these two actresses in the history of French cinema.

The presence in the film of Deneuve's own children, daughter Chiara Mastroianni as Albertine and son Christian Vadim as Albert Bloch, although certainly firmly rooting us in French cinema's present (if not its future), also suggests the lineage of acting aristocracy. The casting of Emmanuelle Béart as Gilberte is also particularly savvy, for Béart is the "successor" to Deneuve's reign as grande dame of French cinema in much the same way that Gilberte is positioned to supplant Odette.

Rather than making a tedious, costume-driven narrative film of a text that poses many challenges to cinematic adaptation, Ruiz wisely chooses to explore the rich metaphorical connections between the reveries and memories evoked by film − the most time-bound of all arts − with those recalled by Proust in *A la recherche du temps perdu*. In *Le temps retrouvé*, Proust writes: "So often, in the course of my life, reality had disappointed me because at the instant when my senses perceived it my imagination, which was the only organ that I possessed for the enjoyment of beauty, could not apply itself to it, in virtue of that ineluctable law which ordains that we can only imagine what is absent" (Proust, 1993: 263). Ruiz pays the ultimate tribute to Proust not only by honoring the author's imagination but also by his own creative imagining of "what is absent" in Proust's text, enriching the film – and inviting the spectator to contemplate the cinematic aspects of *A la recherche* – with his own directorial flourishes. Ruiz fully understands that innovative literature requires an innovative approach to filmic adaptation, one that can illuminate the relevance of the written word by playing with images.

La Captive

Chantal Akerman's *La Captive* (2000), "inspired by" (Akerman's own words) *La prisonnière*, displays the boldest interpretation of Proust's writing. "Interpretation" may be the wrong word here; "meditation" or "rumination" seems more accurate, since Akerman, of all three directors, has taken the most liberties in her adaptation. Her intervention, like Ruiz's, is thrilling: *La Captive* is remarkable for its austere approach to the plot and characters in *La prisonnière*, concentrating instead on the themes of jealousy and possession. When Ruiz and Akerman were making their films (*Le Temps retrouvé* premiered at Cannes in 1999; *La Captive* premiered at Cannes in 2000), interest in Proust and *A la recherche* was quite high. Within the past five years there have been at least three biographies written about Proust; significantly, Edmund White's short biography of Proust, published in 1999, was the inaugural volume of the "Penguin Lives" series. Other books, such as Alain de Botton's *How Proust Can Change Your Life* (1997), wittily find the pragmatic, "how-to" aspects of Proust's writing, reclaiming him as a consummate self-help guru. The resurgence in Proust's popularity may have been the result of wishing to assuage pre-millennial anxiety by following (or, at the very least, studying) the course of introspection so richly articulated by Proust. Ruiz's and Akerman's films turn inwardly, too, illuminating the interior lives of *A la recherche*'s principal players.

Like Ruiz, Akerman realizes that Proust's text lends itself to cinematic references, making the transition from page to screen that much richer. Just as important to Akerman's film is another film: Alfred Hitchcock's *Vertigo* (1958), itself one of the most powerful and indelible treatments of the very Proustian subject of obsessive love. Yet whereas Ruiz made his film time- and costume-specific, Akerman sets hers in present-day Paris. Akerman also forgoes the multiple temporal shifts employed by Ruiz, instead crafting a narrative that transpires over the course of several days. In many ways, *La Captive* echoes the theme of Proust's "Un Amour de Swann": that love is rarely reciprocated. Yet Unlike Schlöndorff's film, which also utilizes a narrative structure, *La Captive* expertly illuminates the mysteries of desire and the anguish of love.

The mismatched lovers in *La prisonnière* are Marcel and Albertine; Akerman changes their names to Simon and Ariane. Simon (Stanislas Merhar), a writer, lives in a sprawling apartment with Ariane (Sylvie Testud), the titular "captive." The first scene in *La Captive* links film to Proust's text, seeing them both as repositories for shards of memory. Simon runs Super-8 footage of Ariane and a group of her female friends (known in Proust's text as "the little band") playing at the beach. The home movie takes on the significance of evidence of Ariane's life before Simon, who scrutinizes it for clues about his lover. "I really like you," he says to Ariane's soundless, flickering image, with a wistfulness that already suggests the melancholy brought on by an impossible love. Ariane seems inscrutable here, just as she will remain throughout most of the film. The opening scene also establishes Ariane's erotic attachments to women; crucial to Akerman's film is Simon's attempt to explore the "mystery" of lesbian desire.

In the scenes that follow, Akerman shrewdly makes the connection between Proust and *Vertigo*, visually quoting moments from Hitchcock's film. "But everywhere my uncertainty as to what she might be doing was the same, the possibility that it was something wrong as abundant, surveillance even more difficult. . . ," writes Proust in *La prisonnière* (1993: 20). Simon, playing private investigator and driven to discover what Ariane does when she is not with him, stealthily follows Ariane in her car, just as Scottie (James Stewart) in *Vertigo* pursues Madeleine (Kim Novak, whose character's name takes on an especially felicitous quality once *Vertigo* is examined *vis-à-vis* Proust).

Simon continues his spying a few scenes later, trailing Ariane in a deserted Musée Rodin, echoing Scottie's surreptitious observation of Madeleine in the Legion of Honor. Ariane, entranced, walks around the marble bust of a woman, increasingly fixated on the sculpture's chignon. Her entranced state mirrors Madeleine's prolonged gazing at the portrait of Carlotta Valdez, during which the camera zooms in on both Madeleine's and the portrait's chignons. That Akerman, like Hitchcock, focuses on the spiral of the chignon is especially apt, for the spiral communicates – almost semaphorically – the trajectory of time, memory, and obsessive desire found in *A la recherche du temps perdu*. (Another point of reference here is Chris Marker's musings on Madeleine's chignon in his film-essay from 1982, *Sans Soleil*.) Similarly, near *La Captive*'s conclusion, Simon dives into the sea to rescue Ariane, who had gone for a late night swim, an instance that recalls Scottie's jump into the San Francisco Bay to save a drowning Madeleine. The ending of Akerman's film is ambiguous, for it is never certain whether the long-suffering Simon actually drowns Ariane. His obsession quite possibly turns into murderous wrath, just as Scottie's rage at being duped by Judy (also played by Kim Novak) and his fixation on re-creating Madeleine's death leads to Judy's death. Akerman's hybridization of Proust's text and Hitchcock's film is particularly perceptive in that her cross-referencing highlights *how* film and literature can illuminate – if not speak to – each other. *La Captive* makes *Vertigo* seem Proustian and *A la recherche du temps perdu* seem Hitchcockian.

Akerman also excels in elucidating the theme of love between women, which occurs throughout Proust's novel, and which she herself has examined quite remarkably in *Je, tu, il, elle* (*I, You, He, She*, 1974), *Les Rendez-vous d'Anna* (*The Meetings of Anna*, 1978), and *Portrait d'une jeune fille de la fin des anneés 60 à Bruxelles* (*Portrait of a Young Girl at the End of the 1960s in Brussels*, 1994). "The daughters of Gomorrah are at once rare enough and numerous enough for one not to pass unnoticed by another in any given crowd," Proust writes in *La prisonnière* (1993: 472). As Elisabeth Ladenson astutely notes in her book *Proust's Lesbianism*, "Proust paradoxically figures Gomorrah as at once exhibitionistic – female sexuality flaunting itself – and invisible, always eluding the male onlooker's efforts to apprehend, visually and conceptually, what women do together" (Ladenson, 1999: 7). Simon's relentless detective work is motivated by his need to demystify what, to him, seems the most enigmatic: sexual attraction between women. "I'm burning to know what goes on between women that doesn't between a man and a woman," he asks Sarah (Bérénice Bejo) and Isabelle (Anna Mouglalis), friends of Ariane's. "It can't be explained," Isabelle responds. It is precisely the inexplicability of lesbian desire that fuels Simon's jealousy, obsession, and possessiveness. As Ladenson explains, "Gomorrah, which flouts the stated laws of Proustian desire according to which love is concomitant with jealousy, acts as a willfully constructed epistemological blind spot, and it offers the novel's unique vision of a sexuality in control of its own representation" (Ladenson, 1999: 7).

Akerman, of course, cannot "explain" lesbian desire either, but she does, in one rapturous scene, marvelously demonstrate the power of its language. Ariane walks out onto the balcony of Simon's apartment, seemingly relieved at being outside her claustrophobic living quarters. From a neighboring apartment she hears a woman singing an extract from Mozart's *Cosi fan tutte*. Ariane sings back to her neighbor, establishing a call-and-response love song. Although Ariane is not a good singer, the ebullience in her performance more than compensates for her weak vocals. It is never clear that the two women can actually see each other; simply *listening* to the other has its own erotic charge. Soon Ariane and her neighbor are singing the lyrics together, and even though the grain of each woman's voice is quite different, there is nonetheless an almost climactic moment during their duet. The spontaneity of this serenade suggests the importance of auditory and verbal recognition in tracing lesbian desire, which, although elusive, is still demonstrable.

So, too, can the rich, dense prose that is the hallmark of *A la recherche du temps perdu* elude meaningful demonstration on film. Yet Ruiz and Akerman imaginatively translate ineffable states of emotion by unearthing the cinematic qualities already found in Proust's writing. Ruiz sees him as a cinematographer; Akerman foregrounds his novel's connection with a canonical film. Both are triumphant achievements over the mis-steps in Schlöndorff's conventional costume drama – and both serve as exemplars for others hoping to adapt the remaining volumes of *A la recherche du temps perdu*.

--------------------------------- Acknowledgments ---------------------------------

A portion of this chapter appeared in *Cineaste* 25: 1. I would like to thank Elizabeth Brown for her helpful comments and Jake Perlin for directing me to *The Proust Screenplay*. Thanks also to Natascha Bodemann at the French Film Office and Gabriel Caroti at Kino.

Proust and Film

Chapter 4

Aciman, André (2002) "Proust Regained," *The New York Review of Books* (July 18), 55–61.

de Botton, Alain (1997) *How Proust Can Change Your Life*. New York: Pantheon Books.

Bowie, Malcolm (1998) *Proust Among the Stars*. London: HarperCollins.

Ladenson, Elisabeth (1999) *Proust's Lesbianism*. Ithaca, NY: Cornell University Press.

Pinter, Harold (1977) *The Proust Screenplay*. New York: Grove Press.

Proust, Marcel (1992–3) *In Search of Lost Time*, trans. C. K. Scott Moncrieff and Terence Kilmartin, rev. D. J. Enright (Modern Library Edition). New York: Random House (originally published 1913–27).

White, Edmund (1999) *Marcel Proust*. New York: Viking.

Melissa Anderson

Chapter 4

Chapter 5

The Grapes of Wrath: Thematic Emphasis through Visual Style

Vivian C. Sobchack

Since its release in 1940, the film version of *The Grapes of Wrath* has attracted enormous and enduring critical and popular attention.[1] Yet, in some ways, it has also remained a neglected film, a film obscured by the shadow of its illustrious parentage (John Ford out of John Steinbeck) and by its generic absorption into that body of culturally significant art representative of and concerned with Depression America. Certainly, *The Grapes of Wrath* was and still is a highly visible film; its popularity as a "classic" is evidenced by its frequent appearance on prestigious commercial television series, at cinema club retrospectives, and in literature, film, and American studies classrooms. In addition, the film enjoys a wealth of critical consideration – as an adaptation of a work of fiction, as a cultural artifact which illuminates various aspects of popular American ideology and myth, and as part of the oeuvre of a major film *auteur*. Paradoxically, however, this widely considered film has suffered from visual neglect. Examined from several critical perspectives, *The Grapes of Wrath* has been more frequently looked *into* than looked *at*. Its visual surfaces have been hardly explored and mapped, its texture and tone have been rarely considered as functions of its imagery, and its dominant thematic emphasis has been only minimally related to its visual style.

The reasons for this literal and figurative oversight can be linked, of course, to the myopia demanded by focused and limited critical discourse. Adaptation criticism, for example, is practiced through a comparison of a novel and film. And, no matter how sophisticated and cinematically literate such adaptation criticism is, its comparisons tend to gravitate toward the literary values and structures which supply common ground between the two art forms. Thus, whether the literature/film critic is ignorant of the complexity of a film's visual text or conversant with film aesthetics, the bulk of adaptation criticism seems to consider a film like *The Grapes of Wrath* almost solely in terms of the literary structures which dictate its narrative action, characterization, and thematic emphasis. George Bluestone's influential *Novels into Film* and Warren French's more recent *Filmguide to The Grapes of Wrath* spend the major portion of their discussion and analysis of the film dealing with its adherence to or departure from Steinbeck's parent work on the basis of dialogue selection, scene deletions or additions, characters maintained, dropped, or synthesized, and the structural arrangement of narrative activity.[2] What the image looks like is neglected for a consideration of what *happens* in it. The subject matter is considered dominant to its visual treatment. Similarly, what happens next is considered more important than how the images happen next. Indeed, images are ignored as affective and cumulative units of meaning and texture which accrue to express the film's theme in conjunction with its verbal and literary devices. Rather, they are regarded as discrete particles of larger dramatic sequences and greatly subordinate in importance to what dialogue and action take place within and through them. Although both Bluestone and French describe various visual aspects of *The Grapes of Wrath*, they have difficulty in their respective methods integrating what they see with what the film says and means. In the final analysis, their differing conclusions about the thematic emphasis of the film and its relationship to Steinbeck's novel both derive from a primarily literary approach to the film text.

A similar approach is taken by those critics whose interest in the film is more cultural than aesthetic. *The Grapes of Wrath* has been praised for its courageous realism and its social relevance as well as damned for its conservatism and timidity in addressing the problems it pretended to tackle. It has also been analyzed and discussed as a cultural and social barometer, expressive of those "meanings and values that were a part of the dominant culture"[3] at the time the film was made and seen. If the cultural approach is not quite literary, it is often too literal in its response to the film's imagery. Content again is predominant and considered independently from its visual treatment. For example, at its release, the fact that the film dealt with relatively contemporaneous subject matter, that it cinematically seemed to articulate the world and the plight of Dust Bowl migrants, and that the material content of its images bore a superficially strong resemblance to the physical world outside the theater attracted far greater critical attention than did the film's stylized and abstracting treatment of its subject matter and physical content. Indeed, the film was initially reviewed and apotheosized more in terms of its relationship to actuality, to documentary realism, than treated as a successful adaptation of a novel or a work of cinematic fiction and art. *Life* magazine called it "bitter, authentic, honest,"[4] and Edwin Locke, a documentary filmmaker, compared the film favorably with the documentary films of Pare Lorentz and the Depression photographs of Dorothea Lange, saying it "set a precedent for contemporary and historical honesty in movie-making."[5]

Certainly, in recent years, cultural criticism of *The Grapes of Wrath* has moved far afield from measuring the film's social worth on the basis of its realism. Now the pendulum has swung the other way and the film's value as a cultural artifact is based on its relation to myth, to its expression of a popular social vision which Charles Maland, for example, sees conveyed through the construction of "a symbolic universe meant to present a pattern of values and meanings in a popular fictional form to a broad audience."[6] But despite the increased sophistication of such cultural analysis, the notion of social vision is linked only rarely to actual vision, to the integration of the film's images and visual texture with the reading of its narrative and cultural content. Thus, while Maland may conclude that *The Grapes of Wrath* is one in a number of contemporaneous films whose concern for the American family "symbolically represents a larger shift in the American film industry at large from a social criticism to affirmation, another indication of the decline of radicalism between 1936 and 1941," that contention is never given the ample and cogent visual support the film could provide.[7]

One might expect that the literary emphasis of adaptation criticism and the literal emphasis of cultural criticism directed toward *The Grapes of Wrath* would be counter-balanced by the more visually oriented attention of film criticism. Not bound through intent or academic discipline to compare the film to the novel or to investigate its place in a cultural and historical *gestalt*, cineastes might be expected to consider the film more freely as an autonomous work of visual as well as verbal art. Unfortunately, such has not been the case. As Steinbeck's novel has obscured the less verbal aspects of the film from literary critics, and as the film's relationship to a particularly fascinating period of social and cultural history has narrowed the focus of cultural critics, so has John Ford's position as a pantheon *auteur* blurred the specific vision of film critics. Rather than being considered on its own merits and discussed on the basis of its aesthetic development and coherence, *The Grapes of Wrath* has been regarded primarily within the context of Ford's entire body of work. As such, it has been either seen as less than a major work and ignored, or discussed less visually than thematically as part of the director's continuing vision of what Andrew Sarris calls a "nostalgic" and "family level of history."[8]

In the first instance, the film is often given short critical shrift because it is not a Western, because it was made at a mid-point in Ford's career which has garnered less attention than his work in the 1930s and after the 1940s, and because it is regarded as somehow less "pure" Ford for being an adaptation of a classic novel. (It is interesting to note that most of the close textual analysis of Ford films is practiced on those not adapted from literature, and that, although Ford used literary sources for ten of his films, only *The Informer* and *Stagecoach* have merited nearly unanimous praise and attention from cineastes.)[9] In the second instance, that film criticism which has dealt with *The Grapes of Wrath* in any detail has done so in terms of its thematic concerns as derived from its narrative structure and its general resemblance to other Ford films. The film itself and its visual specificity have fallen victim to how a given critic feels about Ford. For someone like Sarris, the film's apolitical evocation of nostalgia through its "humanizing Steinbeck's economic insects into heroic champions of an agrarian order of family and community"[10] is clearly one of the film's chief virtues. On the other hand, in a negative "reassessment" of Ford, Michael Dempsey castigates the director and his work for polit-ical conservatism and easy sentimentality and says disparagingly of *The Grapes of Wrath*, "Ford the contemporary of Dreiser and Dos Passos and even Steinbeck gives us . . . a hollow celebration of that emptiest abstraction, The People, along with a cop-out analysis which avoids blaming any individual or interest for the plight of the Okies."[11] These statements, however, whether for or against Ford as a film artist of merited stature, are not backed up by careful consideration of the film's imagery. Unfortunately, that imagery is too often assumed as a given by critics anxious to get on with the job of dealing with Ford's themes. As Pierre Greenfield notes, a great deal of such criticism presents "an exposition of Fordian philosophy without any serious justification of it."[12] Film critics are therefore as guilty as literary and cultural critics in their general neglect of the visual elements of *The Grapes of Wrath*.

This tripartite oversight needs some redress – not necessarily because *The Grapes of Wrath* is a great work of film art (which is arguable), but because it is a film and it is shown on a screen and has a visual presence. The way we read and perceive it is as much a function of its visual imagery as it is of its literary and dramatic and cultural content. Indeed, in most cases the strength and immediacy of a film's visual imagery is at least equal to if not far greater than its literary content, even if its power is not acknowledged or articulated. Because of this power, a film's visual imagery merits as much attention when it is supportive of literary and cultural and thematic analyses as when it is more flamboyantly contradictory or quietly subversive. In the case of *The Grapes of Wrath*, the consensus of critical response has been nearly unanimous in its recognition that Ford's film is different in tone and spirit from Steinbeck's novel and that the film is a politically conservative and poetic work whose major theme is the value and resilience of the American family. That consensus was not arrived at merely by an examination of the film's structural relationship to the novel which was its source, or by a cultural analysis of its place in a *gestalt* of populist art, or by its thematic echo of what its principal creator expressed in his work both before and after it. That consensus of critical response to *The Grapes of Wrath* was also generated by the *seeing* of the film, by the intuitive integration of the film's imagery into the critical act. The apprehension of that imagery and its function needs both appropriate recognition and articulation.

It is agreed that Ford's transliteration of Steinbeck's book to the screen restructures the values of an essentially realistic and political novel and emphasizes those aspects of the parent work which are the most consistent with the filmmaker's own values and personal vision. Although both Steinbeck and Ford do share a common bond in their focus on American institutions and ideology, in their dramatic humanization of those institutions and ideas through the medium of proletariat protagonists, and in their use of humor and folklore, their sympathies and interests are dramatically divergent. Steinbeck's novels emphasize the importance of the present, the harshness of reality, the potential of radical politics, and the need for social and political change. Conversely, Ford's films emphasize the values of the past and soften the harsher aspects of historical reality with nostalgia; his film worlds are apolitical and atemporal and his aesthetic evocation of America revolves around the harmony and established traditions of community. Indeed, his life's work reveals a reverence for those human values that are most simple and universal, a reverence which balks and trembles at the necessity for progress and change. As Andrew Sarris cogently indicates in *The John Ford Movie Mystery*, "Ford never lost his faith in the benign drift of American history . . . and intuitively redirected the pessimistic class conflicts in . . . Steinbeck . . . into relatively optimistic family chronicles."[13]

The novel, however, is less concerned about seven months in the life of the Joad family than it is about the relationship of men to land, about an untenable economic system, and about the inevitable awakening of a communal revolutionary consciousness in the oppressed and exploited. The Joad family is only a sharply focused point from which the novel continually moves out far beyond the limited awareness of its main characters to deal with epic social and political issues, abstractions which — of dramatic necessity — must find embodiment in the concrete and specific, in characterization and action and the details of physical imagery. Although the Joad family takes on the bulk of this dramatic function in the novel, Steinbeck has structured the book in such a way that the reader cannot forget that the family is only one of many families, that it is part of a larger organism composed not only of families but also of land and plants and animals and weather. The Joads are constantly counterbalanced by the equal emphasis given in the intercalary chapters to larger issues than their immediate survival and to larger groups than the family. As a result, their family unit is not metaphorical in function; it is, instead, illustrative. Its importance in the novel is not in its mythic cohesion and endurance, but in its realistic specificity. The Joads comprise only half of the novel's emphasis, enjoy only half its attention. And the universal theme of family solidarity is greatly subordinate to the larger emphasis Steinbeck gives to a cry for the solidarity of men in a definite political and economic context. Indeed, as Warren French points out, the novel charts the progress of the Joads' "growing out of the narrow concept of 'fambly' in the blood-relationship sense to a concept of membership in the entire 'human family.' "[14]

As has been pointed out by many critics including those cited here, Ford is not particularly concerned with the Joads' integration into the family of man. Nor is he particularly interested in relating them to an economic or political milieu. Although there is a great deal of dialogue in the film which relates the family to the land, to a larger population, and to a political climate *verbally*, the visual interest of the film is on the Joads as an isolated and universal family unit which transcends the particularity and specificity of time and place. Certainly, the Joads on screen are specific and particular in their photographic realization; it is the nature of the medium to particularize "characters" and "place" far more exactly and idiosyncratically than written language. But the visual treatment of Henry Fonda's Tom, Jane Darwell's Ma, Charley Grapewin's Grampa, John Carradine's Casey, and John Qualen's Muley softens their physical individuality and resonates photographic specificity into expressive metaphor. Because of the manner in which the major portion of the film has been visually conceived and shot, Steinbeck's multiple themes and simultaneous emphasis have been exchanged for a less epic but equally universal vision, for a scope at once smaller than the novel's in its reduction of politics and economics and social realities to the size of a single romanticized family, and yet also a scope larger than the novel's in its evocation of the survival and endurance of that family against a stylized background which is not limited by time and space. While Charles Maland suggests that Ford's emphasis on the Joads as a familial and communal unit can be linked to the director's natural affinity for Jeffersonian agrarianism, to his belief in independent ownership of land by industrious and hard-working families,[15] the Joads gain their universality from their being dispossessed of their land. Indeed, it is their lack of land (and its lack of photographic reference) which abstracts them into the generalized and poetic space of the montage sequences and places them in cramped close-ups and medium shots isolated in trucks and cars and tents far from communion with anyone but themselves.

Thus, where the novel *moves out* both structurally and imagistically from the Joads to continually emphasize the land, biological presence, and the crush of thousands of migrants on the move, the film's movement visually *closes in* on the Joads, at times to such a degree that they have only a minimal connection with either the land or the rest of society. The characters, of course, do pay lip service to that connection through the dialogue – so much so that a reading of the continuity script alone might result in the impression of a quite different film from the one actually realized on the screen. But that connection is not actually visible through a great portion of the film. Land is not as visible as what French calls "the fresh, temporary look of studio sets."[16] Most of the film was shot indoors or on the studio lot rather than on location in a landscape which might have matched the visual power and presence of the Monument Valley Ford used in so many of his Westerns. Though there are some brief long shots of authentic locations in some of the montage sequences, their open quality primarily serves as a striking reminder of the film's overwhelmingly closed visual construction. If one looks at the film's imagery, it seems rather off the mark to read *The Grapes of Wrath* as a land tragedy.

Some early critics noted this absence of land imagery in the film and remarked on Ford's departure from Steinbeck in this regard. Generally, these astute reviewers were filmmakers themselves, attuned to the visual qualities of film. Edwin Locke, for example, came to the film with a background as a member of the US Film Service, a government agency whose films specialized in evoking the beauty of the American landscape:

It is a pity that Ford's sense of environment has not come through as well as his sense of people. The opening of the picture is greatly weakened because he has given us no feeling of the country or the people's background. Where are the vast stretches of the dust bowl and the tiny houses as lonely as ships at sea? Where is the dust? It is hard to believe that Ford has ever seen *The Plow that Broke the Plains*. It is baffling to hear that a camera crew was sent to Oklahoma along Route 66; certainly but a few feet of their film was used. It is regrettable that the Joads were snatched across the beautiful and terrifying expanses of the country in a few pans and process shots; we could justly have expected more. We could have expected more of what it is like to be tractored off the land, more than the knocking over of a prop house by a Caterpillar roaming at large, more than a hackneyed montage of clanking monsters in abstract maneuvers. We might have all these things, and a richer picture, if Ford had followed a little further the documentary technique that is now being talked about in connection with his work.[17]

he [Nunnally Johnson, the screenwriter] needed to think in terms of skies and brown land and, most of all, wind. He needed only to have written "drought" and then left it to the director to re-create the feeling of those dusty plains tilting from Oklahoma clear up to Canada, with their miserable huts and busted windmills. In fact, he needed only to have gone to the panhandle of Oklahoma and Texas and western Kansas and the Dakotas and eastern Colorado and said: "Photograph this – here is where they came from."

As he did not, then Director John Ford (who, by virtue of going to Zion Park in Utah to photograph his outdoor sequences in *Stagecoach*, made a Western action picture into a thing of beauty) at least might have started his picture with the Great Plains instead of with scenes that, even though they were from the book, did not give you a feeling of the land.[18]

Less important for their recognition of how Ford's film broke a certain faith with Steinbeck's book or with natural history than for their recognition that the visual images of a film are crucial to its meaning, these comments indicate the closed quality that permeates Ford's work, his visual *choice* which omits wide-open spaces and panoramic vistas of either parched earth or pastures of plenty. Indeed, until Ford brings the Joads into Hooverville – halfway through the film – the camera isolates them, disconnects them, perhaps even protects them from larger forces and larger movements which give the novel an epic quality.

The general composition of *The Grapes of Wrath* is consciously controlled and tight. For the most part, the action occurs in visually limited space – limited either by its actual spatial parameters and tight framing or by the amount of it we are allowed to see by virtue of the given illumination. Right from the beginning – after one brief long shot – we move inward. Tom hitches a ride and we are confined for the first of many times in the cab of a truck, cramped in its interior or looking in close-up through the windshield at Tom and the driver. While Maland's comment that the film "consists almost entirely of the Joads riding in their ramshackle truck"[19] is an exaggeration, it is true that the characters are usually cramped into a cluttered screen and limited space. Not only is a good deal of the Joads' odyssey confined and isolated in automotive interiors, but a large share of the dramatic action is also confined indoors: in cluttered or darkly oppressive rooms, tents, or shacks, all of which close in the characters. Out of the 50 "scenes" French describes as comprising the units of the film, a total of 25 are shot (entirely or in part) within the Joad truck or within an oppressive interior.[20]

Those compositions which occur in "open space" are also chafingly contained and limited by their cardboard and set-like quality and by the relative lack of internal movement of both the camera and the characters. Although, for example, Tom's initial encounter with Casey takes place in an "open" field punctuated by an overly aestheticized willow tree, the camera stays in one spot and the characters stand immobile except for occasionally and uncomfortably shifting their weight from foot to foot. Containing their physical movement in such a way, Ford contains the frame as well. The visual effect is that there is no field outside the limits of the camera's vision, no land – rather, there is a non-space, or a studio set covered with false and aestheticized earth. The long long shot which concludes the sequence shows Tom and Casey silhouetted against the darkening sky as they set out for the Joad homestead. But the shot – however long and panoramic – is more closed than open, more memorable for its composed quality and artful lighting and static vision than it is for an evocation of a real world with real earth and dust which is really blowing away. Uncle John's farmyard is no more open spatially than a stage setting which pretends to realism. And both the Keene Ranch and the Wheat Patch government camp seem patently artificial in their respective evocations of squalor and darkness and spanking clean brightness. The effect of this spatial closure on the film is not necessarily negative, but it does communicate the visual message that the world which the Joads inhabit is less than real and vital. *Their* vitality against the cardboard settings, the Edward Hopper skies and contrived grimness and beauty, makes them more important than the problems they face – for they are physically present and dramatically highlighted, while the Depression and the land blowing away and the rest of the world are shown as an abstracted stage set or ignored altogether.

The static compositions, the tableau-like posturing of the characters, and the pattern of the editing also add to the visual elements which lift the Joads out of connection with things immediate and specific and create of their struggle and endurance something universal and iconic. The camera rarely moves, preferring for the most part to look at its subjects from eye-level and mid-distance. This point of view produces images which look at times like the same view of the action one would get watching a stage production or historical tableau; the entire human figure is seen in the frame and so the image does not extend itself imaginatively out into the world, and the relative immobility of the camera creates a sense of the characters entering and exiting from wings as opposed to the camera seeking them out. The one literally jarring exception to the general pattern of composition and camera/subject movement is the visual treatment given to the Joad's entrance into Hooverville, and to the fight which occurs in that tent city. The subjective camera, which moves as a member of the Joad family through the street, visually opens up the film as it, paradoxically, limits its objectivity. Both the subjective vision and the camera movement are more jolting than the supposedly shocking content presented, as is the later fight sequence which contains so much more movement and randomness than we have seen before.

Indeed, generally the dramatic activity or stage "business" within the frame is rarely spontaneous or random, and the relative lack of physical movement by the characters when someone has something important to say (a "speech" such as Casey's on not being a preacher, or Muley's on being "touched," or Ma's on Tom's not becoming mean) makes the dialogue denser than it might otherwise be if lightened by some random motion. Instead, such speeches are met with stillness, are photographed as tableaux removing the characters from a peopled and physically present environment into the realm of archetype and iconography. The settings of the Joad farm, of Uncle John's farm, of the cabin in the pickers' camp, in the tents of Hooverville, in the neat exteriors of the government camp – not one of them has the uncontrolled and extraneous quality of realistic and immediate art or document. Not a chicken stirs, and every object seems to exist for dramatic and atmospheric rather than natural purpose. As a result, the social and political and economic problems which the characters face seem far more dramatic than real, far more aesthetically and narratively functional than immediately pressing.

The way in which the film is edited further stresses the archetypal and iconic aspects of the Joads by creating stylized temporal relationships between shots. The Joads exist in montage time, for example – shots linked together rhythmically or superimposed so as to convey the passage of time without really being specific. In addition, the Joads exist in what might be called "tableau time" – that is, they are seen in set pieces, in scenes which are not dynamically connected or visually continuous to others. Warren French has commented derogatorily on the perfunctory nature of the editing, criticizing not only the narrative puzzles it presents with the disappearance of Noah Joad or Rosasharn's baby, but also with the use of "sharp breaks between scenes" and the lack of associational editing, the "switch from one scene to another by cutting from an object in one scene to a similar object in another." He also notes that Ford "apparently preferred to break the picture into a series of discrete episodes by the use of sharply delineated fadeouts and fadeins." These editorial devices add to the film the "compensating universality" French sees as a substitute for the bite and timeliness of Steinbeck's novel. The lack of simultaneity through cross-cutting, the abstractness of the montages, the measured and highly theatrical fades, and even the one flashback sequence in which Muley "tells" what happened to the land – all are stylistic choices which serve to abstract the Joads.[21]

Whereas the average viewer might not notice the abstracting qualities of the film's composition and editing, it is nearly impossible not to notice that the film is dark. French points out that "almost exactly half the action takes place at night or under dimly lit conditions,"[22] a proportion which might allow one to also argue that almost exactly half the film takes place during the day or in brightly lit conditions. The dramatic weight of the film, however, falls on the dark side, for if one compares those scenes which occur in varying degrees of darkness with those which take place in relatively bright light it becomes obvious that the former are more important to the narrative and more intense in their emotional content than the latter. Casey and Tom's reunion is marked by the dimness of approaching dusk. The long and highly dramatic scene in the deserted Joad cabin is shot in candlelight as Casey and Tom are joined by Muley who relates in the dark present and in the punctuating brightness of a flashback what has occurred to the farmers and their land. Ma Joad's brief but powerful review of her life's souvenirs occurs in the dimness of the stripped house. The Joads' first stay in a campground with other migrants and their encounter with the man who tells them about the false promise of the handbills is at night. The Joads' desert crossing in which Granma dies is also dark. And nearly the entire 22 minutes of the Joads' sojourn at the Keene Ranch is played in the dusky interior of the filthy cabin or at night – as is the important dramatic sequence under the bridge in which both Casey and Tom and their companion strikebreakers fight the Keene guards, a fight which leaves Casey dead and Tom hurt and guilty of murder. Finally, even the climactic scene in the Wheat Patch camp occurs at night: despite the celebratory nature of the Saturday night dance, and its triumphant drama in which the migrants form a cohesive and persuasive group to oust their enemies, the sequence is dark – as is the related scene in which Tom says goodbye to Ma and delivers his "I'll be ever'where" speech before disappearing into the blackness. The drama and narrative impetus in the daylight scenes are anecdotal compared to the force of the night scenes. And, again, it is only in Hooverville that Ford provides a marked exception.

The chiaroscuro lighting of a major portion of the film does more than merely supply atmosphere and support the thematic darkness of the Joads' odyssey. It also functions as a technique which is abstracting, which again brings a sense of closure to the screen image by obscuring the connection between various objects in the frame and turning the viewer's attention inward toward the Joads. The shadows spatially blot out the rest of the world much of the time and are, as well, oppressive and confining. Consider, for example, the sequence in the Joads' abandoned farmhouse near the beginning of the film. Composed quite statically and shot in darkness punctuated only by candlelight and flashlight, the images curl into themselves rather than extend outwards to the corners of the frame and to a consciousness of a physical world in motion beyond its confines. The camera's emphasis is on faces, faces which become not quite real in the semi-darkness, faces which are isolated in cinematographer Gregg Toland's "web of shadows and night," visually reinforcing, for instance, "Muley's belief that he is just 'an ol' grave-yard ghos'."[23]

Either through the actual proximity of close-ups or the masking effect of darkness in the medium shots, the abundance of expressionistic cinematography which emphasizes the pale faces and glistening eyes of the characters is not really counterbalanced to any great degree by an equivalent insistence on realistic and clearly defined imagery. Indeed, the personal intensity and attention of the camera on the faces of the Joads is never matched in kind by equally intense or emphatic shots of the people they meet or the land they supposedly revere – with one exception. Muley's flashback sequence is as stylized and intense and visually compressed as any in the film. The land as a force is visually acknowledged in such a manner that it is made as transcendent and universal as the Joads. In one stylized and uncharacteristic high-angle shot, Muley squats on his land, alone and in dark contrast to the barren lightness of the earth around him. And in another, the final shot of the sequence, the camera moves from Muley and his family to isolate their shadows upon the ground marked with the destructive tracks of the Caterpillar tractor. The confluence in the frame of the men's shadows, the trail of destruction, and the land itself is as expressive and compressed as Charles Maland suggests in his analysis of the sequence.[24]

But the expressive weight and metaphorical force of the flashback's visual articulation is diluted by its early and singular placement in the film. The same is true of the visual style and brighter illumination in the sequence in Hooverville. It is only in Hooverville that Ford connects the Joads visually with a context which unites them with

other people. The tent city is teeming with spontaneous humanity. It is more concret
physical in its presence than any other location in the film — a world of dirt and
and texture which Ford let Toland photograph in daylight. The images of Hoove
are less moody, less artfully shadowed and expressionistic than elsewhere in the film; the
viewer is allowed to see and thereby experience the texture of material things, the gray
and grainy images effectively evoking the feel of grit and dust. Because there is more
light, the composition seems freer and the boundaries of the frame seem larger and more
potentially extendable; our attention is not directed inward to the center of the frame as
it is through a great deal of the rest of the film. Because of the relatively bright illumination, because there is more random movement of more characters who are visually seen
in contiguity with the Joads, and because there is a selection of more spontaneous visual
detail (it is hard to control the flapping of clothes drying on a line), the episode in Hooverville
is singular in its attempt at documentary realism. Although it is memorable, it is also jolting in its contrast to the film's predominant visual style, a style acknowledged by both Ford
and Toland for its "blackness."[25] That blackness is less grim than abstracting, less harsh
than protective; the Joads and the viewer are removed from a visually urgent and engaging context and the result is a predominant imagery which seems highly aestheticized,
staged, and framed.

The lighting in *The Grapes of Wrath* and its abstracting effects derive from the chiaroscuro
practiced by the German Expressionists in their nightmare paintings and films and, indeed,
practiced by Ford himself in two highly expressionist and stylized works which rank among
his personal favorites: *The Informer* (1935) and *The Fugitive* (1947). The visual ambience
created by the lighting in *The Grapes of Wrath* evokes the vague outlines of night and
dream rather than the harsh specificity of daylight and Depression America. In a brief
but cogent discussion of the film's lighting, French concludes that, through the lighting,
"Ford converted what could have been a nerve-wracking social protest . . . into an artful
product that resolves all transient violence in a serene meditation."[26]

That serene meditation is, of course, on the Joads' "coherence as a family . . . not as
a class,"[27] and the film's appeal and emotional force derive from the simplicity and direct-
ness of Ford's focus. Indeed, Maland points out the film's ability to satisfy "the intense
desire of many Americans to be involved, through their sentiments at least, in the human
problems caused by the depression."[28] But one might amend Maland's observation by
suggesting that Ford's film was so satisfying precisely because it involved the contemporaneous viewer primarily on the level of sentiment, because its transcendent vision of
the Joads as an archetypal family freed the viewer from the responsibility for specific
social action. It is not only the lighting (as French suggests) but the whole visual style
of the film which lifts the Joads from specificity and immediacy, which elevates them
far from spatial and temporal urgency. Indeed, the film is most powerful in its use of
what might be identified from today's perspective as the visual shorthand of a Depression
iconography. Through its images it evokes the softened and popularized form of the
Depression — its outline — without assaulting the viewer with the harsh demands of actual
content.

Although he sometimes confuses the content of the imagery with its softened treatment, George Bluestone senses the iconic visual quality of *The Grapes of Wrath*:

> Behind the director's controlling hand is the documentary eye of a Pare Lorentz or a Robert Flaherty, of the vision in those stills produced by the Resettlement Administration in its volume, *Land of the Free* . . . or in Walker Evans' shots for *Let Us Now Praise Famous Men* . . . Gregg Toland's photography is acutely conscious of the pictorial values of land and sky, finding equivalents for those haunting images of erosion which were popularized for the New Deal's reclamation program and reflected in Steinbeck's prose.[29]

While Bluestone seems off the mark in his efforts to prove how the film and novel share a common tone or evoke similar land imagery, he is to the point in noting the film's visual resemblance to the documentary poetry of both Robert Flaherty and Pare Lorentz. Both of these filmmakers dealt in a kind of generalized imagery which has given their work universal qualities. Man's struggles against the landscape of Flaherty's *Nanook of the North* and *Man of Aran* are as primal and timeless as they are physically concretized in specific geography, and the editing techniques of Lorentz combined with his use of abstracting close-ups of water and land and objects give to both *The Plow that Broke the Plains* and *The River* a temporal and spatial vagueness which is powerful and iconic. Indeed, despite Lorentz's criticisms of the absence of land imagery in *The Grapes of Wrath*, Ford's visual abstraction of the Joads parallels in style and effect that documentary filmmaker's timeless and aspatial treatment of the ecological problems of the Middle West. On the other hand, Bluestone displays a visual insensitivity to style when he equates Ford's film and the photography of Walker Evans. The hard-edged clarity, sharp focus, and unsentimental asceticism of Evans's work is removed in both sensibility and style from Flaherty, Lorentz, and John Ford. *The Grapes of Wrath* only superficially resembles the always specific and unsparing definition in either Evans's or Dorothea Lange's Depression photography; if there is a likeness it is in content rather than style. A visual counterpart to the general effect of the film's imagery can be more readily found in the work of a fine artist who tempered the realistic subject matter of his content with a softening of focus, a rounding off of hard edges and sharp contrasts; *The Grapes of Wrath* looks more like the blunted vision of Edward Hopper than the acutely detailed vision of the Depression's most acclaimed photographers.

Indeed, the film derives much of its emotional and aesthetic power from its generalized quality, its use of what Bluestone calls "popularized" images, which are neither realistic nor documentary, as Bluestone's aligning them with documentary filmmakers and photographers would suggest. They serve mythology and metaphor rather than social realism, and while they may often tug at the heartstrings with their sentimental appeal, they rarely incite the viewer to serious thought; they are equivalent not to the harsh prose of Steinbeck's work or the clarity and asceticism of Evans's photographic style, but rather to the emotional appeal of poster art. Thus, much as Ford in his Westerns has used the temporally and spatially circumscribed and compressed world of object and landscape to evoke a mythology which creates its own contained time and space and which owes little to actual history, he has also used the temporally and spatially circumscribed iconography of the Depression to create softened and blunted images which evoke the Depression but which continually contain it in the realm of art. The film abounds with material objects and landscapes which simultaneously concretize and yet abstract the political, economic, and social realities of Steinbeck's chapters about the Joads into poetic and emotional short-hand: the slouched and soiled hats, the caps, the floral print dresses and the haphazardly buttoned sweaters which have come to clothe our emotional associations with the Depression; the static posturing of family groups, stiffly posing for the future with a fascinating self-consciousness which keeps them rigidly facing the camera while they secretly avert their eyes from it; old trucks and jalopies whose geometry is top-heavy as an inverted pyramid – falling apart, choking, and bursting at the seams with material goods gathered together with old clothesline, familiar mattresses, and old kitchen chairs; gas stations and gas pumps somehow evocative of both ordered corporate power in a technological society and the migratory movement of an agricultural people no longer in harmony with the land; industrial machinery glorified by the power conferred by the close-up and low angle, biting into the earth like prehistoric carnivores. The visual imagery of Ford's film uses all this emotional iconography which has come to us generalized out of specific and harsher pieces of Depression art and life.

In the final analysis, the film projects the images of a ritualized world, a world in which change is neither possible nor desirable. Instead, survival and endurance and the continuation of traditional values are apotheosized by the Joads and their odyssey through "a-timeless world that cages men, while allowing them the freedom of movement to dignify and humanize their lives through action and comedy."[30] This is certainly not the world of John Steinbeck. Rather, the film is the result of the legitimate aesthetic choices made by a director with a reputation at least equal to the novelist's whose work he has translated. By choices, Ford's film is powerful in its realization of "family." His style is not miscalculated or unconsidered. And it is not merely derived from the changes made in the literary elements of the film. The static compositions and camera placement, the artificiality of the studio set, the non-dynamic editing, and the chiaroscuro lighting and its resultant softening of harsh contrasts and hard edges, coupled with Ford's neglect of a concrete political and social context and his omission of those sequences which would make the family less attractive than it is – all serve his emotional exploration of the enduring dignity and value of American family life. Rather than choosing to follow Steinbeck's alternation of the abstract with the concrete (something which film is quite able to do despite its constant dependence on material reality), Ford has chosen to make a film equivalent in tone with the intercalary chapters of Steinbeck's novel. That tone, however, is applied to the stuff of Steinbeck's more concretely realized chapters: the Joads. If Ford's film is so enclosed, so reluctant to include the visual feel and evocation of human-ity found in Walker Evans's or Dorothea Lange's Depression photographs so alive with sweat and dirt and particularity, it is consistent with Ford's lack of interest in the specificity of history and politics and social problems. It is no accident that the film's visual style neglects real estate and agriculture for people. We never see the Joads work the land they speak of. At the Keene Ranch, when the men and children go off to pick fruit the images stay behind with Ma and Rosasharn. The only work we see Tom do that has any connection with earth and dirt is laying pipeline. And there is not a single peach in the film.

Asked by Peter Bogdanovich what attracted him to the novel, Ford answered: "The whole thing appealed to me – being about simple people – and the story was similar to the famine in Ireland, when they threw the people off the land and left them wandering on the roads to starve. That may have had something to do with it – part of my Irish tradition – but I liked the idea of this family going out and trying to find their way in the world."[31] The family as the basic unit of community is crucial to Ford's work. Thus, as Warren French notes, the director aims at "abstracting the Joads from any particular context and treating them as ageless figures of dispossessed wanderers."[32] The film image hardly leaves the Joads for more than a few moments. Tom's final speech to Ma about his metaphorical omniscience everywhere articulates his and his family's own position within the context of the film. And Ma's final affirmation ("We'll go on forever, Pa. We're the people") is less an assertion of social consciousness than of the indomitability of the family.

With respect for what it achieves in its own right, as well as for its artistic coherence and its place in a larger body of acknowledged work, Ford's *The Grapes of Wrath* clearly and visually evidences his main interest and main thematic emphasis on the Joads as a family unit – and not as Steinbeck emphasizes them in the novel, as a family of man. Although the same conclusions about the film can be arrived at through careful consideration of the film's literary elements and its place in the culture of a specific period, those conclusions deserve the support of an equally careful visual analysis.

Acknowledgment

This chapter was first published as "*The Grapes of Wrath* (1940): Thematic Emphasis Through Visual Style," in *American Quarterly* 31:5, Special Issue on Film and American Studies (Winter, 1979), 596–615.

Notes

1   John Ford directed *The Grapes of Wrath* (1940) for Twentieth Century–Fox.
2   George Bluestone, *Novels into Film* (1957, reprinted Berkeley, CA: University of California Press, 1973); Warren French, *Filmguide to The Grapes of Wrath* (Bloomington, IN: Indiana University Press, 1973).
3   Charles J. Maland, *American Visions: The Films of Chaplin, Ford, Capra, and Welles, 1936–1941* (New York: Arno Press, 1977), p. 367.
4   Quoted in French, *Filmguide*, p. 59.

Vivian C. Sobchack

Chapter 5

5   Edwin Locke, "Review of *The Grapes of Wrath*," *Films* (Spring 1940), reprinted in Stanley Kauffmann with Bruce Henstell (eds), *American Film Criticism* (New York: Liveright, 1972), p. 389.

6   Maland, *American Visions*, p. ix.

7   Ibid., pp. 169–70.

8   Andrew Sarris, *The American Cinema, Directors and Directions 1929–1968* (New York: E. P. Dutton, 1958), pp. 43–9 (p. 44).

9   The two most detailed textual analyses of specific Ford films are "John Ford's *Young Mr Lincoln*," *Screen*, 13 (Autumn 1972), translated from the original in *Cahiers du Cinema* 223 (1970); and "*The Searchers*: Materials and Approaches," *Screen Education* 17 (Autumn 1975). See also H. Peter Stowell, "John Ford's Literary Sources: From Realism to Romance," *Literature/Film Quarterly* 5 (Spring 1977), 164–5.

10 Sarris, *The American Cinema*, p. 45.

11 Michael Dempsey, "John Ford: A Reassessment," *Film Quarterly* 28 (Summer 1975), 5.

12 Pierre Greenfield, "Print the Fact: For and Against the Films of John Ford," *Take One* 5 (November 1977), 15.

13 Andrew Sarris, *The John Ford Movie Mystery* (Bloomington, IN: Indiana University Press, 1975), p. 161.

14 French, *Filmguide*, p. 27.

15 Maland, *American Visions*, pp. 164–6.

16 French, *Filmguide*, p. 18.

17 Locke, "Review of *The Grapes of Wrath*," pp. 387–8. (*The Plow that Broke the Plains* was made in 1936 by Pare Lorentz for the US Film Service.)

18 Pare Lorentz, "Review of *The Grapes of Wrath*," in *Lorentz on Film* (New York: Hopkinson and Blake, 1975), p. 184.

19 Maland, *American Visions*, p. 154.

20 French, *Filmguide*, pp. 38–56. (I have not included those scenes shot in brightly lit interiors.)

21 Ibid., pp. 35, 33, 38.

22 Ibid., p. 34.

23 Stowell, "John Ford's Literary Sources," 167.

24 Maland, *American Visions*, pp. 156–9.

25 John Ford speaks of this in Peter Bogdanovich, *John Ford* (Berkeley, CA: University of California Press, 1968), p. 78.

26 French, *Filmguide*, pp. 34–5.

27 Sarris, *The John Ford Movie Mystery*, p. 96.

28 Maland, *American Visions*, p. 161.

29 Bluestone, *Novels into Film*, p. 161.

30 Stowell, "John Ford's Literary Sources," 169.

31 John Ford in Bogdanovich, *John Ford*, p. 76.

32 French, *Filmguide*, p. 38.

Chapter 6

Cape Fear and Trembling: Familial Dread

Kirsten Thompson

> "You're scared, that's O.K. I want you to savor that fear. You know the South evolved in fear – fear of the Indian, fear of the slave, fear of the dammed Union. The South has a fine tradition of savoring fear."
>
> Private investigator Kersek (Joe Don Baker)

In Martin Scorsese's *Cape Fear* (1991), Detective Kersek's ominous description of fear is part of a dread rooted in the history of slavery, colonialism, and the faded confederacy. The *mise-en-scène* of fear is everywhere, in New Essex, the small town in the deep South in which the Bowdens, our narrative family live, and in the swamps and mists that surround the Cape Fear River, to which they flee. Kersek expresses a pleasure in the savoring of fear, a fear that attaches to particular national historical repressions, and whose specific objects are those of Native American, black, and Northerner. From William Faulkner to Carson McCullers, the Southern gothic mobilized tropes of stolen land and bartered bodies, hidden burials and family secrets. Embedded in the past, Confederate and National crimes are the repeated revenants that haunt the narratives of American gothic, and in the disavowal of these traumas, historical memory becomes fear itself. The two cinematic adaptations of *Cape Fear* (1962, 1991) are a dialogue with their different cultural and historical production contexts, with the second film as the monstrous return of the repressed desires, fears, and violence, whose threat was contained in the original. Through the central figure of the monster, Max Cady, these secrets and traumas, and their relationship to repressions of race, class, and nation, foreground what Louis Gross (1989: 90) calls "the singularity and monstrosity of the Other; what the dominant culture cannot incorporate within itself, it must project outward onto this hated/desired figure."

In 1962 the first cinematic *Cape Fear* was released amidst the desegregation struggles in the South, and only six months later, its star, Gregory Peck, would appear as Atticus Finch in another key drama which thematically foregrounded race in the South: *To Kill a Mockingbird* (Robert Mulligan, 1962).[1] Nearly thirty years after J. Lee Thompson's eerie portrait of an upstanding family's nightmare at the hands of an ex-con named Max Cady, Martin Scorsese would remake *Cape Fear* in 1991. J. Hoberman has noted the centrality of the historical context to Thompson's portrait of Cady which "conjures up the bogie of a terrifying rapist – albeit white – who proved inconveniently conversant with his "civil rights." In its nightmarish way *Cape Fear* managed to suggest both what terrified the white South and the terror the white South itself inspired" (Hoberman, 1992: 8).[2]

In the epigraph given above, Detective Kersek addresses his invocation of fear to Samuel Bowden, as they lie in wait in a trap to kill the man who is threatening the Bowden family, Max Cady. Kersek suggests that fear is the necessary catalyst for the violence required in the defense of the family. Similarly, in Thompson's *Cape Fear*, Bowden does not fear to use his wife and daughter as bait to catch Cady because they come from "pioneer stock." Both films suggest that the defense of the (white, nuclear) family is parallel to historical actions of violent appropriation and displacement in American history, and recall the paranoid racist fantasies of white women in peril, from the captivity narrative to *Birth of a Nation*. Scorsese's remake is a self-reflexive homage to the Hitchcockian thriller, yet a far different tale from the anxious yet utopian original, with its Eisenhower family threatened by the sleepy leers of a predatory Robert Mitchum. Instead, Scorsese's post-Cleaver narrative presents the Bowden family in a violent Darwinian struggle for survival, which leaves it tenuous and traumatized, in a startling undermining of hegemonic Hollywood representations of the family. The sexuality and violence hinted at in the purring physicality of Robert Mitchum becomes hyperbolically explicit in De Niro's baroque performance of Max Cady. Linking apocalyptic eschatology to Nietzschean *ressentiment*, the rhetorical hubris of Scorsese's Max Cady is horrifying in its megalomaniacal fluency and prophetic urgency. Bearer of the punishments of Judgment Day, Cady is a prosopopoetic law of dreadful revenge.

If the horror of rape, mutilation, and violent death is the obvious threat that Cady bears, the parallels that connect him to his alter ego, the self-righteous lawyer Samuel Bowden, link horror to theology in an ethical interrogation of ethics and law, crime and punishment. Not unlike an Ibsen play for the nineties, this portrait of a flawed, white, middle-class, nuclear family critiques the ideological nostalgia proffered by J. Lee Thompson's original. Scorsese's version exposes the chasms and ideological struggles over the constitution of the contemporary nuclear American family and the repressions necessary beneath its idealized representation as white, suburban, and middle-class.

In *Family Fictions*, Sarah Harwood's (1997) study of popular films of the eighties under Reagan, the family is a central trope ideologically reasserted in its heterosexual nuclear and white hegemonic form, by the Republican Party and the Christian Coalition, amongst others, and yet radically altered in its material formations and cinematic representations. Divorce rates of 50 percent, the rise of single-parent families, extended family parenting, gay marriages, and adoptions are all examples of the contemporary proliferation of different and alternative models to the idealized nuclear family of the fifties. In light of this drastically altered social landscape, Scorsese's remake instituted key character changes in the Bowden family, far from the ethical idealizations of the original, and creating a portrait of a fractured, embittered family unit. Shifting from the unruffled righteousness of Gregory Peck's Bowden to the hysterical self-righteousness

Cape Fear and Trembling

Chapter 6

of Nick Nolte's Bowden, and from the predation of Robert Mitchum's Cady to the monstrous grievance of Robert De Niro's Cady, the remake is a radical change.

Cape Fear (1991) unveils the multiple repressions and disavowals of the past that have a continuing presence in the Bowden family. Here everyone has a secret to hide: the parents, Samuel (Nick Nolte) and Leigh Bowden (Jessica Lange) have a marriage that is evidently in trouble, due to Sam's repeated adulterous affairs. Samuel has also committed legal and professional malfeasance in his original defense of Max Cady by burying a report of the sexual history of the rape victim, a report that Cady will claim later would have mitigated his sentence. Leigh has had a nervous breakdown and "lost time," and is embittered with her husband and disappointed in her teenage daughter Danny (in a breakout role for Juliette Lewis), who, in turn, also has secrets and strange memories of her childhood holidays, of "those days in the boat." In the narrative, she will develop an illicit and dangerous relationship with Max Cady (Robert De Niro).

Adapted by James R. Webb in his screenplay for the first *Cape Fear*, John MacDonald's 1957 novel *The Executioners* depicted the Bowden family as beleaguered in its innocence. In the novel, Samuel Bowden witnesses Cady's rape of a 16-year-old Australian girl during his army service in World War II. Moreover, in the source story Cady's pathology is located in his post-traumatic psychosis as war veteran. J. Lee Thompson's *Cape Fear* omits the war context and updates the historical setting. Bowden (Gregory Peck), a professional prosecutor, and eyewitness to the rape, testifies against Cady, who in turn hunts him down after his eight-year prison term ends. Unlike Scorsese's remake, Bowden has committed no legal improprieties as an attorney nor has he had adulterous affairs with any of Cady's victims. Thus, Thompson's Bowden does not share the legal and ethical crimes of Scorsese's adulterous, unethical lawyer, and this difference is important for the complexification of Max Cady's character in the remake.

Another distinction evident in changes to the story is the impact of feminism in the thirty years between the two films. In Thompson's *Cape Fear*, Cady's second victim is Diane Taylor (Barrie Chase), a "fallen" pageant queen who refuses to testify in a rape trial, not because of any uncertainty as to Cady's conviction (which the narrative implies would be inevitable with her testimony), but *because* of the implied social and familial disgrace as a rape victim. Initially in a catatonic stupor after her rape, Diane refuses to communicate with the police and abruptly leaves town. Similarly, the Bowdens would not let their daughter Nancy testify against Cady for sexual stalking, out of the same fear of social stigma. This is an important ideological distinction from the remake, in which Cady's victim Lori Davis (Illeana Douglas) refuses to testify *because* she is a legal officer and understands the ways in which power functions in the legal system against rape victims: "This time I'm on the other side." She knows that she was drunk and flirting with Cady in a public space and as a result foresees what the defense could do to her public character under cross-examination: "they crucify them on the stand and laugh about it afterwards." Even with contemporary rape shield laws protecting rape victims from interrogations about their sexual history, the prosecution and conviction for rape falls far below estimated offenses. Lori's decision not to file a complaint indicates her professional understanding of the ideological biases of the legal system, notwithstanding the changed social context of two decades of second-wave feminism.

Other significant changes from the novel (see table 6.1) include the two films' foregrounding of Cady's sexual threat to the Bowden's teenage daughter, and their

Table 6.1 Principal differences between book and films

The Executioners (1957)	*Cape Fear* (1962)	*Cape Fear* (1991)
Author: John D. MacDonald	*Director*: J. Lee Thompson *Screenplay*: James Webb	*Director*: Martin Scorsese *Adapted screenplay*: Wesley Strick
Cady rapes Australian girl in WWII. Spends 13 years in jail	Cady rapes American woman. Imprisoned for 8 years	Cady rapes 16-year-old, 14 years in the diegetic past (c. late 1970s). Imprisoned for 14 years
Bowden is witness to rape	Bowden (a prosecutor) is witness to rape and testifies against Cady	Bowden is Cady's defense attorney. Buries report of rape-victim's "sexual promiscuity"
Bowden family: Sam and Carol Bowden, Nancy (15), two sons Bucky and Jamie. Marilyn the family dog	Bowden family: Samuel and Peggy Bowden, Nancy (15). No sons. Marilyn, family dog	Bowden family: Sam and Leigh Bowden, daughter Danny (15). No sons. Benjamin, male dog.
Bowden is not adulterous	Bowden is not adulterous	Troubled Bowden marriage. Sam is having an affair with co-worker Lori Davis
Cady's "combat fatigue" in war suggests a causative factor for his violent behavior. Cady rapes and abducts his ex-wife who has re-married	Cady is raped in prison. On release, Cady rapes, abducts, and beats wife for 3 days. Wife won't press charges. Cady rapes Diane Taylor, a "fallen" beauty queen. She refuses to testify	Cady is raped in prison. Cady is betrayed by his attorney's malfeasance. Cady rapes and mutilates Lori Davis, Bowden's lover. Cady murders Detective Kersek, and Graciella, the family maid. Cady rapes Leigh and intends to rape Sam and Danny
Mother witnesses death of dog	Family witnesses death of dog	Mother witnesses death of dog
No houseboat	Mother and daughter alone on houseboat as bait	Family all on houseboat
Bowden wounds Cady with a bullet and Cady later bleeds to death	Bowden wounds Cady with a bullet but does not kill him	Bowden strikes Cady with a rock, but he dies by drowning

Cape Fear and Trembling

Chapter 6

elimination of the other children. Thompson's version splits the familial reaction to Cady's stalking into two character responses. As Mr Bowden moves from unruffled legal rationalist to methodical vigilante, he is admonished by Peggy – "I can't believe we're standing here talking about, about *killing* a man" – and when her husband runs out of the house with a gun, Peggy Bowden calls the police. Yet, in an earlier dream sequence, their positions are reversed; we hear Peggy say to Sam "a man like that doesn't deserve civil rights." The dream (which may recall an actual conversation) continues with Samuel Bowden's rejection of the law as totalitarian tool: "but darling you can't put a man in jail for what he *might* do, and thank heaven for that." Bowden's comments are an ironic contrast to a later scene in which Chief Dutton (Martin Balsam) scolds Bowden for advocating just that: "I couldn't arrest a man for something that *might* be in his mind. That's dictatorship. Now Sam you're a citizen, would you want it any other way?" These ideological oppositions are symptomatic of the film's Cold War and civil rights' historical context. Instead, Scorsese's remake combines these contradictory positions into the ambivalent thoughts and actions of Mr Bowden.

Intertextual Homage

In one of Scorsese's few ventures into mainstream commercial Hollywood, with its higher budgets, production values, and star casting, *Cape Fear* was a relative commercial success, earning $79,092,000 (more, in adjusted dollars, than the original). Elmer Bernstein reorchestrated Bernard Herrmann's original score, imitating the agitated string motifs and distinctive edginess that were so familiar from Herrmann's scores for Hitchcock. Although sound is often assaultive and anxiety-inducing in the horror genre, Scorsese's sound effects and Bernstein's sound track act with an even greater intensity. Redherring trick shots frighten the viewer with fake threats that are natural or technological, as we see in the abrupt jump cuts to extreme close-ups of the telephone, ringing with a strident loudness. Jarring montages, canted angles, and Herrmann's use of fortissimo horn passages and assaultive score create a heightened spectatorial experience. Scorsese's remake invokes the spectatorial dread and fear that always threaten the limited boundaries of what Isabel C. Pinedo (1997: 5) describes as *recreational terror*, which offers the spectator the illusion of mastery. Both diegetic and non-diegetic sound form part of the texture of the *mise-en-scène*'s evocation of an all-encompassing dread, and signal the Bowden family's increasing loss of control.

Scorsese's uncanny recasting of Robert Mitchum, Gregory Peck, and Martin Balsam in cameo appearances is a dialogical subversion of the first *Cape Fear* in which they all originally starred. Upstanding Sam Bowden in the original, Peck now plays Cady's ingratiating and pompous Southern lawyer, Lee Heller; Mitchum, the original Max Cady, is now a genial yet dodgy detective, only just this side of the law,[3] and Martin Balsam moves from police chief to a sanctimonious Southern judge. The entire court scene in which

Cady seeks a restraining order against Sam Bowden is an ironic study in Cady's manipulation of the law. "In the interests of Christian harmony," the judge (Balsam) grants Cady's petition and admonishes Bowden with a deadpan citation of "that great Negro educator, Booker T. Washington, 'I will let no man drag me down so low, as to make me hate him.'" This ironic casting also foregrounds the dissonance between the words of a former slave espousing a Christian demand for equality and justice, and their enunciation by a representative of the Southern judiciary known for its racist opposition to desegregation in the sixties. Heller congratulates the judge – "King Solomon could not have adjudicated more wisely!" – and vows to bring Bowden to disbarment hearings for "moral turpitude." Although Cady wins, he is also subtly Othered in the judge's mispronunciation of his name as "Maximilian Caddy," suggesting an unconscious association of Cady as a Jew. Adding to the intertextual resonance of Scorsese's casting was Robert De Niro as Max Cady, whose intense performance style and violent psychotic roles in *Mean Streets* (1973) and *Taxi Driver* (1976) offered additional menace to his character.

Scorsese's dialogism continues through stylistic and intertextual references to the interlocking constituencies of horror and melodrama in the family. *Cape Fear* cites two films: the first is *Problem Child* (Dennis Dugan, 1990), a comedy about a monstrous child and comic re-make of *Bad Seed* (Mervyn LeRoy, 1956),[4] which the Bowdens watch in a movie theater. The sadistic comedy of John Ritter performing a father's violence toward his child "Here's Daddy" in turn cites both *The Tonight Show* ("Here's Johnny"), and John Torrance's ironic "Here's Daddy," in *The Shining* (Stanley Kubrick, 1980) in which the father becomes a murderous threat to his wife and child. This intertextual chain of references foregrounds the horror that lies not far beneath the surface of familial dysfunction. The second instance of cinematic intertextuality is a close-up of Jane Wyman's face in Douglas Sirk's melodrama *All that Heaven Allows* (1955), which Leigh and Danny watch on television. Wyman plays a middle-class woman who falls in love with her gardener (Rock Hudson) and subsequently faces social disapproval for her class transgression. The expansion of class as a key component in Scorsese's characterization of Cady intersects with this theme, as we will discuss below. His intertextuality also operates on a cinematographic level: there are a number of shots of the family home (and houseboat) at sunset that are visual citations of Sirk's use of hypersaturated color in his American melodramas of the fifties. The sexual, familial, and class antagonisms in Sirk's and Dugan's films erupt in hyperbolic form in Scorsese's Cady who becomes both monster and figure of desire for Mrs Bowden and her daughter.

--------------------------------- **Fear and Trembling** ---------------------------------

[1] **dread** vb. (ME dreden, Fr. OE draedan) vt. (bef. 12C)
1a: to fear greatly, *archaic*: to regard with awe, **2:** to feel extreme reluctance to meet or face ~ vi: to be apprehensive

Cape Fear and Trembling

Chapter 6

[2] **dread** n. (13c) **1a:** a great fear esp. in the face of impending evil, **1b:** extreme uneasiness in the face of a disagreeable prospect<~ of a social blunder:
archaic : awe 2: one causing awe or fear
[3] **dread** adj. (15c) **1:** causing great fear or anxiety, **2:** inspiring awe

From *Cape Fear*'s (1991) opening credit sequence, designed by Saul and Elaine Bass, a shot sequence of the waters of the Cape Fear River lap-dissolve into each other as Elmer Bernstein's adapted score establishes the tone of an ominous *mise-en-scène*. Reflections of double-exposed inchoate images appear beneath the waters. We see a barely discernible chain of images: a face, a rolling eyeball, a mouth, teeth, a human figure with long hands, a swooping hawk (at the introduction of De Niro's credit), concluding with a drop of water which moves vertically downward as the image fills with a blood-red saturation. This then dissolves into a saturated red close-up of Danielle Bowden's eyes, followed by a gray/white negative photographic image, which finally shifts into color and zooms out (see figure 6.1). From the *mise-en-scène* of the gothic South to Danielle's psyche, the sequence already foreshadows the metastatic spread of Cady's presence. At this moment, the narrative's opening voice-over begins, foregrounding the thematic centrality of memory:

DANIELLE: My reminiscence. I always thought for such a lovely river, the name was mystifying – Cape Fear. When the only thing to fear on those enchanted summer nights was that the magic would end and real life would come crashing in.

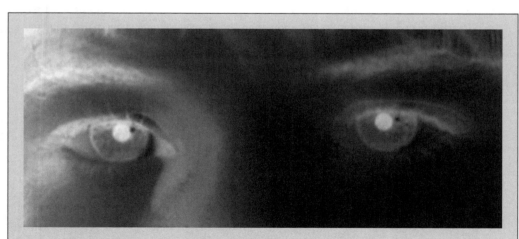

Figure 6.1 Negative image of Danielle Bowden's eyes from Scorsese's *Cape Fear* (1991)

Kirsten Thompson

Chapter 6

Danielle's opening and closing voice-overs bracket *Cape Fear*'s narrative as her own – whether as nightmare, gothic story, or unconscious fantasy, we are never sure. This narrative bracket is unique to Scorsese's version and is literally embodied in the close-ups of her eyes, dissolving from saturated red, to negative gray and white, to color, and in reverse order at the film's end. After we zoom out from her eyes, we see Danny standing in front of what appears to be a classroom blackboard, over which running water is reflected, perhaps from outside rain. Her dress is formal, she appears as a schoolgirl, and so the entire narrative could be the homework assignment that we hear about later: to write a story modeled on the reminiscence formula of Thomas Wolfe's *Look Homeward Angel*.[5] The film's and Danny's last words, "the end," mark her authorship and survival as "final girl." Her childhood memories of the family vacations on a houseboat on the Cape Fear River are the unconscious trauma within the wider familial trauma, and from the start link narratively with Cady's horror. When her father asks what she will write about, Danny replies "the houseboat." Sam's response is a terse "oh, the houseboat," as he continues striking a piano key that will not sound. This silent piano key metonymically suggests repressed secrets in the Bowden family. This scene immediately follows Max Cady's violent rape of Lori Davis, and the key is silent because Max Cady has already been in the Bowdens' house to steal the piano-wire. Later he uses it to garrote Detective Kersek and Graciella (Zully Montero). Thus, the repressions of Bowden's past (whether sexual or legal) return in the avenging figure of Cady, who takes the piano's sound away as the symbolic foreshadowing of his homicidal rage. It is apt that Danielle is this film's narrator, as she is the locus of sexuality in both her own burgeoning desire, and in the unconscious and overt sexual attention she receives from her father and Max Cady. Although Danny, like Nancy in the original, is Cady's principal sexual target, Scorsese's creation of her as narrator foregrounds the psychic dimension of her exploration of "mystifying fear." This exchange suggests further repressions of familial memory in Bowden's (and the piano's) unresponsiveness. It begs the narrative question: just what did happen in Danny's childhood? Was it the magical world that she suggests?

Samuel Bowden's repression of his earlier ethical and legal transgressions (the burial of the report of the rape victim's "sexual promiscuity") masks and encodes his unconscious incestuous desire for his daughter, which remains unspoken like the suggestive piano key. The emotional intensity of Bowden's reactions to his daughter's illicit contact with Cady betrays his unconscious jealousy: "Wipe that smile off your face! Did he touch you?" His growing awareness of her pubescent sexuality is an uncomfortable one: "Put some clothes on, you're too old to be running around like that [wearing underpants]." His unconscious incestuous desires for his child are projected onto Max Cady as the *external* sadistic threat to his family. Danielle quickly becomes the target of Cady's stalking, and as Bowden is aware, she is only one year younger than Cady's first rape victim. It becomes apparent that Sam Bowden understands this sexual threat to his daughter when he is deliberately vague about Cady's criminal history, lying to his wife: "I think it was battery" (instead of the aggravated sexual assault and battery that we know Bowden clearly remembers). Similarly, Bowden lies about his affair to his wife and in an unconscious displacement of what could be a description of his teenage daughter, misleadingly describes his mistress Lori as "a baby. She looks up to me [with an] infatuation." Cady metonymically substitutes for the name of the Father, as a personified threat of sexual violence to all of the Bowden women, yet the real threats are the legal and sexual improprieties that Samuel Bowden has already committed.

The following scene's nod to Freud's *Totem and Taboo* subtly suggests the Oedipal nature of the family's tensions foregrounded by Scorsese. In an exchange between Sam and Leigh as they prepare for bed, the scene is presented in a two-shot reflection in the bathroom mirror. Samuel Bowden's face is reflected in the extreme foreground of the frame, with Leigh Bowden in the background corner, rubbing her skin in a dreamy, erotic manner (as she often does in front of mirrors). The parents fret over Danny's drug bust, as she is required to attend summer school, or risk expulsion:

> BOWDEN: Why'd they have to make such a stink, like she was on heroin or something? I mean marijuana, what's marijuana? You and I smoked a little dope in our time, and y'know in some cultures it's considered almost a sacrament – course I realize in ours it's forbidden. *Leigh (playfully): right up there with incest and bestiality and necrophilia . . .* (my emphasis)

Ethical and personal conflicts are mapped out on a grid of sexuality in which all three members of the Bowden family have illicit sexual desires: Samuel's adultery with Lori, Danny's desire for Cady, and Leigh's unconscious fantasies and vague desire, for someone for whom she puts on her lipstick. One night, after she and Sam Bowden have made love, Leigh is unable to sleep. She rises to sit at her dressing-room mirror, sensually rubbing herself with cream. The mood is quiet, romantically lit with a soft blue light outside the upstairs verandah, where fireworks are exploding on Independence Day. Nevertheless, the shots in this sequence are dissonant – beginning with the shots of the Bowdens making love, which appear as *negative* celluloid images (in the second use of this device), there is already a sense of Leigh's psychological distance, if not derealization. Leigh's reflection, split into three images in her dressing-mirror, suggests the fragmentation of her previous breakdown and her conflicted desires. It is then that Leigh sees that Cady is watching their home from his perch on their wall, and in a repeated editing leitmotif, Scorsese accentuates her horrified gaze, through a triple repetition of rapid zooms-in on Cady. Running outside, she self-consciously wipes off her lipstick as if suddenly defiled by the unknown watcher (later Danny will also wipe her mouth self-consciously after kissing Cady, an action which links mother and daughter in their desire for him). It is as if Cady's supernatural ubiquity has the power to enter into the intimate space of the family home, and recognize her unconscious desire for someone other than her husband. The family are now in a state of siege: Cady's surveillance has become the primary threat.

In both cinematic versions, Max Cady embodies the threat of the specular. Thompson's film shows us repeated shots of Cady watching Nancy, remarking to her father: "She's getting to be almost as juicy as your wife." However, in Scorsese's version the threat of Cady's sexual gaze is even more extensive. In his first encounter with Sam Bowden, Cady leers at some teenage girls walking by – "Great at that age in't they?" – and later describes Danny as "always a firecracker on the fourth of July. You're damn lucky to have her boy." Like the original, in which Cady stalks the family in a bowling alley, Cady haunts the Bowdens' recreational time together. He watches the family at an ice-cream store from across the street, forcing the family to move inside, but when Sam looks again, Cady has vanished into the traffic that obstructs Sam's point-of-view shot. Under the pretense of returning the collar of the family dog he has poisoned, Cady gets a closer look at Leigh. When she realizes who he really is she defiantly acknowledges his predatory gaze: "Take a good look, Mr Cady. Are you happy now?" She also acknowledges her own desire to see the forbidden: "I'd been wanting to see what you looked like, I'd been wanting to see your face. But you know now that I see you, you are just repulsive." Then, unexpectedly, Danny comes out and becomes vulnerable to Cady's gaze. Immediately, Leigh screams: "Danny get back inside." Danny's nascent sexuality links to the horror that threatens the family, as she becomes subject to Cady's chicken hawk sexual desires. Because her parents forbid Danny to look or listen, much of what she does is illicit (her reading of Henry Miller, her use of drugs, her sexual contact with Cady). Danny is told repeatedly to "go back to her room" or "not to listen" when her parents are fighting, and later, "not to look" at the corpses of Graciella and Kersek. When she descends the staircase, she takes a forbidden look at their bodies, and screams when she sees Graciella. The trauma of this bloody visibility is underscored as Sam slips in Kersek's pool of blood, and to his horror, is covered in it.

The most stylized exposition of this specular trope of surveillance is the Fourth of July parade that the Bowden family attends (which does not appear in the original). The wide-angle and close-up shots of the Fourth of July parade with its floats of American military triumphs (Iwo Jima, the American Revolution) are photographed in slow motion: the whole scene is presented as a dizzying visual kaleidoscope of sound, confetti, flags, and faces. The philosophical implications of this portrait of national celebration connects the Bowden family with hegemonic cultural constructions of nationalism, which, in the case of each iconic float, represents the United States in wars for its very survival. In this way, the democratic nation, as represented in its moments of historical triumph, is connected with the Bowdens' own survival under threat. Unseen by them, Cady is on the opposite side of the parade, watching Danny and Leigh. Bowden spots Cady – "the son of a bitch is staring at you!" – and, enraged, confronts him. We do not see Cady

Cape Fear and Trembling

Chapter 6

until Sam does so, but then the camera cuts away to a shot emphasizing Danny's vulnerability, lost in the crowd – "Mom?" We are not sure where Leigh is at this point, nor do we know from whose point of view we see Danny. Cady is the unseen voyeur of Leigh and Danny, until Sam's point of view reveals him to us, almost hidden in a long shot of the crowd. By alternating between privileged and restricted narration, Scorsese's shot structure intensifies spectatorial disorientation and the ubiquity of Cady's specular threat.

> I had the weirdest feeling that he was already in the house.

There are similar ambiguities in what we see, particularly when the image shifts into negative form. On the night of Graciella and Kersek's murders, Sam awakens to see what appears to be Cady in his bedroom, watching him. The image we see is starkly defamiliarized, a photographic negative – the flipside, and literal unconscious of vision. The negative then dissolves into a brief positive image of the same shot. However, when Sam rubs his eyes, the image has uncannily vanished, and it appears that Cady has been a nightmare. At this point in the narrative we do not know that Cady is already in the house, murdering Graciella and Kersek, but this uncanny haunting of familial space is suggested through Bowden's eerie vision. Scorsese's third use of a negative image formalizes the doubleness of Cady's connection to Bowden as uncanny doppelgänger, and is the celluloid trace of the Bowden family's unconscious dreams and fears.

──────────── Max Cady: Body and Text ────────────

> With his long slicked back hair, under a white yachting cap, mouth wrapped around the world's biggest cigar butt, and torso draped in a flaming aloha shirt, De Niro is a cracker from hell.
>
> (Hoberman, 1992: 10)

Max Cady is an *Übermensch* with an agenda. As textual special agent on a self-appointed mission, his first words in Scorsese's *Cape Fear* are "already read 'em" (in response to the prison guard who asks him if he wants his books). With the hyperintellect of the serial killer, and the hard body of fourteen years of prison workouts, his character is a meta-constellation of class, race, Christian iconography, and textual references. Cady, in other words, is our monstrous fetish, a clichéd devil with inhuman strength and spooky ubiquity. Our first image of him is a full-frame close-up of his back, which is tattooed with a large cross holding two scales, labeled "Truth" (holding a Bible) and "Justice" (holding a knife). Cady literally embodies Judgment Day; he is a walking, preaching body metaphor, covered in tattoos of biblical quotations – "Vengeance is mine" – and figures of the cross and the grim reaper. Lieutenant Elgart (Robert Mitchum) recognizes this corporeal semiotics: "I don't know whether to look at him or read him." De Niro's performance as Cady differs from Robert Mitchum's interpretation in its more physical, self-referential, and above all hypertextual dimensions. Cady is always ready with a weighty quotation: "Have you suffered so many things in vain?" (Galatians 3: 4). His physical embodiment of theological text is matched by his performative embodiment of speech; he merges speech and writing. The moments of maximum horror are when Cady's speech moves into an inaccessible language, glossolalia. When he threatens Leigh with her imminent rape, he says: "Ready to be born again, Mrs Bowden? A few moments alone with me and you'll be speaking in tongues." Surrounded by photos of Stalin, Robert E. Lee, and Christian martyrs, which suggest his political sympathies and psychological identifications, Cady is an ironic signifier of Pentecostal Evangelism ("Granddaddy used to handle snakes in church") and the poor, white, working class. Here is another form of folklore, this time rural, Southern, and gothic. By contrast, Robert Mitchum's Cady, less working class than bohemian hipster, greets everyone as "daddy" and "man" and seduces his first victim in a jazz bar. Bowden curses him as a "shocking degenerate." At first, De Niro's Cady mimics the initial psychological subtlety of Robert Mitchum's performance in the original. But where Mitchum's restrained sexual threat is suggested through his breaking an egg near Peggy Bowden, De Niro moves from thumb-sucking (of Danny) to cheek-biting (of Lori Davis). By shifting Cady's monstrosity to a more graphic and violent sadism, Scorsese adds the conventions of slasher horror to the psychological thriller.

Loss and Revenge

Cady is buried alive in an "eight by nine" cell for fourteen years. His imprisonment is the metonymic extension of Bowden's burial of a report that Cady suggests might have prevented or reduced his prison sentence. Hidden books, wills, deeds, and burials alive litter the gothic uncanny, as that which Schelling describes as "everything that should have remained hidden, but has been brought to life."[6] Cady erupts from his burial as the return of the repressed, vowing that Bowden will "learn about loss." His key trauma in prison was rape: as he observes wryly, "I learned to discover ma feminine side."[7] At his sentencing, his wife and child disown Cady and have no further contact with him. Thus, as husband and father, Cady loses his family, for which he blames Bowden. When Sam initially offers to buy him off, Cady is insulted: "What is the formula for compensation, sir? $10,000? Hell that's not even minimum wage!" Rape for rape, wife for wife, and child for child, Cady promises a substitutive retribution (an eye for an eye . . .). As horror collapses boundaries between self and other, both corporeal and psychic, so does Cady seek, as Bowden's double, to take his place. In the first *Cape Fear*, Cady's principal target is his ex-wife, who he kidnaps, rapes, and murders, before he turns to the

Bowdens. By contrast, Scorsese's version makes the Bowden family Cady's only target for retribution:

> CADY: Good, 'cos if you're not better than me I can have what you have . . . a wife, a daughter . . . I'm gonna teach you the meaning of commitment. Fourteen years ago, I was forced to make a commitment to an eight by nine cell. And now you're gonna be forced to make a commitment. You could say I'm here to save you . . .

Max Cady's corporeal revenge is the re-enactment of his trauma and his loss, mapped onto the bodies of Bowden's wife, mistress, and daughter. Cady refers mockingly to his rapes in prison, where he was "some fat hairy ugly hillbilly's wet dream." In return, Cady's crimes are acts of physical and sexual sadism: the rape of a 16-year-old girl, the murder of another inmate in prison (which echoes Hannibal the Cannibal in that he bites the man's tongue off); the poisoning of the Bowden dog; the seduction of Danielle; the rape and cannibalistic-biting of Lori Davis; and the murders of Graciella and Kersek. As Cady rapes Lori he says: "Did [Bowden] hurt you like this, 'cause what he did to me hurt a lot worse than this!," enacting himself as both rapist and rape victim. In the film's dramatic climax on the family houseboat, Leigh pleads with Cady not to rape her daughter, offering herself instead. She claims a bond with Cady based on their mutual betrayal by Sam: "you see, I know about loss, about losing time . . . you see, we have this connection."

In the narrative, fundamentalist Christianity is epistemologically bound up with certain supernatural powers. Not unlike John Doe in *Se7en* (David Fincher, 1995), Cady self-consciously constructs himself as avenging angel of God. As part of this identification, extraordinary strength, knowledge, intelligence, and endurance of pain are crucial. Here is one of Cady's key speeches, which demonstrates his supernatural capacity to withstand pain:

> [Final scene in the houseboat. Danielle throws boiling water over Cady's face]
> CADY: Are you offering me something hot?
> [Cady lights flare and lets it drip all over his arm]
> CADY: Let's get something straight here. I spent fourteen years in an eight by nine cell, surrounded by people who were less than human. My mission at that time was to become more than human. You see, Granddaddy used to handle snakes in church, Granny drank strychnine. I guess you could say I had a leg up, genetically speakin'.

Cady's grandiose preaching of revenge and retribution, aided by his reading *Thus Spake Zarathustra*, enlarges his personal grievances to apocalyptic proportions. Although Cady feels he has created himself as Superman (God is dead, he is god), he more accurately epitomizes Nietzsche's notion of *ressentiment* – as a poor, white, working-class illiterate, shut out from society and power. Cady is the classic autodidact, studying the law and philosophy with equal devotion, and with the completion of his prison sentence, his physical and intellectual training are at an end: "I ain't no white trash piece of shit.

I'm better'n y'all. I can outlearn you, I can out-read you, I can out-think you, I can out-philosophize you, and I'm gonna outlast you. It's gonna take a hell of a lot more than that counselor, to prove you're better than me." Just as Cady has become like Bowden, in terms of his mastery of the law as weapon, so too does he demand its attendant class trappings – the white, middle-class family and home. Like Edmund the Bastard who seethes with resentment at his inferior status, and plots to betray his brother Edgar in *King Lear*,[8] Cady's prodigal reinvention of the Self expands the dimensions of the threat he poses to the Bowdens. In one of the film's horror set-pieces, Scorsese shows Cady following the family to the Cape Fear River by superhumanly clinging to the bottom of their car. Similarly, after triumphing against three men hired by Bowden to beat him, he gleefully shouts:

> I am like God, and God like me,
> I am as large as God
> He is as small as I
> He cannot above me
> nor I beneath him be.
> – Selatius, seventeenth century

Gothic Performances

> I'm from the Black Forest. Maybe I'm the Big Bad Wolf.
>
> *Cady to Danny in the theater*

Cady is a master impersonator of class, race, and gender, and as part of his dramaturgy of terror, he performs multiple roles: innocent citizen, accident victim, pot-smoking drama teacher, nuclear-power protester, Danny's father, sympathetic guidance counselor, and, in literal drag, Graciella, the Bowden's maid. As the epigraph above suggests, Cady is a gothic transvestite, as exemplified in his seduction of Danny in the school theater: "[class is] in the theater today – what better place for drama?" He enacts the discourse of seduction, both sexual (inserting his thumb in Danny's mouth) and textual (citing Henry Miller's *Trilogy*). Cady initiates Danny in a number of taboo acts; meeting and sharing a joint with her, giving her Miller to read, and kissing her. He performs the pedagogy of sexuality, and Danny's naïveté, desire, and vulnerability heighten our spectatorial dread – we don't know what Cady will do next to her.

Cady's seduction of Danny is the eerie echo of his earlier seduction of Lori, Bowden's mistress. Lori, drunk and giggling, meets Cady "by chance" in a bar, and, in spectatorial terms, has an unbearably dreadful conversation with him. It is so agonizingly dreadful because our narrative knowledge is greater than that of Lori, so that we hear every joke as monstrous and foreboding. Cady appears affable (to her) yet sadistically threatening (to us). She tells a joke about an unmarried woman who meets an ex-con who "chopped his wife into fifty-two pieces" (at which Cady laughs uproariously). The punchline is "so the woman asks, are you single?" This leads to him joking: "well, maybe I'll chop you into fifty-two pieces." Cady tells Lori that he is an ex-con, but cleverly pretends he was imprisoned for assaulting a violent cop at a nuclear-plant protest – appealing in its simulated liberalism (and further problematizing the disjunction between law and criminality). A highly intelligent and literate sexual sadist, Cady rhetorically warns her "but you gotta stay sober . . . if you ain't sober, you're takin' your chances, because I'm one hell of an animal." The irony, of course, lies in Lori's interpretation of Cady's words as figurative, and therefore "a joke", but as Cady has already said, "you think I'm joking, but everything I say is the truth." When they return to his home for sex and he handcuffs her, Lori still interprets his actions as performative sexual aggression, laughing, "he's a rough one." However, Cady is a literal man. Just as he embodies theological punishment in his tattoos, he also enacts the unconscious of language (in its textual and oral formations), such that verbal aggression becomes corporeal enactment and figurative aggression becomes horribly literalized. He bites her cheek, mutilates and beats her; "how you like this bitch?" He makes her eat her mocking earlier words, by eating her.

Max Cady's horrific drag impersonation of Graciella the maid invokes Norman Bates (*Psycho*, 1960) or Buffalo Bill (*Silence of the Lambs*, 1991), where, in the horror genre, drag functions as the traditional signifier of gender "perversity." Like Buffalo Bill, Cady takes drag one step further – the monster inhabits the clothes (and sometimes skin) of his previous victim.[9] Not only does Cady figuratively wear the "skin" of Graciella, he adopts her clothes and hair as well, as burnings and beatings progressively strip his own skin away. In the houseboat battles, Danny twice burns Cady's face, and Cady burns himself with a melting flare held as a candle, to show his contempt for pain – his own skin is burnt, melted, and dissolved, as the necessary step in the monstrous flesh made legible. Like Freddy in *Nightmare on Elm Street* (1984), he is the victim of vigilantism, and the horror of that communal violence is a central part of his monstrosity. Cady's display of monstrous flesh is the corporealization of the secret violations, direct and indirect, that he has endured. It also represents Cady's own deracinated transformation from illiterate "Pentecostal cracker" through autodidact to the monster who literally incarnates the return of the repressed.

Unique to Scorsese's version, Max Cady's drag impersonation of Graciella also complexifies the monster as victim, and underscores the class status he shares with a Latina maid. His performance as Graciella functions several different ways. As the maid, he rises up and tries to slaughter his/her class oppressors. As a white man impersonating a working-class Latina immigrant, he transforms her identity into his own, but only through a violent act of appropriation over her body. Moreover, as an act of gender impersonation, his performance links cross-dressing and cross-ethnic identification with his plan to destroy the white, middle-class family. Cady first kills those who are *too close to him* – victims marked by their class or racial differentiation from the white, middle-class family that is his ultimate target and site of identification. After he garrotes

--- The Law ---

The second *Cape Fear* is more baroque, violent, and explicit in its horror, a slasher remake that showcases a family profoundly unstable beneath the façade of its own ethical and law-abiding fictions. Discourses of ethics and justice become central to unveiling Max Cady as the surd,[10] the irrational rage, and conflicts that implode the family from within. As the negative image of Cady suggests, he was always already in the house, haunting their dreams. As tensions rise, the Bowdens fight over the past – the infidelities, the marriage counseling, the shift to New Essex from Atlanta, and Leigh's three-month depression. Sam tries to use the counseling as an excuse to keep his past (and present) affairs buried: "Now isn't this what Dr Hackett talked about? *Digging* up the past." His comment is an uncanny slip, unconsciously echoing his desire to keep other transgressions – whether legal or personal – in a crypt of disavowal.

Ironically, rationality is at the center of the law – a discourse in which both Bowden and Cady trade. The key battles occur over legal issues – harassment, stalking, trespass, assault, threats – and for every extra-legal act that Bowden takes, Cady replies with a legal countermove. As the law proves inadequate to Cady's threat, Bowden's actions become increasingly irrational and violent in his attempts to protect his family. This ideological conflict between justice and the law reveals the corruption of Bowden's own ethical and professional persona. He has transgressed emotionally (his previous adulteries and current affair with his court clerk, Lori Davis), and professionally (his failure as Cady's attorney). Bowden's original crime, the burial of the report about Cady's first victim, is rapidly multiplied by further legal transgressions: (1) he tries to bribe Cady to keep quiet and leave town; (2) he threatens Cady in a café; (3) he hires thugs to beat up Cady; (4) he intends to entrap and kill Cady for trespass (intended murder). Because of these transgressions, he faces professional disbarment for gross moral turpitude. When Bowden admits to his legal colleague, Tom Broadbent (Fred Dalton Thompson), that he buried a report that could have mitigated Cady's sentence, Broadbent lectures Bowden on his breach of the Sixth Amendment: "In every criminal prosecution, the accused shall have assistance of counsel for his defense." In a further irony, the self-righteous Broadbent is also corrupt. His character is also doubly uncanny, given that actor Fred Thompson's career as politician, lawyer, and senator has seamlessly blended with his acting career, in which he specializes in (often corrupt) public official roles.[11]

Cady's first attack on the family is poisoning the symbolically over-determined figure of the Bowden's dog. In the first *Cape Fear*, Marilyn, the family dog, "couldn't bite through a doughnut." The whole family sees her death, but the narrative privileges the distress of Nancy (Lori Martin) through her eyeline matches. Scorsese makes the dog's death an off-screen occurrence, emphasizing its psychological effect on the already vulnerable mother, not the child. Leigh's tearful soliloquy of the dog's death – "He was winding down, like an old clock" – is self-consciously melodramatic in keeping with her Tennessee Williams-like character, always on the verge of another nervous breakdown.[12] Instead, Scorsese translates the castrated weakness of the female dog in Thompson's *Cape Fear* into Bowden's ineffectual masculinity, who is powerless to stop Cady smoking in a movie theater.[13]

Cady's escalating strategies of stalking and intimidation heighten the Bowden family's hysteria without leaving them any protection or solutions. His legal training serves Cady well, as he knows the laws on trespass, harassment, assault, and blackmail, and uses them to hoist Bowden with his own legal petard. In response, Bowden hires Kersek, a private detective and corrupt ex-cop – "This is all fucked up, Kersek. The law considers me more of a loose cannon than Cady" – and, following Kersek's advice, hires some thugs to beat up Cady. Bowden's increasing frustration with Cady's skillful legal manipulations prompts a lecture from Kersek on the realpolitik of the law:

BOWDEN: What good are cops and law and due process . . . ?
KERSEK (interrupting): Sam, Sam, Sam, calm down, let me explain something to you. See the system is set up to handle generalized problems like burglary and robbery. If some lone creep out there targets you for some obscure reason, the system is slow and skeptical, it's pathetic even.

Bowden keeps swinging between vigilante actions and a fading belief in the law (so central to his identity): "Maybe 2000 years ago we might have taken this guy out and stoned him to death, but I can't do that. I can't operate outside the law. The law's my business." Midway through the narrative he takes a belated ethical turn, for fear of getting caught; he refuses Broadbent's offer that his daughter will lie in an unrelated court case – "I won't do it, it's perjury" – and he refuses Kersek's offer of another vigilante action – "No more guys." Even the ironically cast police lieutenant Elgart (Robert Mitchum) is an ambivalent symbol of the law. In the following exchange with Bowden, he gives veiled advice in the form of a hunting metaphor:

ELGART: I can't bust someone for planning to rape your wife, you're a lawyer, Mr Bowden, you know that damn well . . . The way I'd handle it . . . Just think of this fella Cady as a tagger. The trick is to get him out of the brush. And how do we do that? You stake out a couple of your goats, and hide in a tree.
BOWDEN: What are you suggesting Lieutenant, that I use my family as bait? And then what? I'm agonna hope that this psychopath attacks my wife and child, and then what? Blow his head off?
ELGART: I'm a law officer, it would be unethical of me to advise a citizen to take the law into his own hands. So I suppose you must have misunderstood me.
BOWDEN: I guess I must have.
ELGART: Well pardon me all over the place.

An ironic double-entendre, Elgart's rustic hunting allegory metaphorically offers a plan to break the law. Bowden responds with performative sarcasm, not irony (for his meaning accords with his words) but the context demonstrates two officers of the law openly, yet secretly, discussing in uncanny language how to commit premeditated murder.

Bowden finally decides to act on Elgart's advice and, with Kersek's help, fools Cady into thinking he has flown out of state to attend his disbarment hearing. Cady, in another performative disguise at the airport, pretends to be a victim of a car accident, in which "his little daughter Danny" died. Under this ruse, he gets the check-in clerk to break regulations (another ethical impropriety) in order to check if Bowden was on the passenger list for the flight. Thus satisfied, Cady returns to the Bowden house to attack his wife and child, who are seemingly defenseless. Bowden and Kersek wait to lure Cady into the house and kill him in "self-defense." Yet Sam worries: "you know what really disturbs me is killing this guy – dammit, it's premeditated, it, uh, it makes me an accomplice, an accessory, an abettor. It's also excessive force." To which the ever obliging Kersek gothically rationalizes: "the only thing excessive we could do to Cady would be to gut him and eat his liver."[14] Here Cady's dehumanization is made explicit as a Girardian sacrificial figure that requires ritualistic execution and consumption. Kersek ties wire to all the windows, using Danielle's teddy bear as a visual trigger of movement (and an ironic symbol of child-girl sexuality under threat, with its string of pearls around its neck), claiming "I'll know if the Holy Ghost is sneaking in" (but the devil as Cady can). The stakeout fails, ending in Kersek and Graciella's murder. Upon the family's discovery of the bodies, they flee the scene (a legal offense in a homicide), for which Bowden cites a legal defense of exceptionality, and one that is in part theological – *force majeure* – an unforeseen "act of God." The Bowdens flee to their family houseboat on the remote and haunted Cape Fear River, oblivious to the fact that Cady is under their car. By contrast, in the first *Cape Fear*, Bowden attempts to entrap and execute Cady at the houseboat, not the house, and as part of his meticulous plan enlists both the police and a private investigator. Instead, Scorsese's dramatic climax on the houseboat isolates the Bowden family in its final battle with Cady. In an earlier scene, Cady forecast the biblical significance of this final conflict, in his suggestion to Bowden to "read the book between Esther and Psalms" – the Book of Job. However, Scorsese's biblical intertext is ironic for it recasts the family's ordeal, not as a lesson in faith, as with Job, but in mere survival. As Leigh muses "I want to see just how strong – or how weak we really are."

───────── Crime and Punishment: The Mad Trial in the Houseboat ─────────

Scorsese's dramatic climax stages another innovation: Cady places Sam on trial before his wife, daughter, and God, in a mock trial on the houseboat, a trial whose upside-down world recalls King Lear's mock trial on the heath. As part of this upside-down metaphor, Scorsese shows Cady and Bowden hurled upside down, as the houseboat capsizes on the rocks. Cady does not blame his trial judge or prosecutor, "who were only doin' their jobs," but only Bowden for violating his professional obligations as Cady's defender. In direct address to the camera (as God), in a sermon of declamatory fury, Cady rages:

Kirsten Thompson

> I'm Virgil, counselor, and I've gotten you to the gates of Hell. We are now in the ninth circle of Hell, the circle of traitors — traitors to country, traitors to fellow men, traitors to God. You, sir, are charged with betraying the principles of all three. Can you please quote to me the American Bar Association's rules of professional conduct, canon seven?
> BOWDEN: A lawyer should represent his client.
> CADY (interrupting): — should *jealously* represent his client within the bounds of the law and I find you guilty, counselor, guilty of betraying your fellow man, guilty of betraying your country, guilty of abrogating your oath, guilty of judging me and selling me out. And with the power invested in me by the Kingdom of God, I sentence you to the ninth circle of Hell, now you will learn about loss; loss of freedom, loss of humanity, now you and I will truly be the same, counselor.

This revivalist rhetoric has the formal attributes of sermons — repetition, escalating speed and recapitulation, all infused with a righteous sense of divine retribution: "now you will learn about loss . . . now you and I will truly be the same." As Bowden's uncanny doppelgänger, Cady will now take from Bowden the privileges of his white, upper middle-class life, by raping his wife and daughter before his very eyes. Cady's specular threat has now become Bowden's enforced specular retribution. Cady rages that Bowden's unethical actions not only are violations of their professional relationship, but also betrayals of a national order "guilty of betraying your fellow man, guilty of betraying your country," that echo Scorsese's symbolic staging of the Fourth of July parade. These discursive connections are uncanny pointers to what Eric Savoy theorizes in *American Gothic* (1998) as "a discursive field in which a metonymic national 'self' is undone by the return of its repressed Otherness."

By the film's bloody climax, Bowden acts like a caveman, hefting a large rock down onto the head of Cady, in a gesture that underscores his regression to a brutal defender of his family, a man who uses rocks, not the law, as his weapons. He has moved far from the ineffectual study in masculinity we saw at the story's beginning, and in his brutality, has indeed become the same as Cady. By contrast, Thompson's Bowden wounds Cady with a gun but refuses to kill him, instead sadistically promising his gothic entombment: "you're gonna live a long life in a cage . . . and this time for life. Bang your head against the walls, count the years, the months, the hours, until the day you rot!" In the remake, Scorsese uses visual metaphors that recall the Flood in Genesis; slow-motion reverse photography of the houseboat's capsize in the river shows us Bowden and the waters flowing backwards, in an apocalyptic image that suggests the regressive transformation of

Bowden's character. However, unlike Noah's boat, the Bowdens do not survive the Flood unscathed, but are cast ashore in the post-Edenic mud. Although battered by the rock, Cady is not yet dead, but still helplessly handcuffed to wreckage in the rising Cape Fear River. He sings, "I'm bound for the Promised Land" and then "dissolves" into glossolalia, language inaccessible and uninterpretable, the language of "God." Bowden washes his hands of Cady's blood and watches as he slowly sinks beneath the waters. The film's final scenes of Leigh, Sam, and Danny staggering up from the mud are an ironic refiguration of prelapsarian myth, in which God made "man from clay." The bloodiness and destruction of the narrative's final scenes show this middle-class family at a point of near-complete destruction – crawling in the slime in which they have been ethically implicated. The final horror of violence, although so hyperbolically projected onto Cady as Monster, is now explicitly internalized within the family that we see lying muddied, bruised, and bloodied by their Darwinian struggle in the floodwaters after Cady's (final) death. This portrait of a family barely intact segues into a matter-of-fact acknowledgment of the new trauma that must be repressed, with Danny's final voice-over that closes the film. It accompanies the same negative image of her eyes that opened the narrative, but ends this time with a saturated blood-red filter.

> DANIELLE: We never spoke of what had happened, at least not to each other. Fear, I suppose, that to remember his name, or what he did would mean letting him into our dreams. And me, I hardly ever dream about him anymore. Still, things won't ever be the way they were before he came, but that's all right, because if you hang onto the past, you die a little every day. And for myself, I know I'd rather live. The end.

Scorsese's remake of *Cape Fear* is an interrogation of buried secrets and repressed memories of the post-nuclear family of the nineties, and a critique of the nostalgic American image of the family in Thompson's adaptation of the early sixties. In his transformation of Max Cady into an apocalyptic figure of crime and punishment, who becomes the Bowden family's dreaded Other, Scorsese foregrounds the unconscious fears and traumas that were the repressed subtext of the cinematic original. In his complexification and hyperbolization of Cady as monster, he also creates a figure of radical *ressentiment* who would appropriate the benefits of class and race of the white nuclear family. The ambiguous conclusion to Danny's story suggests a desperate desire to forget the primal scene of Max Cady's violence – and that of their own – and signals a return to former and new repressions that have fractured this family. Yet the eerie fairy-tale horror with which Danielle Bowden's "reminiscence" is infused is also a fantasy of terror and desire, a tale of her – and our own – unconscious dread. If trauma is a pathology of a subject's history, epistemologically constitutive by its lack of integration into consciousness as memory, then Danny's flashbacks, memories, and voice-overs are a *tempus interruptus* that have no integrated place in past or present. It is this traumatic temporal "hole" that is at the heart of Martin Scorsese's dialogical remake.

1   At this time, Gregory Peck's star persona is strongly identified with a white liberalism that paralleled his earlier role in the liberal Hollywood film on anti-Semitism, *Gentleman's Agreement* (Elia Kazan, 1947). Another link is production designer Henry Bumstead who worked on *To Kill a Mockingbird* and the 1991 *Cape Fear*.

2   Barry Gifford, in a review of the 1962 version, remarked of *Cape Fear* that "you won't forget this film if you're a Yankee Jew," foregrounding the film's allegorical relationship to the politics of race in the 1960s, and also alluding to the violent opposition to desegregation in which African Americans and Jews were murdered.

3   Roles like Jeff Bailey in *Out of the Past* (Jacques Tourneur, 1947) typified Mitchum's world-weary star persona. Mitchum's deadly performance in *Night of the Hunter* (Charles Laughton, 1955), in which he played an evangelical preacher and killer, has obvious parallels with Max Cady. "Love" and "Hate" are tattooed on his knuckles, an ambivalence mimicked in Cady's "Truth" and "Justice" tattoos.

4   Another allusion to the "bad seed" is when Leigh (annoyed with her daughter's obtuseness) speaks about Danny to her dog, joking "they switched babies on me in the hospital, didn't they?"

5   Thomas Wolfe's (1900–1938) coming-of-age story of a young man, Eugene Gant, and his journey from his rural home in Asheville, North Carolina to Harvard, was autobiographical. Ironically from within the narrative, Danny describes Eugene's journey as "really, um, mystical, almost like a pilgrimage" to which Cady replies "like a cop-out. You can't run away from your dreams." Instead, he gives her another reading assignment: to read Henry Miller's trilogy, *Plexus*, *Sexus*, and *Nexus*. For Cady, Danny's journey is not to be one of escape to other places, but a spiritual journey "into the light" as his companion. He intends that this journey with Danny will be both sexual and violent and end in her torture and death on the houseboat.

6   See Schelling cited in S. Freud, "The Uncanny," trans. James Strachey, in Albert Dickson, (ed.), *Sigmund Freud: Art and Literature*, vol. 14 (London: Penguin, 1985), pp. 339–76 (original work published 1919).

7   This femininity is also suggested by Cady's long hair, often tied in a bun. When he arrives at the Cape Fear River, he enters the woman's bathroom to clean himself up, and uses a woman's mascara brush to darken his gray hair.

8   Edmund rails against his inferior status: "Wherefore should I / stand in the plague of custom . . . For that I am some twelve or fifteen moonshines / Lag of a brother? Why Bastard? Wherefore base? / When my dimensions are as well compact, / My mind as generous, and my shape as true, / As honest madam's issue," *King Lear*, I, ii: 2–9, in K. Muir (ed.), *The Arden Shakespeare* (New York: Routledge, 1991).

9   Judith Halberstam (1995) has noted that skin is a key interstice that shows us what classical horror usually leaves out. The cannibalism of Cady (he bites Lori's face, and spits out her flesh with contempt) is symptomatic of his desire to consume – the law and the Bowden family. It is also revenge for Lori's earlier patronizing mockery for not understanding a word: "debauchery, it's a three-syllable word."

10 Etymologically: irrational number, also deaf, silent, and stupid from the Latin *surdus*. The most common use of surd is the mathematical definition of an irrational number, e.g. $\sqrt{2}$.

11 Initially Sam Bowden is working on a case involving Broadbent's daughter and son-in-law, involving stolen money and a Savings and Loan. It could be a divorce case, or a corruption

investigation into the S&L. Broadbent later offers to get his daughter to perjure herself in this case but Bowden refuses any more legal improprieties. Fred (Dalton) Thompson was a senator for Tennessee from 1994 to 2002, and was chair of the Senate's 1997 subcommittee to investigate campaign fundraising abuses. He was a lawyer on the Watergate committee and appeared in the archival footage of the hearings in Oliver Stone's *JFK* (1991) ironically, a film which is itself an artful blend of fictionalized reality. Prior to *Cape Fear*, Thompson played a succession of roles as government officials and military leaders: *No Way Out* (1987), *Days of Thunder* (1990), *Die Hard 2* (1990), *Flight of the Intruder* (1990), *The Hunt for Red October* (1990), *Class Action* (1991), *Thunderheart* (1992), *Barbarians at the Gate* (1993), and *In the Line of Fire* (1993).

12 This performance is also typical of Lange's star persona built from a multiplicity of melodramatic roles. See her Broadway performances in *Streetcar Named Desire*, in 1994 and TV movie in 1995 respectively, and *Long Day's Journey into Night* and her cinematic performances in *Frances* (1982), *Music Box* (1989), *Men Don't Leave* (1990), *Blue Sky* (1994), *Thousand Acres* (1997), and *The Old Maid* (1998).

13 In the second *Cape Fear*, Leigh's dog Benjamin never obeys Sam Bowden. He also fails to get Cady to stop smoking his cigar in the movie theater, so the family has to move seats. Danny says to him afterwards, "you should have just punched him out" and Leigh says "yeah, you know how to fight dirty, you do that for a living."

14 In a self-conscious allusion to *Silence of the Lambs* (Demme, 1991).

References

Gross, Louis S. (1989) *Redefining the American Gothic*. Ann Arbor, MI: UMI Research.

Halberstam, Judith (1995) *Skin Shows: Gothic Horror and the Technology of Monsters*. Durham, NC: Duke University Press.

Harwood, Sarah (1997) *Family Fictions: Representations of the Family in 1980s' Hollywood Cinema*. New York: St Martin's Press.

Hoberman, J. (1992) "Sacred and Profane," *Sight and Sound* 1: 10 (February), 8–13.

Muir, Kenneth (ed.) (1991) Arden Edition of William Shakespeare, *King Lear*. London: Routledge.

Pinedo, Isabel Cristina (1997) *Recreational Terror: Women and the Pleasures of Horror Film Watching*. Albany, NY: SUNY Press.

Savoy, Eric. (1998) "The Face of the Tenant: A Theory of American Gothic," in Eric Savoy and Robert. K. Martin (eds), *American Gothic: New Interventions in a National Narrative*, pp. 3–19. Iowa City, IA: University of Iowa Press.

Chapter 6

The Carnival of Repression: German Left-wing Politics and *The Lost Honor of Katharina Blum*

Alexandra Seibel

In the German winter of 2001, memories of left-wing terrorism from the 1970s resurfaced in Germany with a vengeance. The German weekly *Stern* published photographic material from a demonstration in 1973 which showed the current vice-chancellor, minister of foreign affairs, and member of the Green party, Joschka Fischer, beating up a policeman lying on the ground.[1] Fischer was wearing a motorcycle helmet and holding a stick, and his attack on the representative of the German state – more than two decades after the fact – caused widespread outrage. The photos unleashed a heated public debate about the activities of the left-wing student movement from 1968 onwards and its stance on the use of political violence, especially since some of its representatives hold important positions within today's government. But what had been at stake in 1976, and suspiciously silenced in 2001, was the uneasy relationship between left-wing activists and a radicalized group of urban terrorists, the so-called Baader–Meinhof group, also known as the RAF (Red Army Faction). Ironically, the person who identified Fischer in one of the photos and who placed the incriminating material into the hands of *Stern* was none other than Bettina Röhl, daughter of Ulrike Meinhof, a founding member of the Baader–Meinhof group.

Röhl's "revenge" at the radicalized end of left-wing politics initiated an ethical discussion about the heritage of the student movement of '68 and its relationship to violence. For many observers, though, this debate mostly served conservative ends by eclipsing once more the complicated history of Germany since 1945. By zooming in on specific violent acts by left-wing activists and by failing to contextualize the complex political and social circumstances that shaped the political agendas of the "'68 generation," the power elite substituted overheated polemics for a thorough political analysis. Fischer apologized to the policeman he had beaten up twenty-five years ago, and was presumably forgiven. But liberal German news magazines noted with sarcasm that these discussions only pointed out German uneasiness about a very recent past with which the public still had not come to grips. As Karl Heinz Bohrer argued in an essay for the German weekly *Die Zeit*, the widespread use of the "metaphor of violence" to identify evil within the history of politics and political activism obliterates historical specificity altogether. This focus on violence as metaphor culminated in the publicly voiced proposition that representatives of the generation of '68 would have to face their own past just as earlier generations of Germans had had to face their Nazi past.[2] This absurd and ahistorical equation of Nazism and left-wing radicalism signified for Bohrer the saddest and most depressing turn in the debate of 2001.

On a different note, Wolfgang Farkas observed in the German newspaper *Süddeutsche Zeitung* that even though the RAF and the semiotics of their guerrilla warfare had become an indispensable part of contemporary pop culture, a thorough confrontation with the political events of that time was still missing. Pushing the point further, Raul Zelik, in the German music and pop-culture magazine *Spex*, recognized an increased fascination with the "radical chic" of the former RAF members whose habits of driving fast BMWs and wearing smart designer clothes inspire features about retro-fashion in glossy Zeitgeist magazines.[3] Zelik also discerned that the RAF phenomenon had become the trendy object of a proliferation of recent films, books, art exhibitions, and even rap songs.[4] Fascination with the urban guerrilla group, Zelik argued, has mainly to do with aesthetic appearances and the re-creation of personal dramas and revolutionary myths. What is missing is a deeper investigation into the decisive role of the German state in the 1960s and 1970s, and especially its self-proclaimed monopoly of violence in the battle against terrorism.[5]

As Olaf Hoerschelmann has pointed out in an essay on postwar Germany and film culture, the struggle over national history and national identity after 1945 was refracted in discursive contests over the representation of a collective history in public memory.[6] In an effort to rebuild a German nation-state after the defeat, official politics had made a superficial break with Germany's fascist past, but at the same time had obscured the continuing fascist legacy within Germany's civil institutions. The older generation still held powerful social positions; for example, as university professors, judges, medical doctors, and even in the government, notwithstanding the fact that they had been Nazi party members during the Third Reich. It was these circumstances that deeply shaped the political climate of the time and ultimately the 1960s' student movement and the formation of the Baader–Meinhof group.

The same forces also decisively shaped the emergence of a German film culture, which came to be known as New German Cinema. In examining the continuing struggles over the construction of public memory at the time, Hoerschelmann shows how some of the films associated with the New German Cinema – films made between 1962 and 1988 – tried to articulate alternative voices to the official language of reconstruction and consolidation. For his first two examples of counter-memorial filmmaking, he turns to the experimental filmmakers Daniele Huillet and Jean-Marie Straub and specifically to their short film *Machorka Muff* (1963) and their first long feature *Not Reconciled* (1965).

Both films take on the issue of fascist remnants within the German political and military elites after 1945, and comment directly on the "problem of residual fascism in West Germany."[7] For Thomas Elsaesser, *Not Reconciled* can be identified even as a "terrorist film" because it offers a violent "solution" to the failures of effective de-Nazification: the female protagonist of *Not Reconciled* attempts to shoot one of the official politicians, a former Nazi who is now the Minister for Rearmament.[8] Interestingly, both Straub/Huillet films are based on the literary works of Heinrich Böll: *Machorka Muff* on *Hauptstädtisches Journal* (Journal from the Capital) and *Not Reconciled* on *Billard um halbzehn* (Billiards at Half-past Nine). *Not Reconciled*, in particular, seems to anticipate the later forms of terrorism aimed at radically protesting the reconstruction and remilitarization of the German nation-state after the war.

Straub and Huillet were not the only filmmakers who turned to the work of Heinrich Böll, however; and it is certainly not a coincidence that writer and essayist Böll became such a decisive public figure in the intellectual life of Germany's culture after 1945. Born in 1917 in Cologne, Böll lived through the Second World War as a common soldier who could assume the role of moral consciousness in postwar Germany. Unlike other writers of his generation, such as Martin Walser or Siegfried Lenz, Böll never bracketed the fascist past from his own writing, but established a clear connection between German guilt and German literature. The authenticity of Böll's novels, in other words, were derived from their direct engagement with issues otherwise glossed over in the material blooming of the economic miracle. After all, postwar German society granted affluence for everybody on the basis of letting the past be the past. But even though Böll identified with the common German soldier as just another victim of Nazism, he displayed the utmost honesty and self-criticism in negotiating historical guilt. As such, Böll was recognized not only as "a decent man" but also as the "most important witness of his time" (Marcel Reich-Ranicky). His literature is commonly characterized as simple, black and white, and rather didactic, depicting a polarized, not very complicated world through moral exempla. Throughout his life he was deeply devoted to Catholicism, but at the same time he relentlessly pointed to the shortcomings of the Catholic Church which he left in protest in 1976. When Böll died in 1985, his books had sold 31 million copies and had been translated into 45 languages. Although he incarnated the image of the "good German" outside his own country, his patriotic "public relations" work did not always meet with gratitude.

In 1972, Heinrich Böll received the Nobel Prize for literature, the very same year he published a famous essay in the weekly magazine *Der Spiegel*, entitled "Does Ulrike Meinhof Want Pardon of Free Conduct?" In this essay, he condemned the vicious polemics of the tabloid press against the RAF, which he equated with a kind of lynch-mob mentality. The public reaction toward his interventions triggered "an unparalleled outbreak of demagogic hysteria."[9] This incident only heightened the repressive climate of these years, which had followed a period of relative openness to change. Between 1966 and 1971 political reforms had seemed possible,[10] but in 1972, the government, with social democratic leadership, passed the so-called "Radicals Decree" which allowed the government to dismiss or refuse a post to any citizen in the civil service whose loyalty to the state could be doubted. This decree was comparable to the witch-hunts of the McCarthy era, since it could be put to use against any progressive or reformer who applied for a civil service job. By 1978, over two million people had been investigated and at least 611 had been rejected for employment in the public sector.[11]

This conservative backlash was partly triggered by the formation of the RAF and its terrorist acts against the German state, which the RAF saw as fascist. The terrorist activities began in 1970 with the liberation of radical arsonist Andreas Baader from prison. They later involved bank robberies, bombings, and kidnappings. All in all, the actors gave the state a perfect excuse for fighting back and mounting full-scale civil surveillance. Public hysteria was fueled by the mass media, most notably the right-wing Springer press and its popular tabloid daily *Bild-Zeitung*, which condemned everything on the left as "terrorist." *Bild* initiated a collective hunt that not only turned every citizen on the left into a potential "terrorist," but also turned every citizen into a potential terrorist-hunter. Böll's intervention on behalf of Ulrike Meinhof, who together with Andreas Baader, Holger Meins, Jan Carl Raspe, and Gudrun Ensslin had been arrested in 1972, tempted *Bild* to accuse Böll of adopting the rhetoric of Joseph Goebbels, minister of propaganda in the Third Reich. Böll was depicted as "blind in the left eye," of inciting people to violence; he was even publicly asked to leave the country. The Springer press subjected him to a campaign of defamation, calling him even more dangerous than the Baader–Meinhof group themselves. As a result, Böll was privately harassed and his house was raided by the police. Furthermore, and this was evidence to prove Böll's claim that the press and the police had collaborated on an illegitimate basis, the Springer press in 1974 reported the raid on the flat of Böll's son in Berlin even before it had occurred.[12]

It was in this context that Böll penned his novel *The Lost Honor of Katharina Blum*. Published in 1974, he himself called it a "pamphlet," aimed directly at the unscrupulous methods of the tabloid press as practiced by the *Bild-Zeitung*. Reid reports that *Lost Honor* was first serialized in *Der Spiegel* before it was published in a hardback edition which sold 150,000 copies in the first six weeks.[13] That this book hit a raw contemporary nerve can also be measured by the fact that, only one year later, German directors Volker Schlöndorff and Margarethe von Trotta – both important representatives of the New German Cinema – turned the novel into a film. In what follows, I shall explore the relationship between these two texts.

The novel's subtitle – "How Violence Can Arise and Where It Can Lead" – brings to the forefront the attempt to locate the origins of violence within the complex relationship between the individual, the state, and the media. The plot itself is rather simple, in many ways comparable to a typical Hitchcockian "wrong man" plot in which an innocent citizen gets caught up in a political intrigue. Katharina Blum, a decent young woman and housekeeper, attends a party during carnival, where she meets a young man called Ludwig Götten. After dancing the whole evening exclusively with him, she takes him home to her apartment were they spend the night together. The next morning, the German police storm her house and accuse her of being the lover of a wanted terrorist. She is interrogated

The Lost Honor of Katharina Blum

Chapter 7

over and over by hostile police, while the journalist Werner Tötges from the newspaper *NEWS* (a clear allusion to the *Bild-Zeitung*) launches a malicious campaign, ruining the reputation not only of Katharina, but also of those close to her. In a final confrontation, she shoots Tötges when he proposes having casual sex.

It is worth noting that, while writing the novel, Böll had toyed with the idea of having his book turned into a film. According to Volker Schlöndorff, Böll approached him with the idea of an adaptation for the screen, and a friendly collaboration between the novelist and the filmmakers followed. Their mutually agreed agenda was to investigate the "structural violence" (Böll) within society which manifested itself simultaneously in the state apparatuses – such as the media, judiciary, police – and which crucially informed not only public opinion, but also shaped the reaction-formation of this very public toward officially "designated" terrorists.[14] Hence, they attempted to construct a contrapuntual history that went against the grain of the official state-dominated discourse on terrorism and left-wing politics.

Despite the friendly nature of the collaboration, however, much of the scholarly writing scrutinized Schlöndorff/von Trotta's film in terms of its fidelity to the literary source – with varying results. In his defense of Schlöndorff's film adaptation of Robert Musil's novel *Young Törless*, Eric Rentschler dismisses *The Lost Honor of Katharina Blum* by posing the rhetorical question: "Is this not the director who – together with Margarethe von Trotta – eradicated the painstakingly exacting narrative persona of Heinrich Böll's *The Lost Honor of Katharina Blum* . . . and turned the ironic documentation into a dramatic and shrill passion play?"[15] Jack Zipes comes to a similar conclusion, arguing in great detail that both Böll's novel and, even more, Schlöndorff/von Trotta's film, diminish the political dimension of their endeavor by limiting the narrative to a moralistic and individualist approach.[16] Others have been less harsh. In their thorough discussion of the relationship between film and novel, William R. Magretta and Joan Magretta demonstrate how the filmmakers have been "faithful to the essential humanism of Heinrich Böll"[17] by taking the novel's reference to "reality" – that is, the aforementioned historical condition of Germany – as their artistic departure. Rather than Böll's treatment of the material, the material itself becomes the most important factor in their translation of the novel to the screen.

With respect to the "fidelity" of the film to its literary source, Schlöndorff/von Trotta introduce new significant sequences in their screen version. First, the opening scene surveys Ludwig Götten's arrival in town through the point of view of a police surveillance camera lens. Thus, the theme of state repression and surveillance technology is introduced from the outset. The collusion between state, church, and capitalism is further highlighted by another, added, scene in which a high clergyman arranges a meeting between Katharina and Alois Sträubleder, an influential industrialist and her unwanted admirer. Thirdly, there is an unforeseen encounter between Katharina and Ludwig on the way to their prison cells: Katharina breaks free from her guards and throws herself at Ludwig. This image clearly reverberates with the infamously inhuman conditions suffered by the RAF members in prison, in which they were kept apart from each other in isolation cells.[18]

Alexandra Seibel

Chapter 7

Finally, the filmmakers change the ending of the novel by closing their narrative with Tötges' funeral, thereby demonstrating once again the hypocrisy of an official media discourse, which claims to protect freedom of speech and the freedom of the individual.

What the filmmakers dropped from the original is as important as the scenes they added. And here the question of the two endings becomes of extreme importance. The Magrettas briefly allude to Böll's closing chapters, where the author traces the effects of the violent events on the supporting characters close to Katharina, most notably on Blorna and Else Woltersheim. Böll's ending, they claim, is "much in the manner of the epilogues of nineteenth-century novels," whereas Schlöndorff/von Trotta "choose a more straightforward chronology."[19] Although this is an absolutely accurate observation, there is more at stake here than simply addressing the literary conventions of the nineteenth century. The divergent endings, it seems to me, point to the most significant differences between the book and its adaptation to film. I would therefore like to flesh out three major themes of crucial importance in Böll's novel, before moving on to a discussion of their translation onto the screen.

One of the major divergences of the film from Böll's text is its deployment of a chronology of suspense, which keeps the viewer within the logic of "what next": the events unfold in a linear manner and culminate in the killing of Tötges. Böll, on the other hand, opens his report with the announcement of the murder, thereby drawing our attention to the question of "why" things happened rather than "how." The basic agenda of the book, then, seems obvious: Böll is attempting to demonstrate in all its excruciating detail the unjust intervention of state apparatuses – press and police – in the life of an innocent citizen. The entire narrative is based on the labor of reconstructing the unfolding events in a meticulous manner and thereby laying bare the difficulty of a truth-finding process. The media, on the other hand, deliberately fictionalize reality by distorting the meaning of people's words and abusing them for reactionary ideological ends. Tötges, for example, changes Katharina's mother's last words from "Why did it have to end like this, why did it have to come to this?" into "It was bound to come to this, it was bound to end like this." He then justifies his "editing process" as "helping simple people to express themselves more clearly."[20] Böll clarifies his intentions in the prologue where he suggests that any resemblances between the practices of his fictional newspaper and the actual *Bild-Zeitung*, rather than being pure coincidence, were actually quite unavoidable.

The title, *The Lost Honor of Katharina Blum*, furthermore, suggests a loss of chastity and alludes to the important fact that the case of the unruly citizen Blum is significantly gendered: becoming a public figure and becoming visible as a woman makes a witness especially vulnerable. Being female adds a further dimension to public humiliation, even more so when the accused person is unmarried and independent. The "lack" of a husband invites the hostile public to target Katharina as a property without owner that can be sexually assessed. Böll poignantly presents a whole spectrum of inappropriate and patriarchal behavior toward the young woman, ranging from the patronizing attitude of the investigating inspector Beizmenne to the pornographic hate mail sent to her by anonymous citizens. Böll's awareness of the feminist movement at the time and their famous slogan "The personal is political" clearly reverberates in a scene where Katharina refuses to distinguish between Beizmenne, the police inspector, and Beizmenne, the "person." After having insulted her with questions such as "Did he fuck you?" during his investigations about Götten, Beizmenne attempts to establish a "friendly" relationship "outside" the hearings. But Katharina refuses: "It was clearly impossible for her – as Hach told it – to separate official from personal relations, to understand the necessity for the interrogation" (p. 27).

Considerable attention has been given to Böll's sympathetic treatment of his female protagonist and the feminist aspects of the novel.[21] J. H. Reid, in particular, examines Böll's engagement with the German feminist movement which emerged almost in tandem with the student movement. Although Böll had little sympathy for the pro-choice movement, Reid points out, he nevertheless rejected the outspoken machismo within society and the Church. He also argues that the character of Katharina is profoundly different from all the other female characters in Böll's work in that she is not defined by motherhood or reliance on a man, but by her own independence, both emotional and professional. But even though contemporary left-wing reviewers of the book regarded her mostly as a somehow angelic and pure figure, an innocent housekeeper who falls prey to a state intrigue, Reid insists on the conservative traits Böll has ascribed to her character as well: she is depicted as a tough, calculating business woman and conformist, who, together with her friends, all read the *Bild-Zeitung*.[22]

This tension in the depiction of Katharina as both a victim of circumstance and a very stubborn and strong-willed person lies at the core of Böll's text and structures its meaning to a greater extent than has been generally noted. Of crucial importance in this respect is the position of the narrator. As the Magrettas have pointed out, the narrator is highly present in the text and comments in a very ironic, detached manner on the material he presents to us. As a narrator-character, he compiles document after document, consisting of transcripts, police reports, newspaper articles, and diary entries which he arranges and organizes like an editor, sometimes even in very cinematic flashback-like terms (p. 44). His own comments on the unfolding events are usually posed in a manner comparable to the character of Trude Blorna who always speaks in a "mock naïve-ironic way" (p. 86). Ultimately, he convinces us to take up his own point of view on the unfolding events. In that manner, he functions as the main character through whose consciousness the entire narrative is focalized. We do not have direct access to the other characters' subjectivity, except in one example of free indirect discourse where the narrator speculates about the sexual desires of prosecutor Hach:

> "In any event, Hach, who was present when the apartment was searched, is regarded by his friends and acquaintances as 'sex starved' and it is quite likely that such a crude idea occurred to him on seeing the extremely attractive Blum girl leaning so casually against her counter, and that he would have liked to ask her that very question or perform the crudely specified activity with her." (p. 21)

Even this small glimpse into Hach's sex-obsessed subjectivity – especially when calling Katharina "the Blum girl" – is placed in quotations marks and provides a rare example of giving access to the character's inner emotional (macho-) life. Usually, though, the narrator oscillates between ironic detachment and excessive objectivity;[23] as, for example, when he meticulously enumerates all the various objects Katharina smashes against the walls of her apartment, or when he tells us the exact down-to-the-minute time of an event. Thus, Böll's presentation of a cause-and-effect narrative sets out to create a Brechtian distanciation vis-à-vis the misfortune of the protagonists. Indeed, the mode of address is certainly more intellectual than emotional; the love story, especially, is presented with a "mild sneer."[24]

The manipulation of words and images, of course, plays a crucial part in determining "how violence can arise and where it can lead." Böll takes great pains to demonstrate the necessity of a proper use of language, which, for him, is a moral responsibility. His entire narrative is focused upon the labor of meticulously reconstructing the events that lead to the final killing of a journalist, who was himself a notorious manipulator of both language and image. The crucial importance of correct language is not only demonstrated, for example, in sexual politics – as when Katharina insists on calling unwanted passes by men "advances" rather than "becoming amorous" (p. 30) – but Böll's concern with language also registers a discontent within the political climate of these years – the early 1970s – that witnessed what Klaus Theweleit has termed the emergence of "abstract radicalism."

The problematic of language becomes of utmost importance here. Theweleit argues that at the core of the German student movement in 1968 lay an "explosion of multiple languages" which challenged the hegemonic discourse of German public speech. These dissident languages were informed by Marxism, critical theory, and psychoanalysis, but, most importantly, they stemmed from the "extra-territorial," the "outside" of official Germany, most notably from the language of expelled Jews (Freud, Adorno, Marcuse). In articulating an alternative public voice, then, the mobilization of a vocabulary residing outside official discourse became of crucial importance. This explosion of language, Theweleit argues further, subsequently slowly died as the student movement and their "extra-parliamentary opposition" broke down into small groups, and the plurality of languages gave way to Marxist jargon and demagogy. The movement left people radicalized, but in a political void, finally leading to the formation of the RAF in 1970. According to Theweleit, the founding of the RAF can be regarded as a desperate response to this void, and their reductive use of language – gestures, slogans, and maxims instead of analysis – closed down the former plurality of speech. Ulrike Meinhof's career, for Theweleit, serves as a salient example of a trajectory from political activism to radicalized "abstractivism."[25]

As already noted, it was Böll's political engagement on behalf of Ulrike Meinhof, and the violent reactions it provoked from the German public, that provoked him to write *The Lost Honor of Katharina Blum*. Obviously, on the level of both content and form, Böll's novel is concerned with the dangers of the improper use of language, especially

The Lost Honor of Katharina Blum

Chapter 7

when abused by a powerful institution such as the tabloid press. But Böll's narrative registers more than his evident outrage against the unscrupulous collusion of the Springer press with the German state in their public hunt for terrorists. There is more at stake: the subtextual undercurrent of the narrative of *Katharina Blum*, the advent of "abstract radicalism" — I would argue — is also very much being negotiated.[26]

Sensitivity to the emergence of an abstract radicalism within the political climate of Germany at the time certainly registers on the level of form, insofar as the narrator takes great pains to compile multiple voices and diverse materials to present his case — even when he has to admit that "too much is going on." There is no univocal truth, but only a truth to be cobbled and patched together from different sources. A speech of subtle differentiation and analysis, it seemed, was losing favor in public discourse in Germany at the time; certainly on the part of the conservatives, but also, if one is to believe Theweleit, on the part of the radical left.

Böll devotes the final seven chapters — absent in the film — to Hubert Blorna, Katharina's ex-employer and attorney, and Else Woltersheim, her godmother and dear friend. They seem to be the characters who suffer most from Katharina's committed crime. Already in the opening pages, the attorney Blorna has pinned down the dialectical forces that lie at the core of the narrative: "Blorna," as the narrator informs us, "could find no explanation for the whole affair and yet, 'when I come to think about it,' found it 'not inexplicable, but almost logical' " (p. 7). This very tension between the inexplicable and the irrational, on the one hand, and a clear order of things creating an almost frightening logic, on the other, comes to an uneasy halt in the final pages. For Katharina, the killing of Tötges has a cathartic impact which leaves her cleansed and optimistic. But this is not what happens to her close friends: "While Katharina, restricted only in her freedom, is looking almost untroubled to the future, Else Woltersheim is on the way to a state of steadily increasing bitterness" (p. 130). On another occasion, in describing the personal and professional fall of Blorna, the narrator informs us that Blorna is in love with Katharina: "he loves her, she does not love him, and he hasn't a hope in the world, since everything, everything, belongs to her 'dear Ludwig'!" (p. 134).

While Blorna seems to lose more and more control over his life, Katharina appears to be of almost uncanny cheerfulness thanks to her unconditional love for "my dear Ludwig." But since the novel (unlike the film) hardly introduces Ludwig as a character, he remains somewhat abstract, and so does Katharina's devotion to him. It seems as if, within the story world (and especially toward the ending), the signifier "Ludwig" has lost its referent. Ludwig becomes more and more disassociated from any particular character; rather, Katharina's insistence on her devotion to him codes the love story — already treated with a "mild sneer" — more and more in fanatic terms. Katharina's happiness in prison, where she can live "under the same conditions as my dear Ludwig" (pp. 128–9), resonates uneasily with her obliviousness to the miseries of her friends (Blorna, Woltersheim).

The narrator's remark that Blorna's attempt to hold hands with Katharina "is purely one-sided" (pp. 134–5) suggests more than unrequited love: the abstract "dear Ludwig" has taken over her actual relationships with the people around her, or so the text suggests.

The emphatic textual accounts, given the social and professional demise of Hubert and Trude Blorna and Else Woltersheim, are pitched against Katharina's cheerful business plans regarding her future life after prison, making her seem more strong-willed and ego-centric than sweet and kind. Admittedly, Böll does conclude with Katharina's personal statement in which she gives a detailed explanation of her reasons for shooting Tötges. But since her confession comes at the end, only after the narrator has informed us about the sad after-effects of Katharina's act on her truly innocent friends, the killing appears less justified and worthwhile than the entire course of the novel might suggest.

Blorna's opening remark, that the whole affair was "not inexplicable, but almost logical," encapsulates the difficulties of Böll's own analysis of "how violence can arise and where it can lead." While openly detesting the rhetoric of the state apparatuses and their methods of persecuting everything deemed "left," Böll's writing also seems to hint at and register the complexities of a political development that inform his writing more deeply than one might assume at first glance. Even though he ultimately takes sides with "Katharina," he adds a further dimension to the "pure and innocent housekeeper" driven to murder, and makes her a more complex, ambiguous, and interesting figure. Thus, his analysis of "how violence can arise and where it can lead" exceeds the obvious, namely the critique of a malicious press which turns innocent people into "killers." Böll also tells the story of the contamination, collusion, and, ultimately, corruption of his main character.

In the end, just before the actual killing, Katharina puts on a Bedouin costume and goes to a café frequented mostly by journalists. There, she spends "an hour and a half, unrecognized, at the reporters' hangout, presumably gathering information on Tötges" (p. 122). By putting on a carnival costume, going undercover, and being able to pass as a "normal" citizen, Katharina becomes one of them. That is what really signifies her "loss of chastity": by buying into the semiotics of the official German carnival which fosters the notion of a surveillance state and encourages the entire nation to go under-cover and spy on each other. Katharina is clearly marked as different from her fellow citizens in the beginning of the narrative. When she is going to the dance and "was dressed neither as a Bedouin nor as an Andalusian but merely wore a red carnation in her hair" (p. 17), she appears to be adorned rather than disguised. When she finally commits the crime and shoots Tötges, though, she appears in a full Bedouin costume like everybody else. However comprehensible, even justifiable, her final violent act might appear on an emotional level, Böll nevertheless demonstrates how Katharina becomes, at least on a structural level, "one of them."

In their screen adaptation, Schlöndorff/von Trotta emphasize the emotional dimension of the narrative and thus render the character of Katharina less ambiguous than she is in the novel. This loss of ambiguity becomes most obvious in the slight changes the directors make with regard to the carnival scenes. But, on a more general level, the narrative of the film, unlike that of the novel, does not give away the murder, and instead follows the classical Hollywood suspense narrative by keeping the viewer anxiously concerned about "what's next." Right at the beginning, when Ludwig arrives in the city, the viewer is cued into the perspective of the police surveillance camera, which observes him through the crosshairs. Throughout, black-and-white footage alternates with color, heightening the suspense by destabilizing the viewer's point of view, switching the spectator back and forth between the perspectives of the observers and the observed. Carefully oscillating between detachment and engagement, the film allows far more emotional access to Katharina's subjectivity than the novel. Not only is she present in almost every shot, she is also granted subjective flashbacks when she fondly remembers her romantic encounters with Ludwig and their intimate conversations at the party. This device not only turns Katharina into the passionate heroine of a love story rather than an agent of structural violence, it also fleshes out the character of Ludwig and his romantic impact on the whole story. Put simply, the film amplifies the emotional ingredients of the narrative beyond its literary source and thus motivates the character's actions more on an individual than a structural level. But this is not to say that alienation and detachment go unregistered. On the contrary, the *mise-en-scène* of *Katharina Blum* effectively conveys an atmosphere of surveillance, repression, and homelessness in a nation-state in which eavesdropping and surveillance penetrate the very fabric of everyday life.[27]

The non-diegetic, uncanny musical score by atonal composer Hans Werner Henze allows no harmonic closure on the sound track.[28] The settings of the film are mostly public institutions like police offices, hospitals, and churches, whereas the private and homely space of Katharina's apartment deteriorates in accordance with the moral demise of the heroine. In the scene where Katharina throws bottles against the walls of her apartment, the *mise-en-scène* clearly visualizes the protagonist's inner destruction. Böll's ironically "gendering" remark about the "immaculate" walls, which get destroyed by a carefully enumerated amount of half-empty bottles, translate in the film into a far more compassionate scene of aggression and desperation. Katharina's lost honor and public humiliation are made palpable by the besmirched walls of her rooms, heightening the sense of her destroyed purity. Significantly, when she finally shoots Tötges in the middle of this very same apartment, the music suggests that this killing restores the lost harmony of her private space. When Tötges enters the apartment in long shot, the atonal and disharmonic music reaches a kind of climax on the sound track, as if to mark out Tötges' actual penetration of her room as the absolute high point of a public invasion of private space. Once he is in the room and closes the door behind him, the restless and nervous music dies down and gives way to an almost peaceful silence. This tranquility is contradicted by the *mise-en-scène* which places the character of Tötges in front of the stained walls, the bloody outcome of his encounter with Katharina already anticipated. But nevertheless the absence of music prevails until the final scene, suggesting at least a temporary relief of tension due to this individual act of violence.

Carnival, finally, plays a crucial part in the film, especially when compared to its use in Böll's novel. Robert Stam, building on the work of Russian theorist Mikhail Bakhtin, has elaborated on the potential subversive pleasures of carnival as "decentralizing (centrifugal) forces that militate against official power and ideology."[29] Carnival in its literal sense refers to a folk tradition of festivity that suspends hierarchical structures, mocks authorities, and undermines socio-hierarchical inequalities. The official German carnival as mobilized both in the novel and in the film, however, serves the exact opposite, but nevertheless helps to lay bare hierarchies and authoritarian structures.

In a comprehensive analysis of the discussion of the RAF within the German public since the "hot autumn" of 1977, Thomas Elsaesser has pointed to the " 'theatricalized' logic of the RAF's argument about 'unmasking' the German establishment."[30] This logic, based on the assumption of the "return of the repressed," perceives Germany as a fascist state in the guise of Western capitalism: "By 'tearing the mask off the face of power' the terrorist expected the public to see what hid behind capitalism and economic prosperity: the old fascist state and its obedient servants."[31] Böll and Günter Grass, especially, both part of the older generation of liberals, very much subscribed to this thesis of a "return of the repressed." They experienced the RAF terror as an uncanny (*unheimlich*) return of the Weimar years with both their left- and right-wing street terror. For the younger generation, Elsaesser argues, the sympathies with the terrorists were not so much inspired by the return of a familiar Weimar history, but rather a "vicarious satisfaction" (*klammheimlich*) in the death of some of the RAF's victims.[32]

It is precisely this distinction between the "uncanny" and the "vicarious" that marks the demarcation between Böll's novel and Schlöndorff/von Trotta's film, and it reverberates in their different alignment of the metaphor of the carnival with its connotation of fascism. Costume in Schlöndorff/von Trotta signifies the "obedient German servant" of the disguised fascist state: "decent" citizens in costume stare shamelessly at Katharina's unmasked face (for example, when she takes a ride in the elevator in her own apartment building) because they feel empowered by their own incognito status. Another explicit reference to the notion of a carnival of repression emerges during the hearings at the police station, where in a long shot the camera discloses a back room of the police building, where an entire unit of officers dresses in carnival costumes in order to disguise their surveillance equipment. More importantly, the line between the police agents and the average German citizen is blurred when the entire nation is attired in carnival costumes, enabling them to act as informants on behalf of the nation-state and its nefarious (fascist?) intentions.

Granted, Böll uses the carnival and costume in the same way as the filmmakers; he, too, foregrounds the official carnival of repression as a reversed metaphor of a "tearing off" of the mask: those who have nothing to hide have no need to wear a mask. But unlike Schlöndorff/von Trotta, Böll lets Katharina don her Bedouin costume and become "one of them." He lets her mingle at the journalist hangout and get away unnoticed. Schlöndorff/von Trotta, in contrast, show explicitly that for Katharina "passing" is not an option. In the scene in which Katharina dresses up to blend with the people in a coffee shop, her costume is immediately torn off; she is recognized, beer is poured on her, and she is thrown out of the restaurant. By deliberately not aligning her with the crowd in costume when committing her crime, the filmmakers share more of the younger generation's "vicarious satisfaction" with the act of terrorism than Böll did. Even though the filmmakers tailor their film more toward the needs of a mainstream audience by foregrounding suspense, romance, and individual character motivation, overall they display greater sympathy with Katharina's act of violence than did Böll in his detached presentation of events.[33] His narrative not only debunks the fascist underpinnings of the German nation-state, it also registers the emergence of an all-pervasive abstract radicalism on the part of the ultra-left and finally reads these symptoms off the character of Katharina.

Twenty-five years after *The Lost Honor of Katharina Blum*, Volker Schlöndorff involved himself again with the German terrorism of the 1970s, tracing its aftermath until the fall of the Berlin Wall. His latest work on the topic *The Legend of Rita* (Germany, 2000), loosely based on a different kind of text, to wit the autobiography of ex-terrorist Inge Viett, sides strongly with the young militant heroine Rita and her investment in radical politics. After accidentally killing a French policeman, Rita "disappears" in Eastern Germany, the then enemy of the West German nation-state, and is provided with a new, forged identity (a so-called "legend"). Rita attempts to engage disillusioned GDR-citizens with her revolutionary socialist optimism, only to fall prey to the revenge of the West German nation-state after the fall of the Berlin Wall. In her effort to escape by motorcycle over the border, Rita is shot down by the border patrol. *The Legend of Rita* is, of course, another of Schlöndorff's powerful passion plays, made to move a large audience. An emotionally accessible character like Rita provides a strong identificatory entry into a narrative which once more tells the story of a failed political project on a purely individual level. Again, Schlöndorff is not an analyst but a sympathizer, although he does tell one story quite accurately. Episodes from that unruly German history keep popping up and disrupting public memory – just as they recently did on the level of official state politics. In other words, Germany and its terrorist past are as yet "not reconciled."

Notes

1 See the detailed interview with Joschka Fischer on his past in the student movement and his use of violence in Tilman Gerwien, Norbert Höfler, and Hans-Martin Tillack, "Ja, ich war militant [Yes, I was militant]," *Stern* (January 4, 2001), n.p.

2 Karl Heinz Bohrer, "Fantasie, die keine war," in *Die Zeit* (August 2, 2001), n.p.

3 RAF-chic even made it into trend magazines on German TV, as for example in Katharina Wenzel's feature, "Die friedensverwöhnte Jugend schmückt sich mit den Accessoires der RAF-Terroristen [The freedom spoiled youth adorn themselves with accessores of RAF-terrorists]," in *Polylux* (ARD), December 2, 2001.

4 Raul Zelik, "German Ghost Stories," in *Spex* 6: 1 (June 2001), 76–80. Zelik in particular refers to the German rapper Jan Delay and his song "Söhne Stammheims [Sons of Stammheim]" (Stammheim being the high-security prison in which the terrorists were held); further, he mentions an exhibition in Berlin, the novel *Rosenfest* by Leander Scholz about the Baader–Meinhof group, and various films on the RAF: Christian Petzold's *Innere Sicherheit*, a film in which Harun Farocki collaborated on the script, and Andreas Veiel's *Blackbox BRD*.

5 Andreas Busche, "Freiheit jetzt!," *Spex* 6: 1 (June 2001), 80.

6   Olaf Hoerschelmann, "'*Memora dextera est*': Film and Public Memory in Postwar Germany," in *Cinema Journal* 40: 2 (Winter 2001), 78–97.

7   Ibid., 83.

8   Thomas Elsaesser quoted in ibid.

9   For detailed documentation of this public debate on the integrity of Böll, see J. H. Reid, "Citizen for Brandt (1969–1976)," in *Heinrich Böll: A German for his Time* (Oxford: Oswald Wolff Books, 1988), pp. 159–89.

10 See Jack Zipes, "The Political Dimension of *The Lost Honor of Katharina Blum*," in Terri Ginsberg and Kirsten Moana Thompson (eds), *Perspectives on German Cinema* (New York: Simon and Schuster, 1996), pp. 403–12.

11 Reid, "Citizen for Brandt (1969–1976)," p. 166.

12 Ibid., p. 182.

13 Ibid., p. 181.

14 See Schlöndorff, quoted in William R. Magretta and Joan Magretta, "Story and Discourse: Schlöndorff and von Trotta's *The Lost Honor of Katharina Blum* (1975)," in Andrew Horton and Joan Magretta (eds), *Modern European Filmmakers and the Art of Adaptation* (New York: Frederick Ungar, 1981), pp. 278–94, p. 280.

15 Eric Rentschler, "Specularity and Spectacle in Schlöndorff's *Young Törless* (1966)," in Eric Rentschler (ed.), *German Film and Literature: Adaptations and Transformations* (London: Methuen, 1986), pp. 176–92, p. 179.

16 Zipes, "Political Dimension," p. 407.

17 Magretta and Magretta, "Story and Discourse," p. 294.

18 See, for example, Margarethe von Trotta's film *German Sisters* (also known as *Marianne and Juliane*; Germany, 1981), where the imprisoned Marianne tells her sister about the psychologically devastating effects of the isolation cells.

19 Magretta and Magretta, "Story and Discourse," pp. 282–3.

20 Heinrich Böll, *The Lost Honor of Katharina Blum*, trans. Leila Vennewitz (New York: Penguin, 1975), p. 105. Subsequent page numbers in text refer to this edition.

21 For a detailed discussion of the feminist aspect in both novel and film, see, for example, Daniel Cetinich, "*The Lost Honor of Katharina Blum*: Who's the Terrorist in West Germany?," in *Jump Cut* 19 (1978), n.p.

22 Reid, "Citizen for Brandt (1969–1976)," pp. 186–7.

23 Magretta and Magretta, "Story and Discourse," p. 291.

24 Ibid., p. 284.

25 Klaus Theweleit, "Das RAF-gespenst [The RAF Ghost]," lecture October 7, 1997 in the Berliner Ensemble, Cologne: supposé, 2001, 2 audio CDs (www.suppose.de).

26 This is certainly not to say that the character of Katharina Blum is modeled on the terrorist Ulrike Meinhof. But contemporary readings of *Katharina Blum* in the press, who mostly agreed upon Katharina Blum being described as a "pure and innocent woman" whose only crime is loving a terrorist (cf. Reid, "Citizen for Brandt (1969–1976)," p. 183), eclipsed a deeper dimension to her character. This becomes most apparent in the ending, when the narrator, in his usually detached and ironic manner, sets out to collect the fragments of his characters after the final blow, that is, the killing of Tötges.

27 For a detailed analysis of the use of glass and mirror to emphasize the notion of surveillance, see Lester D. Friedman, "Cinematic Techniques in *The Lost Honor of Katharina Blum*," *Film Quarterly* 7: 3 (1979), 244–52.

28 See Magretta and Magretta, "Story and Discourse," pp. 284–5.

29 Robert Stam, *Subversive Pleasure: Bakhtin, Cultural Criticism, and Film* (Baltimore, MD: The Johns Hopkins University Press, 1989), pp. 122ff.

30 Thomas Elsaesser, "Antigone Agonistes: Urban Guerrilla or Guerrilla Urbanism? The Red Army Faction, Germany in Autumn and Death Game," in Joan Copjec and Michael Sorkin (eds), *Giving Ground: The Politics of Propinquity* (London: Verso, 1999), pp. 267–302, p. 274.

31 Ibid.

32 Ibid., p. 284.

33 Also, as Hoerschelmann points out correctly, both novel and film were made before the significantly more violent and bloody phase of German terrorism which climaxed in 1977. See Hoerschelmann, "'*Memora dextera est*'," p. 91.

Alexandra Seibel

Chapter 7

Chapter 8

Serial Time: Bluebeard in Stepford

Bliss Cua Lim

---- "Stepford is Out of Step": Fantastic Nonsynchronism ----

Patriarchies are never simply old-fashioned. In *Stepford Wives* – both Ira Levin's 1972 novel and Bryan Forbes's 1974 film – the feminist heroine is implicitly reproached for assuming that modernity is always anathema to misogyny. "Stepford is out of step," she tells her husband, deriding the town's Men's Assocation as "outdated."[1] To her own undoing, she fails to realize – until the eleventh hour – that her "present" is characterized by nonsynchronous patriarchal responses challenged-forth by and contemporaneous with the women's movement.

Retooling a conception derived from Marxist philosophies of history, I use the term "nonsynchronism" to designate a fractured sense of time evoked by the figuration of competing contexts of experience, or discontinuous epistemological paradigms, in fantastic narratives.[2] My work on *Stepford Wives* is part of a larger project on fantastic cinema from various national contexts, including Indian, Chinese, Japanese, and Filipino films. In what follows, I would like to briefly contextualize my discussion of *Stepford Wives* in terms of my interests in fantastic nonsynchronism and historical difference.

Critical consensus holds that the fantastic depicts archaic belief systems re-emerging in the disenchanted present. Freud speaks of the uncanny as the return of "surmounted modes of thought,"[3] and literary scholars and anthropologists alike characterize the fantastic as degraded myth in a post-mythic age, pre-modern beliefs surviving in a rational time. The hegemonic idea of the fantastic as an anachronism in a completely rationalized modernity presumes a complete eclipsing or expulsion of the occult in the current age. I take the opposite view, and suggest that, in representing unsurmounted worlds in a fractious present, the fantastic disquietingly insinuates, not the stability of one time vis-à-vis another, but their co-implication.

The concept of nonsynchronism designates that recurring notion, in the fantastic, that people do not all dwell in the same Now; that there is more than one time in any one time, that past, present, and future modes of being in the world are neither securely moored nor absolutely differentiated, but are mutually entangled. Though I cannot here undertake a full explication of the genealogies of the term "fantastic," I understand the fantastic as a meeting place for the anomalous and the ordinary (frequently, the supernatural and the natural) which, far from upholding an historicist drama whereby mythical or pre-modern thought is surmounted by modern rationality, very often espouses a nonsynchronous view of social life, calling attention to the problematic role of anachronisms and non-contemporaneities in historicist thought.[4] I proffer the concept of nonsynchronism not to advance yet another generalization or definition of the fantastic as a mode or genre, but to describe a certain kind of insight into historical alterity that the fantastic, in its figura-tion of disjunctive worlds and times, has a propensity to disclose.

Several strands of historical nonsynchronism abound in *Stepford Wives*. In the dialogue I quote from Levin's novel at the beginning of this section, the heroine Joanna, deceived by her husband's seeming adherence to feminist views, ridicules the Stepford Men's Association for being "outdated," "old-fashioned," and "out of step" with the current time. The film does not rehearse this scene, but the same characterization of Stepford's sexual politics as anachronistic emerges in the emphasis given to the word "archaic" in the screenplay, the word which Joanna and her best friend Bobbie use to describe the Men's Association and the very word that Bobbie forgets once she has "changed." The nonsynchronous texture of life in Stepford belies Joanna's historicist misprision that patriarchy is outmoded while feminism is contemporary. Instead, Stepford's homicidal husbands employ cutting-edge technology to reprise old-fashioned notions of femininity, embodying a temporally discrepant patriarchal ethos, at once futuristic, coeval, and deeply nostalgic.

My analysis of Forbes's film pursues an intertextual understanding of the film in which Levin's novel is granted little primacy. Intertextuality, Kristeva's own illuminating inter-textual appropriation of Bakhtinian dialogism, names our recognition that every text is "an intersection of textual surfaces rather than a point of fixed meaning," and that every term in narrative is "at least double."[5] Intertextuality is strongly suited to frame a discussion of fantastic nonsynchronism because intertextuality is always temporally discrepant. A radically intertextual method eschews the linear temporality underpinning the assumption that the film "comes after" and is thus obliged to be faithful to its literary "predecessor." Intertextuality cautions us against assuming that meanings can ever be wholly ascribed to a defining, "original" source or intention. It also reminds us that the cacophony at the heart of every utterance is historically nonsynchronous, a juxtaposition of discourses from diverse eras. Bakhtin writes that language is "heteroglot from top to bottom," embodying "the co-existence of socio-ideological contradictions between the present and the past, between differing epochs of the past."[6]

I introduce the concept of intertextuality in order to distance my approach from the source–adaptation dyad that dominates studies of literature and film. Rather than conceiving of Levin's novel as a "source" which the film contests or transforms, this study positions the novel as only one of several discourses through which the nonsynchronous temporality of the Bluebeard tale – the story of a husband who murders a string of wives – is refracted. My discussion mobilizes Levin's book among an assortment of intertexts: centuries-old tropes of misogyny (the seventeenth-century Skull Doctor and the medieval Mill of Old Wives), Disney audio-animatronics, second wave feminism, and the Final Girls and serial killers of Hollywood horror films.

How is it possible to discern Bluebeard's dire visage in sunlit Stepford? Such a construal does not proceed by unveiling evidence of an intention – whether on the part of novelist, director, or screenwriter – to invoke folklore's murderous bridegroom; indeed, neither novel nor screenplay makes mention of him. Intertextuality is not a matter of intentional allusion because intertexts are both "conscious and unconscious quotations, conflations and inversions of other texts."[7] If, authorial intention notwithstanding, it is possible to perceive the Stepford husbands as kin to Bluebeard, it is because the figure of the serial killing husband is not a singular point of meaning but a variegated prism through which other discourses are refracted. The film can be apprehended as a Bluebeard tale because, as Kristeva puts it, "every text is constructed as a mosaic of quotations; any text is the absorption and transformation of another."[8]

If every text is a mosaic, then discursive ownership is impossible to claim. As Bakhtin deftly puts it, "The word in language is half someone else's."[9] Being half someone else's, every discourse is already an adaptation of texts that are themselves not originals. Yet adaptation studies has come under fire precisely for its ideal of fidelity to literary properties.[10] Discourse misconstrued as property underpins both the fallacy of originality and the "chimera of fidelity" in adaptation studies.[11] Creative spectatorship and fan ownership are only the most obvious rejoinders to the claims of copyright, attesting to the difficulty of reining in discourse as property.[12]

In my view, "source novels" are never the measure of "film adaptations." A single novel as a principal yardstick or comparison-text for cinematic meaning forgets that discourses have no fealty to originals, but are echoing chambers whose resonances are difficult to exhaust. The model of novel–film dyad, whether conceived as correspondence or transformation, might unwittingly confine our understanding to "the dungeon of a single context."[13] The source–adaptation paradigm excludes not only other, perhaps more salient intertexts, but more crucially, the "rejoinder" of the spectator, whose response to the film may have little or nothing to do with the novel it adapts, a novel which, in this sense, cannot claim to be the "source text" of the viewer's dialogic response. In Bakhtin/Kristeva's cruciform model, the text lies at the horizontal crossroads of authors and audiences and at the vertical intersection of one work with the corpus of other works among which it is positioned.[14]

In what follows, I first explore the likeness of *Stepford Wives* to Bluebeard tales to emphasize two crucial aspects of this narrative of marital murder: the essentializing, equivalizing gesture of serial killing; and the nonsynchronous temporality of serial victimization as a narrative of fate (the victims recognize their future doom in the past death of their predecessors). The next section explores the significant departures of *Stepford Wives* from the Bluebeard structure: most obviously, its recourse to audio-animatronic doubles specifically attributed to Disney's pioneering work with this technology. At once emblematic of nostalgically pictured femininity and produced by cutting-edge industrial wizardry, the doll-doubles of Stepford are nonsynchronous in the extreme, and point up the uncanniness of Disney's ultra-modern innovations. This section also explores the film's proximity to folkloric tropes of recycling an intractable wife, and discusses *Stepford Wives'* allegorical portrait of erotic domination, evident in its fantasy of remaking women by violence and in its positioning of female mannequins as sexual surrogates. The last section of the chapter juxtaposes the Stepford heroine who dies – Joanna – alongside the triumphant Final Girls of horror. Like these victim-heroines, Joanna attests to the life-saving value of feminist paranoia: why then does she fail to survive? The narrative implicitly chides its heroine for thinking of the Men's Association as "old-fashioned" and "out of date" by revealing that the men of Stepford are never merely obsolescent, but wield the technological arsenal of the present to shocking ends.

On the Threshold of Seriality: Bluebeard and the Temporality of Fate

Bluebeard is folklore's first serial killer. Carol Clover incisively reminds us that "horror movies look like nothing so much as folktales." Like folklore, horror bears "the hallmarks of oral narrative: the free exchange of themes and motifs, the archetypal characters and situations . . . This is a field in which there is in some sense no original, no real or right text, but only variants."[15] Though comprised of countless variants and close cousins,[16] the hallmark of the Bluebeard narrative is its string of unsuspecting wives done to death by a homicidal husband or suitor. Its nucleus is sexualized, sequential murder. This emphasis on seriality perhaps guarantees its continuing relevance to popular culture. Marina Warner notes, "the fairy tale written by Perrault in 1697 thrills like a Hitchcock film before its time, it foreshadows thriving twentieth-century fantasies about serial killers and Jack the Rippers."[17] The Bluebeard figure has "metamorphosed in popular culture for adults into the mass murderer, the kidnapper, the serial killer: a collector, as in John Fowles's novel, an obsessive, like Hannibal Lecter in *The Silence of the Lambs*."[18]

Described as a "wealthy serial bachelor"[19] who entices young women with his affluence, only to subject them, by turns, to his repetitive "project of marital coercion,"[20] Bluebeard is a potent emblem for women's longstanding fears of literal or metaphoric death in wedlock. In most versions, Bluebeard gives his new wife access to his considerable holdings, but sternly prohibits her from entering a certain chamber: "As for this little room, I forbid you to enter it, and my prohibition is such that if you happen to open it, there is nothing you should not expect from my anger."[21] Our heroine's inquisitiveness spurs her to transgression – "Bluebeard" has often been subtitled "The Fatal Effects of Curiosity"[22] – but nothing could have prepared her for what she finds in the forbidden chamber. In his version, Charles Perrault writes:

> At first she saw nothing, for the windows were closed, but after a few moments she perceived dimly that the floor was entirely covered with clotted blood, and that in this were reflected the dead bodies of several women that hung along the walls. These were all the wives of Blue Beard, whose throats he had cut, one after the other.[23]

To the new wife's unspeakable horror, the sanguine mirror both reflects the remains of other women and also augurs her own undoing, for Bluebeard discovers her disobedience. He prepares to murder her in the manner of her predecessors, but she is saved, sometimes through the timely intervention of her brothers, sometimes by her own cunning stratagems.

One writer puts it superbly: "Bluebeard" is a story in which "marrying is brought into association with being butchered."[24] Like "Beauty and the Beast," this folktale does not dramatize a courtship but pursues a marital plot, in the dual sense of narrative and conspiracy. In contrast to Freudian readings of the husband's animal nature as a metaphor for the woman's awakening into sexuality, Warner suggests that the sinister bridegrooms of "Bluebeard" and "Beauty and the Beast" afford brutally candid explorations of the marital dynamic.[25] From the late seventeenth century onwards, women of letters added their voices to the cautionary fables of elderly nurses or low-born women, re-spinning old wives' tales through an overt infusion of feminism, and reworking oral sources to decry arranged marriages and stifling gender roles for women.[26] At its core, *Stepford Wives* is a Bluebeard tale, a story of women serially murdered in marriage.

Stepford Wives traces the increasing alienation-in-marriage of Joanna, a semi-professional photographer in her mid-thirties who undertakes a city-to-suburbs move for her husband Walter. The film specifies that the couple and their two children have relocated from Manhattan to Connecticut, and opens with the family's last morning in Manhattan and their drive to Stepford.[27] The novel, for its part, begins with Joanna already in Stepford, being interviewed for the "Notes on Newcomers" section of the local newspaper. In her interview with the Welcome Wagon Lady, Joanna characterizes herself as "interested in politics and in the Women's Liberation movement. Very much so in that. And so is my husband."[28] The film is less forthright on this point; Walter is never described as actively involved in the women's movement, though Joanna discloses to a friend that she herself "messed around with Women's Lib" back in New York.

Once in Stepford, Joanna strikes up a fast friendship with another "ex-Gothamite," Bobbie, a vibrant, assertive young woman who, like Joanna, was active in the women's movement and recently moved to Stepford at her husband's urging. Their first conversation in the film, which hews closely to the novel, establishes the grounds of their companionable bonding: their shared disapproval of their new female neighbors, Stepford's "compulsive *hausfraus*," as Joanna puts it.[29]

In a tone of humorous frustration, the two friends agree that Stepford women seem cast in the mold of television advertisements' nostalgia for idealized 1950s' femininity. "You see, doctor," Bobbie jokingly says to Joanna in the film, "my problem is that, given complete freedom of choice, I don't wanna squeeze the goddamn Charmin." In the novel, Joanna reflects that the Stepford wives were like "actresses in commercials, pleased with detergents and floor wax, with cleaners, shampoos, and deodorants. Pretty actresses, big in the bosom but small in the talent, playing suburban housewives unconvincingly, too nicey-nice to be real."[30] As newcomers, Joanna and Bobbie feel fenced out by the town's investment in nostalgic femininity, palpable in both their housework-oriented female neighbors, and in the Men's Association which their supposedly women-positive, "liberated" husbands have joined. (In the novel, both their spouses promise that the organization will be "co-ed" in six months' time.)

Convinced that a massive dose of consciousness-raising is in order, Joanna and Bobbie set about trying to organize a women's group in Stepford (in the novel, they make reference to starting a National Organization of Women chapter), but there are no takers save one: Charmaine, the unhappily married wife of a television producer, who loves tennis and hates housework, preferring to leave housekeeping to her maid. In the film, Joanna, Bobbie, and Charmaine manage to put together one consciousness-raising session, with the other Stepford wives in attendance, but the results are as chilling as they are hilarious: Charmaine begins by tearfully disclosing that her husband views her only as a "trophy wife," but when the other Stepford wives chime in, their deepest-felt anxieties concern baking and cleaning. One wife, Kit, is anxious because "It took me so long to get the upstairs floor to shine, I didn't have time to bake!" The other wives console her with enthusiastic testimonials on the virtues of house-cleaning aids. (Marie: "Well, if time is your enemy, make friends with Easy On.")

Despite the humorous overtones of this women's liberation meeting turned group commercial – this incongruous scene may account for Betty Friedan's storming out of the theater, if reports are true[31] – this is the first time we and the heroines truly recoil in horror at the Stepford wives, whose deepest personal priorities include cleaning products. As an upshot of this experience, Bobbie and Joanna realize that their female neighbors cannot be helped simply by conversion to feminism, since these women exhibit a troubling lack of consciousness, a total devolution of agency. The scene plays like a commercial in which a talking mechanical dishwasher extols the virtues of the most effective detergent available. We, like the film's heroines, begin to sense something automated about the Stepford wives, who, as Joanna rhymingly reflects in the novel, "work like robots all their lives."[32]

Todorov's fantastic hesitation rears its head in *Stepford Wives* as a feminist doubting of other women's humanity.[33] At this early stage in the narrative the protagonists waver between rational and preternatural explanations. After the surreal "women's lib" meeting,

Joanna and Bobbie ask each other aloud whether they are going crazy. Their suspicions are further aroused upon learning that seven years ago, Stepford boasted a very active, feminist-identified women's organization. The officers of that women's club, which disbanded when membership dropped and its leaders resigned, are the very women who now have so little interest in anything outside their wifely duties.

Panic rises in Bobbie and Joanna as they begin to see themselves as part of a larger series of feminists who moved to Stepford only to undergo a radical transformation. All the submissive Stepford wives began as women with interests outside the family who moved to the suburbs at their husbands' behest, upper-class, college-educated wives of successful and prosperous men who gave up full-time work in order to raise children and keep house. Within the narrative, the idiosyncratic individualism of each woman gives way to a terrifying equivalence, as first Charmaine, then Bobbie, goes off for a weekend alone with their husbands, only to return more lovely but also completely vapid, no longer interested in anything but servicing their husbands and keeping the house sparkling clean. Terrified and increasingly suspicious of her own husband and his colleagues in the Men's Association, Joanna confides her worst fears to a female psychiatrist in the film:

> Oh Jesus. It's so awful. *If I'm wrong, I'm insane, and if I'm right, it's worse than if I'm wrong* . . . Bobbie my best friend changed in four months and that's what convinced me. That's how long I've been in Stepford. Four months. And I don't know what's going on, I just know something's wrong and *my time is coming* . . . Don't ask me to explain it, I just know. There'll be somebody with my name and she'll cook and clean like crazy but she won't take pictures and she won't be me. She'll — *She'll be like one of those robots in Disneyland*. (emphasis added)

In this agitated monologue, Joanna articulates a clear-sighted understanding of her own entrapment in a plot of serial murder. Like the heroine in Bluebeard's bloody chamber, she sees in the demise of her predecessors the portent of her own, and frantically tries to avert the equivalizing fate the Stepford husbands have in store for their wives.

The investigative heroine has arrived at the brink of truth: the suburban husbands in the Men's Association are in the business of remaking all their wives, conspiring to murder them and install automata in their place. As docile as they are buxom, the Stepford wives are sexually available to every male fantasy (the real women of Stepford, in both film and novel, do not often oblige their spouses' prurience), and undertake thankless household chores with unquestioning enthusiasm. These mechanical dolls (parodically nicknamed "fembots" in *Austin Powers: International Man of Mystery* [Jay Roach, 1997]) literalize serialized uniformity. The ultra-feminine robots, despite pitch-perfect engineering to resemble the ruined wives, are fundamentally indistinguishable from one another, women-made-collectibles by serial killing's erasure of difference, its logic of repetition.

The serial correspondence achieved by murder in Stepford is at the heart of the Bluebeard tale. When Joanna tells her therapist that her "time is coming" she is articulating the selfsame shock of recognition that Bluebeard's bride experienced upon opening the door to the bloody chamber. *Stepford Wives* stages the very threshold of recognition that Casie Hermansson identifies in the Bluebeard plot:

> Bluebeard's tableau of his wives' bodies defamiliarizes the reflection they stage for the viewing wife: *the image is based on the past (they are previous wives, and no longer alive) but encodes the sign of her future (she is to be a dead one).* As one variant Bluebeard says, "as you have seen, so you shall become!" . . . The iconic tableau incorporates *evidence of the serial act,* or repetition-compulsion by another name. The icon feeds itself by physically drawing in newcomers, who have already been encoded there in the abstract, and by *suppressing their individual differences through this use of like-ness.*
>
> The effect of these structures of uncanny likeness infused through Bluebeard's destructive vision is apparent at *the moment on the threshold. As she gazes upon the bodies of her predecessors, Bluebeard's wife realizes (in both senses of understanding and making it happen) that she is now within Bluebeard's serial plot, and she is horrified.* (emphasis added)[34]

Hermansson's acute reading reveals the crux of Bluebeard's "death artistry,"[35] his maniacal work-in-progress. An ever-accreting tableau of dead wives, masculinist design executed upon female corporeality, the bloody chamber as icon of equivalizing vision insinuates the essential homogeneity of women – collectible and quiescent – in the patriarch's eyes. This ghastly tableau is what brings slasher and serial killer movies into the compass of the Bluebeard tale. Whether in *Stepford Wives* or recent films like *The Cell* (Tarsem Singh, 2000), the homicidal lover kills to refashion female identities into the inert similitude of dolls on display.

Hermansson suggests that the implications of the equivalizing gesture of seriality are not exhausted by the motif of collection; rather, the most fundamental (and frightful) consequence of serial logic is its grisly encryption of nonsynchronism. The bloody chamber is a temporally nonsynchronous mirror in which the new wife recognizes, in the downfall of her predecessors, her own impending death. As Hermansson points out, this moment at the threshold of knowledge is crucial. Will she recognize herself in these dead women and collude in Bluebeard's foregone conclusion regarding her essentialized identity, or will she refuse it by artful subterfuge, forging, as in some variants of Bluebeard, another double of herself, not one which prophesies her submission, but one which forfends it?

In moving to Stepford, Joanna, like several women before her, finds herself at the doorway of Bluebeard's fatal chamber, faced with horrific evidence of how her antecedents met their gruesome doom. Nonsynchronous seriality lies in the dissolution of linear past, present, and future in the circular repetition of a fate that is both not yet and always already hers. The heroine of *Stepford Wives*, alongside her counterparts in Bluebeard stories, *stands on the threshold of a prior fate*: in recognizing what has befallen other women, she sets in motion her own impending destruction.

The trope of the fateful threshold and its desperate echoing of disparate but interwoven times and fates are clear to scholars of the Bluebeard tale. Philip Lewis understands the "body-reflecting" pool of blood in Bluebeard's forbidden room as a mirror in which the new wife first identifies with "the corpses on the walls": "she, the present wife, belongs to this group made up of Bluebeard's mysteriously missing previous wives . . . The bruising effect of this self-recognition, in which the live victim is forced to identify with her dead predecessors, is to immerse her experience of identity and desire in anxiety, to relate them to the coming of her own death."[36]

In the Blubeard plot, nonsynchronism is literalized in the mirroring effect of serial temporality. Its logic of inexorable sequentiality belongs to narratives of fate, which serve to cast the present as the already-past of an inevitable future. Put another way, Joanna, who fears that her time is coming, sees, like Bluebeard's wife, the downfall of other women as the portent of her own undoing; in the moment at the threshold, serial temporality fuses with the time of the omen. A bad omen involves a perverse temporality akin to Barthes's "vertigo of time defeated." The inverse of Barthes's punctum (something past and long dead that haunts us with disturbing present-ness due to photographic indexicality),[37] the omen is a present we experience as past at the moment it occurs: a past "construct[ed] in the form of a future,"[38] a feeling that the present is already behind us, already a past that cannot be changed, and hence that the future it augurs is inevitable. For Joanna in Stepford, the terrified would-be victim at the threshold of a serial killer's plot, the present is already past, construed from the vantage-point of a future blighted before it happens.

In *Stepford Wives*, the Bluebeard figure is not a single bridegroom but the husbands of Stepford taken as a diabolical collective. Seriality in *Stepford Wives* lies not in one man's killing a string of wives, but in all of these men colluding to kill each of their spouses. In *Stepford Wives*, the serial bachelor of folklore is replaced by collaborative perpetrators of seriality and sameness: each real wife is dispatched precisely as part of a communal effort to make the women into one same essential Wife. All of these different, vibrant women are being recreated as automata, ageless reiterations of a supposedly quintessential femininity. "The Robber Bridegroom," a Bluebeard variant by the Brothers Grimm, features a collective serial killer (a troupe of maniacal bandits, unlike the wealthy Bluebeard who acts alone), and, indeed, the Stepford husbands seem to draw from both fairytale prototypes, merging the communal homicide of thieves in the woods with the financial privilege of the widower in his castle. The crucial contribution of *Stepford Wives* is precisely the pluralization and abstraction of the Bluebeard figure. The film takes folklore's forerunner to the twentieth-century serial killer and widens the scope of the narrative's indictment: in Stepford, what kills our heroine is not one merciless husband but an entire ethos. The animate but annihilated suburban wives live out a slow death-in-life; in their routine obedience and lives of leisure they are but a torpid shadow of their former selves.

Yet what distinguishes the Stepford husbands from Bluebeard and the Robber Bridegroom is their repugnant audacity, their cynical confidence in putting their death-artistry on conspicuous display rather than totally closeting their crimes. The whole of Stepford is, to borrow Lewis's evocative phrase, a "euphemized sepulcher";[39] the upscale

Bliss Cua Lim

Chapter 8

Connecticut suburb is a strangely bloodless crypt, both undeniably public and terribly private, an open secret, to be precise. The place is a memorial under the sign of erasure, preserving yet obliterating the forever subjugated dead women who are the town's inert center, a sanitized, bloodless chamber, hiding in plain sight, recalling the profile of the serial killer, whose monstrosity is both cloaked and disclosed by his too-normal normalcy.[40]

Like "Sleeping Beauty," "Bluebeard" and *Stepford Wives* disclose a structure of ominous prophecy.[41] In the novel, Joanna feels "a sense of beforeness" touch her when she hears about her best friend's planned weekend getaway with her husband. Once Bobbie "changes," Joanna frantically attempts to take her children and flee Stepford because "it's going to happen to me in January,"[42] thus epitomizing folktale motifs of predestination and the heroine's desperate desire to be delivered from her coming doom. *Stepford Wives* thus reconfigures the fairytale's emphasis on fatalistic pedagogy.[43] Unlike "Bluebeard," in *Stepford Wives* the heroine, despite her knowledge, dies; the cautionary tale proceeds to confirm the omen, to pursue the nonsynchronous, fatal vision glimpsed by the heroine at the threshold of seriality to its bitter conclusion.

In the novel, Joanna meets her end when she asks her best friend, Bobbie, to prove she is human by cutting her finger so Joanna can see if it bleeds. The novel elliptically suggests that Bobbie agrees to do so but turns the knife against Joanna instead. In the next scene, a dutiful Joanna appears at the supermarket, indistinguishable from the Stepford wives she so recently deplored. The novel's narration, heretofore centered upon Joanna's free indirect speech,[44] shifts focalization to Ruthanne Hendry, the first African American woman to move to Stepford and, the novel ominously implies, the town's next fresh kill.

In the film version, Joanna is cannier than her novelistic counterpart: suspecting that the much-altered Bobbie will *not* bleed, she plunges the kitchen knife into her best friend's stomach. The weapon sticks out incongruously, bloodless on the robot's pristine white apron. In the end, it is not Bobbie's double that kills Joanna but her own. Bedraggled and terrified, Joanna watches helplessly as her own idealized mechanical countenance approaches her in a diaphanous nightgown, a stocking held taught between two hands. This ending underscores the likeness-in-difference with which the serial plot has framed her. For the Stepford wife, seriality always implies a rendezvous with fate, the heroine's providential meeting with and becoming her double. On the threshold of epiphany in *Stepford Wives* and "Bluebeard," our heroine finds herself entangled in the nonsynchronous time of fate, the linearity of cause and chance factored out, part and parcel of another temporality of repetition and variation, her future already foregone.[45]

Remaking Wives: The Technologies of Nostalgia

Screenwriter William Goldman emphasizes that *Stepford Wives* must be seen in its historical specificity, as a response to and engagement with what has been called the "second wave feminism" of the 1960s and 1970s:

Ira Levin's novella, on which the film was based, came out in the early seventies, when the Women's Liberation Movement was the hot topic on all the TV talk shows. Betty Friedan's *Feminine Mystique* had opened the floodgates, Gloria Steinem was a magazine cover girl, and all across the country people were echoing Freud's great unanswered question: "What do women want?"[46]

In this light, the Stepford husbands are placeholders for averse reactions to the women's liberation movement. By the late 1960s and early 1970s certain ideals of what has been called the "egalitarian feminism"[47] of the women's liberation movement had become mainstream, and patriarchal convictions regarding masculine superiority had gone underground, so to speak, just as, in the 1990s, political correctness as a kind of received etiquette has not so much eradicated prejudice as dictated its dissimulation.

The disobeyed Stepford husbands are the maniacal vanguard of a patriarchal order contested by the women's liberation movement. The conspiratorial men of Stepford feel themselves to have been wronged by their wives, but have kept silent about their disapproval regarding autonomous women, preferring to work in secrecy. Even more than Bluebeard, who murdered his wife because he could not trust her to keep her word, the Stepford husbands seem all the more motivated by unconscionable masculine pettiness. When Joanna asks the head of the Men's Association why the men executed their wives and replaced them with robots, he replies:

Why? Because we can. We found a way of doing it and it's just perfect. Perfect for us and perfect for you. Think of it the other way around. Wouldn't you like some perfect stud waiting on you around the house, praising you, servicing you, whispering how your sagging flesh was beautiful no matter how you look?

The wifely shortcomings for which the Stepford women must die are tragically banal: they are killed for not keeping a sufficiently tidy house, for refusing to play along with their husbands' sexual preferences, for sometimes neglecting to prepare dinner because they are wrapped up in part-time work. The Stepford wives, then, are executed for their lack of fit with a conception of femininity against which they have been secretly weighed by their husbands, only to be found wanting. Bluebeard's desire for domination, however unjust, was at least forthright. In the folktale, Bluebeard's prohibition was made plain to his wife, his wrath expected. In *Stepford Wives*, however, the women are unaware of their husbands' displeasure. Unlike Bluebeard's wives, the Stepford wives die not because they are curious, not because they have, in spite of themselves, knowingly crossed their husbands, but because they fail to appreciate the depths of their husbands' commitment to certain gender norms. The Stepford husbands meld Bluebeard's iniquity with anti-feminist subterfuge: covertly masculinist, some of the men are even avowed feminists. (In both novel and film, Joanna's husband Walter pretends to differ with the Men's Association's policy of excluding women, only to use his evenings at the organization for

Serial Time: Bluebeard in Stepford

Chapter 8

foul play.) In the age of feminism, none of the husbands openly espouses gender ideals loudly contested by the women's movement. The husbands know better than to argue with a feminist, preferring instead to replace her with a less quarrelsome version of herself.

Bluebeard kills his wives, whereas the men of Stepford murder women in order to "recycle" them. The Bluebeard tale features a nefarious husband, but *Stepford Wives* juxtaposes the inhumane husband with a literally inhuman wife, a doll who borrows a semblance of life. Central to *Stepford Wives*, then, is the folkloric "idea of a man who wants to master the feminine by actually creating it in the image of his desire."[48]

The film and novel take their title from the fantastic conceit of the narrative: the Stepford wives are real women retooled, made more pliant, more comely, and perpetually young. In this, *Stepford Wives* recalls another aggregate of folkloric tropes, the seventeenth-century Skull Doctor, Lustucru, and the medieval Mill of Old Wives, magical smithies and wondrous machines in which one's sharp-tongued, aging missus could be ground up or pummeled, and by such violence transformed into a nubile, subservient wife.

Warner describes one baleful French image: Lustucru (a contraction of *L'eusses-tu cru?*, "Would you have believed it?") is "forging new heads for women brought to him by their menfolk – husbands, chiefly – in order to make them into properly docile wives." Like Bluebeard's bloody chamber, the workshop of Lustucru the Skull Doctor (*Le Médecin céphalique*) is bedecked with the remains of women, row upon row of the female heads he has hacked off. The sign above the workshop displays a decapitated woman along with the words "Everything about her is good." Should we fail to catch the deeper drift of this grotesque scene, Lustucru's centrally framed anvil is inscribed: "*Touche fort sur la bouche. Elle a meschante langue* (Strike hard on the mouth: she has a wicked tongue)." Warner historicizes the popular burlesque sketches of Lustucru, "the champion of henpecked husbands, a hero among men," by pointing out that this trope emerged in response to "the intellectual ambitions of seventeenth-century aristocratic women," "the bluestockings of the Paris salons" who "criticized arranged marriages and the dynastic and social market in wives, and sought instead to cultivate equal, companionable relations between men and women."[49]

I draw attention to the kinship of *Stepford Wives'* conceit of reforging a recalcitrant wife to decapitation at the Skull Doctor's smithy not in order to impute any conscious allusions to seventeenth-century misogyny on the part of Ira Levin. Rather, if we presume Levin's unfamiliarity with Lustucru, the real issue – nonsynchronous heteroglossia – becomes even more pointed: the fantasy of disciplinary violence against women as a means of curbing their desire for self-determination has startling longevity and variety of expression. At once topical and perennial, this poetic invention is neither wholly medieval nor purely modern. It is a recurring figure of anti-feminist tirade continually tailored and reconfigured to the contestations of the moment, but also perpetually encoding chastisement of unruly women. The dark fantasy of the Skull Doctor betokens patriarchal resentment against a nascent feminist consciousness. Lustucru's popularity emerged in the context of a feminist campaign among seventeenth-century literati and aristocrats; similarly, a backlash sensibility against second wave feminism is the context for *Stepford Wives*.

The seventeenth-century Lustucru was himself derived from the medieval motif of the Mill of Old Wives, the theme of "recycling wives when their husbands are tired of them."[50] In burlesque sketches, the mill was portrayed as a mechanical process by which women considered unattractive because of their age and their stridency are first pulverized then refinished so as to emerge young, pliable, and newly amorous to the arms of waiting husbands, who show no signs of having aged. *Stepford Wives* is a dark, twentieth-century echo of the Mill of Old Wives.

Like Lustucru's hammer, which smote women on their heads and on their mouths, and the Mill of Old Wives, which ground women to a pulp in order to remake them, the grotesque notion of recycling one's tiresome wife is a conspicuous fantasy of dismemberment. Violence toward the woman's body is really directed against her mind: the Skull Doctor decapitates and "strikes hard on the mouth" to chastise the wife's "wicked tongue," and similarly in Stepford the uncanny mannequins are feeble-minded and well spoken by design. The word list which the real women are asked to speak into a recorder literalizes this fantasy of women's circumscribed expression, as the "new and improved" Stepford wives are equipped with sweet new tongues and an approved vocabulary from which the word "archaic" is conspicuously absent.

In *Stepford Wives*, the technology that reproduces women in the image of masculinist desire is not a medieval mill but audio-animatronics, pioneered by Walt Disney enterprises in the 1960s. In the novel, Joanna discovers that the serial marital homicides-cum-makeovers begin with the arrival of Dale "Diz" Coba, so nicknamed because he "worked in 'audio-animatronics', at Disneyland, helping to create the moving and talking presidential figures featured in the August number of *National Geographic*."[51] Slowly, other men, necessary accomplices, arrive in town: specialists in optics, microcomputers, sound, biochemicals, vinyl polymers, systems engineering. As male experts in industrial technologies take hold of Stepford, women's organizing in the town experiences a rapid downturn.

Joanna's psychiatrist in the novel is skeptical and slightly condescending when Joanna confides her fears of a conspiracy against women in Stepford. Striving to rationalize Joanna's paranoia, the doctor intones:

> It sounds like the idea of a woman who, like many women today, and with good reason, feels a deep resentment and suspicion of men. One who's pulled two ways by conflicting demands, perhaps more strongly than she's aware; the old conventions on the one hand, and the new conventions of the liberated woman on the other.

But Joanna does not feel her suspicions to be the delusions of a woman caught between worlds old and new; she insists that the Stepford wives resemble nothing so much as audio-animatronic attractions at the Hall of Presidents in Disneyland: "They're like . . . [those] figures of all the Presidents [in Disneyland], moving around, making different facial expressions. Abraham Lincoln stood up and delivered the Gettysburg Address; he was so lifelike."[52]

The uncanniness of the robotic Stepford wives derives from their nonsynchronous constitution: as Joanna's therapist suggested, the women of Stepford are both old *and* new, triumphs of cutting-edge engineering put to the service of vivifying an ideal Woman forged in the fires of nostalgia (as Joanna crudely puts it, "a stay-in-the-kitchen wife with big boobs and no demands.")[53] As one critic notes, nostalgia is key to the husbands' motivations for murder:

> These high-tech executives . . . grow fascinated with the manufactured nostalgia of television: grandmas with homey, clean houses and kitchens, ruffled aprons, homecooking, families staying together watching television. Nostalgia becomes demonic as the men of Stepford, with the power of the new technologies at their disposal, create perfect robot replicas of their wives, programmed to behave like the television grandmas, with which they replace their murdered wives.[54]

Disney products are closely bound up with the drive to "construct and commodify nostalgia."[55] Eric Smoodin writes: "Disney – the entrepreneur, the corporation, and all of the products – signified the homely values of family and country even while demonstrating the possibilities of the future, the inevitability of constant technological innovation."[56] Disney discourse weds a saccharine invocation of an idyllic past to the futurist lexicon of technological euphoria. The historical nonsynchronism of Disney discourse is nowhere more palpable than in audio-animatronics. In the mid-1960s, Disney's version of "Abraham Lincoln-come-alive" was a poster child for the corporation's accomplishments in the new technology. In the selfsame *National Geographic* interview Levin cited in his novel, Disney explains his deployment of cutting-edge audio-animatronics ("animation with sound, run by electronics"). The *National Geographic* reporter is awestruck by the audio-animatronic Lincoln's "chilling realism"; the "illusion was alarming."[57] Like Disney's Lincoln, the mechanical women of Stepford fascinate and frighten because of their constitutive nonsynchronism: they are both nostalgic and futuristic.

Disney-style audio-animatronics gone awry are central to the most powerful moment in the film: Joanna plunges a knife into the doll-that-was-Bobbie and the mechanical mannequin malfunctions. In a brilliantly orchestrated performance, Paula Prentiss as Bobbie becomes a veritable broken record, breaking into a repetitious, failed monologue accompanied by actions that miscarry. "How could you do a thing like that?" she asks over and over, taking one coffee cup after another off its hook, walking toward the counter, and missing it every time, so that each cup comes crashing down on the floor. Tossing one spoonful of coffee after another into the air, and twisting back and forth from the refrigerator, Bobbie says repeatedly, in a voice both wounded and insincere: "I thought we were friends." In this chilling scene of mechanical failure in a Stepford wife's spotless kitchen, we see the automatic woman, the ideal wife, as she truly is, as she was intended to be: one more appliance among others in a beautifully equipped house, of a piece with the gleaming toaster and the new fridge. She is both quintessentially archaic (a woman produced by Lustucru's smithy) and an unquestionably modern apparatus – woman retooled, updated, and instrumentalized as kitchen aid and sex gadget.

--------- Doll-doubles and Domination ---------

At the beginning of the film, Joanna, about to leave Manhattan for Connecticut, sees an incongruous sight, and takes out her camera in order to capture it on film: across the street, a man is carrying an unclothed female mannequin under his arm; her face is featureless and her eyes are covered by a swath. With hindsight, we see that this early scene combines foreshadowing and Sophoclean irony: *Stepford Wives* is a story about the disparity of knowledge-power between husbands and wives. In the city, sharp-witted Joanna notes the titillation, the peculiarity, of a man clasping a comely female dummy, but in Stepford she is too deceived to see the same thing all around her until it is too late. When Walter gets in the station wagon, preparing to push off for the suburb, his daughter tells him what they have seen: "Daddy, I just saw a man carrying a naked lady!" Without missing a beat, Walter replies with a double-entendre: "Well, that's why we're moving to Stepford" – they move both to get away from the tawdriness of Manhattan and to live Pygmalion's dream.

In one sense, the Stepford wives are not so much characters as ideas interacting: they are ciphers for female submission and deadening conformity. The film's presentation of the wives as dolls facilitates this, mobilizing the semantic weight of doll figures as inauthentic for the purposes of social criticism.[58] In the comi-tragic "supermarket quadrille" at the end of the film,[59] we see the wives identically outfitted in floor-length dresses, their flawless faces framed by large summer hats (figure 8.1). Shapely and tractable, the "compulsive *hausfraus*" are more akin to superficial mannequins than they are to well-rounded people, and this allows them to embody that "constriction of meaning" that characterizes the allegorical caricature's "transformation of the real into an abstraction." It has been said that "caricature is allegorical in essence, since it strives for the simplification of character in terms of single, predominant traits."[60] This allows the Stepford wives to depart from the well-rounded characters of realist convention in order to attain the striking iconographic legibility of personified ideas: the fembots are clueless and parochial, exempla of infantilized femininity, doll-like abstractions of Woman.

Stepford's open secret relies on the capacity of a marionette to convincingly "pass" for a woman. The conventional association between dolls and femininity is not owing to the fact that mannequins mirror women, but that women are expected to fashion themselves in accordance with prevailing notions of femininity, to come as close as possible to resembling the *idea* of Woman. In the film, when Joanna first confronts the automaton masquerading as Bobbie, the doll replies: "Nothing's got me. I just wanna look like a woman. And keep the house looking decent, too." The implication, of course, is that

Figure 8.1 Joanna's audio-animatronic double joins the other *hausfraus* in a "supermarket quadrille"
(*Stepford Wives*, dir. Bryan Forbes, prod. Edgar J. Scherick, 1974)

some women do not look like a Woman, that gender does not derive from natural essence but is an exacting performance, a life-work.

The men of Stepford betray a peculiar relation to essentialism. Essentialism is defined by Elizabeth Grosz as "the attribution of a fixed essence to women," the belief that particular traits and practices – "nurturance, empathy, support, non-competitiveness and the like" – are "given," "shared in common by all women at all times" so that a woman cannot "act in a manner contrary to her essence."[61] Although the men of Stepford fashion their new wives in the visage of essentialism, their motives for matrimonial homicide in the first place betray an anti-essentialist recognition that the women in their lives are *not* much inclined to housework and to entertaining their husbands' sexual whims. That is, the husbands' serial murders are a perverse acknowledgment of the distance and difference of real women from whatever the essentialized conception of them (the *hausfrau*) entails. The murders are the husbands' harshest possible response to undeniable evidence that their wives are not universal Woman, and, further, that their wives, sympathetic as they are to the women's movement, are openly critical of this essentialized conception of femininity. The epigraph to the novel, a quotation from Simone de Beauvoir's *The Second Sex,* drives home this point:

Today the combat takes a different shape, instead of wishing to put man in a prison, woman endeavors to escape from one; she no longer seeks to drag him into the realms of immanence but to emerge, herself, into the light of transcendence. Now the attitude of the males creates a new conflict: *it is with a bad grace that the man lets her go.* (emphasis added)[62]

This epigraph suggests that the husbands of Stepford, in their palpable bad grace, their unwillingness to let go, pursue essentialism with bad faith. Although they realize that femininity is not inherent in women, this realization does not result in their abandoning essentialism, but in their insisting upon it. Thus they remake their singular wives into the same icon of womanliness; their Disneyland equivalent of the Mill of Old Wives grinds down difference to produce it as sameness. In these husbands, the Bluebeard *topos* of seriality, their signal lack of compunction toward the newcomers to whom they dispense the same death as their predecessors, is their staunchest expression of their desire to discipline gender difference into uniformity.

The doll-doubles of Stepford are a figuration for the husbands' complete subjection and annihilation of their erotic other. The thematic of domination has always been prominent in the Bluebeard tale, its apparent warnings against the foibles of feminine curiosity notwithstanding. Like *Rosemary's Baby* (Roman Polanski, 1968), another horror film drawn from an Ira Levin novel, *Stepford Wives* features a heroine whose failure to triumph over those who conspire against her is rooted in her inability to distrust her husband until it is too late. In Polanski's film, Rosemary expresses no more than passing annoyance over the marital rape that leads to the conception of the monster in her womb; maternal instincts undo her, leading her to eschew her own convictions against Satanism and agree to raise the child of the devil because it is also her own. Rosemary never once considers leaving her husband, despite the fact that he's raped her, isolated her from her friends, and prohibited her from reading books or seeing doctors of her own choosing. Ultimately *Rosemary's Baby* is not a story of her husband's Faustian compact (the devil's bargain with a struggling actor) but of an entirely more commonplace contract between man and wife, which both Levin novels consider a form of conventional bondage. Only this unquestioned, naturalized marital domination could have allowed Rosemary to carry Satan's child to term, or enabled each wife in Stepford to collude in her own undoing by speaking the entirety of standard English vocabulary into a tape recorder at a man's request. Both films use the motif of devilish conspiracy to forge a cautionary fable about what Jessica Benjamin has called "the bonds of love":

> Obedience to the laws of civilization is first inspired, not by fear or prudence, Freud tells us, but by love, love for those early powerful figures who first demand obedience. Obedience, of course, does not exorcise aggression; it merely directs it against the self. There it becomes a means of self-domination . . . It is a problem that must be defined not simply in terms of aggression and civilized constraints, but as an extension of the bonds of love.[63]

Benjamin asks, "How is domination anchored in the hearts of the dominated?"[64] In other words, what are the erotic means of subsuming resistance? Her answer: obedience, defined by Benjamin as "self-domination," is "first inspired" by love.

In this light, *Stepford Wives* can be seen as an allegory for marital domination in the context of suburban life, a chilling tale of "how domination is anchored in the hearts of the dominated." The Stepford wives have only been metaphorically murdered: the dolls are placeholders for their own utterly dominated selves, whittled into complete submission over the years (unlike the Bluebeard tale, the victims are not fresh brides but wives married about a decade) so that they no longer resemble the autonomous subjects they once were. Their city-to-suburbs move is a figure for a feminized movement away from a public or workplace life toward permanent retirement in the private sphere, a withdrawal into the atomized world of home-keeping and child-rearing, the contraction of the woman's previously wider social circle into the confines of the home or the parochial community.

This is what makes the Stepford wives as disturbing as they are ridiculous. On a literal level, the robotic Stepford wives are so many doubles for women, serial variants of the same sexually available, housework-inclined woman, a perverse simulacra of the women who are made equivalent by their death-transformation into the same mechanical wife. But if *Stepford Wives* has entered popular vocabulary as a cautionary fable for conformity, it is because its figure of feminine doubling, more than its reworking of the folkloric tales of serial *lustmord* (sex murder), hints that the heroines are not entirely antithetical to the compulsive *hausfraus* that replace them. Indeed, as Keppler suggests, the double as a second self is never wholly different from the first identity. Stepford sounds a note of admonition for women: not only to warn against male conspiracy but to counsel against conformity and complacent submission to the breadwinner, which marriage and economic wealth might encourage. (In Perrault's "Bluebeard" the young heroine, after having been wined and dined in grand manner at the monster's estate, agrees to marry him because his wherewithal has made her think that he "had not so very blue a beard after all.")[65]

Joanna and Bobbie are stay-at-home, married women very much in danger of becoming like the "*hausfraus*" they disparage: insular wives with no interests outside home and family. This common ground between the heroines and the *hausfraus* they so detest frames *Stepford Wives* as a story about the marital dynamics of a generation of upper-class, white women at the height of mainstream awareness of the women's movement in the United States. On this semantic register, *Stepford Wives* reads less like a Bluebeard tale about a man's capacity to turn on his wife, and more like an object lesson on how, for aggregated reasons, women enable their own subjection.

In Forbes's film, Joanna's death at the hands of her mechanical double (figure 8.2) is rendered via a shot/reverse-shot: to her horror, the heroine's gaze discloses the monster to be another self. This may be read allegorically as a metaphor for a woman's banal marital demise, a figuration for her succumbing to tendencies in herself which collude in her own oppression, in exchange for creature comforts and male companionship. The novel contrasts the wealthy, duped women of Stepford with an outsider, a working woman named Mary who can see at first glance that the Men's Association is the culprit in the town, changing women's quality of life for the worse: "If my old man was alive he'd have to knock me on the head before I'd let him join!,"[66] she cries, highlighting by contrast the avowed feminists' deference to their husbands, whose membership of the Men's Association they protested against but nevertheless accepted.

Figure 8.2 In the film version, Joanna (above) meets her doom at the hands of her double (below)
(*Stepford Wives*, dir. Bryan Forbes, prod. Edgar J. Scherick, 1974)

The story of Stepford's Bluebeard husbands, tyrannical spouses who do away with their wives in the name of forcing them to submit to their will, does seem to be an allegory for what Benjamin incisively calls the "undertow" of the master–slave dynamic of domination in "'ordinary' intimate relationships."[67] But, in light of her discussion of domination, the question we are prompted to ask of the Stepford husbands is why they should find the lifelessness, inhumanity, and complete numbing obedience of their wives so pleasurable; where is Benjamin's expectation of the master who, having utterly destroyed his partner by bending her to his will, feels a terrible pang of isolation?[68]

To my mind, there are two ways to consider this question in *Stepford Wives*: first, the narrative may be understood as an allegory for the numbing interpersonal dynamics of marriages in which complementarity has given way to a polarization of power. Such a reading would suggest that *Stepford Wives* is too simple a figuration of erotic domination, and Bluebeard, who searched repeatedly for a female other rather than taking up with a corpse, counts as a more textured rendering of how the wife as erotic other can become dehumanized by patriarchal husbands. Lewis writes of Bluebeard's loneliness as an erotic tyrant: "Yet insofar as, lifeless, they [his dead wives] cannot furnish him the active recognition he sought to secure from wifely obedience, his relation to them leads to the disappointment that rekindles his search for satisfaction through marriage."[69]

One might, however, take another view, and see *Stepford Wives* as a categorical departure from the Bluebeard tale: while the folkloric killer may have disposed of his wives, he never took up residence with a sex doll. The fact that the husbands in Stepford do not seem to have any misgivings about taking a lifeless object for a life-long erotic companion suggests that for these men their wives were never fully people in the first place. Personhood, otherness, recognition, and assertion were never things they desired from women because their wives were never, in their eyes, social agents: their social others, those they engaged in the dialectic of mutuality, were other men. In the novel, Joanna expresses surprise that Dale "Diz" Coba worked at Disneyland because "You don't look like someone who enjoys making people happy." To this Diz replies coldly, "How little you know."[70] In the face of his repetitious brutality against women, Diz can only earnestly maintain that he enjoys making people happy if he has never seen a woman as a person in the first place. The serial-killing husbands' dehumanizing logic of misogyny is the secret of Stepford's bloody chamber. The compulsive *hausfraus* of Stepford are, in fact, the remains of the women they resemble in their husbands' eyes, always-already less than human, always-already a means to be mastered and instrumentalized. This is the secret that the wives of Stepford, each in her turn, preserves by embodying.

Paranoia in the Town that Time Forgot

"Something fishy is going on here! We're in the Town that Time Forgot!"
Bobbie, after abortive attempts at women's organizing in Stepford.[71]

The Bluebeard tale has often been framed as a diatribe against female curiosity, but, insofar as the heroine survives *despite* her inquisitiveness, "Bluebeard" and its variants may be seen to uphold the generative effects of female suspicion. (Curiosity, I would argue, is collocated with suspicion and paranoia due to their shared semantic element: inquisitiveness is prompted by a felt imbalance in knowledge that one seeks to rectify.) Indeed, one may well argue that Joanna and her predecessors die in Stepford, as

Bluebeard's wife did not, because they did not exhibit enough of the latter's incorrigible curiosity. Bluebeard's wife knew enough to fear her husband and called out to her sister to ask whether rescue was on its way; but all the Stepford wives except for Joanna do not think to suspect their husbands, to their own great loss.

Terrified and paranoid, but nonetheless stout-hearted and resourceful, Joanna in *Stepford Wives* shares a certain kinship with the female victim-hero of horror and exploitation films, the protagonist that Carol Clover calls the Final Girl. The hold of the Final Girl on the feminist imagination has everything to do with (as Clover put it) this figure's nuanced embodiment of women's anger as well as their fear. Clover is correct to posit the Final Girl's debt to the mainstreaming of feminist discourses: "the female victim-hero['s] . . . status in both roles has indeed been enabled by 'women's liberation.' Feminism, that is, has given a language to her victimization and a new force to the anger that subsidizes her own act of horrific revenge."[72] The heroine-victim is evidence of the historical malleability of even the most rigidly and normatively gendered genres: the woman's movement is troped in the horror heroine's indignation at her vulnerability in the face of attack, and in her concomitant resolve to empower herself and turn the tables on her persecutor.

Clover's Final Girl, "the one who did not die," is an admixture of qualities. As the last remaining survivor of an horrific ordeal — the slasher film, like the plot of serial homicide in *Stepford*, is a longevity narrative powered by an engine of relentless attrition — the Final Girl has survived the longest and learned the most, and as such is more intensely terrified than any other character. She is a wellspring of resourcefulness and slumbering strength, which, once unleashed, vanquishes the monster through means more violent than his own (think of Ripley in the *Alien* tetralogy, or the heroine of the *Texas Chainsaw Massacre* [Tobe Hooper, 1974]). As grim as her nemesis, yet exhibiting extreme vulnerability and paranoia, the Final Girl is quintessentially a shaken woman brandishing a chainsaw. (In *Stepford Wives*, Joanna bests her husband with a ski pole.)

For Halberstam, the Final Girl survives primarily because of her "productive fear:"

> [I]t is precisely the fear of being watched, the consciousness that she may be being watched, that saves the woman and allows her to look back. The women who are not worried about being watched within the horror film very often die; the alternative to paranoia in horror films very often is nothing more than a gullibility and a kind of stupid naïveté.[73]

The productive paranoia that Halberstam reads in the Final Girl is thus a specific articulation of the kind of fruitful disquiet that is often present in grim fantastic narratives. But Halberstam has incisively shown how, in an era profoundly affected by feminism, such necessary apprehension, in a woman, becomes charged with cautious knowledge about a strong woman's precarious footing in patriarchal society.

The panic-stricken heroine of *Stepford Wives* exhibits the Final Girl's feminist paranoia, her productive, life-preserving fear, and her folkloric cunning. Why, then, does she die? Why does she not, like her cousins in folklore or in the slasher film, counter her husband's death-artistry with a symmetrical escape-artistry? I believe Joanna's undoing lies in her inability to grasp the nonsynchronism of patriarchial dynamics: she disparages the Stepford wives and husbands as anachronistic, failing to appreciate the contradictions which make it possible to be both nostalgic and fully in the present (in the case of the husbands), simultaneously modern women and old-fashioned *hausfraus* (in the case of the wives). Like Bobbie, who calls Stepford "the Town that Time Forgot" (Bobbie, even more paranoid than Joanna, like her, fails to survive), Joanna sees the Men's Association and their docile wives as relics of the past. In one scene in the film, Joanna tries to convince a Stepford wife to come to their women's group meeting:

> JOANNA: Doesn't it bother you that the most important organization in Stepford is sexually archaic?
> MARIE: Archaic?
> BOBBIE: Old fashioned! Out of date!
> MARIE: Does it ever bother me? . . . No, it doesn't.

The word "archaic" has a special importance in the film: in the climactic scene between Bobbie and Joanna, Joanna's stabbing of her friend is preceded by her realization that Bobbie no longer knows what "archaic" means. "It's not on the word list, is it?" says Joanna, realizing. For Joanna and the narration, this lapse of vocabulary is telling because it means that the insipid wives in Stepford do not know what they themselves are: sexually archaic, exponents of old-fashioned, out-of-date sexual roles. In the novel, Joanna is surprised to note that the Men's Association is not, in fact, a traditional institution, but an organization newer than the women's club, not yet seven years old. Joanna is mistaken to conceive of the husbands as a simple anachronism, for in their nonsynchronous deployment of technological wizardry in the service of nostalgia, and in the nascence of their response to the contemporary women's movement, they are, in fact, a pernicious social force in the present. In their historicist derision of the Men's Association, our heroines fail to see that patriarchal discourses are never simply retrograde, that modernity does not always only banish, but can often collude with, differing historical forms of misogyny.

In the late seventeenth century, Charles Perrault appended a campy moral to "Bluebeard," one which worked to undermine the warnings against feminine curiosity that the tale was often understood to provide:

> If one takes a sensible point of view
> And studies this grim story,
> He will recognize that this tale
> Is one of days long past.
> No longer is the husband so terrifying,
> Demanding the impossible,

Being both dissatisfied and jealous;
In the presence of his wife he is now gracious enough,
And no matter what colour his beard may be
One does not have to guess who is master![74]

In this reflexive, self-ironic epilogue, Perrault shifts the emphasis from moralizing to temporalizing. The narrator tells us that "overbearing husbands" like Bluebeard, and their harsh "abuse of male privilege,"[75] no longer exist: there is, then, no longer any need to revisit this outdated cautionary fable regarding women's vulnerability in marriage. As one scholar remarks, in Perrault's "historicizing commentary," the moral "no longer claims to apprehend the sense of the events; rather, from its transcendental standpoint it claims only its anachronism, its complete obsolescence."[76] Yet along with twentieth-century serial killers and other inheritors of the Bluebeard narrative structure, *Stepford Wives* belies Perrault's droll insistence that patriarchal domination in marriage is a thing of the past. Rather, *Stepford Wives* as a Bluebeard narrative conveys the nonsynchronous texture of gender norms, a field of contestation characterized not by obsolescence, but by a discontinuous collocation of essentialism, feminism, and patriarchal rejoinders to the women's movement.

Halberstam has insightfully commented that the horror audience often "worries that what it consumes will later consume it."[77] Indeed, despite three decades' distance from the novel and the film, "Stepford" continues to command immediate legibility as a cipher for "narrow self-definition" and "dim conformity," invoked as a warning against Martha Stewart fans, planned communities, and the fitness-obsessed, upper-class culture of certain gay communities. One acerbic critic writes: "contemporary gay life and lifestyle is total Stepford;"[78] another notes: "It didn't take long for the term 'Stepford Wife' to go into the lexicon as shorthand for a clueless, zombie-like lady of leisure with an empty head."[79]

Stepford Wives is more than an indictment against retrograde male malevolence: it is a memorable warning against historically tenacious forms of internalized domination and upper-class complacency. Its nightmare vision is not easily shaken off, which may account for its longevity in the popular imagination. Like Perrault's moral to "Bluebeard," *Stepford Wives* begins by framing patriarchy as a throwback to less sexually enlightened times, but I have argued that it ends by insinuating the nonsynchronous tenacity of sexual oppression. Erotic domination subtends the essentializing logic of serial murder and is well served by its fatalistic temporality; as the Stepford fembots demonstrate, it thrives in futuristic fantasies nostalgic for feminine marionettes.

Acknowledgment

I am extremely grateful to Bibi Tinio for her illuminating comments on an earlier version of the essay that forms this chapter.

Serial Time: Bluebeard in Stepford

Chapter 8

Bliss Cua Lim

Chapter 8

1   Ira Levin, *The Stepford Wives* (Greenwich, CT: Fawcett, 1972), pp. 17–19.

2   See Ernst Bloch, "Nonsynchronism and the Obligation to its Dialectics (1932)," *New German Critique* 11 (Spring 1977): 22. For a fuller discussion of my reformulation of this term, see Bliss Cua Lim, "Spectral Times: The Ghost-film as Historical Allegory," *Positions: East Asia Cultures Critique* 9 (2) (Fall 2001), 287–329.

3   Sigmund Freud, "The Uncanny (1919)," in James Strachey, in collaboration with Anna Freud (ed.), *The Standard Edition of the Complete Psychological Works of Sigmund Freud*, vol. 17 (1917–1919) "An Infantile Neurosis and Other Works" (London: Hogarth Press, 1955), p. 247.

4   By historicism, I mean a linear, universal, and evolutionary view of history. Dipesh Chakrabarty defines historicism as "the idea that things develop in historical time, that this time is empty and homogeneous, that history is layered and contains what Marx called the 'unvanquished remnants of the past' . . . [It] consists in a very particular understanding of the question of contemporaneity: the idea that things from different historical periods can exist in the same time (the so-called simultaneity of the non-simultaneous) but belong to different worlds. Thus we may have a 'medieval' object before us, but it is [a] relic from a past world that is no longer there. One could, in historicism, look at peasants in the same way: as survivals from a dead world." Chakrabarty underscores the pernicious ethical implications of historicism: it enables one to deny the contemporaneousness of others, positioning them as backward or anachronistic. See Dipesh Chakrabarty, "The Time of History and the Times of the Gods," in Lisa Lowe and David Lloyd (eds), *The Politics of Culture in the Shadow of Capital* (Durham, NC: Duke University Press, 1997), pp. 48–50.

5   Julia Kristeva, "Word, Dialogue and Novel" (1966), trans. Alice Jardine, Thomas Gora, and Leon S. Roudiez, in Toril Moi (ed.), *The Kristeva Reader* (New York: Columbia University Press, 1986), pp. 36–7.

6   M. M. Bakhtin, "Discourse in the Novel," trans. Caryl Emerson and Michael Holquist, in Michael Holquist (ed.), *The Dialogic Imagination: Four Essays by M. M. Bakhtin* (Austin: University of Texas Press, 1981), p. 291.

7   Robert Stam, Robert Burgoyne, and Sandy Flitterman-Lewis, *New Vocabularies in Film Semiotics* (London: Routledge, 1992), p. 204.

8   Kristeva, "Word, Dialogue and Novel," p. 37.

9   Bakhtin, "Discourse in the Novel," p. 293.

10 Dudley Andrew, "Adaptation," in James Naremore (ed.), *Film Adaptation* (New Brunswick, NJ: Rutgers University Press, 2000), p. 31.

11 Robert Stam, "Beyond Fidelity: The Dialogics of Adaptation," in James Naremore (ed.), *Film Adaptation* (New Brunswick, NJ: Rutgers University Press, 2000), p. 54.

12 See, for example, Henry Jenkins, "Star Trek Rerun, Reread, Rewritten: Fan Writing as Textual Poaching," in C. Penley et al. (eds), *Close Encounters: Film, Feminism, and Science Fiction* (Minneapolis, MN: University of Minnesota Press, 1991), pp. 171–204.

13 Bakhtin, "Discourse in the Novel," pp. 273–4.

14 Kristeva, "Word, Dialogue and Novel," pp. 36–7.

15 Carol J. Clover, *Men, Women and Chainsaws: Gender in the Modern Horror Film* (Princeton, NJ: Princeton University Press, 1992), pp. 10–11.

16 Charles Perrault's and Marie-Jeanne L'Héritier's versions in the 1690s, the Grimms' in 1810, and the operas of Maurice Maeterlinck/Paul Dukas and Béla Bartók in the early twentieth century, to name a few. See Marina Warner, *From the Beast to the Blonde: On Fairy Tales and their Tellers* (New York: The Noonday Press, 1994), p. 268.

17 Warner, *From the Beast to the Blonde*, p. 241.

18 Ibid., p. 269.

19 Casie Hermansson, "Reflecting Revision: Bluebeard and the Uncanny," paper presented at a panel on "The Uncanny in Contemporary Horror" at the Eighteenth International Conference on the Fantastic in the Arts, Fort Lauderdale, March 19, 1997, p. 2.

20 Philip Lewis, *Seeing Through the Mother Goose Tales: Visual Turns in the Writings of Charles Perrault* (Stanford: Stanford University Press, 1996), p. 198.

21 "*Pour ce petit cabinet, je vous défends d'y entrer, et je vous le défends de telle sorte, que s'il vous arrive de l'ouvrir, il n'y a rien que vous ne deviez attendre de ma colère.*" Charles Perrault, *Contes*, ed. Marc Soriano (Paris: Flammarion, 1989), p. 258, trans. by and quoted in Lewis, *Seeing Through the Mother Goose Tales*, pp. 207–8.

22 Warner, *From the Beast to the Blonde*, p. 244.

23 Charles Perrault, "Blue Beard," in *Perrault's Complete Fairy Tales*, trans. A. E. Johnson et al. (London: Penguin, 1961), p. 73.

24 James M. McGlathery, *Fairy Tale Romance: The Grimms, Basile, and Perrault* (Urbana, IL: University of Illinois Press, 1991), p. 71.

25 Marina Warner, *The Absent Mother, or Women Against Women in the "Old Wives' Tales"*, lecture delivered as Tinbergen Professor at the Erasmus University Rotterdam, Faculty of Societal History and Study of the Arts, on January 18, 1991 (Hilversum: Verloren, 1991), pp. 38–9.

26 "[F]eminism and the fairytale have been strongly associated . . . in the writings of the French 'prècieuses' Cathèrine d'Aulnoy, Gabrielle-Suzanne de Villeneuve, and Jeanne-Marie Leprince de Beaumont, who all campaigned in their different ways for women's greater independence, and against arranged marriages through their fairytales." Warner, *Absent Mother*, p. 23.

27 Stepford was not explicitly identified as Connecticut in Levin's novel; the specificity of setting is something injected by director Bryan Forbes, who shot the film in Westport, Connecticut. When interviewed, Forbes maintained, "I didn't shoot in any sets at all. I didn't build any sets. That's Connecticut – the white picket fences, the manicured lawns, etc. etc. I wanted to keep that normality." *The Stepford Life: Interviews with Director Bryan Forbes, Producer Edgar J. Sherick, and Stars Katharine Ross, Paula Prentiss, Nanette Newman and Peter Masterson* (dir. David Gregory, 2001), *The Stepford Wives* Silver Anniversary Edition DVD (dist. Anchor Bay Entertainment, Inc., 2001).

28 Levin, *The Stepford Wives*, pp. 12–13.

29 Ibid., p. 22.

30 Ibid., pp. 70–1.

31 Susan Brownmiller writes: "I wasn't among them, but according to a gossipy report in the *New York Times*, Betty Friedan, the mother of us all, walked out in a huff, and Lois Gould, whose novel 'Such Good Friends' had been a 1971 screen hit, pronounced it 'junk.' Rattling her sabers in the *New Yorker*, the rambunctious film critic Pauline Kael, no friend of feminism, took an opposite tack and eviscerated 'Stepford' with words like 'boobish' and 'cruddy' in a passionate defense of hardworking, misunderstood men." See Susan Brownmiller,

Serial Time: Bluebeard in Stepford

Chapter 8

"Domestic Engineering: A Feminist Deconstructs *The Stepford Wives*," AMC About the Movies (available at http://amc.thoughtbubble.com/about/stepfordwives1.html).

32 Levin, *The Stepford Wives*, p. 102.

33 For Tzvetan Todorov, the fantastic appears in the instant when one nearly believes, but does not fully believe; when one nearly rejects, without entirely dismissing, that event which scandalizes one's frames of reference. In his view, hesitation lies at the core of the fantastic: "'I nearly reached the point of believing': that is the formula which sums up the spirit of the fantastic. Either total faith or total incredulity would lead us beyond the fantastic: it is hesitation which sustains its life." Tzvetan Todorov, *The Fantastic: A Structural Approach to a Literary Genre*, trans. Richard Howard (Ithaca, NY: Cornell University Press, 1975), p. 31.

34 Hermansson, "Reflecting Revision," pp. 2–3.

35 Ibid., p. 2.

36 Lewis, *Seeing Through the Mother Goose Tales*, pp. 213–14.

37 Roland Barthes, *Camera Lucida: Reflections on Photography*, trans. Richard Howard (New York: Hill and Wang, 1981), pp. 78–9, 96–7.

38 Johannes Fabian, "Of Dogs Alive, Birds Dead, and Time to Tell a Story," in John Bender and David E. Wellbery (eds), *Chronotypes: The Construction of Time* (Stanford: Stanford University Press, 1991), p. 192.

39 Lewis, *Seeing Through the Mother Goose Tales*, p. 212.

40 Mark Seltzer astutely remarks that the emergence of the category "serial killer" in the mid-1970s is a "naming event" possessed of "its own internal 'torque.' It involves the positing of a category or type of person as a sort of point of attraction around which a range of acts, effects, fantasies and representations then begin to orbit." One aspect of the serial-killer profile with which actual serial killers have come to "over-identify" is the notion of "abnormal normality." One self-confessed serial killer described himself as "an average-looking person with a family, job, and home, just like yourself." In popular discourses on the serial killer, it is this typicality, this "sheer ordinariness," that makes the idea of serial killers so unnerving. Mark Seltzer, "The Serial Killer as a Type of Person," in Ken Gelder (ed.), *The Horror Reader* (London: Routledge, 2000), pp. 97–9.

41 Max Lüthi, *Once Upon a Time: On the Nature of Fairy Tales*, trans. Lee Chadeayne and Paul Gottwald, introduction by Francis Lee Utley (Bloomington, IN: Indiana University Press, 1976), p. 30.

42 Levin, *The Stepford Wives*, pp. 113, 131.

43 For Warner, folktales are distinguished by their cautionary fatalism. See Warner, *Absent Mother*, pp. 18–19.

44 A character's internal monologue in the guise of narrator's discourse, for example, "Was she dreaming?" See Dorrit Cohn, *Transparent Minds: Narrative Modes for Presenting Consciousness in Fiction* (Princeton, NJ: Princeton University Press, 1978).

45 Keppler argues that fate opposes "Timelessness to Time" – fatalism refutes an understanding of time as simple forward progression. For him, fatalistic time is a nonsynchronous "all-at-onceness." C. F. Keppler, *The Literature of the Second Self* (Tucson: University of Arizona Press, 1972), pp. 196–8.

46 William Goldman, *Adventures in the Screen Trade: A Personal View of Hollywood and Screenwriting* (New York: Warner Books, 1983), pp. 203–7 (available at http://www.gynoid.com/goldman.htm).

47   Elizabeth Grosz, "Sexual Difference and the Problem of Essentialism (1989)," in *Space, Time, and Perversion: Essays on the Politics of Bodies* (New York: Routledge, 1995), pp. 50–3.

48   Marina Warner, "Women Against Women in the Old Wives' Tale," in Duncan Petrie (ed.), *Cinema and the Realms of Enchantment* (London: British Film Institute, 1993).

49   Warner, *From the Beast to the Blonde*, p. 29. See p. 28 for an eighteenth-century rendering: a woodcut from Normandy showing the Skull Doctor at work in his smithy.

50   Ibid., pp. 43–4. See p. 43 for a nineteenth-century Danish woodcut of the Mill of Old Wives.

51   Levin, *The Stepford Wives*, p. 153.

52   Ibid., pp. 146–7.

53   Ibid., p. 162.

54   E. B. Daniels, "Nostalgia: Experiencing the Elusive," in Don Ihde and Hugh J. Silverman (eds), *Descriptions* (Albany, NY: State University of New York Press, 1985), pp. 77–8.

55   Eric Smoodin, "Introduction: How to Read Walt Disney," in Eric Smoodin (ed.), *Disney Discourse: Producing the Magic Kingdom* (New York: Routledge, 1994), pp. 1, 10.

56   Ibid., p. 10.

57   Robert De Roos, "The Magic Worlds of Walt Disney (1963)," in Eric Smoodin (ed.), *Disney Discourse: Producing the Magic Kingdom*, reprinted from *National Geographic*, August 1963, pp. 159–207 (New York: Routledge, 1994), pp. 65–6.

58   On the doll as a metaphor for subjective inauthenticity and lack of autonomy, see my article, "Dolls in Fragments: *Daisies* as Feminist Allegory," *Camera Obscura* 47 16.2 (Fall 2001), 37–77.

59   Brownmiller, "Domestic Engineering," n.p.

60   Angus Fletcher, *Allegory: Theory of a Symbolic Mode* (Ithaca, NY: Cornell University Press, 1964), pp. 32–4.

61   Grosz, "Sexual Difference," p. 48.

62   Simone de Beauvoir, *The Second Sex*, quoted in Levin, *The Stepford Wives*, p. 5.

63   Jessica Benjamin, *The Bonds of Love: Psychoanalysis, Feminism, and the Problem of Domination* (New York: Pantheon Books, 1988), p. 5.

64   Ibid.

65   Perrault, "Blue Beard," p. 71.

66   Levin, *The Stepford Wives*, p. 79.

67   Benjamin, *The Bonds of Love*, p. 65.

68   For Benjamin, human relationships are characterized by a dialectic of assertion and recognition; when the relations are mutual, these two terms exist in a reciprocal balance. Domination is the opposite of mutuality: it is the polarization of these two terms, so that one partner in the dynamic exhibits pure assertion (the master) while the other exists only to recognize him (the slave). Domination and submission are a breakdown of necessary tension between self-assertion and mutual recognition that allows self and other to meet as equals. Domination, in polarizing assertion and recognition, dehumanizes the person who only ever submits; the master finds the recognition, however total, to be unsatisfying because it does not emerge from a true other. The complete dependency and recognition-without-assertion of the slave dehumanizes her; on his part, the master finds himself acutely alone "because the person he is with is no person at all." Benjamin, *The Bonds of Love*, p. 53.

69   Lewis, *Seeing Through the Mother Goose Tales*, p. 211.

70   Levin, *The Stepford Wives*, p. 53.

71 Ibid., p. 42.

72 Clover, *Men, Women and Chainsaws*, p. 4.

73 Judith Halberstam, *Skin Shows: Gothic Horror and the Technology of Monsters* (Durham, NC: Duke University Press, 1995), pp. 124–7.

74 Perrault, "Blue Beard," p. 78.

75 Warner, *From the Beast to the Blonde*, p. 244.

76 Winfried Menninghaus, *In Praise of Nonsense: Kant and Bluebeard*, trans. Henry Pickford (Stanford: Stanford University Press, 1999), p. 69.

77 Halberstam, *Skin Shows*, p. 159.

78 Tim Teeman, "Down with the Stepford Gays," *New Statesman* 129/128: 4427 (March 12, 1999), 23–4 (available at http://newfirstsearch.oclc.org). For other examples of Stepford's valence in popular media, see Christina Shea, "Planned Communities: The Good Life or Stepford Revisited?," *USA Today* (September 1999) (available at http://newfirstsearch.oclc.org).

79 Brownmiller, "Domestic Engineering," n.p.

Bliss Cua Lim

Chapter 8

Chapter 9

Boyz N the Hood Chronotopes: Spike Lee, Richard Price, and the Changing Authorship of *Clockers*

Paula J. Massood

Nothing is experienced by itself, but always in relation to its surroundings, the sequences of events leading up to it, the memory of past experiences... Every citizen has had long associations with some part of his city, and his image is soaked in memories and meanings.

Kevin Lynch, *The Image of the City*[1]

In the closing scene of Spike Lee's *Clockers* (1995), Strike Dunham – the film's young, ulcer-prone protagonist – escapes from the life-threatening dangers of urban life. In the film's final frames we witness both an emigration and a migration as Strike concurrently leaves behind his past and heads toward a more promising future. This in and of itself is neither new nor innovative. We are familiar with Hollywood's happy endings, designed to let audiences walk out of the theater with a satisfying feeling of narrative closure. The way the scene is shot adds to its redemptive qualities: infused with a golden light, Strike heads into the sunset before the screen fades to black.

In a variety of press releases and interviews, Lee stated that he wanted *Clockers* to be more than just another "hood" film: what he referred to as the "black gangster, hip-hop shoot-'em-up . . . drug genre."[2] One of Lee's primary concerns was to differentiate *Clockers* from hood films such as John Singleton's *Boyz N the Hood* (1991) and the Hughes Brothers' *Menace II Society* (1993), films with similar subject matter and settings. As Lee stated after the film's release, "It was always our intention that if we succeeded with this film, that this might be the final nail in the coffin and African-American filmmakers would try telling new stories."[3] While *Clockers* is wholly self-conscious of, and reliant upon, the hood films immediately preceding it, the film occupies a different position from those with which it is most closely aligned. For instance, its self-conscious appropriation and revision of many of the conventions of the hood film problematizes a clear-cut alignment of it with earlier examples of the genre. Its much more self-consciously reflexive use of hood conventions is apparent in the film's narrative, style, and shifting character identification. *Menace II Society* is arguably also a self-referential text, especially in its conscious appropriation of many of the narrative elements of *Boyz N the Hood*, yet while *Menace*'s self-consciousness accepts hood conventions while expanding upon them, *Clockers* deconstructs and problematizes them.

But rather than examine all the ways in which *Clockers* either succeeds or fails to fulfill generic requirements, here I would like to begin from the understanding that *Clockers*'s iconography resembles that of a number of other films set in African American urban spaces in the 1990s. But, I would also suggest that Lee broadens this urban sign system in discrete ways. In fact, Lee's film fuses the hood with the traces of another time and space by linking contemporary Brooklyn to an African American past, and he accomplishes this linkage through specific changes in Richard Price's original story. This chapter focuses on the ways in which Lee's adaptation of *Clockers* reconsiders and revisions the hood film, in particular, and cinematic representations of the African American city in general.[4] In the process, I examine how the film's spatiotemporal parameters dialogue with the traces of another time and space through the motif of the train. The presence of the train in *Clockers*, I would argue, inserts the tropes of migration, mobility, and settlement in the narrative in order to reinsert history, especially African American history, into a dialogue with contemporary African American filmmaking. But unlike more identifiably "historical" films, such as Mario Van Peebles's *Posse* (1993) and Bill Duke's *Hoodlum* (1997), *Clockers* is set in a contemporary location and uses the conventions of a contemporary genre. Ironically, this is accomplished primarily by referencing the mode of transportation so central to the establishment of an urban black population.

A knowledge of the production circumstances of *Clockers* clarifies the significance of Lee's role in the final product. *Clockers* was adapted from Richard Price's novel of the same name. The novel focused on the experiences of two very different characters: Strike, a small-time drug dealer, and Rocco Klein, a New Jersey homicide detective. Both men are brought together when Rocco is assigned to investigate the murder of a local drug-dealer. The original story was optioned by Martin Scorsese, with Robert De Niro slated to star as Rocco. Price, already well known for other scripts based on his novels, adapted the screenplay. When Scorsese and De Niro left the project to work on *Casino*, Lee was hired to direct, with Scorsese continuing his involvement as co-producer. Lee, as co-producer, rewrote the script, significantly altering the film by amplifying specific elements of the novel and muting others. In these alterations and amplifications are located the most telling links to what I am calling the "hood chronotope," after Mikhail Bakhtin's concept of the literary (narrative) chronotope, and to the historical foundations of the cinematic urbanscape.

As defined by Bakhtin, a "chronotope" is a "unit of analysis for studying texts according to the ratio and nature of the temporal and spatial categories represented."[5] The chronotope functions as "materialized history," where temporal relationships are made literal by the objects, spaces, or persons with which they intersect.[6] Often a particular chronotope is linked to a certain genre or subgenre, and helps to define it. This has certainly been the case with hood films from the early 1990s, which have been characterized by their relationship to particular spaces (Los Angeles, New York) and particular times (contemporary). It is my assertion here that *Clockers* draws on elements of the hood chronotope – urban setting and contemporary time-frame (aided by sound-track, costuming, and extratextual references) – but revises them by setting up a dialogue between the hood's present and its past, a dialogue non-existent in the original novel. This chronotopic translation is visible in three of the most important modifications made to the original story, having to do with main character, setting, and conclusion.

First, in reconceptualizing the narrative, Lee focused on Strike (Mekhi Phifer), a young drug dealer, or clocker, a change from both the novel and the original screenplay. The novel alternates point of view between Strike and Rocco (Harvey Keitel). This shuttle approach helps develop the psyches of both characters and provides background informa-tion for the tension informing the pair's interactions as Rocco first investigates Victor (Strike's brother), but then changes his focus to Strike. In his screenplay, Price changed the novel's original structure by shifting primary point of view to Rocco alone. The effect was to provide Rocco with a more fully developed psychology, at the expense of Strike's, a change most likely influenced by De Niro's casting. Lee's change, however, expanded audience identification with (and thus sympathy for) a character traditionally left psychologically underdeveloped in most of the films focusing on similar protagonists, with the possible exceptions of Tre in *Boyz* and Caine in *Menace*.[7] Like Caine, Strike often seems unsympathetic. Unlike the Hughes Brothers, however, Lee wanted to more thoroughly explore the trials and tribulations, the pressures and the motives behind Strike's choice to clock rather than starting from the presumption that such a decision is made inevitably or comes "naturally."[8] Furthermore, Lee's film more fully and sympathetically acknowledges the effects of Strike's and his crew's presence on the surrounding com-munity and, in particular, on his family and his neighbors.

Clockers focuses on the same subject matter as many hood films; however, Strike's characterization – as a young, black man coming of age in the inner city – is more three-dimensional (at least with regard to his motives, doubts, and limitations) than the majority of related characterizations in that he comes equipped with a well-defined psychology. The film's more sympathetic Strike is not only charismatic but also plagued by enough of a conscience that he is literally eaten up from the inside by ulcers from the stress of his daily activities. Also, in an interesting expansion and explication of street morality, Strike becomes even more sympathetic when he has trouble carrying out orders to murder another dealer. This shift reframes the more cold-blooded characterizations of Caine, Doughboy, or Bishop from *Juice* (Ernest Dickerson, 1992), who show no remorse over similar murderous acts.

The fact that Strike is not a conventional drug-dealer is further emphasized by the scenes in which he interacts with authority figures. Unlike earlier cinematic renderings of gangsta' characters, but like Rusty Cundieff's satirical *Fear of a Black Hat* (1993),

Clockers problematizes the "hard" exterior associated with both the cinematic and musical variations of thugs.[9] Strike is relatively soft (he drinks a Yoo Hoo-like soft drink called Moo Moo rather than the ubiquitous "forties" malt liquor), he collects and plays with model trains, and, most importantly, he is often emasculated in the face of authority. In almost all of his interactions with authority figures, Strike is inarticulate (in the novel he even stutters when tense), ineffectual, and childlike, behaviors that hint at his youth and inexperience. All the authority figures complicating Strike's life, interestingly, are distanced from him by generational factors (with André the housing cop coming the closest in age), as well by the more obvious structural and ideological factors. Generational miscommunication and disappointment reside at the core of many of the tensions of hood films, with agency and neighborhood control often ceded by ineffectual elders to a younger generation. *Clockers* inverts this relationship, less as a critique of Strike than as a reinsertion of elders back into contemporary African American popular culture.

——————— Living in the City: Brooklyn's Many-storied Pasts ———————

Lee also shifts the novel's setting – the second major change – from the Roosevelt Houses in Dempsy (a fictional New Jersey location roughly based on Jersey City) to the "Nelson Mandela Houses" of Brooklyn (in actuality the Gowanus Houses, located in the Boerum Hill section of Brooklyn). Despite Lee's claim that "projects are projects," the effect of this move is quite significant.[10] First, by relocating the narrative to Brooklyn, Lee situated the film in the already storied and familiar spatial parameters of both his own films and of hood films in general. While the majority of hood films were set in Los Angeles, a few important examples, such as *Straight Out of Brooklyn* (Matty Rich, 1991) and *Juice* were located in New York City, and only one, *New Jersey Drive* (Nick Gomez, 1995), was set in New Jersey. Lee's location shift contributes to the film's already complex interweaving of references and temporalities. On the one hand, the film's frenetic camera techniques, identifiable urban location, rap-based soundtrack, up-to-the-minute fashions, and references to contemporary African American popular culture announce its affiliations with hood films and the hood chronotope, especially as developed in *Menace II Society*. But this change must also be viewed in the context of Lee's entire cinematic oeuvre, which, almost from the beginning, has explored the present in the context of the past – symbolized most often by references to particular characters' (and by extension the city's) Southern roots. This motif appears in Lee's work as early as *Joe's Bed-Stuy Barbershop: We Cut Heads*, and has continued throughout his career, most notably in *School Daze* (1988), *Do the Right Thing* (1989), *Malcolm X* (1992), and *Crooklyn* (1994). Thus, the move to Brooklyn locates *Clockers* in a particular urban history which acknowledges the effects of migration and ghettoization on black neighborhoods.

Understanding this motif requires some understanding of Brooklyn's history as an African American community, a history often overlooked in most studies of urban African

American migration as it pertains to metropolitan areas such as Los Angeles, Chicago, Detroit, and even New York City where discussion is often limited to Harlem. During the Great Migration, Harlem, especially, played a crucial role as a black city within a city – a "promised land" – for many rural migrants. However, Brooklyn also has its own concurrent history as a home for a large African American population, a result of the same demographic shifts that helped constitute Harlem. As early as the turn of the century, Brooklyn – and specifically the Bedford and Stuyvesant neighborhoods – was home to an established black, predominantly middle-class population. In addition, through the 1920s many Harlem blacks crossed the short distance to Brooklyn "seeking social mobility and escape" from the social forces that were already turning their area into a ghetto.[11] The expansion of the New York City subway system (specifically the A-train) to the borough in 1936, facilitated the migration of Harlemites to Brooklyn. This local migration, combined with the continuing addition of new arrivals from the rural South and the Caribbean, expanded the neighborhood's black population.[12] The area's demographic growth continued through the mid-century (especially with the employment offered by the Brooklyn naval yards) and into the 1980s. At this time Bed-Stuy became synonymous with black.[13] Not coincidentally, this last development also coincides with Lee's career, so much so that, in the 1980s, cinematic representations of black Brooklyn became synonymous with Spike Lee.

With the expansion of Brooklyn's African American population, the Bed-Stuy, Brownsville, and Boerum Hill sections of Brooklyn, among others, were transformed from relatively integrated neighborhoods into increasingly isolated and marginalized ones as other ethnic groups emigrated to different parts of the borough (Bensonhurst), to other New York City boroughs (Queens, Staten Island), or to the suburbs (Long Island, Westchester County, New Jersey). Property speculation, absentee landlords, and governmental disinterest in the 1960s and 1970s resulted in the destruction of the area's property values and the increasing ghettoization of the black community – a ghettoization also experienced in Los Angeles, Detroit, Chicago, and other major metropolitan areas. This was complicated by the construction and subsequent abandonment (through decreases in funding and governmental interest) of low-income housing projects, of which the Gowanus (Nelson Mandela) Houses are a prime example. As Ernest Quimby observes, "anti-blockbusting campaigns, urban renewal, and the construction of exclusively low-income housing projects . . . erode[d] the sense of community, prevent[ed] social mobility, thwart[ed] economic and political mobilization, and allow[ed] the containment and administrative manipulation of Blacks."[14] Price, himself a product of the projects, expounds a similar view. He observes: "What was amazing to me was how the projects went from launching pads for working-class families to just terminals where generations are stacked up in the same apartment because there's no place to go."[15] Both the Quimby and Price observations echo the concerns of many contemporary African American filmmakers who use similar metaphors of entrapment in depicting discrete city spaces.

All of this complexifies Lee's seemingly simple or innocent choice of relocating *Clockers* to Brooklyn, especially the area's significance as a terminal point of sorts. While it may also be true that it was cheaper and easier to shoot in Brooklyn, or that Lee was more comfortable working in a familiar location, neither factor diminishes the importance of the choice of Brooklyn as the film's setting. On the one hand, the borough is the final destination of the majority of New York's subway lines that run southeast. Brooklyn is where you get off, unless you want to head all the way back through Manhattan to Queens – though characters in *Clockers*, except for Victor (Isaiah Washington), never head in that direction.[16] As I have suggested, Brooklyn was also the end point for many who had experienced the superimposed dislocations and migrations inherent in the African diasporic experience: the Middle Passage, the South, Harlem. In this history, Brooklyn is more than just a stopover or transitional point, as places such as Memphis were for many migrants. Brooklyn is the literal end of the line after many shifts and movements. And, as Price's observation regarding the transformation of housing projects suggests, Brooklyn became a metaphorical terminal point as well, as what was once the hope of moving from the poverty of the rural South, or the urban decay of Harlem, became the stagnation of the projects and economic displacement. In this sense, the ultimate irony of all this mobility is that its end result is only entrapment.

The architectonics of *Clockers* clearly makes this point. Most of the film is shot in the projects' central courtyard, a tree- and bench-lined circular plaza with a raised concrete platform that the community has ceded to Strike, his crew, and the crack business. According to Georgia Brown and Amy Taubin, this area "is both stage and prison – an inversion of Foucault's panopticon. Trapped within it, Strike is under constant surveillance, vulnerable to aggressors who enter from all sides."[17] This aspect of the projects is also noted in the novel: "Strike scanned the canyon walls of the Roosevelt Houses. There were thirteen high rises, twelve hundred families over two square blocks, and the housing office gave the Fury [Housing Police] access to any vacant apartment for surveillance, so Strike never knew when or where they might be scoping him out."[18] Furthermore, the construction of this particular *mise-en-scène* is illustrative of Foucault's concept of the "spatialization of power," as formulated by Edward Soja, in which cultural hierarchies are mapped onto specific landscapes.[19] Here, the projects become a carceral city, where the surrounding buildings act as sentries, looking down on the activities taking place below, guarding the boundaries of the projects, and barring movement from within their perimeter.

As a socially constituted space, the Mandela Houses both reflect and refract their neighboring communities, societies, and histories. *Clockers*, especially through its focus on boundaries, indicates that the projects (and most of their residents) may abut the surrounding communities, but they are not necessarily "of" the community. True, they contain social relations that mirror the society constituting them, but the projects are roped off from the community, with most pro-filmic events occurring within their highly conscripted borders. What lies beyond the Mandela Houses is an urban frontier, not freely accessible to the characters imprisoned within the projects' visible and historic barricades. Most of the characters show little inclination or desire to leave their immediate surroundings. The majority of characters seem to have been stripped of the ability to even envision

Paula J. Massood

Chapter 9

an alternative existence. Strike and Victor differ from the other characters because they, especially Victor, can see beyond the projects. Victor works in two demeaning and underpaid jobs in order to save enough money to move his family out of the projects, a desire based on the possibility of a literal shift out of their present environment and, in a more figurative sense, for social (and economic) mobility from the underclass to the working/middle class. Strike's flight, on the other hand, is mostly imaginary; his fantasies about trains carry him away from his surroundings only in his mind. Strike does not experience real movement until the end of the film, though it is at least foreshadowed by these earlier scenes. The paradox of this situation is frustratedly articulated by André to Strike: "There's more than just these projects out there, you know. Don't you want to go someplace you've never been before? . . . you love trains but you've only ridden the subway." Here, the stasis of the projects is clearly contrasted with the movement of subways and trains. At this point, however, subways offer no real escape – a clear reversal of their role earlier in the century. It may be that Strike's knowledge of trains – and the fact that he has already moved out of the projects – will be his ticket out of the ghetto.

Before moving on to a discussion of the third change from the novel, I would like to consider the ways Lee reframes the film's city spaces in relation to the conventions of the hood chronotope. On the one hand, as already pointed out, the shift of settings brings the narrative into a closer relationship to the familiar boundaries of the hood as seen in films like *Juice, Straight Out of Brooklyn, Just Another Girl on the IRT* (Leslie Harris, 1993), and *New Jack City* (Mario Van Peebles, 1991). The *mise-en-scène* has the spatial integrity of many of its antecedent hood films, especially in the way that it calls attention to its location through prominently placed "signage," the Nelson Mandela Houses and the references to Brooklyn and "Crooklyn" being the most obvious. Yet the film reworks the hood films' emphasis on "real" space (real streets and street signs, and the calling out of specific urban areas, for example) by constructing a space that is concurrently real (shot on location) and manufactured (announced by the self-referentiality of the film's editing, camera movement, cinematography, and *mise-en-scène*). In its reworking of these conventions, *Clockers* transforms the hood chronotope into dispersed chronotopic traces, which then dialogue with other generic and historical traces or motifs. According to Gary Saul Morson and Caryl Emerson, a chronotopic motif serves as an "aura" of another genre, a reminder of another space and time.[20] In *Clockers*, the train, a reminder of another place and time, is the central chronotopic motif dialoguing with the hood.

The film's locations are indisputably recognizable to most of its targeted audience. However, it is the ways in which the film breaks down this a priori generic spatial integrity that make it interesting for my analysis, and indicate how the hood gradually diminishes in importance in black-directed films released after *Clockers* (or, alternatively, it returns as a trope or trace in a selection of these later films, for instance F. Gary Gray's *Set it Off*, 1996, and John Singleton's *Baby Boy*, 2001). As suggested earlier, almost all of the action occurs within the confines of the projects, even though the two main characters,

Rocco and Strike, are not themselves currently residents (though Strike was raised there). Most of the scenes are exterior shots, filmed on location in the projects' central plaza. The film rarely shifts to interior shots, instead centering its narrative attentions on the activity in this park-like area. In Lee's articulation of the space, especially in the opening shots, the plaza differs from more conventional renderings of inner-city space. For example, it is green, lush, and infused with a rich light that calls attention to the colors found in both the space's vegetation and the clothing worn by the clockers. Furthermore, it is lively and filled with the comings and goings of members of the community; a pleasant and ironic setting for crack entrepreneurs. Yet even in this shift away from the more dystopian and desolate urbanscape of the hood film, the plaza maintains an integrity with its real location, the Gowanus Houses. It appears to be "authentic."[21]

The film's excursions outside of this space draw attention to the constructed nature of its *mise-en-scène*, and, by relation, foreground the constructedness of representation as a whole. Lee's experimentation with filmic form is well known, and *Clockers* is no exception. In fact, *Clockers* deploys certain "signature" techniques, such as the effect of placing characters and camera on a moving dolly while taking care to keep the changing background in focus. The film foregrounds its own processes of manufacture, especially in its camera movement, editing, *mise-en-scène*, and cinematography. In particular, the variety of film stock and lighting techniques calls attention to the tactile aspect of the film's images. The film's *mise-en-scène* also draws attention to Lee's experimentation. Lee has always been known for constructing specific sets to meet his diegetic needs, a fact that provoked rather misguided criticism in the mainstream press for *Do the Right Thing* because he had changed the look of an existing city block in Bed-Stuy. In *Clockers*, the projects remain virtually untouched. It is the surrounding spaces – Ahab's, the bar, Strike's apartment, the train – that are differentiated from the Mandela Houses.

The bar and Ahab's are distinguished from Strike's apartment and the train through changes in setting, sets, and lighting. The Kool Breeze and Ahab's are defined through their relationship to pro-filmic violence: they are the sites in which violence is first planned and then performed. In effect, they enable the entire narrative in that the actions that take place in these spaces set off the remaining chain of events. Both sites, which we only see at night, are characterized by brightly lit and colorful signage – Ahab's complete with a revolving whale that blows out steam through its airhole. The spaces are also the sites of some of the film's most aggressive and virtuoso cinematography. First, Strike confronts Darryl (Steve White) before presumably murdering him. The scene is introduced by a self-referential allusion – a close-up of a tabloid headline reading "Crooklyn" – before the camera tracks back to reveal a deep-focus shot with Strike in the foreground (from a low angle) and a billboard announcing "No More Packing." Significantly, Ahab's – and this scene in particular – will be revisited in various characters' flashbacks, but with a gritty image quality diluting the hypersaturated colors of the original scene.

The Kool Breeze is also introduced by its brightly lit sign, which appears in an establishing shot prior to a cut first to television images of a rap video, and finally into the interior of the bar. Once inside, the editing and cinematography are quite conventional, with Victor and Strike framed in a two-shot as they discuss Darryl. Similar editing and cinematography are maintained when Rocco and his partner (John Turturro) enter the bar to question its patrons. In both of these examples time occurs in the narrative present and the Kool Breeze is introduced through the rap images on television. The rap images link the activities presented in the videos and malt liquor advertisements with those taking place in the bar. Later, the film returns to the bar and to Ahab's in flashbacks. In these flashbacks, the cinematography is gritty, the colors are diluted, and the rap images have disappeared.

These spaces, articulated through their relationship to violence, differ from those that are more closely associated with Strike – his apartment and the train. Strike's apartment is a run-of-the-mill tenement space, characterized by aged woodwork and walls, and installment-plan furniture. As such, the apartment is indistinguishable from other spaces of lesser narrative importance, such as Victor's apartment in the projects. Yet it is the way in which the space is shot that makes it so interesting. As in the later scenes with the train, the scenes set in the apartment are fused with a golden, glowing light, streaming through two windows in the background and suffusing everything in the middle- and foregrounds with a slight halo. But no narrative necessity dictates this use of lighting. In fact, the narrative undercuts this haloed treatment through the kinds of activities that take place in these scenes; one time Strike, in a misguided attempt at mentoring, is teaching Tyrone (Peewee Love), a neighborhood kid, how to cut and weigh crack cocaine, and the second time Strike is preparing to leave town. In both examples a direct narrative link is made with the trains, foreshadowed in these scenes but not realized until the film's conclusion. First, prior to teaching Tyrone about the drug business, Strike shows him his collection of model trains and teaches Tyrone their history, a history that will be reiterated by Tyrone to his mother at the film's conclusion. Second, when Strike is preparing to leave town, he pauses long enough to write a note to his landlord, leaving his trains to Tyrone. The rendering of the train in the film's conclusion has already been foreshadowed here.

It is only *Clockers'* cinematic articulation of the Mandela Houses – and a few other scenes (mostly street scenes, especially around Rodney's store and the police station) – that reveal the cinematographic traces of the hood chronotope. These scenes define and articulate the urbanscape, a space already identified in earlier films as the "hood." Yet, the scenes outside the boundaries of the projects show that *Clockers* does more than merely appropriate hood film conventions. Its manufacture of these heterotopic "other spaces" indicates a self-conscious attempt to suggest that the cinematic city might be more manufactured than it first appears.[22] The city might be, like Ahab's, the Kool Breeze, and Strike's apartment, an entirely constructed terrain. This sense of constructedness distinguishes *Clockers* from the "hip hop . . . drug genre." But it is at the point where the traces of the hood chronotope and Lee's self-conscious image-manufacturing start to dialogue with the train that the polyphony of the text expands to acknowledge history, especially the links between the city and African American migration.

Paula J. Massood

In classical narrative cinema the train was generally given the role of integration and linkage, of stabilization, especially in terms of American national identity: the mythology of assimilation to a "universal" American identity.[23] The significance of the shift in setting, and its relationship to what Paul Gilroy refers to, in another context, as "movement, relocation, displacement, and restlessness,"[24] is evidenced in Lee's third and most crucial change from the novel *Clockers*: Strike's fascination with trains. In the novel, Strike's interests are limited to making money and dealing drugs. He "had never really liked music. He had never cared about sports, even girls that much if he thought about it" (p. 622). Strike's world revolves solely around his relationship with Rodney and the other clockers. This conforms with the novel's strategy of splitting point of view between Strike and Rocco, together with its less sympathetic approach to Strike's character. In the film, however, Strike's hobby of collecting model trains humanizes his character: who would expect a drug dealer to have any interests outside the criminality that defines and limits him (the same criminality that defined and limited him in the novel, and that wholly limits Caine in *Menace*)? Lynne Kirby suggests that between 1880 and World War I the "cult" of toy trains "firmly linked masculinity with railroading."[25] However, she continues, African American boys "were barred" from fulfilling dreams of "glamorous railroad careers as engineers because of skin color," ironically undercutting the mythology of assimilation Kirby discusses in the comments opening this section. The most that young, black men could hope for was to become Pullman porters, though Kirby notes that this was also a position of "esteem."[26] What is interesting here is that it is Strike's hobby, rather than his gun or his drug dealing, that defines him as a man. Yet Strike's knowledgeable fascination with the history of trains was viewed as insignificant by most viewers and critics, if it was mentioned at all. For the more cynical viewers, the trains were nothing more than the enabling metaphor for the film's "rapturous" finale, or, worse, as just another detail of the *mise-en-scène*, simply an excuse for Strike's outfit of overalls at the beginning of the film.[27]

While the trains humanize Strike, they also alter the novel's conclusion. Rather than leaving town on a Greyhound bus from the Port Authority bus terminal as in the novel, the cinematic Strike flees on a train from Penn Station. The change is made more powerful by the way Lee shot the final scene: filtered with golden light and soft-focus lenses, a marked difference from the gritty cinematography constituting most of the film. The combination of Strike's hobby and *Clockers'* conclusion enables Lee to further historicize contemporary cinematic representations of the black city.[28] *Clockers'* metonymic use of trains references the interconnected histories of African American migration, the rise of inner-city ghettos, and the subsequent demise of a black middle class, and gives ironic import to Taubin's observation that "no one can escape from the past."[29] The train references the related tropes of mobility and entrapment, two of the most recurrent themes in African American cultural production in the twentieth

Chapter 9

century and in African American films from this time period, and a central theme of hood films.

To understand all this it is important that we remain aware of the complex historical role that migration has played as a central trope in African American cultural production, in particular, and the African diaspora as a whole. For Gilroy, among others, an understanding of the construction of identity, and a politics of identity, is directly related to the concepts of location and dislocation. "It would appear," he suggests, "that there are large questions raised about the direction and character of black culture and art if we take the powerful effects of even temporary experiences of exile, relocation, and displacement into account."[30] While Gilroy is discussing the influence of freely chosen travel experiences on particular individuals such as W. E. B. DuBois and Richard Wright, his observations regarding the significance of movement are relevant to the experiences of African Americans in general. The question thus becomes not only how travel affects an individual's ideological outlook and sense of self, but also how massive migration affects or transforms cultural production and reception and how both are shaped by limitations on movement and agency. In short, how have "successive displacements, migrations, and journeys (forced and otherwise) . . . come to constitute . . . black cultures' special conditions of existence"?[31]

Arthur Jafa's notion of "primal sites" is also relevant here, especially as it relates to the ways in which time, especially history, has a complex relationship to space in African American cultural production. In a review of *Menace II Society*, Jafa stresses the importance of understanding the role of primal sites in "black film practices grounded in African-American cultural assumptions." According to Jafa, primal sites are "those group experiences, such as the Middle Passage, that have determined so much of the psychic makeup of the African-American community." Furthermore, it is only through an understanding of such sites that we can begin to comprehend the ways in which African American filmmakers reconfigure "hegemonic norms into conventions and methodologies better suited to African-American expressivity."[32] In his historically informed understanding of African American aesthetics, Jafa importantly links space and time. In this attempt to define what is fundamentally a temporal metaphor, Jafa relies on spatial terms. In effect, what he accomplishes in this link of spatial and temporal boundaries is parallel to my understanding of the cinematic chronotope, especially as it pertains to representations of urban space and its relationship to black culture and history.

Keeping in mind the history of migration and how it is related to the film's Brooklyn location, Strike's fascination with trains is a particularly telling addition, especially if we understand the train as a chronotopic motif. In *Clockers'* narrative, the train forms a sort of spatiotemporal unity that fuses the history of twentieth-century African American migration, the growth of an identifiable black city space, and the ghettoization of the black city together into a single sign. In this context the train symbolizes the contradictions and contestations of African American mobility by signifying a past, a present, and – in the case of the film's conclusion – a possible future that is immeasurably intertwined with the city.

The Changing Authorship of *Clockers*

Chapter 9

Paula J. Massood

Chapter 9

It is no accident that Lee's addition of the train chronotope to *Clockers* logically helps link the film's urban present with both its urban and rural pasts. However, the train also raises important questions regarding African American mobility, both in terms of the literal movement from place to place and in the figurative sense as a symbol of African American social mobility. Mobility and entrapment have been themes in African American films from almost their very inception and have increasingly become a central thematic concern (in both film and literature), simultaneously with the increasing urbanization of the nation's black population and the city's emergence as a dystopian site, a kind of economic and social prison. In short, the focus on mobility thus becomes more pressing as the urbanscape changes from promised land to ghetto.

Like the hood films it references, *Clockers* focuses on the sense of entrapment and lack of agency that the projects' prison-like spaces engenders in its characters. Most of the characters are content to remain in the confines of the hood, living (and often) dying in the same limited spaces. In fact, they have trouble envisioning any other alternative existence. But some of the characters – Victor and Strike in particular – do look beyond the hood, and desire (in Strike's case belatedly) to escape from their surroundings. Victor and Strike thus provide the link with the second aspect of the film's concern with mobility, that which is concurrently linked to the literal mobility of escape, and to a more figurative social mobility and agency. This expands our understanding of the role of the train chronotope in the film. Not only does the train represent a form of travel – Strike's escape – but it also references social mobility, especially in the links it makes to African American history and the Pullman porter.

In this regard, I would like to return to Paul Gilroy's discussion of the train chronotope and its relationship to the Pullman porter. According to Gilroy, "the porters worked in ways that both continued patterns of exploitation established during slavery and anticipated the novel forms of debasement and humiliation associated with contemporary service work." In other words, the seeming social mobility of the porter's position was severely circumscribed. Paradoxically, the porter's movement illustrates the curiously constructed and conscripted terms of progress as experienced by African Americans – and, by extension, black diasporic peoples – in what Gilroy defines as early modernism. For in this moment of massive industrialization (of which the train and film are by-products), and its attendant opening of new frontiers, some boundaries – however much they may appear to shift – may have ultimately remained the same. For Gilroy, the history of the train presents a significant mediation of the contradictions and limitations of African American mobility, specifically as it relates to the experiences of the Pullman porter and the Jim Crow car. Gilroy identifies the porter as "an important symbol of the new opportunities and the new constraints that fell upon blacks in the 19th century."[33] In a similar way, the city symbolized new opportunities and constraints, or as Charles Scruggs has outlined, "the city as a symbol of community, of home" and "the city of brute fact in which blacks in the 20th century have had to live."[34] Porters "enjoyed" increased mobility – both physical and economic – but this was always mediated by their position as servants. And African American passengers who were not porters were segregated to the Jim Crow cars.

An important facet of the porter's existence was that his job equipped him with the often problematic ability to move between worlds – to cross borders. While serving the train's white passengers, the porter also possessed a "freedom" that allowed him to move into (though never to occupy) cars not allowed to other African American passengers. In this position, porters mediated the tension between two segregated poles. Strike's position in the narrative, because it is so closely aligned with trains and the concurrent references to migration and mobility, is similar to that of the porter, but it is a similarity that is not unproblematic. At the beginning of the film, there is little to differentiate Strike from his clocker counterparts. The murder of a local dealer linked with his boss, Rodney Little, and Victor's subsequent confession marks Strike for the unwanted attention of the homicide detectives. As Rocco and his partner increasingly interact with and harass Strike, his safety within his community and with Rodney drastically diminishes because he is increasingly forced out of this world. The detectives, Rocco in particular, purposely pursue Strike and their most effective weapon is to "out" him by talking to him in full view of the community. In effect, Strike is forced to become an unwilling and literal border-crosser, rather than just an imaginary one with his trains. But, the more he is insinuated into the detectives' world, the more his life is endangered. Ultimately, Strike's movement between the two worlds becomes the threat – he is imagined to have crossed a line – that forces Rodney to order his execution. The end result of this maneuvering is that Strike is compelled to leave town, and is rejected by his family, the community, the police, and Rodney.

Strike's experiences are indicative of the danger inherent in African American border-crossing, a danger, however, that is more fully exemplified in Victor's experiences. In a discussion focusing on Chester Himes's *A Rage in Harlem*, Manthia Diawara identifies the train's ability both to offer mobility and to contradict that which it symbolizes. As he notes:

> The train's power . . . coincides with the devaluation of Black life. The train is also powerful because of its mobility; nothing hinders its traversing of Harlem, and its movements into the white world which connotes power, economic prosperity, and freedom. Mobility empowers the train . . . and the lack of mobility constitutes a check on the freedom of Black people.[35]

Nowhere are the pressures of these contradictions more apparent than in Victor's struggles to break free.

Everyone, especially Strike, is surprised when Victor confesses to Darryl's murder. In the course of his investigation, Rocco is convinced that Strike committed the murder, not Victor, because, in Rocco's words, "Victor's a good kid; not the murdering type."

Victor is presented sympathetically throughout the narrative: a family man, he is supporting a wife, two kids, and his mother on the income from two jobs. In addition, he is trying to save enough money to move his family outside the projects by purchasing a co-op and becoming a property owner. By all accounts, Rocco is correct to look to Strike for the murder as Strike is the homeboy, the clocker, the criminal with a record.

Cracks start to appear in Victor's near-perfect façade, cracks that are directly linked to his ambitions. In the course of his investigation, Rocco hears nothing but praise for Victor. But Rocco also learns of incidents in which Victor had disputes with different young men from the neighborhood, all of whom flash large piles of cash at Victor and verbally demean him. By the film's conclusion, we learn that Victor was responsible for Darryl's death, and that the motive is what Diawara, among others, has referred to as "Black rage . . . a set of violent and uncontrollable relations in Black communities induced by a sense of frustration, confinement, and White racism."[36] In Mrs Dunham's flashback version of events, we see Victor succumb momentarily to his rage, which is then directed at Darryl, a representative of every frustration preventing Victor's dreams from coming to fruition, of every obstacle stripping him of his agency. While Darryl is the target, the cause of his death is related more to Victor's realization that his dreams of mobility are undervalued, even in his own community (or at least by the youth that control it). Strike, on the other hand, is a porter figure because he shifts between two worlds; however, unlike the porter, Strike is eventually forced to choose a new world, since he no longer fits into either. Thus, Diawara's and Gilroy's identification of the contradictions inherent in the role of the porter indicates the cultural context from which the trains in *Clockers* emerge, and establishes the train as an important primal site of African American movement.

The film concludes with golden shots of Strike riding on a train, literally heading into the sunset. These shots are intercut with images of Scientific (Sticky Fingaz), one of Strike's clockers, lying dead in a pool of his own blood, as Tyrone plays with Strike's trains (now located in his apartment) while passing on their history — Strike's legacy — to his mother. It would be easy to read this ending as overly optimistic, "rapturous," or moral. Or, one could conclude that the film lapses into a nostalgia or a pessimism "which views the city as bad."[37] But to do so would be to miss the point. To paraphrase Gilroy again, there are important questions to be raised about black culture if the effects of experiences of even temporary movement and displacement are taken into account. While Strike's train ride might lead out of the city, it signifies the themes of mobility and escape at the roots of many contemporary African American cinematic, especially hood, narratives, themes altogether absent from Price's rendering of African American experiences in the novel. To leave the city is perhaps in the final analysis not an act of nostalgia or a form of anti-urbanism, for the film does not suggest that Strike is returning to his rural roots or that he is fleeing from urban life in general. Lee's ending perhaps illustrates Gilroy's linking of "the association of self-exploration with the exploration of new territories," at least for Strike.[38] In relocating his version of events to Brooklyn, and by utilizing the train in a metonymical manner, Lee constructs a version of the contemporary African American city that concurrently acknowledges its history of migrations while avoiding the nihilism of many contemporary hood films set in similar locations. In the process of changing the novel, Lee expands the boundaries of current African American cinema and provides at least one of his protagonists with a vital resource – agency.

Acknowledgment

A longer version of this chapter entitled "Taken the A-Train: The City, the Train, and Migration in Spike Lee's *Clockers*" appears in Paula J. Massood, *Black City Cinema: African American Urban Experiences in Film* (Philadelphia: Temple University Press, 2003).

Notes

1   Kevin Lynch, *The Image of the City* (Cambridge, MA: MIT Press, 1960), p. 1.
2   Quoted in Stephen Schaefer, "Spike Makes 'Clockers' Timely," *New York Post* (August 25, 1995), 47.
3   Quoted in Jonathan Bernstein, "Spike Lee," *The Face* (December 1997), 202.
4   I am using the term "African American city" to refer to those specific areas of cities that have been historically the centers of African American residency and culture. For instance, New York City's Harlem and certain areas of Brooklyn (and Manhattan's San Juan Hill and Little Africa before them), Los Angeles's Central Avenue district and Watts, and Chicago's South Side. At issue here is the way in which the phrase demarcates more than just a specific and locatable geographic area; it also signifies black cultural *ownership* (often only symbolic) and *occupancy* of certain urbanscapes.
5   M. M. Bakhtin, *The Dialogic Imagination*, ed. Michael Holquist, trans. Caryl Emerson and Michael Holquist (Austin: University of Texas Press, 1981), p. 425.
6   Ibid., p. 247. For a discussion of the chronotope in the cinema, see Robert Stam, *Subversive Pleasures: Bakhtin, Cultural Criticism and Film* (Baltimore, MD: The Johns Hopkins University Press, 1989).
7   *Boyz* offers perhaps the 1990s' most sympathetic rendering of an inner-city African American youth. But Tre does not apply here because he neither deals nor uses drugs, nor is he involved with gangs. In fact, as a college-bound over-achiever, Tre is the epitome of the American Dream.
8   As Lee states: "I really wasn't interested in telling a cop's story. I was much more passionate about telling the story of this young African-American kid who comes from a strong family, who's gone off the straight and narrow and has turned to a life of drugs" (quoted in Bernstein, "Spike Lee," 202).
9   On this phenomenon, see Todd Boyd, *Am I Black Enough For You?: Popular Culture From the 'Hood and Beyond* (Bloomington, IN: Indiana University Press, 1997); S. Craig Watkins, *Representing: Hip Hop Culture and the Production of Black Cinema* (Chicago: University of Chicago Press, 1997); E. Michael Dyson, *Reflecting Black: African-American Cultural Criticism* (Minneapolis, MN: University of Minnesota Press, 1993); and Lisa Kennedy, "Natural Born Filmmaker: Quentin Tarantino versus the Film Geeks," *Village Voice* (October 25, 1994),

32. In Kennedy's piece, Tarantino observes: "Someone said to me at Sundance when *Reservoir Dogs* was there, 'You know what you've done, you've given white boys the kind of movies black kids get. You know like *Juice,* and . . . *Menace II Society,* looking cool, being bad, with a fuck you attitude.' "

10 Quoted in David Bradley, "Spike Lee's Inferno: The Drug Underworld," *New York Times* (September 10, 1995), 32.

11 Ernest Quimby, "Bedford–Stuyvesant," in Rita Seiden Miller (ed.), *Brooklyn USA: The Fourth Largest City in America* (New York: Brooklyn College Press, 1979), p. 229.

12 Ibid., p. 232.

13 David McCullough, *Brooklyn: And How It Got That Way* (New York: Dial Press, 1983), p. 212.

14 Quimby, "Bedford–Stuyvesant," p. 236.

15 Quoted in Laurie Werner, *USA Weekend* (September 15–17, 1995), 10–11.

16 Almost all the film's action is set in Brooklyn. In fact, the story shifts only once to another location: when Rocco visits the Manhattan boutique that had previously employed Victor as a security guard.

17 Georgia Brown and Amy Taubin, "Clocking In: Two Critics Rate Spike Lee's Ultimate Hood Movie," *Village Voice* (September 19, 1995), 71.

18 Richard Price, *Clockers* (Boston: Houghton Mifflin, 1992), p. 4. Subsequent quotations in text will be referenced by page number to this edition.

19 Edward Soja, *Postmodern Geographies: The Reassertion of Space in Critical Social Theory* (New York: Verso, 1989), p. 21.

20 Gary Saul Morson and Caryl Emerson, *Mikhail Bakhtin: Creation of a Prosaics* (Stanford: Stanford University Press, 1990), p. 375.

21 The film's concern with the intersections between the manufactured and the real are introduced in its opening credits, which appear over photographic recreations of the victims of actual drug-related homicides. This, more than Singleton's statistics opening *Boyz N the Hood,* graphically points to the dangers of inner-city living.

22 Michel Foucault, "Of Other Spaces," trans. Jay Miskowiec, *Diacritics* 16: 1 (Spring 1986), 24.

23 Lynne Kirby, *Parallel Tracks: The Railroad and Silent Cinema* (Durham, NC: Duke University Press, 1997), p. 10.

24 Paul Gilroy, *The Black Atlantic: Modernity and Double Consciousness* (Cambridge, MA: Harvard University Press, 1993), p. 133.

25 Kirby, *Parallel Tracks,* p. 78.

26 Ibid., p. 80.

27 Brown and Taubin, "Clocking In," 71.

28 *Clockers* is not the first use of the railroad in contemporary African American film. The train is significant in *Posse* as a symbol of both promise and demise, and links the film's late nineteenth-century setting with its contemporary context. A more interesting use of trains appears in Charles Burnett's *To Sleep with Anger* (1990), which itself references his earlier *Killer of Sheep* in its characters' journey along the rails. In *Sleep* the train injects a Southern rural past, in the form of trickster Harry Mention, in the Los Angeles' family's modern present. The train also appears symbolically in *Boyz*'s opening vignette, in which Tre, Ricky, Doughboy, and friends walk along the tracks in South Central on the way to look at a dead

body. The most obvious reference for this was the earlier *Stand by Me* (Rob Reiner, 1986); however, it can be traced back even further to Burnett's *Killer of Sheep* (1977), which contains similar scenes of young boys playing on the tracks. In fact, the shots are so similar (complete with throwing rocks) that I would go so far as to suggest that the scenes in *Boyz* are quotations of the earlier film. Significantly, the possibilities for and limitations of young boys living in the inner city are directly linked to the railroad.

29 Brown and Taubin, "Clocking In," 76.
30 Gilroy, *The Black Atlantic*, p. 18.
31 Ibid., p. 111.
32 Arthur Jafa, "Like *Rashomon* but Different: The New Black Cinema," *Artforum* (June 1993), 11.
33 Gilroy, *The Black Atlantic*, p. 133.
34 Charles Scruggs, *Sweet Home: Invisible Cities in the Afro-American Novel* (Baltimore, MD: The Johns Hopkins University Press, 1993), p. 4.
35 Manthia Diawara, "*Noir* by *Noirs*: Towards a New Realism in Black Cinema," *African American Review* 27: 4 (1993), 530.
36 Ibid., 528.
37 Ibid., 535.
38 Gilroy, *The Black Atlantic*, p. 133.

The Changing Authorship of *Clockers*

Chapter 9

Chapter 10

Defusing *The English Patient*

Patrick Deer

In the publicity for the transnational collaboration that produced *The English Patient* (1997) for the screen, a compliant and enthusiastic author, a visionary writer–director, and a wily, worldly producer teamed up to transform a contemporary "classic" into a movie that achieved both critical acclaim and immense popular success. According to this fantasy of collaboration, like Count Laszlo de Almásy and the intrepid band of internationalist explorers their movie celebrates, Michael Ondaatje, Anthony Minghella, and Saul Zaentz led their cast into the Tunisian desert (and to the lush Tuscan landscape near the producer's villa) to outfox the Hollywood war machine. A British director had battled the odds to realize his vision of a group of exiles gathered in a ruined monastery in Northern Italy at the close of World War Two, allowing his audience to eavesdrop on the romantic recollections of the burned, dying English patient. In the process, the production appropriated both Ondaatje's literary reputation, as winner of the 1992 Booker Prize and author of a contemporary "classic," and his status as glamorous, transnational cosmopolitan, a Sri Lankan living in Canada. Its success also transformed irrevocably the novel's conditions of reception. The result was an independent film celebrated for aesthetic rigor, seductive romance, and epic box-office appeal. Transported by the film's unabashed imperial nostalgia, the London press proclaimed the "sun rises on a new empire" and forecast another new era for the British film industry.[1]

Despite the fantasy of a therapeutic, "blessed collaboration" offered by its creators,[2] the fault lines and wounds opened up by the passage from book to film refuse to heal. The film adaptation of *The English Patient* is at once a faithful transposition of elements of Michael Ondaatje's book, and a systematic betrayal of its dominant obsessions. The film not only defuses the anti-imperialist critical charge of the novel, it also bleeds Ondaatje's text of color and drains it of its historical specificity. The result is a peculiarly symbiotic and unstable relationship between film and novel, author and production. In their presentation of generational conflict, film and novel offer very different visions of the struggle to excavate and work through knowledge of a traumatic imperial past. Flirting with romance and melodrama, they question masculinity, along with the sovereign, imperial gaze, and come up with conflicting answers. The abrasive, unassimilable ethnicity of the Indian sapper Kip is displaced by the erotic whiteness of the European lovers' skins. The historical frames of 1930s' Egypt and Libya, and of Second World War England and Italy, are diffused and spatialized in the film's stunning panoramas of North African desert and its hypnotic Egyptian and Italian interiors. The novel's subversive treatment of the role of art in wartime and of gendered reading strategies is reduced, like the character of the Canadian nurse, Hana, to the handmaiden of patriarchal narrative.

Most damagingly, the film presents the depoliticized internationalism of Count Laszlo de Almásy and the "desert Europeans" as a tragically misunderstood alternative to the violent political commitments of the Second World War. Viewed as a narrowly nationalist conflict, rather than as a world war against fascist aggression complicated by a struggle to maintain control over colonial possessions, World War Two no longer represents the end of the line for British imperialism, after which the struggle for national independence and decolonization would become inevitable. In this revisionist narrative, decontextualized and aestheticized, European imperialism no longer represents one of the contributing causes of World War Two, but a possible alternative to global war, a road not taken.

Yet, for all this, the film is only partially unfaithful to a novel dealing in seduction, betrayal, collaboration, and the deliberate manipulation of identity. Indeed, these novelistic themes were deployed and flaunted by the film's production team in their remarkably successful campaign to mask the drastic revisions and excisions in their screen version of this contemporary "classic."

Seduce, Collaborate, Betray

To adapt the book required the studied betrayal of a "difficult" literary fiction. According to Anthony Minghella's account of the collaboration, Ondaatje's novel was like an unexploded bomb that needed defusing and translating into a clearer and more transparent medium. Self-consciously deploying Ondaatje's dominant themes of seduction and complicity, Minghella declares in the introduction to his screenplay that he took pains to defend himself against its mesmerizing "richness," researching the film in "purdah" in rural England with a car load of history books but not the novel itself.

I decided the only possible course available was to try and write my way back to the concerns of the novel, telling myself its story . . . I hope the army of admirers of [his] novel forgive my sins of omission and commission, my misjudgments and betrayals; they were all made in the spirit of translating his beautiful novel to the screen. (SP, xiv–xv)[3]

Patrick Deer

Chapter 10

Like the characters in the film, director, writer, and producer gathered at an Italian villa to spin their story, holding script conferences in Zaentz's "cool aquamarine pool, our chins bobbing on the surface of the water, punctuated by bouts of what we called water polo but which was essentially a form of licensed violence to work off all our various pent-up hostilities, and at which Michael proved to be the master" (SP, xiv).

According to his own version of the collaboration, Michael Ondaatje signed on enthusiastically from the start, knowing what he was getting himself into: "None of us wanted a faithful echo. I knew my story's shape and various swerves and plots would not go unscathed."[4] In interview at London's National Film Theatre, he acknowledged the film's painful excisions, especially of the Indian sapper, "Kip" Singh, who provides the novel with its most powerful critiques of colonialism and Englishness.

> My mythology growing up in Sri Lanka and in England in my teens, was the second world war. English films, novels, biographies. But I also knew there was another version of that history, not just the English at war or Americans at war, but Asians at war. There weren't films that had the number of Indians killed in the second world war – not that that was my thesis in writing the book. But I didn't want Kip to be a background figure. I wanted him to be a central character.[5]

In the same interview he expresses unease at the removal of Kip's angry reaction to the news of the allied bombings of Hiroshima and Nagasaki:

> A book can do some things a film can't and vice versa. Some people in the States didn't like the Hiroshima section in the book, they thought it was tacked on, that it didn't work. That's their problem – I thought it worked. But in a film to focus on a group of people for so long and suddenly have news from abroad just doesn't work emotionally.

The film's postcolonial critics have been less forgiving with the drastic downsizing of Kirpal Singh's screen character.[6] But in print the author maintained the united front: "There were other losses in the translation to film but in each case they were understandable choices. They made the film better" (SP, viii). Appropriately for a writer strongly associated with the postmodern and postcolonial, Ondaatje accords each version its own ontological authority: "What we have now are two stories, one with the intimate pace and detail of a three-hundred-page novel, and one that is the length of a vivid and subtle film. Each has its own organic structure. There are obvious differences and values but somehow each version deepens the other" (SP, ix). Yet his invocation of the organic formal relationship between them is closer to James than Jameson.

Saul Zaentz, veteran producer of One Flew Over the Cuckoo's Nest (1975) and The Unbearable Lightness of Being (1988), also drew on tropes of intimacy and betrayal to describe his own involvement in the collective, international endeavor to "transform an incredibly complex novel into film . . . ploughing between several drafts, the screenplay continued to shed pages, characters and scenes that we loved. And it kept improving" (SP, xi). More prosaically, he recounted to an interviewer from *Première* magazine that he had told Ondaatje as early as 1993, "Michael, we're going to fuck up your book."[7]

The collaborators were less open about their own experiments in the manipulation of identity. Despite its mainly British lead actors, director, and its indebtedness to David Lean's *Lawrence of Arabia* (1962), *The English Patient* was not exactly English. In the run-up to the film's Oscar triumph, much was made of the fact that Twentieth Century Fox had nearly killed the project, rejecting it as too European. Yet, though the movie was proudly championed in the US as part of an independent film resurgence against Hollywood, the Weinstein Brothers' distribution company Miramax Films was also a subsidiary of the Disney Corporation. While Fox is owned by Rupert Murdoch's News Corporation, with 2001 annual revenues of $11.6 billion, the Walt Disney Company is currently the third largest global media conglomerate, with annual revenues in 2001 of $25.4 billion.[8] To further complicate matters, according to UK and EC financial regulations, with its American finance capital and post-production work, *The English Patient* could be classified as neither "British" nor "European."[9] Nor was the title character quite the dashingly straight figure Ralph Fiennes portrayed: the real Count Laszlo de Almásy was a Nazi collaborator and a homosexual.[10]

But, according to the logic of the film, none of this should really matter. In its celebration of a tragically romantic fusion of identities, its projection of a nebulous, portable Englishness, the depoliticized internationalism of its desert "expeditioners," and the amnesiac evasions of the patient, the film offers the vision of a seducing, transnational adventure in which bodily and national boundaries were an inconvenience and colonialism a matter of archaeology and eroticism.[11] As the opening sequence suggests, in which Nazi gunners abruptly open fire on Almásy's plane in its final epic flight over the desert, the real threat to the film's exhilarating, mobile vision is the violence that comes from nationalist allegiances, like that which culminated in World War Two. In its blurring of boundaries, the film stages the pre-1939 age of empire as romantic desert spectacle, its nostalgic, meticulously ordered *mise-en-scène* ended by the confusion of World War Two. In its celebrated flight sequences over the vast depopulated Sahara, it also erases the long history of connections between air power and empire.[12] European imperialism becomes instead the brilliant, doomed precursor to the era of globalization. This is a long way from the critical, skeptical vision of Michael Ondaatje's novel.

The Patient under the Knife

The adaptation turns the novel's narrative frame inside out. Michael Ondaatje's *The English Patient* begins in the closing weeks of World War Two, as Hana, a shell-shocked Canadian army nurse, takes refuge with one of her patients from the victorious Allied advance through Northern Italy. The man was rescued, burned and amnesiac, by Arab nomads in the North African desert and is identified only as English, and Hana begins unraveling his memories by reading to him from the library of the ruined villa. The narrative is composed of ten sections, roughly chronological, filtered through the consciousnesses of Hana, the thief-turned-spy Caravaggio, and the Indian bomb disposal expert, Kip, as they gather around the burned man to listen to his story and to confront their own psychic war wounds. The fragmented point of view of the patient finds its expression in the scraps of personal, historical, and geographical anecdote collected in his well-thumbed copy of Herodotus' *Histories*.

Embedded at the novel's center, like one of Herodotus' inset stories, are two chapters dedicated exclusively to recounting a doomed love affair during an expedition in the Libyan desert in the 1930s. Unusually for a novel in which constant shifts of perspective are the norm, these sections are focalized almost entirely through the perceptions of the English patient and his lover, Katharine Clifton. Thereafter, the narrative present of Hana, Caravaggio, and Kip is interlaced with the increasingly intense and disturbed romantic memories of the patient, who is forced to confront his own complicity in the deaths of the Cliftons and the brutal consequences of his collaboration with the Nazis.

The term "flashback" is not really adequate to describe the English patient's recollections, since for the most part they are fragmented and dispersed throughout the story. Since his recollected narrative is embedded and dispersed within the novel, it becomes difficult in narratological terms to distinguish between the patient's external analepses (or flashbacks), which refer to a time prior to the opening of the text, and his internal analepses, which move back in the story but do not involve crossing the text's opening.[13] Ondaatje's novel deliberately blurs these boundaries. Rather than the self-contained retrospective sections that the visual metaphor flashback suggests, they are predominantly oral and "literary" performances, frequently prompted by the act of reading aloud. They are thus thoroughly mediated by the book's narrative frame, self-consciously staged and performed for Hana, Kip, and Caravaggio. The patient's palimpsest of memories, often literally enfolded within his copy of Herodotus, thus becomes another kind of intertext for the novel, in addition to the abundant literary, classical, historical, and geographic citations.

Suspense is generated in the novelistic present by the erotic tension between Hana and Kip, and by Caravaggio's relentless desire to unmask the patient as Count Laszlo de Almásy, the traitor responsible for his torture and mutilation by the Germans. The narrative momentum is interrupted by a section which recounts Kip's early training in England at the hands of the eccentric Lord Suffolk, and shows the origins of his continuing romance with Englishness despite his brother's anti-colonial activism in India. The romances end variously: the patient/Almásy recollects repeatedly Katharine's death in the Cave of Swimmers; Caravaggio forces the revelation of the patient's identity but abandons his revenge against him; enraged by the news of the dropping of the A-bomb on Hiroshima, Kip breaks with Hana, attacks the English patient and leaves. The patient dies alone in darkness as the others prepare to leave the villa. The narrative closes with a brief proleptic scene in which Kip and Hana are shown back in their native lands, still connected by shared memories of listening to the patient.

In striking contrast, the film seals off the novel's non-linear and unstable temporality, beginning and ending within a closed, temporal loop. This twisting of narrative structure encloses the novel's shifting temporalities and perspectives solely within the frame of the recollected romance between the patient and Katharine. It open and closes with scenes of Almásy's plane flying over the desert carrying Katharine's body. After this visually spectacular opening over the deserts, with its clear echoes of David Lean's *Lawrence of Arabia*, the action shifts to Italy and to Hana's traumatic war experiences. Once she and the patient take refuge in the villa, the cast is assembled and the focus shifts onto the English patient whose recollections will dominate the rest of the film. The romance is unfolded in linear fashion, in about a dozen flashbacks to the exotic locales of North Africa in the 1930s. In stark contrast to the novel, there are no flashbacks for Hana or Kip. Only Caravaggio's past is also presented directly, as in the novel, in a flashback to his betrayal, capture, and torture by the Germans after the fall of Tobruk. In sharp contrast to their novelistic counterparts, Kip and Hana are reduced to spectators, as the younger generation is shown receiving its sentimental education at the hands of the old. Once the romance kicks into gear, Hana's war traumas fade into the background. Deprived of his colonial past and imperial education, Kip serves a similarly secondary role as loyal spectator to the patient's performances.

The romance thus becomes not the enigmatic absent center of Ondaatje's narrative, but the entire purpose of the film's diegesis which is dedicated to excavating the love affair in a relentlessly linear fashion. The audience is thus encouraged to identify largely with the romantic leads, Ralph Fiennes (the patient/Almásy) and Kristin Scott Thomas (Katharine), instead of with the younger generation's struggle to break with a seductively lethal past. The novel's constant questioning of masculinity is displaced in favor of the erotic fixations and duplicities of the love triangle, and on Caravaggio's own narrowly focused desire for knowledge and revenge.

That Dangerous Supplement

Both versions of *The English Patient* have been praised for their artistry. Yet while Ondaatje's novel rapidly attained "classic" status,[14] the film version works more strenuously to project the aura of the work of art. It does this by promoting the legend of the difficulty of the literary "text," which must be contained, defused, and disposed of like one of Kip's unexploded bombs. Many of the book's critics, including Minghella himself, have commented on the filmic quality of the novel, stressing its constant cross-cutting and mosaic-like style and disorienting demands on the reader.[15] Ironically, though, the screen adaptation is far more formally conservative, masking its own artifice and manipulation with a sacrosanct vision of the art object and "the book." Through its nostalgia for the trappings of empire and its middlebrow fantasy of reading, the film stakes its own claim to be the guardian of "classic" art and literature.

Just how difficult, then, is Ondaatje's novel? The distressed shape and surfaces of the text, with its splintered perspectives, unsteady framing, and fragmented narrative structure, can be read as a highly ambitious mimetic attempt to represent the shattering effect of wartime violence on the novel form. Despite the self-conscious non-linearity of the text, *The English Patient* nevertheless offers many of the traditional novelistic satisfactions of the classic realist text. In this respect, while the novel is situated in the postcolonial moment, it flirts only marginally with postmodern narrative strategies. Ondaatje's text is thus closer to the gentler, British versions of "historiographic metafiction" practiced by writers like Graham Swift, Kazuo Ishiguro, or Angela Carter than to the more epistemologically skeptical and less filmable visions of Salman Rushdie, Thomas Pynchon, or J. M. Coetzee. While the novel shifts gears unpredictably between grammatical tenses and disrupts syntax, it nevertheless preserves the reader's faith in the ultimate determinacy of the narrative.[16]

As Bronwen Thomas has observed, the screen adaptation of *The English Patient* goes to great pains to try to produce a filmic "mirage" that reproduces some of the disorienting textual mosaic of the novel.[17] Yet neither the film nor the book really produces the disorientation in the reader or audience of the kind she or the book's other critics suggest. This simulation of disorientation is one of the most seductive achievements of the film. In this respect, it mimics the novel's evocation of the shattering epistemological effects of wartime trauma within the ruins of a stable narrative frame, which is one of the text's chiefest pleasures.

In Ondaatje's text the indeterminacy that haunts the patient and Caravaggio is contained and anchored in the determination of the younger generation to outlive the end of war. Hana and Kip the sapper may both be damaged by the deforming masculine violence of total warfare or by colonialism, but they remain subjects who possess the ability to penetrate the opaque surfaces of the past. Their emotional lives may be temporarily numbed and stunted, but their hermeneutic faculties are unimpaired. They know that the fantasy of fused identities offered by the patient or by the British war machine that consumed their mentors will also destroy them. Thus Kip and Hana may be postcolonial, but they have admirably centered egos and psyches. In this respect they are closer to Vikram Seth or Zadie Smith's casts of characters, than to the decentered fragmented figures of Rushdie or Ishiguro, or of Will Self, Jeanette Winterson, and James Kelman.

This epistemological confidence at the heart of Ondaatje's novel, despite the projected mirage of experimentalism or disorientation, no doubt accounts for its great popularity and readability, despite its supposed "difficulty." This is signaled most tellingly in Anthony Minghella's extraordinary description of *The English Patient* as "a mosaic of fractured images, as if somebody had already seen a film and was in a hurry to remember all the best bits" (SP, xiv). The text has now become the dangerous supplement of the film: needing not only to be translated, but also defused.[18] In another temporal loop, Minghella's film version turns out to be not only temporally, but ontologically, prior to the novel. Thus the screen adaptation can claim to be the truer "original," more "classic" than the novel.

Faced with this audacious claim, it is not possible simply to reassert the priority of the literary, seductive though that might be for admirers of Ondaatje's novel. Here an old-fashioned, high-culture formalism might collaborate harmoniously with a more newly minted postcolonialism, both uniting to bemoan the fall from Ondaatje's plural, polyvocal, hybrid, and indeterminate text to Minghella's monologic, formally conservative, and determinedly low-brow production. As Robert Stam has noted, this kind of approach to film adaptation places us in a cul-de-sac, forced to argue for the inherent superiority and priority of either one medium or the other.[19] I am suggesting instead that the case of *The English Patient* reveals to an extraordinarily rich degree the complicity of both mediums, novel and film, in shaping and re-envisioning narratives of war and of empire for the global culture markets.

The novel has its own supplementary logic, which protects the younger generation from the epistemological damage of the old, by deferring Kip's anti-colonial epiphany almost to the last minute. Unlike Hana's gender critique or Caravaggio's cynical demystification of romance, his critique is not woven into the book's fabric. It is a shadow held in suspension by the spell of romance and imperial nostalgia that surrounds that patient, not allowed to fully emerge until the end. The novel's structural peculiarity thus made it far easier for Anthony Minghella to make a film which almost completely ignores Ondaatje's powerful demystification of Englishness and imperialism.

The novel's younger generation is in a much better position than either the patient or Caravaggio to critique the imperialist militarism of wartime: most strikingly in Kip's horrified reaction to the bombing of Hiroshima, or Hana's quieter rejection of patriarchy and the masculine codes of violence that fuel and sustain the war. But these judgments are also supplementary to the logic of the narrative. Kip's epiphany about the exterministic, racist violence of the British war machine for whom he has been patiently defusing bombs comes only at the end of the novel. Up to this point, unlike his brother, he has remained faithful to the aristocratic fantasy of Englishness taught him by Lord Suffolk. While he refuses to become "the replacing vision" after his mentor's death (*The English Patient* [EP], 196), his response is to disappear into the Italian campaign, rather than to break with British imperialism. His *non serviam* is more of a gesture than anything else. For her part, Hana puts her own rebellion on hold: after her breakdown at the news of her father's death, she deserts from the war, but fills the vacuum with her fantasy of devotion to the English patient at the villa (EP, 41). Again, she possesses the knowledge but cannot act on it; the epiphany restores consciousness rather than fracturing or decentering it.

In this respect, Ondaatje's representation of the damaged lives of Caravaggio and the patient/Almásy is considerably more subversive than that of the younger characters. Caravaggio clearly sees Hana's self-deluding fantasy of fusion with the patient's burned-out husk, but he cannot act on this knowledge. The English patient, for his part, has suppressed the ugly consequences of his collaboration and complicity with the Nazis. He is consumed by his disastrous, monstrous role in the old love affair that killed Katharine and Geoffrey Clifton and burned himself beyond recognition. This romance is more real to the dying man than is the war that has raged on around him; in much the same way, he continues to project an archaic imperial romance onto Kip, an "international bastard" (EP, 176) like him, despite the manifest falseness of his orientalist vision. For the patient, Kip will always be like Rudyard Kipling's Kim, and empire will always be a nostalgic international expedition to discover and preserve the treasures of the Orient. By going along with this, Kip's passivity and complicity in the patient's fantasy are exposed for the reader early on. But it takes the biggest bomb of all to shake him out of his complacency. By then, of course, it is too late. The patient is dead, Hiroshima incinerated, and he is relegated to the margins of the British war machine he has served, just another relic of the Raj.[20]

In the logic of the film, because they are somehow more naïve and less worldly wise, Kip and Hana become mere onlookers to the spectacle of romance and imperial nostalgia. The adaptation of *The English Patient* turns the novel's logic on its head: instead of an overthrow of the illusions and confusions of the old by a more skeptical younger generation, the film stages the sentimental aesthetic education of youth by middle age.

Art and Crime

Film and novel alike are preoccupied with the transforming force of the aesthetic and with the need to preserve art from the ravages of war. The shattering decentered perspectives of psyches fractured by war are not only contained by a generational logic, but by the redemptive play of art. This confidence in the power of the aesthetic is signaled in the novel by the rich intertextual play of references from the classics. Each of its main sources of citations represent foundational texts: Herodotus, the "father of history"; the Italian Renaissance art and architecture of the villa and its surrounding churches; Kipling's *Kim* as one of the master narratives of empire. The friezes in the Cave of Swimmers that the patient discovers at the Gilf Kebir in the Libyan desert offer the spectacle of a marvelous lost civilization that predates the nomadic culture of the Bedouin or the European nationalist race to "own the desert." Alternating between its lavishly detailed desert, Cairo, and Tuscan *mise-en-scènes*, the film clearly strives to emulate Ondaatje's lavish visual imagination and wealth of citations.

In addition to the "classical," there is another radical vision of art and artists in wartime in Ondaatje's novel. On the one hand, there is the archaeological impulse to preserve, to hoard, to collect that the film celebrates. On the other, there is the far more subversive play of appropriation, desecration, and disfiguring in the novel, which is connected to a libidinal energy of seduction and violence. The boundaries between high and low are constantly transgressed. Hana uses the villa's rare books to repair the shattered staircase, plays Bach on the villa's booby-trapped piano, and dances to the patient's 1920s' jazz and ragtime records. His copy of Herodotus is stuffed with heterogeneous mementoes, like cuttings from the Bible, song lyrics, journal entries, the wrapper of a Christmas cracker, the leaf of a fern. His great archaeological discovery, the cave friezes of swimmers in the desert, also becomes a recurring motif for the illicit love affair, including the patient's necrophiliac reunion with Katharine.

There is also a strong association between art and crime. The thief and spy, David Caravaggio, shares his "absurd name" with the rebellious seventeenth-century artist, triggering a digression from the patient on his painting *David with the Head of Goliath* (EP, 116). Caravaggio appears in Ondaatje's earlier historical novel, *In the Skin of a Lion*, where he is a painter imprisoned in Toronto during the 1930s with Hana's father, Patrick. In a moment of comic absurdity, he is painted blue by his cell mates so that he can escape across the prison roof. As Douglas Barbour notes, he is thus literally part of the "moment of cubism" evoked in Ondaatje's postmodern historical novel.[21] Little of this carries over directly to *The English Patient*, and none at all in the film, but Caravaggio retains a disturbingly fluid and subversive persona. As Hana declares surreally, "When I was a child I thought of you always as the Scarlet Pimpernel, and in my dreams I stepped onto night roofs with you" (EP, 55). Working for British intelligence "in Cairo during the early days of the war, he had been trained to invent double agents or phantoms who would take on flesh . . . Just as some in Cairo he worked for invented whole platoons in the desert. He had lived through a time of war when everything offered up to those around him was a lie" (EP, 117). Skilled in lies and deception, he watches Hana falling in love with her fantasy of the English patient's identity, and makes it his business "to reveal him for Hana's sake. Or perhaps invent a skin for him, the way tannic acid camouflages a burned man's rawness" (EP, 117). Little wonder that in the novel Caravaggio never fully manages to establish the patient's identity as the collaborator Almásy.

In the film the only real residue of this Bohemianism is Caravaggio's morphine addiction. He is clearly motivated to steal the drug in order to numb the pain of his mutilated hands, his thumbs amputated by SS torturers as a result of Almásy's treachery, but the film's most transgressive scene shows Caravaggio shooting up to the near orgasmic pleasure of the English patient. Caravaggio's screen persona is given an extra aura of potential danger by Willem Dafoe, an actor who has played both Jesus, in Martin Scorsese's controversial *Last Temptation of Christ* (1988), and haunted drug-takers, in *Platoon* (Oliver Stone, 1986) or Paul Schrader's marvelous *Light Sleeper* (1991).

The lines between art and the technologies of violence are also blurred in Ondaatje's work. In the novel, the English patient is kept alive by the Bedouin because of his encyclopedic knowledge of their stolen weaponry, which he caresses and fondles like a true connoisseur. As Kip discovers, he is "a reservoir of information about Allied and enemy weaponry" (EP, 88). The retreating German army seems to have taken delight in booby-trapping everything, including the villa's piano, or a monumental statue at the film's conclusion. Indeed, Kirpal Singh spends much of his time trying to anticipate the demonic inventiveness of his Axis counterparts. The sapper is shown developing his skills at the hands of an English eccentric genius, Lord Suffolk, who sees bomb disposal as a delicate and labyrinthine art. In unforgettable sequences in both versions, which would presumably gray the hair of art preservers, Kip uses his engineering skill to hoist Hana up into the eaves of a Tuscan church so that she can inspect Renaissance frescos by flare light. Indeed, Ondaatje's characters like works of art best when they have been disfigured or shattered by war, reconstructed as assemblages of shards and fragments like the wounded Buddha at the close of *Anil's Ghost*.[22] The genius of the film is to project the aura of preservation and of the sacrosanct, while desecrating the literary original.

---------------------------- Reading Lessons ----------------------------

In both *English Patients*, Herodotus' *Histories* functions as an analogue for these contradictory attitudes toward the function of art, and for two very different kinds of intertextuality. On the one hand, Herodotus stands as an authorizing master narrative, a palimpsest which can encompass and contain both the history of the north African desert and the master code to "the world of cities . . . ancient and modern" (EP, 246, see also p. 150).[23] To Kip, in his negative epiphany at the end of the novel, it is the patient's "holy book" (EP, 294). Yet the only story quoted directly from the *Histories* calls authority into question. Katharine's inset narrative of Candaules and Gyges, read to the desert Europeans, is a story of infidelity and regicide that anticipates her own adulterous liaison. And, indeed, this is the other side of reading in Ondaatje's novel, a continual process of vandalism and defacing, which turns the ancient text into a commonplace book into which are pasted a random assortment of other found textual objects. This is a decidedly unstable, open text which is in a constant state of revision and addition, never finished, even after its owner's death. The characters can read into this book whatever they would like; the patient's bad habits as reader and writer encourage Hana, for one, to read voraciously and haphazardly to him from the villa's library. Following his meandering reading practice, she pursues her own unscholarly path, defacing the antique volumes with her own marginalia, even using them as lumber to repair the shell-cratered staircase.

Significantly, the film adaptation has Katharine quoting the Candaules–Gyges story from memory, instead of quoting it as a promiscuous reader from Almásy's copy of the *Histories*. This is the version of Herodotus that the film prefers, a sacralized book with an aura of exotic mystery; like Ondaatje's novel, it supplies another textual supplement for the filmic *English Patient*. Little wonder that the film's popularity boosted sales of Herodotus, or that the text features largely as an opaque, monolithic object for its characters. For the adaptation, Herodotus functions as an authorizing cover story that can distract viewers from the drastic revisions and elisions of Ondaatje's novel. It is the literary analogue for David Lean's "epic" *Lawrence of Arabia*, the chosen intertext for a film that brazenly claims "classic" status from its very first frames. What better than Herodotus, a lost classic that the novel demonstrates can be all things to all men, to fill the vacuum left by Minghella's adaptation, to staunch the wounds left by his drastic surgery?

In the film, reading is a social activity, never solitary. Here reading is almost always an activity triangulated by desire: people read for, or read to, they never just read. Hana at first uses the villa's library to repair the war damage to its staircase. Reproved by the invalid she is nursing, she reads to the English patient. Kip reads *Kim* for him, or mis-reads it, according to the patient. But he is the only one to really hold his own. Katharine is seen recounting the inset story of Candaules and Gyges to the desert Europeans (known in the film as the "International Sand Club") after Hana reads from the episode to Almásy. Katharine offers to add her paintings to the book and is at first snubbed. Then, watching Almásy, she reads about herself in the book. At last, dying in the cave, she adds her own final testament to the marginalia in his Herodotus. Caravaggio later uses the book to identify Almásy, hunting him from Cairo to Northern Italy (SP, 133). The expedition's maps are read by the Germans in order to give Almásy his chance to return to Katharine at the Gilf Kebir, and to get their spies across the desert. Almásy creates his personal map of the ridge near the Gilf in conversation with an Arab and uses it to share his discovery of the Cave of Swimmers with the whole expedition, Europeans and Arabs. The book reads the patient into his final sleep after Hana delivers him a lethal overdose of morphine. In the film, after his death, a shot of its crowded pages fills the entire screen for a moment as Hana returns for the last time to his now empty room to retrieve it.

By "making you want to read" the film gives its spectators the illusion that they are part of a community of readers as much invested in learning about history, the Middle East, or the classics, as about the English patient's doomed love affair with Katharine Clifton. But there is no attempt to show the other side of colonial rule, and a singular lack of interest in the non-Western perspective of any of the film's Arab characters.[24] This staging of reading as an instrumental activity restricts its possibilities to a paternalistic preordained script overshadowed by the "father of history." Two scenes from the film involving the younger generation suggest how strictly their elders are controlling their reading practices.

When Hana first reads to the English patient, she is placed in the position of the naïve reader, the vessel through which the flashback emerges, without her knowledge. She is shown reading the story of Candaules and Gyges, stumbling over the names and being scrupulously corrected by the patient; the scene cuts to Katharine Clifton confidently recounting the episode from memory around the campfire to the "International Sand Club." In the novel, Katharine had self-consciously chosen the episode from Almásy's Herodotus and recounts it as a provocation to him and a warning to her husband. Hana's off-screen narration continues the story, but she is ironically unaware that her words have transported the patient and the audience to another time and place. It is a particularly ironic reversal as the story is about a woman unwittingly displaying her nakedness to an unseen suitor with her husband's consent. This first episode of book reading ends with the patient falling asleep and the nurse closing the book, kissing him goodnight, and blowing out the candle. She has been transformed from a veteran frontline army nurse to a children's nanny, like Almásy's childhood *daijka* in Hungary (SP, 91). Again, at the end of the film, Hana is shown reading Katharine's last words, and the older woman's voice takes over. When Hana reads the last words, both Katharine in the past and the patient in the present have already breathed their last, leaving her ultimately as only a spectator to the romantic mystery she has patiently unraveled.

The most explicit moment of postcolonial critique – and of imperious masculinity – comes during another key reading lesson, appropriately from Rudyard Kipling's *Kim*. This is the one scene where a character is shown matching the patient/Almásy in both resonance of voice and in critical insight. Kip sits magisterially over the open book on a bedside table as the patient corrects his phrasing. Having read the opening of Kipling's novel, the Indian sapper breaks off, saying "I can't read these words. They stick in my throat" (SP, 74). In tune with his somatic, instrumental reading practice, the patient takes him literally and responds, "Because you're reading it too fast," oblivious to Kip's critique of this imperialist classic. Kirpal Singh's defiant reply, "Not at all," is lost in a scene focalized through the amused gaze of Hana, who has come in to serve them. The patient pedantically rattles through the Kipling passage, stagily inserting the word "*comma*" at appropriate intervals, declaring "You have to read Kipling slowly! Your eye is too impatient – think about the speed of his pen" (SP, 74). The irony of his complete blindness to the content of the words is almost lost in the busy scene in which Hana tracks through the space as if ignoring the exchange. Kip's voice is not as loud as the patient's, but he gets his revenge by contextualizing Kipling's passage about "the gun Zammzammah" on which Kim is sitting "in defiance of municipal orders" as the novel opens.[25] Kip, like Kim, the scene reveals, was born in Lahore: "It's still there, the cannon, outside the museum. It was made of metal cups and bowls taken from every household in the city as tax, then melted down. Then later they fired the cannon at my people *comma* the natives. *Full stop*" (SP, 75).

Somewhat obtusely, for such a sensitive reader and orientalist, the patient is not sure if Kip is objecting to "the writer or what he's writing about?"[26] But Kip's explicit critique of the aestheticizing and legitimizing of colonialist violence in Kipling's text is defused in a shift from witty irony to crude "stage Indian" slapstick, as he declares:

> What I really object to, Uncle, is your finishing all my condensed milk.
> (*snatching up the empty can*)
> And the message everywhere in your book – however slowly I read it – that the best destiny for India is to be ruled by the British. (SP, 75)

This strikingly powerful critique of the ideological function of literature in the service of empire is lost amidst the good-natured, manly banter. Through Hana's point of view, the spectator is placed on the outside of the exchange, an effect reinforced by the patient's cheerful paternalism. Ignoring Kip's declaration about British imperial hegemony in India, he declares to her: "Hana, we have discovered a shared pleasure – the boy and I" (SP, 75). She refuses to be drawn in:

> HANA: Arguing about books.
> THE PATIENT: Condensed milk – one of the truly great inventions.
> KIP: (*grinning, leaving*) I'll get another tin.
> [*Hana* and *The Patient* are alone.]
> THE PATIENT: You like him, don't you? Your voice changes. (SP, 75–6)

In miniature, the audience is given an object lesson in the power of reading to divide and rule. Like the erotics of eating, which is sensually evoked throughout the film, the pleasure of the text acts to defuse and distract from the tasteless distractions of political engagement. The master reader, like Almásy, can move effortlessly from literature to food to sex without distraction, just as the European "internationalists" may roam freely across the desert without attending to petty national boundaries. In one fell swoop, the patient manages to ignore both Kip's critique of colonialism and Hana's dig at masculinity. Neither character is allowed to hear the other's critical opinions.

This defusing of a dangerous moment is particularly striking given that, in the novel, the original reading lesson is given to Hana, not to Kip (EP, 93–4). Ironically, for a film that celebrates reading as a sensual, social act, the scene makes "arguing about books" seem an insular, almost blindly, masculine pursuit from which women are excluded except as silent handmaidens or potential sexual partners, and in which knowledgeable "boys" like Kirpal Singh must defer to the older, wiser, and whiter. Perhaps it is arguing about the books, rather than just consuming them, that is the problem. The scene ends with Kip returning to make another joke about food: condensed milk sandwiches, a staple of British public-school life. His wry closing remark, "They taste very good with salt," which does not appear in Minghella's screenplay, is an appropriate coda to a scene in which the Indian sapper is shown taking the patient's reverential reading lesson with an unusually large pinch of salt.

—————— Cold Fusion: Masculinity Rearmored ——————

The following scene in the screen *English Patient* flashes back to Katharine Clifton's return from her romantic sojourn in the desert. As fez-wearing boys carry her luggage back into the film's "wonder house," Shepheard's Hotel, Almásy is shown refusing to follow her in. Instead he petulantly demands his book back from "Mrs Clifton." The ironic temporal juxtaposition suggests that in his sexual and intellectual romance with Katharine Clifton Almásy runs up against boundaries he cannot pass. Here, in response to a highly skeptical feminine reader, he retreats behind the armor of a fortified masculinity holding his Herodotus.[27]

In the novel, from the first, Katharine clearly detects a monstrous violence in her lover. Listening to the patient/Almásy's erudite monologues about "propinquity in the desert," she is infuriated by his pretentious worldliness:

> When he talked like that she hated him, her eyes remaining polite, her mind wanting to slap him. She always had the desire to slap him, and she realized even that was sexual . . . He assumed he was experienced in the ways of the world he had essentially left years earlier, struggling ever since to explore a half-invented world of the desert. (EP, 150)

Enraged by his "pose of courtesy, graciousness," she thinks of him as a "dog in clothes" (EP, 151). Later she wounds or bruises him during every sexual encounter. This devastating critique of Almásy's illusions is largely absent from the film, which presents Ralph Fiennes's character largely without irony as an unimpeachably intellectual, even saintly figure.

In addition to the literary, the screen adaptation mobilizes its cinematic intertexts to further fortify the patient's masculinity. The "Production Notes" to *The English Patient* proudly invoke Fiennes's affinities to both Almásy and Lawrence, while carefully erasing the Count's unfortunate Nazi past: "In early 1994, the script was sent to Ralph Fiennes who, as soon as he read it, committed himself to play the role of Count Laszlo de Almásy, a noted linguist and noted expeditioner who has charted unexplored regions of the Sahara and bears a kindred [sic] to T. E. Lawrence (Lawrence of Arabia)."[28]

The "Notes" make clear the film's ambitions to stake a claim in the "great tradition" of imperial heritage film by also invoking the name of David Puttnam, producer of *Chariots of Fire* (1982), which, with *Gandhi* (1983), was supposed to usher in a new epoch of British filmmaking. The "Notes" point out that after his classical stage training at RADA and the Royal Shakespeare Company in the 1980s, Fiennes appeared in Puttnam's TV special *A Dangerous Man: Lawrence after Arabia* (1991), emerging in the mid-1990s "as one of his generation's leading actors."

In David Lean's *Lawrence of Arabia* (1962), Peter O'Toole's character is framed in controversy from the very start. The film opens with a long shot of the steps of St Paul's cathedral showing mourners leaving his state funeral. Asked by an American journalist, "You knew Colonel Lawrence, didn't you?" they give totally conflicting judgments. O'Toole's virtuoso performance is full of excess and self-deprecating irony, frequently verging in the English sections of the film on high camp. It is only when T. E. Lawrence is allowed to don his flowing Arab robes in the panoramic desert sequences that his character transforms pantomime into epic grandeur. But Fiennes's Almásy is not a dangerous man, compared to his "icon shattering interpretation" of Heathcliff opposite Juliette Binoche in *Emily Brontë's Wuthering Heights*.[29] Nor does he display the compellingly boorish psychosis that won Fiennes an Oscar for his portrayal of the SS Commandant Amon Goeth in *Schindler's List* (1993), another Nazi role subject to drastic revision in the process of adaptation.[30]

Ralph Fiennes has thus had both the blessing and curse of appearing in two films that seemed to demand almost absolute loyalty from their contemporary audiences. The British press, never loath to tear down successful icons, published a series of attacks on *The English Patient* in advance of its Oscar sweep, which pointed out the duplicity of its production team in declaring the film as either independent or British.[31] Exposés also appeared revealing the film's whitewashing of Almásy's Nazi past, but this did little to dent the film's appeal to British audiences, the majority of whom were old enough to know something about World War Two and the Holocaust.[32] In the United States, there was far less open criticism of the film, which proved enormously successful at the box office and boosted sales of both Ondaatje's novel and of Herodotus' *Histories*.[33] As one British journalist observed:

> *The English Patient* has been out six months in America and is still a hot potato. Here it has been in the cinema just six weeks. There are still dinner parties to be spoilt by it, marriages waiting to be wrecked, and embryonic relationships that will founder on the rocks of this siren of the picture house.[34]

This combined lack of irony and aura of reverence was memorably satirized in "The English Patient" episode of the US situation comedy *Seinfeld*, in which Elaine Benes is ostracized by friends and acquaintances for refusing to like the movie. Retribution is delivered at the hands of her Lawrentian boss, J. Peterman, whose mail-order catalogue specializes in marketing orientalist kitsch to a public hungry for the kind of exotic imperial nostalgia offered by the film. As punishment, Elaine is banished to a cave in the Tunisian desert until she relents and purifies her soul.[35] Yet again complicity is at the heart of the matter. The *Seinfeld* critique of the film version poses flippantly a serious question: how was the novel's challenge to bourgeois sexuality transformed into a strongly heteronormative romance with mass audience appeal?[36] As I have suggested, the key lies in its exploitation of nostalgia, amnesia, and its refusal of irony in relation to the crisis of masculinity interrogated by Ondaatje's novel.

The most overtly retrograde screen character is Geoffrey Clifton, played by Colin Firth, who is purged of the homoerotic aura projected onto him by Almásy and his companions in the novel. The lovers' desire, the book hints, is triangulated around the boyish figure of Geoffrey; the patient at first bitterly resents Katharine's intrusion into the homosocial world of the desert Europeans. Though Katharine warns Almásy that he is driving all of them mad (EP, 156–7, 173), there is no real preparation for the murderous violence with which he tries to kill all three in the desert at the Gilf Kebir. As the patient comments laconically, "We would have devoured him" (EP, 230). The homoerotic desire that Almásy shares with Madox, Clifton, and the Arabs who save him after his fiery descent into the desert is projected in the film onto only one member of the desert explorers, who flirts with one of the Arab boys serving the expedition. In the novel, a British explorer, Fenelon-Barnes, had kept a "small Arab girl" tied up in his tent: a far more disturbing staging of colonial sexual violence.[37]

Colin Firth is thus given the unenviable task of playing exactly the unreconstructed public school masculinity that so many of his other roles have critiqued, from the homoerotic sensitivity of Judd in *Another Country* (1984) to the ambivalent "new men" of Mr Darcy in the BBC adaptation of *Pride and Prejudice* (1994) or Paul Ashworth in the screen version of Nick Hornby's *Fever Pitch* (1997). Indeed, Firth's career was launched by the stage play of *Another Country* in which he acted the part of the queer schoolboy and spy, Guy Bennett, later played on screen by Rupert Everett.[38] In *Another Country*, like *The English Patient*, the critique of Englishness, masculinity, and homophobia is also linked to themes of espionage and betrayal. Yet there internationalism has a specific politics, connected explicitly to the anti-fascist struggle of the Republican side in the Spanish Civil War. The protagonists' brutalization at the hands of the fascistic public-school hierarchy ultimately results in Judd's death in Spain and in Guy's betraying England and spying for the Soviets. Typical of much British Cold War culture, however, the frame of empire is otherwise absent.

The film's Geoffrey Clifton closely resembles one of the bullying prefects who thrashed Firth so soundly in *Another Country*. Unlike his celebrated portrayal of Jane Austen's Mr Darcy, reprised in *Bridget Jones's Diary* (2001), his bluff, armored exterior conceals no inner reserves of sensitivity. Clifton belongs instead to the laddish world of British soldiery in the film, a slightly parodic zone populated by familiar character actors straining to give depth to stereotypes. Kevin Whateley's presence as Sergeant Hardy, for example, shamelessly recalls his cheerfully deferential Sergeant Lewis from Granada Television's *Inspector Morse* series, an iconic Englishness tried and tested on the export market.[39] The scenes of British officers in Tobruk under siege, for example, echo countless World War Two movies in their brisk evocation of the call of duty amidst the chaos and confusion of wartime. The crisis of British imperial power in North Africa is transformed into another heritage film spectacle. The German soldiers, by contrast, seem more at home in this treacherous Orient, a point emphasized by the gratuitous presence at Caravaggio's interrogation and torture of an attractive Arab nurse who has no counterpart in Ondaatje's novel. As Josef Pesch observes, this brief addition to the scene puts a Moslem on a level with the Nazis.[40] This revision of the text has been justly criticized, but it is consistent with the treatment of Arabs in Minghella's film adaptation, who barely feature except as an objectified, near-invisible labor force.[41] As stubborn, barely acknowledged presences whose point of view is never focalized, they reveal momentary glimpses of the film's exploitation of the "new international division of labor," which led the production to use Tunisia as a source for cheap labor and exploitable locations that could be transformed without the interference of environmental regulation.[42]

Ironically, the only character in the film who displays a sensitive "new masculinity" is Naveen Andrew's Sikh sapper, Kip. His long, flowing hair released from his turban in the gentle love scenes with Juliette Binoche's Hana, he represents a strong counterpoint to Fiennes's rigidity or Firth's machismo. A British-born South Asian actor, who has appeared in the television adaptation of Hanif Kureishi's *The Buddha of Suburbia* (1993) as well as *Karma Sutra* (1996), his screen presence brings an unconventional coding of masculinity and a witty and quietly critical postcolonial subjectivity into the otherwise white and bourgeois world of the film. However, there is little sign of the hybrid ethnic and sexual positionings celebrated in *The Buddha of Suburbia* and characteristic of much black British culture in the late 1980s and 1990s.[43] At the climax of his almost sexless romance with Hana, the screen Kip is shown as a child-like innocent who declares "I do want you to find me. I do want to be found. I do. I do" (SP, 122). As the verb tense shifts to the passive voice, his agency drains away as he repeats an ironic echo of marriage vows that the rigid racial and gender coding of the film could never allow to stand. In the next scene, he is shown defusing the German bomb "with his name on it" (SP, 123), but he displays little of the confident mastery of the novel's bomb disposal scenes. At the climactic moment he is shown paralyzed by indecision, needing Sergeant

Hardy's paternal, butler-like advice: [*Hardy*]: "You've got to cut, sir, that frost won't last." / [*Kip*]: "Go away." / [*Hardy*]: "Yessir" / [*Kip*]: "This is making me incredibly angry" / [*Hardy*]: "I know sir . . . Cut it, sir, you've got to cut it!" (SP, 127). As any viewer of *Inspector Morse* knows, if you depend on the good sergeant to tell you what to do, you are indeed in trouble. After Hardy is killed by a booby-trapped statue, Kip makes final his eulogy to Englishness.

> KIP: I was thinking yesterday – yesterday! – the Patient and Hardy: they're everything that's good about England. I couldn't even say what that was. We didn't exchange two personal words, and we've been through some terrible things, some terrible things . . . and us – he never once . . . He didn't ask me if I could spin the ball at cricket or the Karma Sutra or – I don't even know what I'm talking about.
> HANA: You loved him. (SP, 154)

Instead of his blistering anger at the militarist racism that incinerated Hiroshima, Kip's sudden departure from the film and from Hana is explained as a grief-stricken return to a self-contained, laconic masculinity. In a further reduction, Kip possesses neither full access to his own emotions nor to the now-obvious knowledge that the patient is neither "good" nor English. Both the Indian sapper and his lover, the Canadian nurse, are placed on the outside, as spectators of the fortified "English" masculinity represented by the patient and by Hardy.

Global Maps and Imperial War

Despite the collective efforts of Hana, Caravaggio, and Kip to excavate the full details of the English patient's identity and memories of war and romance, the novel keeps the question open to the last. Ondaatje's Almásy is shown deliberately exploiting ambiguities about his nationality and wartime allegiances to seduce his audience and to evade justice. In this way, Ondaatje is able to use narrative indeterminacy to distance his title character from the historical Almásy, a Nazi and homosexual. The film resolves these questions early on, making sure that the audience identifies the burned, bedridden patient as Count Almásy and the woman in the plane flying over the desert in the opening sequence as Katharine Clifton. Yet it carefully blurs the question of nationality by celebrating the internationalism of Almásy's "expeditioners;" Englishness, in the film, becomes a nebulous aura that can include both the demotic Geordie Sergeant Hardy and the Hungarian aristocrat Almásy.

Ondaatje's text not only critiques the Western narrative of the relationship between World War Two and decolonization, but it also participates self-consciously in the recent memory boom in which the Second World War itself, like the Libyan desert in the novel, has become an enormously resonant imaginative territory to be fought over and remapped. The novel's success thus depends on both resistance to and accommodation with the neo-imperial mythology of the post-Cold War era. Novel and film belong to two different moments in the millennial memory boom.[44] The first, into which the novel intervened, bloomed from the thaw that followed the collapse of the Soviet Union in 1989, in which national histories deep frozen and repressed during the Cold War could at last emerge and be confronted. In Western Europe this unleashed an obsessive return to the aftermath of the nationalisms of World War Two, to forgotten collaborations with the Nazis during the war, hasty denazification, and accommodation with war criminals; in the East, with the aftershocks of decades of totalitarian rule, state violence, and official and private surveillance. The European Union and the United States's long-delayed response to the genocidal civil war in Bosnia dramatized the failure of Western modernity to contain the atavistic power of these buried histories when they emerged virulently onto the post-Cold War stage. Beyond Fortress Europe, most notably in Latin America and South Africa, other client states of the US and Soviet Union sought some measure of official truth and reconciliation as a way of containing the fallout of decades of political repression and state-sponsored racism, torture, murder, and disappearance.[45]

The second memory boom of the mid- to late 1990s, into which the film version of *The English Patient* so triumphantly emerged in 1997, sought to leave national ghosts behind, recuperating the supranational and making the world safe for a new global order. It was to be more short lived. Here the Second World War could be represented as not merely the site of archaic nationalist violence, but also as a global event in which multinational cooperation, presided over by a benign US superpower, won out over the narrowly sovereign. Despite the rhetoric of globalization, however, agency remained tightly controlled by a sovereign power acting in the name of the new world order, and masquerading as the true spirit of internationalism. Steven Spielberg's *Saving Private Ryan* (1998) is a crowning example of this kind of repossession of world war as a narrowly American narrative. After the shocking events of September 11, 2001, the Middle East and Islam were remapped by the ideologues of a permanent global war on terrorism, demonized as the originary site of atavistic violence and terror. The failure of the new global order to accommodate the neo-imperialist designs of the Bush doctrine would lead to yet another desert war, against Iraq in 2003, despite widespread international condemnation. In the ubiquitous images from this second Gulf War, history and memory are remapped and emptied out into empty spaces, like the exoticized, feminized desert of *The English Patient*'s opening and closing sequences, opened up for traversing and penetration by the commanding, mobile gaze of the transnational spectator.[46]

Michael Ondaatje's novel *Anil's Ghost* (2000), which assembles a group of characters similar to those in *The English Patient*, each damaged and struggling to recover from the consequences of traumatic violence at the end of a civil war, has enjoyed far more modest success. Certainly, the story is more localized, centered around an Americanized forensic archaeologist returning to her native Sri Lanka to investigate state terrorism and to engage in a quest for truth, if not reconciliation. But its far more modest success suggests that more is at stake. Though it lacks *The English Patient*'s intertextual wealth and literary self-assurance, and refuses the seductions of romance, *Anil's Ghost* does offer Ondaatje's trademark exotic settings and ambitious archaeological scope. But this more recent novel is positioned far more precariously in theme and content in relation to the Western culture markets. Its insistence on charting the specificity of postcolonial violence and on state terrorism is far less assimilable to the Hollywood version of truth and reconciliation, which prefers its excavations of genocide to be located amongst the old nationalisms of the First World, in a traumatic European past that has finally been put to rest. There has as yet been no screen adaptation of *Anil's Ghost*.

Maps are the figures for both memory and colonization in both *English Patients*. They are also weapons of war. Idealized as works of art, "drawn by desire," as in the map of deep England that Kip admires at Lord Suffolk's manor (EP, 190), they stand as the symbolic markers for a depoliticized world of imperial exploration and romance.[47] As the patient lyrically declares, "Give me a map and I'll build you a city. Give me a pencil and I will draw you a room in South Cairo, desert charts on the wall. Always the desert was among us . . . But you do not find adultery in the minutes of the Geographical Society" (EP, 117). Yet they are also clearly associated in the novel's plot with their strategic and instrumental function as potential instruments of war that allow the ownership and "rape" of the desert. This is the crucial knowledge that the traitor Count Almásy sells to the Germans in exchange for passage back to the desert, though the precise details of the transaction remain hazy (EP, 253–4).

The film makes clear the link between mapping and war by staging a literal scene of betrayal that does not appear in the novel. It takes place in melodramatic fashion in the desert next to Madox's Tiger Moth plane: "*Almásy carries a mapcase and hands it over to the German officer, who salutes him and walks towards his car. Almásy turns to the plane, rips off a sign Madox has pinned to a wing. It reads* SEE YOU IN DORSET" (SP, 153). The betrayal is personalized yet simultaneously diminished by the patient/ Almásy's off-screen voice-over: "I did get back. I kept my promise. I was assisted by the Germans. I had our expedition maps. And after the British made me their enemy, I gave their enemy our maps" (SP, 152–3). His act of collaboration, which will kill thousands by getting German spies and troops across the desert to Tobruk, is elided as Almásy the doomed romantic takes flight into apolitical international space over the desert, leaving behind a war between enemy and enemy. "So I got back to the desert and to Katharine in Madox's English plane with German gasoline. When I arrived in Italy, on my medical chart, they wrote 'English Patient.' Isn't that funny, after all I became English" (SP, 153).

Despite its attempt to locate its war story in time and space, the film ultimately prefers to draw its own maps of desire on visually stunning but empty landscapes. The desert becomes a feminized space to be exotically and erotically explored and conquered. The patient/Almásy is shown finding the Cave of Swimmers by comparing the rocky landscape to a sketch map of a ridge that the screenplay claims looks "*exactly like a woman's back*" (SP, 59). Though he gets the information from an elderly Bedouin in the first flashback to the desert, the conversation is not translated and Bedouin culture remains, like the desert's seemingly endless sand dunes, objectified and mysterious, off limits to the film's audience. In one of the most striking of its drastic revisions, the film puts the patient's climactic speech about cartography into the mouths of Hana and Katharine. The ironic juxtaposition between his confession of his collaboration with the Nazis, his complicity in the murder-suicide that kills his lover and her husband, and his morphine-inspired homoerotic vision of "an earth that had no maps" (EP, 261) is entirely lost. Despite the fact that in the novel Katharine Clifton herself had earlier mocked this very solipsistic escapism, the film gives these lines to her. The message seems to be that she has joined him in this noble, if romantically doomed alternative to the chaos of World War Two: "I want all this marked on my body. We are the real countries, not the boundaries drawn on maps with the names of powerful men . . . That's all I've wanted – to walk in such a place with you, with friends, an earth without maps" (SP, 159). By having Katharine, and Hana in voice-over, identify her body with the desert, the film mobilizes and recycles a familiar orientalist trope.[48]

Clearly, the film seeks to place the spectator in exactly the position of this "you," as a "friend" to the romantic lovers who will also embrace their utopian vision of "an earth without maps." The screenplay makes explicit that the final shot, which closes the opening frame of Almásy's doomed last flight over the desert with Katharine, is designed to communicate exactly this image of boundlessness: "*The plane banks over the dark ravines of the Gilf Kebir, and then suddenly, the rocks have gone, giving way to the earth without maps – the desert – stretching out for mile after mile. Almásy, the English Patient, looks down on it / THE END*" (SP, 161). This can be read as a subversively molecular Deleuzian vision of Katharine or Hana as "becoming woman," as Barbara Kennedy argues.[49] But its boundless, spatializing vision depends on a radically depoliticizing amnesiac version of internationalism that the novel clearly ironizes and critiques.[50] Both the agency of Katharine and of the Arabs who populate the desert is finally erased in favor of the patient's sovereign, imperialist gaze over the desert. No sooner does this embodiment of imperial air power take to the skies over North Africa than he and his plane are consumed in flames and plunge earthward, trapped in a closed loop of nostalgia and repetition.

Notes

1   *Evening Standard* (March 18, 1997), 3. Recalling the false dawn of 1981, when Colin Welland declared "The British are coming" as he collected his Oscar for *Chariots of Fire*, the article proclaims: "Not since the days of the 'Hollywood Raj', the golden age of the thirties and forties – when Charlie Chaplin, Cary Grant and a host of other Brits shone in front of the camera – has this nation's stock been so high."

2   Anthony Minghella, cited in Maya Jaggi, "Journey to Hollywood: Michael Ondaatje Reveals Why He Welcomes the Screen Adaptation of *The English Patient*," *The Guardian* (March 6, 1997), 9. Minghella's screenplay for the film was published with a carefully arranged trinity of testimonials: a "Foreword" by Michael Ondaatje, a "Preface" by Producer Saul Zaentz, and an "Introduction" by the director, each attesting to the authenticity and harmony of the

collaboration. See Anthony Minghella, "Introduction," *The English Patient: A Screenplay by Anthony Minghella* (London: Methuen Drama, 1997), pp. vii–xvi.

3   Minghella, "Introduction," *The English Patient: A Screenplay*. The screenplay is cited in the text as SP. All quotations from the novel are from Michael Ondaatje, *The English Patient* (New York: Vintage, 1992), referred to in the text as EP.

4   Michael Ondaatje, "Preface," *The English Patient: A Screenplay*, p. viii.

5   Jaggi, "Journey to Hollywood," 9.

6   For an incisive critique of the film's excision of any reference to Hiroshima, see Josef Pesch, "Dropping the Bomb? On Critical and Cinematic Reactions to Michael Ondaatje's *The English Patient*," in Jean-Michel Lacroix (ed.), *Re-constructing the Fragments of Michael Ondaatje's Works: Le diversité déconstruite et reconstruite de l'œuvre de Michael Ondaatje* (Paris: Presses de la Sorbonne Nouvelle, 1999), pp. 229–46. See also the important critiques of Jamal Mahjoub, "Review of *The English Patient*," *Wasafiri* 26 (Autumn 1997), 76; and Raymond Aaron Younis "Nationhood and Decolonization in *The English Patient*," *Literature/Film Quarterly*, 26: 1 (1998), 5–8.

7   *Première* 10: 4 (December 1996), 100.

8   Mark Crispin Miller, "What's Wrong with This Picture?," *The Nation* (December 20, 2001), 1–2. See also Toby Miller, Nitin Govil, John McMurria, and Richard Maxwell, *Global Hollywood* (London: British Film Institute, 2001). For useful resources on global media concentration, see the Center for Digital Democracy's website (www.democraticmedia.org).

9   Toby Miller discusses the changing British government regulations in "The Film Industry and the Government: Endless Mr Beans and Mr Bonds?," in Robert Murphy (ed.), *British Cinema of the 90s* (London: British Film Institute, 2000), p. 39. The EU's definitions of "European" film identity are discussed by Ian Christie, "As Others See Us: British Film-making and Europe in the 90s," in Murphy (ed.), *British Cinema of the 90s*, p. 75. For the Department of National Heritage's strenuous attempts to reinterpret both sets of regulations to restore the Britishness of *The English Patient*, see "DNH Bends own Rules to Claim Patient as British," *Screen Finance* (March 23, 1997), n.p.

10 The first British exposé of the Count's collaboration with and spying for the Nazis was Sebastian O'Kelly's "The Real Laszlo de Almásy," *The Daily Telegraph*, Weekend Section (March 11, 1997), 19.

11 Raymond Aaron Younis ably critiques this logic in "Nationhood and Decolonization," 3–5.

12 On the seductive claims of imperial air power to discipline and oversee colonial subjects and territories, see, for example, David E. Omissi, *Air Power and Colonial Control: The Royal Air Force 1919–1939* (New York: Manchester University Press, 1990); or Sven Lindqvist's provocative survey, *A History of Bombing* (New York: New Press, 2001). The same old-fashioned imperial logic can be seen at work in the recent deployment of US and British air power in Kosovo, Afghanistan, and Iraq to discipline and punish large numbers of intransigent, and largely Muslim, bodies by using high-tech weaponry and surveillance in the name of "postmodern" humanitarian warfare, in order to reduce the exposure of its own massed ground forces on the field of battle.

13 For elaborations of Gérard Genette's influential discussion of "analepsis" in *Narrative Discourse: An Essay in Method* (Ithaca, NY: Cornell University Press, 1980), see Shlomith Rimmon-Kennan, *Narrative Fiction: Contemporary Poetics* (London: Methuen, 1983), pp. 46–51; and Michael J. Toolan, *Narrative: A Critical Linguistic Introduction* (New York: Routledge, 1988),

pp. 50–4. Edward Branigan offers a useful discussion of the specifically filmic functions of the flashback in his *Narrative Comprehension and Film* (New York: Routledge, 1992), pp. 172–9; see also Robert Stam, Robert Burgoyne, and Sandy Flitterman-Lewis, *New Vocabularies in Film Semiotics: Structuralism, Post-structuralism and Beyond* (New York: Routledge, 1992), pp. 118–22.

14 Erica Sheen uses the work of Michel Foucault and Pierre Bourdieu to discuss the rapid accumulation of "consecrated" cultural capital by both novel and film in her "Introduction" to Robert Giddings and Erica Sheen (eds), *The Classic Novel: From Page to Screen* (New York: Manchester University Press, 2000), pp. 9–10.

15 See, for example, Bronwen Thomas, "'Piecing Together a Mirage': Adapting *The English Patient* for the Screen," in Giddings and Sheen (eds), *The Classic Novel*, pp. 197–232.

16 One remarkable readerly response to the novel's narrative logic is Lisa Mirabile's marvelously ordered intertextual index to the novel, "An Index to the Vintage 1993 edition of *The English Patient* by Michael Ondaatje," June 1998 (http://people.ne.mediaone.net/gbirch/epindex.html).

17 See Thomas, "'Piecing Together a Mirage,'" esp. pp. 215–17 on the "difficulty" of the film.

18 On the logic of the "dangerous supplement," see Jacques Derrida's discussion of the play of speech and writing in Rousseau's *Confessions*, in *Of Grammatology*, trans. Gayatri Spivak, corrected edn (Baltimore, MD: The Johns Hopkins University Press, 1998), pp. 141–67.

19 Robert Stam, "Beyond Fidelity: The Dialogics of Adaptation," in James Naremore (ed.), *Film Adaptation* (New Brunswick, NJ: Rutgers University Press, 2000), pp. 54–76.

20 For postcolonial critiques of the adaptation, see Pesch, "Dropping the Bomb?," pp. 229–46; Mahjoub, "Review of *The English Patient*," 76; and Younis, "Nationhood and Decolonization," 5–8.

21 Douglas Barbour, *Michael Ondaatje* (New York: Twayne, 1993), p. 199.

22 See the closing section of Michael Ondaatje, *Anil's Ghost* (New York: Alfred A. Knopf, 2000), pp. 299–307, in which a religious statue blown up during Sri Lanka's violent civil war is carefully reconstructed under the supervision of the artisan Ananda. Ondaatje's narrator clearly prefers this scarred and broken Buddha, which had been ransacked and destroyed by thieves, to the seamless concrete replica being erected nearby.

23 For a discussion of the ambivalent status of the *Histories* as the work both of "the father of history" and of a notorious liar, see Thomas Harrison, "Herodotus and *The English Patient*," *Classics Ireland* 5 (1998), 1–10.

24 See Edward Said, *Culture and Imperialism* (New York: Alfred A. Knopf, 1993), pp. 190–281 and 326–36; and Ella Shohat and Robert Stam, *Unthinking Eurocentrism: Multiculturalism and the Media* (New York: Routledge, 1994), pp. 248–337. On the historical conjuncture in the Middle East during the twenties and thirties, as well as a lucid discussion of the political and cultural impact of the Second World War, see Albert Hourani, *A History of the Arab Peoples* (Cambridge, MA: Harvard University Press, 1991), pp. 315–49 and 351–65.

25 Rudyard Kipling, *Kim*, ed. Edward W. Said (London: Penguin, 1987), p. 49.

26 For a discussion of exactly "what" Kipling is writing about in relation to the discourses of British imperialism, see Edward Said's expansive discussion of *Kim* in *Culture and Imperialism*, pp. 132–62.

27 To reinforce this literary armoring of Almásy's masculinity, which verges at moments on misogyny, Anthony Minghella requested that Ralph Fiennes also read Philip Larkin before playing

the role. As Fiennes recalled to an interviewer: "He thought there was an austerity in some of Larkin's poems . . . Something remote, bitter, hard, removed and astute that might be useful." See "Patience Pays," *The Daily Telegraph* (February 6, 1997), 14. For a discussion of the deployment of armored bodies in the fascist *Freikorps* literature of the 1920s and 1930s against the intolerable softness and feminine "flow" of the "molecular," see Klaus Theweleit, *Male Fantasies*, vol. 2: *Male Bodies: Psychoanalyzing the White Terror* (Minneapolis, MN: University of Minnesota Press, 1989), pp. 75–6 and 191–7.

28 "Production Notes," *The English Patient* (Miramax, 1997), p. 20.

29 Ibid., p. 20.

30 I am grateful to Tawia Ansah for his insights on the aestheticizing transformation of the historical Amon Goeth in both Thomas Kenneally's novel and Spielberg's screen adaptation.

31 The British assault on the film was led by the novelist Frederick Forsyth, who published a critical piece in *The Spectator* in March 1997, after which the media followed suit. For a lively overview of the controversy, see Jonathan Margolis, "'Biggles Meets Barbara Cartland: Is There a Backlash against *The English Patient*?," *The Sunday Times* (April 27, 1997), 4–5. See also, for example, Alison Boshoff, "Oscar Knives are Out for The Un-English Patient," *The Daily Telegraph* (March 24, 1997), 5; Magnus Linklater, "For an Oscar, Play it Safe," *The Times* (March 29, 1997), 20.

32 As Stuart Hanson notes, despite the dominant presence of 15–34-year-olds amongst British cinemagoers, 61 per cent of the audience for *The English Patient* was over 35. Hanson cites figures from *Screen Finance* (March 19, 1998) in his "Spoilt for Choice? Multiplexes in the 1990s," in Murphy (ed.), *British Cinema of the 90s*, p. 55.

33 London's *Time Out* reported that, by May 1997, "Herodotos . . . whose name has been misspelt by everyone since the film came out" had sold "a massive 100,000 copies;" "Making History," *Time Out* (May 7–14, 1997), 6. Ondaatje's novel had sold 600,000 copies in the US as a "tie-in book" within three months of the film's release there and was already a "top 10 seller" in Britain even before the movie's opening (Jaggi, "Journey to Hollywood," 9).

34 Margolis, "Biggles Meets Barbara Cartland," 5.

35 *Seinfeld*, 8th series, episode 151, "The English Patient," broadcast March 13, 1997 (produced by Shapiro/West Productions in association with Castle Rock Entertainment, distributed by Sony Pictures Television).

36 See, for example, Douglas Sternberg, "A Firmament in the Midst of Waters: Dimensions of Love in *The English Patient*," *Literature/Film Quarterly*, 26: 4 (1998), 255–62.

37 On the connection between images of archaeological excavation, the desert, and the "dark continent" of femininity and imperialist discourse, see Shohat and Stam, *Unthinking Eurocentrism*, pp. 148–52; see also Anne McClintock, *Imperial Leather: Race, Gender and Sexuality in the Colonial Conquest* (New York: Routledge, 1995), pp. 28–31.

38 The duo are reunited on-screen in the film adaptation of Oscar Wilde's *The Importance of Being Ernest* (dir. Oliver Parker, 2002), in which Firth plays the duplicitous dandy Jack Ashworth.

39 Part of Anthony Minghella's "apprenticeship," after he quit his lectureship in English at the University of Hull in 1981 and made his first feature film, *Truly, Madly, Deeply* (1991), included work on "several witty episodes of *Inspector Morse*." See Jonathan Coe, "From Hull to Hollywood: Anthony Minghella Talks about his Film, *The English Patient*, and Denies that He is Turning into David Lean," *New Statesman* (March 7, 1997), 38–9.

40 Pesch, "Dropping the Bomb?" pp. 232–4.

41 Jack G. Shaheen gives the film a fairly positive assessment in his *Reel Bad Arabs: How Hollywood Vilifies a People* (New York: Olive Branch Press, 2001), pp. 184–5. But the objectification of the Arabs in the film clearly follows the contours of the objectifying and potentially dehumanizing logic outlined by Edward Said, for example, in *Zionism from the Standpoint of its Victims*, reprinted in Anne McClintock, Aamir Mufti, and Ella Shohat (eds), *Dangerous Liaisons: Gender, Nation and Postcolonial Perspectives* (Minneapolis, MN: University of Minnesota Press, 1997), pp. 15–38. See also Shohat and Stam, *Unthinking Eurocentrism*, pp. 23 and 148.

42 The film's "Production Notes" report that in order for the production's "army of transport vehicles and equipment trucks" to traverse the miles between Tozeur, Tunisia to the desert locations "the line producer Alessandro von Normann supervised the extension of the road while also widening the sandy camel/donkey path." They note with affectionate irony that the new road was named "the Saul Zaentz Imperial Highway" in honor of the film's producer (Notes 24–5). The film was also reported to have had a profound impact on the Tunisian tourist economy, which brought its own environmental consequences. For an invaluable discussion of the "new international division of labor," see Miller et al., *Global Hollywood*, esp. pp. 44–82.

43 An essay by Karen Alexander suggests that the problem is not limited merely to heritage productions like *The English Patient*, noting that during the 1990s black British films have failed to follow through on the work begun in the late 1980s by films like *My Beautiful Launderette*: "It seems ironic that the complexities of black British culture can be encapsulated in a love song or a dance track but fail to find articulation in one of the most modern art forms, cinema." See Karen Alexander, "Black British Cinema," in Murphy (ed.), *British Cinema of the 90s*, pp. 112–13.

44 On what he calls the post-Cold War "memory boom," see Andreas Huyssen's highly provocative analyses in *Twilight Memories: Marking Time in a Culture of Amnesia* (New York: Routledge, 1995).

45 For a definitive overview of the origins of truth commissions as instruments of state in Latin America, South Africa, and elsewhere, see Priscilla B. Hayner, *Unspeakable Truths: Confronting State Terror and Atrocity* (New York: Routledge, 2001).

46 Mary Louise Pratt discusses the "monarch-of-all-I-survey" scene in her *Imperial Eyes: Travel Writing and Transculturation* (London: Routledge, 1992), pp. 201–8. David Spurr uses the term "commanding view" to describe the broader tropes of surveillance in imperial discourse, in *The Rhetoric of Empire: Colonial Discourse in Journalism, Travel Writing, and Imperial Administration* (Durham, NC: Duke University Press, 1993), p. 18. Spurr, like Mary Pratt and Edward Said, traces the survival and persistence of these tropes in much contemporary discourse about the developing world.

47 Younis, "Nationhood and Decolonization," 6–9.

48 Stam and Shohat, *Unthinking Eurocentrism*, pp. 148–50; McClintock, *Imperial Leather*, pp. 28–31.

49 Barbara M. Kennedy, *Deleuze and Cinema: The Aesthetics of Sensation* (Edinburgh: Edinburgh University Press, 2000), pp. 147–62. Douglas Sternberg takes a similarly euphoric view of erotic fusion in the film; see his "A Firmament in the Midst of Waters," 255–62.

50 David Aaron Murray critiques the political isolationism of *The English Patient*, contrasting it to the overtly interventionist logic of *Casablanca*, from which it cites, in "*The English Patient* Plays *Casablanca*," *First Things* 73 (May 1997), 10–12.

Chapter 11

Carnivals and Goldfish: History and Crisis in *The Butcher Boy*

Jessica Scarlata

> Carnival is for Bakhtin the "antibody" living within a pathological social body, always threatening to rupture the latter from within. In other words, carnival is simultaneously continuous with the contemporary social world and desperately at odds with it. It is not therefore a species of "bad utopianism," for Bakhtin clearly believes that a carnivalistic culture of the people actually existed in the not-too-distant past, and that it continues to be a potent (albeit rarely appreciated or understood) force in the present.
>
> Michael Gardiner, *The Dialogics of Critique*[1]
>
> When you roll into the carnival, anything can happen . . .
>
> Wyclef Jean, "Anything Can Happen," *Wyclef Jean Presents the Carnival*

In arguing against the accusation that Mikhail Bakhtin's theorization of the carnival offers merely a version of naïve utopianism, Michael Gardiner expands Bakhtin's celebration of the carnivalesque and the comic grotesque to a context in which they may have a profound and lasting effect on the society from which they emerge. In Gardiner's explanation, carnival is no longer a safely contained utopian moment of free contact and the inversion of social hierarchies — a moment cordoned off by holidays and quarantined to the marketplace and fairground — it becomes a force that can be mobilized in everyday culture, in literature (as Bakhtin's own analysis demonstrates) and in film.[2] In emphasizing the disruptive over the euphoric aspects of carnival, Gardiner opens up a space in which the carnivalesque may be rendered dystopian but remain an "antibody" within a moribund and repressive social order. Or, as demonstrated throughout *Wyclef Jean Presents the Carnival* (1997), "anything can happen," including playful subversion, celebration, violence, death, unemployment, and revolution.

Both Gardiner and Wyclef present a way to consider the potential and the limits that a Bakhtinian understanding of carnival offers a postcolonial Irish text and context. Put simply, how do you speak of the carnivalesque of a not-too-distant past in a country where the comic grotesque has often been used in the service of racist colonialist caricatures and where carnival freedom has a history of being violently repressed? At the same time, it is this potential for radical rupture from within a repressive culture that gives the carnivalesque imagery in Patrick McCabe's *The Butcher Boy* its dynamic power for critical readings of Ireland's colonized history.

This chapter will look at the ways in which McCabe's novel and Neil Jordan's film adaptation use actual carnivals, carnivalistic excess, the grotesque, garbage, and kitsch to engage with Ireland's colonized history and to critique Irish postcolonial cultural nationalism. *The Butcher Boy* can be read – and seen (and heard) – as a national allegory structured around fragments of history and culture which constantly disrupt any sort of continuity – of time, space, genre, emotion – and in so doing force open a space for critique within the monologic discourses of two historically opposed official cultures: British colonialism and Irish postcolonial nationalism.

The Butcher Boy: Synopsis and Criticism

Set in the early 1960s in the small town of Clones, Co. Monaghan, *The Butcher Boy* centers on Francie Brady, the pre-adolescent son of a volatile and alcoholic father (Benny) and a psychologically shattered mother (Annie). Events in Francie's life are told filtered through his own chaotic consciousness, narrated in both novel and film in his piercing, wounded, unstable voice. The initial bucolic moments Francie enjoys with his best friend Joe are threatened early in the story by the Nugent family, recently returned to the town from England. Francie's rivalry with the Nugents, particularly with Mrs Nugent, begins shortly after he and Joe swindle her son Philip out of comic books. Mrs Nugent visits Francie's home to chastise Annie Brady, ending the confrontation by calling the Bradys pigs, and screaming "Pigs – Sure the whole town knows that!"[3] The epithet of "pig," recalling a long English tradition of cruel anti-Irish caricatures, sticks to Francie for the rest of the story, often as a marker of difference between his family and the Nugents.

In addition to his continuing rivalry with the Nugents, Francie's life is broken by frequent loss and recurring violence and structured by his constant return to the town square ("the diamond"); with each return to the diamond, Francie relentlessly hopes that his life will somehow be made whole. Shortly after Mrs Nugent's visit, Francie's mother suffers a nervous breakdown and is taken to an asylum. She is released in time for Christmas, when his parents fight bitterly, and Francie runs away to Dublin, returning to find that his mother has committed suicide in his brief absence. After his mother's death, Francie's antagonism toward the Nugents escalates. He breaks into their home, vandalizing it in a comically grotesque way, and is promptly sent to a reform school run by Catholic priests, one of whom molests him. Because of the potential embarrassment Francie's experience holds for the school, he is released early for his silence. Throughout the rest of the story,

Francie continues to yearn for and hate the TV-perfect life of the Nugents as his own life is further marred by his father's death and Joe's growing friendship with Philip Nugent. When the town doctor and police sergeant discover that the body of Benny Brady has been left where he died — in the home — Francie is sent to another "reforming" institution, an asylum, where he is drugged and given shock treatment, and from which he eventually escapes.

Back at the diamond again, Francie begins working for the town butcher, collecting "brock" (bits of rotting food for feeding pigs), delivering meat, and cleaning the slaughterhouse. He learns that Joe has gone away to a boarding school near the seaside holiday town of Bundoran, where Francie's parents spent their honeymoon. He heads off to Bundoran in search of both the halcyon days of his parents' honeymoon stories and a renewed purity of friendship with Joe. He arrives only to find out that his parents' idyllic stories were lies and that his friendship with Joe is over for good. This ultimate loss of Joe to Philip Nugent leads him back to the town one last time, and into the Nugent home, where he kills and butchers Mrs Nugent on the day the town is preparing for a visit from the Virgin Mary. Francie buries the pieces of Mrs Nugent's body at the bottom of the brock heap, hides from the town and eventually surrenders. The novel ends with a tearful Francie in a madhouse thinking of Joe. In one of its few departures from the plot of the novel, the film ends with Francie as an adult released from the asylum into a green world dotted with sheep and snowdrops.

Much of the criticism of *The Butcher Boy* focuses on the individual psychology of Francie Brady, understanding the story almost as a cautionary tale about the damage that years of abuse can do, turning children into murderous pre-adolescents, and the dynamic of abused-becoming-abuser is central to both the novel and the film. In Francie, McCabe creates a mass of complexities; his disjointed thoughts fly at the reader, bringing both riotous laughter and crushing pain, often within the same sentence or paragraph. In the novel, Francie's devastating loss of his mother, his peaceful love of "the beautiful things of the world," and his increasingly violent fixation on Mrs Nugent and her son all contribute to a densely textured story that merits a critical examination of the individual psychology of Francie. Although the film maintains Francie's disjointed voice (primarily through voice-over narration), it also reduces and eliminates many of the complexities surrounding the novel's other characters and events. In the film, a version of the story emerges that is given audiovisually in broad strokes, rendering the text's fragmentary elements — carnivals, garbage, kitsch objects, Hollywood "B" movies and threshold spaces — jarringly discordant.

In his essay on *The Butcher Boy*, "The Abused Child of History," film historian Martin McLoone argues for a more political and less psychological reading of Jordan's film.[4] Taking into account the film's specific national and historical context — rural Ireland in the midst of modernization and Americanization — McLoone explains that the concept of the abused child functions as a metaphor for the brutality of Irish history, a history that includes centuries of violent colonization. In this reading, the fact that Sinéad O'Connor plays Francie's hallucination of the Virgin Mary becomes significant given O'Connor's outspokenness about child abuse in Ireland and her own use of this metaphor in her song *Famine*: "I see the Irish as a race / that's like a child that got itself bashed in the face."[5] The connection between child abuse and the Famine is not accidental; the "Famine hovers in Irish consciousness as a great tragedy that, like childhood trauma, has been suppressed and remains strangely unacknowledged."[6] McLoone's argument that, in *The Butcher Boy*, trauma extends beyond Francie's personal ordeals brings out complexities in the film not visible in a strictly psychological reading. But, at the same time, it remains focused only on Francie and his place within an incomplete, dysfunctional family – a metaphor for the sickness of the nation.[7] While the pathological Brady family is at the heart of the novel and film, other characters and events play a significant if less central role. This chapter is an exploration of those peripheral, neglected aspects of *The Butcher Boy* which become important to understanding how the film and novel can be read together as parts of a larger text which addresses the pain of a colonized history and the disappointment of a postcolonial state.

McLoone's analysis of the film reveals some of the ways in which it is critical of Irish history and Irish cultural nationalism, and his reading can be expanded by examining the film and novel together as a kind of third text that has a greater complexity than either of its two components alone. McCabe co-wrote the screenplay with Jordan and was closely involved with the film's production, even appearing as the debauched "Jimmy the Skite" (a character like the "drunk lad" in the novel), who follows Francie around, hitting him up for cash. While film adaptations are often misunderstood as flattened and/or corrupted versions of their "pure" literary "sources," McCabe's collaboration with Jordan undermines such an understanding and blurs the boundaries between the literary "original" and its filmic "copy." His presence in the film as a drunk and ragged character who milks Francie (his own creation) for money further carnivalizes his own authority as *The Butcher Boy*'s only creator. When both versions of *The Butcher Boy* are looked at together, what emerges is a kind of national allegory that radically critiques not only the violent colonization of Ireland, but also the brutality of the postcolonial state which broadcast an impossibly Catholic and idealized image of the nation, an image that contrasted sharply with the abject conditions of many of its citizens.

National Allegory

Film theorist Ismail Xavier has examined the resurgent critical interest in allegory and the different historical uses of allegory in culture.[8] In "Historical Allegory," he explains that allegory reveals the gap between words and their meaning; an allegorical reading of a text acknowledges the non-transparency of language.[9] The gulf between what is spoken and what is meant has a particular resonance for countries with colonized histories, not only because the people of those countries were depicted as liars by their colonizers, but also because of the interdiction on speech that the colonizer imposed, be it the use of the native language in official colonial institutions, the prohibition of verbal protest and organization, or the censorship on television and radio of certain political parties. Allegory can also speak of historical trauma where direct representation fails. As Xavier writes: "the accumulation of historical experience related to cultural shock, slavery, repression, and violence has shown its central role in the interaction of different cultural systems."[10] Adapting his list to an Irish context, I would add the Famine.

Xavier concludes his essay with a type of national allegory that critically engages with issues and questions relating to the nation and nationalism. This kind of allegory is "effectively engaged in reflecting on the crisis of the category of nation as a social and political framework . . ." Xavier writes: "Allegories . . . often emerge from controversies, conflicts of interpretation, confrontations related to struggles for hegemony . . . So allegory is bound to emerge . . . as a privileged signifying practice that brings to light all the ambiguities related to national identity and interests, or related to the omnipresent mediasphere shaping our everyday life."[11] *The Butcher Boy* addresses the ambiguities of national identity in many ways, most often by setting up, playing with, and subverting stereotypes of Ireland and the Irish. Xavier's "omnipresent mediasphere" becomes literal in the novel and the film, as Francie constantly looks to comic books, film, and TV for the language in which to articulate his desire and pain.

Looking at *The Butcher Boy* as a critical national allegory shifts the focus away from Francie's psychology and the abused-child metaphor, foregrounding other aspects of both the film and the novel that have often been marginalized in analyses of both texts: the treatment of time in the narrative, the beauty of the images, the ubiquity of garbage and other abject matter that violates core/periphery boundaries, the recurrence of kitsch objects, the prevalence of pig imagery, the different institutions of "correction" or "healing" that fail both Francie and his mother, and the casting of Sinéad O'Connor as Francie's vision of the Virgin Mary.

Reading the film and novel together as a national allegory foregrounds how *The Butcher Boy* examines Irish nationality diacritically, not as defined against another nationality (like English or US American), but against itself. A major strength of *The Butcher Boy* as a national critique is that it refuses to circulate an unproblematic sense of Irishness. The Nugents are anglicized and watch American TV. Francie and Joe read British and American comics and spend most of their time in the forest pretending to be American Indians. Benny Brady is a frustrated trumpet player and an abusive drunk, whose theme song in the film is "Oh Mein Papa." Annie Brady is insane – a walking, trembling reminder of the damage that a national cult of stoic maternal sacrifice can do to women. And characters like the townspeople and Father Bubble engage in typically Irish small talk and spout rustic wisdom, but do so in an excessively stereotypical and disturbingly ineffective way. In the film, even the Blessed Virgin Mother is played by an internationally known rock star with a Dublin accent, who has been publicly chastised for her outspoken critiques of nationalism and religion. The tension in the film and the novel between an idealized hegemonic conception of Irish national identity – which appears in excess at several points in both film and novel – and the failure of the characters and even the landscape to embody that ideal produces a text that is able to problematize "Irish" without sacrificing a sense of national cultural specificity.

An allegorical reading of *The Butcher Boy* begins to make sense of its disparate elements – its "fragmentary utterances, apparently interrupted messages, suggestive juxtaposition of images."[12] A striking example of this occurs in the novel, during one of Francie's careening pub conversations with "the drunk lad:"

> We went up to the Diamond Bar and he says I know you and you know me with his arm round me. Dink donk went the music take me back to Mayo the land where I was born. You're only a pack of baaastaaards! shouts the drunk lad. There was darts and this government is the worst yet and will you have another ah I won't ah you will and here is the news crisis in Cuba it all twisted in and out of itself till I got a pain in my head on top of everything else where are you going he shouts come back! (p. 149)

The line "this government is the worst yet" seems almost a throw-away and is followed by the question "will you have another?" On the surface, the question seems to be asking "Will you have another drink?" but, in his prose, McCabe uses sentence fragments in a style similar to cinematic montage, where the juxtaposition of two fragments has a deeper and more politicized meaning than either part alone. "Will you have another?" could also mean "Will you have another government?" In this exchange, drinks and governments become interchangeable; the imagined grandeur of the latter is equated with the banality and corrupting influence of the former.

This literary montage mixes official and popular cultures – the government and the pub – in carnivalesque fashion. The dazzlingly chaotic style of the prose is translated into an audiovisual style through which the film indifferently represents both the mundane details of life in Clones and the more horrific and spectacular moments in the story. Slick, over-saturated images complement the sound track's warped carnival theme, which at times resembles music from the horror film *Carnival of Souls* (1962) – tinkling bells, organ music slightly off-kilter, the tempo just a beat too slow – finding moments of both beauty and horror in Francie's world.

Carnival in its many manifestations dominates *The Butcher Boy*. Pigs, excessive amounts of food and drink, garbage and defilement, religious parody, threshold spaces, anti-grammaticality, role-playing, and violations of core/periphery boundaries reappear and recur throughout both novel and film. However, many of these carnivalesque elements were also stereotypes grafted onto the Irish by their English colonizers. Carnival in *The Butcher Boy* is rarely utopian (of the naïve or radical kind), but it often maintains the power to rupture official discourse. The frenetic energy of both novel and film derive from these carnivalesque elements, but that energy is often paired with anxiety, as when a real carnival comes to town while Francie is away in the reform school. Joe writes Francie a letter recounting the fun he and Philip had together, and telling Francie that Philip won a goldfish and gave it to Joe. Francie is tormented by this threat to his bond with Joe, obsessively returning to the question of *why* Joe took the goldfish. He finally decides to stop thinking about it, declaring, "Carnivals and goldfish, the end," but then instantly begins worrying again about the possibility of losing Joe. When Francie finally attends the carnival himself, it offers no release, only beatings and drunken hallucinations (from liquor procured by McCabe/Jimmy the Skite). That a dystopian carnival permeates *The Butcher Boy* raises questions about the death of the carnivalesque in Ireland and the limits that a Bakhtinian analysis of carnival and the grotesque has for an Irish context.

Oppressive Laughter

Bakhtin writes that laughter, with its link to the internal aspects of subjectivity, "could never become an instrument to oppress and blind the people. It always remained a free weapon in their hands."[13] While Bakhtin may not be offering a naïve utopianism in his theories of the carnivalesque, his work is overly optimistic about the liberating potential of laughter, which, along with the comic grotesque, was used to ridicule the colonized and to justify their continued oppression. Images of the grotesque body – fat bellies, noses elongated to resemble snouts, and voracious open mouths – were appropriated by British Victorian magazines to depict the Irish and Africans as porcine or simian and therefore greedy and impulsive and unfit for self-governance.[14] The chaotic domestic inversion and reversal of gender hierarchies that elicits carnivalesque laughter were used in cartoon representations of the colonized to characterize them as incapable of understanding the basics of "civilization" as defined by their middle-class colonizers. Irish popular festive forms were translated by the British Empire into evidence of a Celtic aversion to sobriety and reason. In opposition to these caricatures, Irish cultural nationalism invented and essentialized its own stereotypes: the noble, poetic, heroic Gaelic lord, whose descendants were pious and sober Catholics. The comic grotesque was occluded.

Bakhtin's analysis of laughter and the carnivalesque grotesque fails to consider the many uses of laughter in the service of oppression. As Anne McClintock explains, the laughter behind caricatures and stereotypes used to sell British imperial commodities repeatedly placed the white, Victorian middle-class on a higher plane of civilization than its comic others – the colonized, the working class, servants – the people made abject by the imperial culture.[15] But while the absence of oppressive laughter from Bakhtin's analysis limits its applicability to a colonial context, the power struggle he examines between an official hegemonic culture and the dialogic fragments it excludes *is* relevant to countries like Ireland in which the arrival of the postcolonial state brought a new and only slightly less suffocating construction of the nation.[16] This constricting national image defined "Irish" within the boundaries of orthodox Catholicism and rural, patriarchal traditionalism. The urban, working-class Irish were excluded from conceptions of the nation as were women who did not fit a domestic maternal ideal derived from Mother Ireland and the Virgin Mary. The traditional patriarchal family was enshrined in the constitution of 1937 which stated that women's greatest contribution to the Irish nation was to be made from within the home, and it received a more recent affirmation with the 1983 constitutional ban on abortion.

With specific historical references to (US) American television, Hollywood "B" films, and the Cuban Missile Crisis, *The Butcher Boy* is set during the social and political transitions of the early 1960s, when Irish society was supposed to have undergone rapid modernization and internationalization. In an earlier version of his essay, Martin McLoone writes that this historical shift provokes Francie's breakdown and ultimate act of violence. Finding himself caught between the hollow parochial society in which he lives and the emptiness of "modernization's excesses," which also bring about the loss of an older Irish identity, Francie has no coherent voice with which to speak and turns instead to violence.[17] Gibbons points out that this transition was not the revolutionary moment it has been mistaken for. Although "with revisionist hindsight, 1959 is taken as the *annus mirabilis* of modern Ireland," all that was declared to be dead – religious and cultural traditionalism, unemployment, and even nationalism – returned with a vengeance in the 1980s.[18]

The Butcher Boy is set during a moment of crisis that was understood to be a progressive break with the past but was merely a momentary repression of it, and the story is structured around crises in the linear aspect of time. Each time Francie leaves his home town of Clones to travel through "the wastes of time and space," he ends up back in the center of town, at the fountain built for a promised visit from Queen Victoria that never occurred. Each time Francie ends up back in town he hopes to recapture what he remembers as the happiness of his early days with his best friend Joe, but each return to the fountain brings him a step closer to losing Joe forever. In this complex structuring of time around linearity, suspension, and repetition, *The Butcher Boy* invites Irish history from all eras to haunt the text and becomes an artistic wedge driving open Irish historiography and questioning stagnated assumptions at its core.

History and Timeless Ireland

Through its particular use of time, *The Butcher Boy* is able to address the prevalence of the past in Irish culture and to criticize Irish postcolonial cultural nationalism by hinting at similarities between the colonial and postcolonial states. In the novel and its film adaptation, time is unbounded and confused, largely through Francie's narration. The story unfolds across multiple planes of time and space, which his mind occupies all at once. He imagines himself traveling thorough "the wastes of time and space" at different points in the story, and his own movement through time and space on a narrative level is mirrored on a formal level in both the novel and the film, although in different ways. Francie's gleeful disregard for the boundaries of temporality is made clear in the opening line of the novel, in which he is not merely imprecise about how far back in the past the story begins, but hyperbolically, comically vague:

> When I was a young lad twenty or thirty or forty years ago I lived in a small town where they were all after me on account of what I done on Mrs Nugent. I was hiding out by the river in a hole under a tangle of briars. It was a hide me and Joe made. Death to all dogs who enter here, we said. Except us of course. (p. 1)

Francie's deliberate vagueness about when he was young and his meandering away from the tantalizing allusion to what it was he did to inspire the animosity of the *whole town* play on stereotypes of temporal inexactitude and loquaciousness that have their roots in theatrical caricatures of the comically unruly Irish, who often "fail" to appreciate the "finer points" of grammatical and temporal exactness and of industriousness.[19]

The stereotype of the perpetually late or incurably lazy Irishman is connected to another pervasive stereotype involving time and Ireland, one that is used (although to different ideological ends) by English colonialist discourse, Irish-American nostalgia, and Irish cultural nationalism: the representation of Ireland as a land outside time, an ahistorical or mythic land. In *The Butcher Boy*, stereotypical images of timeless Ireland abound in descriptions (in the novel) and shots (film) of bright, rich green hills and embankments. In the opening of the novel Francie sits calmly by a stream while waiting for the town to find and punish him for the murder of Mrs Nugent:

> Then I stuck my nose out to see what was going on. Plink – rain if you don't mind! But I wasn't complaining. I liked rain. The hiss of the water and the earth so soft bright green plants would nearly sprout beside you. This is the life I said. I sat there staring at a water-drop at the end of a leaf. It couldn't make up its mind whether it wanted to fall or not. It didn't matter – I was in no hurry. Take your time drop, I said – we've got all the time we want now. We've got all the time in the world. (pp. 1–2)

Francie lingers in a postcard world where raindrops have time to decide whether or not to fall off leaves, and where the soil is so rich that plants can grow almost in minutes. Rain and the growth of plants – two ways to mark the passage of time – have as little regard for temporal exactness as Francie. In this fantastically green Ireland, time has ceased to be a reliable factor; we are in a suspended time, similar to the time associated with the carnival.

Film adaptation involves a visual and aural manifestation of a novel's descriptions, and, however far from "realism" an adaptation may be, the fact of the image would seem to pose a problem for maintaining the kind of temporal vagueness more easily rendered in literature, if only because age is visible and audible in the faces and voices of the characters. But the adaptation of *The Butcher Boy* cleverly maintains the novel's chaotic temporal pastiche primarily by splitting the character of Francie into two manifestations that often speak to each other: twelve-year-old Eamonn Owens who plays Francie on screen and Stephen Rea who narrates in voice-over. The film further complicates Francie's placement in time in that Rea (whose voice is easily recognizable on the sound track) plays Benny Brady on screen in addition to doing Francie's voice-over, and he also appears at the end of the film as the adult Francie released from the asylum. Furthermore, while the use of Rea over Owens for the voice-over fixes Francie's narration far into the future, that voice is frequently dislodged from its chronological position and literally put into dialogue with the on-screen events in the film's present, as in the "pig school" sequence discussed below.

In the film, the story begins with the same line, "When I was a young lad . . ." spoken over an image of Francie (Owens) and Joe made-up as American Indians, running through a rich green forest and standing on either side of a large, crystal-blue lake nestled between lush, green hills under a bright, clean sky. A more beautiful image of Ireland the *Bord Fáilte* (Irish Tourist Board) itself could not imagine. In a line that does not exist in the novel, the loss of this Eden is blamed on Mrs Nugent: "If she hadn't of poked her nose in between me and Joe, everything would have been alright." The name "Nugent" may carry with it echoes of the Famine, as it was also the name of an Anglo-Irish Famine landlord,[20] and Francie is quick to point out that Mrs Nugent has been anglicized, having come back from England with newly acquired "airs and graces." That Francie blames the anglicized Mrs Nugent for the loss of his paradise implies that this color-saturated world belongs to the imagined precolonial Ireland of cultural nationalism, a tie tightened by the postcard perfection of this shot.[21]

Luke Gibbons explains that postcards overflow with a specific type of nostalgia which "is not simply an evocation of an idealized past, but a very distinctive form of longing . . . the painful desire to restore the sense of belonging that is associated with childhood, and the emotional resonance of the maternal." In *The Butcher Boy*, this occurs on the personal, psychological level with Francie's painful longing for his mother. But given the historical allegorization of Ireland as a mother and the prevalence of female imagery in descriptions and allegories of the Famine, it could also be understood within the context of cultural nationalism's attempt to recover a past destroyed by colonialism, famine, and emigration. Gibbons explains that while Hollywood films like *The Quiet Man* can fulfill this desire by having American Sean Thornton return to and purchase the cottage lovingly described by his mother's voice, "in John Hinde's Irish postcards, there is an uneasy feeling that we are getting a last glimpse of a world that is lost. It is as if the emigrant's break with the past has been internalized *within* Irish culture, forming its popular image of itself."[22] Later in the film, this same shot reappears in one of Francie's hallucinations (induced by a doctor's sedative), only to be lost forever to an atomic bomb.

Famine and Carnivalistic Excess

In outlining the basic carnival imagery, Bakhtin focuses quite a bit on food, both the elaborate banquets of Rabelais' work, but also the centrality food had to the medieval carnival. Bakhtin writes, "Man's encounter with the world in the act of eating is joyful, triumphant . . . Sadness and food are incompatible . . . The banquet always celebrates a victory . . . It is the triumph of life over death."[23] In the novel, Francie frequently describes excessive amounts of food. When he runs away to Dublin, he spends a great deal of time eating: he goes to a candy store and buys thirty Flash Bars, eating "as many of them as I could" (p. 41). He continues eating his way through Dublin, ordering "a slap-up feed" at the Gresham Hotel and briefly taking on the alias of Algernon Carruthers, a boy in Philip's comic books who spends most of his time traveling "and eating big dinners" (p. 41). Francie then goes to a science fiction movie and loads up on candy at the concession kiosk, and, as he watches the film, he pushes "Maltesers into my mouth one after the other" (p. 42). But the exuberance associated with candy is sharply curtailed when one of the priests at the reform school – Father Tiddly, as Francie calls him – lures him into being sexually molested with excessive amounts of Rolos.

While feasting may be joyful and triumphant for Bakhtin, *The Butcher Boy* often juxtaposes excessive food with hunger, sadness, humiliation, and emptiness in that the food that exists in excess is not nourishing. Even the feast of Christmas – a celebration of an infant king – offers no safe haven from sorrow. Just before Christmas, Francie's mother has a nervous breakdown and is sent to an asylum (which Francie refers to as the garage, pretending not to understand the severity of his mother's illness). When she returns, she immediately sets to baking cakes and buns for the upcoming Christmas party. Francie explains: "The cakes were stacked in towers on the chairs. There were some on top of the wardrobe and the washing machine. There were ones with icing and without, all decorated with hundreds and thousands and marzipan and different kinds of designs" (p. 27). In translating this description into images, the film takes Francie's hyperbole seriously. On screen, the Bradys' kitchen literally overflows with cakes, and there is also not a trace of any other food in the house. Annie puts all the eggs, milk, and butter straight into the cake batter, singing and mixing the batter to the incessant repetition of the ballad "The Butcher Boy."

The sadness and violence that lurks behind food in the novel is layered under the cakes on the film's sound track. The film cuts to a shot of Francie sitting on his bed upstairs as his adult voice-over complains, "Well if I heard that record once, I heard it a hundred times," preventing us from clearly hearing the argument that is brewing between his parents down among the cakes in the kitchen. The *only* bit that filters through unmuffled is Benny yelling to Annie, "I'm fuckin' *starving*!" followed by more shouts and the clatter of breaking dishes. Francie later comes down the stairs, and the camera follows him but includes his point of view as he steps over broken plates, looks at cakes stuck to the wall by their icing, and watches one cake spin around on "The Butcher Boy" record which continues to play. Although the cakes on the walls and furniture are the result of a violent argument, there is something absurdly comical about the single, upturned cake spinning round and round, the cake fragments stuck to the unconscious Benny's face and hair, and the cake shrapnel lodged in the wall. The cakes elicit laughter, but they are also a sign of excess without nourishment. Here the celebratory food that marks a festive time is rendered dystopian. The carnivalesque in the form of excessive cakes is used to evoke the Famine in the form of hunger from having nothing nourishing to eat.[24]

McCabe's juxtaposition of the laughter of carnival with the sorrow of the Famine is significant as Gibbons has connected

> "the killjoy morality of post-Famine Ireland" to the eradication of the poorest of the poor and with them a system of religious practice that bordered on the riotous. The re-division of the land in the wake of the Famine enabled the rise of a wealthy, indigenous land-owning class which built churches, supplied religious orders with its younger sons and daughters, and could draw on recent example to illustrate that sexuality and sin and death were inextricably linked.[25]

While the Famine was not planned by the British colonial administration, that government also did little to ease its toll on the population. Potato blight also occurred in Scotland, England, and Wales, but only in Ireland did it cause a famine because only in Ireland did a large portion of the indigenous population rely solely on the potato for its sustenance. The Famine had the effect of aiding the processes of centralization that had begun before it with the gradual repeal of the Penal Laws, eventually legalizing Catholicism and thus allowing the Irish Catholic church to be brought into line with Roman Catholic orthodoxy.[26] It also helped to speed up the colonial project of land clearance, making the middle class (both Catholic and Protestant) wealthy in the process. In Ireland, the carnivalesque culture of the "not too distant past" that Bakhtin believed in was killed off both by the death and emigration of actual people and by the entrenchment of a traditionalist middle class, part of which would eventually help to shape the national image of the postcolonial state.

Bakhtin's theorization of carnival is, as Gardiner writes, not simply a version of simplistic utopianism, but rather a way of making room for the radical potential of ambivalence to drive a wedge into the monologic discourse of official cultures. However, despite Bakhtin's embrace of ambivalence, there remains very little room in his theorization for the oppressive historical shocks that can also accompany the carnivalesque. In Ireland, the loss of life and culture from the Famine and its wake hover ominously over the carnivalesque as spectral reminders of the violence of colonialism. As discussed above, the comic ambivalence associated with the grotesque — pigs, drunkenness, idiocy, filth — has a more negative resonance given the oppressive use of the grotesque to characterize the Irish. The grotesque carries with it a history of physical, cultural, and psychological violence rooted in the history of colonization, but enduring far beyond the moment of decolonization, as these stereotypes persist in more recent moments of English, American, and Irish culture, especially in cinema.[27] In *The Butcher Boy*, the grotesque is not washed clean of its oppressive history, but instead uses those associations to reveal the violence lurking beneath the staid patronizing smile of the official culture. In both the novel and its film adaptation, the grotesque is simultaneously comic *and* oppressive and remains always dangerous, dystopian, and toxically explosive.

Hybridization or adulteration resists identification both in the sense that it cannot be subordinated into a narrative of representation and in the sense that it plays out the unevenness of knowledge which, against assimilation, foregrounds the political and cultural positioning of the audience or reader.[28]

In *Anomalous States*, David Lloyd examines artistic forms that had been discarded by Irish cultural nationalism as disruptive to its constructed monologic image of an Irish identity. Much of his book looks at these fragments as they relate to the writing of an official Irish nationalist historiography which marginalized certain aspects of the culture in order to forge a unified identity with which to confront the colonizer. As he explains in his introduction, his point is "not simply to revalue marginal elements of Irish culture, but to reinsert them into the dynamic of identity formation and to restore to them some of the critical force for which they had to be expunged as 'unrepresentative.' "[29] For Lloyd, a critique of official postcolonial historiography is inseparable from a critique of colonialist historiography. The dynamic tensions within identity formation and the violent struggle in culture between an official historiography and one that disrupts and fragments is important to *The Butcher Boy*, which materializes this struggle through its use of threshold spaces and liminality. In *The Butcher Boy*, pigs and garbage often function as allegories of what is "trashed" by both colonialist discourse and anti/postcolonial cultural nationalism.

Pigs run rampant throughout the novel and film versions of *The Butcher Boy*. Mrs Nugent, having recently acquired "airs and graces" in England, first hurls the slur of "pig" at the Brady family, but rather than try to refute it, Francie takes the insult to an extreme, calling himself a pig throughout the story and using the label of pig to unmask the brutality behind the concerned smile of reforming state institutions. And, as Francie reminds us in the novel, Mrs Nugent is herself a pig, try as she might to disguise her identity with proper middle-class manners: "Then what does she do only lean right into me she was so close I could see the wiry hairs on her chin and the pink make-up and powder on her cheeks. The smell of it turned my stomach" (p. 46). Even the title – *The Butcher Boy* – evokes Francie's job in a slaughterhouse and his eventual butchering of Mrs Nugent. In positing Francie as both pig *and* butcher, the story also avoids the simple binary opposition between victim and victimizer – a binary upheld by cultural nationalism at the expense of a more complex and fragmentary view of Irish history.

Peter Stallybrass and Allon White describe the pig as a hybrid creature characterized as "almost but not quite," which transgresses the boundaries of human/animal and domestic/wild. Its pink, easily sunburned skin makes it almost but not quite human, its proximity to the house and diet of table scraps makes it almost but not quite domestic.[30] Friedrich Engels associated the Irish with pigs through their spatial proximity in the cities, but, as Stallybrass and White explain, the English kept pigs in their city homes as well.[31] The connection made in British colonialist discourse between the Irish and pigs stems more from the need to portray the colonized as existing on the border between human and animal. The Irish were constructed as almost human but not quite, or "almost the same but not white."[32] Like the inhabitants of other colonies, the Irish were also the servants of the British Empire, thus strengthening their association with dirt and liminality.[33] Pigs and dirt cross boundaries and disrupt categorization. In wearing the identity of pig, Francie resists assimilation into the society around him and acts as a stumbling block to the institutions that seek to produce citizens homogeneous with the official image of the nation. In this sense, Annie Brady's return from the garage as a hyperbolization of Irish domesticity is just a hint of what the Brady/Pig family is capable of.

When Francie arrives at the reform school, the priest he calls Father Bubble (though not to his face, of course) asks him what he thinks of his new home, and Francie replies that it is a fine school, for pigs. He needles the priest a little further, "*The Incredible School for Pigs!*, I said in my telly voice" (p. 73), and Bubble responds by preparing to beat Francie:

> He tried to get a hold of me, but I was too slippery for him and when I went down on all fours he couldn't manage it at all. I crawled around and it drove him mad. I let a few snorts out of me. There was an old priest above at a window. I went up on my hind legs and begged a bit for him. Snort I said and a big grin. Then Bubble caught me a rap on the side of the head and I saw stars. That's nothing to what you'll get, he said. I was glad he did it. I wanted him to give me a proper hiding. (p. 73)

Francie's performance as a piglet provokes the priest's outrage. While his reasons for instigating this violence stem partly from a desire to be beaten, possibly in order to alleviate the guilt and pain associated with his mother's death, the film omits this masochistic aspect and shortens the sequence so that Bubble hits Francie after fewer provocations. Francie follows Father Bubble (Brendan Gleeson) through the dormitory, and the priest seems at least twice Francie's size. He answers Francie's first provocation ("It's alright for pigs") by firmly but calmly saying, "I'm afraid you'll find no pigs here," but after Francie announces "The Incredible School for Pigs," Bubble responds with a whack that knocks Francie to the floor. That the priest's approach to schooling moves instantaneously from smile to stick becomes even clearer in the film, and Francie's urge to provoke violence seems to stem more from a desire to reveal the violence of assimilation than a drive to be punished. This is, after all, the second time Francie has been in a pig school. The first occurs in the school he conducts at the Nugent home, and, again, the film flattens out the novel's psychological detail so that we are left only with McCabe's parody of official state education.

In *Inventing Ireland*, Declan Kiberd examines the nature of postcolonial education in Ireland and other former colonies. He characterizes it as a system based on learning by rote and repetition designed primarily to teach students to pass national exams. "[Ireland's] schools remained obsessed with a hyperacademic form of learning, derived from the colonial period, which tested new recruits for the swelling civil service."[34] Religion took the place of English literature as the central object of study, which meant that the accomplishments of Irish writers in the English language went largely ignored. Kiberd states: "It may even have suited certain dogmatists in the Department of Education to misrepresent English culture . . . since that helped to feed a pet theory that Irishness was only to be found within the Gaelic tradition."[35] This is yet another way in which the postcolonial state answers one monologizing discourse with another, continually narrowing the definition of what constitutes Irishness so that the majority of the country is excluded from its hegemonic national image.

The film parodies this method of teaching when Francie breaks into the Nugents' home through the kitchen window while they are away. He smashes Mrs Nugent's cakes and grinds them into her gleaming, black-and-white linoleum floor. Francie eats a cake in front of the Nugents' TV, watching an American educational program demonstrating the "duck and cover" drill that will supposedly save lives in the event of a nuclear attack (clipped from *Atomic Café*, a carnivalesque treatment of nuclear warfare). As the camera abruptly zooms to a close-up of Francie, his adult voice-over announces, "Right, enough about bombs, today we're going to do the farmyard." Francie's voice-over plays the role of schoolmaster and Francie becomes his pupil Philip. The schoolmaster asks "Philip" which animals are found in the farmyard, guiding his answers along until they satisfy him. The instructor then tells his student to write twenty times, "Philip is a pig." In this "pig school" sequence, where Francie controls both ends of the dialogue, he reminds the Nugents that he is not the only pig in town. Francie also *becomes* Philip, writing "Philip is a pig" on the mirror/chalkboard.

In addition to parodying academic learning, this scene unmasks the face of the educational system, giving us a glimpse of the process of self-hatred that students learned in both the colonial state – which openly told them that England, not their own country, was the center of culture – and the postcolonial state which made abject anything beyond the scope of the official image of the nation. When the pig schoolmaster asks his student the final question, "And what do pigs do, Philip?" "Philip" gives several answers to which the schoolmaster replies, "Yes, but that's not quite the answer I'm looking for . . ." until, as men on the television put pigs into an atomic shelter and a bomb explodes, Francie-as-Philip-and-Mrs Nugent defecates on the living-room floor. *That* was the answer the schoolmaster wanted. In the novel, he explains, "They'll tell you that pigs are the cleanest animals going. Don't believe a word of it. Ask any farmer! Yes, pigs are poo animals. I'm afraid they simply will cover the place in it no matter what you do" (p. 66). While the film makes it clear that, in the eyes of the state, the "pigs" of Ireland will not produce anything worthwhile, the novel brings the idealized image of cute Irish farms back down to earth by reminding us of the shit that lies below the green.

Ultimately, Francie's power to provoke crisis is limited. After Joe ends their friendship, Francie returns to the town which is preparing for the end of the world and a visit from Our Lady. In the film, Francie sweeps up the slaughterhouse floor and has a conversation with the hanging dead pigs about whether Mary will show. He packs up the tools, and the film cuts between Francie's actions and the town's preparations, finally cutting to a shot of Mrs Nugent kissing her rosary beads in her home. Francie steps out from behind a door, shoots her with the captive bolt gun used to kill pigs, and butchers her body shouting, "One little piggy went to market, one little piggy stayed home," with each blow. Although this scene is utterly horrifying, a comic one follows on its heels. It begins with a chilling shot of the word "PIG" written repeatedly in Mrs Nugent's dripping blood over the floral wallpaper; the image is accompanied by a scream and a long discordant saxophone note. One of the women in the town comes screaming out of the Nugents' home, and is asked "Did you see her? Did you see Our Lady?" The townspeople take her inability to answer as a yes, and excitedly rush into the house, only to exit covering their mouths in horror. Francie's voice-over cuts in saying, "Well Our Lady never did show up, but Francie Brady didn't let them down, and it was the best show that town had ever seen." Francie then hides and dumps Mrs Nugent's dismembered body at the bottom of the brock heap, where flies buzz over bits of rotting food and garbage.

Robert Stam has described garbage as the "ideal . . . postcolonial metaphor . . . [a] radically decentered social text,"[36] and garbage pervades *The Butcher Boy*, violating core/periphery boundaries, blurring the distinction between human and non-human, and constantly destabilizing coherence because this radically decentered matter refuses to stay on the periphery. In the novel, garbage clings to Francie, staining him despite his best attempts to get clean: when he goes to Bundoran in search of his parents' idealized past, his jacket is stained with a spot of pig guts that attracts flies. In the film, trash and dirt seem to be everywhere except within the Nugent home. And in both film and novel, the greatest violation of core/periphery boundaries is the rotting corpse of Benny Brady sitting in the very center of the home – in front of the hearth.

There may be no flies or garbage in the Nugent home, but Mrs Nugent is hardly safe from the dangers of trash. Francie is constantly pushing against the front door of her home, trying to get in. When he finally does, he defiles first her home and then her. When Francie buries her under the brock, he could be "returning" her to the trash heap fit for pigs. The film's treatment of Mrs Nugent's murder amplifies whatever misogyny there may be in blaming Mrs Nugent for all of Francie's woes, in that, although shocking and gruesome, her murder becomes the material for the comedic scene that follows.

At the same time, the film features an important change from the novel that also functions as a critique of the "heart and home"[37] attitude of the postcolonial state in its gleeful parody of the mother of all sacred images (forgive the pun): the Virgin Mary. In the novel, when Francie has his religious "visions" at the reform school, he meets with a host of saints, or, as he puts it, "dozens of the fuckers" (p. 83). In the film, Francie talks only with the Blessed Virgin Mother, and to make matters more carnivalesque, this paragon of Irish feminine virtue is played by Sinéad O'Connor.

The (brilliant) casting of Sinéad O'Connor as Mary gives the film a critical force that it may not have had otherwise. O'Connor's background remains audible in her speech: Mary is not only no longer saintly silent (like the Virgin at Knock), but speaks with a Dublin accent. She is not a remote and impossible ideal for Irish women, but a member of multiple populations made abject by postcolonial nationalism (women, urbanites, abused children) which continue to be positioned in opposition to a "natural" Irish identity in films like *Into the West*.[38] Furthermore, O'Connor has also been vocal about issues that the state and church would rather avoid, such as women's reproductive rights and child abuse, appearing in Margo Harkin's *Hush-a-Bye Baby* (1989, made in the wake of the abortion debates in Ireland) and speaking out against the church's cover up of abuse perpetrated by members of the Catholic clergy.

O'Connor's appearance as the Virgin in *The Butcher Boy* is an instance where the carnivalesque functions "in order to 'defamiliarize' the present state of affairs, to historicize that which is generally taken to be immutable and eternal, and to relativize abstract claims to truth through a 'gay parody of official reason . . .' "[39] Mary appears in liminal, profane spaces to Francie. They have mundane conversations about his life and how "things" are going; she never instructs him to build a shrine or spread the "Word of God." These factors and the possibility that the "visions" may be just the hallucinatory products of a deranged mind shake the image of the Virgin Mary out of its unquestioned place at the core of Irish society. It destroys the staid, distant image of Mary as a role model whose state of grace can never be achieved by real women. It creates (or restores) an image of her as a guardian of the dispossessed rather than a contradictory identity (*virgin* mother) that women should spend their lives trying to imitate. Mary's kindness toward Francie and the humor in the film serve to remind an often authoritarian, centralized Roman Catholic church of the anti-hierarchical strains in its history that it tries to repress. Sinéad-as-Mary *is* the return of the repressed, and this is why Mary appears in liminal, dirty spaces to a dangerous and wounded child.

The Butcher Boy itself is a hybridization, bringing together the opposing linguistic consciousnesses (or genres) of comedy and tragedy within the single utterance of a paragraph, a shot or the whole novel or film. The humor in reviews of the film was classified as "sick" or "dark," and reviewers repeatedly expressed their amazement at laughing at certain scenes. *The Butcher Boy* destabilizes generic categories and elicits ambivalent laughter. In having the Famine and traditional Irish culture coexist in the same time and space as Flash Bars, Hollywood, and the Kennedys, the story begins to resemble Irish culture: a hybridization marked by the pervasiveness of the past, the unbroken threads of diaspora, and a disregard for temporal and spatial borders. But this continuity in no way lessens the sense of crisis. Rather, crisis, like carnival, disrupts official monologic culture and makes visible the continuity in time and space of a plurality of Irish voices.

--------------------- Acknowledgments ---------------------

I am indebted in this chapter to the work of several authors in postcolonial studies whose influence is present even when not directly cited. They include Luke Gibbons, David Lloyd, Anne McClintock, and Robert Stam.

History and Crisis in *The Butcher Boy*

Chapter 11

1   Michael Gardiner, *The Dialogics of Critique: M. M. Bakhtin and the Theory of Ideology* (London: Routledge, 1992), pp. 139–40.

2   See Robert Stam, *Subversive Pleasures: Bakhtin, Cultural Criticism, and Film* (Baltimore, MD: The Johns Hopkins University Press, 1989) for an excellent in-depth analysis of the relevance of Bakhtin's theorization of the carnivalesque to cinema, especially in a postcolonial context.

3   Patrick McCabe, *The Butcher Boy* (New York: Dell, 1992), p. 4. Subsequent references to the novel will be by page number in brackets in the text.

4   Martin McLoone, "The Abused Child of History," in *Irish Film: The Emergence of a Contemporary Cinema*, pp. 213–23 (London: British Film Institute, 2000).

5   Ibid., p. 219.

6   Ibid., p. 220.

7   Ibid., p. 223.

8   Ismail Xavier, "Historical Allegory," in Toby Miller and Robert Stam (eds), *A Companion to Film Theory*, pp. 333–62 (Oxford: Blackwell, 1999).

9   Ibid., p. 337.

10 Ibid., p. 333.

11 Ibid., p. 360.

12 Ibid., p. 340.

13 Mikhail Bakhtin, *Rabelais and his World*, trans. Helene Iswolsky (Cambridge, MA: MIT Press), p. 94.

14 Of course, these caricatures were not limited to Ireland and Africa. However, in the history of racist colonialist discourse, Ireland and Africa were often compared to each other, in part to gloss over the crisis that Ireland provoked in the categories of "white" and "native," which were constructed by colonialist discourse as two opposite and discrete categories, aiding in the constructed division of people into different "races." See Luke Gibbons, *Transformations in Irish Culture* (Notre Dame: University of Notre Dame Press, 1996); Noel Ignatiev, *How the Irish Became White* (New York: Routledge, 1995).

15 Anne McClintock, *Imperial Leather: Race, Gender, and Sexuality in the Colonial Contest* (London: Routledge, 1995).

16 Cf. Bakhtin, *Rabelais and his World*, p. 101.

17 Martin McLoone, "The Abused Child of History: Neil Jordan's *The Butcher Boy*," *Cineaste* 23: 4 (1998), 32–6. Cf. also David Lloyd "Violence and the Constitution of the Novel," in *Anomalous States: Irish Writing and the Postcolonial Moment* (Durham, NC: Duke University Press, 1993), for an interesting analysis of the relationship of violence to coherent/incoherent narratives of national identity and historiography.

18 Gibbons, *Transformations in Irish Culture*, p. 82.

19 These "stage Irish" caricatures have also been used in film representations of Ireland such as *The Quiet Man* (John Ford, 1952). The film playfully links an inability to see the value of time efficiency to an inability to "get to the point" when telling a story. *The Quiet Man* begins with the paradoxical situation of a train's being "three hours late *as usual*," and the town shaughran and drunk, Michaeleen Og Flynn, often interrupts his own stories with digressions or requests for drink. Luke Gibbons and Martin McLoone have both written extensively on Ford's reflexive use of stereotypes, arguing that he knowingly and winkingly offers an image

of Ireland saturated with an émigré's nostalgia for home (embodied in the film by John Wayne's Sean Thornton). Cf. Luke Gibbons, "Romanticism, Realism and Irish Cinema," in Kevin Rockett, Luke Gibbons, and John Hill (eds), *Cinema and Ireland* (Syracuse: Syracuse University Press, 1988); and McLoone, *Irish Film*, pp. 52–9.

20 Anne McClintock, "*The Butcher Boy*," Graduate Seminar, New York University, New York, December 8, 1998.

21 McLoone describes the shot as one "which resembles a postcard from the John Hinde collection (nature ever so slightly airbrushed and embellished)" in *Irish Film*, p. 214.

22 Gibbons, *Transformations in Irish Culture*, pp. 39, 40.

23 Bakhtin, *Rabelais and his World*, pp. 281, 283.

24 It is hard not to think of Marie Antoinette's "Let them eat cake." In addition, the other form of abundance-without-nourishment that surrounded the famine victims was grass, and one of the most chilling images of the famine is that of dying and dead bodies with grass-green stains around their mouths.

25 Ruth Butler, "Famine" (Review), *Film Ireland*, 50 (December 1995/January 1996), 39.

26 Luke Gibbons "The Colonial Sublime," Graduate Seminar, New York University, New York, March 31, 1997.

27 For example, the simian town mute in *Ryan's Daughter* (David Lean, 1970), Bull McCabe's inarticulate and impulsively violent son in *The Field* (Jim Sheridan, 1988), and the bungling, often drunk characters in *The Matchmaker* (1997) and *Waking Ned Devine* (Kirk Jones, 1999).

28 Lloyd, *Anomalous States*, p. 114.

29 Ibid., p. 5.

30 Peter Stallybrass and Allon White, *The Politics and Poetics of Transgression* (Ithaca, NY: Cornell University Press, 1986), p. 47.

31 Ibid., p. 132.

32 Homi Bhabha, *The Location of Culture* (London: Routledge, 1995), p. 89.

33 Cf. McClintock, *Imperial Leather*, on domestic work, racialization, dirt, and danger.

34 Declan Kiberd, *Inventing Ireland: The Literature of the Modern Nation* (Cambridge, MA: Harvard University Press, 1995), p. 552.

35 Ibid., p. 555.

36 Robert Stam, "From Hybridity to the Aesthetics of Garbage," *Social Identities* 3: 2 (1997), 283.

37 Anne Crilly, dir., *Mother Ireland* (Derry Film and Video Workshop, 1988).

38 *Into the West* (1992) offers the return to Celtic mythology and a wild West of Ireland as a cure for what it imagines as modern and purely urban (and therefore not naturally Irish) social problems. Orla Ryan has addressed representations of Dublin working-class people and neighborhoods in both her writing and her artwork; I am grateful for her insights.

39 Gardiner, *The Dialogics of Critique*, p. 139.

Chapter 12

Passion or Heartburn? The Uses of Humor in Esquivel's and Arau's *Like Water for Chocolate*

Dianna C. Niebylski

In her first novel, *Like Water for Chocolate* (*Como agua para chocolate*, 1989), Laura Esquivel attempts to maintain a cook's measured view of the real and metaphorical ingredients needed to survive in a world on the brink of exploding with domestic and historical tensions. While the generic balancing act results in a stylistic and generic pastiche that mixes together historical nostalgia and naïve sentimentality, the novel's pro-feminist revisionism is tempered by a bourgeois respect for culinary traditions. In this manner, revolution is shown to be compatible with nostalgia-filled romance. Turning culinary experiments and major life experiences into recipes with particular ingredients and specific measures has the effect of taming the novel's parodic revisionism, and hence taking the edge off the novel's antagonistic ideological agenda.

Culinary recipes can delight by subtle substitutions of ingredients, yet any attempt to experiment with a revisionist re-telling of history must be willing to offend traditionalist sensibilities on a larger scale. Returning to the novel almost a decade after I first wrote about it, what strikes me as most surprising, in a work that pays lip service to excess (to be at the point of "like water for chocolate" is to be at boiling point, either metaphorically or literally), is its consistent reluctance to be anything less than conciliatory in its treatment of potentially polemical topics, such as gender revolt or class revolution. In Esquivel's *Like Water for Chocolate*, revisionism and reconciliation ultimately cancel each other out.

Parodied Romance or Comic Melodrama?

Both the love story and the cooking lesson in Esquivel's *Like Water for Chocolate* take place in the rural and border town of Coahuila during the decades of the Mexican Revolution (the principal events of the story take place roughly from the early 1900s to the late 1930s). Most of the action in the novel revolves around the long-suffering and much-maligned Tita, the youngest daughter of a family of wealthy ranchers. Lacking her dead father's protection, Tita becomes the victim of a peculiar and peculiarly matriarchal tradition, one that requires that she give up romantic love for familial duty. Mamá Elena, a strong-willed matriarch reminiscent of García Lorca's Bernarda Alba (but with more than a touch of the classical evil stepmother of children's books), forbids her youngest daughter to marry the young suitor who pursues her because in her family the youngest daughter must sacrifice her future in order to take care of her aging mother. No match for Mamá Elena's strength or determination, the lovelorn suitor quickly agrees to the matriarch's suggestion of marrying elder sister Rosaura instead, presumably so he can stay a room away from the woman he craves. It is unclear whether Pedro, the suitor, lacks the imagination or the rebel instinct to think of other ways to be with his beloved, but Tita's attraction for this domesticated but resourceless Pedro is one of the novel's unresolved mysteries.[1]

Rosaura, the elder sister who gets a husband, and eventually a child, out of the family's tradition, suspects that Pedro is in love with Tita but decides that an arranged marriage is better than no marriage. Witnessing the failed love story and troublesome triangle developing under the ranch's big roof is Gertrudis, a second daughter born of the matron's illicit affair with a black slave and who, unlike her sisters, manages to escape maternal tyranny and other forms of domesticity altogether by joining the Mexican Revolution. A second suitor, John Brown, politically and racially "correct" as the soft-spoken, liberal, and light-skinned descendant of European and Native American grandparents, enters the novel to test Tita's love for Pedro, but perhaps merely to ignite Pedro into a jealous rage and hence into action for the first time in the narrative. A few revolutionaries come in and out of the ranch – and the narrative – with predictable but minor consequences. In the kitchen and on the sidelines, female Indian servants (as well as John Brown's Indian grandmother) by turns provide maternal affection, secrets of healing, and comic relief.

If the details listed above are not convincing enough to detect the comic, and potentially parodic, touches in the novel, here are more. The insensitive sister Rosaura, mirroring the evil sister in fairytales, is subjected to the punishments befitting evil sisters in such stories, modified to reflect contemporary women's fears as dramatized by the popular media: chronic bad breath, a body that swells and softens like bloated Jell-o, and death from indigestion, but not before suffering a prolonged and noisy attack of flatulence. Countering Rosaura's increasing bitterness is happy and wild Gertrudis, destined by her mulatto heritage to a sensuality and a taste for freedom so boundless that she takes up prostitution for a while, then joins Pancho Villa's armies, where she soon climbs up the ranks of *generala*. Then there is the unlikely "resolution" to the novel's principal story, where the lovers do not ride off into the sunset or even walk down the aisle but instead die during a sexual act so consuming that Pedro suffers a stroke, and Tita, eager to follow him to his death, ingests enough matches to set herself, the ranch, and the land on which it stands, on fire.[2] In what is undoubtedly the finest comic touch in this novel about recipes and revolution, the ending of the novel burns the main characters of its love story to a crisp.

Because they caricature or otherwise carnivalize traditional conventions of romance, and especially of romantic melodrama, one is soon tempted to read the novel's clichés, hyperboles, and other fantastic apparitions or events as parodic rather than merely comic. Film theorist Mary Ann Doane has noted that wild exaggeration is a tactic to which feminist narratives sometimes resort in order to expose and destabilize the absurd, or absurdly dated, tropes of femininity endorsed by popular melodrama. By rendering these tropes "*fantastic*, literally *incredible*, women authors, artists and performers can subversively appropriate the conventions and structure of the genre in order to show the need to resist, or reject them" (Doane, 1991: 180).[3] For Doane, the intervention of the fantastic in melodrama means the possibility of turning the heat on outmoded clichés so that expressions of sentimentality, already hyperbolic in melodrama, become overblown beyond belief. Thus, while traditional romantic rhetoric describes a woman's discovery of sexual desire by resorting to similes and metaphors that describe her body in various degrees of heat, Esquivel *shows* us what happens when the cliché is rendered literal. Gertrudis's body nearly burns up with sexual desire after eating her sister's most combustible dish. Rendering Gertrudis literally out of control of her body and her senses, the scene thumbs its nose at the traditional expectation that a woman must not let her desire overwhelm her body and her senses.[4] The image of naked, lusty Gertrudis running out of the burning shower stall shows us just why traditional romances must guard against both uncontrollable desiring women and the possibility of unleashing this kind of excessive behavior in their reading public.[5]

Tita's explosive death at the end of the novel reveals similar parodic strategies. While Pedro's death of a stroke from a sudden release of long-deferred desire is merely comic (unless one insists on reading the ending in a seriously romantic way), Tita's suicide exaggerates and mocks another staple of melodrama and (tragic or tragicomic) romance. Rendering "real" the metaphorical fireworks of romantic comedies and melodrama, *Like Water for Chocolate* ends with enough sparks to set to rest any doubts about the carnivalized appropriation of a stereotypical romantic ending. Since interrupted sexual consummation occurs after the big banquet at her niece's wedding (the novel's *real* happy ending), Tita's "inflamed" and "in-flames" body becomes the novel's last rite, but this does not obscure the fact that her exaggerated death, which could also be read as another death by poisoning in the novel, is a comic-parodic foil of a romantic and melodramatic ritual: dying for love.[6] These instances of exaggeration are both carnivalesque and fantastic. Although they do not reproduce the kind of "serious" masquerade or aggressive vamping that Doane describes, and as a strategy for exposing the phallocentric gaps and crevices in the representation of traditional (and culturally prescribed) femininity is beyond this novel's bawdy but momentary flashes of carnivalesque humor, the use of fantastic elements (some critics see it as a form of magical realism) does have at least temporary parodic and desacralizing effects on this otherwise orthodox tale of love, subservience, and mild rebellion.

For Kathleen Glenn, what makes *Como agua para chocolate* a convincing parody rather than a poorly edited pastiche is Esquivel's hyperbolic rendition of cultural and colloquial clichés. The "deliberate" attempt "to emphasize the ironic distance that exists between [her novel] and the formulaic ones she recasts," says Glenn, becomes especially obvious against the novel's historical and geographical background (Glenn, 1994: 41). Like Glenn, most scholars who read *Like Water for Chocolate* as an example of a gendered appropriation of popular genres through exaggeration or other deconstructive tactics insist that the novel's comic treatment of the popular and conventional frameworks it mirrors is both ironic and intentionally parodic.[7]

The comic imitation of certain concrete types of behavior is easily recognizable, making a wholly parodic reading of the novel indeed plausible, at least initially. The scene in which Pedro is stopped dead in his tracks by the sight of Tita's breasts exposed as she grinds almonds on the famous *metate* (earthen stone) capitalizes on a convention shared by the *costumbrista* tradition of Mexican nineteenth-century painters and twentieth-century muralists, both of which showed barely covered women's breasts as they knelt or bent over the *metate* stone in preparation of a meal.[8] Mamá Elena's fears that her daughter might be poisoning her undoubtedly echoes a long-established phobia in Mexican history, one that goes back to colonial legal and Inquisitorial records and that associates the subversive potential of women's cooking with the infinite possibilities a woman has of poisoning her husband.[9] And in her incarnation as a Mexican *generala*, Gertrudis is obviously modeled not on any historical woman general (Pancho Villa's armies had none), but on María Felix's celebrated erotized renditions of this improbable historical figure.[10]

Yet, while all of these examples of fantastic or hyperbolic imitations of conventional characters and events may be proof that Esquivel's handling of the popular genres she imitates forces readers to question the gender and cultural prejudices inherent in the modus operandi of these same genres, the interpretation of the novel as genre parody runs into some significant obstacles. To begin with, the parodic intent is compromised by the inconsistent tone of the narrative, which shifts from comic carnivalesque to comic sentimental and sometimes openly maudlin and nostalgic, often within a single sentence.[11] It is conceivable (as some critics have argued) that these tonal inconsistencies are themselves a parody of the careless semantic and stylistic abuses of popular *telenovelas* or romances quickly written and badly edited for publication in monthly women's journals, but such a tactic would require a sustained pattern to appear parodic, and there is no evidence of such a pattern to these noticeable and often patronizing tonal inconsistencies.

"Generic fiction may be a site for the allegorical description of social injustices displaced in time and/or place from the reader's own society," notes Anne Cranny-Francis in *Feminist Fiction: Feminist Uses of Generic Fiction*, but she warns that attempts to use these genres may backfire, or "be reappropriated by the discourses against which [these are] written," when the writer fails to be aware of, or fails to portray, "the ideological significance of generic conventions" (1990: 9). Applying Cranny-Francis's sound observation to parodic versions or inversions of generic fiction, one could argue that the parodied edge begins to crack, or at least to lose its sharpness, when the parody fails to suggest a sufficiently ironic distance from the original. A merely comic intent to interrogate the ideologies that feed the conventional models is not enough to render them objectionable. The danger of using comic tactics devoid of satiric "bite" in any parodic appropriation lies in the risk that the humor may actually render the parodied model harmless, albeit in a comical manner.[12]

It is precisely when considering the failure of *Like Water for Chocolate* as an ironic rendition of multiple traditional genres that an argument for a unilaterally parodic reading of the novel becomes unsustainable. While the novel's inconsistencies in terms of its uneven carnivalization or exaggeration of formulaic characters are troublesome on an aesthetic level, the fact that these inconsistencies happen to reinforce rather than subvert the misogynistic notions behind the conventional generic formulas is highly problematic on an ideological level. Mamá Elena's character is a good starting-point for analyzing the ideological problems behind the novel's inconsistencies when read as a parody of generic conventions and cultural stereotypes. Described from the first as a castrating or phallic mother, Mamá Elena is blatantly uncaring, unjust, and downright nasty in her treatment of her youngest daughter. Yet she is also presented as a paragon of strength when seen standing up to the men around her, including the revolutionaries who come to attack the ranch for the first time. As a woman in charge not just of a family but of a wealthy ranch, she is able to keep her own at a time when bigger and better men than she – the *hacendados* or landowners against whom the Mexican Revolution was fought – lost everything, their lives included. The image of the elder widow made bitter by the need to hold her own in a man's world already provides at least a partial explanation for her black bile, but the novel gives us two more built-in justifications for her harsh – and at times openly sadistic – treatment of her daughter: (1) she is following a family tradition; and (2) she herself has been the victim of a frustrated love. Yet, despite all this, the narrative revels in turning Mamá Elena into the image of an hysterical harpy.

The fact that Mamá Elena becomes a victim of her own emetics halfway through the novel, and that Tita's cooking is unintentionally but directly responsible for her death, may be proof of the novel's intent to turn this traditional enmity between mothers and daughters into a comical version of a dark fable. But the proof turns out to be insufficient as well as belated. The representation of the phallic mother is especially problematic when one considers that Mamá Elena's more admirable traits are precisely those traits her daughter would need if she ever hoped to escape the limiting spaces of the kitchen and/or the bedroom. Equally problematic is the fact that implicit in the narrative's Manichean contrast between Mamá Elena's bad and Nacha's good mothering is the suggestion that phallic mothers should be replaced by servile (and indigenous?) women with magical cooking secrets (but no recipes for their own, or other women's, independence).

Dianna C. Niebylski

Chapter 12

In her discussion of Hollywood romantic comedies, Kathleen Rowe divides the films she examines into the categories "comedian comedy" and "romantic comedy." Where romantic comedy "at least demands a place for women . . . in its vision of a social order that is not only renewed but . . . transformed" (1995: 102), comedian comedy sides with the case of the father and is often guilty of "symbolic matricide" (1995: 104).[13] In this way, adds Rowe, "comedian comedy" often "direct[s] its corrective laughter onto the matriarch, displacing the hostility it is licensed to level at the father onto the repressive, phallic mother" (1995: 105). Following Freud on this point, Rowe convincingly argues that such a tactical move not only deprives women of a serious role in (melo)drama but turns them, instead, into "fearsome or silly symbols of repression and obstacles to social transformation" (1995: 105). In *Like Water for Chocolate*, Mamá Elena's caricatural treatment fits the model of the phallic mother outlined by Rowe and prefigured by Freud in disturbing ways. Although Mamá Elena is capable of standing up to a whole army of soldiers and of raising three daughters largely by herself, the novel turns her into a laughing stock: a screaming, angry hysteric while alive; a scary ghost after death. In the meantime, the family man (or men) is depicted as an ineffectual but ultimately harmless victim of conniving women like Elena.[14]

Mary Russo (1994) has forcefully argued that the grotesque depiction of the female body (usually through some form of failure of containment, as is the case with Rosaura) can be used by women, or by feminist texts, to "destabilize idealizations of female beauty or to realign the mechanisms of desire" (1994: 221). Yet as Russo, critiquing Bakhtin, also notes, the carnivalized tactics of the grotesque can also be used to turn females into objects of social denigration and cultural rejection. Rosaura's treatment as a female grotesque in the novel falls into the latter category. By projecting grotesque qualities onto the elder sister, Esquivel not only reproduces the Cinderella story without questioning the complex social motives and cultural fears that turn women into "ugly stepsisters," she also reproduces the pernicious cultural prejudices that turn pregnant, unloved, and overweight women into women who "explode" because they cannot control their urges (when, in fact, Rosaura is the most repressed of the three sisters), and thus deserve their miserable fate.

Contrasting sharply with Mamá Elena's and Rosaura's hysterical, choleric, or grotesque bodies, Tita's body remains trapped within the confines of idealized femininity. Not only does she not break her mother's ironclad control until after the matron's death, but she also remains the persistent victim of the author's refusal to let the novel's heroine enter the sphere of the properly carnivalesque. In the early parts of the novel she is identified – and identifies herself – with whiteness and winter, a color and a season anathema to the carnivalesque.[15] While preparing the mix for her sister's wedding cake, Tita fears that she will be swallowed up by the whiteness of so many kilos of granulated sugar, and the whiteness of the sugar sends her back to childhood memories where she remembers going to church dressed in white, walking amidst white candles in the white chapel where she offered her white flowers to the Virgin.[16] Although the narrative does not editorialize on the passage, what Tita seems to fear on this occasion is the anti-carnivalesque containment to which the novel subjects her.

Significantly, Tita's longest episode of revolt and rebellion is cast in terms of empti-ness, self-annulment, and the denial of bodily pleasures. While refusing to eat and to speak are legitimate forms of rebellion, they both turn with masochistic force on the subject's own body. While Tita's magical lactation at hearing her nephew's cries for food might put her in the tradition of the hysterical *ilusas* or deluded women described by Jean Franco (1989) in her discussion of Ana de Aramburu in the early nineteenth century, in Tita's case the lactation is kept secret (a secret she shares only with Pedro) and presented as proof of yet another of her "magical" tricks to feed those around her.[17] Only her death by ingesting enough matches to make herself combustible belongs to the realm of the carnivalesque, largely because, for once, she decides to give control to and to defile her body simultaneously. In keeping with the strategies of purity and contain-ment that define her throughout the novel, however, neither Tita nor her attempts at asserting independence are cast in comic terms. It is indeed ironic that, while her alchem-ical powers in the kitchen result in some of the novel's most memorable carnivalesque scenes, Tita herself is depicted with the same bland sweetness that turns good heroines (*la buena* [the good woman] of the popular romances and soap operas) into bores. It is tempting to speculate that, exaggerated to comic or carnivalesque proportions, Tita would have been a much livelier and more entertaining parody of a romantic heroine.

I do not mean to ignore those moments in which Tita expresses disagreement and perhaps even gradual revolt. She does indeed violate the home-making rules codified by the often-mentioned *Carreño's Manual* by refusing to baste before she embroiders; she flirts egregiously with the married Pedro despite her mother's punishing gaze and some-times more punishing hand; she takes a vow of silence and keeps it for months after her mother refuses to let her mourn for her dead baby nephew; she tells John Brown (in writing) that she does not speak because she "doesn't want to" ("*porque no quiero*"); she engages in illicit and passionate sex with Pedro after having all but promised herself to John Brown in marriage; and she refuses to let her sister Rosaura turn her niece Esperanza into yet another victim of the family's anachronistic and cruel tradition. Yet despite all these moments of revolt, Tita remains the family's cook as well as the family man's concubine for most of the novel. In other words, these gestures of revolt fail to add up to a "revolution." Content with glimpses of furtive satisfaction and deferred happiness, she never develops a conscious awareness of her own status as the family's sacrificial lamb.

Addressing the problems of writing generic fiction from a feminist perspective, Anne Cranny-Francis notes that "feminist generic fiction" must "(re)negotiat[e]" the subject position by "deconstruct[ing] femininity [and] revealing it as an ideological construct" (1990: 192). Furthermore, the critic adds, gendered generic fiction must also "construct a . . . reading position which involves a particular negotiation of the discourses inflected by the traditional text and those discursively indicated by the revision of traditional conventions" (1990: 192). Failing to deconstruct traditional models of femininity except through the largely absent character of Gertrudis, and neglecting to comically expose not just the phallic mother and the sadistic sister but also the social and cultural mechanisms that turn mothers into ogres and "uglier" sisters into grotesques, Esquivel's narrative stops short of proposing an alternative system of values to those of the traditional genres she imitates. And, what is more, she frames the story with images of a young woman whose world seems to be confined to the kitchen despite her great-aunt's sacrifice. It is important to note that it is not only Tita (who is, after all, a woman who lives in the early part of the twentieth century) who remains caught in the frames of traditional femininity. Evidently so does her great niece. Based on the only images we have of her, there is no reason to believe that the young female narrator whose memories encase the novel has an existence independent of the kitchen to which her great aunt was banished. In fact, although born two generations after the Revolution and Tita's "revolt," Esperanza's daughter appears to be dependent on food and tears as her only weapons in what may still be a man's world.

Culinary Subversions, Poisonous Encounters

The discourse of bawdy, grotesque, and steamy bodies in *Like Water for Chocolate* is influenced not only by the popular culinary tradition that the novel imitates and seeks to join,[18] but also by a popular discourse of bodily and bawdy humor, a practice much in evidence in Mexican film, television, and even popular song. The combination of these two distinct but related semantic and thematic discourses results in an innovative and regionally infused version of the carnivalesque. Adding both spice and an extra measure of aggression to this already combustible combination is the presence of a third historical and cultural discourse, one composed of legal and anthropological records relating stories of women's homemade poisons or of the supernatural powers of women's fluids, a discourse with a history almost as long and as established in Mexico as that of culinary manuals or recipe books.

Linking the body and its functions with all sorts of edibles are the novel's ubiquitous homespun similes and metaphors, most of which display a kind of easy and teasing humor about them. When told that Tita understands her own body's reaction to first meeting Pedro's gaze by likening it to "how dough must feel when it is plunged into boiling oil" ("*lo que debe sentir la masa de un buñuelo al entrar en contacto con el aceite hirviendo*": Esquivel, 1989: 15), we laugh both at the touchingly domestic honesty of the image and in recognition of what it is imitating. By contrast, the metaphor that describes Tita's sense of loneliness and disappointment upon realizing that Pedro would never be brave or rebellious enough to elope with her (as the soldier on horseback does with her sister) graphically captures a gourmet cook's sense of shameful waste: "One lone chile in walnut sauce left on the platter after a banquet couldn't feel any worse than she did" ("*un chile en nogada olvidado en una charola después de un gran banquete no se sentiría peor que ella*": Esquivel, 1989: 57). A newborn is to be wrapped "like a taco" ("*envuelto como taco,*" 1989: 74).

When Rosaura has the bad taste of imposing on her young daughter the same curse that Mamá Elena imposes on Tita (forbidding her to marry), her words are "repugnant, foul-smelling, incoherent, pestilent, indecent and repellent" ("*repugnantes, malolientes, incoherentes, pestilentes, indentes y repelentes*": Esquivel, 1989: 162). One wishes that the author had left out "incoherent" and "indecent," abstract adjectives that undermine the malodorous image conjured up by the other adjectives. Yet the piling up of the other four adjectives, all olfactory, fits the halitosis-prone, gaseous Rosaura to perfection. In their ubiquitousness, these overblown analogies inevitably refer us to the clichéd simile so abused by the popular romance or the *novela rosa*. Significantly, the comic parody that results from these exaggerated clichés does not obscure the celebration of a descriptive and analogical taxonomy that is fully grounded on bodily, even visceral, experience.

Along these lines is the cliché that woman reaches man's heart through his stomach, though it would be more accurate to say that what the heroine reaches through her gourmet recipes is not Pedro's heart but his senses. Against Tita's disclaimer that her knowledge of the kitchen makes her a poor student of the world, a statement which sounds like a direct (if perhaps unintentional) inversion of Sor Juana Inés de la Cruz's famous claim that the kitchen was her laboratory to the world, Tita's power is, indeed, rooted in her alchemical relationship to the food she cooks, a relationship that in turn yields other, even more magical, alchemies.[19] Whether during preparation or ingestion, food is Tita's ally and her most powerful weapon, much more so, in fact, than her luscious body. Because her intimacy with edible ingredients reaches magical proportions, her tears cause massive longing at her sister's wedding, her happiness at the fullness of her nursing breasts causes euphoria among the guests at the baptismal banquet, and her passionate blood mixed with the rose petal sauce induces a kind of vicarious sexual, or at least psycho-somatic, intercourse between Pedro and Tita at the memorable family dinner that, not so incidentally, leads to Gertrudis's escape and escapades.

This last passage is a good reminder that, while cooking may be a space for feminine experimentation, it becomes a place for female transgression only when a daring combination of ingredients leads to sex, or to escape, or even to (comic and carnivalesque) death. The first "death by chocolate" story recorded in the New World appears in Thomas Gage's 1648 *Travail by Sea and Land, or A New Survey of the West Indies*, a work in which the English Dominican writes about the much-publicized murder of the Bishop of Chiapas at the hands of one of his female parishioners. The cause of death was declared to be "death by chocolate" (Coe and Coe, 1996: 184–6). It turns out that the bishop had forbidden his women parishioners to consume the thick, sweet, liquid during mass. He quickly became a casualty of his own prohibition when an outraged wealthy parishioner (Doña Magdalena de Morales) decided to take revenge by giving him a (poisoned) taste of his own medicine: no more chocolate for the bishop, either.

No one dies in Esquivel's novel by ingesting poisoned chocolate. Yet the way in which *Like Water for Chocolate* sustains its decidedly carnivalesque fascination with chronic indigestion and self-poisoning introduces a much more subversive strain in the novel's appropriation of the culinary discourse. And it is not just the cook who determines the effects of the meal. In Mamá Elena's case, the poisoning is a result of the emetics she ingests when she becomes convinced that her daughter is trying to poison her. Like Mamá Elena, who complains that Tita's food is unpalatably bitter, Rosaura too dies a victim of her own bitterness or bilious "humors." In this sense, her death too is a form of self-poisoning. For that matter, Tita's death by ingesting enough matches to set herself on fire can be read within this same context, even if the motivation for Tita's fatal in(di)gestion is love rather than hate.

-------------------- ## Explosive Encounters, not so Comic Repressions --------------------

Besides linking the novel's multigeneric parody to yet another historical discourse, as I noted (that of women's poisons), the episodes of self-poisoning link the narrative to the theme of violence, a theme the author chooses to treat from a distance and without turning it into either an object of comic laughter or serious criticism. Nevertheless, the recurrence of violence at the domestic level prefigures the violence to which the country is exposed through the Revolution. Unfortunately, and following the patterns already established by popular romances or televised melodrama, the novel brings in the reality of both private and public violence only to give the story additional local flavor. Although there are many opportunities in the novel for contextualizing (comically, ironically, or seriously) the violence in and outside the ranch, no effort is made to explore the links between this violence and the class and race conflicts that are tearing the nation apart, or the gender struggles that, unrecognized, will keep family and cultural institutions in a pre-revolutionary state.

In this context, the treatment of Chencha's rape at the hands of the revolutionaries, and the complete indifference to the event or the servant girl's trauma on the part of the family, is a highly problematic moment in the novel. Dismissed from service by Mamá Elena, who becomes more and more impatient with Chencha's cooking, the narrative notes that Chencha went home because she needed "to forget the rape incident" ("*necesitaba olvidarse del asunto de la violación*": Esquivel, 1989: 1350). The use of the casual word *asunto* (matter) in reference to something as serious as rape appears to convey the same indifference to the misfortunes and violent incidents of the marginalized poor. In another telling passage earlier in the novel, Chencha has just returned from the town center and is telling Tita about reports of people hanged in the plaza, but Tita ignores her and the news of the revolution's proximity because she is too caught up in her memories of Pedro gazing at her breasts. As in other passages that record important historical details as mere local color resting passively in the background, Tita's indifference to Chencha's news of the public hangings is not related ironically, so the reader has no choice but to assume that the authorial voice is equally indifferent to the historical events narrated and more interested in following the melodramatic love story.

Failing to use Chencha's news to comment on the public acts of terror taking place in the town's plaza, the novel misses an easy opportunity to link the repressive hangings with the repression taking place at home. In fact, the narrative only foregrounds the symbolic or metaphorical importance of violent acts in scenes where violence is perpetrated in the name of a delectable dish (or pleasure). It is only in these less polemical or less overtly political scenes (as when Tita kills the quail by twisting its neck, for example) that the novel draws parallels between the real act of violence and the repression and violence Tita must suffer under her mother's tyranny. In some instances (and the quail incident is one), however, even the parallel between metaphorical repression of the young woman by her mother and Tita's act of culinary violence is incomplete or puzzling. In the example mentioned above (see the preparation for the quail dish in chapter 3), the fact that Tita equates her mother's "murderous" tyranny with her killing of the tender quail neglects the fact that the chapter will soon celebrate the consequences of Tita's killing of the bird.

As scholars and theorists of carnivalesque practices have noted, bawdy humor and irreverent discourses derive much of their power from the antics and (dis)functions of bodies that are out of control and from equally uncontrolled, and uncontrollable, appetites. At its weakest, this type of unmannered humor breaks rules of decorum. At its best, it topples the social codes on which those rules of decorum, etiquette, and social hierarchies are founded. But what these critics also note is that in order for this bodily, deep-bellied humor to begin to wreak havoc on its targeted surroundings, it must be willing to offend. Esquivel's reluctance to offend is what keeps the potential of her carnivalesque transgressions partially in check (but never entirely); what keeps them, in other words, from blowing up in the reader's face — an explosion that could lead to laughter and celebration or to embarrassment and anger.

By resisting the temptation to offend sensibilities and test the limits of decorum in aiming for deeper belly aches and thereby harsher laughter, Esquivel's novel undermines the questioning, oppositional potential of its most effective humorous strategy, as described above. In this respect, the hyperbolic details that accompany some of the kitchen or eating scenes do not belong to the transgressive humor of comic irony or parody but to the affirmative humor of celebration. And, while in many women's comic writings, celebratory humor is often a liberating humor, or a humor that affirms new forms of liberation, in *Like Water for Chocolate*, this celebratory humor ushers in a sense of liberation only on a limited scale: the women who live in the domestic rooms assigned to them rarely laugh out loud, and Gertrudis's laughter is often only an echo.

Alfonso Arau's *Like Water for Chocolate*: Disarming Revolutions, Sweetening Home Revolts

Directed by Alfonso Arau and based on Laura Esquivel's script, the film version of *Like Water for Chocolate* became the biggest-grossing Spanish-speaking movie import of all time.[20] Although it failed to win any major awards, the film did garner modest critical acclaim during its box-office heyday. With the film's runaway success came new paperback editions and reprints of Esquivel's novel. While the earlier editions of the novel marketed *Like Water for Chocolate* on the basis of its unusual cookbook–romance format, the reprints and new editions that hit popular bookstores after the film's release sported scenes from the film on its covers, aiming to sell the novel for the same market-proven combination of exoticism and sensuality that turned the film into an unexpected box-office success.

In one of the few unfavorable reviews of the film published in the US, Jonathan Romney (1993) noted the complete absence of irony in the film, speculating that this very lack of irony could help explain the film's success with general audiences normally resistant to art-house or foreign films. Noting the missed opportunities for revisionism and subversion in a film genre (the food film) that has produced brilliant, if few, examples of social satire, Romney damns Arau's production as "shmaltzy," "overglazed," and self-congratulatory (1993: 33). As the following paragraphs make clear, the film's lack of interest in sustaining the novel's uneven but interesting revisionist tendencies, and its failure to capitalize on the potential of a carnivalesque humor that could have rendered the novel's story both more comical and more openly rebellious, meant that the movie version of *Like Water for Chocolate* was a much less internally conflicted artistic production than Esquivel's text. Film critic Romney is right on this point. By depicting both the Mexican Revolution (what little we see of it) and the heroine's personal revolt (never more mild in the novel) in sepia-colored hues and without irony or self-parody of any kind, the film marketed the culinary romance into a sensual story with exotic, ethnic flavor. The source of its appeal to mainstream audiences was in figuring out a recipe for attracting a public hungry for a sterilized shot of exoticism from south of the border. But both the south and the border presented in the film were even less connected to historically specific circumstances than was Esquivel's novel. The two adjectives most commonly seen on adverts for the film in the US were "sexy" and "sensual."

Although Romney considered this film in the context of the food film, Arau's *Like Water for Chocolate* fits squarely within the generic frame of the ranch melodrama (or *comedia ranchera*) in Mexican cinema. The longest-running and most ubiquitous subgenre in popular Mexican cinema, the ranch melodrama is obsessed with patriarchy, power, and class differences, all of which must be negotiated through the bodies of good and bad women. Yet an overview of some of these films shows that women's roles in traditional *comedias rancheras* are mere accessories, signposts that the leading men must yield to or avoid in their journey toward testosterone-fueled games for and among men. From its inception, the *comedia ranchera* is a melodramatic genre rampant with hyper- but unresolved masculinities. One of the earliest and most famous films of this genre is Fernando de Fuentes's *Allá en el rancho grande* (*On the Big Ranch*, 1936), a film that spawned a slew of imitators.[21] Often centering on box-office mega-draws like Fernando Soler, Pedro Infante, Jorge Negrete, and Dolores del Río, these films revolve obsessively around the figure of patriarchal authority. Although many of these films have the Mexican Revolution as their backdrop, just as many seem to long for a pre-revolutionary time when life on the big ranch (always a microcosm for the nation) was hierarchical, orderly, and predictable.[22]

Dependent on a largely female cast, director Arau's take on the *comedia ranchera* would appear revisionist. Like the novel, the film's story revolves around a matriarch rather than a patriarch, turning to the matriarch's daughters, rather than the patriarch's sons, for its source of story. Yet, where Esquivel's novel struggles to maintain what may be an impossible equilibrium between a reverence for tradition and a desire for charting new fictive spaces by exploring feminine spaces previously ignored or devalued by both popular culture and the popular genres that depict it, Arau's film insists on keeping the figure of the benevolent patriarch (or its substitute) on the margins of the visible frame at all times. In fact, it should be noted that almost every important scene in this nearly all-woman cast revolves around the figures of the three principal males, one of whom dies at the beginning of the novel: Pedro, the passionate lover undone by his inability to turn his back on the past and break with tradition; John Brown, the affectionate but dyspeptic northern suitor who gets to watch his son marry Tita's niece as his consolation prize; and the dead father, whose absence is mourned more in the film than in the novel.

Seldom are the movie's key scenes reserved exclusively to the women or to women's issues unrelated to women's desire for a male body or for male approval. Even the cooking scenes, which in the novel are often framed by Tita's great-niece's narration, become, in the film, another avenue for watching women's bodies work up a sweat in some state of undress. Seen thus, the cooking lesson, which has the effect of diverting readers' attention away from the tense sexual passions of the novel, become another setting for the raw (if highly mediated) sensuality for which the film was marketed. Julia Tuñón Pablos (1994: 141) has noted that the dining room is often the focal room in ranch melodramas. Arau's preference for featuring the dining room over the kitchen (where many of the novel's most important scenes take place) in the film is indicative of the director's own preference for public spaces within the family ranch. The dining room is much less threatening to a male member of a patriarchal family than is the servant- and women-filled kitchen.

An illustration of the way in which Arau's film co-opts the novel's feminine spaces, reducing these to spaces of waiting rather than portraying them as vitally creative spaces, can be seen early on in the film, when the director decides to merge two scenes that the novel narrates separately (they are separated by a space of two years in the novel). One of the earliest memorable scenes in Esquivel's novel is the scene of Tita's birth. While Esquivel fails to capitalize on the Rabelaisian power of this particular scene, her interest in anchoring the story to the feminized space of the kitchen is made conspicuously and powerfully clear in this episode.

The movie also includes the scene of Tita's birth in the kitchen, but it distracts the viewer from paying too much attention to it by flashing back and forth between this scene and the scene in which Tita's father, standing amidst other successful, hard-drinking males, learns of his wife's infidelity. Preferring to emphasize the more stereotypical and verbal humor of the male joke (Freud's model of joke work can only be an exchange between men over an absent woman's body), the movie offers this scene both as a condemnation of the "bad" mother giving birth below, but also as an alternative model of authority (lost but not forgotten with the patriarch's death), one which Tita will yearn for, first as a child and then as a young woman. By having the scene in which women's bodies lose their boundaries in a space reserved largely for women pre-empted by a scene full of respectable men clad in black, the movie forces us to choose between the private ways of the kitchen and the public life of the dining room, but there is no doubt where the director's preferences lie, and it is not with the women in the kitchen.

Neither the novel nor the film allows women characters (or women viewers) to envision a life away from men, one without desire for their libidos or their approval, but the film's nostalgic tone rests on the premature death of the patriarch and the inescapable orphanhood which must follow. Syntagmatic of the way in which Arau will treat the figure of the absent patriarch in the film, the scene featuring Tita's father's death seems to hang on the director's promise that the patriarch will be neither exiled nor replaced (by younger sons). He will simply be preserved on the edge of the frame. In this way, no matriarch may ultimately have her corrupt way with power. But no daughter will be permitted a way out of the tradition, either.

The film's anti-realist approach to history is further illustrated in its anti-realistic approach to women's bodies. Aiming to reach mass audiences both at home and abroad, the film tones down both the potentially offensive scatological humor of the novel and the even more potentially problematic libidinousness of some of the novel's sexual scenes. In so doing, it once again reduces the importance of feminine spaces as explored by the novel. Whereas the novel celebrates its Rabelaisian moments by describing them in detail, in Arau's film the scenes that feature bodily secretions of various sorts are filmed with a wide angle lens and from a safe distance, thus blurring any disturbing details for the more squeamish viewers. The catastrophe at Rosaura's banquet, for example, is not only shown from a distance in the film but also depicted in safe (non-carnivalesque) sepia-hued pinks. Viewers respond with laughter but not disgust to the collective vomiting. The novel's image of Rosaura rolling in her own and everyone else's vomit, for instance, is replaced with the image of Rosaura retching, but, again, seen from a safe distance. A similarly cautious treatment of Rosaura's death, in the film, misses – and purposefully so – the concretely detailed humor of the novel's description of it.

Similarly, even the most overtly sexual scene in the novel, the scene in which Tita serves her *pièce de résistance* and Gertrudis becomes the happily lusty medium of Pedro and Tita's consuming desires, acquires a more comical tone in the film that it has in the novel. Though the actress who portrays Gertrudis is sexy enough, the whole sequence is ultimately more hilarious than erotic in the film. We see red-headed Gertrudis galloping off into the sunset as she embraces her first revolutionary, but the film stops short of suggesting the stunt-like copulation the novel's lovers engage in as they ride away. Thus, though the film keeps some of the sensuality (and nudity) of the novel's scene, it tastefully blurs and humors it so as to make it more palatable to its more puritanical viewers. The comical tone of the scene turns Gertrudis's transgression (a huge one, where tradition is concerned) into a mere social and sexual *faux pas*. Consequently, while in the novel Pedro and Tita pant with their own internal combustions as they watch this dual demonstration of rebellion and lust, film viewers are more apt to smirk than smolder at the corresponding scene.

Nowhere is the film's predictable use of comic figures and situations more evident than in its treatment of the revolutionaries as consistently humorous, if occasionally dangerous, figures. If one had any questions about the film's potential for subversion, its portrayal of the Mexican Revolution (and its revolutionaries) should set those questions to rest. Without distinguishing between the federal and the rebel troops, as the novel does quite clearly, the film casts even the scene in which Chencha is raped and Mamá Elena killed – a scene which has no counterpart in the novel – in a questionably comic light. By contrast, Esquivel's novel grants the rebels a measure of respect. Polite and disciplined, the captain is able to keep his troops in check and *disconcert* Mamá Elena, who had, until then, shared her class's views of the rebels as killers and thieves. By contrast, the film melts all of its revolutionary figures into one stock *bandolero*: lusty, comical, and ignorant.

Rather than presenting a revisionist image of both the revolution and the lower classes, Arau's film conveys an almost reactionary ideology. This may simply be an indication of the director's indifference to the sociopolitical context of the story. Although the film forces viewers to remember the revolutionary horizon against which Tita and Pedro's story unfolds, the historical backdrop is there mostly for local color. While the same observation could be made of the novel, it is only fair to note that when Esquivel does take the time to remember the revolutionary figures who gallop in and out of the story, she is sympathetic to some of them. Arau, who received his first taste of Hollywood playing gunslingers in B-grade westerns, includes them only for their stereotypically comic benefit. In fact, Arau's *Villistas* are depicted as even more ignorant and crude than Hollywood's most negative depictions of Mexican revolutionaries. Contrasting Esquivel's with Arau's perspective on the revolutionary figures in their treatment of Sergeant Trevino proves useful. Forced to cook Gertrudis's favorite fritters on orders from the *generala*, the mustachioed, illiterate soldier is a ridiculous simpleton in the film, but a tragicomic and sensitive recruit, hopelessly in love with his beautiful *generala*, in the novel.

Although both the novel and the film work with cultural and generic clichés, the novel presumes to question the values that underlie those clichés, and at least partially succeeds. Aimed strictly at mass audiences and forced to simplify its comic strategies, however, the film makes no attempt to do so. The best example of this reliance on the operable cliché is the film's treatment of the young servant Chencha. No popular Latin American melodrama could afford to be without such a stock character, but the film makes sure that Chencha, like the revolutionaries whose class status she shares, will be seen strictly as laughing stock. By choosing a comic actress with less than good looks, director Arau makes sure that Chencha will inspire little pity and provide comic relief whenever on screen.

As mentioned earlier, the novel's quick gloss on Chencha's rape is offensive in its minimalism, yet the film's depiction of Chencha is troublesome indeed. A few scenes after she is raped by revolutionary rebels, the movie portrays Chencha cavorting with Gertrudis's soldiers at the family Christmas dinner. Since the film makes no effort to distinguish between revolutionary troops, film viewers must ask themselves if the soldiers she is cavorting with are the same soldiers who raped her earlier. Given that the soldiers are with Gertrudis, they probably are not, but the film is either ignorant of this potential misreading or it is perversely entertained by it. Lastly, while in the novel's final banquet Chencha is, like everyone else present, overcome with lust after eating Tita's *chiles*, she responds to this by going to look for her husband, who is in the village building a house for their new family. In the corresponding movie scene, however, the servant, having loudly announced that her husband is away, raunchily (and indeed comically) flirts with John Brown, then with most of the other men present. Predictably funny to mass audiences because it panders to a long history of stock characters who fit this particular type, Chencha's character in the film is nevertheless highly problematic and almost reactionary in its insensitivity.

The film's treatment of Mamá Elena is further proof of the director's lack of interest in treating complex female types in the film. As the novel's most vicious but most powerful figure, Mamá Elena is understood to be as much victim as victimizer in the narrative. Under Arau's direction, however, the character loses whatever complexity it had and operates merely at the level of caricature. In Esquivel's novel, Mamá Elena's death occurs considerably late in the story, guaranteeing that her presence in the novel will be both enduring and real. Convinced that her daughter is putting poison in her food, she poisons herself with emetics over a brief period of time. A highly appropriate end for a woman whose treatment of her dutiful daughter, and almost everyone else, has been bilious indeed, Mamá Elena's death is highly reminiscent, but also parodic, of poisoning scenes in cheap romantic thrillers and fairytales. By contrast, in the film she is killed quite early on and at the hands of rebel soldiers. This is a major loss in the conception of the character, but predictable given the fact that Arau is too busy mourning the loss of the good patriarch to be interested in exploring the intricate complexities of matriarchal power, or matriarchal corruption. By reducing the most complex female character in the novel to a Disney-like witch, the film resolutely refuses to place the issue of women's power and women's freedom at the center of the film. Yet in dismissing Mamá Elena as an evil stepmother, the film refuses to engage in a discussion of the oppressive traditions for which she stands.

Whereas a reader will circle Esquivel's novel in an attempt to decipher both the intended tone and its intended audience, the film gives us no such difficulties. Unlike Esquivel, Arau is neither indeterminate nor undecided about his medium or his film's message, and critical parody with revisionist intent is clearly not what he is after. Indeed, it is only the film's felicitous insistence on returning to the joys of Mexican cooking that keeps its nostalgic portrayal of the story from sinking into a made-for-TV sentimentality. In this lies the Arau film's only claim to a revisionist aesthetic of the *comedia ranchera* or ranch melodrama. Despite the filmmaker's insistence on reducing women's passions in the story to games of passion around the elusive figure of absent, unavailable, or unsuitable males, the kitchen imagery slowly takes over this most testosterone-prone of genres. What results from the tension between wishing to maintain the masculinist stamp of the ranch-melodrama and the uncontainable sounds and images of a kitchen that remains a force of creativity and sustenance (although not of true revolt) is not a revisionist historical melodrama but an emasculated *comedia ranchera*.

Interestingly, the emasculating motion originates in the kitchen, not in the bedroom, and herein may lie the novel's revenge on the film that cannibalizes it. Even as the director seeks to stamp a patriarchal zeal of ranch-style melodrama on a history remembered and told mostly by women, kitchen gossip, or gossip coming from the novel's ubiquitous kitchen, wafts into the main frame of the cinematic melodrama. As it does so, it has the effect of turning these would-be epic spaces into spaces of lyrical experimentation that have little to do with melodrama and even less with Arau's resistance to an openly feminized melodramatic tale. Not surprisingly, the movie's best scenes are scenes in which women are allowed to take pleasure in the banal activities of the household: playing with food, dancing, laughing: moments, in other words, where the patriarch is not only not there, but no one is missing him. Unfortunately, the film has too few of these scenes, and the novel would need many more to be convincing.

Conclusions

Given the wildly successful reception and distribution of both Esquivel's novel and Arau's film, one would have to admit that both the director's and the author's refusal to engage seriously with the personal or collective histories addressed only superficially in *Like Water for Chocolate*, proved to be a cool recipe for success. Almost a decade after first considering these issues, however, I am saddened yet not surprised to see that Esquivel's novel is already disappearing from graduate reading lists and course syllabuses. When I first wrote about Esquivel's novel's insufficiently revisionist tactics, I speculated that the author's desire to occupy a middle ground may, in retrospect, explain the novel's relatively short popularity (especially among Latin American cultural critics). A reconsideration of both Esquivel's and Arau's versions of *Like Water for Chocolate* only strengthens my conviction that, while playing safe (that is, opting for compromise rather than polemical resistance or disruption) may be a good recipe for popular bestsellers, it is rarely a good strategy for making a lasting mark. A good chef knows that the price she pays for not burning a few meals while revising the menu is culinary boredom. Too many compromises and too much reconciliation are bad ingredients for revisionist art: they fail to stir things up sufficiently.

An earlier version of this chapter appeared as "Heartburn, Humor and Hyperbole" in Shannon Hengen (ed.), *Performing Gender and Comedy: Theories, Texts and Contexts* (Australia: Gordon and Breach, 1998). For an extended discussion of Laura Esquivel's novel *Like Water for Chocolate*, see chapter 2 of my book *Humoring Resistance: Laughter and the Excessive Body in Latin American Women's Fiction* (Albany, NY: State University of New York Press, 2004). I am grateful to SUNY Press for allowing me to reprint portions of that discussion in this chapter.

————————————————— Notes —————————————————

1 Mirroring rather than parodying the romantic cliché of first love's ferocious hold, the novel casts its female protagonist in the role of Penelope. Although not always patient, Tita is trapped into the role of the largely passive woman, even if she is also the "other' woman.

2 It is interesting to note that this "literary" practice of committing suicide by ingesting matches appears already in Ricardo Palma's *La camisa de Margarita* (in *Tradiciones peruanas*, 1872), where the heroine is said *not* to have committed suicide only because matches had not been invented yet.

3 It is important to note that Doane does not include comic or carnivalesque genres as a possible site of "textual intervention." Adopting an almost exclusively Freudian view of humor, she fears that the "joke" will be on the woman if/when women use jokes. As Kathleen Rowe (1995: 6) notes in her own assessment of Doane's theories, Doane seems to miss "an obvious site of fantasy and masquerade [in] comedy."

4 Upon feeling Pedro's gaze on her breasts, Tita also likens her new awareness of her awakened sensuality to " how contact with fire can alter the shape of things, how formless cornflour dough is transformed into a tortilla" ("*supo en carne propia por que el contacto con el fuego altera los elementos, porque un pedazo de masa se convierte en tortilla*"). This image too is one of burning up, but Tita's metaphor for describing her emerging sexuality retains the clichéd version of traditional romantic description of female desire by allowing the metaphor to mitigate and displace the desire described.

5 In keeping with the carnivalesque aspect of the scene, the young revolutionary officer who "rescues" her from the burning shower stall has been led to the ranch by his good nose for scenting a woman's body-in-heat ("he was led there by Gertrudis's body" ["*lo guiaba el olor del cuerpo de Gertrudis*"]: Esquivel, 1989: 52).

6 Tita's death could be read as the novel's "last meal," but this implies a comic grotesqueness to the ending that is contradicted by the ending's melancholy tone.

7 Beatriz González Stephan, Kristine Ibsen, Gastón Lillo, and Monique Sarfati-Arnoud are among these critics.

8 See Jeffrey Pilcher's fascinating book on Mexican cuisine for more on this subject (Pilcher, 1998: 58).

9 Ruth Behar (1986: 178–206) has amply documented the early history of this fear in her studies of the Mexican Inquisition.

The Uses of Humor in *Like Water for Chocolate*

Chapter 12

10 The *soldaderas* were a reality of the Mexican Revolution. What is improbable was that any of these women ever reached the kind of stature depicted by María Felix in these movies, or by Gertrudis in Esquivel's novel.

11 Nearly every paragraph in the novel contains examples of this tonal instability. One relevant example here is Tita's response (and the tone used to describe it) to Gertrudis's steamy escape. In one of her moments of revolt, Tita blames Carreño's *Manual of Manners* and the culture of "decency" that has condemned her body "to wilt little by little" ("*a marchitarse poco a poco*": Esquivel, 1989: 57). She begins to express her outrage in a tone that indicates comic anger but ends by lapsing into conventional romantic lyricism. The sentence in which she judges Pedro's lack of determination encapsulates this unevenness in the course of a few phrases: "And damned Pedro, so decent, so polished, so manly, so . . . so loved!" ["*Y maldito Pedro tan decente, tan correcto, tan varonil, tan . . . tan amado!*"] While the "damned Pedro, so decent, so polished" conveys irony and outrage, the end of the sentence loses sight of irony and humor altogether and returns to the conventional (but non-parodied) register of cheap and badly written romance.

12 It should be clear to my reader that by parody here I mean parody with ironic intent. Linda Hutcheon (1985), who argues that parody need not be comic, insists that in order for an imitative discourse to be parodic it must be able to show ironic distance. At the same time, Hutcheon discusses the category of "parody of homage," where the intent is not to mock the model parodied but to celebrate it.

13 Rowe credits Lucy Fischer's article, "Sometimes I Feel Like a Motherless Child: Comedy and Matricide," for this insight.

14 Although one might be tempted to argue that Esquivel's novel narrates the story of a daughter's liberation, the treatment of the mother–daughter struggle in *Como agua para chocolate* is too traditional, and too insufficiently parodic, to warrant this conclusion. Brought to relief not only through the relationship between Tita and Mamá Elena but between Esperanza and Rosaura, the imminent threat of the aggressively phallic mother is indeed at the center of the story.

15 Esquivel (1989: 19). When she hears that Pedro is betrothed to her sister, we are told that she feels as though winter had entered her body: "*como si el invierno le hubiera entrado al cuerpo de golpe y porrazo*" (1989: 13).

16 This revealing and symbolically powerful passage is unfortunately compromised by the trivial revelation that what Tita dreamed of while walking toward the altar was that someday she would be walking down that aisle on a man's arm.

17 See Jean Franco, "The Power of the Spider Woman: The Deluded Woman and the Inquisition" (Franco, 1989: 55–76).

18 For a discussion of nineteenth-century cookbooks, nationalism, and gender in relation to this novel, see Kristine Ibsen's chapter on *Like Water for Chocolate* in *Latin American Literature and its Times* (Moss and Valestuk, 1999).

19 However, the novel also subverts this claim by never allowing Tita a voice or a destiny of her own (independent of the men she loves, or who love her).

20 Esquivel and Arau were married at the time the film went into production. They divorced shortly after the film was completed.

21 So popular was this particular film that even the original director was unable to resist the temptation to remake the film in 1948, this time with even bigger actors playing the main roles.

22 I have found Julianne Burton-Carvajal's (1997) and Carlos Monsiváis's (2000) comments on this particular genre of Mexican film particularly helpful.

──────────────────── References ────────────────────

Behar, Ruth (1986) *The Presence of the Past in a Spanish Village*. Princeton, NJ: Princeton University Press.

Burton-Carvajal, Julianne (1997) "Mexican Melodramas of Patriarchy: Specificity of a Transcultural Form," in Anne Marie Stock (ed.), *Framing Latin American Cinema: Contemporary Critical Perspectives*. Minneapolis, MN: University of Minnesota Press.

Coe, Sophie D. and Coe, Michael D. (1996) *The True History of Chocolate*. London: Thames and Hudson.

Cranny-Francis, Anne (1990) *Feminist Fiction: Feminist Uses of Generic Fiction*. New York: St Martin's Press.

Doane, Mary Ann (1991) *Femmes Fatales: Feminism, Film Theory, Psychoanalysis*. New York: Routledge.

Esquivel, Laura (1989) *Como agua para chocolate*. México: Editorial Planeta Mexicana.

— (1994) *Like Water for Chocolate: A Novel in Monthly Installments with Recipes, Romances and Home Remedies*. New York: Doubleday.

Franco, Jean (1989) *Plotting Women: Gender and Representation in Mexico*. New York: Columbia University Press.

Glenn, Kathleen M. (1994) "Postmodern Parody and Culinary-narrative Art in Laura Esquivel's *Como agua para chocolate*," *Chasqui* 23 (2): 39–47.

Hutcheon, Linda (1985) *A Theory of Parody: The Teachings of Twentieth-century Art Forms*. London: Methuen.

Monsiváis, Carlos (2000) *Aires de familia: cultura y sociedad en América Latina*. Barcelona: Editorial Anagrama.

Moss, Joyce and Valestuk, Lorraine (1999) *Latin American Literature and its Times*. Detroit: Gale.

Niebylski, Dianna (2004) *Humoring Resistance: Laughter and the Excessive Body in Latin American Women's Fiction*. Albany, NY: State University of New York Press.

Pilcher, Jeffrey (1998) *Que vivan los tamales! Food and the Making of Mexican Identity*. Albuquerque: University of New Mexico Press.

Romney, Jonathan (1993) "Eating her Gut Out: Film Review of *Like Water for Chocolate* directed by Alfonso Arau," *New Statesman and Society*, October 1: 33–4.

Rowe, Kathleen (1995) *The Unruly Woman: Gender and the Genres of Laughter*. Austin: University of Texas Press.

Russo, Mary (1994) *The Female Grotesque: Risk, Excess, and Modernity*. New York: Routledge.

Tuñón Pablos, Julia (1994) "La silueta de un vacío: imágenes fílmicas de la familia mexicana en los años cuarenta," *Film-Historia* 4 (2): 137–47.

Chapter 13

Beloved: The Adaptation of an American Slave Narrative

Mia Mask

Although the term "magic realism" has been used primarily to categorize a Latin American literary practice, it is also relevant, I would argue, to the African American novel *Beloved* (1987).[1] Mingling the mundane with the fantastic, Toni Morrison's Pulitzer Prize-winning novel[2] superimposes one perceived reality upon another, treating the fantastic as quotidian. It uses magic and fantasy to recuperate the real and reconstruct histories that have been obscured or erased by political and social injustice.[3]

Gabriel García Márquez's *One Hundred Years of Solitude* (1967) epitomizes the magic realist style. Márquez locates the roots of magical realism in the African Caribbean coast of Colombia. The concept of magical realism persists because it retains explanatory value, but also because it describes the common historical and cultural conditions shared by African and Latin American authors. Such writers are familiar with transition, border-crossing, and ambiguity, as well as with the mingling of capitalist and pre-capitalist modes within societies that have been postcolonial since the nineteenth century. They deploy the carnivalesque-grotesque – one complex theme of magical realism – to convey the notion of unfinished metamorphosis, the idea of something aborted, or incomplete. In *Beloved*, Toni Morrison uses magical realism as the structuring device to syncretize the supernatural with a realistic historical perspective. *Beloved* addresses the historical moment at which a newly manumitted African American community found itself between slavery and freedom, terror and safety, antebellum tradition and Reconstructive modernity. In the filmed adaptation of *Beloved* some aspects of magical realism and the "carnivalesque-grotesque"[4] come to the forefront more vividly than in the novel.

On October 16, 1998, Touchstone Pictures released the Harpo Films/Clinica Estetico Production of *Beloved*. Directed by Jonathan Demme, the film starred producer Oprah Winfrey as Sethe and Danny Glover as Paul D. Oprah Winfrey worked on the adaptation of *Beloved* to film for over a decade, having purchased the film rights shortly after the book was published in 1987. Although Winfrey considered the production of *Beloved* as a theatrical feature a "personal triumph," the film was considered a commercial failure (by Hollywood industry standards) for earning $24 million at the box office against a $65 million investment. When the additional $15–20 million for marketing and advertising campaigns are considered,[5] the film's production deficit was larger still. *Beloved* continues to return incremental profits as a video rental, but with only one Oscar nomination – for best costume design – it was unlikely to gain much momentum as a rental commodity. Herein resides the crucial difference between the novel and the film: as the product of commercial culture (and society) the Hollywood commodity must earn a profit. To make a profit, it *must* entertain consumers. Where a novel can sell 20,000 volumes and yield a reasonable return, the film must reach millions.[6]

It is a long-standing truism that there exists no valid correlation between box-office performance and artistic value, and *Beloved*'s box-office performance is certainly not an indication of the film's artistic merit. In the 1940s, Frankfurt School Marxists Max Horkheimer and Theodor Adorno challenged the correlation between conspicuous production and cash investment in the culture industry. Investment, they argued, bears no relation to the meaning or merit of the products themselves.[7] In the 1960s, political modernism and revolutionary "Third Cinemas" demonstrated that Hollywood films are popular precisely because they are ideologically complicit with dominant ways of seeing and understanding the world.[8] Political modernism offered a theory of counter-cinema: an independent and avant-garde praxis motivated by political concerns and by the critique of illusionism. Manthia Diawara, Michele Wallace, and Clyde Taylor critiqued ideological forms of signification and spectatorship in mainstream films.[9] These scholarly communities (the Marxists, modernists, Third Worldists, and African Americanists) proved that ideology involves not only the "message" of films but includes forms of looking, hearing, and the biases in perception and identification that spectators bring to the cinema. *Beloved* presents aesthetic and ideological challenges to conventional forms of signification, readership, and spectatorship because it intermingles past and present, the everyday and the supernatural, objective historical material and subjective emotional perspective in art-house cinema. These challenges to traditional spectatorship are what make *Beloved* a unique filmed spectacle.

As an object of mainstream film criticism *Beloved* fared poorly. In the mainstream press, it was the subject of extensive media promotion. Media concentration escalated into a contentious debate about the impact of canonized literature on feature film production. Contradicting the media hype, however, several reviewers faulted *Beloved* for infidelity to its source novel and especially for its inability to translate the complexities of the original narrative. Film historian Natalie Zemon Davis wrote: "In the movement from the miraculous prose of Toni Morrison to the screen, the story of *Beloved* has lost some of its breadth, complexity and imaginative range."[10] But we should be wary of moralizing and reductive readings, situating literature as miraculously highbrow and film as degenerately low-grade. Many of *Beloved*'s reviewers – proponents and detractors alike

– failed to take into account the complicated conversion process by which a novel becomes a screenplay and the screenplay, in turn, becomes a film. This conversion is an artistic endeavor involving the *aesthetics of transcription* from novel to film, or part of what has been called "the dialogics of adaptation."[11]

Advising against reductive approaches focusing on "fidelity" to the source material, Robert Stam proposes "intertextual dialogism" as an analytical paradigm in which adaptation is part of "the infinite and open-ended possibilities generated by the discursive practices of a culture, the entire matrix of communicative utterances within which the artistic text is situated."[12] Dialogism is an appropriate framework for evaluating film adaptation as it facilitates analysis of the diverse extra-diegetic texts, discussions, and ideological debates informing the critical discourse about a film adapted from a novel. Stam's insights dovetail with Pierre Sorlin's and Robert Rosenstone's discussions of historical film.[13] Much of the scholarship on the representation of historical events in film compare the filmed account with a written description of those same events, presupposing the written description as always-already more accurate and therefore superior. But this approach implies two problematic, logocentric assumptions. First, it suggests that the practice of written history is the only legitimate way of understanding the relationship to the past; and, second, that written history mirrors reality.

Intertextuality is also an appropriate framework for interpreting a multivocal, magically realist novel like *Beloved*, which engages the interweaving of time-frames, states of consciousness, discourses, linguistic codes (for example, standard English, rural black vernacular English, black feminist discourse, black patriarchal discourse)[14] and genres (slave narrative, gothic, horror, historical melodrama). This matrix of utterances encompasses history as a discursive formation and history's dialogic relationship with literature. This chapter examines the adaptation of *Beloved* from novel to film through the prism of intertextual dialogism. The communicative utterances within which the film *Beloved* is immersed, meanwhile, include (but are not limited to) the media campaign around the film (which shaped the commercial reception and public discourse); the intertext of Winfrey's boundless celebrity (which helped bring the film to fruition but adversely affected its reception); and the competitive Euro-American centered cultural terrain upon which African American films must forge a marketplace for themselves.

Toni Morrison gathered source material for *Beloved* from fragments of slave narratives she discovered while editing *The Black Book* (1974), a scrapbook of African American history. Particular historical details came from the real-life story of Margaret Garner, a slave, who in January 1856 escaped from her owner Archibald Gaines in Kentucky, crossed the Ohio River, and sought refuge in Cincinnati. Gaines and a party of officers pursued her. Margaret Garner, her husband Robert, and their four children were surrounded and overtaken. Realizing hopes for their freedom were bleak, Garner seized a butcher's knife and with one stroke cut the throat of her little daughter – probably the most "beloved" of them all. Garner chose death for herself and child rather than return to the state of chattel slavery. Implicit in the "herstory" of *Beloved* is a fusion of the past and the future in a single act of death. Garner was tried *not* for attempting to kill her child, but for the supposedly "real" crime of stealing property – herself and her children – from her master. In *Beloved*, Morrison leaves some of this historical material behind, for although Sethe kills her child, Beloved, Sethe is freed and ostracized from the black community.[15]

In the 1970s, historians began re-examining both the status of family life under slavery and the variegated forms of resistance to slavery, ranging from subtle sabotage to outright revolts. Earlier schools of scholarship viewed slavery as devastating to black family life and genealogy. Newer research on the history of women and family examines how African Americans tried to lessen or outwit the dehumanizing effects of slavery. Although slaves had no formal right to marry or develop kinship ties, for example, running away constituted a major challenge to the slave system. Family loyalties were factored into the decision to flee and risk patrols, dogs, recapture, punishment, and harsher enslavement. Reviewing this history, Morrison read extensively about slavery, abolitionists, fugitives, and Cincinnati in the mid-nineteenth century.[16]

Morrison re-writes African American history as literature in her novels. The dialogic relationship between literature and history evident in her work reverberates with Hayden White's claim that history too is a form of *ecriture*, an interpretive form of narrative enplotment. Historians choose, on aesthetic grounds, different plot structures by which to endow sequences of events with various meanings.[17] Morrison has often stated that the history and literature of the United States are "incoherent" without an understanding of the African American presence. Much like Jewish Holocaust literature – also known for its forms of magical realism – *Beloved* gives expression to intricacies, erasures, and surrealist disjunctions of conflicting histories. The film *Beloved*, for its part, reflects on these disjunctions through innovative formal techniques (for example, Expressionist, Surrealist, magical, and postmodern) in order to re-vision what is meant by history.

Given Morrison's literary objectives and Winfrey's personal commitment to the historical material, Jonathan Demme seems an unlikely choice of director for surrealist-experimental African American cinema. Directors Julie Dash (*Daughters of the Dust*, 1991) or Charles Burnett (*To Sleep with Anger*, 1990), for instance, seem like more obvious choices, especially since both are well known for successfully mingling the mundane, the spiritual, and the historical realms in magically realist renditions of African American cinema. This is not to suggest that a director's racial identity determines his/her ability to effectively direct a film. Such an assertion implies racial essentialism. Besides, Demme brought some unique flourishes to the film. Speculating about what Dash or Burnett might have brought to the film is merely to question why Winfrey did not employ a director known for rendering the African American experience in magically realist images. Furthermore, it is to note that *Beloved* was Demme's first historical film to address African American issues, although he had made two documentaries about the black diaspora in other contexts (*Haiti: Dreams of Democracy*, 1987, and *Cousin Bobby*, 1991).

Winfrey's decision to select Demme as director articulates one of the tensions in making and marketing an experimental-historical black film that is part slave narrative, part magically real ghost story, and part maternal melodrama. The film innovatively combines disparate genres, non-linear narrative construction, and an Afrocentric vision

Beloved

Chapter 13

of American history to create what is (in some way) an avant-garde (read art-house) film. Winfrey and the producers (Ronald Bozman, Kate Forte, Gary Goetzman, and Edward Saxon) may have been compelled to employ an "A" listed, white male director whose Hollywood status and commodity-sign value would lend the picture prestige and name recognition and balance its art-house qualities with a commercial trademark. Unfortunately, Winfrey failed to anticipate the extent to which this directorial selection could adversely affect viewer's perceptions of what the film would entail. In other words, while the choice of an "A" director lent the film celebrity name recognition, it also raised serious questions of credibility for black and white audiences. Was Demme familiar with the politics of racial representation and the necessity for re-visioning African American history? Was it clear that this film presented a relationship between literature and history? Finally, would Demme understand Morrison's long-term project of examining constructions of blackness?

Revising constructions of African American history and identity constitutes a central form of resignifying for Morrison. As she suggested in *Playing in the Dark*, the examination of constructions of literary "blackness" make it possible to discover the nature – even the tacit grounds – of literary "whiteness."[18] Morrison's criticism of literary whiteness broadens the critique of intellectual Eurocentrism by foregrounding the biases inherent in Euro-American literature and literary criticism. Second, this critique under-scores the intertexual relationship between African American literature and American historiography; it reminds us that judgments about data, verifiability, argument, and evidence are always constructed and historically situated. Third, her literary criticism serves as an intertext for film criticism. By examining cinematic blackness, we can begin to dismantle the hegemony of cinematic whiteness. *Beloved* exemplifies the way in which African American history written as cinematic narrative can present an intellectual and ideological critique of dominant cinema.

The novel and film versions of *Beloved* begin with tropes of dismantled blackness. The narrative opens precisely where Toni Morrison's other narratives end: with the individual and the community sundered. This point of narrative departure forms an aesthetic link between Morrison's other works of fiction: the recurring emphasis on protagonists and characters who are separated from the larger community. Having learned of the infanticide, the black Cincinnati community has turned its back on Sethe (Oprah Winfrey) and her remaining family.

When the film starts, Sethe's two sons Howard (Emil Pinnock) and Buglar (Calen Johnson) take their belongings and leave their haunted home in turmoil. The film then flashes forward eight years to the summer of 1873. Until this point Denver (Kimberly Elise) and Sethe have lived at 124 Bluestone Road alone, isolated from society. One summer day, Paul D (Danny Glover) walks into Sethe's front yard and together they recount the years since escaping Sweet Home plantation. After a few days, Paul D agrees to live with Sethe and Denver, beginning a new life. As the summer moves into autumn, Paul D and Sethe grow closer together. But their newly laid plans to bond as family are thwarted by the arrival of a mysterious young woman, Beloved (Thandie Newton).

Beloved offers the strongest expression of the harrowing experience individuals undergo at the hands of the community even while trying to be reconciled with it.[19] Separation from the community is almost always a consequence of some appalling, horrifying, or un-representable act. The un-representable – or what Morrison terms the "unspeakable" – manifests itself prominently in the author's other novels (for example, *The Bluest Eye*, 1970 and *Song of Solomon*, 1977) in the form of betrayal, abuse, and the presence of ghosts.[20] Maintaining much of the novel's plot structure, the film centers on Morrison's female protagonist, Sethe. The central narrating voice, in both the novel and the film, belongs to Sethe, since the story revolves around her maternal confrontation with the incarnated ghost of her murdered, woman-child daughter, Beloved.

The tropes of "unspeakable" and "un-representable" acts render *Beloved* particularly challenging material to adapt for the screen. A novelist's portrayal induces us to imagine characters and events. A film, by contrast, designates specific performers, props, settings, and landscapes. The selection of these signifiers imposes limits, restricting the imagination each spectator brings to the cinema.[21] In making *Beloved*, the filmmakers not only manipulated concrete signifiers, they also concretized magical and supernatural events already un-representable, unspeakable, or difficult to signify. *Beloved* as a film, therefore, assumes a double "burden of representation," beyond that incumbent upon a novel.

The eponymous Beloved (Thandie Newton) instantiates this un-representability. Morrison wrote Beloved as a supernatural character that transcends epistemological and ontological bounds. "In magical realist texts," as critics point out, "ontological disruption serves the purpose of political and cultural disruption: magic is often given as a cultural corrective, requiring readers to scrutinize accepted realistic conventions of causality, materiality, motivation."[22] As the fulcrum of magical realism, Beloved as character is an oxymoronic literary construction that troubles convention and captures the paradox of uniting opposites. Simultaneously a corporeal presence and an ethereal ghost, she is also the matrilineal connection between indigenous black Africa and colonizing white America. As a symbol, she is the haunting avatar of *many* Beloveds – generations of mothers and daughters hunted down and stolen from Africa. A parapsychological epiphenomenon of slavery, invulnerable to barriers of time, space, and place, Beloved is both vacant and omnipresent.[23] As Sethe's offspring, she incarnates the newly formed black collective body, a hopeful populace reborn on the cusp of Reconstruction and bent on democratic participation.

Regrettably, critics hastily dismissed Thandie Newton's performance of Beloved as camp and farcical. Some cited Newton's Beloved as proof of the novel's un-translatability, an inevitable calamity in the passage from novel to film. But Newton's performance should not be dismissed as an inevitable betrayal of the source material, or as a symptom of the film medium's intrinsic incapacity to capture the characteriological complexity. The disparity is actually a matter of emphasis rather than translation. Precisely because the film foregrounds Beloved's actual return, her physical presence, and her life with Sethe, she becomes less the symbolic ghost of the written text than the corporeal reality of the film. More specifically, the film calls attention to the growth and development of her

Beloved

Chapter 13

body, to its fluids and functions. She is Sethe's unformed, uncontrollable, woman-child, blurring the boundaries between self and other.

To understand Beloved's prominent function in the film, it is useful to discuss her corporeality in terms of Mikhail Bakhtin's concept of the grotesque body, and Mary Russo's notion of the female grotesque. Their interpretations of the grotesque inform (and overlap with) the category of magical realism. For Bakhtin, the unfinished and open body (dying, bringing forth, and being born) is not separated from the world by clearly defined boundaries; it is blended with the world, with animals, with objects. The grotesque body is an incarnation of this world at the absolute lower stratum, as the life of the belly, the reproductive organs, and the acts of defecation, copulation, conception, pregnancy, and birth.[24] "Bakhtin found his concept of the grotesque embodied in the laughing pregnant hags of the Kerch terracotta figurines, which combine senile, decaying flesh with fresh new life, conceived but as yet unformed."[25] In the enslaved body, which was a vehicle for white enjoyment and coerced festivity, one finds a negative, non-festive version of Bakhtin's grotesque. For in the carnivalesque pageantry of the coffle, the enforced dancing on slave ship decks, and the obligatory live stepping on auction blocks, we see spectacles of black pain, which entangle terror and enjoyment.[26] Perhaps because the magical realism of the story is encoded into the story narrative itself, both the novel and the film share equally in these twin realms of the carnivalesque and the grotesque.

Mary Russo critiques Bakhtin for failing to incorporate the social relations of gender in his semiotic model of the body politic.[27] Bakhtin's grotesque, pregnant hags, for Russo, remain under-analyzed, representing only paradox: pregnant death, senility and nubility, aged and new flesh. Within Russo's feminist perspective, the female grotesque can be used to destabilize idealizations of female beauty, realign desire disrupting the familiar world, and, I would add, to introduce the state of cognitive dissonance typical of *Beloved*. I interpret young Beloved as a grotesque female body, one in the process of becoming. Beloved's arrival even coincides, it is implied in the novel, with carnival in the narrative.[28] At first she is the haunting ghost, but she later materializes into the grotesque corporeal body, representing the return of the repressed, and the re-emergence of Sethe's horrific maternal past as an irrepressible present. Once impregnated, she grows like the pregnant hag whose body symbolizes both young life and aged death. Beloved's continual physical metamorphoses parallel the narrative's aesthetic traversals between carnivalesque and grotesque realms.

The trope of the female grotesque aptly describes mother and daughter, as Beloved's grotesque body mirrors Sethe's. Toni Morrison's text and Akosua Busia's screenplay are replete with examples of abused, enslaved bodies. Sethe's body exemplifies the subjected, abused, and tortured corpus. In the film, the abuses endured by her are particularly visible. She is on display as the primary object of terror and victimization. Her body, bloodied feet, pregnant womb, growing back and incontinent bladder comprise what Saidiya Hartman terms the "scenes of subjection" – the site of terror and violence perpetrated under the rubric of pleasure, paternalism, and property. We can extend Hartman's concept to an analysis of the film. The abuses perpetrated against Sethe – both overtly and covertly – constitute the very *mise-en-scène* of subjection in the film.

Recall, for example, Amy Denver (Kessia Randall) who stumbles upon pregnant Sethe (Lisa Gay Hamilton), as she lies stranded in the woods, oozing, bleeding, birthing, and lactating with a blossoming cherry tree on her back. Throughout the novel and film Sethe's body is associated with beasts of burden, blended with the world of animals. Schoolteacher chastises his nephews for beating Sethe as if she were a horse (p. 149). Learning of the infanticide, Paul D tells Sethe she's "got two feet not four" (p. 165). At one point, Schoolteacher tells the boys to write Sethe's "human characteristics on one side, and her animal characteristics on another" (p. 193). Then, there is the terrorizing day "two boys with mossy teeth, one sucking on [her] breast the other holding [her] down," took her milk (p. 70). All of these incidents are foreshadowed by the description of Sethe's arrival at Sweet Home. When she arrived: "The five Sweet Home men looked at the new girl and decided to let her be . . . They were young and so sick with the absence of women they had taken to calves" (p. 10). These incidents in the story evoke the grotesqueries of slavery, as written upon the enslaved body. Moreover, these incidents parallel the way Sethe literally and figuratively bestowed them upon baby Beloved's body (i.e., "with one stroke of the knife"). Taken collectively, these textual moments evoke the magical realist intermingling of man and beast, trading places within the slippery hierarchy of a grotesquely carnivalized world.

As a consequence of the film's emphasis on Beloved's developing self, Newton's performance does seem camp and comedic rather than solemn and severe. But the sounds and images of young Beloved drooling, defecating, burping, vomiting, and mumbling are clearly intentional, even unavoidable. Whereas readers of the novel move quickly through descriptions of Beloved's offensive physical fluidity, spectators of the film are confronted with lingering, embodied spectacles of her amorphousness, her protuberances, triggering a much more visceral kind of disgust. The grotesque body in cinema is usually a generic concomitant of slapstick comedy (for example, Jerry Lewis's and later Eddie Murphy's "Nutty Professor"). It is not usually a component of historical melodrama. Consequently, Newton's performance seems "excessive" and difficult to assimilate. Newton's Beloved stands out as generically incongruous with other aspects of the film. Whereas descriptions of Beloved's grotesque body in the novel are simply components of the verbally constructed character, the live performance of Beloved's grotesque body in the film enters into intertextual dialogue with other performances in *Beloved*, which, by contrast, appear more measured. Her performance also enters into dialogue with other genres and individual films in which the grotesque is synonymous with comedy and/or horror.

As a film, *Beloved* dialogues with the vast genre of maternal melodramas also known as "women's films," and specifically with a subset of films, functioning as a counterbalance to the dominant male genres, called "the woman's weepie."[29] These Hollywood genre films typically depicted women as subordinated to the Law of the Father. Tragic mother–daughter melodramas have enjoyed commercial success in American theaters since the 1930s. In the transcription from novel to film, director Jonathan Demme, producer

Beloved

Chapter 13

Oprah Winfrey, and screenwriter Akosua Busia were cognizant of the novel's potential relationship to classical Hollywood films scripted to address predominantly female audiences. As a film, *Beloved* could be categorized as an African American maternal melodrama (rather like such films as *A Raisin in the Sun*, 1961; *Sounder*, 1972; *Crooklyn*, 1994). Like classical melodrama, *Beloved* reveals how the mother strives to gain unmet gratifications by establishing an intimate relationship with her child. Sethe's yearning to merge with her children as love-objects exposes this desire as excessive, uncontrolled. The social, moral, legal, and racial system is unable to accommodate her excessive love, a point Paul D expresses when he says: "Your love is too thick . . . what you did was wrong, Sethe" (p. 165).

One key difference between *Beloved* and classic Hollywood melodrama is that the former overturns the trope of the sacrificial mother. Here the mother's personal sacrifice is the life of the child itself. Another important difference is that Hollywood's typical tragic, maternal melodrama usually exploits sensational or sordid subjects like sexual jealously (for example, *Mildred Pierce*, 1945), class mobility (*Stella Dallas*, 1937), the tragic mulatto (*Imitation of Life*, 1934, 1959; *Lost Boundaries*, 1949; *Pinky*, 1949), interracial marriage (*Guess Who's Coming to Dinner*, 1967), or trans-racial adoption (*Losing Isaiah*, 1995) in ways ultimately complicit with the dominant ideology. The denouement of these pictures – mainstream and African American – inevitably reasserts the Law of the Father, since the mother is ultimately revealed as excessive, overbearing, or somehow inadequate.

Due to the painful memory of slavery, *Beloved* approaches its maternal themes with more solemnity than most filmed melodramas. It raises questions of historiography in the context of maternal melodrama by treating the brutal genealogical legacy of slavery with high artistic seriousness. The cinematic *Beloved* even deploys a level of gravity and impact that surpasses the literary *Beloved*. After all, the cinema has a greater capacity to engage various senses and synthesize antecedent arts.[30] These resources for expression enable it to attain more emotional weight when the arts are synthesized with generic coherency. Whereas the novel offers description, the film presents *mise-en-scène*. More effectively than the novel, the film graphically (and acoustically) presents horrific representations of brutalized black bodies, of the enslaved body as the inscribed surface of historical events. Sounds of whips cracking, sights of bloody skin flayed open, the nooses around necks, and imprint of the chokecherry tree on Sethe's back momentarily conjure up the horror of chattel slavery in ways unavailable to novels. Even Baby Suggs's (Beah Richards) sermonizing plea for recovery and celebration of the black body are more vivid in the film than the written depictions of sermons at The Clearing.

One problematic consequence of the film's narrative emphasis on the tragic, domestic drama, however, is the partial erasure of Paul D's (Danny Glover) post-Sweet Home survival story. Paul D's role in the film is limited to that of the man who re-enters Sethe's life, who drives the ghostly spirit out of 124 Bluestone Road, and who later is in turn "moved out" by Beloved. His post-slavery traumas are abridged in the motion picture in favor of emphasis on Sethe's self-sabotage, trauma, re-memory, and guilt. Consequently, *Beloved* as a film becomes a "woman's film," focusing on efforts by Baby Suggs (Beah

Richards), Denver (Kimberly Elise), and Sethe to transcend the trauma of the past still threatening in the present.

Paul D's internment experience in Georgia, and his work on the chain gang, carefully described in the novel, is notably absent from the film. In the novel, Morrison recounts that Paul D was sent to prison after trying to kill Brandywine, the man to whom Schoolteacher had sold him. Brandywine was leading him, in a coffle with ten others, through Kentucky into Virginia. "He didn't know exactly what prompted him to try – other than Halle, Sixo, Paul A, Paul F, and Mister . . . but the trembling was fixed by the time he knew it was there" (*Beloved*, p. 106). Just as Sethe's relationship with Beloved represents the link between many mothers and daughters, Paul D's incarceration and work on the chain gang represents the literal and figurative link between himself and many African American men who shared an abusive history of internment during Reconstruction. His subjugation at the hands of Reconstruction-era correction officers parallels Sethe's subjection at the hands of antebellum authorities. Relaying "his story" and setting it in Georgia is central to the historiographic intervention Morrison initiates.

Historians continue to unearth the relationship between slavery and mass incarceration. Prior to the 1920s African Americans convicted of breaking the laws – petty and grand – in the New South found themselves "farmed out" to the highest bidder, and destined to labor for the duration of their sentence or their life, whichever came first. Convicts built railroads, mined coal, manufactured brick, forested lumber, paved roads, and picked cotton. According to Alex Lichtenstein, convict leasing remained the predominant form of punishment until the closing years of the nineteenth century and contributed to the region's industrial expansion and postbellum economic transformation.[31] Various states, including Mississippi, Tennessee, Florida, and Alabama, relied heavily on convict-lease (chain gang) penal systems. The penal system in the New South was not only a corrupt system of labor recruitment, control, and exploitation, it was also suited to the political economy of a post-emancipation society. "From a purely penological point of view, the convict lease was a fiscally conservative means of coping with a new burden: ex-slaves were emancipated from the dominion of the slaveholder only to be subject to the authority of the state."[32] Benefiting from the scholarship on slavery of writers as diverse as John Edgar Wideman, Randall Kennedy, Horace Cayton, and St Clair Drake, Loïc Wacquant writes: "On the morrow of Emancipation, Southern prisons turned black overnight, as 'thousands of ex-slaves were being arrested, tried and convicted for acts that in the past had been dealt with by the master alone' and for refusing to behave as menials and follow the demeaning rules of racial etiquette."[33]

The racial disproportionality of imprisonment in the United States can only be understood against the backdrop of the full historical trajectory of racial domination in the US. Morrison recounts the internment experience of Paul D as a way of recuperating the historical experiences of incarcerated black men. Sexual abuse was a routine concomitant of this imprisonment. Thus, the author recounts the daily practice by which black inmates were forced to fellate white prison guards (for example, "Hungry, nigger?," *Beloved*, p. 108) as a way of re-presenting a variant of sexual racism that has long been suppressed.

Enslaved men (and newly freed men) were sexually vulnerable both to the wanton abuses of their owners and to those operating as punitive agents for the state. Hayden White's assertion that narrative broadly defined "has to do with the topics of law, legality, legitimacy, or more generally, *authority*,"[34] calls attention to the strong political intervention implicit in this aspect of Morrison's text.

The filmmakers may have omitted Paul D's story from the screenplay for any number of reasons. Including Paul's story material may well have earned the film an NC17 rating from the Motion Picture Association of America. Second, some of the novel's material had to be eliminated to narrow the film's scope. Third, *Beloved* was made in order to appeal to female audiences. Retaining *something* of Paul D's perspective, however, enables the film to preserve facets of the gendered multivocality of the novel and the "multivalence of subjection" as endured by Morrison's characters.

When the film actually does include Paul D's perspective, it is rendered through unrestricted narration and perceptual subjectivity. The latter refers to the internal and psychological; it includes thoughts, dreams, fantasies, and sensory experience.

Although both the novel and the film are multi-voiced, the film is more adept at showing spectators the internal psychological states of characters. Flashbacks to Sweet Home, haunting memories, and encounters with ghosts, for example, are communicated in the film via focalized perceptual subjectivity. When Paul D first enters 124 Bluestone Road, for example, the camera aligns the spectators with his point of view. What we see is his inner-subjective experience of the ghostly presence in Sethe's home. As he walks through the corridor, it appears as if he is walking through the annals of slave life at Sweet Home. That Demme reportedly borrowed this eruptive memory technique from the death camp flash memories of Sidney Lumet's *The Pawnbroker* forges a subliminal link between two forms of holocaust. First, Paul D sees visions of family and friends bloodied and chained. Then, he is startled by the image of Sethe's murdered daughter. Finally, he takes his last steps through a barn door to enter her home. Throughout the foyer he is confronted with flesh and blood memories of abuses perpetrated on the plantation. Here the film develops the synthetic properties of the medium (close-ups, wide angles, zoom-in shots, props, make-up, ambient sound and point of view) to rouse our horror at the atrocities of slavery by conveying a subjective experience. In the novel, by contrast, Paul D's entry into Sethe's home is described rather subtly:

Paul D tied his shoes together, hung them over his shoulder and followed her through the door straight into a pool of red and undulating light that locked him where he stood.

"You got company?" he whispered, frowning.

"Off and on," said Sethe.

"Good God." He backed out the door onto the porch. "What kind of evil you got in here?"

"It's not evil, just sad. Come on. Just step through." . . .

She was right. It was sad. Walking through it, a wave of grief soaked him so thoroughly he wanted to cry. It seemed a long way to the normal light surrounding the table, but he made it — dry-eyed and lucky. (pp. 8–9)

Mia Mask

Chapter 13

While this description aptly details Paul D's actions, it does little to convey the subjective experience of his character, or communicate his startling encounter with the ghostly presence haunting Sethe's home. Here the film effectively enlivens the original source material by synthesizing the various antecedent arts into focalized perceptual subjectivity. The film actually allows you to see more than the novel. It renders aspects of magical realism vivid. Whereas a reader of the novel pauses to contemplate the sentence "a pool of red and undulating light that locked him where he stood," the film shows you images of bloodied corpses, chained bodies, and slaughtered children in startling succession. Because spectators are aligned with Paul D's perspective, they momentarily share his fear, dismay, and alarm at the sight of these images. This amplification suggests that film – rather than being inferior to the novel – can actually enrich written texts in ways that go far beyond what a prejudiced view would have us believe about the cinematic medium.

Literary critics have discussed the way the novel created an aesthetic by playing against and through the cultural field of postmodernism. Both *Beloved* the film and the novel are polyperceptual: they engage numerous voices and narratives by telling and retelling the same event from Sethe's, Denver's, and Paul D's perspectives.[35] Like the novel, the film is innovative in linguistic ways that originate in the black tradition of oral narrative.[36] It mixes vernaculars and modes of response. Thus, another key difference between the novel and the film is that the latter translates narrative voice into focalized perceptual subjectivity, bringing spectators and characters into closer relation.

The film manifests another hallmark of a kind of resistant postmodernism. By eroding the boundary between high (literary) culture and (low) mass television or popular culture, the film collapses a boundary, for example, between Toni Morrison, the erudite cultural producer and Nobel Prize winner, and Oprah Winfrey, the TV icon and arbiter of bourgeois taste. The novel's story of slavery (invoked by *Beloved* and endured by Baby Suggs) is premised on the absence of power, the quest for self-determination, the loss of a homeland, and of a language.[37] But the film – at the level of its production at least – comes wrapped in the aura of Winfrey's career success, as media mogul, a career marked by the presence of power, the realization of self-determination, the existence of a cinematic language. As producer and star in the transcription of novel to the screen, Winfrey's approach is "inevitably partial, personal and conjectural."[38] In what follows, I explore the reception of *Beloved*, in general, and the impact of Winfrey's star persona on the media's response to *Beloved*, in particular.

Do the Media Matter?

The critical discourse around the film influenced the reception of the picture. More specifically, the reception presents another set of texts with which the film exists in dialogic relation. Three salient issues regarding the media coverage stand out. First, the media saturation appeared to backfire: the excessive hype hindered rather than helped the film financially. Second, the racial polarization of the critical discourse indicated blatant ethnic and racial partisanship in film reporting. Third, the African American press coverage (in an attempt to overcompensate for, or pre-empt, critical dismissal of *Beloved* by the white, mainstream press) was overly celebratory. Contrasting the various public dialogues about the film contextualizes *Beloved*'s box-office performance. It also reveals how reviewer commentary became part of a discursive struggle over the reception of dramatic black films by critics and audiences.

The reviews and promotion of *Beloved* revealed distinct trends, and, more specifically, two types of media coverage: promotional magazine stories (for example, *Vogue*) and evaluative film reviews (for example, *The New Yorker*). By and large, evaluative reviews appearing in the mainstream news publications (the predominantly white press) were respectful of the efforts to bring *Beloved* to fruition, but overly critical of the final product (*The New Yorker, The New York Times, The Village Voice, Variety, Sight and Sound*). Conversely, commentary in African American periodicals (*Ebony, Jet, Essence, The Amsterdam News*) was explicitly celebratory. A concerted effort on the part of black issue-oriented publications (and African American journalists working at predominantly Euro-American publications) was aimed at encouraging audiences to support *Beloved*.

However positive the African American media campaign may have been, it did not translate into ticket sales or approval from black audiences. Not only did African American audiences fail to support the film, a larger black bourgeois community denied the film artistic recognition. This aesthetic negation was clearly articulated at the 1999 NAACP Image Awards. Despite receiving six nominations, *Beloved* lost to *How Stella Got Her Grove Back* (36 percent), which took Outstanding Motion Picture over *Beloved* (17 percent), *Down in the Delta* (15 percent), *Enemy of the State* (22 percent) and *He Got Game* (10 percent).[39] So, despite the film's relatively high production value, positive reviews in the black press, an expensive advertising campaign, a story based on a Pulitzer Prize-winning novel, and a cast of stars, *Beloved* was unable to gain recognition from *black* audiences.

The mainstream press coverage began with a *Time* magazine cover story featuring the film's star-producer in costume. As *Time* covers are usually reserved for persons (and events) reflecting the tenor of the Zeitgeist, the cover itself seemed to mark a milestone because (like the *Time* cover featuring recording artist Lauren Hill with the caption "Hip Hop Nation") it appeared to substantiate the claim that black cultural idioms are continually moving from margin to center. Oprah Winfrey's image on the cover marked a milestone because it announced that a theatrically released African American film about the legacy of slavery and the reality of Reconstruction was a significant cultural event.

The four *Time* articles in this issue were so celebratory as to prod *The New Yorker* critic David Denby to begin his censorious review of *Beloved* by admonishing *Time* magazine. Denby wrote: "Weeks before the movie opened, *Time* unfurled the ceremonial bunting in a journalistic package so elevated in tone that the magazine seemed awed by the importance of its own coverage. When the public gets a proper look at the movie, the bunting may turn out to be a crêpe."[40] While Denby's dismissive tone is certainly problematic, he was correct in predicting audience response. As the *Time* magazine cover demonstrated, the Disney Company was banking on the cultural capital invested in Winfrey's celebrity sign. Clearly, the studio, director Jonathan Demme, and Oprah Winfrey herself were under the false impression that charismatic devotion to her celebrity would translate into audience enthusiasm – in much the same way that a book "translates" into a screenplay. The pun of *Time*'s cover, "*The Beloved Oprah*," itself hinged on linguistic slippage between Winfrey's televisual and film personae, even as it paralleled the textual shift from novel to film. But what Disney, Demme, Winfrey, and others failed to realize is that Oprah's celebrity charisma constitutes entertainment charisma not political charisma. Motivating black, white, and other ethnic audiences to support postmodern, avant-garde-inflected black cinema is fundamentally a difficult political and aesthetic challenge.

Beloved-as-film, more than *Beloved*-as-novel, elicits a particular political and ideological sensibility of viewers, a sensibility generally not found at the multiplex. In fact, rather than help the film, this kind of media coverage – like the casting of a TV celebrity instead of a trained actress – clearly hindered the film by discouraging viewers who erroneously dismissed it as more of Winfrey's self-indulgent, commercial populism. Media saturation made it difficult to separate Oprah's making of *Beloved* from the commercial self-help agenda presented on *The Oprah Winfrey Show*. More than one reviewer commented on the connection between themes addressed on the show and Winfrey's interest in producing the novel as a film. *The Village Voice* critic Jim Hoberman suggested that the movie might well be a platform for the issues Winfrey pursues in the context of her show:

> *Beloved* is less Oprah's vehicle than her time machine. Even more than Morrison, Winfrey – who sees herself as a medium for the spirits of specific Negro slaves – has assumed the role of a tribune. *Beloved*'s oscillating tone and close-up driven absence of perspective become more coherent once the movie is understood as an epic version of *Oprah!* – a show in which the star naturally shifts between autobiographical confession and maternal advice, reliving personal adversity and offering the model of her own empowerment as New Age therapy.

Writing for the *Chicago-Sun Times*, Roger Ebert echoed Hoberman's observations: "Her whole persona is about controlling her own destiny – owning herself. No wonder she was powerfully attracted by *Beloved*, which is about a woman who tastes 28 days of what freedom feels like and is willing to kill her daughter rather than see her taken back into slavery." Writing for the British Film Institute's glossy *Sight and Sound*, Charlotte O'Sullivan made a similar observation. Even Winfrey herself made connections between her talk show and the film when she shrugged off criticism of *Beloved*'s limited commercial appeal by contending that America's current race problem is rooted in its failure to honestly confront its emotional issues and history. "If you don't acknowledge the pain in truth, then you carry forward the pain in distortion . . . It's no different from your own personal history and wounds. If you don't heal your personal wounds, they continue to bleed. And so we have a country of people who have continued to bleed."[41]

Beloved

Chapter 13

Thus, in her own proselytizing plea, Winfrey pursued the project as a partial extension of the themes, ideas, and technologies of self-help presented on the program. In making an African American holocaust film, she attempted to impart the profound results and persistence of racism. Yet the way in which the film was discussed in the media (including her own show) undermined the gravity of the picture. Her appeal manifests the intertextual impact of television stardom on an American literary classic.

On one level, the *Beloved* project was matured by a progressive desire to provoke American audiences to consider the dehumanization at the core of the nation's foundation. On another level, the film was based on a profoundly naïve and commercial premise: that viewers would heed Winfrey's clarion call to "heal" the American family of its dysfunctional race relations. And, that all that was necessary for this "healing" to begin – if not occur – was for the "mother-of-America" to tell her adoring public to "*go see this film.*" However, if it is naïve for a celebrity like Winfrey to expect audiences to support an aesthetically and ideologically progressive project, it is worth asking another question: what does it take to get audiences (mainstream and ethnic) to support innovative, historically audacious black films?[42] What does it take to motivate African American audiences to support films other than *Blade* ($23 million) or *How Stella Got Her Grove Back* ($29 million), films which earned more in two weeks than *Beloved* earned during its entire theatrical run? I believe audiences avoid such pictures for two reasons: because they perceive them to be "high art" projects, and they stay away because they – understandably – do not want to confront their feelings about slavery.

The tension around *Beloved*-as-epic emerged in the racially polarized struggle for discursive control of its reception. Consider, for example, reviews by the African American *New York Press* critic Armond White and *The New Yorker* reviewer David Denby. White's complimentary review lauds every aspect of the film. White correctly notes: "Demme achieves in a commercial format what avant-gardists Carl Dreyer, Jean Cocteau, Maya Deren and Jean Genet could communicate to their intimates." But White's praise of Demme rises only to eventually fall into the trap of simplistic racial and aesthetic essentialism, as when he offers Demme's "black heart" as the explanation for his sensitivity to African American cultural idioms. White's own paradoxical racial essentialism is implied in the statement that lumps together dissimilar black-oriented films like the aesthetically innovative *Beloved* and the narratively conventional Steven Spielberg film, *The Color Purple* (1985). He writes:

> To be inured to the faces in *Beloved* is to be indifferent to the lives they represent; their history, ethnicity and humanity. There's no way around the fact that film critics are pitifully subject to affirming themselves by praising such questionable talents as Woody Allen, Merchant Ivory or this week's Atom Egoyan. When films with African-American subject matter like *The Color Purple, Amistad* or *Beloved* are dismissed while trash like *The English Patient* or *Titanic,* or *Your Friends and Neighbors* is praised, it only means that white people are loving what has historically been their cinematic privilege.[43]

While we ought to be skeptical of White's appraisal of Demme, he makes a valid argument about the hegemony of Euro-American cinema and white film criticism, which participate in the exclusion and erasure of black cultural production. White describes what Cornel West has aptly depicted (in another context) as a history of "racist bombardment at the level of aesthetics." Moreover, White's insightful sensitivity to the role of film criticism in the reproduction of taste rearticulates the fact that film criticism – a concomitant of cultural criticism – is always already a political enterprise.

If mainstream critics were unfairly disparaging of *Beloved*, this raises several questions. Was *Beloved* a poor adaptation? Were critics racially biased in their evaluations? How could the film have been cast or directed differently? The deeper we probe, the wider the critical divide. In opposition to White, for example, David Denby demonstrated considerable political partisanship in his assessment. The author of a polemical book against multiculturalism, Denby's dismissal went so far as to challenge the validity of multicultural education. For Denby, the question was far greater than whether this was a successful adaptation. In his view, excessive praise for Toni Morrison's novel forced what he saw as the ogre of multiculturalism to raise its ugly head. In *The New Yorker* Denby wrote:

> *Beloved* is not an event to be enjoyed; it's an event to be endured, rather like the dedication of a new building on the Washington Mall . . . Still, media attention of this proportion is bound to electrify the Morrison industry in the universities and the schools; one can only squirm in sympathy for all the seventeen-year-olds who will be forced to sit through the movie."[44]

It is hardly surprising that a critic with Denby's conservative sensibility (and traditional readership) would dislike *Beloved*, especially since he refers to the novel as "ornery" (translation: angry black women produce angry black novels that make conservative viewers uncomfortable and are therefore unworthy of critical praise). Denby's comments questioning Morrison's rightful place in the American literary canon indicate cultural backlash and crude intellectual protectionism. As if inspired by Allan Bloom's *The Closing of the American Mind*, Denby attempts to protect the genealogy of Euro-American cultural capital – the very cultural hegemony Armond White challenges. Denby's review underscores the important intervention of Morrison's literary criticism. Her book, *Playing in the Dark: Whiteness in the Literary Imagination*, eloquently critiques such assumptions, accepted by literary historians and circulated as knowledge. This perspective maintains that traditional, canonical American literature is free of, uninformed and uncontaminated by, the four-hundred-year-old presence of African Americans. "The contemplation of this black presence," Morrison writes, ". . . is central to any understanding of our national literature and should not be permitted to hover at the margins of the literary imagination."[45]

Denby may have been unaware of Morrison's argument as presented in *Playing in the Dark*. Nevertheless, her thesis could also be extrapolated to cinema and popular culture. Contemplating the black diasporic presence is also central to an understanding of our national cinema. It is important for a host of reasons, including the significant role of blackness in the semiotic construction of villainy. Even in the era of African American "firsts" like Condoleeza Rice, Colin Powell, and Clarence Thomas – not to mention the cross-over celebrity of rap stars like Eminem who evince the performativity of race – blackness is still the definitive threatening racial signifier. This demonstrates the enduring nature of anti-black racism in the US. Films from the 1990s and the early twenty-first century are replete with representations of menacing black drug lords, gang leaders, welfare mothers, prostitutes, crack addicts, violent prisoners, pushy pimps, and husky hooligans. Examples from popular cinema include Tony Scott's *True Romance* (1993), Quentin Tarantino's *Pulp Fiction* (1994), the Hughes Brothers' documentary *American Pimp* (1999), Darren Aronofsky's *Requiem for a Dream* (2000), Steven Soderbergh's *Traffic* (2001), Antoine Fuqua's *Training Day* (2001), and Todd Solondz's *Storytelling* (2002) to mention only a few. In cinema today, movies still present menacing black characters as the primary threat to white people's innocence. A century after W. E. B. DuBois declared "The problem of the twentieth century is the problem of the color-line . . . ," we are still addressing "the relation of the darker to the lighter races."

While dialogue over the aesthetic merit of *Beloved* in mainstream publications was profoundly biased, discussions in the African American press were naïvely uncritical. Aside from Armond White's review, there was little in the African American press of substance, with the exception of Talise Moorer's *New York Amsterdam News* review. Moorer acknowledged the film's significance, situated it historically, yet questioned casting decisions while still encouraging viewers to see the movie.[46] Writing for *Essence Magazine*, Pearl Cleage published a fluffy interview with the star, which recounted Oprah's "journey to make the film," described the project as "her labor of love," and explained that "re-enactments of slavery" had helped Winfrey prepare for the role. These production experiences turned out to be part of Oprah's process of spiritual self-renewal. And, Cleage reported, this religious sensibility would now permeate the star's other projects. Black press coverage allowed the intertext of Winfrey's stardom to govern evaluation of the film.

Aware of *Beloved*'s limited commercial viability, Winfrey asserted that this film was her "gift" to the black community. "I give it as a gift, and I know that every person who receives it and really gets it is transformed in some way." Articles in the Johnson Publications (*Ebony* and *Jet*) chronicled her so-called journey. These emphasized the challenging shift Winfrey made from an epistemological to an ontological understanding of slavery during the process of *Beloved*'s production. For example, in *Ebony* magazine, Laura Randolph wrote of Winfrey saying:

> that her emotions were so raw it surprised her. After all, [Oprah] knows Black history almost as well as she knows the book. "I thought I knew it," Oprah says, "But what I have come to know is that I had just intellectually understood it – the difficulty, the sorrow, the pain. You can talk about it on an intellectual level, but during the process of doing *Beloved*, for the first time, I went to the knowing place."[47]

Unfortunately, media coverage in African American publications can also be dismissed as publicity — engaged less in the quest for discursive authority than in propagating the culture of black celebrity. Film criticism becomes a form of ethnic cheerleading. In some ways, Oprah Winfrey's journey to the terrible place of "knowing" slavery may undermine a basic premise of the book. It may undermine Morrison's premise that slavery was so epistemologically dissimilar from twentieth-century life as to confound the mind with the unfathomable reality that would lead a person to the unknowable desire to choose death over life. Fortunately, the film successfully communicates this premise even if Winfrey's experience of making the film does not. Further, *Beloved* the film communicates something profound about black modernity born of revolutionary struggle against the political economy of slavery.

Beloved as a novel and as a film presents a rich and revolutionary story. It articulates a reconstructive feminist voice within the fields of revisionist history, contemporary fiction, and feature film. *Beloved* is the product of, and a contribution to, an historical moment in which African American literature, historiography, and film production are in a state of fervid revision.[48] Morrison (in her novels and criticism) and Winfrey (in her show and the making of *Beloved*) are signifying, albeit quite differently, on academic and aesthetic traditions. For these reasons, I think the best way to interpret the cinematic *Beloved* is as a re-constructive text, seeking to open up new dialogues and new filmmaking possibilities. Viewing the film merely as a political football blinds us to the film's intellectual and aesthetic intervention against Hollywood's global hegemony.

Notes

1   Franz Roh, a German art critic, first used the term "magical realism." To him it was a way of representing and responding to reality depicted in the Post-Expressionist art of the 1920s. The introduction of Roh's magic realism to Latin America occurred through the Spanish translation of his book by the *Revista de Occidente* in 1927. Within a year, magic realism was being applied to the prose of European authors in the literary circles of Buenos Aires. The cultural migration from Europe to the Americas in the 1930s and 1940s probably played a role in disseminating the term. Various scholars have speculated as much. See P. Gabrielle Foreman, "Past-on Stories: History and the Magically Real, Morrison and Allende on Call," and Irene Guenther, "Magic Realism, New Objectivity, and the Arts during the Weimar Republic," both in Lois Parkinson Zamora and Wendy B. Faris (eds), *Magical Realism: Theory, History, Community* (Durham, NC: Duke University Press, 1995).

2   See Brian Finney, "Temporal Defamiliarization in Toni Morrison's *Beloved*," in Barbara Solomon (ed.), *Critical Essays on Toni Morrison's Beloved* (New York: G. K. Hall, 1998). Finney writes: "The novel was received with adulation (it topped the best-seller lists and was awarded the 1988 Pulitzer Prize) and reserve (she was passed over for both the National Book Award and the National Book Critics Circle Award, leading to a protest in the *New York Times Book Review* by forty-eight Black writers)."

3   Zamora and Faris (eds), *Magical Realism*, p. 9.

4   David Danow, *The Spirit of Carnival: Magical Realism and the Grotesque* (Kentucky: University Press of Kentucky, 1995), p. 64. Danow traverses from the carnivalesque to the grotesque, defining the latter as a contradiction in terms that suggests a range of ideas in expression. It is an irresolvable paradox that is universal and archetypal, that subverts an established value system in order to institute one of its own. It creates language and behavior codes in the work of creating new ones and superimposes one paradox upon another.

5   See *Variety* data March 1, 1999. Also, according to *The New York Times*, the Disney Company is estimated to have spent as much as $75–80 million to produce and market the film. See Bernard Weinraub, "Despite Hope, 'Beloved' Generates Little Heat Among Moviegoers," *The New York Times* (November 9, 1998).

6   George Bluestone, *Novels into Films: The Metamorphosis of Fiction into Cinema* (Berkeley, CA: University of California Press, 1957), p. 34.

7   Max Horkheimer and Theodor W. Adorno, *Dialectic of Enlightenment*, trans. John Cumming (New York: Continuum, 1991). One of the most celebrated texts of the Frankfurt School, this work endeavors to answer why modernity, instead of fulfilling the promises of the Enlightenment, has sunk into a new barbarism. Drawing on their work on the "culture industry," as well as the ideas of key thinkers of the Enlightenment project (Descartes, Newton, Kant), Horkheimer and Adorno explain how the Enlightenment's orientation toward rational calculability and man's domination of a disenchanted nature evinces a reversion to myth, and is responsible for the reified structures of modern administered society, which has grown to resemble a new enslavement.

8   D. N. Rodowick, *The Crisis of Political Modernism: Criticism and Ideology in Contemporary Film Theory* (Berkeley, CA: University of California Press, 1988).

9   See Manthia Diawara, "Black Spectatorship: Problems of Identification and Resistance," *Screen* 29: 4 (1986), 66–76; Michele Wallace, *Invisibility Blues: From Pop to Theory* (New York: Verso, 1990); Clyde Taylor, "The Re-birth of the Aesthetic," in Daniel Bernardi (ed.), *The Birth of Whiteness: Race and the Emergence of US Cinema* (New Brunswick, NJ: Rutgers University Press, 1996).

10 Natalie Zemon Davis, *Slaves on Screen: Film and Historical Vision* (Cambridge, MA: Harvard University Press, 2000), p. 108.

11 Robert Stam, "Beyond Fidelity: The Dialogics of Adaptation," in James Naremore (ed.), *Film Adaptation* (New Brunswick, NJ: Rutgers University Press, 2000), pp. 54–76.

12 Ibid., p. 64.

13 Pierre Sorlin, "How to Look at an Historical Film," and Robert Rosenstone, "The Historical Film: Looking at the Past in a Postliterate Age," both in Marcia Landy (ed.), *The Historical Film: History and Memory in Media* (New Brunswick, NJ: Rutgers University Press, 2000), pp. 25–49 and 50–66, respectively.

14 See Bernard W. Bell, "*Beloved*: A Womanist Neo-slave Narrative; or Multivocal Remembrances of Things Past," in Solomon (ed.), *Critical Essays on Toni Morrison's Beloved*, p. 173.

15 Henry Louis Gates, Jr and Nellie Y. McKay, *The Norton Anthology of African American Literature* (New York: W. W. Norton, 1997), p. 2097.

16 Davis, *Slaves on Screen*, p. 95.

17 Hayden White, *Tropics of Discourse: Essays in Cultural Criticism* (Baltimore, MD: The Johns Hopkins University Press, 1985), p. 53.

18 Toni Morrison, *Playing in the Dark: Whiteness and the Literary Imagination* (New York: Random House, 1992), p. 9.

19 Marc C. Conner, "From the Sublime to the Beautiful: The Aesthetic Progression of Toni Morrison," in Marc Conner (ed.), *The Aesthetics of Toni Morrison: Speaking the Unspeakable* (Jackson: University Press of Mississippi, 2000), p. 64.

20 Ibid.

21 For instance, this is allegedly why Alfred Hitchcock avoided using an actress's image for the eponymous character of *Rebecca* (1940). Hitchcock surmised that each spectator would visualize (in his/her mind's eye) a more enigmatically beautiful woman than any real actress could render.

22 Zamora and Faris (eds), *Magical Realism*, p. 3.

23 Deborah Horvitz, "Nameless Ghosts: Possession and Dispossession in *Beloved*," in Solomon (ed.), *Critical Essays on Toni Morrison's Beloved*, p. 93.

24 Mikhail Bakhtin, *Rabelais and his World*, trans. Helene Iswolsky (Bloomington, IN: Indiana University Press, 1984), pp. 21–7.

25 Robert Stam, *Subversive Pleasures: Bakhtin, Cultural Criticism, and Film* (Baltimore, MD: The Johns Hopkins University Press, 1989), p. 160.

26 Saidiya Hartman, *Scenes of Subjection: Terror, Slavery and Self-making in Nineteenth-century America* (New York: Oxford University Press, 1997), p. 23. See also Danow, *The Spirit of Carnival*, p. 50.

27 Mary Russo, *The Female Grotesque: Risk, Excess, and Modernity* (New York: Routledge, 1995).

28 Toni Morrison, *Beloved* (Plume Contemporary Fiction Series, New York: Penguin, 1988), p. 235. Subsequent references by page number in the text will be to this edition.

29 E. Ann Kaplan, *Motherhood and Representation: The Mother in Popular Culture and Melodrama* (New York: Routledge, 1992), p. 66. Kaplan also cites Janet Staiger's essay "Mass-produced Photoplays: Economic and Signifying Practices in the First Years of Hollywood," *Wide Angle* 4: 3 (1980), 12–27.

30 Stam, "The Dialogics of Adaptation," p. 61.

31 Alex Lichtenstein, *Twice the Work of Free Labor: The Political Economy of Convict Labor in the New South* (London: Verso, 1996), pp. 1–17.

32 Ibid., p. 3.

33 Loïc Wacquant, "From Slavery to Mass Incarceration: Rethinking the 'Race Question' in the US," *New Left Review* 13 (January–February 2002), 41–60.

34 Hayden White, "The Value of Narrativity in the Representation of Reality," *Critical Inquiry* (Autumn, 1980), 17. See also Brenda Cooper's discussion of White's work in *Magical Realism in West African Fiction: Seeing with a Third Eye* (London: Routledge, 1998).

35 Rafael Perez-Torres, "Knitting and Knotting the Narrative Thread: *Beloved* as Postmodern Novel," in Nancy Peterson (ed.), *Toni Morrison: Critical and Theoretical Approaches* (Baltimore, MD: The Johns Hopkins University Press, 1993), p. 105.

36 Brian Finney, "Temporal Defamiliarization in Toni Morrison's *Beloved*," in Solomon (ed.), *Critical Essays on Toni Morrison's Beloved*, p. 104.

37 Perez-Torres, "Knitting and Knotting the Narrative Thread," p. 94.

38 Stam, "The Dialogics of Adapation," p. 62.

39 See the NAACP Image Awards website and the *New York Amsterdam News* arts and entertainment section December 31, 1998. Three hundred industry professionals and NAACP leaders decide the forty-one categories.

40 David Denby, "Haunted by the Past: Toni Morrison's Lyricism Encounters Oprah's Blunt Common Sense," *The New Yorker* (October 26 and November 2, 1998).

41 Ron Stodghill, "Daring to Go There," *Time* (October 5, 1998).

42 I am not suggesting that black audiences do not support black film. *Blade, How Stella Got Her Grove Back*, and *Dr Do Little* were tremendous commercial successes in part because of black audience support.

43 Armond White, "*Beloved*: Directed by Jonathan Demme," *New York Press* (October 21, 1998).

44 Denby, "Haunted by the Past," *The New Yorker* (October 26, 1998).

45 See Morrison, *Playing in the Dark*, pp. 1–29.

46 Talise D. Moorer, "Oprah's *Beloved* Personalizes Impact of Slavery," *The New York Amsterdam News* (October 15, 1998), 24.

47 Laura B. Randolph, "Sizzle: In her First Love Scenes in the Powerful Film *Beloved*," *Ebony Magazine* (November 1998), 36–42.

48 Ashraf Rushdy, "Daughters Signifyin(g) History: The Example of Toni Morrison's *Beloved*," in Linden Peach (ed.), *Toni Morrison Contemporary Critical Essays* (New York: St Martin's Press, 1998), pp. 140–53.

--- Bibliography ---

Ayer, Deborah (1998) "The Making of a Man: Dialogic Meaning in *Beloved*," in Barbara Solomon (ed.), *Critical Essays on Toni Morrison's Beloved*. New York: G. K. Hall.

Bell, Bernard W. (1998) "*Beloved*: A Womanist Neo-slave Narrative; or, Multivocal Remembrances of Things Past," in Barbara Solomon (ed.), *Critical Essays on Toni Morrison's Beloved*. New York: G. K. Hall.

Bloom, Harold (ed.) (1990) *Modern Critical Views: Toni Morrison*. New York: Chelsea House.

Bobo, Jacqueline (ed.) (1998) *Black Women Film and Video Artists*. London: Routledge.

Conner, Marc (ed.) (2000) *The Aesthetics of Toni Morrison: Speaking the Unspeakable*. Jackson: University Press of Mississippi.

Corey, Susan (2000) "Toward the Limits of Mystery: The Grotesque in Toni Morrison's *Beloved*," in Marc Conner (ed.), *The Aesthetics of Toni Morrison: Speaking the Unspeakable*, pp. 31–48. Jackson: University Press of Mississippi.

DaMatta, Roberto (1991) *Carnivals, Rogues and Heroes: An Interpretation of the Brazilian Dilemma*. Notre Dame: University of Notre Dame Press.

Danow, David (1995) *The Spirit of Carnival: Magical Realism and the Grotesque*. Kentucky: University Press of Kentucky.

Davis, Natalie Zemon (2000) *Slaves on Screen: Film and Historical Vision*. Cambridge, MA: Harvard University Press.

DeKoven, Marianne (1997) "Postmodernism and Post-utopian Desire in Toni Morrison and E. L. Doctorow," in Nancy Peterson (ed.), *Toni Morrison: Critical and Theoretical Approaches*, pp. 112–30. Baltimore, MD: The Johns Hopkins University Press.

Diawara, Manthia (1993) *Black American Cinema*. New York: Routledge.

Dickerson, Vanessa (2001) "Summoning SomeBody: The Flesh Made Word in Toni Morrison's Fiction," in Michael Bennett and Vanessa D. Dickerson (eds), *Recovering the Black Female Body: Self-representations by African American Women*. New Brunswick, NJ: Rutgers University Press.

Fitzgerald, Jennifer (1998) "Selfhood and Community: Psychoanalysis and Discourse in *Beloved*," in Linden Peach (ed.), *Toni Morrison: Contemporary Critical Essays*, pp. 110–27. New York: St Martin's Press.

Foreman, P. Gabrielle (1995) "Past-on Stories: History and the Magically Real, Morrison and Allende on Call," in Lois Parkinson Zamora and Wendy B. Faris (eds), *Magical Realism: Theory, History, Community*. Durham, NC: Duke University Press.

Gates, Henry Louis, Jr and Appiah, K. A. (eds) (1993) *Toni Morrison: Critical Perspectives Past and Present*. New York: Amistad.

Hartman, Saidiya (1997) *Scenes of Subjection: Terror, Slavery and Self-making in Nineteenth-century America*. New York: Oxford University Press.

Hudson-Weems, Clenora (1991) "Toni Morrison's Use of Mysticism in *Beloved*," *Abafazi: Simmons College Journal* 1: 1 (Spring), 2–5.

Kaplan, E. Ann (1992) *Motherhood and Representation: The Mother in Popular Culture and Melodrama*. New York: Routledge.

Landy, Marcia (ed.) (2000) *The Historical Film: History and Memory in Media*. New Brunswick, NJ: Rutgers University Press.

Lichtenstein, Alex (1996) *Twice the Work of Free Labour: The Political Economy of Convict Labour in the New South*. London: Verso.

McKay, Nellie (1988) *Critical Essays on Toni Morrison*. Boston, MA: G. K. Hall.

Massey, Douglas and Denton, Nancy A. (1993) *American Apartheid: Segregation and the Making of the Underclass*. Cambridge, MA: Harvard University Press.

Mobley, Marilyn Sanders (1990) "A Different Remembering: Memory, History and Meaning in Toni Morrison's *Beloved*," in Harold Bloom (ed.), *Modern Critical Views: Toni Morrison*. New York: Chelsea House.

Morrison, Toni (1992) *Playing in the Dark: Whiteness and the Literary Imagination*. New York: Random House.

Peach, Linden (ed.) (1998). *Toni Morrison: Contemporary Critical Essays*. New York: St Martin's Press.

Perez-Torres. Rafael (1997) "Knitting and Knotting the Narrative Thread: *Beloved* as Postmodern Novel," in Nancy Peterson (ed.), *Toni Morrison: Critical and Theoretical Approaches*, pp. 91–109. Baltimore, MD: The Johns Hopkins University Press.

Plasa, Carl (ed.) (1998) *Toni Morrison*: *Beloved*. New York: Columbia University Press.

Rodowick, D. N. (1988) *The Crisis of Political Modernism: Criticism and Ideology in Contemporary Film Theory*. Berkeley, CA: University of California Press.

Rosenstone, Robert (2000) "The Historical Film: Looking at the Past in a Postliterate Age," in Marcia Landy (ed.), *The Historical Film: History and Memory in Media*, pp. 50–66. New Brunswick, NJ: Rutgers University Press.

Rushdy, Ashraf (1998) "Daughters Signifyin(g) History: The Example of Toni Morrison's *Beloved*," in Linden Peach (ed.), *Toni Morrison: Contemporary Critical Essays*, pp. 140–53. New York: St Martin's Press.

Russo, Mary (1995) *The Female Grotesque: Risk, Excess, and Modernity*. New York: Routledge.

Sale, Roger (1990) "Toni Morrison's *Beloved*," in Harold Bloom (ed.), *Modern Critical Views: Toni Morrison*. New York: Chelsea House.

Samuels, Wilfred and Hudson-Weems, Clenora (eds) (1990) *Toni Morrison*. Boston: Twayne.

Solomon, Barbara (ed.) (1998) *Critical Essays on Toni Morrison's Beloved*. New York: G. K. Hall.

Spillers, Hortense (1990) "A Hateful Passion, a Lost Love," in Harold Bloom (ed.), *Modern Critical Views: Toni Morrison*. New York: Chelsea House.

Wacquant, Loïc (2002) "From Slavery to Mass Incarceration: Rethinking the 'Race Question' in the US," *New Left Review* 13 (January–February), 41–60.

White, Hayden (1985) *Tropics of Discourse: Essays in Cultural Criticism*. Baltimore, MD: The Johns Hopkins University Press.

Wideman, John Edgar (1995) "Doing Time, Marking Race," *The Nation* (October 30).

Zamora, Lois Parkinson and Faris, Wendy B. (eds) (1995) *Magical Realism: Theory, History, Community*. Durham, NC: Duke University Press.

Mia Mask

Chapter 13

Chapter 14

Oral Traditions, Literature, and Cinema in Africa

Mbye Cham

The landscape of creative practice in Africa today is marked by, among other things, the coexistence of multiple forms and media of artistic expression, some of which claim indigenous ancestry in Africa itself, while others trace their origin to cultures outside Africa. Artistic creativity expressed through the medium of oral performance, for example, is accorded indigenous African roots, but that transmitted through the media of writing (the novel) and the visual (film) is usually thought of as forms or media introduced into Africa in the wake of her encounter with Euro-Christianity and Arab-Islam. Different origins notwithstanding, and setting aside the oft-repeated error of denying and erasing a written tradition in Africa prior to her contact with Europe, in particular, these three forms of imaginative expression continue to exist side by side, influencing, confronting, and interacting with each other dialogically and in mutually transformative ways in terms of subject matter, theme, style, technique, and political significance.

Coexistence within the same creative landscape cultivates and promotes an interesting dynamics of exchange, to borrow a phrase from Keith Cohen,[1] one predicated on varying degrees of repetition, revision, subversion, parody, "betrayal," and change, as well as a blurring, conflation, or even erasure of singular artistic labels. The latter refers to the trend (elaborated below) whereby many artists are shedding singular designations as novelists or filmmakers to take on plural or compound labels as griot–filmmaker or writer–filmmaker to expand the more prevalent earlier label of writer–storyteller/oral performer.

Various aspects of this dynamics of exchange in Africa are the subject of increasing critical attention in some quarters of African cultural studies.[2] In particular, the focus has been predominantly on the relationship between the oral and the written, and only scant attention has been paid to the complex of interactions between the latter two (oral narrative performance and the novel) and film, a relatively recent phenomenon in Africa.

Where such interactions have been examined, the tendency has been to focus on written forms of literature (the novel and short story, for example) to the exclusion and marginalization of oral narratives.

Perhaps this is a function of the background and perspectives of scholars and critics, some of whom hail from cultures and settings where oral performance and oral narrative traditions have lost both the vigor of their practitioners and the attention of their audience, and where oral narratives themselves are encountered, appreciated, and "experienced," paradoxically, through their written transcriptions and translations, which render only the verbal aspects of what are complex creations that depend on a wide array of non-verbal elements and strategies. Nevertheless, many fine studies on the links between the oral and the written, as well as a few on the written and the filmic, have produced insights that can be synthesized and adapted to generate highly productive descriptions and analyses of the modes and implications of exchange and dialogue between oral traditions, written literature, and film in Africa. This chapter is a brief survey of the constantly shifting nature and meanings of this interaction and exchange in African film culture.

There hardly exists an African writer or filmmaker whose work or pronouncements have not articulated or posited some kind of relationship with his or her indigenous oral and creative culture and tradition.[3] Similarly, some African writers have clearly defined relationships with African filmmakers and vice versa. This rapprochement between oral traditions, written literature, and film has produced a film practice in Africa that has entertained, courted, and cultivated, in varying degrees, significant ties among practitioners in the three domains, particularly between writers and filmmakers.

The patterns of relationships – hierarchical, collaborative, adversarial, love, hate – between literature and film that have marked the history of adaptation in Euro-American film cultures at different points in time have been largely absent from African cinema practices to date. The reigning tendency here has been one of mutual cross-fertilization, exchange, and acknowledgment of equality, importance, and complementarity of discursive and signifying systems on the part of both individual artists and the organizations and institutions of cinema. For example, the Comité Africain des Cinéastes (CAC), formed in the mid-1980s by filmmakers such as Med Hondo, Ousmane Sembène, Souleyeman Cissé, and others, highlighted as one of its pillar principles and action agenda items the encouragement of productive relations between literature and film. During its short life-span, the CAC established a fund to aid the financing of film productions by Africans, and contributors to this fund were urged to identify an African literary text of their choice which they would like to see adapted to the screen. Although this project, as well as the CAC itself, did not survive long enough to implement these and other goals, it nevertheless points to an awareness of literature as a fertile source for African film culture, and the desire of African filmmakers to connect productively with fellow cultural workers who use a different medium. The work of the two leading figures of the CAC, Med Hondo and Ousmane Sembène, provide some of the most interesting cases of adaptation in African film culture. I shall return to them later.

The CAC was not alone in advocating close ties between writers and filmmakers in Africa. Institutional actions on this score are also significant. The biggest and most important film festival in Africa is the biennial Festival Panafricain du Cinéma et Television de Ouagadougou (FESPACO), which takes place in Ouagadougou, the capital city of Burkina Faso in West Africa. Since its inception in 1969, FESPACO has consistently promoted a strong awareness of the inextricable links between cinema and other media of creative practice in Africa. In 1985, the ninth meeting of FESPACO highlighted a three-day UNESCO-sponsored colloquium on "African Literature and Film" at which African writers in attendance, Mongo Beti and Francis Bebey of Cameroon, as well as writer–filmmakers such as Ousmane Sembène, joined with scholars, critics, and public officials to draw attention to and debate the imperatives, benefits, and possible directions of closer collaboration between literary artists and filmmakers. The first in a series of FESPACO programs on the ties that bind African cinema to a whole spectrum of African artistic practices and systems, this colloquium was followed in the next gathering of FESPACO in 1987 by another major focus on the theme of "Oral Traditions and the New Media." This was also the theme of the tenth festival of FESPACO which featured artists and others working in the oral media and their relevance to new media such as film and television. The seventeenth festival in 2001 renewed this focus by choosing as its theme "Cinéma et Nouvelles Technologies."

Such individual, organizational, and institutional efforts have gone some way to promote a film culture in Africa in which oral artists, novelists, and playwrights collaborate with each other and write for film. In some cases, they become filmmakers in their own right. They are also increasingly establishing in Africa a cinema of adaptation of literary texts and drama pieces that are themselves, in some cases, adapted from narratives, myths, and legends in the oral traditions. Thus, what one is likely to encounter in general in this cinema of adaptation are "thrice-told tales," films whose point of creative departure can be traced in one way or another to the oral traditions, as well as films that are adapted from original literary texts. Analyses of such works will gain much from a critical aware-ness of the creative trajectories of such narratives, trajectories that also reinforce the notion of a dynamic continuum in African artistic cultures. What Millicent Marcus dubs "cinemorphic" novels,[4] that is, novels whose narrative and other structural elements approximate and are influenced by film technique, as well as novels that are inspired by films, are also a presence in African film culture. Before engaging a survey of such film adaptations in Africa, let me briefly consider how African writers and filmmakers see themselves, each other, and their oral traditions. This will go some way to illuminate the modes of interaction that mark adaptive practices in Africa.

--------- Of Griots, Novelists, and Filmmakers ---------

Ousmane Sembène, the "father of African cinema," is credited with popularizing the notion of the African filmmaker as the modern-day equivalent of the *griot* or traditional storyteller. Refusing the conservative and exploitative tendencies, as well as the anachron-isms, associated with certain forms of "*griotage*," Sembène, nevertheless, reworks and appropriates the griot label to create a cinema that engages a broad range of the personal, social, cultural, historical, political, and imaginative experiences and challenges of his society. When Sembène calls himself a "*griot-conteur*" he is speaking for a number of African filmmakers who also position themselves in similarly critical ways vis-à-vis their traditions of creative practice. His journey from writing to filmmaking, as well as the constant shuttle between these in his practice, are by now well known. A poet, novelist-turned-filmmaker, Sembène's experience with and accomplishment in multiple creative media are replicated in the case of many other African filmmakers.

Many African filmmakers came to cinema with varying degrees of experience and accomplishment in drama and fiction. Equipped with knowledge of their respective oral traditions, many of these dramatists, novelists-turned-filmmakers bring this background to bear in important ways in their work. Med Hondo of Mauritania was, prior to becoming a film director, a man of the stage, a director, producer, and actor. He was one of the founding members of "Les Griots," a theater group formed in Paris in the 1960s which included African and Caribbean actors, such as Ababacar Samb Makharam and Sarah Maldoror, some of whom later took up filmmaking. Samb Makharam is the Senegalese director of *Jom: histoire d'un peuple* (1981), a film about workers' resistance to labor exploitation in contemporary Senegal, inspired by a popular oral legend of early Senegalese resistance to French colonial intrusion.

Sarah Maldoror is one of the pioneers of African filmmaking and is the Guadeloupean/Angolan director of *Sambizanga* (1972), a film adapted from the novel *The True Life of Domingos Xavier* by Angolan writer José Luandino Vieira. Ethiopian filmmaker Haile Gerima also came to cinema from the theater. He credits the writings and plays in Amarigna of his father as some of the most important influences on his own film work. In a conversation I had with Gerima in 1983, he pointed out that "some of the best work we filmmakers need to pay attention to is really in the novel form, like the work of Ayi Kwei Armah, Ngugi and even Chinua Achebe . . . Of course, adapting these written works into film will be the most progressive marriage."

After a short stint as actor with the Daniel Sorano Theater Company in Senegal, Djibril Diop Mambety turned to filmmaking, and in a nod to the potential of African artistic tradition in contemporary practices, he argues that "What *le masque nègre* did to advance modern art, it can do for cinematic writing."[5] Finally, we can cite the example of the young filmmaker Dani Kouyaté from Burkina Faso who, like his father who plays leading roles in his films, is also a dramatist and an actor who has directed and acted in many African as well as European plays. A griot by caste, Dani Kouyaté confesses his luck at being a part of what he calls the "*siècle du cinéma; c'est un instrument fabuleux pour un griot.*"[6] His two feature films, *Keita: Heritage of the Griot* (1995) and *Sia, le rêve du python* (2001), which I shall refer to again below, are clear examples of what we are dubbing "thrice-told tales" here.

While Sembène is clearly the most cited figure in the category of novelist-turned-filmmaker in Africa, there are several others with similar levels of distinction and achievement in this category. Assia Djebar of Algeria readily comes to mind. Celebrated for her fine work in fiction in French, Djebar took up filmmaking to complement and extend her work on issues of gender, history, politics, religion, and social justice. Unlike Sembène who adapts his own fiction to film, Djebar has thus far preferred to do original screenplays which draw in other ways from her own fiction. She has directed films such as *La Nouba de femmes du Mont Chenuoa* (1979) and *La Zerda ou les chants de l'oubli* (1982).[7]

Nobel laureate Wole Soyinka of Nigeria flirted for a brief moment with film, directing a feature film in 1979 entitled *Blues for a Prodigal*, which he wrote himself. For reasons not quite clear to me, this film about politics and military intervention in Nigeria was yanked out of circulation a few months after its release. Prior to his directorial debut, Soyinka was involved as writer and leading actor in the 1970 film adaptation of his 1965 play *Kongi's Harvest* directed by African American actor, Ossie Davis. From Soyinka's point of view, this project was a disaster as a result of distortions of and deviations from the screenplay that Soyinka wrote, among many other issues. He dissociated himself from the final version of the film, going to the extent of taking out an advertisement in *The New York Times* to denounce it, according to Nigerian film critic Onookome Okome.[8]

Soyinka's experience with film seems an unhappy one and is, perhaps, an exception. However, his novels and plays have exerted their weight in productive ways on other film-makers. Fellow Nigerian filmmaker and playwright Segun Oyekunle (*Parcel Post*, 1982) pays tribute to Soyinka in a 1983 interview as "my earliest strongest influence. I love *The Road* very much. It is his play that has influenced me the most." It is a paradox, though, that the work of the first black African winner of the Nobel Prize for Literature (1986), so rich in its artistry and so insightful and sincere in its commentary on African politics, culture, history, and change, as well as the human condition in general, has yet to be adapted significantly for cinema. In contrast, Nagib Mahfouz, another African Nobel laureate from Egypt, has seen some of his novels taken to the screen, even if they have had to travel, as was the case with *Midaq Alley* (1947) which was adapted in 1994 as *El callejon de los milagros* by Mexican filmmaker Jorge Fons. (I shall return to this category of traveling texts in African literature and film.) We can also point to the case of Nadine Gordimer, a South African Nobel laureate, whose collection of short stories, *Six Feet of the Country* (1982), about the experiences of people under apartheid, was adapted to the screen in the early 1980s by Barney Simon, Peter Chapelle, Lynton Stephenson, and Richard Green, with Gordimer herself writing the screenplay for two of the films.

Among the recent arrivals in this category of novelist-turned-filmmaker is Senegalese novelist Khady Sylla, author of the novel *Le Jeu de la mer* (1992), several short stories, and one short fiction film based on an original screenplay, *Les Bijoux* (1997), as well as a documentary entitled *Colobane Express* (1999). She joins Tsitsi Dangarembga from Zimbabwe, author of the critically acclaimed *Nervous Conditions* (1988), a novel about gender, struggle, and growing up in colonial Rhodesia, which she has adapted into a screenplay, but has yet to secure the funds to produce. Dangarembga directed her first feature film in 1996 entitled *Everyone's Child*. This 90-minute feature film about AIDS orphans in Africa is based on a story by fellow novelist and compatriot Shimmer Chinodya who is best known for his novel *Harvest of Thorns* (1989) about the liberation struggle in Zimbabwe. Before directing her first feature, Dangarembga wrote the story for another Zimbabwean film, *Neria* (1992), and was also involved in theater as a playwright and director while at the University of Zimbabwe.

It is evident from the preceding overview that what we tend to see as discrete, fixed, autonomous and, at times, rival entities are so mainly in certain theoretical and conceptual formulations that lock creative practices into rigid, mutually exclusive, generic categories. Broader perspectives, however, will show that they constitute, not a seamless complete whole, but rather an intricate and closely knit web of interlocking units and codes, constantly in motion, interacting with, wrestling with, influencing, and changing each other in many ways and on many levels, thus creating a sense of continuity and change across the three creative media of oral narrative performance, written literature, and film. What are the modalities of this exchange? Do the formal particularities of oral narrative performance, written literature, and film allow a triangular multi-directional bridge to permit and facilitate movement and exchange between the three? If so, on what levels? Can one speak of uniformity in the African writer's approach to and referencing of the oral traditions or in the African filmmaker's creative engagement with African oral traditions and literature? What have been the fortunes out of Africa of some African literary texts as far as adaptation is concerned? And of what literary sources outside Africa have African filmmakers availed themselves? I do not intend to engage these questions fully in the limited space at my disposal here. What I want to do in the rest of this chapter is to provide a brief survey of adaptation in African film practice, convinced that such an exercise will broach and, in some cases, provide perspectives on these questions and their implications for theory and critical practice.

Oral Traditions and Film

Adaptation of oral narratives and novels has been a part of African film culture from the start. Filmmakers looked first to their respective oral narrative traditions for stories as well as styles and techniques to tell these stories in film, and then to short stories and novels written in European languages, for the most part. Some of these are themselves adapted from specific oral narratives or inspired in other ways by elements of the oral narrative tradition. In its early stages, the turn toward the oral tradition was motivated in some measure by a desire and perceived duty to preserve in another medium this rich heritage of narrative and art, thought to be in danger of disappearing under the encroaching weight of writing, visual media, and technology. Hence, the tendency to reproduce and repeat, as closely or faithfully as possible, the original oral texts. I should point out here that this original is by no means a singular, fixed, finished entity, as numerous studies on the dynamism and flexibility of oral narrative performance traditions have shown. Other motivations and modes of engagement, beyond mere preservation, have since emerged, so that today what one encounters in African cinema's relations to both the oral and the written traditions are relations of repetition, revision, and transgression.

One of the first films directed by an African filmmaker from the Sub-Saharan region was made in 1955 by Mamadou Touré from Guinea, West Africa. Entitled *Mouramani*, this film is an adaptation of an oral narrative from Guinea and it paved the way for the practice of going to the oral narrative traditions for specific stories for film. *Mouramani* is driven by the impulse to repeat in order to preserve, not unlike the work of other filmmakers such as Paulin Vieyra and Momar Thiam of Senegal whose early films were basically adaptations of Wolof narratives as re-narrated in the writing in French of fellow compatriot, poet-veterinarian, Birago Diop. Responding to the Negritude urge to "return to the source," Diop dipped into his memory of traditional, pre-colonial oral narratives performed by the griot Amadou Koumba to transcribe and re-tell these stories in his highly acclaimed *Contes d'Amadou Koumba* (*Tales of Amadou Koumba*), which has proved to be a most fertile source for a good number of Senegalese filmmakers, in particular. It is to this collection of Senegalese oral narratives that Paulin Vieyra turned for his first short fiction film *Ndiongane* (1965), adapted from the story entitled *Petit Mari*, and Momar Thiam for his *Sarzan* (1965) and *La Malle de Maka Kouli* (1969), all from Birago Diop's stories of the same titles. Mansour Sora Wade's short 1989 film, *Fary L'Anesse*, is also based on a story of the same title from Diop's *Contes d'Amadou Koumba*. These films constitute the prototypes of the "thrice-told-tale" films that have been appearing with increasing frequency and in different forms in African film culture.

South African Palesa Letlaka-Nkosi's 1997 short film, *Mamlambo*, takes its inspiration from the South African oral narrative of the same title, as well as the short story in English by fellow South African writer, Bheki Maseko. While Letlaka-Nkosi's film references these prior texts in terms of title and other story elements, she revises and transgresses the myth and trope of the reptile *femme fatale* (characteristic of the prior texts) to engage a discussion of gender and power in contemporary South Africa.[9] Although a "twice-told-tale" in the sense that it is based more on the oral myth than directly on Maseko's adaptation, Letlaka-Nkosi's *Mamlambo* is emblematic of the relations of revision and transgression that define many contemporary African films that mine the oral traditions and literature as sources. The work of Dani Kouyaté from Burkina Faso is equally telling in this respect.

By caste, Dani Kouyaté is traditionally a griot, and he sees cinema as a great tool for the contemporary griot. Known more for his two critically acclaimed films, *Keita: Heritage of the Griot* (1995) and *Sia, le rêve du python*, than for his work in theater, Kouyaté's fiction films represent some of the most fascinating and provocative examples of adaptation practices predicated on repetition, revision, insertion, transgression, subversion, and transformation. As a griot, Kouyaté puts a premium on the value of tradition, but a renovated tradition in sync with the imperatives of the moment. Hence the importance of continuity for him. At the same time, there are entrenched elements of tradition and structures of thought that are outdated, and he employs transgressive adaptation to this end.

Kouyaté's first feature film, *Keita: Heritage of the Griot*, takes on the Mande oral epic of Sundiata Keita, founder of the thirteenth-century Mali empire in West Africa. A master narrative that is known and revered by most Mande griots and the general population at large, the epic legend of Sundiata occupies a special place in Mande history, narrative traditions, and definitions of self and other. The epic has been transcribed and translated into many versions and languages by scholars, the most well known being by Djibril Tamsir Niane of Guinea.[10] Also, the legend has inspired artists, writers, musicians, and dramatists who have produced works based on this story.

Kouyaté's film approaches the epic with respect, adoration, reverence, and confidence tinged with trepidation. Rather than re-tell the legend in its entirety, from birth to the return from exile of Sundiata to establish the Mali empire, as is the case in Niane's text, Kouyaté's *Keita* limits itself to the events up to the moment of departure for exile. Thus, the film re-tells only a third of the epic. It defers the rest for another time and to another griot. This is a significant departure from the original, and such a move allows him to insert into this partial story of past greatness and achievement the contemporary invented story of Mabo, the young boy negotiating the desire and expectations of modernity and the pull and obligations of tradition. By inserting the story of young Mabo into the story of Sundiata, the filmmaker revises the epic text into the present and enlists it in contemporary debates around questions of education, culture, history, and relevance. As pointed out by Christopher Miller, versions of the epic "are produced dialectically, in a conscious, symbolic relation to changing political and cultural circumstances. This is to say that *Sunjata* is always allegorical, always implying, inciting, insinuating, and teaching."[11] Kouyaté's second film, *Sia, le rêve du python*, takes this approach a step further.

Perhaps the most subversive and transgressive film thus far in African film practice vis-à-vis its source, *Sia* explodes a myth that is deeply entrenched in the worldview and cultural belief systems of many societies in West Africa. While *Keita* reproduces tradition and a usable past through repetition, insertion, and revision, *Sia* undermines and exposes the misuse and exploitation of tradition through repetition, insertion, and transgression. It invokes the myth only to explode it. *Sia* is an adaptation of the seventh-century Soninke legend of Wagadu, the tale of the python deity to which a virgin (in this case, Sia) was to be sacrificed every year for the welfare of the society. Like Sundiata, this legend commands a great deal of belief and reverence among its Soninke adherents, and it is also one that has inspired numerous re-workings in other media such as drama, novel, poetry, music, and art. Prominent among these is the play, *La Legende du Wagadu vue par Sia Yatabéré*, by Mauritanian playwright, Moussa Diagana, who worked with Dani Kouyaté on the screenplay to adapt the play for film. Thus, *Sia* is also a "thrice-told-tale."

The film evokes the main story line of the legend and play, narrating the decision-making process and debates regarding the issue of the ritual of sacrifice as a matter of tradition and obligation. However, it also departs from the prior texts in several ways, using insertion and transgression as principal strategies. As he did in *Keita* with Mabo's story, Kouyaté invents and inserts here a story of power and intrigue within a palace setting that mirrors in no uncertain terms the power structures and relations between state and civil society of many a contemporary African nation-state. There is a palace coup d'état and a counter coup in which the king, his loyal soldiers as well as civilians, especially those who voice opposition to the established regime, are eliminated. There is also a love story between Sia, the virgin selected to be sacrificed, and Mamadi, the head of the military guard, as well as the revolt and refusal of Sia to be part of a regime founded on lies, oppression, and the denial of free speech. Kouyaté stitches this story of contemporary Africa into the legend to radically subvert it, thus making apparent its status as an allegory on the abuse of power and the complicity of people in their own subjugation. In the place of a ritual sacrifice which legend and tradition uphold, Kouyaté inserts a gang rape of the woman selected for sacrifice. There is no seven-headed python deity. Instead, Kouyaté's camera exposes seven royal priests who mask habitual gang rape and murder in ritual sacrifice.

Also interesting in both *Keita* and *Sia* is the manner in which Dani Kouyaté engages a self-reflexive discourse on the role of griot as practice and institution. *Keita* reiterates the importance and relevance of the griot in contemporary Africa as the guardian of history and culture. On the other hand, *Sia* presents us with a palace griot, who opportunistically goes with the flow of power, privilege, and authority, instead of being the voice of conscience and morality that is the hallmark of the true griot.

While early filmmakers like Vieyra and Thiam were oriented toward preserving in film aspects of the oral narrative tradition and heritage, a more recent filmmaker like Kouyaté is interested less in re-telling an African legend on screen than in producing an allegory on the nature and misuse of power, both in the past as well as in the present. He invokes the tradition to renew and transcend it at the same time. As Moussa Diagana, the author of the play on which *Sia* is based, said at a post-screening press conference in Ouagadougou, "*Il faut d'abord rentrer dans le mythe pour en sortir*" ("You have to go through the myth first in order to come out of it.")[12] Kouyaté's transgressive move in *Sia* struck a responsive chord in the Burkinabe audience at the film's premiere in Ouagadougou when someone in the theater shouted "*Mais ça c'est Zongo!*" at the point where the madman in the film, the most vocal, consistent, and fearless voice of opposition and criticism to the established regime, was secretly eliminated by the king's henchmen. This person, as well as journalists reviewing the film in the local press, drew parallels between the elimination of this voice of dissent in the film and the recent killing, allegedly by the Burkina authorities, of Burkinabe journalist Norbert Zongo, an outspoken critic of the regime. Thus, for Kouyaté, adapting a legend like Sia becomes an act of cultural criticism at the same time as it constitutes an intervention in and commentary on current politics of governance, gender, and freedom in Africa, in particular.

Literature and Film

African filmmakers also draw from African novels and short stories written both in African as well as European languages. As pointed out earlier, some of these are themselves adapted in one way or another from narratives from the oral tradition, and others are original stories that reference the tradition in other ways. Recent activity seems to point to a trend toward more and more adaptations of novels, building on the foundation set by pioneers like Ousmane Sembène and Med Hondo. However, compared to film cultures elsewhere, much remains to be done in this area of African cinema, as the following overview will indicate.

It is perhaps appropriate to begin with the work of Ousmane Sembène, who personifies the novelist–filmmaker in African film culture. Of the fifteen films of various formats and length attributed to Sembène, four – *Niaye* (1964), *La Noire de . . .* (*Black Girl*, 1966), *Mandabi* (1968), and *Xala* (1974) – are adapted from his own literary work, and two – *Taaw* (1970) and *Guelwaar* (1992) – form the basis of a short story and a novel published after the release of the films. His second short fiction film, *Niaye*, is the first film adapted from a literary work by Sembène. Based on his novella *Vehi Ciosane ou Blanche Genèse* (1964), this film, which uses a griot as narrative vehicle, was never released for general circulation. Sembène's first feature-length film, *La Noire de . . .*, is also one of the first African feature films to take a literary work as its source material. Adapted from Sembène's own short story entitled "La Noire de . . ." (translated into English as "The Promised Land") in the 1962 collection of short stories, *Voltaique*, this film marked the start of what has now become a most prominent trait of the film work of Sembène. *La Noire de . . .* was followed in 1968 by another critically acclaimed film, *Mandabi*, which Sembène adapted from his short novel, *Le Mandat*, and in 1974 by *Xala*, based on the 1973 novel of the same title. Sembène also writes short stories and novels based on his screenplays. This is the case with films like *Taaw*, the 1970 short film which was to appear as a novella with the same title in 1987. Such is the case also with his 1992 film *Guelwaar* from which Sembène wrote the 1996 novel of the same title. A detailed analysis of the relations between his literary work and films is not within the purview of this overview. However, a general glance will show few differences – omissions, additions, varying degrees of emphasis – in terms of characters, situations, and other such elements, and much continuity in terms of story line (despite changes in narrative sequence), plot, theme, political analysis, and ideological perspective.

It is interesting to note also that Sembène is the only one who has thus far adapted his literary work to film. No other filmmaker, with the exception of his close associate Clarence Delgado, has used a Sembène novel or short story for film. After a long period of apprenticeship under Sembène, Delgado made his first feature film in 1992 entitled *Niiwam* (1992), based on a 1987 novella of the same title by Sembène. What accounts for this is the subject of some speculation. However, the testimony of Sarah Maldoror may provide some clues, on one side of the story, as to why other filmmakers have not taken on Sembène's literary work. Maldoror has been quite vocal and open about her experience with Sembène. At a film and literature conference that I organized in April 1980 at the University of Illinois at Urbana-Champaign, Maldoror lamented and denounced the fact that she was at first granted then denied the rights to adapt Sembène's novel, *Les Bouts de bois de Dieu* (*God's Bits of Wood*, 1962), a novel which many consider a masterpiece and which Maldoror admires a great deal. Why this novel about the 1947 railway workers' strike in Senegal and Mali has not been adapted to cinema remains a mystery.

A few other filmmakers from Senegal and elsewhere have built on the foundation set by Sembène. In fact, a number of early Senegalese films looked to Senegalese novels and short stories for narrative material. *Kodou* (1971) by Ababacar Samb Makharam of Senegal is based on a story of the same title by one of the pioneer women writers in Africa, Senegalese poet, writer, and activist Annette Mbaye d'Erneville. After obtaining the rights in 1959, Momar Thiam took his compatriot Ousmane Socé's 1937 novel, *Karim*, as the basis of his 1971 feature film, *Karim*. Still in Senegal at this early period, Mahama Johnson-Traoré came out with *Lambaye* in 1972, a feature film on political corruption, adapted from a play, *Pot de vin*, by his compatriot, Maurice Sonar Senghor, who himself adapted the play from *Revizor* (*The Government Inspector*, 1836) by Russian writer Nikolay Gogol.[13] This initial trickle of literary adaptation in 1970s' Senegalese cinema dried out in the mid-1970s, the 1980s, and much of the 1990s. It was only quite recently, with Delgado's *Niiwam* (1992), Cheick Oumar Sissoko's *Battù* (2000), and Mansour Sora Wade's *Le Prix du pardon* (2001), that we began to see the beginnings of a return to literary texts in any significant way in Senegalese cinema.

Although he hails from neighboring Mali, Cheick Oumar Sissoko redirected the spotlight on Senegalese literature as a fertile source for cinema when he came out in 2000 with his fifth feature film, *Battù*, based on the novel *La Grève des battù* (*The Beggars' Strike*, 1979) by Senegalese novelist Aminata Sow-Fall. Featuring, for the first time in African cinema, a famous Hollywood and a black independent cinema actor, Danny Glover and Issach de Bankole, *Battù* follows the original text in its main plot line, but departs from it in terms of omission, addition, and conflation of characters, as well as its elaboration of police brutality, repression, and resistance. Sissoko extends the political and moral scope and significance of the novel by inserting into the film the issue of African immigration in France. He creates the character of Saar, the rebel-activist daughter of the minister, who draws a parallel between the Senegalese official treatment of the beggars in Senegal and the French government's brutalizing of illegal and clandestine immigrant workers in Paris. Saar's character, coupled with the revisions in the character and actions of the female leader of the beggars, enabled Sissoko to elaborate the gender discourse in the text which he links in more direct ways to issues of agency and youth. The revision and elaboration in *Battù* vis-à-vis Sow-Fall's novel are also evident in Mansour Sora Wade's engagement of Mbissane Ngom's novel *Le Prix du pardon*.

Wade's 2001 film, entitled *Ndeysaan* in Wolof and *Le Prix du pardon* (*The Price of Forgiveness*) in French, is a liberal adaptation of a novel of the same title by Senegalese writer, retired school teacher, Mbisaane Ngom. Both novel and film narrate the story of a close friendship which turns into rivalry and ends up in tragedy followed by reconciliation and forgiveness. However, Wade's film also builds on and extends the text by effectively using a griot as narrative vehicle, not unlike Cheick Oumar Sissoko's other film, *Guimba the Tyrant* (1999) and Ababacar Samb Makharam's *Jom, histoire d'un peuple* (1981). In relation to the novel, Wade observes that he "took a few aesthetic liberties

Oral Traditions, Literature, and Cinema in Africa

Chapter 14

in the creation of the different moods . . ." He also links both the novel and the film to the oral tradition, "Indeed, before becoming a book, this story is that of a griot who creates a tale by talking about real events and passes it on to future generations. Therefore, the film aims to respect this oral tradition by finding a cinematic equivalent and, like the griot's tale, blends triviality and symbolism, and pays attention to detail and metaphor."[14]

African cinema's adaptation of African literary texts may have had its start in Senegal, but the practice is equally prominent and significant in other places on the continent. As indicated above, Med Hondo of Mauritania stands out in African cinema as one who has always articulated the importance of literature as source material for African cinema. Pan-African in perspective and outlook, Med Hondo draws from sources and engages issues both in the continent of Africa and the diaspora. Although not an adaptation of a specific text, his first major film on colonialism and black and other immigration in France, *Soleil-O* (1973), is profoundly shaped and influenced by a variety of black creative, scholarly, and political texts, as well as a wide array of black verbal styles and forms.

Building on this seminal work, Med Hondo turned to a specific text in 1979, *Les Negrièrs*, a play by Martiniquan writer Daniel Boukman, for his second major film, *West Indies: Les Nègres marrons de la liberté*. Transposing the setting of the film to a boat, a replica of a slave ship built expressly for the film set, the film reiterates the experience of enslavement and the resistance that Boukman narrates in the play. It also links this historical experience with the mid-twentieth century experience of emigration toward the European metropolis and the experience of immigration, racism, and labor exploitation. Med Hondo's other major work, which took the grand prize, the "Etalon de Yenenga," at the 1989 FESPACO in Ouagadougou, is the epic historical film, *Sarraounia*, adapted from the novel, *Sarraounia: Le Drame de la reine magicienne*, by Abdoulaye Mamani from Niger. As was the case with *West Indies*, *Sarraounia* revises Mamani's novel while sticking to the basic outlines of the narrative, and Med Hondo inflects the latter in ways that foreground and stress the reconstruction of African history and French colonial and military history that he undertakes in the film. This also enables the film to go beyond the historical context of the turn of the nineteenth century to comment on contemporary challenges in Africa.

Sarah Maldoror took up cinema after a very active period as a leading player in the 1950s' black theater group, "Les Griots," in Paris. She brings to African cinema perhaps the most diverse baggage of literary texts and personalities, ranging from Africa, the Caribbean, and France to Russia. She has also documented some of the leading literary figures of the Caribbean, such as Aimé Césaire (*Aimé Césaire: un homme, une terre*, 1976), Léon Damas (*Léon Gontron Damas*, 1991), and René Despestre (*René Despestre*), who were instrumental in the Negritude Movement of the 1940s in France. Maldoror has played a key role, from the very beginning, in promoting and advancing the use of novels and other literary texts in film, and her choice of source materials conveys in no uncertain terms her political and ideological perspectives and leanings.

Her first feature film, *Sambizanga* (1972), is adapted from the novel *A vida verdadeira de Domingos Xavier* (1961) (*The True Life of Domingos Xavier*) by Angolan writer, José Luandino Vieira. The story of the search by Maria for her husband, Domingos, who is suddenly arrested by the Portuguese secret police (PIDE) for subversive activities, forms the basis of both the novel and the film about Portuguese colonialism in Angola and the incipient resistance of Angolans. While following the novel fairly closely, Maldoror also effects a few changes in the film in order to more effectively capture and convey the growing activism among Angolans in the early 1960s that signaled the start of the armed struggle. Given the temporal context of production of the film (1971–2), at the height of the armed struggle which was to culminate in independence in 1975, the shift from victimhood and rage, evident in the novel which was written in 1961, to active resistance in the film becomes clear. The novel portrays Maria as someone who wavers and despairs in her search when confronted with the intransigence of the PIDE, but the film presents her as one who is determined, against all odds, to find her husband.

A pioneer female filmmaker, who has, perhaps more than any other African filmmaker, documented and worked on other documentation of the liberation struggles of Africans against colonialism (in Algeria with Pontecorvo's *Battle of Algiers*, her other films on Guinea-Bissau and Angola), and the struggles of workers and minorities in other places (*L'Hôpital de Leningrad,* 1982, based on Victor Serge's *L'Hôpital de Leningrad*), Maldodor appropriately revises Vieira's novel in order to place the role that women played in these struggles into proper perspective. Her interest in the struggles of ordinary people to affirm their humanity and to forge a genuine multiculturalism, particularly in the context of immigration, also pushed her toward the short story, *Un dessert pour Constance*, by French writer Daniel Boolanger, which she adapted in 1980 into a light comedy with the same title.

Other African filmmakers who have turned to African novels and short stories include Ola Balogun of Nigeria, who adapted Kenyan writer Meja Mwangi's 1974 novel, *Carcase for Hounds*, about Kenyan armed struggle against British colonialism, into a feature film entitled *Cry Freedom* in 1979. Balogun's compatriot, Adamu Halilu, took the novel *Shaihu Umar*, written in 1955 in Hausa by Alhagy Sir Abubakar Tafawa-Balewa, the future first Prime Minister of Nigeria, and made an historical epic film based on the novel in 1976. *Shehu Umar* has been dubbed the first African historical costume drama. From Côte d'Ivoire, we have Yéo Kozoloa's *Petanqui* (1984), a feature film about corrupt public officials who sell food donated to assist drought victims. The film is adapted from a novel, *15 ans, ça suffit (Enough, 15 Years)* by Amadou Ousmane from Niger.

Cameroonian filmmaker Daniel Kamwa is also well known for his social satires and parodies of social climbers. His two films, *Boubou cravate* (1973) and the later *Notre fille* (1981), are both based on the work of two well-known Cameroonian writers. *Boubou cravate* is adapted from Francis Bebey's short story, *Jimmy et l'égalité*, and *Notre fille* from Guillaume Oyono-Mbia's play, *Trois pretendents, un mari*. Equally important is the work of Bassek Ba Kobhio, also of Cameroon, who is both a novelist and a filmmaker. Ba Kobhio's well-received 1991 first feature film, *Sango Malo*, is adapted from his own novel, *Le Maître du canton*. He has also collaborated recently with Central African filmmaker Didier Ouenangaré to direct the feature film, *Silence de la forêt* (2003), based on a 1984 novel of the same title by Central African writer Etienne Goyémidé. Ba Kobhio also announced at the Cannes film festival in May 2003 that his next film project is an adaptation of the novel *Allah n'est pas obligé* by Amadou Kourouma of the Côte d'Ivoire.

The dismantling of formal apartheid in South Africa has encouraged the beginnings of what could become an important wave of the future in South African cinema, in particular. The rich corpus of novels and short stories by South Africans, particularly those in the indigenous languages, has yet to be tapped by filmmakers. However, there is cause for optimism when one takes notice of the fact that the first feature-length film directed by a black South African turned to a short story by a celebrated black South African writer for its source. Ramadan Suleiman's *Fools* (1997) is an adaptation of the award-winning (Noma Prize for Literature) short story of the same title by Njabulo Ndebele.

In spite of a few technical shortcomings and anachronisms, and the fact that the film sticks a bit too closely to the original and stays in the apartheid era, *Fools* constitutes an important step in the development of productive relations between literature and film in Africa. Other significant adaptations to come out of South Africa in the post-apartheid moment include Zola Maseko's *A Drink in the Passage* (2002), based on a short story of the same title by South African writer, Alan Paton. Another one is Mickey Mododa Dube's *A Walk in the Night* (1994). Adapted from the 1962 novella by Alex LaGuma about life in 1950s' District Six in Cape Town, Dube's adaptation operates on a somewhat radical revision in time, geographical setting, characters, and story line. Without going into detail, suffice it to say that Dube takes the story out of the 1950s and out of Cape Town, and makes it unfold in and comment on the challenges of life in the new South Africa. Issues of gender, black activism, resistance, and challenge, which were somewhat muffled in the text, assert a presence in the film in ways that subvert the pervasive sense of paralysis, passivity, and popular resignation to environmental and social decay that dominates the novel. These revisions resonate much with present-day challenges in South Africa.

Traveling Texts: *Into Africa*

In more recent times, there has emerged a trend whereby non-African texts make their way into African narrative and expressive cultures through adaptation in cinema. A cursory glance at the history of African intellectual, creative, and political cultures will reveal the openness of Africans toward other cultures and individuals with perspectives, values, ideas, and ideals deemed relevant, useful, and adaptable to specific African struggles and projects, as well as humanity at large. Too many to enumerate and elaborate here, this brand of appropriation has worked in Africa principally on the basis of what the late poet-president of Senegal, Léopold Senghor, dubbed "*enracinement et ouverture*" ("rootedness and openness)," revision and transformation. For example, while rooted in their "*Africanité*," Negritude called upon the Harlem Renaissance and Surrealism, Wole Soyinka's drama beckons toward Euripides and other products and aspects of Greek dramatic culture, and Sembène winks at Italian neo-realism and Marxism and cognate frames to speak of Africa and a global humanity.

A similar outlook informs the recent work of a few African filmmakers who have looked outside Africa, this time for specific texts. The late Senegalese filmmaker Djibril Diop Mambety went to Switzerland and picked up *Der Besuch der alten Dame* (*The Visit of the Old Lady*), a 1956 play by Swiss playwright Friedrich Dürrenmatt, and made it travel to the Sahel as a feature film entitled *Hyènes* (*Hyenas*, 1992). Similarly, in 2001, Diop Mambety's compatriot and protégé, Joseph Ramaka Gaye, took Georges Bizet's opera, *Carmen*, itself inspired by the Prosper Mérimée story, and made of it what perhaps comes close to being the first full-fledged African musical feature with the title *Karmen Gei*. Prior to adapting Aminata Sow-Fall's novel, *La Grève des battù*, in 2000, Malian filmmaker Cheick Oumar Sissoko looked to the Bible in 1999 for his film *La Genèse*, an African re-interpretation of chapters 23 and 27 of the book of Genesis three hundred years after the Flood. Young Egyptian filmmaker Ossama Fawzi journeyed to Brazil for a story by Jorge Amado (*A morte e a morte de Quincas Berro d'Aqua* [*The Man who Died Twice*], 1961) and, in his words, "betrayed" and "disfigured" the novel he took to *fin de siècle* Cairo as *Gannat Al Shayateen* (*Fallen Angels' Paradise*, 1999). In general, African films adapted from non-African texts repeat, revise, radically transform, and even betray and disfigure (in the case of *Gannat Al Shayateen*) the original texts which serve as points of departure for allegories on post-colonial African political and cultural economies.

I also want to stress the important work of Sarah Maldoror in relation to this category of traveling texts. Although different in their use of settings outside Africa – in France, in particular – her two films, *Un dessert pour Constance* and *L'Hôpital de Leningrad*, provide additional insights into the breadth and depth of African cinema's appropriation of non-African texts to speak to both Africans and humanity at large. *Un dessert pour Constance*, adapted from a short story from the collection *L'Enfant de Bohème* (1978) by French novelist and scriptwriter Daniel Boolanger, tells the story of the efforts of a group of African immigrant workers in Paris to raise money to send an ailing colleague back to Africa by studying to enter a TV game show. Maldoror takes Boolanger's very short story, of little more than 12 pages, and weaves into it a light-hearted narrative and a biting commentary on black immigration in the French metropolis.

Maldoror's work transcends racial categories by speaking to issues of humanity at large, especially in contexts of domination and resistance. In *L'Hôpital de Leningrad*, she adapts the short story of the same title by Belgian-born Russian dissident writer and political activist, Victor Serge, to examine and interrogate Soviet mental asylums as mechanisms of state repression and, by extension, processes of containment and denial of dissent by state powers the world over.

Oral Traditions, Literature, and Cinema in Africa

Chapter 14

While there has been a steady trickle of non-African texts into African film culture, the record in the opposite direction is negligible. To date, African novels and short stories have largely been confined to Africa, as far as cinema goes. With the exception of Euzhan Palcy's Hollywood-produced adaptation of South African novelist André Brink's *A Dry White Season* (1989), Hans-Jurgen Pohland's 1971 adaptation of Chinua Achebe's classic *Things Fall Apart* and *No Longer at Ease*, and a few others, such as Alan Paton's *Cry the Beloved Country* (1948), African source texts are absent in much of world cinema, even if some of these cinemas appropriate forms and styles that are African and diasporic. As pointed out above, one of the few African texts to be adapted by a non-African filmmaker is *Midaq Alley* (1947) by Egyptian Nobel Prize laureate, Nagib Mahfouz, which was adapted in 1994 as *El callejon de los milagros* by Mexican filmmaker Jorge Fons.

What Millicent Marcus dubs "cinemorphic" novels, that is, novels that evoke and move in some fashion toward the condition of cinema, can also be counted, however few, among the corpus of African literature. Film references and techniques in the fiction of African writers are not many, but the few that can be identified point to an imagination highly responsive to the possibilities and potential of film in literature. Ngugi wa Thiong'O of Kenya characterizes his novel in Kikuyu, *Matigari ma Njirugi* (*Those Who Survived the Bullets*), as "a series of camera shots." He also argues that "film or cinema as a medium is very important for us to master." Along with Manthia Diawara, Ngugi went in search of fellow writer/filmmaker, Ousmane Sembène, and came up with a documentary, *Ousmane Sembène: The Making of African Cinema* (1995).

In his 1969 novel, *Fragments*, Ayi Kwei Armah of Ghana provides a glimpse of film sensibility through Baako, the principal character, whose film scripts and treatments, reproduced in parts in the novel, form an integral and important part of the narrative approach. South African novelist, Alex LaGuma, also stands out as one whose sensibility and sustained attention to cinema translate into subtle and highly effective stylistic twists and ideological purposes. His last novel, *Time of the Butcherbird* (1979), provides many occasions where film allusions function as indices of temporal shift and as a device for character portrayal and development. Equally telling is my own experience with LaGuma's work in the classroom. My students habitually point out the affinity between his novel, *A Walk in the Night*, and a film script. Little wonder that it became one of the first black South African novels to be adapted to the screen in the new South Africa, and a clear example of what Marcus describes as a paradox of film "borrowing from itself."[15]

African literature has much to offer to African and world cinema. This brief survey of film adaptation of African literary texts shows how much more remains to be done, particularly in light of the strong degree of convergence and complementarity in the ways in which writers and filmmakers see and define their practices, and their attitudes toward the oral traditions. The classic novels of Chinua Achebe like *Things Fall Apart*, *Arrow of God*, *A Man of the People*, and *Anthills of the Savannah*, for example, cry out for significant screen adaptation. The same is also true of the fine novels and short stories of Ama Ata Aidoo of Ghana (*Changes*), Nurrudin Farah of Somalia (*Maps* and *Gifts*), Mariama Ba of Senegal (*So Long a Letter*), Bessie Head of South Africa (*Maru* and *A Question of Power*), Ben Okri of Nigeria (*Famished Road*), Calixthe Beyala of Cameroon/France (*Les Honneurs perdues* and *La Petite Fille du Réverbère*), Bealu Girma of Ethiopia (*Oromaaye*), Ngugi wa Thiong'O of Kenya (*A Grain of Wheat* and *Petals of Blood*), Maryse Condé of Guadeloupe/France/Guinea (*Segu*, *Heremakhonon*), and many other younger and lesser-known writers. The example of Senegalese filmmaker Mansour Sora Wade's turn to the novel of a relatively unknown writer for his critically acclaimed film, *Le Prix du pardon*, may tell us a thing or two about the magic that can result when filmmakers search creatively and run toward texts and also, as indicated by Sarah Maldoror, when texts run toward filmmakers. For his film, Wade also called on the imagination and skill of established Senegalese writer, Boubacar Boris Diop, and equally talented novelist/actor, Nar Sène, to write the script for the film. Such collaboration signals a progressive step that can only enhance the dialogical and mutually transformative relations that have always marked the relationship between the African novelist and filmmaker, on the one hand, and between these two and their oral traditions, on the other.

In accounts of relations between writer and filmmaker in Western cinema culture, one frequently encounters the anecdote of the writer and the filmmaker traveling on the same boat, but each harboring a secret desire to throw the other overboard. Events over the years may have altered such adversarial tendencies in the West, tendencies which have largely been weak or absent in relations between the African writer and filmmaker. As we witness the progressive undermining and dismantling of rigid generic boundaries in current creative practices, we see a movement in the direction of dynamic, dialogic, and mutually transformative multi-directional flows and shuttles between the various forms of creative practice that populate our modern world. This brief overview provides a perspective on modes of production and performance of this dynamic in African oral traditions, literature, and cinema practices, as well as the important role they play in a broader and deeper understanding of such a movement.

Notes

1   Keith Cohen, *Film and Fiction: The Dynamics of Exchange* (New Haven, CT: Yale University Press, 1979).

2   See Isidore Okpewho, *African Oral Literature: Backgrounds, Character, and Continuity* (Bloomington, IN: Indiana University Press, 1992), and "Myth and Modern Fiction: Armah's *Two Thousand Seasons*," *African Literature Today* 13 (1983), 3–20; Harold Scheub, "A Review of African Oral Traditions and Literature," commissioned by the ACLS/SSRC Joint Committee on Africa Studies, and presented at the 27th Annual Meeting of the African Studies

Association, October 25–28, 1984, Los Angeles, California, and *Story* (Madison: University of Wisconsin Press, 1998); Keyan Tomasselli and Maureen Eke, "Secondary Orality in South African Film," *Iris* 18 (Spring 1995), 61–9; Nokwenza Plaatjies, "Ubuntu: A Study of Women's Representation and Identity in South African Creative Media," unpublished PhD dissertation, Department of African Studies, Howard University, Washington, DC (May 2001); Dudley Andrew, *Concepts in Film Theory* (New York: Oxford University Press, 1984); Joseph Gugler, *African Film: Re-imagining a Continent* (Bloomington, IN: Indiana University Press, 2003).

3   See Mbye Cham, "Ousmane Sembène and the Aesthetics of African Oral Traditions," *Africana Journal* 13: 1–4 (1982), 24–40.

4   Millicent Marcus, *Filmmaking by the Book: Italian Cinema and Literary Adaptation* (Baltimore, MD: The Johns Hopkins University Press, 1993), p. 2.

5   June Givanni, "African Conversations: A Conversation with Djibril Diop-Mambety," *Africa '95 Screen Griots Publication* (from *Sight and Sound*), mimeo.

6   See the Internet site: www.dani-kouyate.com.

7   See Sada Niang (ed.), *Littérature et cinéma en Afrique francophone: Ousmane Sembène et Assia Djebar* (Paris: L'Harmattan, 1996).

8   See Onookome Okome, "Cinema and Social Change in Nigeria: The Political Imperative," in Onookome Okome and Jonathan Haynes (eds), *Cinema and Social Change in West Africa* (Jos: Nigerian Film Corporation, 1995, 1997), pp. 73–83.

9   See Plaatjies, "Ubuntu."

10 See Djibril Tamsir Niane, *Soundiata: une épopée mandingue* (Paris: Presence Africaine, 1963), translated into English by G. D. Pickett, *Sundiata: An Epic of Old Mali* (London: Longman, 1965).

11 Christopher Miller, *Theories of Africans* (Chicago: University of Chicago Press, 1990), p. 98.

12 FESPACO, Ouagadougou, Burkina Faso, February 27, 2001. You can read this interview and others on the website of *Africultures* (www.africultures.fr).

13 See Paulin Vieyra, *Le Cinéma Africain: dès origines à 1973* (Paris: Presence Africaine, 1975), p. 185.

14 Press pack for *Le Prix du pardon*.

15 Marcus, *Filmmaking by the Book*, p. 2.

Chapter 15

Memory and History in the Politics of Adaptation: Revisiting the Partition of India in *Tamas*

Ranjani Mazumdar

Tamas is not entertainment, it is history.

Bombay High Court (January 23, 1988)

The broadcast of the television series *Tamas* (*Darkness*) on Indian television in the late 1980s was a public media event that fused the politics of nation and memory, revisiting submerged sites of conflict around India's birth as a postcolonial entity.[1] The very public nature of the debate on *Tamas*, waged in courts and street demonstrations, in the columns of newspapers, and in buses and trains raised the televisual event in South Asia to a new high. Present in the *Tamas* debate were intimations of emergent struggles over national identity and the resurfacing of a more aggressive and culturally contemporary radical Hindu nationalism.[2]

Tamas was based on Bhisham Sahani's novel of the same name, which received India's highest literary award (Sahitya Academy) in 1976 for its portrayal of the horrors, violence, and psychological dislocation unleashed during the riots that accompanied the Partition of India in 1947. The story moves around the period just before and after the borders between India and Pakistan were drawn up. While the novel was respected as an important book, it never circulated beyond the literary public in the decade following its publication. In 1987–8, Govind Nihalani, an important figure of the "Indian New Wave," directed and screened the adaptation of the novel on national television as a five-part tele-series.[3] It was an immensely popular series that immediately ran into controversy as Hindu fundamentalist groups across the country demanded a ban on its broadcast. A petition for a public interest writ was filed in the Bombay High Court to prevent the telecast of the series after two of the episodes had already been shown. The petition argued that public order would be disrupted since *Tamas* was an incitement to violence and communal hate. On January 23, 1988, two judges vacated the court injunction, hours before the third part was to appear on television.[4]

Unlike the book, the television series rekindled the memory of Partition for a whole generation of people displaced from their original homeland. *Tamas* was one of the biggest events for Indian television, screened about five years before the cable boom of the 1990s changed the perceptual economy of television watching in India.[5] The Partition narrative entered the homes of millions, triggering the memory of a dark period that had been relatively silenced in the official history of the freedom struggle. Both the novel and the tele-series looked at the themes of violence, loss, revenge, political formations, honor killings, and physical displacement. This chapter seeks to understand the cultural politics of adaptation in the context of the public response to the television series.

I will look at the series from three vantage points. The first is the series itself as a narrative on the Partition of 1947, its relationship to the novel, and the specific differences between the novel and the film. Second, I will move briefly through the debate on *Tamas* as reflected in the media. Finally, I will bring all the arguments together in the last section of the chapter to see how the televised version of *Tamas* became a "national event" located at the interstices of several fractured histories: the memory of the past, the contemporary juncture of communal violence, and the role of television in the formation of a new public that moved between the intimate private spaces of the home to the shared visual economy located outside the home. As James Naremore (2000: 10) has suggested, it is important to move beyond just the formal impulse that has dominated the discourse on adaptation to an approach that locates the role and function of adaptation within a broader terrain of social, economic, and cultural contexts. It is this approach that guides the tenor of the argument in this chapter. The formal dimension is certainly not ignored here, but is located within a set of historical and political concerns that shaped the production and reception of *Tamas*.

Literature, Cinema, and the Shadow of Partition

In 1929, the writer Rabindranath Tagore wrote: "the core of cinema is the continuous movement of the scenes. The beauty and glory of this mobile form should be expressed in such a way that it should remain self-sufficient without the help of any uttered sentence . . . cinema is still playing second fiddle to literature" (Singh: 1995). Despite this vision of the cinematic form as distinctly different from that of literature, the tussle between writers and filmmakers has dominated discussions on adaptations. Issues of original form, authenticity, and resemblance are usually controversial, particularly in a context where the form of Indian cinema is a musical one, while many of the novels display a realist structure. Mahasweta Devi's novel *Rudali* (*The Mourner*) was made into a film of the same name by Kalpana Lajmi (1992). The writer was deeply unhappy with the adaptation because she saw the musical form as alien to the novel's realist drive. More recently, the controversy over the adaptation of Tagore's *Char Adhyay* (*Four Chapters*, 1997) by the experimental film director Kumar Shahani has drawn attention to the hostile approach

Ranjani Mazumdar

Chapter 15

the literati can sometimes have to cinema, to innovation, and to creative interpretations of original texts. The debate over *Char Adhyay* also raised interesting issues around intellectual property and copyright concerns since the Visva Bharati University, which had exclusive rights over Tagore's work, decided to challenge Shahani's adaptation.[6] Gulzar, another well-known filmmaker and writer, has referred to the relationship between literature and cinema in India as an affair between good neighbors.

The adaptation of novels and short stories into films has been widely prevalent all over the world and India is no exception to the rule. Satyajit Ray's filmography has a substantial number of films based on novels by Rabindranath Tagore such as *Charulata* (*The Lonely Wife*, 1964), *Ghare Baire* (*Home and the World*, 1984), and *Teen Kanya* (*Three Women*, 1961). Ray's *Pather Panchali* (*Song of the Road*, 1955), *Aparajito* (*The Vanquished*, 1956), and *Apur Sansar* (*The World of Apu*, 1959) were based on Bibhutibhusahan Bannerjee's novels. The Bengali filmmaker Ritwick Ghatak has also used literary texts as the basis for some of his films, such as *Titas Ekti Nadi'r Naam* (*A River Named Titash*, 1973), which was based on a novel by Advaita Mall Burman. The relationship between literature and cinema in the state of Bengal has been deeply linked primarily to the emergence of the film industry within a vibrant cultural and intellectual milieu in the early part of the twentieth century.

The many adaptations of Sarat Chandra Chatterjee's *Devdas* all across the country also speak to this relationship. In the countless sea of *Devdas* adaptations (Pramathesh Chandra Barua, 1935; Bimal Roy, 1955), director Sanjay Leela Bhansali of the Bombay film industry came out with yet another one in 2002. Other major adaptations include *Ek Chadar Maili Si* (*The Dirty Sheet*: Sukhwant Dhadda, 1986) based on Rajendra Singh Bedi's novel, and *Chemeen* (*The Wrath of the Sea*: Ramu Kariat, 1965) based on a novel by the Malyalam writer, Thakazhy Shivashankar Pillai. There are also many examples of films based on Western literature. *Maya Memsaab* (Ketan Mehta, 1992) was based on Gustave Flaubert's *Madame Bovary*. Similarly, *Bees Saal Bad* (*Twenty Years Later*: Biren Naag, 1962) was an adaptation of Conan Doyle's *The Hound of the Baskervilles*. Literature and cinema have therefore had a prolonged and interesting relationship in India.

The literary world has also seen the production of powerful narratives on the Partition of India. Ravikant and Tarun Saint (2001) have elaborated in great detail on the range of literature that has explored and reflected on the texture of violence experienced during the Partition. Literary texts moved from images of dismemberment and mutilation to abduction and rape "as if in a sensorium" (Ravikant and Saint: 2001: xv). And yet there has been only one short story that made its way into a fully fledged film. *Garam Hawa* (*Hot Winds*, 1973), directed by M. S. Sathyu, was based on Ismat Chugtai's short story. It was the story of a Muslim family's gradual disintegration and displacement in the wake of the division of India. But *Garam Hawa* does not deal specifically with the violence of the Partition. The silence on this issue in film raises intriguing questions, the answer to which can only be tentatively traced in the dislocation between the event and the discourses on it.

The Partition of India was one of the most catastrophic events in the history of the country, with violence continuing for a period of 15 months from August 16, 1946. More than a million people were affected as Hindus, Sikhs, and Muslims killed each other in the most inhuman way. As a frenzy of killing spread over large parts of the country, violence, destruction, rape, and looting left two emergent nations scarred with the despair and trauma of tortured memories. Given the scale of the violence, the historiographical enterprise on the Partition has been enormous. Much of this political and nationalist historiography has focused on the political ramifications of the division and the causal chain of events that finally led up to the assassination of Mahatma Gandhi. There exists a plethora of writing dealing directly with the events, the political tussle for power between Jinnah and Jawahar Lal Nehru and other maneuverings that finally culminated in the division of India (Page, 1982; Jalal, 1985; Hasan, 1993; Chatterjee, 1995). However, the past two decades have witnessed a renewed but distinctly different approach to uncovering and understanding the trauma of what some have called the "invisible holocaust" (Butalia, 1998; Menon and Bhasin, 1998; Nandy, 2001; Pandey, 2001). It was primarily the assassination of Indira Gandhi, and the pogroms of Sikhs immediately after the killing, that brought back with a sudden jolt the memory of a tragic past. In the renewed look at this dark period of South Asian history, memory and the writing of history have been the main focus.

The overwhelming question of silence and the stoking of individual memories to rewrite a nationalist history that organized a violent moment only around a series of events have formed the primary agenda of much recent scholarship. While the journey of women in the Partition has been the concern of some, others have looked deeply at the conflictual site of memory and its constant slipping away from the historian's grasp (Pandey, 2001). Still others have tried to understand the silence that overwhelms this violent moment. How do we represent the past, particularly a violent and traumatic past? What is the language deployed to represent this? Can the social scientist grasp the enormity, complexity, and spectacular nature of the Partition? These questions have led many to look at a body of fictional literature dealing with the Partition to see how literary forms deal with the issue (Ravikant and Saint, 2001). The collection of short stories on the Partition (Bhalla, 1994) testifies to this, along with the detailed analysis of particular literary texts such as Sadat Hassan Manto's *Toba Tek Singh* (Das and Nandy, 1985). The literary form has been seen as more appropriate and powerful in its ability to grasp the intimate and macabre nature of Partition violence. Within the diverse range of available writings, Bhisham Sahani's *Tamas* (1976) remains an important book. However, what made Sahani's novel popular was its adaptation for television in 1988. The teleseries emerged as a major public site of controversy and memory, a journey into a sea of human hatred and brutality whose ugliness has never really disappeared.

Ashis Nandy (2001) has referred to the idea of the journey as a central aspect of the South Asian imaginary. The journey functions as a popular trope that enables us to understand both personal and collective experiences. It is a metaphor that has inspired philosophers, scholars, and mystics in South Asia for centuries. For Nandy (2001: 99), journeys that seek to alter the cartography of the self tend to acquire epic proportions. The Partition of India involved such a journey through violence, finally ending in Mahatma Gandhi's assassination. But few talk openly about the exact nature of this journey. The Partition remains embedded in South Asian consciousness as a journey that gave birth to the Indian nation-state. This particular deployment of the journey, suggests Nandy (2001: 10), in some ways justifies the violence and suffering as inevitably required for a larger cause. It was the television production and controversial reception of *Tamas* that fractured this journey, bringing to the fore, for the first time in public, the embedded narrative of dislocated and tortured memories. The Bombay High Court judgment referred to the series as "a memorabilia of a cursed past when man was taught to be wolf to man" (*The Indian Post*, January 24, 1988). In a sudden surreal dance of violent memories, television became the site for a deeper journey that played both with the past and with what Nandy (2001: 10) calls the "future of the self."

The Literary Form and the Televising of *Tamas*

Tamas is the story of Nathu (played by actor Om Puri) and his wife Karmo (played by actress Deepa Sahi) caught in the maelstrom of violence just before and after the Partition of India. The story begins with an extended killing sequence where Nathu (a low-caste tanner) is asked to kill a pig for someone. Nathu is promised the sum of five rupees for his work. Killing a pig is not part of his profession, but the lure of the money makes him agree. Nathu finds it very hard to kill the pig but finally the job is done and someone takes the pig away in the morning. This action seems almost irrelevant to the story until we discover a little later that the dead pig has been left outside a mosque, triggering off tension in the area between Hindus and Muslims. The rest of the novel deals with Nathu's guilt as he sees the town caught in the grip of bloody violence. While clearly having been used as a pawn by someone with political connections, Nathu's guilt remains overwhelming. When the violence starts spreading like wildfire, Nathu decides to leave town with his pregnant wife and elderly mother. During the journey across the border, the mother dies. Subsequently, the couple meet up with another, older Sikh couple, Harnam Singh (played by the writer Bhisham Sahni himself) and Banto (played by Dina Pathak). The four, together, come to represent the formation of a new family, even in the midst of violence and uprooting. The journey ends with Karmo discovering Nathu's body at a refugee camp in the midst of violent cries of hatred.

Tamas is written in a classic realist mode with both small and large events woven together to create the plot for the main characters, who become the subjects of its quasi-historical narrative. Throughout the novel, a series of episodes that resemble the causal impulse of the traditional documentary form are deployed. So, while the protagonists form the heart of the novel, a narrative of factual details saturates all the personal stories. The theme of ordinary people as pawns in the larger game of political intrigue immediately after independence remains the guiding thread of the narrative. This essentially humanist quality prevails throughout the novel, presented as a dialectic of hope and despair, tragedy and happiness, birth and death. The eternal cycle of rejuvenation surfaces throughout the novel, and is most explicitly brought out at the end of the series when birth follows death as symbols of the eternal dynamics of time and reality.

There are three levels on which the novel functions. First, there is the story of four principal characters who come to represent the trauma of the Partition. The second level of the novel tries to situate the four characters within a series of political, social, and cultural contexts. The third level is the undying humanism of the novel, which ultimately makes *Tamas* a novel about the birth of the Indian nation. Unlike the novel, which is woven around a simple episodic narrative structure, the tele-series presented the audience with a visible tension between its narrative and performative drives. It was this tension that enabled the series to emerge as a powerful document, shedding the somewhat rationalist discourse of the novel.

Historians like Gyanendra Pandey (1992: 32) have referred to *Tamas* as a narrative that:

> marks a return to a less subtle nationalist statement in which agent-provocateurs and mysterious evil folk pulling the strings from behind the scenes misled an innocent and bewildered but brave people. Partition is represented here, moreover, in the likeness of a natural disaster in which human actions play little part, far removed from the run of daily life.

This analysis is elaborated upon in Purnima Mankekar's analysis of the text. Mankekar echoes Pandey's reading and also feels that, ultimately, *Tamas* makes a rather crude separation between politicians and the elite on one side and the "common people" on the other. As the violence spreads, the "common people" are shown as victims who become pawns in the hands of the elite. They are robbed of their own subjectivity and thus remain outside the narrative of nationalist history. For Mankekar (1999: 304–5), *Tamas* is ultimately about the birth of the nation. Unlike the novel, the tele-series culminates in the birth of Nathu's child at a refugee camp.

While I do not disagree with this reading of *Tamas*, it seems to me that the tele-series differs somewhat from the overwhelming humanism that saturates the novel. It is easy to be ideological about a narrative when it is taken and analyzed in its totality. Yet we all know that the performative and diegetic space of any visual medium complicates verbal narrative structures. The visual narrative demands that we concentrate on detail, *mise-en-scène*, and performance to complicate general ideological assumptions. Both Pandey and Mankekar rush to critique *Tamas* without making any distinction between the novel and its televised version. Filmic representations of novels always tend to be different. While characters in the novel are like "verbal artifacts" created primarily through the use of words, the cinematic character "is an uncanny amalgam of photogenie, body movement, acting style, and grain of voice, all amplified and moulded by lighting, *mise-en-scène*, and music" (Stam, 2000: 60). While in the novel we only have characters, the cinematic medium has both character and performer, creating a series of tensions and contradictions that are essentially denied in a purely verbal medium (Stam, 2000: 60). Analysis of particular sequences convinces me that the differences between the two mediums made *Tamas* the tele-series into a more complex text on the violence of Partition. While the series remained committed to the novel for its overall emphasis and structure, the performative space and *mise-en-scène* evoked in its visual structure brought about a series of associations that complicated the novel's somewhat simplistic narrative.

The Partition of India involved unimaginable violence. The adaptation of *Tamas* to the screen brought out a visceral experience that was missing in the novel. The experience of pain and trauma acquired a tactile form in the series as violence became both performative and cathartic. One of the immediate differences between the novel and the tele-series lies in the elaborate soundtrack mounted for the latter. Vanraj Bhatia's evocative music track succeeds in producing a sense of experiential terror not so clearly delineated in the novel. The soundtrack's ability to evoke the uncanny as against the descriptive violence of the novel clearly points to the differences between the literary and filmic mode. It also succeeds in capturing the experience of communal violence as something that is constantly felt in the air.[7] A sophisticated combination of silence, loud intrusive shouts, and an expressive musical score heightens this experience in *Tamas*. The music sets the tone for the narrative, marking a major departure from the novel.

Director Govind Nihalani is also an accomplished cameraman well known for his skills in lighting. The dramatic high contrast tone of his frames both within the home and outside made the tele-series a specifically cinematic text. Nihalani's overwhelming focus on the texture of Nathu's face, his play with light and shadow, and his concentrated drive to understand "interiority" within the visual *mise-en-scène* of the series made the tele-series textually different. The heavy use of misty nights, violent slogans rending the air, combined with silence, showed the effort put in to produce a visceral experience of terror. It was this peculiar ability to foreground the cinematic aspects of terror, as against the terror described in the novel, that made the tele-series so important as a vehicle for the rekindling of suppressed memory. And, again, it was the psychological exposé of violence and fear presented through a skilled narrative of cinematic terror that enabled the series to transcend the rational, humanist discourse evident in the novel.

While attempting a realistic portrayal of the period, clearly *Tamas* relies heavily on studio sets and backdrops created specially for the film. A distinct quality of the series is the use of architectural lines and movements to evoke terror. Low-key lighting in all the night sequences helped to create light and dark spaces and sharpen the lines of steps, street corners, and doorways. The foreboding quality of the spreading violence is presented through a constant use of corridor space, stairways, and shadows combined with a soundtrack of bloodcurdling cries coming from outside the home. The notion of the uncanny is repeatedly projected through a very evocative soundtrack, spatial claustrophobia, and expressive performance. The sound of the bell at the center of the town square, for instance, is dramatically cut with the expression on a Muslim tailor's face.

Here the sound brings back a moment from the past for the tailor as he almost predicts a cyclical return to a violent time through his worried and concerned expression. Such expressivity in both the aural and visual ensemble highlights the differences between a literary mode and film. It also shows Nihalani's particular talent in the evocation of cinematic terror.

Nihalani's use of architectural space to express a psychological disposition takes us to the relationship between space and fear, something that is uniquely created in cinema. Anthony Vidler (1992: 11) suggests that "in each moment of the history of the representation of the uncanny, and at certain moments in its psychological analysis, the buildings and spaces that have acted as the sites for uncanny experiences have been invested with recognizable characteristics." This approach is deployed interestingly when, early on in the series, Nathu is shown walking down a narrow, empty street (a familiar street for Nathu). While there are houses on both sides of the street, a sense of desolation is brought out by the use of early-morning light and the camera tracking behind Nathu as he walks. The constant tracking and movement, combined with music, produces a sense of foreboding as Nathu suddenly tramples over an earthenware bowl full of religious totems. Nathu's expression here is similar to the Muslim tailor's later on in the film. Nathu sees in his trampling a bad omen for the future as a moment from the past flits by. In the novel, Nathu's walk down the street does not acquire the dramatic aura evident in the televised version. The constant use of objects, sounds, and space to create a sense of the uncanny takes the violence of the Partition to something beyond social analysis. While there exists a parallel narrative that is almost sociological in its approach, it is the expressive sections of the series that stay with the audience. The playing out of this tension makes the series more open in its narrative address.

One of the most powerful moments in the tele-series is the mass suicide of Sikh women when an attack seems imminent on the Gurdwara (Sikh temple) where they have taken shelter. The men go out in search of missing friends. The women are waiting inside. Once the violence becomes imminent, the women's sexual honor becomes central for the protection of the community. As an extremely tired and confused Karmo (who, along with Nathu, has taken shelter in the Gurdwara) watches, Jasbir (played by actress Uttara Bawkar), the daughter of Harnam Singh and Banto, leads all the women and children to a nearby well. Through a misty haze of clouds and darkness, Nihalani makes this walk to the well look like an epic sequence imbuing it with dramatic significance. Each woman shouts the Sikh war cry *Jo Bole So Nihal, Sat Sri Akal* just before she jumps into the well. The power of the internal violence of this sequence resides in the visual darkness of the night. The long shots of the women walking against the night sky look like a painting. The painting-like quality of the sequence imbues the image with a sense of embeddedness in a specific cultural context. Suddenly the image recalls other forms of honor killings. This violence has an old history that goes back to the tradition of *Johar*.[8]

In her reading of this suicide sequence, Mankekar expresses a discomfort with the connection made with *Johar* as a medieval form of protection against invading "Turks." For Mankekar, the sequence evokes a fear of the Muslim and has communal overtones.

In a personal interview with Sahani, Mankekar asks the writer why the sequence was conceived in this manner. In his reply Sahani links the mental state of the women during the suicide mission to "a trance of religious ecstasy" where they "link themselves with the past but it's not a rational linking" (Mankekar, 1999: 312). Elaborating on Jasbir's role in leading the women to the well, Sahani says that her actions were "not the result of a conscious choice but of early influences of childhood, religious influences. So you don't rationalize. She's been told Muslims are your enemies, so she follows her training" (1999: 312).

While this is a dramatic moment in the novel, the tele-series takes it to a fever pitch that is both powerful and evocative. By saturating the image with a mythical and epic quality, Nihalani manages to take the violence into the realm of the philosophical and historical. There is a certain timelessness introduced in the nature of internal violence here. While clearly Sahani himself wants to evoke the "irrational" quality of the violence, Nihalani's visual imagery draws on the iconography of late nineteenth- and early twentieth-century calendar art[9] to give the sequence a mythical and expressionistic aura. The muted color of the women's clothing, the landscape, and the texture of light are compositionally organized against the cloudy sky evoking an almost epic-like grandeur. The inevitability of death is evident in both the elaborate staging of the sequence and the melancholic tone of the music. Sahani's projection of the "irrational" acquires a premodern grandeur in the tele-series, displacing the novel as a rational text to suggest the very complicated nature of violence experienced during the Partition. The subtext of Johar, which is evident in the image, connects with an historical cultural/communal memory, thus endowing the image with allegorical significance.

Nathu and Karmo's travel across the border is also like an epic journey during which they encounter many hurdles. This is also a journey where the two meet the older Sikh couple, Banto and Harnam Singh. The movement across the border is presented as a journey across wilderness. The couple travel through forests, they cross river streams and then spend the night beneath the open sky. The absence of any built structure or transportation system gives the journey and the fear associated with it an almost "primitive," premodern quality. This is not a violence just of modern times, but a violence that has a long history.[10]

The conscious use of "untamed" space and natural locations is dramatically different from the studio-like sets used in the rest of the series. The claustrophobic use of space in the town is contrasted here with the violence embedded in open space. This dual use of space establishes both the modern nature of this violence as well as its so-called "irrational" history located within an almost unknowable context. The rush for political analysis that is evident in the city and town sections is absent when the journey across the border starts. This is the moment of contradiction and displacement where Tamas the series engages with the violence of the Partition as a force that escapes easy analysis. As Nandy (2001: 99) says, "all landscapes are, by definition, landscapes of the mind." While the novel describes the journey as arduous, painful, and difficult, in the televised version the natural landscape is given an almost classical contour evident in the heavy use of mist and fog. The expressionism of this landscape imbues the journey with a mythical quality evoking a series of journeys embedded in the myths and legends of the sub-continent. The journey here is clearly a premodern journey. The presence of a gun and a vegetable vendor's cart are the only relatively modern objects used in the sequence.

Tamas was written on the basis of a fragmented account of certain sites that Bhisham Sahani remembered from his childhood in Lahore before the Partition of India. Describing his perceptions as the reflections of a writer, Sahani's thoughts express a complex approach:

> Whenever I reminisce about those far off days, many a face flits across my mind. I see myself, walking along a long, metalled road in Jalandhar Cantonment after the riots, and by my side is Bahadur Singh, a Sikh neighbor of my Rawalpindi days. He walked along with me, but he was in a kind of daze. He told me that he had killed 86 Muslims during the days of the riots. He bragged about it, but it appeared to me that he was already sick at heart, and had not been able to get over the sense of acute depression and frustration that his cold blooded butchery had engendered . . . He walks in the streets of Delhi now, living a bedraggled existence, knocking at the doors of old Rawalpindi friends and acquaintances and asking for monetary help. (Sahani, 1994: 2)

Clearly there is a sensitivity to despair in Sahani's reflections here. His interest in the psychic make-up of a person who has participated in the violence reveals the author's desire to understand the violence rather than judge people on the basis of their actions. The interest in the actions of a perpetrator suggests that Bahadur Singh was not a "victim" created by the larger force of history but someone who intricately rests within the conflictual unfolding of history. And yet these thoughts do not make their way into the novel with the same force.

There is a section in *Tamas* where both readers and spectators are exposed to the relationship between masculinity, violence, and religious identity. This is clearly revealed in the sequence on the initiation of young men into the Hindu fundamentalist RSS (Rashtriya Swayam Sevak Sangh).[11] The men have to display their bravery and courage before they can enter the organization. The initiation rites involve the killing of a hen with bare hands. One young man, Ranbir, finds it difficult to do this the first time, but later succeeds in his mission to join the organization. The young men of the organization are ordinary people with their own anxieties and insecurities. In an interesting section of the series, the men prepare to go out and kill someone from the other community. They are not completely sure how to go about it. Their clumsiness, hesitancy, and anxiety are on display. And then Ranbir provides the dramatic force of the RSS's ideological conviction. By linking masculinity to violence and to the politics of the RSS, Sahani expresses a desire to understand this process of human transformation. But the overwhelming focus on the RSS as evocative of a masculine violence makes Sahani narrowly locate this relationship only within the political ideology of the RSS. And yet there are innumerable examples of men involved in the violence on both sides of the religious spectrum who had little involvement with any religious or political organization.

There is some effort to understand the relationship between masculinity and violence in the uncanny transformation of Shah Nawaz, a Muslim man close to a Hindu family living in a predominantly Muslim neighborhood. When the violence escalates, Shah Nawaz comes to escort the Hindu family to his own house in a different neighborhood. The family forgets to get a jewelry box from their house. Shah Nawaz offers to fetch the box. In the novel, the jewelry box belongs to a childhood friend of Shah Nawaz; in the tele-series, two different moments and characters are encapsulated in a charged sequence. We see Shah Nawaz ring the bell at his friend's house. A crippled boy (the servant of the house) limps across to the door. The servant's clumsy limp is shot against dark corridors and staircases. The door opens to reveal the servant boy, a foolish smile on his face. The servant's stupidity is contrasted here with Shah Nawaz's poised and restrained demeanor. Shah Nawaz goes to a room and finds the jewelry box. From the window of the room, he sees the body of a dead man in front of a Mosque as a crowd gathers to pray for him. Something changes from this point onwards. Shah Nawaz follows the servant out of the room and suddenly pushes him down the flight of stairs. Shah Nawaz's volte-face is a moment of surprise in *Tamas*. His masculine aura is contrasted with the servant boy's foolishness and crippled body.

It is difficult to establish the combination of forces that may have led Shah Nawaz to push the servant. The image of the dead man seen from the window seems as important as irritability with the servant's clumsy manner. In a flash, various tendencies come to the fore, leading to the violent action against the boy. This moment in *Tamas* stays with the audience because here the psychology of violence goes beyond a simple causal question of identity. In the novel, the build-up to Shah Nawaz's action is causally mapped out through a series of street and personal encounters. The violence in the town is visible for him to see. The tele-series, on the other hand, compresses this moment in a single encounter. The use of darkened stairs and the slow build-up creates an uncanny aura, again contributing to the feeling that the Partition violence was at times too complex to comprehend.

The Media Controversy

The broadcasting of *Tamas* on national television spurred on a major media debate. *The Hindu*, a national daily reporting on the controversy around the series, titled its article "The Veil of Darkness Lifts" (February 21, 1988). A flurry of letters to the editor of *The Times of India* expressed a range of responses. One writer said: "Our people should be exposed to the reality of history very carefully. *Tamas* should be shown exclusively in libraries and international conferences. Its screening on Doordarshan[12] should be stopped immediately in the larger interests of the nation." Another person said "To witness the horrible riots of 1947 before going to bed is no way of learning history or of learning lessons in how to correct one's attitudes towards others" (January 30, 1988).

Chandan Mitra, a well-known journalist with *The Times of India*, said "It may however be argued that this is the view of the author, Bhisham Sahani, and that *Tamas* does not claim to be an accurate portrayal of history. But that precisely is the problem with the serial. It is neither history nor fiction" (Mitra, 1988). Reacting to Mitra's diatribe against *Tamas*, Badri Raina wrote:

> Bhisham Sahani's novel was published as far back as 1974. Nothing happened then. The fact cannot but prompt the question as to why the turbulence now. Sadly, Mr Mitra misses the configurations of the present historical moment within which Mr Nihalani astutely reopens matters that we, perhaps, believe constitute a finished past. Dearly as one might wish that were so, the painful fact is that *Tamas*, like most other historical reconstructions, is not just about then but about our contemporary polity. More than Mr Mitra, it is organized communal opinion which has been quick to recognize this and has accordingly lost no time. (Raina, 1988)

In a somewhat similar vein, Sudhish Pachauri (1988) offers a parallel narrative to Raina's. Pachauri suggests that the debate about whether *Tamas* is history or fiction lies in the articulation of the narrative through a new form of communication.

> *Tamas* may or may not be a very high class serial but the way it communicates ideas is fundamentally different. For nearly one hour every week, it recreates the reality of riots with expressionistic methods. It does not intend to provide the answers to the foolish questions posed by the RSS as to who started the riots, Hindus or Muslims? It just analyses the effects of the riots – the barbarity and dehumanizing process, the guilt of the common man, the helplessness of the political groups, etc. It is very tense viewing. There has been no other serial so far which demands so much attention. (Pachauri, 1988)

Clearly, the telecast of *Tamas* triggered off a series of complex associations that needed to be analyzed. Cultural memory, as many have suggested, is produced through mechanisms that are not easy to understand. The catastrophic event is never over. It always resurfaces in different contexts through objects, images, and representations. The past, as Andreas Huyssen (1995) tells us, is not contained within memory but articulates itself in order to become memory. The tension or dislocation produced between the actual experience of the catastrophic event and its memory within representation is a "powerful stimulant" that can provide enormous energy for cultural and artistic practice (Huyssen, 1995: 2–3).

In a sense, television became the technology for the production of memory, creating in its wake a tension between the representation of memory and the experience of the event. For the millions who watched the series, the experience of the Partition became a shared "national" memory. The context of both the production and reception of the series blurred the boundaries between the image of history and the history of the image. Marita Sturken (1997: 44) suggests that in "acts of public commemoration, the shifting discourses of history, personal memory, and cultural memory converge." The televising of *Tamas* was therefore like a public acknowledgment and commemoration of a catastrophic event that had ripped Northern India apart. Images of the series allowed spectators the chance to experience a collective witnessing of a past event. As a prime-time show on national television, with no alternative channel, the context of watching *Tamas* was an overwhelming experience, something that may not be possible today, given the fragmented perceptual economy that has emerged after the cable boom of the 1990s.

Much of the media controversy around the reception of *Tamas* was located within the debate about whether *Tamas* was history or fiction. To understand the moment of this controversy and the reasons for it, we need to look beyond the simple narrative elements of the television adaptation. *Tamas* was broadcast at a particular moment in India's history. The 1980s saw the aggressive face of Hindu nationalism in India as a major political force. Thus the role of television in engendering a collective witnessing of the past, where the lines between history, memory, event, and the contemporary moment blurred, needs to be investigated through a complex interrogation of the role of television in creating what Vivian Sobchack (1996) calls the "persistence of history." It is this particular experience of the televisual apparatus that made the serialized reception of *Tamas* so different from the original novel.

The Persistence of History through Television

History and memory are always embroiled in a unique relationship. Television, as we have now seen, is one of the most powerful sites for the articulation of memory within the public sphere. In a similar situation, the telecast of the American television show *Holocaust* (produced by NBC) in Germany provoked a nationwide debate on the issue. The hype around the show, both prior to and after the telecast, ensured that the series turned into a public event through television, enabling the production of history as collective memory. There are, of course, differences between the two situations. First, a US show was being broadcast in Germany where the Jewish population is virtually absent. Second, it was shown on one of the many German channels. *Tamas*, on the other hand, was telecast on India's only existing, state-controlled channel at the time. The similarity of the debate, however, lies in the fact that people sympathetic to the telecast of *Holocaust* felt that it had a pedagogical and political role. Despite its lack of aesthetic appeal, the show was seen as a vehicle through which audiences experienced the Holocaust at an emotional level, breaking the silence around the past (Markovitz and Hayden, 1980: 53–80).

The entire debate in the media in India centered on the authenticity of the series. While the defenders of *Tamas* lauded the realistic and "correct" portrayal of an historical time, the critics of the series said it was pretentious, not needed, unrealistic, and biased. Both sides were ultimately debating the factual accuracy of the violence around the Partition. Clearly, both his own experiences and those of others who lived through the period heavily influenced Sahani's novel. In that sense Sahani at no point denies the source of his imagination as something he himself lived through. The presence of the "event" as a shared and remembered experience, embedded within the personal and public stories that have circulated since the Partition, is rekindled by the telecast of *Tamas*. The narrative differences and issues involved in the adaptation of the book therefore ceases to be important in a situation where television was, in many ways, turning an historical event into another public event which was charged with the schisms and tensions simmering beneath the contemporary polity. The tele-series became a performative space at once disturbing and cathartic. Suddenly, after years of silence, a nation was collectively engaging with the horrors of a past that was equally relevant within the contemporary moment. A performative visual saga that was at once provocative and tragic broke four decades of silence.

The story of the Partition of India has by and large been treated as an aberration in the nationalist march against colonialism. Official nationalist history has rarely placed much emphasis on the study of this violent past, burying it instead in official silence. It was only after the violence of 1984, the anti-Sikh pogroms following the assassination of the then prime minister Indira Gandhi, that the reality of communal violence pushed many historians to look at the violence of the Partition, not as an "event" that was over, but as one that continues to live through both public and personal memories.

The fear of remembering the past made it difficult for writers, filmmakers, and other artists to do any creative exploration of the issue for it was seen as "sensitive" and therefore inappropriate within a climate of rising fundamentalism and communal violence in the country. The televising of *Tamas* therefore became an event that shattered the silence around the past, forcing a huge population to confront its own memories. An estimated 35 million viewers eagerly watched the series. It became a "poignant moment of collective encounter – brought about for the first time in the nation's history by an immensely powerful and unique audio-visual medium, leaving a countrywide audience stunned" (Ravikant, 2001: 162).

Memory resides in objects, memorials, texts, talismans, and images. And yet it is the photographic image that is the most emblematic receptacle of memory, constantly responding to the gaze of the viewers (Sturken, 1997: 19). *Tamas* was like a mimetic interpretation of the Partition in which historical fact and memory converged to create a unique site of tension. The retelling of the Partition violence through the adaptation of a modest novel may have enabled the filmmaker to present the series as a form of creative expression, but the audiences received it across the country as "documentary evidence" of what had transpired more than four decades ago. The televised version's ability to rekindle the memory of the horrors of the past lay in its reception as the "reality" of the violence of Partition. The debate in the media therefore focused almost overwhelmingly on whether the series was fair, historical, factually correct, or biased. It was the discomfort created through visuals that were too close to home that led to the court injunction and the rising protest against the series. The tele-series ceased to be just an adaptation of the novel. Instead, it was hotly debated as a story of the Partition itself. The allegorical significance of the series lay in the past standing in for the present. The controversy resulted from this immediate connection between what was seen as a violent historical past and the contemporary context of rising Hindu fundamentalism.

Discussing the complexities involved in the writing of history as fiction, Hayden White suggests that the twentieth century is marred by holocaustic events that are difficult to comprehend through the language of the traditional historian. In traditional history, "human agents are conceived to be in some way fully conscious and morally responsible for their actions and capable of discriminating clearly between the causes of historical events and the effects over the long as well as the short run in relatively commonsensical ways . . ." (White, 1996: 21–2). In a different mode, Veena Das and Ashis Nandy pro-blematize the language of silence that usually exists around issues of violence. Violence, say the authors, tends to be viewed with a certain degree of ambivalence in all cultures. Because this ambivalence is rooted in philosophical doubt, "it invites not only elaborate structures of representation but may also be surrounded by silence and the break-down of signification" (Das and Nandy, 1985: 177). The writers look at Sadat Hassan Manto's short story *Toba Tek Singh* where Toba Tek Singh is a "mad man" who is unable to make sense of the madness that has gripped the collective community of people involved in the riots. The very people who had kept Toba Tek Singh at a distance from their "normal" world were now involved in the violence of the riots. Das and Nandy ask the question "Could Manto be suggesting that the voice of the madman is the only sane voice that could be heard in the midst of these events?" (1985: 190). Clearly, the authors pose a question that pushes us to think through the difficulties of representing violence. The story of *Toba Tek Singh* deploys the language of madness, which allows Manto a certain ability to communicate terror, horror, and fear. During a moment of historical crisis, the "sane" and the "insane" exchange places. The formally insane are now endowed with the power of perception that seems to have escaped rational "normal" communities.

In some ways there is a similarity between Das and Nandy's question and White's perception. All three writers see the difficulty in negotiating the "experiential history" of violence through the "rational" discourses of the social sciences and traditional history. However, while Das and Nandy do turn to literary storytelling forms as an archive of experience and memory, White displays a radical skepticism about storytelling forms. Instead, fragmented, avant-garde techniques of modernist representational forms are seen to provide the answer to this crisis of representation (White, 1996). Clearly, this takes us to the issue of how the adaptation of a violent event can take place within the sphere of cultural representation. All three writers are looking for "evidence" in the textual dynamics of representational strategies to see which could be the most suitable for nego-tiating painful and violent memories.

While this will remain a debate for years to come, clearly it is not just the "pure" resonance of the represented text that triggers a rekindling of suppressed memory. The *Tamas* controversy amply demonstrates the complex network of practices and histories that governs the field of visual perception. The audience became involved in the production of "history in the making," challenging the secluded domain of the historian. History, as Sobchack (1996) says, happens now, in the public sphere, creating in its wake a new historical sense. The televising of *Tamas* presented its spectators with "history" as "fiction" and worked primarily through the engaged responses of the audience. More than just the textual dynamics of the series, it was the audience reception and subsequent debate within the public sphere that enabled the rekindling of a dark memory of the past. With the public debate, *Tamas* functioned as the explosive vehicle through which an older journey, culminating in the birth of the Indian nation, was interrogated for the first time in such an unprecedented manner. The television adaptation of a relatively ordinary novel at a crucial point in India's history also brought to the fore the complexities that govern the cultural politics of adaptation in our times.

Acknowledgments

I would like to thank Sabina Kidwai, Ira Bhaskar, Ravikant Sharma, and Ravi Sundaram for their support, comments, and suggestions.

Notes

1   To be sure there were earlier public media events linked to television broadcasts such as the mythological Ramayana. But none opened up immediate questions of national identity and politics as did *Tamas*. For a detailed account of the relationship between the telecast of the *Ramayana* and the politics of contemporary Hindu fundamentalism, see Rajagopal (2001).

2   The 1980s saw the disruption of older forms of "nationalist identity" (the "secular citizen") and the rise of a right-wing Hindu fundamentalist movement seeking to radically reconstitute the nationalist community. While the older nationalist imaginary was also attacked by new social movements, it has been the Hindu nationalist force that has posed the most serious challenge to the political order. Hindu nationalism has sought to recast the framework of the old "nationalist community" through a series of conflations: those of modernity, of citizenship, and a reinvented Hindu imaginary within an emerging global cultural/political economy.

3   The New Wave was a movement that emerged in the early 1970s as a counter to the institutionalized commercial film industry in India. A coming together of various independent filmmakers, the New Wave was a diverse stream trying to find a cinematic language that would be radically different from mainstream cinema. The movement comprised both realist and avant-garde filmmakers.

4   For a detailed account of the circumstances that led to the court injunction, see Loomba and Kaul (1994), Ravikant (2001), and Simeon (2002).

5   The cable television boom of the 1990s destroyed the monopoly of the state television network with the entry of private players into the market. Suddenly, Indian television changed from a two-channel state run network into a situation where scores of private channels competed for viewers.

6   Sahani's film was initially barred from screening by a civil court in Kolkata. This led to a national debate on issues of intellectual property. See *Asian Age* (February 26, 2002) and Patil (2001).

7   There are innumerable stories of people taking refuge in Gurdwaras (Sikh temples) and mosques. At regular intervals both Muslims and Sikhs would chant their religious slogan – *Allah o Akhbar* and *Jo Bole So Nihal, Sat Sri Akal*, respectively. These cries filled the air as a warning to both sides.

8   A medieval Rajput practice where upper-class women committed suicide by collectively jumping into fire to avoid capture by the enemy. In Hindu nationalist mythology, stories of *Johar* are narrated in the context of Turkish (Muslim) attacks on Hindu Rajput kingdoms. The woman's body becomes the repository of the community's honor and as such cannot be defiled by the other.

9   A form of popular art described as a combination of fine art and bazaar sensibilities. The subjects of calendar art have primarily been popular gods and other mythical figures. It is called calendar art because these paintings are mass-produced as calendars that circulate widely in the country (see Jain, 1997).

10 Interestingly, *Tamas* does not include many shots of the *Kafila* – a procession of thousands of people walking with their belongings, bullock carts, and camels across the border. Many have noted the violence that escalated when the *Kafilas* of Hindus and Sikhs encountered *Kafilas* of Muslims moving in the opposite direction. The *Kafila* is a vivid image evoked in many Partition narratives. Yet in *Tamas*, Nathu, Karmo, Harnam, and Banto travel on their own through isolation.

11 The Rashtriya Swayam Sevak Sangh (RSS) was founded in 1925 as a Hindu nationalist move-ment. Partly sympathetic to German fascism, the RSS developed as a cadre based organization that led attacks on Muslims during and before the Partition. The RSS was hostile to secular nationalist groups like the Congress, though some Congress leaders were partially sympathetic to the Hindu nationalist agenda. The RSS was briefly banned after 1948 when someone asso-ciated with the organization assassinated Mahatma Gandhi.

12 India's national television network controlled by the central government. In 1987–8, this was the only existing channel in India.

References

Bhalla, Alok (ed.) (1994) *Stories about the Partition of India*, vols 1–4. New Delhi: Indus.

Butalia, Urvashi (1998) *The Other Side of Silence: Voices from the Partition of India*. Harmondsworth: Penguin.

Chatterjee, Joya (1995) *Bengal Divided: Hindu Communalism and Partition 1932–1947*. Cambridge: Cambridge University Press.

Das, Veena and Nandy, Ashis (1985) "Violence, Victimhood and the Language of Silence," *Contributions to Indian Sociology* 19 (1): 177–95

Hasan, Mushirul (ed.) (1993) *India's Partition: Process, Strategy and Mobilization*. Delhi: Oxford University Press.

Huyssen, Andreas (1995) *Twilight Memories: Marking Time in a Culture of Amnesia*. New York: Routledge.

Jain, Kajri (1997) "Producing the Sacred: The Subjects of Calendar Art," *Journal of Arts and Ideas* 30–1 (December).

Jalal, Ayesha (1985) *The Sole Spokesman: Jinnah, the Muslim League, and the Demand for Pakistan*. Cambridge: Cambridge University Press.

Loomba, Ania and Kaul, Suvir (1994) "Location, Culture, Post-coloniality," in Ania Loomba and Suvir Kaul (eds), *Oxford Literary Review*, special issue *On India: Writing History Culture, Post-coloniality* 16, no. 1–2.

Mankekar, Purnima (1999) *Screening Culture, Viewing Politics: An Ethnography of Television, Womanhood, and Nation in Postcolonial India*. Durham, NC: Duke University Press.

Markovitz, Andrei and Hayden, Rebecca (1980) "'Holocaust' Before and After the Event," *New German Critique* 19 (Winter).

Menon, Ritu and Bhasin, Kamla (1998) *Borders and Boundaries: Women in India's Partition*. New Delhi: Kali for Women.

Mitra, Chandan (1988) "Why *Tamas*," *The Times of India, Sunday Review*, February 7.

Nandy, Ashis (2001) *The Ambiguous Journey to the City: The Village and Other Odd Ruins of the Self in the Indian Imagination*. New Delhi: Oxford University Press.

Naremore, James (ed.) (2000) *Film Adaptation*. New Brunswick, NJ: Rutgers University Press.

Pachauri, Sudhish (1988) "Disturbing the Culture of Serials," *The Times of India*, February 14.

Page, David (1982) *Prelude to Partition: The Indian Muslims and the Imperial System of Control 1920–1932*. New Delhi: Oxford University Press.

Pandey, Gyanendra (1992) "In Defence of the Fragment: Writing about Hindu – Muslim Riots in India Today." *Representations* 37: 27–55.

—— (2001) *Remembering Partition: Violence, Nationalism and History in India*. Cambridge: Cambridge University Press.

Patil, Vrinda (2001) "Whose Music Is It?," *The Tribune*, January 28.

Raina, Badri (1988) "*Tamas* has touched us in the Raw," *The Times of India*, February 14.

Rajagopal, Arvind (2001) *Politics after Television: Religious Nationalism and the Reshaping of the Indian Public*. Cambridge: Cambridge University Press.

Ravikant (2001) "Partition: Strategies of Oblivion, Ways of Remembering," in Ravikant and Tarun K. Saint (eds), *Translating Partition*. New Delhi: Katha Books.

—— and Saint, Tarun K. (eds) (2001) *Translating Partition*. New Delhi: Katha Books.

Sahani, Bhisham (1994) "Images of Communities: Reflections of a Writer," *Studies in Humanities and Social Sciences* 1 (November).

Simeon, Dilip (2002) "Venue for a Speech on *Tamas*," in Tarun K. Saint (ed.), *Bruised Memories*. Calcutta: Seagull Books.

Singh, Brij (1995) "Still Playing Second Fiddle," *Financial Express*, March 26.

Sobchack, Vivian (ed.) (1996) *The Persistence of History: Cinema, Television and the Modern Event*. New York: Routledge.

Stam, Robert (2000) "Beyond Fidelity: The Dialogics of Adaptation," in James Naremore (ed.), *Film Adaptation*, pp. 54–76. New Brunswick, NJ: Rutgers University Press.

Sturken, Marita (1997) *Tangled Memories: The Vietnam War, the Aids Epidemic, and the Politics of Remembering*. Berkeley, CA: University of California Press.

Terdiman, Richard (1993) *Present Past: Modernity and the Memory Crisis*. Ithaca, NY: Cornell University Press.

Vidler, Anthony (1992) *The Architectural Uncanny: Essays in the Modern Unhomely*. Cambridge, MA: MIT Press.

White, Hayden (1996) "The Modernist Event," in Vivian Sobchack (ed.), *The Persistence of History: Cinema, Television and the Modern Event*. New York: Routledge.

Chapter 16

The Written Scene: Writers as Figures of Cinematic Redemption

Paul Arthur

> You will see that this little clicking contraption with the revolving handle will make a revolution in our life — in the life of writers.
>
> *Leo Tolstoy*
>
> I had a hunch that the talkies would make even the best selling novelist as archaic as silent pictures.
>
> *F. Scott Fitzgerald*

On the surface, it is hard to imagine an activity less given to cinematic representation than a writer's struggle to transform observations or ideas into a finished manuscript. Writing is mostly solitary, static labor performed in dull locations over excruciating stretches of time; its dramas, such as they are, tend to be internal matters of confusion, frustration, and the pressures of the unconscious. Despite a venerable mythology of writers as dissolute misfits operating at the margins of bourgeois society, Hollywood has understandably focused its attention on vocations offering greater opportunities for visual dynamism — exceptions to this preference include musty biopics such as *The Life of Emile Zola* (1937) or film-industry cautionary tales on the order of *Sunset Boulevard* (1950). Lacking clear generic formulas for the development of writer-protagonists, and bearing in mind the *a priori* commercial resistance to such figures, a virtual stampede of recent Anglo-American films boasting a spectrum of intrepid scribblers is, as it were, startlingly out of character. In a period dominated by blood-soaked blockbusters and hi-tech computer effects, writers have been vying for center stage with cops, space cowboys, and the usual roster of (male) screen heroes. Since 1997, writers, or more cogently, the travails of creative authorship, have been a primary focus in nearly twenty mainstream releases: *Love and Death on Long Island*, *Wilde*, *Shakespeare in Love*, *Henry Fool*, *Deconstructing Harry*, *Lolita*, *Topsy-Turvy*, *The*

Muse, Fear of Fiction, Cradle Will Rock, Wonder Boys, Quills, Finding Forrester, Almost Famous, The End of the Affair, Joe Gould's Secret, Croupier, Before Night Falls, and *Girl, Interrupted*.[1]

Although generic idioms within this group range from romantic comedy to crime thriller to costume drama, there are certain similarities in production and marketing as well as shared patterns of characterization and theme. Roughly half were so-called independent productions made on relatively small budgets and marketed for niche audiences, and even the higher-profile studio films were presumably aimed at older, upscale viewers. A half-dozen won major press or industry awards – including *Shakespeare*'s Oscar blitz – and nearly all received substantial critical accolades. Not surprisingly, the majority were adapted from popular novels, plays, or memoirs; in addition, *Shakespeare* and *Topsy-Turvy*, despite original screenplays, incorporate extended scenes from existing theatrical works.[2] Hence, as a group, they can be said to borrow cultural capital accorded not only to writers in general but to specific authors and their signature creations. In doing so, their disparate box-office appeals were often couched in affirmation of a perennially endangered "literate" cinema. Regardless of the financial success or failure of a given film, this strategy marks a form of product differentiation intended, like the mounting of literary "classics," to signify values of complex characterization and sophisticated, if not necessarily highbrow, dialogue – an ideal rhetorically distinct from the pleasures of spectacle-driven entertainment. Part of the cachet surrounding stories centered on writers, whether real or fictional, is that they illuminate personal struggles between an "inner" world of the creative psyche and particular "external" circumstances that feed, inhibit, or otherwise inform the writing process. Such stories therefore propose in some sense to mediate and explain an otherwise recondite, mystified act of creation.

Undoubtedly our most fashionable, prestigious, and culturally resonant literary role is that of novelist, the vocation of choice in nine different films. The same dramatic problems of blocked inspiration, outside interference, or misunderstanding that distress novelists are similarly present in films depicting playwrights, poets, journalists, a screen-writer, and a librettist. Nonetheless, writing would appear to be a tumultuous calling pursued predominantly by unmarried, mature men for whom romantic passion is a drive shared, or reciprocated, between written text and extra-textual entanglements (only *Girl, Interrupted* is focused on a female writer). Every film is punctuated by obligatory scenes in which a wordsmith cogitates or paces, hesitates, then commits thoughts to paper. A seemingly trivial gesture, the motif of blank surfaces beginning to bristle with words and sentences in fact undergirds a larger, meta-thematic discourse concerned with relations between word and image, page and screen.

In ten films, images of writing are augmented with snatches of voice-over narration filtered through loosely applied frameworks of restricted, at times overtly subjective, first-person authority. The presence of intra-diegetic narrators calls attention to a storytelling process ostensibly framed as a literary work-in-progress; typically, what is conveyed in voice-over speech is stipulated or implied as isomorphic with the written page, although the temporal sequence of speaking and writing is often ambiguous, neither simultaneous nor consecutive (in *Wonder Boys*, a novelist's internal musings are revealed only at the very end as fragments of a completed manuscript).

Thirteen films feature ancillary authorial figures, one or more characters who function in relation to the protagonist as rivals (*Lolita*), mentors (*Finding Forrester*), protégés (*Wonder Boys*), advisors (*The Muse*), love interests (*The End of the Affair*), even doppelgängers (*Joe Gould's Secret*). Although their roles vary in size and dramatic importance, the resulting "palimpsest" of writerly activity not only underscores the theme of creative work and interpersonal bonds of authorship – providing opportunities for characters to discuss creative anguish, economic stress, or the calculus of Art and Life (topics such as craft or literary influence rarely surface on the screen) – but can threaten to expose the protagonist's arbitrary position in the narrative as focalized subject or primary agent of enunciation. In other words, the addition of secondary authors or, as in *Topsy-Turvy* and *Cradle Will Rock*, artistic collaborators opens a cluster of films to issues of artistic reliability, autonomy, and originality. To be sure, a common project in these films is to dramatize and celebrate the transformation of imaginative impulses into commercially viable art, a bohemian success story. Yet, in doing so, questions concerning the limits of written texts, and the interchange between a writer's vision and alternative or competing sources of cultural production, tend to be embedded as subtexts.

An important motif that foregrounds, at times destabilizes, the Romantic baggage of isolated, individualist creativity is the dialectical play of high and low culture. Typically, the public's adulation of pulp novels, movies, TV, or pop music is deemed suspect or even malign, antithetical to the codes and aspirations of canonical literature, a "critique" planted then usually recuperated later, as mass culture is shown to be essentially coterminus with high-cultural agendas. Gestures of medium-specific self-validation are familiar features in Hollywood movies, from *Singin' in the Rain* (1952) to *The Player* (1992). Here the crux of cultural juxtaposition is the relationship between cinema and, especially, novelistic prose. Legible as allegories on the status of movies in contemporary literature, and the position of literature in contemporary cinema, a subset of writers' films argue for a harmonious fusion of the two practices. Rather than claim cultural efficacy or aesthetic superiority of one over the other, they simultaneously validate literature via the mass appeal of commercial movie-making and grant to cinema the potential for constructing "complex" novelistic experiences out of moving images.

The allegorical dynamic is particularly salient in films adapted from contemporary American and British fiction. In the past decade or so, the storied animosity of novelists toward commercial adaptations of their work, often buttressed by charges of cinema's usurpation of the novel's cultural prestige, has softened considerably.[3] Writers such as Russell Banks, Michael Ondaatje, Nick Hornby, and John Irving have touted both their active participation in screenwriting projects and their hearty endorsement of the end results. Admittedly, a few literary purists have continued to weigh in on the depredations of movie language and its narrative "shorthand." E. L. Doctorow, a prime combatant, claims that the prospect of movies "unseat[ing] linguistic composition as our major communicative act is . . . only slightly less dire than global warming."[4] The brunt of his and fellow defenders' complaints is that many younger novelists have abandoned nineteenth-century realist traditions of dense description, intricate characterization, and multiple plot strands in favor of approaches that mirror techniques of screenwriting, thus making their books more accommodating to film producers and directors.[5]

Addressed from another angle, the current synergy between novel writing and movie writing reveals distinct advantages for both sides. When novelists disport themselves in books as if they were crypto-screenwriters, and in turn are rewarded by having their work translated for the screen, they tap into a domain of profits and mass reception otherwise inaccessible to the world of publishing.[6] Led by a younger generation of independent filmmaker *auteurs*, many of whom write or collaborate on screenplays as well as direct, a sizable chunk of recent movies forge crossover identifications with contemporary novelists, symbolically appropriating the relative freedom of writers along with the veneer of postmodern experimental energies associated with the likes of Hornby, Rick Moody, and Jeffrey Eugenides.[7] This cozy alliance between the prerogatives of filmic and literary storytelling takes on a decidedly reflexive dimension in films where the protagonists are themselves writers.

Love and Death on Long Island, written and directed by Richard Kwietniosky from Gilbert Adair's 1990 novel, expresses a poignantly desired reconciliation of high-bourgeois novels with what is ostensibly the lowest rung of popular cinema, teen gross-out comedies. Giles De'Ath is a starchy, defiantly mandarin English novelist who, upon making a rare visit to the cinema to peruse an E. M. Forster adaptation, wanders into the wrong theater and becomes instantly infatuated with a minor heart-throb in *Hotpants College II*. Having lived a secluded existence as an erudite writer, he is compelled to enter the low-rent world of popular culture in order to indulge his scopophilic passions. Immersion in teen fan magazines leads to the purchase of a TV and VCR on which he fetishistically replays the vulgar hi-jinks of the beloved movie star. Not content with mere images, he flies to America and comically inserts himself into the actor's life. Like the novel, Kwietniosky's film is studded with allusions to lofty art — Shakespeare, pre-Raphaelite painting, Walt Whitman, Chantal Akerman (on whom former critic Kwietniosky wrote an erudite analysis for *Sight and Sound*) — that are balanced with references to Stephen King, Axel Rose, and sitcoms.[8] Brief parodies of trashy Hollywood genres intermingle with subjectivized dreams and fantasies; even the writer's subconscious has been colonized by mass culture. De'Ath romances his young acquaintance with archly nuanced evaluations of his screen performances and, although their relationship is never sexually consummated, the film's symbolic mandate carries a double valence: even frivolous movies can foster moments of sudden, revivifying beauty, and commercial cinema can successfully rework the themes and aesthetic discourses of classic literature.

Curtis Hanson's *Wonder Boys*, adapted by Steve Kloves from Michael Chabon's 1995 novel, is infused with a similar lesson in cultural convergence. Tripp, a middle-aged, ex-hippie novelist and writing professor with an unhealthy fear of completing a huge, traditional family saga, initiates a prize student into the picaresque adventures of seasoned men of letters — what Chabon calls "the praxis of alcoholism and reckless living."[9] During the college's annual "Wordfest" conference, the novelist, his editor, academic colleagues, and students share troves of arcane knowledge about soul music, baseball, and, above all, Hollywood movies; as artistic role models, Douglas Sirk or George Sanders are as valued by this coterie as Hemingway or Faulkner. In contrast to *Love and Death*, snippets of movies and TV shows wryly comment on Tripp's tangled romantic and professional woes. If melodrama and the musical lend individual scenes an apposite emotional register, the overall narrative structure mines the rhythmic lilt and running gags of 1930s' screwball comedy. The point here, as elsewhere, is that as boundaries between previously distinct cultural modalities continue to erode, the hypothetical antagonism between literature and movies looms as unproductive as it is snobbish; "Wordfest" is now "Imagefest." The film's opening shot furnishes a subtle visual emblem for their reciprocity: as the protagonist recites in voice-over a line from a student story, then switches abruptly into first-person exposition, the camera performs a tricky movement and rack-focus that slides from hazy blank screen to a manuscript page held by Tripp to the page's reflection in an adjacent window.[10] As this is happening, Bob Dylan's original soundtrack tune, "Things Have Changed," gradually fades into the background. The effect is to meld the bedrock resources of written text, film image, and pop anthem. By the end of *Wonder Boys*, the beleaguered novelist has dispensed with his 2,600 page opus in favor of the movie story we have just witnessed, a story whose style and accessibility bears unabashed allegiances to Hollywood and to pop music.

The stakes are rather different in *The End of the Affair*, Neil Jordan's reworking of Graham Greene's novel, less geared to high–low symmetries than metaphysical conundrums. An embittered, atheistic novelist, Maurice Bendrix, attempts to exorcize through prose a recently concluded wartime romance with the wife of a friend. He refers to his venture as "a diary of hate." Jordan mobilizes a compass of subjective effects, from extensive voice-over narration to point-of-view camera angles to flashbacks within flashbacks, in portraying the writer's self-destructive ambivalence toward his work and its living subject, ex-lover Sarah. Unable or unwilling to separate art from life, Bendrix oversteps Flaubert's famous dictum, not only playing god in his fictive universe but trying to gain omnipotence over Sarah's actual life. He hires a private detective to track her movements and, eventually, steal her diary containing alternative versions of key events in the dissolution of their affair.

Greene explores a sort of aesthetic-theological problem which Jordan extends in an unexpected manner. Is a writer's control over his material a matter of free will or is it, if not predestined, shaped by external forces? The book generates a series of metaphoric comparisons in which the act of writing segues with a lover's helpless passion: "I had looked forward to [making love] as a writer looks forward to the last word of his book;" "my mind was a blank sheet of paper on which somebody had been on the point of writing a message of happiness."[11] Writers and lovers share an anxious dynamic of power and/as submission. They are, as it were, compelled to enact, and re-enact, their private obsessions. In the second half of Greene's book, the narrator's dyspeptic description of events and his emotional responses are broken up by entries from Sarah's diary. The same thing happens in the film except that her embedded story is realized through multiple narrational channels: images of the diary, Bendrix's voice reading selected passages, her voice-over, enacted flashbacks of incidents already seen from Bendrix's perspective, shot and edited in a different visual idiom. In addition, the private detective, a writer of "factual" reports, chimes in with his own rendering of the same basic events, complete with *his* flashbacks. Thus the book's effect of univocal, or at worst contrapuntal, authority – in which the intrusion of other voices is consistently contained by the writer's subjective consciousness – is shattered by the film in a hodgepodge of clashing, at times redundant, narrational levels.

David Bordwell maintains that "personified narrators are inevitably swallowed up in the overall narrational process of the film, which they do *not* produce."[12] Yet in *The End of the Affair*, as in numerous examples of *film noir* – to which Greene's novel owes a considerable debt – the dispersal of narrational authority acts to foreground, as it destabilizes, the narrator/protagonist's struggle for control. Rather than getting lost, the narrator's function is made pivotal through the articulation of limits and blindspots. In this sense, the transposition from novel to film further problematizes the central theme of individual autonomy. Jordan adds yet another layer to the fabric of competing enunciative sources and intertexts by paying homage to Greene as historical subject. Greene was a dedicated *cineaste*, critic, and film collaborator, many of whose books had already reached the screen – including several important *films noirs* – and *The End of the Affair* was at once his most autobiographical and overtly modernist novel. As a director with a proven fascination for *l'amour fou* and its spiritual correlative, belief in the supernatural, Jordan lays claim to Greene as kindred spirit, honoring the writer's late religious convictions at the expense of his earlier humanist skepticism. The vehicle of Jordan's "conversion" is of course cinema, with its inherently more porous and divided narrational structure. In the process, Greene's agonized, self-excoriating exercise is turned into a film-modernist house of mirrors in which narrator, author, director, genre, and historical period meet at parallel angles of reflection.

At least two basic kinds of internal validation are discernible in recent writers' films: sweeping affirmations of cinema as partner, cultural equal, or potential redeemer of high literary values; and more personal or parochial agendas involving subtextual endorsements of specific writers, artistic shibboleths, or industrial practices. Albert Brooks's screenwriter in *The Muse*, like Woody Allen's novelist in *Deconstructing Harry*, engages in a thinly veiled autobiographical bid for public sympathy organized around self-deprecating, comic skirmishes with philistine taste and unreasonable commercial expectations. Brooks's film, co-written with Monica Johnson, features a studio hack without a contract and devoid of salable ideas. With the encouragement of a successful friend, he employs a demanding muse who traces her lineage to the ancient Greek tutelaries. He discovers that inspiration is indeed fickle, devouring, and largely an offshoot of dumb luck. As Robert Stam reminds us, "With a novel, questions of material infrastructure enter only at the point of distribution, whereas in the cinema they enter at the phase of production of the text itself."[13] Thus *The Muse*'s parade of dramatized clichés about the nature of creativity are constantly mediated, and frustrated, by pressures of commodification. Chasing ideas for the sake of material gain is shown to be analogous to an endless bout of coitus interruptus; the writer attends to his muse's every whim – from Tiffany baubles to gourmet foods to luxurious hotel suites – but is denied the aura of ecstatic release long associated in Western culture with the fruits of artistic achievement. The point is less that screenwriters lack the exhilarating freedom of literary authorship than that the myth of autonomous invention rings hollow under our current regime of mass entertainment.

Philip Kaufman's *Quills*, adapted by Doug Wright from his stage play, limns a narrower, more urgent polemic. After the Marquis de Sade is incarcerated in Charenton mental asylum, he continues to write his scandalous tracts in the face of increasing institutional threats and physical deprivations. He is abetted by an innocent country laundress who smuggles his work out to be published in cheap back-alley editions. The newly appointed director of the hospital hypocritically spouts religious condemnations of de Sade's sexual perversion while concealing his sadistic pleasure in punitive torture and the brutal treatment of his young wife. De Sade is confected as a literary freedom fighter, a martyr to the cause of free expression, who writes with wild abandon in part as a substitute for actually committing the acts he describes. The film's cultural politics could not be clearer. In a period of renewed conservative attacks on Hollywood for promulgating sex and violence to, especially, younger viewers, Kaufman's spirited defense of a canonical, if deeply contested, author is in essence a defense of cinematic freedom coupled with a plea for openly erotic representation as counterweight to repressed America's overindulgence in sadistic violence. Although *Quills* flaunts an anti-authoritarian, anti-censorship rhetoric, it is not immune to gnawing discursive contradictions – not least of which is a commercially prudent muting of sexual displays. Nonetheless, its strongest barb is reserved for opportunistic bureaucrats who secretly turn a profit from the posthumous sale of de Sade's manuscripts.

Quills is one of a half-dozen writers' films that recruit literary history in order to allegorize contemporary issues and the social dynamics of creativity. In *Shakespeare in Love*, directed by John Madden from a script by Tom Stoppard and Marc Norman, connections between Elizabethan theater and current cinema are too plentiful to ignore. Dramatic literature, in its performative leap to stage presentation, supplies opportunities for kinship not available to fiction writing. Indeed, this portrayal of the Bard is so thoroughly modernized and de-sacralized, so attuned to the thrum and malice of the marketplace, that Shakespeare could be mistaken for Albert Brooks in a velvet jerkin. Moreover, slippages between stage and screen are a two-way street, harboring prescriptions for cinematic renewal as they recuperate Shakespearean drama as entertainment for the masses. Theater is celebrated as a civic arena capable of temporarily suspending differences in class, age, profession, and sexual orientation among both performers and spectators. Couched as the "Dream Factory" of 1593, it is replete with scheming producers, coercive moneylenders, internecine competition (a friendly rivalry between Shakespeare and Christopher Marlowe), and pat formulas for box-office success: "action, romance, comedy . . . dogs" – to which the movie itself adds nudity, pratfalls, and cartoon villainy.

In a manner similar to Stoppard's early play *Rosencrantz and Guildenstern are Dead*, *Shakespeare* spins an intricate backstory for the narrative and thematic genesis of *Romeo and Juliet*. There is at its core an assertion about the power of expressive language to provoke heightened emotions, in this case to literally invent the terms of romantic love.[14] Creative labor is shown as a source of personal as well as collective elevation in which the playwright, blocked at first by a lack of romantic stimulation, rediscovers the potency of his "quill" as a function not of mercantile demands but the endearments of his "leading lady." However, the reciprocity between Elizabethan romance and modern movie conventions — ultimately the compatibility of Shakespeare with summer blockbusters — is fraught with disclaimers and special pleading. Not all types of filmic spectacle are worthy of the Elizabethan legacy. Gratuitous violence, represented by the casual cruelties of an adolescent John Webster, is implied as inimical to humanistic values, and consequent social cohesion, imputed to Shakespeare's work. Additionally, an element of nationalistic preening links sixteenth-century theater, and the London environment which nurtured it, to a specifically English tradition of "literate" screen drama and eloquent verbal performance.

Mike Leigh's *Topsy-Turvy* is also set in the world of London theater, albeit absent of utopian social appeals. In spite of the fact that *Shakespeare*'s protagonist adopts ideas suggested by Marlowe, cribs dialogue from an itinerant street preacher ("A plague on both your houses"), and listens attentively to the requests of theatrical cronies, he is basically a one-man show. By contrast, Leigh focuses on W. S. Gilbert and his some-times fractious relationship with composer Arthur Sullivan, yet the emphasis is on the hardships of ensemble collaboration. Gilbert is no paragon of Romantic genius but a complex, not entirely sympathetic, man of his time: curious, repressed, autocratic, insecure, plagued by misogynist and ethnocentric impulses common to the Victorian era. The dedicated, talented performers he diligently rehearses are afflicted by alcoholism, drug abuse, sexual duplicity, and racism. *Topsy-Turvy* balances private against public exigencies of production, revealing a dense web of biographical and historical factors informing *The Mikado*, an opera so ensconced in our culture that it now seems utterly transparent. A reflexive intertext points to Leigh's own well-documented approach to film directing, a labor-intensive commitment to a democratic community of dramatic exploration. In this light, the contemporary significance of Gilbert and Sullivan's theatrical process — encompassing actors, choreographer, costume designer, theater owner, and so on — is simultaneously the ways in which it parallels and diverges from the director's aesthetic ideals and their political underpinnings. His film, like Gilbert's libretto, will inevitably reflect, restate, and potentially resist dominant ideologies. To the extent that Leigh self-consciously exposes social relations enforced by Victorian theater, he also implicitly validates cinema as harboring possible alternatives to the blind reproduction of reactionary values.

Joe Gould's Secret addresses the relationship between film and literary history from a more familiar, bohemian perspective. Adapted by Howard A. Rodman from two of Joseph Mitchell's signature profiles — published twenty-five years apart in *The New Yorker* — and directed by Stanley Tucci, the film is a tale of two writers with uncannily similar ambitions whose lives otherwise could hardly be more incongruous. Mitchell's journalistic beat entailed intimate observations of New York's marginal subcultures: gypsies, street people, eccentric collectors, bartenders, strippers, "the has-beens and the might-have-beens and the would-bes." Using first-person techniques of point of view, voice-over narration, and nested flashbacks, the film recounts Mitchell's unusually personal entanglement with a garrulous, scruffy Greenwich Village misfit who survived off small "donations" from local artists and gained considerable notoriety for his supposed multi-million word "oral history" of city life. Gould is everything Mitchell is not – aggressive, disorderly, destitute, utterly unreliable, and probably deranged – except that Gould's obsessive undertaking is patently analogous to Mitchell's own writings in both content and style (impossibly long skeins of remembered dialogue, a belief in the voices of ordinary people as "secret" historical record).[15] Moreover, Mitchell confesses to initiating an urban novel that exists entirely in his imagination, like Gould's illusory opus.

Rodman and Tucci expand the framework of Mitchell's stories to include the writer's stable domestic life, of which a key element is his wife's creative work as a still photographer of urban street scenes. They also expand the role of painter Alice Neel, whose portraits of bohemian figures stand as yet another mode of informal urban documentation. These two characters underscore what is tacitly expressed in the opening montage of archival New York City footage: that cinema not only complements the written word as historical account but can incorporate and fuse qualities of prose, spontaneous speech, painterly and still-photographic images. Curiously, Joe Gould's tone of giddy optimism, a faith in film's ability to transcend aesthetic boundaries, is contrary to Mitchell's written profiles which engender a calculus of literary failure and self-deception, absence and obscurity.

In lieu of a conclusion, it is instructive to turn briefly to a recent European art film which, arguably, also functions as a requiem for that faded tradition. Time Regained (1999), Raúl Ruiz's adaptation of the final volume of Marcel Proust's Remembrance of Things Past, co-written with Gilles Taurand, is divorced from the commercial anxieties and sectarian justifications animating recent Anglo-American writers' films. As a consequence perhaps of this relative autonomy, and in keeping with the historical context of the source novel, its allegorical mandate is steeped in cinematic ontology. A meditation on the interdependence of modernist writing and motion pictures, Time Regained implicitly links the twin birth of the modern novel and movies with the aftermath of cinema's 1995 centennial. Proust's fiction has frequently been cited as at once impervious to and solicitous of filmic translation. As Ruiz's earlier work clearly demonstrates, movies are uniquely equipped to capture the sinuous imaginary of time and memory inscribed in the labyrinthine coils of Proust's language. The analogy between Proustian structures of consciousness and film's vivid, fleeting succession of images is realized by Ruiz in long gliding camera movements evoking the ephemerality and instability of memory. In a number of shots, a single movement incorporates disparate first-person time-frames, just as Proust was able to switch tenses within a single sentence – indicative of what Henry James disparagingly called "the terrible fluidity of the 'I'."

The character of Marcel is proposed as an exemplary camera eye drifting through his decadent environment, physically detached yet psychically engaged. Just as Marcel affirms the beauty and significance of past events while recognizing the debased motives of their participants, Ruiz pays tribute to cinema as reservoir – and toxic waste dump – of twentieth-century memory, a coequal source of private fantasy and public imagination. A plethora of sly intertextual references to French culture mesh Cubist and Surrealist painting styles with echoes of Renoir, Buñuel, Resnais. But as is often the case in Ruiz films, there is also recognition of an overblown sentimentality and absurd narrative gambits associated with movie melodrama and other genre formulas.

Historically, film augured a new conceptual order of time – a predicament at the forefront of late nineteenth-century philosophical and scientific inquiry – which the modernist novel would increasingly exploit. According to art historian Arnold Hauser, "The agreement between technical methods of the film and the characteristics of new concepts of time is so complete that one has the feeling that time categories of modern art altogether must have arisen from the spirit of cinematic form."[16] *Time Regained* acknowledges film's long productive exchange with the written word – in particular, the dilemma of subjective enunciation common to all writers' films, the elusive effort to visualize what goes on inside an author's head – while registering certain crucial limitations inherent to both mediums. Specifically what is masked, and in turn signaled, by the illusion of visual plenitude is precisely Proust's remarkable catalogue of tactile, olfactory, and related sensory impressions recruited during his retrieval of the past. Haunted by a shadow world of cinema's inimical version of reality, Ruiz's film is less shamelessly optimistic about the marriage of word and image than the bulk of films discussed above. Despite their mutually enhancing embrace over time, and cinema's unspoken promise of literary redemption as/and/through the fleeting image, there are realms of experience that novels routinely adumbrate which movies cannot touch – and, as Ruiz might concede, so much the better for both mediums.

Notes

---

1 Although I am concerned here exclusively with films that take writing "seriously," in several recent films characters are declared writers but this mantle proves either gratuitous or superfluous. For example, in *28 Days* a blithe spirit confined to a drug and alcohol rehab facility calls herself a writer, although little is made of this far-fetched claim. In *Snow Falling on Cedars* and *True Crime*, the vocation of newspaper journalist is subsumed under well-heeled movie conventions of the private investigator; writing itself takes a back seat to the solution of an enigma. On the other hand, a surfeit of enacted, "non-professional" writing appears in *You've Got Mail* (e-mail correspondence), *Mansfield Park* (letter writing), *The Cider House Rules* (local historiography), and *Bridget Jones's Diary*. Nonetheless, its functions are largely instrumental, a source of exposition or revelation or dramatic anticipation. In none of these cases is the process or ontology of writing sufficiently thematized to sustain the kind of analysis I offer in this chapter.

2 The number of Hollywood literary adaptations in any given year is frequently cited as between 20 and 30 percent, and this figure has remained fairly constant from the 1930s to the present; see George Bluestone, *Novels into Film* (Berkeley, CA: University of California Press, 1957), p. 3; see also Josh Chetwynd, "Hollywood Re-scripts Book Deals," *USA Today* (June 29, 2000), sec. D, p. 1. Both writers find that annual Ten Best lists and Academy Award nominations for Best Picture clearly privilege adaptations: Bluestone reports that, from 1935 to 1947, 47 percent of films on Ten Best lists were drawn from novels; Chetwynd calculates that in the previous twelve years, Oscar nominations for Best Picture included at least one book adaptation.

3 Richard Maltby provides a brief account of the hostility of writers toward Hollywood in rehearsing Theodore Dreiser's infamous attempt to suppress the 1932 version of *An American Tragedy*: "'To Prevent the Prevalent Type of Book': Censorship and Adaptation in Hollywood, 1924–1934," in James Naremore (ed.), *Film Adaptation* (New Brunswick, NJ: Rutgers University Press, 2000), pp. 79–82.

4 E. L. Doctorow, "Quick Cuts: The Novel Follows Film into a World of Fewer Words," *New York Times* (March 15, 1999), sec. E., p. 3. Doctorow made similarly disparaging comments during a panel discussion of Hollywood adaptations, as reported by Dinitia Smith in "Novelists get Back at Hollywood, Mostly Gently," *New York Times* (September 25, 1999), sec. B., pp. 9, 14. His most recent novel, *City of God* (New York: Random House, 2000), extends his strange diatribe against cinema in several long passages of invidious comparison between books and movies.

5 Lewis Cole, a writer and professor of screenwriting, offers an early and intelligent overview of the novelistic trend toward movie language – "condense, simplify, and dramatize" – in "Screenplay Culture," *The Nation* (November 4, 1991), 560–6. Although this argument has received much recent attention, it is at least as old as Edmund Wilson's celebrated 1941 essay, "The Boys in the Back Room," in which he chides Steinbeck's *Grapes of Wrath* for its capitulations to Hollywood narrative, asserting that "the novelist seems, consciously or unconsciously, to be going part of the way to meet the producers"; reprinted in *A Literary Chronicle, 1920–1950* (Garden City, NY: Doubleday Anchor Books, 1956), p. 231.

6 An example of the gross disparity between book readership and movie audiences is the fate of Toni Morrison's *Beloved*. Spurred by its selection to the Oprah Book Club, the novel sold a remarkable 500,000 copies between 1989 and 1997; the 1998 film version was, by Hollywood standards, a complete flop, yet it was seen by considerably more viewers in its opening weekend than the novel's entire projected readership: Chetwynd, "Hollywood Re-scripts Book Deals," p. 1. Publishers have exploited the potential interest of movie audiences in serious literature in unprecedented ways. Going beyond the familiar use of production stills and the tag-line, "Now a Major Motion Picture," a recent anthology, *Writers at the Movies: 26 Contemporary Authors Celebrate 26 Memorable Movies* (New York: Harper Perennial, 2000), recruits novelists such as Julian Barnes, Robert Coover, and Rick Moody to discuss films that in some sense reflect back on their own writerly pursuits, thus encouraging movie fans to seek out new, presumably compatible, literary experiences. In another fascinating move, John Irving, who was so distraught over the – admittedly ludicrous – movie treatment of *A Prayer for Owen Meany* that he requested, and got, a change in the title and renaming of major characters, penned a best-selling memoir of his work on the screenplay to *The Cider House Rules*.

7　Unfortunately, as Robert Stam points out, source novel and adaptation are rarely innovative in the same aesthetic terms or degree; indeed, most of the recent films made from postmodern novels "borrow from novelistic invention without themselves posing new film forms": Robert Stam, "Beyond Fidelity: The Dialogics of Adaptation," in James Naremore (ed.), *Film Adaptation* (New Brunswick, NJ: Rutgers University Press, 2000), p. 73.

8　Gilbert Adair's book is more detailed in its cultural references and more explicit about the social power and personal erotic lure of movie images. Publicized as a reworking of *Death in Venice*, with shades of *Lolita*, the novel's convoluted syntax also has strong affinities to Henry James, a writer who, like Forster, has been embraced by queer theory for his homosocial themes: *Love and Death on Long Island* (New York: Grove Press, 1990/1998).

9　Michael Chabon, *Wonder Boys* (New York: Picador USA, 1996), p. 132.

10　Elegant as it is, this page/screen trope – which recurs in slightly different poses in *The End of the Affair*, *Quills*, and *Shakespeare in Love* – has its origins in the countless opening credit sequences of Golden Age studio adaptations, and achieves sublimity in *Citizen Kane* (1941) in the dissolve from Thatcher's manuscript to Charlie playing in the snow.

11　Graham Greene, *The End of the Affair* (New York: Penguin Books, 1951/1999), pp. 11, 70 respectively.

12　David Bordwell, *Narration in Fiction Film* (Madison: University of Wisconsin Press, 1985), p. 61; see also Edward Branigan, *Point of View in the Cinema* (New York: Mouton, 1981), pp. 40–9.

13　Stam, "Beyond Fidelity," p. 56.

14　The title of a recent Stoppard play, *The Invention of Love*, could also serve for this film.

15　Mitchell's essays draw the doppelgänger connection in more precise literary form. His lengthy quotations of Gould's rambling monologues evidence the same syntax, rhythms, propensity for list-making, that characterize Mitchell's prose style; see "Professor Seagull" and "Joe Gould's Secret," in *Up in the Old Hotel* (New York: Vintage Books, 1993), pp. 52–70 and 623–716 respectively. Lacking the same discursive tools, Tucci nonetheless creates visual parallels through crosscutting, extensive use of medium two-shots, and voice-over readings that occasionally slide from Mitchell's voice to Gould's voice.

16　Arnold Hauser, *The Social History of Art*, vol. 4 (New York: Vintage Books, 1951), p. 253. Keith Cohen expands on Hauser's insight in his useful book-length study, *Film and Fiction* (New Haven, CT: Yale University Press, 1979).

Index